THE ROAD TO
RIVOLI

L'Historia si può veramente deffinire una guerra illustre contro il Tempo, perchè togliendoli di mano gl'anni suoi prigionieri, anzi già fatti cadaveri, li richiama in vita, li passa in rassegna, e li schiera di nuovo in battaglia.

[History may truly be called an illustrious war against time, because by taking from his hands the years he has made prisoner, nay, already reduced to corpses, it brings them back to life, passes them in review, and ranges them in battle once again.]

— Alessandro Manzoni.
Introduction to *I promessi sposi* (The Betrothed).

THE ROAD TO
RIVOLI

NAPOLEON'S FIRST CAMPAIGN

Martin Boycott-Brown

CASSELL&CO

Cassell & Co
Wellington House, 125 Strand
London WC2R OBB

Copyright © Martin Boycott-Brown 2001

First published 2001

British Library Cataloguing-in-Publication Data
A catalogue record for this book is available from the British Library.

ISBN 0-304-35305-1

Distributed in the USA by
Sterling Publishing Co Inc
387 Park Avenue South
New York
NY 10016-8810

Edited by Michael Boxall.
Cartography by Steve Longland.

Printed and bound in Great Britain.

To all my friends in Italy

CONTENTS

Acknowledgements		9
Introduction		12
1	The Origins of the War	15
2	Weapons and Tactics	23
3	The Austrian Army	33
4	The French Army	47
5	Learning the Trade	62
6	The Planner	84
7	Preparations	123
8	Opening Moves	167
9	The Austrian Offensive	194
10	Bonaparte's Reply	219
11	Defeating Piedmont	258
12	Crossing the Po	286
13	Lodi	309
14	Lombardy	328
15	Mantua to Castiglione	360
16	Into the Tyrol	406
17	Arcole	438
18	Rivoli	482
19	Aftermath	521
Bibliography		527
Index		547

ACKNOWLEDGEMENTS

I suppose the first seeds for this book were sown when my (then) girl-friend told me her brother worked in Rivoli and I innocently asked if he knew where the battle had taken place. A couple of years later I was casting round for a new direction to take and realised I had a potential research project almost literally staring me in the face. If I looked out of the window (on a clear day) I could see the cleft of the Adige valley that can be seen in Philippoteaux's painting of the battle. It looked a long way away in the haze, slightly mysterious, yet so near. We went up to Rivoli one day, stood on the top of Monte Pipolo and thought that it did not look much like a battlefield. If I had known then what I was starting, I would have given up the idea straight away.

The immense amount of source material has been truly daunting. I now have a list of over 650 titles of published books, articles, maps, and so forth, which in some way relate to Napoleon's first campaign. Some of the works are voluminous to say the least: Bouvier's book on the campaign is over 700 pages long, and only covers the first couple of months. Not surprisingly, reducing all the information in the sources to a single volume has not been easy, and I sometimes think I may go down in history as the first man to make a molehill out of a mountain. Not only that, but material continues to turn up in the most unexpected places with worrying regularity. No doubt the process will continue, and further discoveries will give us a better understanding of events. I shall try to make some extra material available on the internet site www.historydata.com.

A book such as this one is naturally based largely on the work of other people, and had it not been for the memoirs, the collections of letters, and the work of historians in both the 19th and 20th centuries, it would have been impossible for me to write it. The notes will, I hope, show how much I am indebted to the work of remarkable historians like Félix Bouvier, Gabriel Fabry and the phenomenally industrious Johann Baptist Schels.

There are many people whom I should like to mention for helping more directly with the writing of this book. First I should like to thank Graham Howes of Trinity Hall for many things, especially for reading so many drafts of the text. Thanks also go to a number of well-known experts who have generously shared their knowledge and also shown interest in the project. Among them are David Chandler, Christopher Duffy, Philip Haythornthwaite and Gunther Rothenberg. I received some useful comments and criticisms from Adam Cobb, who was good enough to read one of the many drafts of the book. John Leigh kindly helped with some of the French. My thanks to Steve Longland for drawing the maps.

The staff of Cambridge University Library (particularly in the Rare Books Room, the Map Room, the Photography Department, Inter-Library Loans, Official Publications, and the all-important Tea-Room) must also be thanked for their friendly and efficient service, and so must the staff of the Kriegsarchiv in Vienna, who provided me with so much material and seemed untroubled by my staggering inefficiency. The library in Cuneo also provided me with copies of articles, and more than one *Assessore alla Cultura* has been helpful with maps and local information.

Many friends in Italy gave all kinds of help for which I am grateful. Particular thanks go to: Franco Corsini, Jenny Gascoigne, Rob Hill, Alex Martin, Gabriella Montini and Laura Polato. Mario Marangoni supplied me with some interesting titbits of information about Rivoli. I was also lucky when carrying out research in Liguria to meet many people who readily gave assistance. Paolo Bazzano did much more than a hotel-keeper needs to by taking the trouble to drive me to Montenotte, and also sent me a number of photocopies. Roberto Marchisio accompanied me on my walk over the site at Montenotte and has supplied me with several books. Leonello Oliveri gave me copies of his fascinating articles on the war in Val Bormida, while Ernesto Saroldi gladly shared his profound knowledge of the history of the same area. I should like to thank those who organised and participated in the conference at Cosseria in 1996, where I learned many useful things. Most of all I have to thank Pier Giorgio

Calcagno, who gave up a great deal of time to drive me to all the most important sites from Altare to Mondovì. Without him I would never have seen most of them.

I should also like to make special mention of Rod Dymott, who showed a saintly patience while I re-wrote the book several times. I am most grateful for his kindness, and I hope he will think the effort was worthwhile. Barry Holmes has been similarly tolerant, for which I offer him my thanks.

Last but not least, my thanks to all the members of my family, who have provided various kinds of help, particularly my parents, who gave me somewhere to live while I did the research and writing.

A professor of my acquaintance once told me that it was important to include a few deliberate errors in a book to keep the pedants happy, but I fear that my unintentional ones will be more than sufficient. I only hope there are not too many.

M.B.B.
Cambridge, 2000

INTRODUCTION

In the early spring of 1796, an almost unknown young general named Napoleon Bonaparte was given command of one of the armies then engaged in fighting the enemies of Revolutionary France. It was an appointment that must have seemed extraordinary at the time.

Not only was Bonaparte a mere 26 years old, but he had negligible experience of campaigning. He was an artilleryman by training, and had never led so much as a company of infantry in the field, much less a whole army of tens of thousands of men of all arms. In addition to this he was faced with making war in difficult terrain, leading a starving, disorganised rabble that was on the verge of mutiny, riddled with sickness, and reduced to the last extremity by lack of clothing, weapons and equipment. Any sober observer would have rated his chances of success as practically non-existent.

It was in these unfavourable circumstances that Napoleon Bonaparte set out to fight his first campaign as commander of an army in the field. The results staggered his contemporaries and still seem amazing two hundred years later. The weaker of his adversaries, Piedmont, which had been at war with France since September 1792, only resisted for two weeks before having to surrender. Austria, a much more powerful enemy, held out considerably longer, but suffered the indignity of having its army chased and harried half-way across northern Italy in the space of a month and a half. By the time twelve months had gone by, Bonaparte's army was only 100 miles from Vienna, and the Austrians sued for peace. The War of the First Coalition was effectively at an end, after five long years of suffering.

The shock-waves from this phenomenal and unexpected success continued to reverberate for many years – indeed, some would say they have not yet completely died away. The campaign not only changed the course of the war, but also laid the foundation for the legend of Napoleonic invincibility, and provided a spring-board to propel Bonaparte to even greater influence and power. In this way it profoundly influenced not only the history of France, but also of Europe as a whole. Many military historians would argue that it also marked a turning-point in the history of warfare itself.[1] Whatever one's opinion, it is undeniable that the campaign is a historical event of great importance.

It is therefore somewhat surprising to find that it has been largely neglected by historians in recent times, notwithstanding the fact that its bicentenary has just passed. The English-speaker, in particular, has been reduced to reading rapid summaries of the campaign in general works dealing with the whole of Bonaparte's career. This neglect is difficult to understand. Not only is the campaign fascinating in itself, with its richness of incidents and personalities, but it also provides clear examples of the methods that Bonaparte was to use throughout his career. It is also revealing on a personal level, and shows the future Emperor dealing for the first time with some of the people who were to become his most prominent lieutenants, as well as struggling to cope with his new wife, Josephine, who seems to have caused him much more anguish than the enemy. In short, anyone who seeks an insight into the force that dominated Europe in the first decade of the 19th century, could do worse than examine this campaign.

The purpose of this book, however, is not to provide a systematic study of Napoleon Bonaparte's methods, nor look at the wider ramifications of his successes in 1796 and 1797. It merely aims to tell the story of the campaign, concentrating on the military aspect. While doing this, it attempts to say something about the experiences of the local civilian population, whose sufferings have largely been ignored by non-Italian historians, who tend to portray the campaign as if it occurred in a place where nobody lived. The book also includes information from various Austrian and Italian sources which have not been well covered in English.

NOTES

1. See, for example, Jackson, W. G. F. *Attack in the West.* London, 1953, p. 78, where that author looks upon Montenotte as marking the end of

the era of classic 18th-century warfare of the kind practised by Marl-borough. Some judgements of Bonaparte's achievements have been even more positive (or negative, if you prefer to read them that way). The authors of one work go so far as to say that Bonaparte's Italian campaign demonstrated 'the first coherent new concept of warmaking to manifest itself since Genghis Khan.' Dupuy, R. E., and Dupuy, T. N. *Encyclopedia of Military History*. London, 1970, p. 740

1

THE ORIGINS OF THE WAR

Before examining Napoleon Bonaparte's first campaign itself, it would seem advisable to take a look at the events that led up to it. The 1796–7 campaign in Italy was the culminating phase of the War of the First Coalition, a conflict in which Revolutionary France was opposed by a temporary alliance consisting of a bewildering array of major and minor European powers which joined and left at various times during the five years of fighting. The most constant member of the Coalition was Austria – which is a convenient shorthand term for the sprawling empire ruled by the head of the House of Habsburg.

Its constancy is hardly surprising. Indeed, enmity between the Habsburgs and France (or its rulers) had been an almost unchanging feature of international relations in Europe for several hundred years. As far back as the 15th century, the complications of dynastic marriages and uncertain lines of succession had given rise to bloody disputes between them over the 'ownership' of certain territories in Italy. As time went on a climate of intense competition was established, so that it became almost automatic for each to look upon the other as an enemy, and there were continual clashes, many of which were fought out in the Italian peninsula.

It should, of course, be borne in mind that Italy was not a unified country at this time, but was divided into a considerable number of kingdoms, duchies, republics, city states and the like, some of whose rulers had more or less direct links with the ruling families of France, Austria and Spain. This partly explains Italy's popularity as a campaigning ground, but a further reason was that large areas of the peninsula, mostly in the north, were rich and productive, which meant that they were capable of feeding large masses of soldiery as well as being desirable territorial possessions.

The competition between France and the Habsburgs continued to be intense during the first half of the century in which Napoleon Bonaparte was born and grew up. By 1700, France had established herself as perhaps the dominant power in Europe, and also had significant possessions overseas, while the Habsburgs held sway over Austria, Spain, the Spanish Netherlands, Hungary, Bohemia, Moravia, large tracts of Italy, and a vast overseas empire. When the Habsburg King of Spain died without a direct heir, and the grandson of King Louis XIV of France was nominated to succeed him, a collision was inevitable.

The details of what happened during the twelve years of the War of the Spanish Succession need not trouble us here, but it is worth noting that northern Italy was initially one of the major campaigning areas, and there was some important manoeuvring and fighting in districts that would be fought over again in 1796. Napoleon Bonaparte was an insatiable reader of history, and it is certain that he studied and learned from these campaigns, which were remarkable for some outstanding successes obtained by the young Imperial commander, Prince Eugene of Savoy, whose brilliant manoeuvres led to more than one humiliating defeat for the French.

A further noteworthy feature of the campaigning in Italy was the decision by Piedmont (the northern Italian state that was also a member of the anti-French alliance in the 1790s) to switch sides during the course of the war. Such fickleness became something of a characteristic of Piedmontese foreign policy over the next few decades, and its reputation for inconstancy caused manifold difficulties in its relationship with Austria during the War of the First Coalition.

The result of the War of the Spanish Succession was that the Habsburgs lost Spain, but retained most of their Italian territory, while France found herself drained by her efforts. Among the minor players, the ruler of Piedmont was made King of Sicily, thus placing the extreme ends of Italy under the same monarch. This odd situation did not last for long, and six years later he was given Sardinia instead. Unfortunately, this kind of swapping around was typical of the way that the major powers treated Italy, whose duchies and kingdoms were used like gambling chips to settle up debts, to the confusion of historian and reader alike, who are faced with threading their way through sudden multiple changes, and coping with the fact that the names

Savoy, Piedmont and Sardinia are at times used interchangeably to refer to the same state.

Regrettably, the strife-torn opening of the 18th century was but a sign of things to come, and the situation in Europe did not stabilise. The 1720s were relatively peaceful, but another upheaval overtook Italy when in 1734 the War of the Polish Succession spread there, with Franco–Spanish invasions of Lombardy, Naples and Sicily, supported by Piedmont–Sardinia. Mercifully, the fighting did not last long, but the diplomatic negotiations went on for three years, after which it was 'all change' again, with Naples and Sicily going to the Spanish, and the duchies of Parma, Piacenza and Tuscany to the Austrians.

The ink was hardly dry on these agreements when a much more serious explosion of violence upset the precarious equilibrium of Europe and cast a shadow over its affairs for several decades. It started in 1740 when the new King of Prussia, Frederick the Great, greeted the accession of Maria Theresa to the throne of Austria by seizing the province of Silesia. This sparked off eight years of loosely connected conflicts known as the War of the Austrian Succession, in which various states took the field against Maria Theresa in the hope of carving up her possessions between them. Among these opponents were Spain, France and Piedmont, so Italy inevitably found itself reluctant host to the warring factions again, although in the wider context of the war it was really little more than a side-show compared to the theatre in central Europe, where Frederick's Prussia convincingly demonstrated its military superiority. Nevertheless, some of the situations in which the opponents found themselves in Italy, particularly during the period 1745–6, proved to be very similar to those of the 1790s, and provided much material for historians and military theorists of the time, including some who were to have a profound influence on Napoleon Bonaparte. It is quite clear that some of his strategic planning in the 1790s draws on his knowledge of this earlier campaign.

The wider consequences of the war were substantial. In Austria, the defeats and losses that had been suffered had a marked influence on domestic and foreign policy for the next forty years, causing much work to be done on strengthening the army, and inspiring a radical re-think of diplomatic relations with the other powers. It now seemed clear that the most serious threat to Austria was no longer posed by France, but by Prussia. Accordingly, Austrian diplomats went to work to see what could be done to isolate Prussia by detaching her main continental ally, France. It took some time, but eventually the Austrians reached their goal in May 1756, with a treaty of friendship between themselves and France. In view of the previous relations between them, this was such an astonishing turn-round that it has been called the Diplomatic Revolution. Predictably, Frederick saw the alliance as threatening, and as a direct consequence another war broke out, but this time with the French and Austrians on the same side.

Since this state of hostilities lasted from 1756 until 1763, it came to be known as the Seven Years War, and it was significant in a number of ways. For one thing it became so wide-ranging that it has been called the first 'World War', its campaigns being fought in America, India, Europe and on the oceans. Paradoxically, it was one occasion when Italy remained untouched, largely because France and Austria were allied. It was also such a bloody and expensive war that it left most of the participants dangerously weakened, and discouraged them from acts of belligerence for many years thereafter. It was almost catastrophic for France, which suffered some shattering defeats at the hands of the Prussians and English. Particularly far-reaching in its consequences was the spectacular rout at Rossbach, near Leipzig, in 1757, when Marshal Soubise's army lost 10,000 men against a Prussian loss of 548. As far as the French army was concerned, there seems little doubt that the sense of humiliation engendered by this débâcle caused a great deal of soul-searching and theorising among the more intelligent military men, and a great determination to do something to remedy the defects they perceived. Their work formed part of the military heritage that came down to Bonaparte in the 1790s.

In political terms, the ramifications are difficult to assess, but some felt they were very great. Indeed, in 1814, Bonaparte went so far as to tell the British Commissioner on Elba, Neil Campbell: 'The battle of Rossbach ... produced the Revolution in France, more than any other of the causes to which it was ascribed.'[1] This may be thought an exaggeration, but it seems fair to say that the war helped to create conditions that were conducive to the Revolution. What is more certain is that the war did great damage to the new Austro–French alliance, though neither side really had any alternative but to continue with it. It therefore limped along, despite mutual suspicion and dissatisfaction, bringing no benefit to anyone, awaiting circumstances that would either improve it or destroy it.

Although there was the odd brief outbreak of warfare in the decades that followed, the next really significant upheaval in Europe was not a war, but the French Revolution of 1789. To begin with, it was largely ignored by the other powers, some of whom saw it as a purely internal matter, while others, including the Austrian Emperor, Leopold,[2] actually welcomed the early reforms. Leopold's attitude was partly influenced by the fact that Austro–French relations had been so poor under the *ancien régime*, and it was hoped that changes in France would bring an improvement. Ironically, the alliance, and the attendant links between the French and Austrian royal families, were to contribute much to bringing about the War of the First Coalition.

Although Leopold received secret requests for help from the French Queen, Marie-Antoinette, who was in fact his sister, he did nothing. There was some justification for his attitude in that the situation did not seem dangerous at the time, and anyway, he had not seen his sister for twenty-five years. It is true that when the French royal family almost escaped to Germany in June 1791, Leopold agreed to issue the Declaration of Pillnitz together with the Prussians. This celebrated document appealed to all the sovereigns of Europe to restore the rights and position of the monarchy in France. To this end, Frederick William of Prussia and Leopold stated that they were placing their armies in a state of readiness until such time as they should receive the support of the other monarchs.[3] The latter proviso was apparently inserted as a get-out clause, for Leopold was not keen on direct action and was convinced that international support would not be forthcoming. Instead, he hoped that the declaration would succeed in frightening the Revolutionaries into treating the royal family carefully.

The Prussians, on the other hand, were more keen on definite action. They had shown regrettably piratical tendencies in the recent past, and the chaos in France seemed to present an excellent opportunity to seize some territory from a debilitated opponent who would probably be able to do very little about it. But this was something that Prussia could not undertake without the support of an ally. In September, General Hohenlohe was sent to Vienna to plan military action against France, but Leopold was not prepared actually to agree to anything.

The Declaration of Pillnitz was initially greeted by a resounding silence on the part of the French, who were much more concerned with the introduction of their new constitution, a measure that also met with Leopold's approval. But the new constitution created a new Legislative Assembly,[4] which was very different from its predecessor, there being fewer nobles and clergymen among its members, who were mostly younger and much more radical, and who felt that the Revolution still had far to go. Among them were a number of men who favoured renewing the ancient hostility with Austria because they believed that a war would help them to achieve their domestic political aims.

One such was the Marquis de Lafayette, who had been a companion of Washington during the American War of Independence. He believed that war would enhance the prestige of the King, and of himself as the commander of the army. Another group, led by Jacques Pierre Brissot de Warville, had quite different ends in view. Brissot hated the monarchy, for he had been the victim of political persecution before the Revolution, and his ultimate hope was to found a republic. He believed that a war against Austria would put intolerable pressure on the royal family, with its personal links with Vienna, and that their divided loyalties would bring them to do something that could be construed as treason and used to destroy them.

On 20 October 1791 Brissot, a wonderful orator, made his first great speech on foreign affairs, launching his campaign for war. His main theme, which he was to return to again and again in the coming months, was that there was a plot to destroy the Revolution and restore the former régime, and that it was backed by the other European powers. Brissot insinuated that measures were already being taken by them, citing the Declaration of Pillnitz and the new agreement between Prussia and

Austria, such confirmed enemies, as incontrovertible evidence of this. He suggested that military preparations were already under way and expressed a wish that the Assembly should ask the foreign powers to state their intentions openly. If they refused to do so, he intimated, the French would know what to think. Brissot also put forward the dangerous but attractive theory that France's enemies were weak, and that if they did not give satisfactory answers, France should attack them first. Brissot deliberately tried to inflame passions, appealing to the sense of French honour and speaking of national pride and glory, emphasising the danger to the Revolution posed both by the counter-revolutionaries within France and their supporters beyond the borders. After a while, the debates in the Assembly were being held in an atmosphere approaching collective hysteria.

As relations between the French and Austrians deteriorated, the latter made a serious miscalculation by taking a hard line, evidently hoping that some threatening noises would intimidate the Revolutionaries into better behaviour. The effect was the opposite, for the pro-war party gleefully seized the ammunition it had been given, and the exchanges of threats became ever more serious. Even so, it was some months before the climax was reached.

Eventually, on 20 April 1792, the unfortunate King Louis was obliged to go to the Assembly and listen to the Foreign Minister, Dumouriez, recite a catalogue of Austrian misbehaviour. Then, no doubt with death in his heart, Louis had to tell the Assembly that these were also his views, and ask the Assembly to vote for war. What followed could hardly be called a debate for there was almost no dissent, and in an atmosphere of wild enthusiasm the measure was voted through with only seven votes against.

We shall deal in a later chapter with the vicissitudes of the war itself, and how these led to Napoleon Bonaparte being given command of an army.

NOTES

1. Campbell, N. *Napoleon at Fontainebleau and Elba*. London, 1869, p. 316
2. At the very start of the Revolution the Emperor was Joseph, but he died

soon after, in February 1790, and was succeeded by his brother Leopold, who only ruled for a short period, dying in March 1792.

3. See Blanning, T. C. W. *The Origins of the French Revolutionary Wars.* London, 1986, p. 86

4. There were several changes of constitution during the Revolution, and the main governing body of France changed its form and name correspondingly. The Estates General transmuted into the National Assembly, followed by the National Constituent Assembly, which then gave way to the Legislative Assembly. This was replaced by the National Convention in September 1792, which was in its turn replaced by the Directory in 1795.

2

WEAPONS AND TACTICS

A full understanding of the events of Napoleon Bonaparte's first campaign would not be possible without some knowledge of contemporary military practice and weaponry.

In the 18th century the single most important type of weapon was the infantry musket. This was a smooth-bore muzzle-loader of such spectacular inaccuracy that it was deemed pointless to give it proper sights. At over 150 yards it was scarcely worth aiming at anything smaller than a house, which explains the legendary instruction Israel Puttnam gave to his men at the battle of Bunker Hill in 1775: 'Don't one of you fire until you see the whites of their eyes'.[1] It also led the British Colonel Hanger to comment that a soldier was most unlikely to be wounded from 150 yards' range 'provided his antagonist aims at him' and 'as to firing at a man at 200 yards with a common musket, you may as well fire at the moon'.[2]

A further limitation was that the process of loading was convoluted and slow. The soldier held his musket balanced horizontally in his left hand, and took a cartridge from the pouch on his right hip. The cartridge was a cylinder of paper about the size of his finger, and contained the powder and the lead ball. He gripped the ball in his teeth and ripped off the rest of the cartridge. From this he tipped a small amount of the powder into the trough (called the priming pan) which was positioned on the side of the barrel in front of the hammer. He closed the hinged cover of the pan so that the powder would not fall out, and placed the butt of the musket on the ground in front of his feet. The rest of the powder could now be poured down the barrel, the ball was dropped after it, and the paper stuffed on top as wadding. To complete the process he drew the ramrod from its housing under the barrel, inserted it in the barrel and tamped down the charge. The ramrod then had to be slid back into its housing.

To fire the musket, the hammer was pulled back to 'full cock', the weapon was seated on the shoulder and the trigger pulled. The hammer then snapped forwards, so that the flint that was held in its jaws struck a metal extension on the cover of the priming pan. This simultaneously flicked open the cover and struck sparks that would ignite the priming. This in turn ignited the main charge in the barrel through a touch-hole. Ignition was accompanied by a flash and a puff of smoke from the pan, and a much larger flash and a veritable grey cloud from the muzzle, which could hang about for minutes in still air.

Naturally enough, the many stages of the procedure could lead to errors while carrying it out, and these coupled with the crudeness of the firing mechanism meant that even under good conditions the weapon not infrequently refused to go off when the trigger was pressed. Even if everything went well, in the difficult conditions of a battlefield a soldier would only manage to fire about two rounds a minute at best.

As far as tactics were concerned, conventional 18th-century methods used massed formations of a kind that today are only seen on the parade-ground, with the troops marching shoulder-to-shoulder, in step, and carrying out all the movements of firearms drill, including loading and firing, in unison.[3] Although such formations look suicidal to an eye accustomed to the tactics of the 20th century, they did have certain advantages. The close physical proximity with numbers of colleagues provided some reassurance for the nervous, as well as being a defence against cavalry in open country. Moreover, the packed ranks made it more difficult for the reluctant soldier to absent himself, and allowed greater control on the part of the officers and NCOs, who not uncommonly pushed and pulled men into line, or belaboured them with whatever weapons they were using at the time. Lastly, with some types of formation, it afforded greater firepower.

For much of the century the preferred combat formation was to arrange the troops in a long line only three or four ranks deep, with intervals between the battalions for their supporting cannon. This gave maximum firepower, for it meant that (with the ranks staggered instead of directly behind one another, and the front rank kneeling) it was possible for almost all the muskets to be brought to bear on the enemy. The fire tactics of the period demanded that the troops fire in volleys, though the intention was not usually for whole battalions to let fly at once. Instead, the individual ranks or platoons could fire in various different sequences and combinations, each of which was believed to confer some kind of tactical advantage in certain circumstances, and gave the very real safeguard of keeping a proportion of the weapons loaded at any one time. (This of course was only theory: what tended to happen in battle, as all experienced soldiers knew, was that the men would eventually start firing on their own accord instead of in volleys.) Before long they would probably be able to see only a few yards through the smoke from their own firing, and might have very little idea of what was happening only a short distance away.

The use of linear formations offered great firepower, therefore, but was attended with significant difficulties. If a unit that was on the march had to deploy into line for combat it was faced with performing some evolutions not wholly unlike those of a massive country dance. It could easily go wrong, and the danger was that the unit would become completely disordered. This possibility of falling into disorder and losing control of the men was one of the major worries that haunted officers of the time. If cohesion were lost, a formation became much less than the sum of its parts and could easily disintegrate into a fleeing rabble at the mercy of enemy cavalry. Once the line had been success-fully formed, it was extremely difficult to move. It tended to curve in the middle, and would concertina, so that gaps would appear in some places (leading to cries of 'Close up!'), while overlaps and bunching would appear in others. Movement in line therefore had to be painfully slow if it was to be orderly. Just how slow is demonstrated by the fact that during an action in the Seven Years War, the army under Prince Ferdi-nand of Brunswick took five hours to move a distance that was equal to one hour's march.[4]

These problems caused some theorists to champion the use of a narrower battle formation called the 'column' which sacrificed firepower but offered greater speed and control of movement. Despite its name, this type of formation was not shaped like a battering ram, but instead the troops were arranged in a succession of lines at intervals of about five or six paces. A single battalion in column could easily be seventy yards wide, but it was still a narrow formation compared with the line. (A battalion deployed in line could have a front of about 150 yards.) Since the lines were shorter it was easier to keep them straight, and a column could also change direction more easily and go through smaller gaps without the need to change formation. It was believed by some that an attack in column could succeed without the use of firepower by exploiting 'shock', or momentum, and the bayonet.

Most bayonets of this period were simple spikes about eighteen inches long, and they were known to be useful for digging up potatoes or other root vegetables. On the field of battle the damage they did was often more psychological than physical, since one side normally ran away before bayonets could be crossed. Many nations laid claim to being masters in the use of the weapon, which would strike terror into their enemies, but were actually just as likely to run away as anyone else. Some contemporary observers went so far as to say that they had never seen mass bayonet fights except when troops ran into each other unexpectedly in the dark or at the top of a hill. But although most casualties in fighting were caused by gunfire, bayonets were used with great ferocity when necessary, particularly when defending or attacking fortifications.

Most Austrian troops were also issued with short swords, a practice that was usually limited to grenadiers or other specialist troops in the majority of armies. Once again, the experienced soldiers found these were handy for domestic chores, like chopping up firewood, if the sergeant and the officer were not looking, but probably used them relatively little for fighting — unless they were Hungarians or Croats, who seemed to favour the weapon.

Although mass formations dominated the art of warfare in the 18th century, the period saw a gradual increase in the use of irregular or light troops, who usually fought in a different style. In pitched battles they were most useful as 'skirmishers'. Typically, they would fan out, sheltering behind cover if they could find it, while keeping up a 'nuisance fire' which would peck away at the edges of the massed formations. Their dispersal caused them to be much less vulnerable to enemy fire, and while they did less damage than a mass volley at close quarters, they still caused considerable disturbance among the closed ranks. Troops who were experienced at this sort of independent fighting were also useful as scouts, in isolated outposts, and in raiding parties. An advantage of light troops was that they could be trained much more quickly than regular infantry, who had to learn all the intricacies of drill before they could march in a mass formation without reducing it to mayhem. It was considered that it took two or three years to produce a good regular, but perhaps as little as two months for light troops.[5] On the other hand, the light infantryman probably had to be more intelligent, not to say more willing, to be truly effective.

Most armies also had various sorts of élite troops, of whom the most common were the grenadiers. Usually each regiment had two companies of grenadiers, who were picked from among the best men in the regiment. They were expected to inspire the ordinary soldiers by their bravery, and would often be called on to deal with the most critical situations in combat. Since the hand-grenade had gone out of fashion in the first half of the century, their weaponry was the same as that of other infantrymen, though some of them carried short sabres. It was quite common for the grenadier companies to be detached from their parent regiments and combined to form élite battalions.

The weapons used by the cavalry were, like infantry weaponry, much the same in all European armies, and had changed little since ancient times apart from the adoption of firearms. The latter usually consisted of one or two pistols, with the addition of a carbine for the ordinary troopers. Needless to say, they suffered from the same kind of performance as the infantry muskets, but were even less accurate because the barrels were shorter. Generally speaking, firearms were only used by cavalrymen on outpost or sentry duty, though pistols were sometimes used in a mêlée.

The principal weapon of most cavalry was the sword. They were often about the length of a man's leg, and tended to be straighter for the heavy regiments, which was best for thrusting, while light cavalry commonly used very curved swords suitable for slashing. These fearsome weapons were quite capable of severing limbs or cutting off heads. The main weapon of the Uhlan was a lance about eight or nine feet long. In the hands of an expert it could be a dangerous weapon, with a longer reach than a sword or a musket with a bayonet, but at very close quarters it could be a liability because its length became a hindrance.

The characteristics of the two basic types of cavalry, heavy and light, should be self-evident. The former were big men on large horses, and they were mainly intended to be a battering device for use on the battle-field.[6] Some heavy cavalry wore a cuirass or breastplate, which was proof against musket balls, but was very heavy and uncomfortable, especially in hot weather. Light cavalry consisted of smaller men on more nimble horses. They were really supposed to be used for scouting, raiding, guarding the flanks and rear of the army, pursuing and harrying a beaten enemy after a battle, and collecting stragglers both of their own and the enemy army. Despite this, they were quite often pressed into performing charges on the field of battle when the occasion demanded. In some armies the dragoons became a kind of medium cavalry who could fulfil both roles. They had originally been the predecessors of motorised infantry, and had used their horses only as transport from one battlefield to another, dismounting to fight on foot. But in the course of time their role changed, and by the 1790s almost the only time a dragoon was forced to walk was when he lost his horse.

As with the infantry, conventional cavalry tactics were based on mass formations. But if manoeuvring infantry on the battlefield was difficult, evolutions with cavalry were a nightmare and demanded prodigious skill. This was not always appreciated by members of other arms. Obstacles that might pose no difficulty to infantry could force cavalry to make long detours, and choosing the right formations for any set of circumstances took considerable knowledge and experience. Simply turning to face in a different direction was fairly involved, since a horse is three times as long as it is wide, and cannot merely pivot like a man when standing in line. The problems got worse with larger formations, and moving a division of thousands of men was a task requiring forethought and judgement if you were not to end up with a shapeless mass milling around in disorder. The need to preserve order meant that a cavalry charge was not just a flat-out dash. It began at a walk, and accelerated by stages until a gallop was reached some fifty to a hundred yards from the enemy. If the horses had been exhausted by such repeated efforts, a 'charge' might never rise much above a weary walk.

The cannon that were in use in the 18th century were unsophisticated weapons basically consisting of a metal tube on a wooden carriage. Like the small-arms of the time they were muzzle-loaders, and every shot took time to load and fire. The guns also had to be aimed after each shot because the recoil would disturb their alignment. Other factors such as the wind affected their accuracy, and they were not reliable for hitting small targets. Despite their limitations, however, they were the most destructive weapons on the battlefield. At longer ranges they were used to fling out an iron ball that might weigh anything between two and fourteen pounds, even larger shot being used in sieges. The velocity of these projectiles was not great, so that they could often be seen flying through the air, but the damage that they did when they met human or animal bodies was appalling, smashing bones, knocking off heads and limbs, and even cutting bodies in two. The medium calibres had a range of about half a mile, and if the ground was hard, the ball would bounce and roll some way further. The ball was dangerous even while rolling along the ground shortly before stopping, and the inexperienced soldier who put out a hand or a foot to stop it often had the misfortune to suffer serious injury. Exploding shells were also used, fired by howitzers, which had short barrels designed to throw the shells high in the air. When the powder inside the shell ignited, the casing would fracture into lethal fragments which would spread out for a maximum of forty or fifty feet.

At short range the cannon became a veritable instrument of carnage and slaughter, and was used not unlike a giant sawn-off shotgun or blunderbuss. It could fire grape-shot, a number of smaller balls loaded into the gun simultaneously (usually inside a linen bag), which would not fly so far as round shot, but would spread out after leaving the muzzle and hit numerous targets. Canister could also be used. This was a cylinder the same size as the bore of the gun, made of thin metal sheet and packed with small iron or lead balls. As it left the barrel it broke up, scattering the balls in all directions. A discharge from a single gun was therefore not unlike a volley from a large number of troops, and was fearfully destructive at close range.

Artillery was one of the major restrictions on the mobility of an army. A field gun could vary in weight from about three hundred pounds to a ton, depending on the calibre, and was pulled from place to place by a team of two or more horses, while the crew accompanied it on foot. Ammunition was carried in long wagons also drawn by teams of horses. Vehicles of such weight could only use certain roads and bridges, and the heavier the gun the better the road it needed. Artillery was virtually impossible to move in many hilly or mountainous areas, although some light guns were intended to be dismantled and carried on mules. Not surprisingly, it was quite a frequent occurrence for guns to be left behind in a hasty retreat, and they were costly to replace.

During the 17th and 18th centuries, fortifications had reached a high level of sophistication, particularly in the hands of Marshal de Vauban, the celebrated French engineer, though some of the earliest and best examples of 'artillery fortifications' were constructed around Italian fortress cities, such as Alessandria. The usual arrangement was for the corners of a fortress to be furnished with bastions, which had straight walls that could be raked by defensive fire from above. Between them were straight walls called 'curtains'. In front of the whole complex the terrain was carefully 'land-scaped' to make life difficult for any attackers trying to approach the main walls. There would usually be a wide, steep-sided ditch, and on the far side of this would be an area known as the 'covered way', which was sheltered by an embankment and a palisade. This space was used by infantry as an outer line of defence. In front of the palisade of the covered way, the ground was cleared of obstacles and sloped away gently, so as to expose any attackers to the fire of the defenders. This area was known as the glacis.

Formal sieges were generally systematic affairs which proceeded according to well-established methods. A summons to surrender, accompanied by various threats, would almost invariably be disdainfully rejected, whereupon the besiegers began their work. First, this involved blocking the access roads, to prevent an easy break-out by the defending garrison. Meanwhile, the engineers would study the fortifications to determine the weakest points, which would then become the main targets for the heavy artillery fire, with the goal of opening a breach in the wall through which a storming party could enter the fortress. Work would then begin on constructing gun emplacements in suitable positions from which to carry out the bombardment. Siege artillery was of very large calibre and the pieces were physically heavy, so the emplacements needed to be properly constructed. The guns were also difficult to move about, which often meant a delay before they arrived.

Naturally, the defenders would try to disturb all the enemy preparations by making occasional sorties and using every weapon at their disposal. Apart from the usual artillery and muskets, there were rampart pieces, which were large calibre muskets, or swivel guns. When the besiegers had constructed their batteries they would begin their bombardment using various types of ammunition. Round-shot could be used in its natural state to batter down the outer walls of the fortifications, or it might be heated over a fire until it was glowing red in order to cause fires among the buildings inside the fortress. Shells were also used, fired from mortars, whose high trajectory made it easy for them to clear the walls. These large calibre bombs caused big enough explosions to bring down small buildings.

Under cover of the bombardment, work would begin on the trenches that would permit the attackers to get near the walls in relative safety before they stormed them. The first step was a 'sap', which was a small trench dug by about four 'sappers' working as a team. They used baskets of earth, called 'gabions', to protect them from small-arms fire, and continually pushed forwards, leaving others to deepen and widen the sap into a proper trench. Eventually a system of trenches would be dug, starting with access trenches, which went towards the walls, but zig-zagged to give protection from enemy fire. At diminishing distances from the walls there would be two or three 'parallels' lying concentrically with the walls, in which the storming parties could stay under cover until the moment of attack. This would almost inevitably be horribly expensive in terms of human life, and both sides would often prefer to conclude a siege with a capitulation when the result seemed to be inevitable.

NOTES

1. Also attributed to W. Prescott.
2. Hanger, G., Col. *Colonel G. H. to all Sportsmen ... etc.* London, 1814, p.

205. There is also an interesting comment by Marshal Berthier on the inaccuracy of muskets in Rothenberg, G. E. *The Art of Warfare in the Age of Napoleon*. London, 1980, p. 65–6.

3.   It was a style of warfare that was eventually rendered obsolete by improvements in the range, accuracy and rapidity of small-arms fire, though such formations were still occasionally used during the First World War, as is proved by a photograph in Keegan, J. *The Face of Battle*. London, 1976 (plate 8).

4.   See Mauvillon, J., von. *Geschichte Ferdinands Herzogs von Braunschweig-Lüneburg*. Leipzig, 1794, II, p. 281. Quoted in Duffy, C. J. *The Military Experience in the Age of Reason*. London, 1987, p. 201.

5.   See ibid., pp. 95 and 274.

6.   It should be pointed out that the word 'big' probably did not mean quite the same then as it does now. It is noteworthy that the minimum height for a cuirassier in the French army during the Empire was 5 pieds 4 pouces, or just over 5 feet 8 inches (see Johnson, D. *Napoleon's Cavalry and its Leaders*. London, 1978, p. 160). Napoleon Bonaparte, who is often referred to as being 'small', stood about 5 feet 6½ inches (see Cronin, V. *Napoleon*. London, 1990, p. 179).

3

THE AUSTRIAN ARMY

It would be impossible to comprehend fully the successes and failures of the adversaries during the 1796–7 campaign in Italy without knowing something about the general characteristics of the opposing armies.

The difference between the French and Austrian armies of the Revolutionary Wars could be summarised by saying that they were essentially facing in opposite directions: the French towards the future, and the Austrian towards the past. This is not surprising if one considers the conditions that moulded them.

The Austrian army was effectively the product of a whole series of reforms begun during the 1740s and 50s, when the main task facing its leaders was to mould a force capable of protecting Austrian territory from that most dangerous opponent, the Prussian army of Frederick the Great. The awful string of defeats to which Frederick had subjected them at the beginning of Maria Theresa's reign had amply demonstrated that the army was in no fit state to contend with an adversary of this calibre, and would have to be drastically improved if it were not to be swept away. A process of reform was therefore begun which touched almost every aspect of military life and continued throughout the reign.

The reforms were largely successful. By the time of the Seven Years War the army had improved enough to hand out one or two authentic drubbings to Frederick, and in the War of the Bavarian Succession it managed to neutralise him almost completely by taking up defensive positions so formidable that Frederick dared not attack it. But this period of adaptation was followed by one of stagnation. In the 1790s the army therefore found itself stuck with a set of attitudes and methods that had been adopted to suit the style of warfare of forty years previously. Much to its dismay, it was to be faced with yet another period of adaptation in order to counter the threat posed by Napoleon Bonaparte.

Before we examine the reforms carried out under Maria Theresa, and their consequences, it will be as well to look at one of the unchanging aspects of the Austrian army. That is to say, the fact that it was hardly 'Austrian' at all. Indeed, it was as heterogeneous as the Habsburg empire itself, and drew its troops from a wide variety of nations and linguistic groups. This was not unique in the 18th century, and many armies had their quotas of troops who were more or less foreign. But no other army had quite such a range, with its extraordinary amalgam of Austrians, Germans, Belgians, Hungarians, Poles, Bohemians, Moravians, Italians, Croatians, Transylvanians, Irishmen, and sundry others,[1] all trying to speak 'army German', with varying degrees of success.

In the regular army, some order was brought to this chaos by putting the men into two basic types of regiment, 'German' and 'Hungarian', though these were very loose categories. German regiments included those recruited in Belgium and Italy, while the Hungarian included units that were largely Croatian and Slavonian. Apart from the areas where they were recruited, the difference between German and Hungarian units was largely one of uniform, although Hungarian infantry regiments were larger and had a total of four battalions instead of three. In the cavalry, all the Hungarian regiments were hussars. There was a great deal of rivalry between the two 'nationalities', and troops of one kind often disliked being put under the command of a general from the other.

Apart from the regular troops, the Austrian army was able to call on a number of less conventional types of soldiery: the Grenz (Border) regiments, and the Frei-Corps. Collectively, they were often referred to as 'Croats', though they were not all of Croatian origins. Earlier in the 18th century they had garnered a fearsome reputation for their wildness and readiness to loot and plunder, though it is debatable whether or not they were any worse than the rougher elements of other armies. They sometimes wore red cloaks, which became symbolic of their bloodthirsty and turbulent nature. General Bigarré, who calls them 'eaters of raw meat', said that 'at that time, the Red Cloaks, who were nearly all Turkish deserters, did not take prisoners at all'.[2] This was probably something of an exaggeration, caused by rumour. However, there is no doubt that the Croats were extremely tough and brave soldiers, and in the case of the Grenzers, also very loyal to the Habsburgs.

The Grenzers came from what were called the 'Military Borders', which were zones of Hungary, Transylvania, Croatia and Slavonia that were subject to attack by the Turks. Any man living in these areas was expected to participate in their defence, so effectively the entire adult male population was militarised. When there was no war against the Turks, the Military Borders were a useful source of manpower for service elsewhere, and a number of composite battalions served in Italy, where they generally did well. The Grenzers provided the army with a kind of light infantry and were particularly suited to scouting and skirmishing in open order as well as having their uses in mountain warfare, in which the regular regiments did not excel.

The Frei-Corps were short-lived units, raised in time of war and recruited in the provinces, being disbanded when peace came. In a few cases they were very irregular troops, and it has been said that their conduct and appearance was sometimes reminiscent of bandits from the wilder fringes of Europe. In fact their dress was very varied, and while some units had costumes that were more Turkish or Albanian than Western, others wore uniforms that were identical in style with those of the regular army. This reflected the diversity of the areas where they were recruited, from Dalmatia to Holland. Like the Grenzers, they provided light infantry, though some units were mixed, and had cavalry as well. Two battalions of Frei-Corps Gyulay were prominent in many actions in Italy during the campaign of 1796–7. This corps was composed of Montenegrins, Liccaners, and recruits from the Austrian littoral, and had been formed in 1789 by Josef Vukassovich, of whom we shall hear more later.

Let us now deal with the reforms carried out in the middle of the century, of which it will be necessary to limit ourselves to examining a few of the most significant.

One of the single most important reforms was the issuing of new infantry regulations in 1749. These established uniformity of drill, tactics and words of command where previously every regiment had used its own version. They were modified in 1769, but they laid the foundation for the drill and tactics that the infantry was to use during the Revolutionary Wars. The initial reform was introduced partly in an attempt to replicate what were seen as the key factors in Prussian success, namely precise, rapid movement and intensity of fire, deriving from superiority in drill. It was not quite as simple as that, but more than one army imitated Prussian drill and discipline in the hope of equalling their fighting record.

When the new Austrian drill appeared, Frederick's ambassador informed him that: 'In general it is modelled according to the drill of Your Majesty's troops, but several officers have assured me that the Austrians are going about things in such a way that they will never come near, let alone equal, the success of the Prussians.'[3] They were largely right, and some years later, the French Count de Mirabeau made the following observations:

The Austrian army looks splendid under arms. It is well dressed, well equipped and well armed. It is composed of tall and active soldiers. Yet with all this it is deficient in co-ordination, uniformity and training. It simply does not know how to move. You cannot see an Austrian line advance three hundred paces without losing its alignment and intervals and falling into grievous disorder — something which would be inconceivable in the Prussian army. An Austrian column cannot march without getting strung out, or form into line without having to extend or close itself up.[4]

There were various possible reasons for these failings. Mirabeau himself thought that it was largely due to the fact that an Austrian company had only four officers and fourteen NCOs to control some 230 men (wartime establishment), whereas a Prussian or French company had roughly half that number of men but a similar total of officers and NCOs. If the Austrian arrangement was less than ideal on the parade-ground, it was a recipe for disaster in combat. It is clear that even a small number of casualties could leave a large number of men without anyone to lead them, with potentially catastrophic effects. Units where the ratio of leaders to led was more favourable would be less susceptible to disruptions in the chain of command, and would adapt to setbacks caused by casualties more easily.

Another culprit was the regulations themselves. Indeed, in common with many reforms they went too far, and from being in a situation in which there was too little uniformity, the Austrian army now became obsessed with it. In fact the regulations proved to be far too complex and went into a lot of useless detail. The instructions for volley firing were staggeringly complicated, with drills for every situation, including some rather unlikely ones. There were procedures for firing from inside trenches, ramparts or sunken roads, in thick woods, when crossing bridges, and even when in a street during a riot – evidently different from firing in a street in other circumstances.

Others put the blame on training, which had never been one of the strengths of the Austrian army. It seems there was a tendency to concentrate on the wrong thing, a desire to achieve the polished appearance which had so mesmerised people when looking at Frederick's Prussians. An Austrian officer who was captured in Italy in 1795 made some telling remarks on the subject:

> From Loano I watched the manoeuvres in which the [French] troops were being prepared for warfare on the plain. I could have wished that an Austrian general had been present. He would have sadly missed what was in his eyes the mark of the real soldier, smartness of bearing. In the Austrian service every one of these men would have had to be taught for a whole year before reaching the required standard and many a poor devil would have been beaten to death before he could have been called a soldier ... Apart from this the evolutions went off well and to the purpose. What with us is unattainable by long practice and stark fear is accomplished here naturally and simply on a mere word.[5]

He also had illuminating things to say about the consequences of too rigid insistence on conventional drill and the problems this gave the Austrian troops in mountain warfare:

> On such occasions the clumsiest were the new troops accustomed only to stiff mechanical order, who having no idea of fighting

beyond what they had learned on the drill ground, regarded the slightest disorder as the end of all things.[6]

Although they sustained a number of defeats during the 1790s against French armies using unconventional tactics, the Austrians remained wedded to the idea that the methods that had served Frederick so well were still the best. In 1800 a senior officer stated his conviction that their troops were most likely to be successful by advancing 'courageously in close formation, with bands playing, and keeping their formation'.[7] Insistence on this factor could have extensive repercussions. In January 1797, when the Austrians were preparing to attack Bonaparte's army, even strategic choices of great importance were influenced by the belief that the Austrian troops' standard of drill was not good enough to permit them to face the French on the open plains.

If the reforms of the infantry did not quite give the results that had been hoped for, that of the artillery was an outstanding success. It was supervised by Field Marshal Liechtenstein, a veteran of the Italian campaign of 1745–6, who drew on his immense personal fortune to finance experiments with new designs of cannon. The fruits of these were seen in 1753, when an entirely new range of guns was introduced, making the Austrian artillery the best in Europe for a time. Perhaps the only omission was that improvements in hardware were not accompanied by equal developments in tactics, and the Austrians were to persist in the old-fashioned system of dispersing their guns to give close support to the infantry, instead of massing them in batteries, a more effective method which was adopted earliest by the French and English.

The overhaul of the army's administration was less than successful. At the centre of the problem lay an organisation called the Hofkriegsrath (Court Council of War), which was responsible for the routine administration of the army. It was over-large, and usually directed by semi-senile generals who had rather lost touch with the needs of armies in the field. An example of the difficulties of working with the Hofkriegsrath and the contempt it aroused are to be found in a letter that the Austrian chief minister, Baron Thugut, sent to Count

Colloredo in July 1795. He notes that a request had been made to supply money for cannon-balls and other necessaries for the siege train:

> Our sublime Hofkriegsrath replies to Baron Lilien that, not knowing the plan of operations, it cannot say if cannon-balls will be needed, that he must ask Field Marshal Clerfayt, but in any case it will not be able to give him any money. If I were to wish to give myself the pleasure of mocking these people, it would no doubt be easy to reply to the note of the honourable Hofkriegsrath: 'Gentlemen, as to whether there will be any sieges or not, I think nobody knows, and myself less than others, because this absolutely depends on events. But as by order of His Majesty you have already bought for the service of this artillery many horses, I think that you might, or might have, concluded, without asking Field Marshal Clerfayt to give his opinion on his honour and on his conscience, that the intention of His Majesty was that this artillery was in any case to be provided with the necessary, in order that, if the occasion should offer, one might be able to use it, because what will you use it for if there are no cannon-balls?' It seems to me that there is absolutely no need to be a Grand Cross of the Order of Maria Theresa to conceive or divine such a thing![18]

Although efforts were made to streamline the bureaucracy, it is no exaggeration to say that the whole army was overwhelmed with paperwork. By the 1770s a company of Croats was obliged to keep 72 different files and send out two weekly reports, ten monthly, two quarterly, and a half-yearly return. During the Seven Years War an officer even complained that Field Marshal Daun's effectiveness as army commander was being jeopardised by the amount of report-writing he had to do. Most armies have had trouble with excessive bureaucracy from time to time, but the Austrian army had more than most, with predictably deadening effects.

Maria Theresa and her advisers also made attempts to improve the officer corps. It was here that they encountered their greatest difficulties, and registered their most important failure. The fundamental problem with the officers was that there were not enough of them, and those they had were often not good enough. Something had to be done to encourage volunteers of the right kind, but as there was not much money available other incentives had to be sought.

These included a number of measures that were intended to increase the standing of the officer class in the eyes of Austrian society, who did not view them with much favour. In 1751, officers were permitted to attend court wearing uniform under court dress. Later the need to wear court dress was removed altogether for officers in uniform. Six years later Maria Theresa decreed that noble status would be awarded to officers with 30 years' good service, and in the same year a new decoration, the Order of Maria Theresa, was instituted especially for outstanding service by officers in the field. Nevertheless, there was no great rush of applicants for commissions, and that same year her chief minister, Kaunitz, could still point out that 'the lack of officers is one of the principal defects of the Imperial army'. It continued to be so in the 1790s.

An attempt was also made to regularise promotion when, in 1765, the Hofkriegsrath took over the appointment of all officers above the rank of captain. This removed a source of corrupt practices whereby wealthy officers could hasten their progress up the ladder at the expense of poorer colleagues, but it also made promotion a cumbersome, bureaucratic affair and meant that the general commanding an army had little scope for advancing those who were making a good showing during a campaign. Overall, it has to be said that the Austrian army seems to have been poor at recognising and rewarding meritorious officers with promotion, a characteristic that was hardly likely to attract enterprising and ambitious men to the service.

A further initiative was the opening in November 1752 of the military academy at Wiener-Neustadt, under the direction of Leopold Daun. The promise of free board and education did little to entice pupils from among the high nobility, who continued to regard military service as unattractive, and the academy's effect on the intellectual quality of the officer corps seems to have been limited. Here, perhaps, we find ourselves faced with one of the more puzzling characteristics of the Austrian officers, which is their attitude to book-learning. A

Frenchman remarked that 'they look upon study as a tacit avowal of incapacity',[9] and they seemed to have no interest in committing their thoughts about their profession to paper. Strangely, the period of reform was accompanied by almost nothing in the way of published memoirs, histories or works dealing with the theory of warfare. This contrasted strongly with the French and Prussians, who wrote a great deal about military affairs.

Given the prevalence of such attitudes, it is not surprising that generalship made no great strides during the period of reform. Ideas of how to conduct a war were dominated by the cautious methods of Daun and Lacy, who both favoured the defensive and avoidance of battle unless there was an overwhelming chance of success. This approach was also encouraged by the habit of calling a council of war to discuss any significant course of action, a procedure which militated against spontaneity. The calling of a council of war was made a formal requirement in the army regulations of 1769, so even the most enterprising generals found themselves obliged to bring together their colleagues for a discussion before they could proceed to act. Councils of war were made all the more ineffective by the personal feuds and cliques that riddled the officer corps, such that, on occasions, it seemed that more attention was devoted to ruining the plans of some fellow-officer than to defeating the enemy.

The ineffectiveness of the attempts to improve the quality of the Austrian officer corps as a whole may perhaps be judged from a contemporary letter. In April 1795, Colonel Dietrichstein, an engineer officer who was one of Baron Thugut's most valued informants, wrote the following comments about the army in Germany:

The soldiers, though they lack everything, have the best spirit and the best will possible. The officers put up with the misery, and the fact that they have not yet received the pay for this army, less patiently. The officers, above all of the infantry, argue a great deal, get mixed up in politics, and express improper and reprehensible opinions in front of the soldiers, and publicly among themselves. The generals give them the lead. Where does all this come from? In part from our misfortunes, but above all from the bad choice of officers, from the excessive number of officers of fortune, from promoted NCOs, from the bad education of our people of quality and from our ruinous system of promotion by seniority, which means that we do not have any generals and few colonels who are active. It also means that when entering the service, one can be sure, provided one does not steal, to go through all the ranks, and even arrive at high command. This stifles talent, discourages merit, and takes away all emulation ... His Majesty wrote to Monsieur de Clerfayt that he would be master to choose and employ, but the General finds that there is not much to choose. We do not have anyone who is inventive among our highest in rank. On the day of battle, Alvinczy and Wartensleben will second Monsieur de Clerfayt perfectly, and will lead the troops into Hell, if necessary, on his orders. Among the generals, La Tour, Werneck and Kray distinguish themselves, but at Ourte the first showed that he must not be left master of the dispositions. Messieurs de Kinsky and Colloredo are rather for staying on the defensive.[10]

To add to this unhappy picture, it has to be said that more than a few officers seemed to have little sense of duty, and some were even seriously suspected of treason. In the same month that the letter above was written, Thugut complained of one such:

The journey of this man is in effect firstly a new proof of the indiscipline that reigns in the army, where the senior officers, at the moment of the opening of the campaign, leave their corps to tour around and make journeys. And what is he going to do in Switzerland? Is this the time to go and visit his relatives, when he should be in the saddle? Is it more solidly to arrange his correspondence and communications with the interior of France, as he was violently suspected of during the first campaign on the Rhine under Mr de Esterházy?[11]

42

A further problem was that the officer corps was generally backward-looking. Many of the officers had grown old in the service, and the generals were mostly veterans of the Seven Years War. Their previous experiences naturally coloured their views on how to fight a war, and many of them proudly preserved attitudes that had been formed when war was touched with a certain chivalry. A classic example of this code of behaviour is provided by a well-known incident from the battle of Fontenoy in 1745:

> This engagement took place at such close quarters that the English officers, at the moment of halting their troops, saluted us with their hats in their hands. Ours having replied in the same way to this courtesy, a captain of the English guards, who was Lord Charles Hay, stepped out of the ranks and advanced. The Comte d'Auteroche, lieutenant of the grenadiers, then went to meet him. 'Monsieur,' said the captain, 'have your men fire.' – 'No, Monsieur, replied d'Auteroche, 'we never fire first.' And having saluted each other again, they each went back to their ranks. The English fire began immediately, and with such liveliness, that it cost us more than a thousand men in one go, and a great disorder resulted from it.[12]

It took a long time for some Austrian officers to realise that noble behaviour needed to be tempered with pragmatism, especially when your opponent was hell-bent on gaining every possible advantage from a situation. The message had clearly still not got through to General Kienmayer when, in 1805, he informed Marshal Murat, Napoleon's cavalry commander, that his troops desperately needed a rest, and therefore requested him not to advance on Vienna too rapidly.

These old-fashioned attitudes also contributed to the slowness with which the Austrian army moved. In the middle of the century the aristocratic officer had always maintained a lifestyle in the field that was consonant with his social position. This meant transporting large amounts of gear such as tents, and even porcelain, accompanied by the necessary servants to look after them. The Duke of Cumberland, for example, travelled around with 145 tons of baggage. This was not looked on as showing off, but rather as necessary for a man of high position, and to do otherwise would have brought contempt rather than admiration. While everybody else did the same thing, it had little effect on the army's performance, but once the enemy started to do things differently, it had grave consequences, as an Austrian noted:

> Almost every day our army loses half a march to the French. Their soldiers carry the same load as our men, but what an effort it takes us to get under way! The French officer accompanies his troops on foot, and if necessary he carries his pack himself. In our army, on the other hand, every company had a whole tail of carts just to transport the officers' baggage. If possible, these gentlemen would like to bring along warm stoves and arm-chairs as well.[13]

The slowness with which the army moved was probably also a consequence of slow decision-making on the part of the commanders, but once again this was no doubt influenced by the style of war of the middle of the century which tended to be more leisurely and more predictable. Some Austrian officers, who had not fought a European power since 1779, were disturbed to find that things had changed in the 1790s. Bonaparte himself provides an illustration of their bewilderment with an anecdote concerning the early part of his 1796 campaign. It is taken from his memoirs, which were written in the third person:

> Napoleon, in his nightly rounds, encountered a bivouac of prisoners, where there was a garrulous old Hungarian officer, whom he asked how matters went on with them. The old captain could not deny that they went on very badly. 'But,' he added, 'there is no understanding it at all. We have to do with a young general who is this moment before us, then again behind us, then again on our flanks — one does not know where to place oneself. This manner of making war is insufferable and violates all usage and custom.'[14]

This was rather like the cry of a gentleman who had gone to fight a duel in the proper ritualised fashion, and found an opponent who insisted on firing before he was told to, and hid behind trees to make a more difficult target. Unfortunately, in this case there was no umpire.

This no doubt paints a rather negative picture of the Austrian officer class, but the better officers should not be forgotten. They were courageous, hard-working, devoted to the service, and often gave a good account of themselves under unfavourable conditions. Nor were they idiots: if their decisions sometimes seem faulty, in many cases they were acting according to a professional training and experience that was no longer in tune with the times. If they had still been fighting Frederick they might well have done much better.

NOTES

1. Just to illustrate the point, Duffy, C. J. *The Army of Maria Theresa*. London, 1977, p. 50, has an interesting table showing the origins of the 110 men in one of the companies of IR (Infantry Regiment) Marschall (no. 18) at the end of November 1756. There were: one Dutchman, one Slavonian, three Swiss, four Hungarians, eight Silesians, eight Austrians, twelve Moravians, thirty Germans and forty-three Bohemians. Seven of them were Lutherans, five were Calvinists, and the rest were Catholics.

2. Bigarré, A.-J. *Mémoires du général Bigarré: aide de camp du roi Joseph, 1775–1813*. Paris, 1893, p. 78.

3. Quoted in Duffy, op. cit., p. 76.

4. Système militaire de la Prusse, London 1788, p. 226. Quoted in Duffy, op. cit., pp. 80–1.

5. Wilkinson, S. *The Rise of General Bonaparte*. Oxford, 1930, p. 89.

6. Ibid.

7. Baron Zach, quoted in Haythornthwaite, P. J. *Austrian Army of the Napoleonic Wars (1): Infantry, Men-at-Arms*. London, 1986, p. 9.

8. Vivenot, A., Ritter von. *Vertrauliche Briefe des Freiherrn von Thugut*. Vienna, 1872, I, pp. 243–44.

9. Quoted in Duffy, op. cit., p. 45.

10. Vivenot, A., Ritter von. *Thugut, Clerfayt und Wurmser. Original-Documente aus dem k. k. Haus-, Hof-, und Staats-Archiv und dem k. k. Kriegs-Archiv in Wien vom Juli 1794–Feb 1797*. Vienna, 1869, pp. 119–20.

11. Vivenot, 1872, op. cit., I, p. 204.

12. Fournier, E. *L'ésprit dans l'histoire. Recherches et curiosités sur les mots historiques*. Paris, 1879 p. 356.

13. Arndt, E. M. *Reisen durch einen Theil Teutschlands*. Leipzig, 1804, p. 180. Quoted in Duffy, C. J. *Austerlitz, 1805*. London, 1977, p. 29.

14. Napoleon. *Mémoires pour servir à l'histoire de France, sous le regne de Napoléon, écrits sous sa dictée à Sainte-Hélène, par les généraux qui ont partagé sa captivité*. Paris, 1829, I, p. 212.

4

THE FRENCH ARMY

The French army that Bonaparte served in was, like the Austrian army of the time, also the product of reforms. But, those which had the greatest effect on the French army were political or social, not technical, and they gave birth to an organisation that was in many ways the total antithesis of the Austrian army. While the latter was deeply conservative, the French army was, in spirit if not in equipment and tactics, one of the first modern armies. It was an army like no other in Europe, and owed its existence to the Revolution.

Before we deal with the changes brought about by that great social upheaval, however, we should look at some of the work done by reformers and theorists in the period leading up to it, some of which was indeed technical in nature, and some of which addressed issues that would be brought to the fore by the Revolution.

The first development really dated from the middle of the Seven Years War, when one of the French commanders took the step of split-ting his army into sub-units called 'divisions'. Something like this had been done before, but the system now began to evolve into a perma-nent arrangement by which certain units were placed together under the command of a particular general for the duration of a campaign, instead of the army being a single amorphous bloc, from which marching columns were formed on a day-to-day basis, commanded by whoever happened to be available at the time. The divisional system encouraged teamwork, and made the organisation of movement easier and more flexible, thereby contributing to the speed at which the whole army could move. Not only that, but the system was to be central to Bonaparte's strategic method, which exploited carefully timed and co-ordinated manoeuvres by the various component blocs of the army in order to deceive the enemy as to his intentions, to make rapid switches of his main strength from one place to another, and to execute turning movements.

The period during and after the Seven Years War also saw plentiful discussion of tactical matters, much of it focused on the respective merits of the column and the line, and a number of books were published championing various theories. The most famous was Hippolyte de Guibert's *Essai général de tactique*, published anonymously in 1770. It was a work that Bonaparte held in high consideration, and, as we shall see later, it was more than just a book about how to move troops around. This theoretical discussion was backed up by practical work of a surprisingly modern kind, which sought to assess the worth of the different arrangements that were being propounded. This was supervised by Marshal de Broglie, one of the leading reformers in the army, who conducted a number of experiments involving realistic situations, with troops designated to play the enemy. These experiments were not limited to an investigation of formal tactics, and trials were also conducted using skirmishers, thus anticipating a style of warfare that was to be very important to the Revolutionary army. The outcome of these manoeuvres was adjudged by umpires, and reports were written for the illumination of participants and others.

The eventual result was not a victory for either the line or the column. Instead, the advantages and disadvantages of each were admitted, and a tactical arrangement combining elements of both, called *ordre mixte*, was devised. This refusal to be restrictive chimed in with the views that Bonaparte was later to express, commenting: 'One cannot and must not prescribe anything absolutely. *There is no natural order of battle among modern armies.*'[1] Eventually, *ordre mixte* made its way into the drill book of 1791, which was the basis of formal French tactics during the Revolutionary and Napoleonic Wars.

The lessons of the Seven Years War also brought major improvements to the equipment of the artillery. By the time of the Revolution the French artillery was arguably the best in Europe, thanks partly to the efforts of General de Gribeauval, whose new designs came into use in 1777. De Gribeauval had served with the Austrian artillery, and the designs he produced were very similar to the guns he had seen during his time with them. They had one significant advantage over the Austrian weapons, in that they were all of slightly larger calibre, but it was not just the weaponry that was superior. In terms of organisation and tactics, France had moved ahead of other nations. This was largely due to the influence of Baron Du Teil, who ran the artillery school at Auxonne, where Napoleon Bonaparte spent a vitally important part of his early career. It was here that he learned that artillery should be used in large batteries, and that its work had to be co-ordinated with that of the infantry and the cavalry.

It may also have been at Auxonne that Bonaparte first came across the work of another great French theorist, Pierre Bourcet. He had served in Italy from 1733 to 1735 and again from 1745 to 1746, and was the military adviser and companion of both Marshals de Broglie and de Maillebois. He is particularly remembered for his *Principes de la guerre de montagne*, which was written in about 1766 but never published, and for some important work on the organisation of the French staff. As we shall see in a later chapter, Bonaparte's knowledge of Bourcet's writings was crucial to his success.

As we have mentioned, some of the French theorists of the time did not limit their written discussions to purely technical matters, but went far beyond them, ranging into the territory of politics and social questions. The two most noteworthy examples were de Guibert in his *Essai*, and Joseph Servan.[2]

Among the ideas de Guibert put forward, one that greatly interests historians foreshadows developments during the Revolution: it seemed to de Guibert that the army needed to change its fundamental nature, and what was needed was an army that was closer to the people and had their patriotic spirit. He saw advantages in a mass army using new tactics that would make the best use of weight of numbers and the enthusiasm of the soldiers. He also advocated fighting a war of manoeuvre, which was precisely the type of warfare favoured by Bonaparte and shunned by the Austrians.

Servan disagreed with the idea of mass armies, but still saw the need for a new type of soldier. The title of his work, *Le soldat citoyen*, published in 1781, gives a clue to his thinking. When he wrote it, the military were usually seen as being outside normal civilian society, and often antagonistic to it. Servan wished to see the soldiery not estranged from this society, but part of it. He felt that when there was peace the soldier should be engaged in normal civilian work, so that he was seen to be making a useful contribution to society instead of being a burden. In other words, the soldier ought to be a citizen first and a soldier second. To make this a reality would obviously have required considerable changes in the law and raised the issue of how to give the soldiers the same rights as civilians while conserving military discipline.

There was no shortage of ideas about political reform of the military, therefore, but it was not until the Revolution that those ideas were seriously discussed in government circles, and political change in the army was made reality. Three months after the fall of the Bastille a special Military Committee of the National Assembly was formed. Among its members was Mirabeau, one of the most influential figures of the early stages of the Revolution, and the committee rapidly became a well-spring of reforms, theories and the legislation to put them into practice.

The principal goal of these was not just to create an army that was better at doing its job, but also one that was in harmony with the new state that was being born, in which certain basic rights were guaranteed, while privilege and social distinctions were being rapidly eroded. Initially two things were deemed important: to give the soldiers the same rights as other citizens, and to create a national army in which the soldier's primary allegiance would be to France, not to a region or an individual. In fact the idea of serving the country was one of the recurring themes of the reforms.

The legal rights were not obtained all at once, but a series of changes gave the French soldier basic freedoms, such as the right to marry without the permission of his commanding officer, and to be active in political clubs, which soldiers belonging to other armies in Europe did not have. A new disciplinary code also followed, so that the French army was one of the few that did not rely on a host of medieval punishments like running the gauntlet and breaking on the wheel. The soldier's contract was also changed. Under the former régime, when a soldier joined the army he engaged in a personal contract with his captain, an arrangement that had a feudal smell about it and was soon thrown out by the Military Committee. From 1791 the contract became one between the soldier and his country.

Each of these reforms had its own importance, but possibly the most significant alteration the French army underwent concerned the relationship between officer and soldier. The new government favoured *égalité* and *fraternité*, and that was not consistent with the officer being in any way superior to, or different from, the troops. This created many problems, as the political goal of equality was basically incompatible with military efficiency, but eventually it became obvious that an efficient army could not stop and take a vote on everything, and radicalism was rejected in favour of a conventional system of ranks.

The big difference was that there was no longer an impassable barrier between those who commanded and those who obeyed. Before the Revolution, an officer candidate had had to produce a certificate showing four generations of noble ancestors, whereas now anyone could be an officer, provided he could read and write. Among the National Volunteers, officers were chosen by the unusual method of election by the soldiers. Those who came to prominence as a result included Joubert, one of the heroes of Italy, and there were many others of similar ilk who rose to the highest ranks. Among the regulars, the removal of social barriers meant that NCOs could be promoted, which was not unknown in other armies, but was certainly rare. In France it became commonplace. In this shake-up there were some men who had been sergeants for years who quite suddenly became generals, and proved to be good ones (like Massena) and also, perhaps more surprisingly, noble officers who were stripped of their rank but re-enlisted as common soldiers and worked their way up again (Lasalle being one example).

The results of this innovation were variable, at first. Favouritism and corruption were just as common then as they have always been where some men wield power and others seek advancement, so promotion was not always on merit. In particular, the highest ranks were often given to those who were loudest in support of the government of the moment. Notwithstanding, the cream mostly floated towards the top, a process that was partly assisted in 1793–4 by the drastic measure of removing the heads of generals who were deemed to have failed.

Voltaire had sarcastically commented that in England it was necessary to shoot an admiral from time to time in order to encourage the others, but the English had never been as drastic as the French were during the Terror. Among those who died were Josephine's first husband, Alexandre de Beauharnais, while others defected to the enemy to avoid the same fate. This period of extremism did not last, but the general principle of promotion on merit became an accepted feature of the army. It proved to be a useful tool for Bonaparte, and allowed him to effect a gradual and subtle reshaping of his army in Italy while the campaign was in progress.

Thus, the network of relationships in the French army was fundamentally different from that in any other in Europe, and it may be assumed that professional soldiers were probably more energetic and enthusiastic than in many other armies because they felt that they could achieve advancement through their own efforts. The Revolutionary army could, perhaps, be called one of the first modern armies officered by professional *fighting* men. The aristocratic officers of the early 18th-century army served because it was a habit or a tradition for the nobility to provide officers, and they frequently tried to maintain their aristocratic lifestyle in the field, even going so far as to take furniture with them. Such men were aristocrats first and officers second. The Revolutionary army had officers who had made their way up through fighting, expected to have to carry on fighting, and in many cases even hoped to carry on because it was their only chance of rapid advancement.[3] Antoine-Marie Lavallette, who became Bonaparte's ADC during the Italian campaign, showed these tendencies in strong measure. He had originally gone to Italy to serve another general and was very upset when he found he was not in the middle of the fighting:

> I was persuaded that General d'Hilliers was employed in the active army, and on the way I caressed the most brilliant illusions of glory and advancement. What was my consternation to find him governor of Lombardy! Once more I would have to bury myself in the paperwork of the staff, condemned to distribute the bulletins of our victories, busy myself with the thousand details

of office-work, which is so annoying to a military man, and end up by not daring to say that I had been with the Army of Italy, because I had never shared its dangers or its triumphs. I only had my sword for my fortune, and could I hope for advancement if I had never merited it? These thoughts afflicted me deeply, and made me solicit the command of a company of infantry in a demi-brigade of the advance-guard.[4]

Generally speaking, there was plenty of drive in the French officer corps, and men expected to be appreciated for their energy and dedication. Some of the officers of other armies who felt that French officers were 'not gentlemen' were entirely missing the point. War had become a profession, not a gentlemanly sport, and the French were more interested in winning than in creating a good impression. Because of this, technical expertise at all levels of command also became more important than it had ever been before, and French commanders rarely handled their troops anything but competently.[5]

What applied to the officers was equally true for the men. The ordinary soldier knew that higher ranks were not closed to him and he therefore had incentives for joining the army and fighting hard. Before the Revolution the ordinary soldier usually joined out of desperation, had nothing to gain from war apart from a little plunder, and everything to lose – which was still the case in most European armies. But in the Revolutionary army the ordinary soldiers were the other part of the new equation, and if the officers were a different breed of men, so were the troops. As the Revolution progressed, there was an influx of people who would not previously have chosen to be soldiers, most of whom went into the infantry. They came into the army either by volunteering, or through conscription.

At critical moments of the war, when it looked as if France might be overwhelmed by her enemies and the gains of the Revolution lost, the government made appeals for volunteers. These brought in large masses of 'citizen soldiers' who were very varied in their abilities and level of enthusiasm. The politicians of the period habitually speak of the troops as being imbued with Revolutionary zeal, but this is clearly a somewhat simplified picture. Not all of them found themselves in the army because of their 'pure and enlightened patriotism', and any generalisations about their attitudes can always be contradicted by specific examples of individuals who held different beliefs. To what extent the members of the army shared the ideals of the Revolution, or felt a patriotic urge to defend their country, is a thorny question. Undoubtedly some of them did go to war for patriotic reasons, and others for reasons concerned with a code of honour that is no longer understood by most people. A proportion would have gone because they had to, and some would have gone because a war offered an opportunity for advancement and financial gain. Some, no doubt, would have gone because they actually enjoyed fighting. Probably, many had mixed motives, including Bonaparte, who undoubtedly wanted to serve his country, but probably wanted to further his own career more than anything.

None the less, the French army was, to some degree at least, inspired by a patriotic spirit and sense of nationhood. The decree of *la patrie en danger* had at least some success in mobilising the people in defence of the country. By contrast, this kind of involvement was lacking on the Austrian side in the 1790s, and still had not developed at a later period. The French invasion of Austria in 1809 did not cause any surge of popular desire to take arms and defend the country, as had occurred in France during the Revolution. In similar vein the Austrian volunteer battalions of 1797 were enthusiastic in words, and not so forward when they had to act. It is illuminating of their attitudes that one battalion set off for war, marched two miles, then decided to go home for the night.[6]

The influx of enormous numbers of volunteers, and later of conscripts, presented the French army with the difficulty of training them. The American War of Independence had shown that in times of emergency a man could be taught to load and fire a musket in a fairly short time, and then you had some kind of soldier. He was certainly not the kind who could go through the elaborate manoeuvres of classic 18th-century warfare, but that was not always a disadvantage. If his commander was able to exploit the strengths and cover the weaknesses of this type of soldier, the results could be very good. If complex battle manoeuvres were totally beyond them it was necessary to improvise.

Improvisation led to the adoption of what David Chandler has called 'horde tactics' with the widespread use of great clouds of skirmishers provided by the volunteers, while the old regular troops manoeuvred and fought in classic formations, marched in step, and went through the usual evolutions according to the drill book. A general impression of how these tactics worked is given in a rather idealised passage by General Foy:

> The action was opened by a cloud of sharpshooters, some mounted, some on foot, who were sent forward to carry out a general rather than a minutely-regulated mission; they harassed the enemy, escaping from his superior numbers by their speed, from the effect of his cannon by their dispersal ... It is rare for an army to have placed its flanks in impregnable positions; in any case every position has within itself, or in the arrangement of the troops that defend it, some gaps that favour an attacker. The sharpshooters would fall on them through inspiration ... Once the chink in the armour had been discovered, everyone concentrated his effort there. The horse artillery ... would gallop up and open fire with canister at point-blank range. The attacking force would move off in the indicated direction, the infantry in column (for it had little fire to offer), the cavalry in regiments or squadrons, ready to make its presence felt anywhere or everywhere as required. Then, when the hail of enemy bullets or cannon-balls began to slacken ... The soldiers would begin to run forwards ... the drums beat the charge; the sky would ring to a thousand battle-cries constantly repeated: '*En avant! En avant! Vive la République!*'[7]

The results obtained by these unusual methods were better than might have been expected, and proved disconcerting for the enemy. A French émigré who was on 'the other side' watched in amazement as a division of the Army of the Moselle made an attack:

> We saw the plain suddenly covered by an immense number of soldiers scattered over the ground, who, starting from the crest

of the heights occupied by the Republicans, made full speed for
the village of Berstheim. Hardly had they got within pistol-
range when they formed in squads, even in battalions, to rush
the attack on this locality which had become so important to
them ... This bold stroke nullified in an instant all the effects
of our artillery fire.[8]

Although such tactics could be successful, they were not the whole
answer. Generally speaking, they were better suited to broken terrain. In
flat, open country, troops that were dispersed were extremely vulnerable
to cavalry. It was in these situations that the value of more traditional
tactics made itself felt, for classic formations such as the square were
really essential to repulse cavalry when the landscape provided no other
cover. Similarly, the new tactics were rather better for attack than
defence. All in all, it was clear that some ability in the old style of doing
things was needed, while being careful not to lose the best of the new.
This blend was partly achieved by combining elements of the regulars
and volunteers.

Such a course of action had become necessary because France was
in danger of finding herself with two armies instead of one. The old
regular units not only dressed differently (in the white coats that the
royal army had always worn, whereas the volunteers wore blue), they
were paid less and their administration was different. The regular
troops of the line army had experience and training in the old ways of
doing things, and were proud of their expertise, while those of the
volunteer battalions had none, but felt superior because they were
volunteers and therefore patriots. The differences produced friction
between the two elements, who were contemptuous of each other —
hardly a good basis for military efficiency.

Something needed to be done to mould the two rather disparate
elements together into a logical coherent force, but what? As there
were about twice as many volunteer battalions as regulars, it was
simply decided that new units should be formed consisting of one
regular battalion and two volunteer battalions. It was also hoped that
this would give roughly the right mixture of well-trained regular

elements and enthusiastic but untrained volunteers. This arrangement was the famous *amalgame* decreed on 26 February 1793, which has been called the most important of all the efforts to restructure the army during the Revolution.

It was also decided to give the new units an identity that was in line with Revolutionary policy. Since the word 'regiment' was associated with the bad old days when the aristocratic colonel was lord and master, the term was abolished. So were the old regimental names, such as Médoc and Touraine, which were associated with ideas of feudal fiefdoms and regionalism. In future there were to be 'demi-brigades' instead of regiments, and they were to have numbers rather than names. The rank of colonel, which also had unpleasant associations of aristocratic privilege, not to say virtual slave-ownership, was also abolished and replaced with the simple title of *chef de brigade*. For similar reasons the rank of *chef de bataillon* was substituted for the aristocratic grade of lieutenant-colonel.[9]

Efforts were made to bring the new units up to a reasonable level of proficiency, and even here the French showed a strange blend of professionalism and amateurishness. François Roguet recounted that in early 1793 he was put in charge of training for his demi-brigade, though he knew nothing about it because it had always been in the hands of another officer, who had been promoted. With four hundred recruits on their way, Roguet pretended to be ill and spent three days in his tent reading the drill manuals. On the fourth day he began instructing the newcomers, 'with success'.[10]

A few months after the *amalgame*, the French government took perhaps the final step in the creation of a national army by decreeing universal conscription: the *levée en masse*.

The 'citizens' army' which was the result of all these changes continued to be highly unconventional if looked at from the standpoint of the 18th century. For one thing, it had soldiers who sometimes argued publicly with their generals, or expressed doubts about their political reliability. For another, it had the inestimable advantage that the soldiers could mostly be relied on to go out foraging and come back of their own accord, instead of deserting to the enemy at the first opportunity. This was just as well, because the army was often so short of transport for supplies that the soldiers were obliged to 'live off the land' – or plunder it thoroughly, to put it bluntly.

The lack of transport wagons was not wholly negative, for they tended to block the roads and slow down movement, and an army that was used to depending on reliable supplies found itself in difficulty when they did not arrive. The French were never lucky enough to have thoroughly regular supplies and developed quite an ability to live by their ingenuity at sniffing out sources of food on their own. The mobility of the army was also clearly helped by the fact that the often poverty-stricken officers had no baggage and therefore had no carts to add to the traffic on the roads.

Certainly, seeing the French army on the march seems to have been a unique experience. In 1805 a French officer with the Bavarian army described its progress:

> Ulm taken and negligently occupied, the army of Bonaparte, the victorious army, was disbanded, and appeared to me no longer anything but an army in rout; but in rout in advance instead of in retreat. This torrent took the direction of Vienna, and henceforth there was nothing but an *arrive qui peut* by roads full and encumbered. Our German army alone marched like regular troops.[11]

This impression of organised chaos is confirmed by the recollections of a pastor who saw the army in Germany advancing to attack in 1796. Compared to the Austrian Army, he said:

> One did not see so many wagons or so much baggage, such elegant cavalry, or any infantry officers on horseback below the rank of major. Everything about these Frenchmen was supple and light – movements, clothing, arms and baggage. In their ranks marched boys of fourteen and fifteen; the greater part of their infantry was without uniforms, shoes, money and apparently lacking all organisation, if one were to judge by appearances

alone. But each man had his musket, his cartridge box, and cockade of national colours, and all were brave and energetic.

The French were later obliged to fall back, and the good pastor was treated to another sight of French improvisation:

> Their dress was truly bizarre: most marched barefoot; for clothing they had rigged themselves out with bed curtains, tapestries, peasants' smocks; some had mantles of various colours; some women's and choirboys' clothing, with surplices and albs which they had taken from the churches; some of them were wearing young girls' stockings. You could call it a masquerade.[12]

This lack of conventional discipline and order, indeed the army's general scruffiness and air of destitution, not to mention the undernourished appearance of some of the soldiery, seems to have led its enemies seriously to underestimate its fighting potential. In a letter to his wife written shortly after the Austrian defeat at Loano in 1795, Horatio Nelson, whose ships were patrolling the Riviera, relayed a description of the troops Bonaparte was about to command:

> [Few of the] soldiers are more than twenty-three or twenty-four years old; a great many do not exceed fourteen years, all without clothes; and my officers add, they are sure my barge's crew would have beat a hundred of them, and that, had I seen them, I should not have thought, if the world had been covered with such people, that they could have beat the Austrian army.[13]

He was to have ample proof of the contrary.

NOTES

1. Quoted in Tulard, J. *Dictionnaire Napoléon*. Paris, 1987, p. 1616.
2. It is intriguing to note that of the reformers and theorists mentioned

here: de Broglie, de Guibert, Bourcet and Servan, the first three were all at Rossbach, while the last three were all in Corsica in the year of Bonaparte's birth.

3.   See Forrest, A. *Soldiers of the French Revolution.* Durham, 1990, p. 5.

4.   Lavallette, A.-M. C., comte de. *Mémoires et souvenirs du comte Lavallette, aide de camp du général Bonaparte, conseiller-d'état et directeur-général des postes de l'Empire; publiés par sa famille et sur ses manuscrits.* Paris, 1831, pp. 185–6.

5.   Their progress through the ranks also allowed them to pick up some unexpected but useful accomplishments. There is a story told by Charles Parquin of General Laroche-Dubouscat, who, finding the duty trumpeter at lunch, once reacted to an emergency by grabbing a trumpet from the weapons rack and sounding boots and saddles himself. He had been a boy trumpeter and had not forgotten the trade. See Jones, B. T., ed. *Napoleon's Army: The Military Memoirs of Charles Parquin.* London, 1987, p. 10.

6.   See Haythornthwaite, P. J. *Austrian Army of the Napoleonic Wars (1): Infantry, Men-at-Arms.* London, 1986, p. 41, and Rothenberg, G. E. *Napoleon's Great Adversaries: the Archduke Charles and the Austrian Army, 1792–1814.* London, 1982, p. 139.

7.   Foy, M. S., Gen. *Histoire de la guerre de la Péninsule sous Napoléon, précédé d'un tableau politique et militaire des puissances belligérantes ... publiés par Mme la Comtesse Foy.* Paris, 1827, I, pp. 102–4.

8.   Phipps, R. W. *Armies of the First French Republic and the Rise of the Marshals of Napoleon I.* Oxford, 1926–39, quoted in Rogers, H. C. B., Col. *Napoleon's Army.* London, 1974, pp. 69–70.

9.   The Republican army was also notable for having only two ranks for general officers: General of Brigade and General of Division. The officer commanding an army held the rank of General of Division, but was referred to as the General-in-Chief.

10. See Roguet, F. *Mémoires militaires du lieutenant général comte Roguet (François), colonel en second des grenadiers à pied de la Vieille Garde, pair de France.* Paris, 1862, I, pp. 87–8.

11. Comeau de Charry, S. J. de, Baron. *Souvenirs des guerres d'Allemagne pendant la Révolution et l'Empire.* Paris, 1900, p. 219.

12. Anon. 'Les Français en Allemagne.' *Carnet de la Sabretache* X (1902):

pp. 139–40. Quoted in Elting, J. R. *Swords Around a Throne.* London, 1989.

13. Laughton, J. K., ed. *Letters and Despatches of Horatio, Viscount Nelson, K. B., Duke of Bronte, Vice Admiral of the White Squadron.* London, 1886, pp. 93–4.

5

LEARNING THE TRADE

It is now time to turn our attention to the steps by which Napoleon Bonaparte rose from obscurity to a position of trust and prominence. It is essential to look at these steps because his successes in 1796, like most 'overnight successes', were to a great extent laid on foundations that had been put down much earlier, and a knowledge of these will help us to understand his achievements. At the same time we shall briefly trace the development of the politico-military situation which he faced when he was given command of the Army of Italy in 1796.

When the war broke out in 1792, Bonaparte had been an officer for some six years. His career had been unremarkable and likewise his education. Indeed, one of the few things that distinguished him from his fellow officers was that he was Corsican, and therefore a product of a culture and society that were very different from those of mainland France. In fact he had been born a little over a year after the French had purchased the island from its previous owners, the Republic of Genoa, who had got tired of trying to govern a troublesome outpost that had managed to make itself largely independent under the leadership of a former officer called Pasquale Paoli.

The French had to make two attempts to take control of the island, on the second occasion landing a sizeable army of 22,000 men. One of those who fought against the invaders was Napoleon's father, Carlo, a lawyer and prominent supporter of Paoli. When the French landed for the second time, in the spring of 1769, and Carlo once again took to the mountains to help lead the resistance, he was accompanied by his wife Letizia, who was already visibly pregnant with Napoleon. This time the French were too strong, Paoli was defeated, and Carlo was obliged to surrender. Just three months later, on 15 August, Napoleon was born on an island that now belonged to France.

Culturally speaking, however, the island remained more Italian than French, and the young Napoleon grew up speaking that language, a facility that was to be of some use during his campaigning in 1796. His own family background was also distinctly Italian, and his distant forebears were from Tuscany and Lombardy. On his father's side they had shown a preference for the legal profession, while on his mother's side a number of them had been army officers, including her own father.

If Napoleon's father had been more idealistic or less pragmatic, or a single man without a young family, he might have followed Pasquale Paoli into exile in England, just as his ancestors had left Tuscany for Corsica in difficult times hundreds of years before, but as it was, Carlo decided to stay in Corsica and successfully adapted to French rule. As a member of one of the most prominent families in this little community (the population of Corsica was only 130,000) Carlo was able to make some useful contacts, and became friendly with the French governor. This led to the family receiving an advantageous offer, because of their relative poverty, to complete the education of the two eldest sons, Joseph and Napoleon, in France. It was decided that the former would be prepared for the priesthood, and the latter for a career in the army. The two boys therefore left Corsica, and on Christmas Day in 1778 they set foot in mainland France for the first time. Napoleon was nine and a half years old.

After a few months adapting to his new environment and trying to learn to speak French, he was taken to the so-called Military Academy in Brienne, which was in fact run by Franciscan friars and had very little that was military about it. Here he completed his basic education, showing an aptitude for history, geography and especially mathematics, for which he displayed a deep fascination. These were key interests, which were essential to his success as both politician and general. Afterwards, in October 1784, he went to the Ecole Militaire in Paris for proper military training prior to obtaining a commission. Since he had expressed a desire to go into the navy, he followed the artillery course, which included subjects that were thought to be potentially useful to navigators, such as hydrostatics and calculus.

The course was supposed to last two years, but when his father died prematurely in February 1785, leaving a large family with very little means of support, Bonaparte may have been motivated to graduate as soon as possible and earn some money. In any case, he completed his course in a year, and graduated in the autumn of 1785. As there were no vacancies in the navy, he was obliged to accept a commission in the army. He was too poor and too lowly in social status to go into a prestigious regiment, so it was fortunate that his aptitude for mathematics made him highly suitable for the 'mechanic' artillery, which tended to be looked down upon in fashionable circles as a rather bourgeois, purely technical arm, with none of the associations of nobility and chivalry enjoyed by the cavalry and infantry.

There were several regiments of artillery that Bonaparte could choose from, and he opted to begin his career in the La Fère regiment. It was a good regiment, but there were also practical reasons for his choice. It was garrisoned in Valence in the Rhône valley, about a hundred miles north of Marseille, which meant that he would be relatively close to his family. He took up his duties towards the end of 1785 at the age of sixteen and a half, a fairly common age for a new officer in the 18th century, and settled down to the routine existence of a regular soldier.

This was not particularly arduous if one was an officer, and included entitlement to very extended periods of leave, which Bonaparte exploited to the full, always spending his time at home with his family. In the first six years of his career about half his time was spent away from his regiment. There was nothing unusual in this, and officers frequently spent a long time away from their units, but the fact that he took every opportunity to return to his home and family does suggest that Bonaparte was still deeply attached to them. He had only been in the army ten months when he took his first leave, and departed for Corsica, where he stayed for a year.

According to Jean Colin, who wrote probably the most important work on Bonaparte's military education, he arrived in Ajaccio in September 1786 with a box of books among which were Plutarch, Plato, Cicero, Cornelius Nepos, Livy, Tacitus, Raynal, Montesquieu and Montaigne.[1] This was absolutely typical of him, and all his life he was to be a voracious reader, particularly of history and geography, commonly travelling with a veritable library of such works. He absolutely devoured information, making copious notes, and storing everything away in his remarkable memory. This was not an activity that was restricted to his periods of leave. From the summer of 1788 Bonaparte spent fifteen months in Auxonne with his regiment, and there is ample proof of the unrelenting studies he made during this time in the form of thirty-six notebooks filled with his summaries of what he had been reading.[2]

This period in Auxonne was of fundamental importance for his military career, because it was here that he came under the influence of the great artillerist, Baron Jean-Pierre Du Teil. He was a veteran of the War of the Austrian Succession and the Seven Years War, and commanded the artillery school in Auxonne. He seems to have been an extremely effective teacher, who had the habit of taking his pupils for walks in the country, picking out a piece of terrain, and making them come up with plans for attack and defence of it. This was followed by discussions of the defects and merits of all the possibilities. Such exercises were obviously highly useful to officers who had never actually been on campaign, and were an important method of introducing them to the kind of work they would have to do in a real war.

Du Teil must also have introduced his pupils to the writings of his brother, Chevalier Jean Du Teil, who had produced a modest little book, claiming to be based to a great extent on the work of de Guibert, some six years after the publication of the latter's *Essai*. Whether or not Bonaparte knew the writings of this brother before, he must certainly have encountered them at Auxonne. Colin remarks that they were partly an admirable distillation of the most important principles of de Guibert's work, and eliminated its over-complicated, paradoxical and impractical elements. However, there was more to the work than that:

> He only dedicates a few pages to the subjects already dealt with by Guibert. The rest is by him alone: the excellent précis on the defence of coasts, siege warfare, outpost warfare, etc. And here everything is new, everything is personal, everything is linked to a single doctrine, to those principles of concentration and mobility which we see brought out for the first time.[3]

They were principles of fundamental importance for Bonaparte's style of war, and were used by him to great effect in 1796. So was another idea that was closely linked to them, that of the use of as large an army as could be mustered. Some theorists had seen advantages in using smaller armies, but Du Teil made a number of criticisms of this view, saying, among other things '... can one ignore the fact that a numerous army, being able to subdivide itself, it is possible to oppose a sufficient part of it to that of the enemy, and use the surplus to harass him, turn him, and secure his defeat?'[4] Just how much Bonaparte was to exploit this technique will also appear in the account of the 1796 campaign. Colin concludes his comments on Du Teil by saying:

> In summary, good sense, perceptiveness, and clarity distinguish Chevalier Du Teil from the other military writers of his time. Everything that he wrote is exactly related to the type of war that would be conducted from 1792 to 1815, and the few essential principles which he brings out are precisely those which would form the essence of the Napoleonic method: having superiority of numbers, concentrating one's efforts, attacking the enemy on the flank or in the rear, and surprising him, both by ensuring secrecy of preparation and by rapidity of execution ...[5]

Chevalier Du Teil was not the only theorist that Bonaparte would have come across at Auxonne, and it is highly probable that it was here that he was introduced to the ideas of Bourcet, whose writings were less accessible due to the fact that they had not been published, and were limited to manuscript copies. But the Du Teil brothers were from the same part of France as Bourcet, and the Baron had served in the same army during the Seven Years War. It therefore seems highly unlikely that Baron Du Teil would not have been in a position to pass on to his pupils the most important lessons contained in Bourcet's writings. Again, they were lessons of central importance for Bonaparte's style of war.

Although Bourcet's work was ostensibly about mountain warfare, it actually went far beyond that, and dealt with the highest questions of strategy. Moreover, many of his ideas were not just applicable to situations in the mountains. For example, one concept that was generally valid was the preference for offensive rather than defensive warfare. In this, Bourcet was in agreement with many military theorists of his time, such as Guibert, Du Teil and Frederick the Great. Most of these cited the advantages of the disquiet that it caused the enemy, and the better morale engendered by successful offensive operations. Bourcet, however, also saw more tangible advantages. He remarks:

> The power that acts offensively has only the chord to travel over, while that which is forced to defend itself has the whole extent of the arc ... whatever care the defender may take to prepare his communications and his orders of march to reinforce the parts which are attacked, his troops will never arrive in time if the general of the attacking army has taken care to conceal his movement and his plan, because whatever confidence one may have in the faithfulness of spies or in the reports of deserters, it is necessary to have the time to be warned, time to give the necessary orders, and time to march the troops, even the nearest, to the critical point.
>
> The attacking general will always be able to arrange his movements in such a manner as to gain one or two days' march on his enemy, or only several hours, which may suffice for the execution of his plan. Moreover he will know positively the number against which he will have to fight, without it being possible for he who is defending to foresee any part of his plan, nor the number against which he will have to resist. From this one may generally conclude that the offensive has decisive advantages over the defensive ... *Whatever the manner in which a defending general may place his troops in the mountains, he will never prevent a stronger army from penetrating* [his line].[6]

What Bourcet had grasped was that it was pointless to try to defend a particular strip of ground, except as a temporary measure. Instead, he recommended an indirect and active defence. For this it was necessary to concentrate one's forces, and take the fight to the enemy by manoeuvring into positions that would make his life difficult. In short, it meant defending by attacking, and attacking meant outflanking the enemy positions, or manoeuvring in such a manner that the enemy was forced to abandon them without a fight. Once again, Bonaparte was to make full use of this idea.

It is perhaps in the area of planning that Bourcet may have made the most vital contribution to Bonaparte's methods. Bourcet was aware of the essential unpredictability of military operations, and that nothing could ever permit a commander to have complete control of what was happening. If unpredictability could not be eliminated, it had to be accepted and, as much as possible, prepared for. There was only one way to do this. The commander had to think through *every possible* scenario, and what he was going to do in each and every one of them. In Bourcet's own words, 'One must necessarily foresee all the operations that the enemy may carry out, and on this subject make all the suppositions possible ...'[7] Naturally enough, one also had to cater for one's own operations miscarrying. It was therefore essential to have an overall plan that catered for variations in the operations according to circumstances. Bourcet spoke of a plan having several branches – what might nowadays be called alternative scenarios. This was also useful for the purpose of keeping the enemy guessing. However, it meant that the initial positioning of the elements of the army required great care:

> It is necessary, as much as possible, to dispose the assembly of the army in such a way that it can respond to the different branches that the plan embraces, so that the principal one remains unknown, and, consequently, the first directions of the movements of the troops ... The disposition of the food and the beginnings of the marches will be wasted, but nothing must be spared when it is a question of deceiving one's enemy.[8]

As Colin points out, 'The difficulty consists above all in determining a plan of action which lends itself equally to the execution of the different branches of the plan.'[9] It took a formidable brain to calculate all the possibilities, but of course Bonaparte excelled at calculation. The worth of the method was not lost on him, and it was later to form the foundation of his planning procedures. As he told the economist Pierre Roederer in a conversation of 6 March 1809: 'If I am always ready to face anything, it is because ... I have foreseen what may happen.'[10] He might almost be quoting Bourcet.

To sum up, Colin comments that 'the more one goes into the *Principes de la guerre de montagnes*, the more one discovers a close analogy with the procedures of Bonaparte, and notably with those which he employed in 1794 and 1796.'[11]

The months that Bonaparte spent in Auxonne were crucial for his professional development, but they were even more critical for the future of France, as the clock ticked away the last year before the Revolution destroyed its old ways and habits. There were ample signs of trouble. In January and February of 1789 there were bread riots in the towns. The spring brought peasant insurrections in Flanders, Franche-Comté and the Mâconnais. There was unrest in Brittany, on the northern frontier, in the Paris region, and in Provence. On 1 April, Bonaparte himself was sent with a detachment of 100 soldiers to maintain order in the little town of Seurre, where there had been a riot. He was to remain there for about two months.[12] At the end of April there were riots in Paris, and on 5 May the Estates General finally met in Versailles.

The explosion was just about to come, and on 14 July it duly arrived, with the storming of the Bastille, the old fortress-prison in Paris. News of the event did not travel slowly. The day after it happened, Bonaparte wrote to his great-uncle in Ajaccio, 'I have just received news from Paris ... It is astonishing and singularly alarming.'[13] Not that Bonaparte was a supporter of the status quo, and found change alarming. Quite the contrary, for he was a supporter of the Revolution from the start, but he always hated mobs and disorder. He was, after all, the son of a lawyer, and he wanted change to be achieved through normal legal processes.

With this immense political upheaval creaking into motion, Bonaparte thought first of Corsica. Only a month earlier, he had sent a letter to Paoli saying that he was writing a work on the unjust government of the island.[14] Now that the Revolution had finally broken out he did not think of staying in France at the hub of affairs, but rather of going to see what contribution he could make to improving the lot of the oppressed Corsicans. Thus, in the first few days of September, Bonaparte departed to go home on leave.

For the next two years his time was taken up with almost unremitting political activity in support of the Revolution, either in Corsica, or on the mainland, where he was obliged to spend some time with his regiment from February to September 1791. Towards the end of that period, from 26 to 29 August, just before departing for Ajaccio again, he stayed at Du Teil's home in Pommier. The baron's daughter recalled him 'working constantly with the General, talking with him of the military art or studying maps spread on large tables',[15] so he had evidently not wholly put aside his profession.

Corsica continued to be the main focus of his attention, however, and it was quite fortuitous that he found himself in Paris during the critical period after the declaration of war in the spring of 1792. He had managed to get himself elected lieutenant-colonel of a battalion of the Corsican National Guard on 1 April, and a week afterwards, his new position was to propel him into the middle of a violent clash between opposing political factions on the streets of Ajaccio, in which a lieutenant was killed at his side. By this time, things in Corsica were gradually turning sour for the Bonapartes. Paoli had returned to the island in the summer of 1790, and although he worked with the new French government, he never ceased to envisage an independent Corsica. He does not seem to have taken to the young Bonapartes, with their driving ambition, new ideas, and French education, and gradually they had drifted further and further apart. There was plenty of factional intrigue in Corsica, and it looked as if Bonaparte's actions in the riot would be used against him, so he went to Paris to make sure that his side of the story was heard by those who were charged with investigating the affair.

He arrived on 28 May, right in the middle of one of the most desperate times of the Revolution. A week after the declaration of war, three columns of the Army of the North had advanced to invade the Austrian Netherlands (Belgium). Their offensive had been accompanied by an impassioned, perhaps unwise, proclamation:

AUSTRIAN SOLDIERS, OPEN YOUR EYES!

How are you led? – Like slaves, or rather like animals. The Negroes of America are happier than you … How are you fed? – You are fed worse than dogs in France … How are you clothed? – You are clothed like fools, like Harlequins … How do you sleep? – You sleep like pigs, on straw, and more often on the earth … And you are men, and you are like us, and you are ten paces away from the country where liberty reigns … Soldiers of Austria, Hungary, the Tyrol and others, leave your tyrants! …[16]

The attack had been a disaster, and the soldiers of liberty had shown themselves to be rather less happy than the propaganda suggested. Two columns had panicked during the advance to Tournai, though not in contact with the enemy, and General Dillon, commanding one of the columns, was murdered by his own troops during the retreat to Lille. On 18 May, the army commanders (Rochambeau, Lafayette and Luckner) held a meeting at Valenciennes, came to the conclusion that the condition of the armies made an offensive impossible, and advised telling the King to make peace. Rochambeau resigned as commander of the Army of the North, to be replaced by Luckner. A couple of days later, General Valence sent the Minister of War, Joseph Servan, a disconcerting report:

The state of this Army of the North makes one tremble. It lacks everything, especially order and method in the administration of the staff. It is above all desirable that the general officers be attached to the troops, and, for that, we must have some … I pray you, Sir, with insistence, not to suffer, under any sort of pretext, that MM. Berthier and La Jarre are sent to another army. These two men are indispensable in M. Luckner's [army] and cannot be replaced.[17]

Apart from showing us that the French army was far from battle-worthy at this time, it also tells us that when Bonaparte was to ask for this same indispensable M. Berthier as his chief of staff in 1796, he was following a well-worn path.

Writing of the situation he found in the capital, Bonaparte himself told Joseph: 'Paris is in the greatest convulsions … The news from the frontier is still the same. It is probable that they will withdraw to conduct a defensive war. The desertion among the officers is excessive. In every way the position is critical.'[18]

During the next few months the convulsions and the military crisis intensified. At the end of June, Austria and Prussia formed the First Coalition and a large allied army under the Duke of Brunswick (a Prussian general) began to assemble across the German border at Coblenz. In these circumstances it is no surprise that the army made no difficulty about getting one of their regular officers back, and on 10 July the Minister of War reinstated Bonaparte in the artillery, with the rank of captain as from 6 February.[19] Five days later the desperate situation caused the government to issue the decree of *la patrie en danger*, calling for volunteers. Bonaparte was encouraged to rejoin his regiment, as one might expect, but while he was waiting for his papers to come through, circumstances turned his path in another direction.

On 10 August, the Tuileries Palace was stormed by a ferocious mob, the Swiss Guard was massacred, and the King suspended from his functions. A shocked spectator to this violence was Bonaparte, who managed to save one of the guardsmen. 'Never, after that', he wrote later, 'did any of my battlefields give me the impression of so many bodies as the masses of the Swiss presented to me.'[20] Less than a week later, the aristocratic school that Bonaparte's sister, Marie-Anne, was attending near Paris, was closed down. The day after that, Lafayette defected to the Austrians. In this climate of instability and violence Bonaparte put his sister first and the war second, and whisked her off to safety in Corsica.

On 9 September, when brother and sister left Paris, the Austrians were at Lille, and the Prussians were closing on the capital from the north-east. It looked as if the Revolution was finished, about to be crushed by the might of foreign bayonets. Then the miracle happened. On 20 September, on a low hill at Valmy, a hundred miles from Paris, the combined forces of Generals Dumouriez and Kellermann turned back the Prussian army, the heirs of Frederick the Great. In the evening, as the Prussian officers tried to work out what had happened, they turned to the poet Goethe, who had been with them as a spectator, and asked what he thought. 'At this place, on this day,' he said, 'a new epoch in the history of the world has begun, and you can all claim to have been present at its birth.'[21] This was rather overstating the case, but if the French had lost the battle it hardly seems likely that Brunswick could have been stopped before he reached Paris. The Revolution had gained a breathing space, if nothing else.

These events were closely followed by the opening of hostilities on the Italian front, where Bonaparte was to gain his first experience of war. On the cold and rainy night of 21/22 September, the day the National Assembly voted to abolish the monarchy, a French army invaded Savoy. For the King of Sardinia, the head of the House of Savoy and ruler of Piedmont, this was the unpleasant conclusion to a couple of years of diplomatic manoeuvring in which he had skilfully painted himself into a corner. A mild and principled man, firm in his religious beliefs and with a strong sense of duty, Victor Amadeus was not of a cast of mind to see anything but dangerous innovation in the Revolution. Nevertheless, on its outbreak he was careful not to get involved in France's internal affairs, despite the fact that King Louis's brothers, the Count of Artois and the Count of Provence, were his sons-in-law. Artois had fled to the Piedmontese capital of Turin in late 1789 – taking his mistress as well as his family – and exasperated Victor Amadeus with his anti-Revolutionary intrigues, before leaving at the beginning of 1791 to carry on his work elsewhere.

This removed one possible source of tension between Piedmont and France, but sadly there was another and more serious one. Piedmont stood on the border with France, and two of its possessions, the Duchy of Savoy and the County of Nice, actually lay on the French side of the Alps. Their geographical position had, in previous centuries, made them the object of French ambitions to extend their control to the 'natural frontiers' of France: the Rhine, the Pyrenees and the Alps. Any renewal of this policy would put their security in grave danger, and there were many people in France who supported the idea of annexing them. The Piedmontese were acutely aware of this, and of the fact that it would be very difficult to defend territories that were on the other side of a high mountain chain. Moreover, Piedmont had a problem in that it was really too weak to defend itself alone against a major power, and therefore had to play the risky game of obtaining the support of a stronger state while not leaving itself open to being used for its ally's own ends. Austria, which possessed the neighbouring Italian territory of Lombardy, was an obvious choice of ally, though dependence on the good faith of such a powerful neighbour, who had not been averse to swallowing a chunk of Poland when it was convenient, was not likely to give a feeling of complete security.

Whatever his doubts, in July 1791 Victor Amadeus had asked the Austrians for support if his lands should be invaded, but he also continued to hold talks with the French. A more astute player of the diplomatic game might have been able to stall for longer, and avoid getting sucked into an impossible position, but Victor Amadeus was not quite shrewd enough for that. The Portuguese ambassador in Turin commented: 'The King, indecisive in character, listens to the opinions of everyone, mistrusts everyone apart from himself, and makes no decision.'[22] This may explain why he is reported variously as having said 'I do not try to provoke anyone, but I shall defend myself like a devil',[23] and 'If the Emperor gives me 15,000 men to add to my army, I will invade France.'[24] The Portuguese ambassador added: 'The knowledge of the King, and the intellect of the Prince of Piedmont, rendered useless by the poor education that both of them have received, will be insufficient to hold them back from the bad step to which, in the end, they have let themselves be led.'[25]

Eventually, during the spring of 1792, the Piedmontese managed to offend the French before they had actually secured any help from the Austrians, and the French government ordered General Montesquiou to invade Savoy before 15 May. This attack was long delayed because Montesquiou felt that his army was not ready, but there was ample evidence that it was being prepared. During this waiting period, a Piedmontese envoy was sent to Milan, the capital of Lombardy, to secure the support of an Austrian Auxiliary Corps of 8,000 men, which was to be commanded by General Strassoldo. As on almost every other occasion, the Piedmontese were out-negotiated by the Austrians and came away with a fairly unsatisfactory agreement. The Convention of Milan stipulated that there was to be no offensive war, the Austrian corps was to enter Piedmont when the situation was deemed to require it, and the Piedmontese agreed to supply it with whatever it needed. Ironically, the agreement was signed on 22 September, as hordes of French soldiers were surging into Savoy, sweeping aside its defenders.

The resistance was pitiful. The commander, General Lazary, was over 70 years old and clearly incapable of doing his job. Much to the anguish of the Piedmontese troops, they had to withdraw almost without fighting. On the 24th, Montesquiou entered Chambéry in triumph, and the revolutionising of Savoy began. Five days later the French took Nice, which was abandoned before any serious attack had been made. Among the first to enter the city was a native of the area who was to become one of Bonaparte's most important subordinates – André Massena. From Nice, the Piedmontese troops retired north-east, along the main road towards Cuneo and Turin. They then proceeded to perch high in the Maritime Alps, at Saorgio, just short of the Colle di Tenda, the 6,000-foot-high pass that leads into Piedmont. Thus began three and a half years of mountain warfare on this border, in which Bonaparte was to take a leading role.

In addition to these French successes in the south, the remarkable turn-round in their fortunes continued on the northern frontiers, and armies under Dumouriez and Custine pushed into Belgium and Germany during October and November, winning a major engagement at Jemappes. It was the turn of the allies to complain about their armies, and a Piedmontese general, Count de Saint-André, commented: 'Our War Office is badly constituted, badly directed and nothing in it is secret … Disorder, incompetence, the lack of secrecy and agreement, and perhaps even treason will bring down the throne.'[26] Piedmontese misery was compounded when a French naval squadron bombarded their port of Oneglia as a reprisal for firing on a flag of truce, then landed and sacked the city. It was not the only occasion when the civilians suffered at the hands of the French. Joubert, who was to take a leading role in the 1796 campaign, saw too much of it: 'What pillaging in the towns, what cruelty in the country! The country people will have had great pleasure in becoming French.'[27]

Eventually the winter weather put a stop to campaigning both in the Alps and on the northern frontiers. The lull until the spring was used both in making preparations for the next campaigning season, and in diplomatic negotiations. Victor Amadeus, alarmed by the ineptitude shown by his generals, asked Vienna to send him someone to take overall command. The choice fell on *Feldzeugmeister*[28] Joseph Baron de Vins, a 61-year-old veteran of the Seven Years War. He had been born in Mantua, the son of a general who was killed at the battle of Piacenza in 1746. Having also served against Turkey, he had been commander-in-chief in Croatia before going to Italy. His nomination came through on 21 December. However, Victor Amadeus's problems were not solely military, and he was already experiencing financial difficulty due to the cost of the fighting. This was no secret to his ally, and Gherardini, the Austrian ambassador in Turin, commented in a letter of 16 January 1793 that Victor Amadeus could be pushed into declaring himself neutral, which would expose Lombardy to attack. A few days later his doubts about the firmness of Piedmont increased, and he noted that the French had already made overtures to the Piedmontese, suggesting that they could join forces and take Lombardy.[29] This was not the limit of French efforts to break up the alliance facing them, for as early as September they had approached Prussia with the offer of a separate peace. Attitudes against France hardened, however, when King Louis was found guilty of treason, and went to the guillotine on 21 January. Isolated as they were, the French still dared to declare war on England and Holland, and Spain was to follow in March. Among the Italian states, Naples also entered the war against France in July, while the Papacy, Parma and Modena maintained positions of more or less open hostility.

While these events had been taking place, Bonaparte had been far away from the action, immersed in Corsican politics. He was not to remain on the sidelines much longer, though, and during 1793 various developments were to change his life for ever, and pitch him headlong into the war that was to make his name. To begin with, he had his first experience of real military action in February, when he participated in an attempt to capture a fine natural harbour on one of the islands between Corsica and Sardinia. It was an utter fiasco, though Bonaparte himself had no responsibility for the failure. Weak leadership on the part of the commander of the operation, and unnecessary delays in making the attack were the main reasons behind it, and Bonaparte must have come away with the strong impression that these were things to be avoided in war.

An event that had much greater consequences for Bonaparte took place four months later, when the anti-French party took control of Corsica, and he and his family had to flee for their lives. He left Corsica for Toulon on 11 June, and hardly visited the island again. For some time, Bonaparte had been a relatively large fish in a small pond, and most of his political involvement had been in Corsican affairs. He now found himself relegated to being one amongst millions in mainland France, with no obvious political role to fill. This left him with his military role, and he soon rejoined the part of his regiment that was detached in Nice, serving under General Dujard, whom we shall meet again in 1796. It was not to be long before Bonaparte was catapulted from the routine duties of a lowly captain to sudden and surprising prominence.

There was plenty of work for a soldier to do, as the war had not been going well for the French. In the north, there had been various setbacks, including serious defeats for Dumouriez, who had lost Belgium, and then followed Lafayette's example by defecting to the enemy. The entry of Spain into the war had also meant that another front had opened in the Pyrenees, which caused an unwelcome drain in manpower. The need for more troops to cope with the situation resulted in the decree of the *levée en masse* on 23 August. As far as the war against Piedmont was concerned, there had still not been much progress. An ill-conceived French attack had been mounted on the positions around Saorgio in June, but it had proved a disaster.

After this, the Piedmontese took an inordinate time to organise a reply. De Vins was slow and methodical by nature, but some of the Piedmontese began to suspect him of serving Austrian interests more than their own. Eventually, he produced a plan to attack both Nice and Savoy at the same time. This dispersal of forces was disapproved by many, but even if the plans had been unexceptionable, the chances of carrying them out effectively were reduced by the unwillingness of the generals to co-operate with one another, not to mention some truly bizarre command arrangements. For one thing, De Vins suffered from gout, and intended to direct operations from the comfort of Turin, roughly 90 miles from the defences at Saorgio, and half that distance from Savoy. Incredibly, although the attack in Savoy was to be personally led by the Duke of Monferrato, his daily movements were to be overseen by De Vins. Arrangements in the County of Nice were even more unsatisfactory, because it was stipulated that General Colli (another Austrian officer on loan to the Piedmontese) was to obey Saint-André, his superior, only if De Vins agreed. A further difficulty was that relations between Saint-André and Colli were very poor. There was also immense friction between the Piedmontese officers and De Vins's chief of staff, Argenteau (yet another Austrian officer), who was cordially disliked.

The incredible slowness of the Austro–Piedmontese meant that they were unable to take advantage of the increasing French internal problems, which drew off substantial numbers of troops in the south of France. Indeed, Bonaparte found himself in a distinctly 'hot' area that summer, with rebellions in Marseille, Avignon and Lyon. Piedmontese operations against the French did not begin until the middle of August, which was too late considering the fact that the cold weather would begin early in the high mountains. Notwithstanding his age (he was 67), Victor Amadeus wished to be present during operations in Nice, and left Turin on 21 August with his two youngest sons. He slept in a tent while with the army, visited the camps accompanied by De Vins and his sons, and went as far as the entrenchments at Col de Raus, 6,000 feet up in the mountains north of Nice. The beginning of Piedmontese operations was fixed for 7 September, the anniversary of Prince Eugene of Savoy's victory at Turin in 1706.

Bonaparte was not to take any part in opposing these operations, because he found himself with another job to do. In fact it was the task that was to launch his military career. On 29 August, Toulon, one of France's most important naval bases, went over to the allies and allowed an Anglo–Spanish fleet of 21 ships under Admiral Hood to enter the harbour. The naval arsenal was taken and so were some 70 vessels, 30 of these being ships of the line, half of them belonging to the French navy. On 7 September the Republicans invested the city.

Fortuitously, the commander of the besieging artillery, Dommartin, was wounded on the same day, leaving the technical arrangements in the hands of the overall commander, General Carteaux, who had been a court painter, and was not well versed in siege warfare. His approach consisted of trying to bombard the fleet with a few guns that were placed too far away. This unsatisfactory state of affairs had lasted just over a week when Bonaparte, who was on his way to Nice, passed near Toulon, and stopped off to visit Antoine Saliceti, a fellow-Corsican and family friend with whom he had been much involved in local politics. He got no further. All French armies were now accompanied by 'Representatives' of the government, who kept an eye on things, and sometimes used their enormous political power to get unsatisfactory officers arrested or guillotined. Saliceti was now a Representative attached to the besieging army, and this time he used his power to get Bonaparte employed to direct the artillery. Gasparin, one of the other Representatives, noted: 'Citizen Bonaparte, captain of artillery, was destined for the Army of Italy. But the wounding of Dommartin has forced us to keep him here.'[30]

Bonaparte, despite his total lack of experience, brought an immense analytical superiority to bear on the problem of how to capture the town. He rapidly saw that a direct approach was pointless. The town was supplied and reinforced by sea, and if it were possible to dominate the harbour and make it untenable for enemy shipping, the town would have to surrender. Dominating the harbour meant taking possession of certain heights that overlooked it, and building batteries there from which to bombard the shipping. In particular, there was a promontory at the entrance to the harbour, called L'Eguillette, where it was essential to place a battery. This was a bit too advanced for Carteaux, and according to Bonaparte, when he pointed to these vital heights on the map, and exclaimed 'There is Toulon!', the General took the view that he was not too strong on geography.[31]

Nevertheless, Bonaparte threw himself into his new job and began to collect artillery. On 18 September he fitted out the battery that was to be called La Montagne (after the dominant political faction in the National Assembly), and on the following day it began its bombardment. The English were soon forced to move their ships, but countered by considerably strengthening their occupation of L'Eguillette. To support this position they built a formidable defensive work which they called Fort Mulgrave, and which the French came to know as Little Gibraltar. This meant that the reduction of Toulon was bound to take longer.

Way up in the mountains, the Piedmontese had proceeded so slowly that they had achieved nothing, and were finally frustrated by the first falls of snow. Eventually Victor Amadeus realised that no more could be done, and left for his capital, where he arrived on 14 November. A month later, Gherardini commented:

> The King, despite the evidence to the contrary, is persuaded that he has an army of sixty thousand men, and that his officers and soldiers can rival those of the Austrians. He himself believes he is a great general, and he speaks and acts as if the epoch of today resembled that when fortunate strategies made the House of Savoy shine ...[32]

At Toulon, dissatisfaction with Carteaux had led to changes, and overall responsibility for the siege was finally put in the hands of General Dugommier, who arrived on 16 November. Nine days later there was a council of war and Bonaparte's plan to concentrate efforts on L'Eguillette was discussed and adopted. However, it was not until the night of 16/17 December that the decisive attack on the English positions was made, and Fort Mulgrave captured. Bonaparte was in the forefront of the assault on these heavily defended emplacements, and was wounded in the thigh by a thrust from a half-pike. One of his aides, Muiron, was also badly wounded. Next day the English, aware that the harbour could no longer be safely used, evacuated the city.

The importance of the siege in Bonaparte's career is self-evident. It was here that he began to make a modest name for himself, both as an artilleryman and a planner, and reached a rank that gave him some influence (he was appointed General of Brigade on 22 December). Moreover, for the first time we see him collecting people around him who will be his faithful helpers. It was here that he met Andoche Junot, who was to be his ADC in Italy, and a close companion, as well as Jean-Baptiste Muiron, who met his death at Bonaparte's side in November 1796. He also met Auguste Marmont, possibly not for the first time, but it was here that the younger man astutely attached himself to the Napoleonic bandwagon, which he was so dramatically to abandon in 1814, by going over to the enemy. Another who was at Toulon, and was to have a significant role in Bonaparte's career, was the Representative Paul Barras, who was to be one of the senior members of the French government in 1796. In short, with a high rank and a new network of contacts, some of whom held quite prominent positions, it looked as if the next year would see great things for Bonaparte.

NOTES

1. See Colin, J. L. A. *L'éducation militaire de Napoléon.* Paris, 1900, p. 111.
2. The text of these was published in Masson, F., and Biagi, G. *Napoléon inconnu.* Paris, 1895.
3. Colin, op. cit., pp. 97–8.
4. Ibid., p. 98.
5. Ibid., p. 99.
6. Ibid., pp. 83–4.
7. Ibid., p. 94.
8. Ibid., pp. 94–5.
9. Ibid., p. 93.
10. Quoted in Bouvier, F. *Bonaparte en Italie, 1796.* Paris, 1899, p. 185. He also wrote: 'In forming the plan of campaign, it is requisite to foresee everything the enemy may do, and to be prepared with

the necessary means to counteract it. Plans of campaign may be modified *ad infinitum* according to the circumstances, the genius of the general, the character of the troops and the features of the country.' Napoleon. *The Military Maxims of Napoleon, translated by Sir G. C. d'Aguilar.* London, 1987, p. 55.

11. Colin, op. cit., p. 95.
12. See Garros, L. *Quel roman que ma vie! Itinéraire de Napoléon Bonaparte (1769–1821).* Paris, 1947, p. 37.
13. Ibid., p. 37.
14. See Masson and Biagi, op. cit., II, p. 63.
15. Colin, op. cit., p. 131.
16. From a proclamation attached to a letter sent by Metternich to Kaunitz from Brussels, 30 April 1792. Vivenot, A., Ritter von, and Zeissberg, H., Ritter von. *Quellen zur Geschichte der Deutschen Kaiserpolitik Oesterreichs während der Französischen Revolutionskriege. 1790-1801.* Vienna, 1873–85, II, p. 17.
17. Derrécagaix, V. B. *Le maréchal Berthier.* Paris, 1904, p. 22.
18. Masson and Biagi, op. cit., II, p. 387.
19. See Garros, op. cit., p. 51.
20. Masson and Biagi, op. cit., II, p. 405.
21. Quoted in Hibbert, C. *The French Revolution.* London, 1982, p. 179.
22. Rossi, G. C. 'Vittorio Amedeo III di Savoia nei dispacci inediti di un diplomatico portoghese (agosto 1789–giugno 1790).' *Rassegna storica del Risorgimento,* 39 (1952) p. 10.
23. Gerbaix di Sonnaz, C. A., de. 'Gli ultimi anni di regno di Vittorio Amedeo III re di Sardegna.' *Miscellane di storia italiana,* 49 (1918), p. 296.
24. Bergadani, R. *Vittorio Amedeo III (1726–1796).* Turin, 1939, p. 171.
25. Rossi, op. cit., p. 10.
26. Bergadani, op. cit., p. 188.
27. Chevrier, E. *Le général Joubert d'après sa correspondance.* Paris, 1884, p. 5.
28. The Austrian army had a unique set of titles for its generals, and a handy set of abbreviations for them. In ascending order, they were: *General-Major* (GM), *Feldmarschall-Lieutenant* (FML), *Feldzeugmeister* (FZM) or *General der Cavallerie* (GdC) according to arm, and *Feldmarschall* (FM). The lower three ranks were often referred to simply as 'general'.

29. See Bergadani, op. cit., pp. 217–18.
30. Garros, op. cit., p. 63.
31. See Las Cases, E. A. *Mémorial de Sainte-Hélène.* Paris, 1983, I, p. 112.
32. Vivenot and Zeissberg, op. cit., III, pp. 452–54.

6

THE PLANNER

The next two years were to see a new phase of Bonaparte's career, in which his skills as a strategist were to be exploited by various superiors who called upon him to draw up campaign plans for them. This provided him with a golden opportunity to try out in reality many things that he had previously only read about and provided him with an invaluable practice run for the initial phase of the 1796 campaign. The operations actually carried out were quite limited in scope, which may perhaps have been useful to a young man developing his skills and experimenting with methods, though we shall never know what he might have achieved had he been given more freedom to pursue his objectives. Nevertheless, there is no denying the significance of his contribution on the Italian front, where very little had been achieved after the initial success in the autumn of 1792.

The New Year of 1794 found the armies in Italy, Germany and Belgium in much the same areas they had occupied for the previous twelve months, having drifted back and forth over the same ground without any decisive breakthrough for either side. On the southern front, this situation of stalemate existed despite the fact that the Piedmontese were in an abject financial condition. In April 1793, De Vins had asked for funding of eight million lire for the war effort, but the cost of the campaign that year had been forty-seven![1] At the beginning of 1794, Piedmont's public debt had reached fifty million lire,[2] and drastic measures had to be taken to raise money. These included ordering the churches in the threatened areas to hand over some of their treasures. A document in the parish archive of Cosseria shows that it alone gave up 18 pounds 2 ounces of silver.[3]

It was also necessary to think the unthinkable, and Gherardini informed Thugut on 13 January that there had been a Royal Council meeting a week before, during which there had been a discussion of the possibility of making a separate peace with France. Gherardini also commented on 'the weak intellect of the King, which sags more every day, in proportion to the physical decay of his health and his strength ...'[4]

As they had done so many times before, the Piedmontese tried to extract more help from the Austrians. Since an Austrian force was to be placed between Alessandria, Tortona and Acqui, to protect the outlets from the Riviera to Lombardy, Victor Amadeus sent an emissary to Milan to see the Archduke Ferdinand (the governor of Lombardy) to get the co-operation of this corps with the Piedmontese army. With Piedmont now in a critical position, the Austrians agreed to give more help, but strings were attached. One proposition was that the Piedmontese would return the territories on the west of the River Ticino that the Austrians had lost to them in previous wars, in exchange for any territorial acquisitions made at French expense. Alternatively, such acquisitions would be restored to the French at the end of the war after the payment of an indemnity that would be shared in equal parts by the Emperor and the King. It was not until 10 April that the King agreed to the second proposal, and by that time the French had made a considerable dent in the Piedmontese defences, thanks mainly to Bonaparte.[5]

Here, it is necessary to give a brief description of the geography of the area that would be the scene both of the next bout of fighting, and some phases of the 1796 campaign. Broadly speaking, the north of Italy consists of a largely featureless flood plain, surrounded on three sides by some of the highest mountains in Europe. The waters that flow from these heights gather to form the Po, Italy's largest river. The Po runs for about 400 miles, from the slopes of Monte Viso, past Turin and across the whole width of Italy to meet the head of the Adriatic Sea just south of Venice. The western part of the plain is aptly called Piedmont, the centre (roughly speaking) was occupied by Lombardy and part of the Duchy of Parma, while the rest belonged, in the 18th century, mainly to the Republic of Venice, with some parts going to the Duchy of Modena and the Papal States. Piedmont was therefore protected on three sides by an imposing natural bulwark formed by the Alps and the Apennines. The weaker points in this defensive wall, where there were passes and roads over the mountains, were guarded by fortified towns, of which some of the most important were Susa (to the west), Cuneo (to the south), Tortona, and the great citadel of Alessandria (both to the east). It was on the southern flank of this daunting natural barrier that the main French efforts were to be made against Piedmont over the next two years, in the country bordering the Mediterranean.

The strip of land that runs along the coast of the Mediterranean from Nice to Genoa is known as the Western Riviera. It is between those two cities that the Maritime Alps join the Ligurian Apennines. The sea is thus bordered by a spectacular chain of mountain peaks which rise to a height of anything between 6,000 and 2,000 feet at ranges from fifteen to as little as two and a half miles from the coast. The eroded spurs of the mountains form numberless pale cliffs plunging vertically into the water, so that the road along the coast was forced to make frequent detours inland.

From the crest of the chain of peaks, the land slopes down more steeply towards the sea than it does towards the inland plain, but on the landward side the terrain is deeply cut by the valleys of a number of streams which eventually swell into substantial rivers that flow into the Po. Among the most important of these tributaries are the Tanaro, the Bormida di Millesimo and the Bormida di Spigno. It is a peculiarity of the lie of the land in this area that the upper parts of these river valleys lie almost parallel with the coast and with one another, the ridges between them forming a succession of barriers to movement inland.

It was extremely difficult country for communications, due to the exceedingly broken nature of the terrain, the poor quality of many of the roads, and the caprices of the weather. In the winter, the slopes could be covered with large quantities of snow for weeks or months at a time, after which the melt waters could cause catastrophic flooding, washing away roads and bridges in the valleys. Crossing from the coast to the inland plain of Piedmont was possible on many mule-tracks that led over difficult mountain passes, but between Colle di Tenda above Nice, and the Bocchetta Pass above Genoa, there were almost no roads that could be used by wagons or artillery. (The exception was the road that led westwards from Savona by Colle di Cadibona, as Bonaparte was later to discover.) Nevertheless, the dense network of minor paths and tracks, many of which passed along the crests of the ridges, provided many alternative routes for people on foot, but they were often steep, narrow and rocky – hard going for a heavily laden soldier.

Navigation in the area was not easy. Many of the rounded foothills and lower peaks were entirely covered with trees, which made one look much like another. An observer standing on a crest and looking around him would often be faced with a rolling sea of vegetation stretching as far as he could see. Moreover, the higher peaks could frequently be covered in mist and cloud, hiding their distinctive features. Although the larger valleys provided a broader view over flatter, more cultivated land, the view from the bottom of the smaller valleys or from among the trees was extremely limited. Existing maps of the area were lacking in detail and accuracy, and there were not many habitations at which one could ask the way. It was therefore essential to have first-hand knowledge of the area, or reliable local guides.

The national borders that existed along the Riviera at the end of the 18th century have been called 'bizarre', snaking as they did up and down valleys and along mountain crests, and taking strange twists and turns around old feudal boundaries or natural features. However, stated in simple terms, the Genoese Republic, which was officially neutral during the war, owned most of the strip of land between the watershed and the Mediterranean from the border of the County of Nice (the River Roia) to beyond Genoa itself. The exception was a small area around Oneglia, which belonged to Piedmont. This tiny principality, which constituted Piedmont's only port, now that Nice was lost, was linked to the inland plain by a road of sorts that went over the mountains at Colle di Nava (the 3,000-foot-high pass twelve miles east of Colle di Tenda), and into the Tanaro valley. The road passed through Ormea, then went to the sizeable and strategically important fortress of Ceva, which also guarded the road that came from Savona. Beyond Ceva, the road went on to Mondovì, on the edge of the plain.

On 30 January 1794, Lazare Carnot, the member of the Committee of Public Safety who specialised in military matters, wrote a plan for the new campaign season which advised against operations through Savoy in favour of the Riviera:

The chain of the Alps presents the same difficulties to the attacker and the same advantages to he who is attacked. The outlet in Piedmont across this chain is problematic due to the lack of roads, and in any case it would be necessary to undertake the siege of Susa, a very strong city, before reaching Turin, and take into account the snows that would block our communications. If, therefore, we wish to attack Piedmont, it will be necessary to act from the department of the Maritime Alps, first taking Oneglia, which cuts communications with Sardinia and facilitates instead the arrival of foodstuffs at our army by the Riviera of Genoa. From Oneglia then it will be easy to penetrate into Piedmont, taking Saorgio from behind, and besieging Cuneo.[6]

The defensive line centred on Saorgio, which had served the Piedmontese so well since September 1792, was a considerable natural rampart more than 20 miles long, whose high points were in the order of 6,000 feet above sea level. On one side it extended roughly from Roquebillière in the west, via Col de Raus, Authion and Colle Basse to Saorgio. This stretch was almost parallel with the coast and at right-angles to the road from Nice to Tenda. On the other side of Saorgio, the ridge curved away north-east then north, to Cima di Marte, the pass of Colle Ardente, and Monte Saccarello, where it was almost parallel with the road to Colle di Tenda. Its strategic points, usually the peaks, were punctuated by defensive redoubts that were difficult to reach, never mind attack. It is no wonder that the French now sought to turn the position.

The Piedmontese were expecting this, as the King revealed to Gherardini on 5 February. In particular, General Dellera believed that the French might try to take Colle di Nava, as Marshal de Maillebois (who was assisted by Bourcet) had done in 1745. This was certainly perceptive, because in March, Saliceti asked the War Depot in Paris for some copies of papers and documents relating to the campaign of 1744–5, clearly showing that the French were thinking in the same way. Unfortunately for the Piedmontese, De Vins did not share Dellera's views and would not allow the preventive occupation of Briga, to the north-east of Saorgio.[7] However, at the instance of Dellera, it was planned that an

Austrian corps would advance from Lombardy through Alessandria to the strategically important position at Dego, in the valley of the Bormida di Spigno, and a corps of 4,000 Piedmontese would occupy the Tanaro valley to protect Oneglia and cover the flank of Dellera's troops. A certain Count Moretti, who lived near Dego, noted in his memoirs that the first Austrian troops began to arrive in the area at the beginning of April. They were elements of Frei-Corps Gyulay and an unnamed battalion of Croats.[8]

The French had originally wanted to attack Oneglia by sea, to avoid violating Genoese neutrality, but news of the Austrian troop movements from Lombardy encouraged them to investigate a more rapid method. Bonaparte, who had just been nominated artillery commander of the Army of Italy, was particularly eager to see some progress made, for he had recently expressed the view that it was shameful to have remained at the gates of Italy for a year. He now found himself putting forward a plan for an overland attack on Oneglia combined with a movement outflanking the position of Saorgio.

The inspiration for it seems likely to have been Bourcet's writings on an imaginary campaign set in precisely this area. In particular, Bourcet pointed out that the defending general could not cover both Colle di Tenda and the Riviera at the same time. The plans for the offensive therefore had to be flexible enough for the main effort to made either in the direction of Colle di Tenda, or along the Riviera, according to the reaction of the defender. He adds:

> The best course for the defensive general seems to be to defend the Colle di Tenda, but in that case he leaves it open to the offensive general to move by the sea coast, and ... to advance to Pigna, Triora and Rezzo and thence seize Ponte di Nava [in the Tanaro valley, just over Colle di Nava]. He is then in a position to continue his advance via the Tanaro valley ... whatever arrangements may be made by the defensive general he cannot prevent the offensive general from reaching the neighbourhood of Cuneo and Demonte either via the Colle di Tenda or via the Upper Tanaro and Mondovì ...[9]

The routes proposed by Bonaparte were slightly different, and so were some of his other dispositions, since the actual positions of the troops in 1794 were different from those envisaged by Bourcet, but there seems little doubt that he was thinking of Bourcet when he put his plan together. It was written out in Junot's fine hand (Bonaparte's handwriting was appalling) and after being discussed with the Representatives, it was accepted on or just after 2 April.[10]

The expedition began on 6 April: the same day that Victor Amadeus decided to entrust the command of the Piedmontese troops in the County of Nice to General Colli. The right-hand French column, which was to move down the coast, was accompanied by Bonaparte, and the Representatives: Saliceti, Ricord and Maximilien Robespierre's younger brother, Augustin.[11] The commander of the Genoese frontier garrison at Ventimiglia, Colonel Bacigalupo, had only 160 soldiers under his command, and had to limit himself to making a protest at the violation of Genoese neutrality, as he could do nothing to stop a whole French column marching into his territory. Things progressed smoothly on the coast, and Oneglia was taken on 9 April – without firing a shot, according to Marmont. Indeed, many people had fled, and the city was more than half deserted. Inland, the French advance proved much more difficult, with swollen rivers and blizzards of snow hampering movement.

Resistance to the advance on Oneglia had been almost non-existent, but on 10 April Argenteau, who was now commanding the Piedmontese force in this area, reached Ormea and prepared to defend the Tanaro valley. He placed his troops (ten battalions) along the frontier in an attempt to link Colli with the Austrians who were marching from Alessandria towards Cairo Montenotte, in the valley of the Bormida di Spigno. His efforts were ineffectual. By 17–18 April Bonaparte was in Ormea, and on the 19th he watched while Massena's forces entered Garessio, which Argenteau abandoned. Having pushed as far as was advisable in this direction, the French now turned back to deal with the positions below Colle di Tenda.

In part, however, Bonaparte's goal had already been achieved, because he had rendered the position at Saorgio almost irrelevant, as De Vins recognised. On 20 April, the latter wrote to Colli and told him to pull back all the troops that were not needed for defence into Piedmont. On 23 April, Colli also received orders from the King to hold the County of Nice until the snows melted, then move back to Colle di Tenda.

These setbacks had done nothing to improve relations between the allies. On 25 April, Thugut told Colloredo that 'as always, I only have a very slender idea of the good faith of the Court of Turin'.[12] At the same time, Colonel Costa, Colli's chief of staff, wrote to his brother from the army saying: 'You have no idea of the consternation that reigns here ... the remarks are detestable, but a unanimous curse against M. De Vins. As for me, I judge him incorrigible, because what happens is wanted, not owing to stupidity. Whatever the Austrians promise, we only have treason and bad faith to expect from them.'[13]

The French, meanwhile, were preparing to give the Piedmontese the last shove that would push them out of the high part of the County of Nice. Marmont says that the commander of the Army of Italy, who was then General Dumerbion, had never left the city during these operations because of his age and health,[14] and on 25 April Bonaparte returned there to press him to exploit the advantage they had gained. French pressure was duly maintained, and at dawn on the 27th, a column attacked the entrenchments of Monte Tanardo, north-east of Saorgio. Attacks were also made to the west of the town, and in order to avoid being cut off, the Piedmontese retired. On 28 April, the French entered Saorgio.

The efforts of the allied armies continued to be hindered by lack of co-operation between them. On 30 April, Argenteau wrote to Colli saying: 'I inform you that the Austrians, who are at Cairo, will not help me on any occasion, because they are ordered to defend their position and not to detach a single man to assist me.'[15] Eventually, the Piedmontese fell back to Limone, on the northern side of Colle di Tenda, but were obliged to go even further when the French Army of the Alps also pressed forward. By early May the Piedmontese had been forced to retreat to Borgo San Dalmazzo, a stone's throw from Cuneo.

When taken in the context of the meagre achievements that had been made on this front in the previous year, these rapid advances into enemy territory have to be seen as extraordinary. The position at Saorgio had resisted since the first French invasion of Nice, but had now fallen, to be followed immediately by that of Colle di Tenda. The Army of Italy was now well positioned for either attack or defence, and Massena established a very strong line on the mountain ridge between Ormea and Loano, while General Macquard placed himself at Colle di Tenda. The whole balance of the war on the southern front had been changed in a matter of a month, largely due to Bonaparte. But, naturally enough, it was not the limit of Bonaparte's ambitions. He regarded this as only a start, and so did the Representatives with the army.

On 20–21 May, Bonaparte was in Colmar for a conference at which he presented his 'Plan for the Second Preparatory Operation at the Opening of the Campaign in Piedmont'. It began by stating: 'We can only present ourselves in the plain of Piedmont with forces superior to our enemy. To obtain this superiority it is necessary to unite the armies of the Alps and of Italy.'[16] The area where this concentration was to be achieved was the valley of the Stura, in the area of Cuneo. The plan went on to detail the various movements to be made every day, including the all-important feints designed to deceive the enemy as to the method of effecting the junction of the armies. It was duly signed by the Representatives, Augustin Robespierre, Ricord and Laporte, and sent off to Paris for approval. Here it met the opposition of Lazare Carnot, who was not in favour of offensive operations at that time, and the plan was not carried out.

This was undoubtedly a missed opportunity, as Austria and Piedmont were only just beginning to take steps to achieve better co-operation. A treaty of alliance between them was finally signed at Valenciennes on 29 May. In this, Austria promised to send to Italy the greatest number of troops possible considering the demands of the other fronts. It was agreed that the Piedmontese army would defend the exits from the Alps, and the Austrian would limit itself to preventing a French advance along the Riviera, while acting as a reserve in case the French penetrated into the Piedmontese plain. It was also agreed that General de Vins would remain commander-in-chief of the two armies, subordinate to the King as far as the Piedmontese troops were concerned, and to the Archduke Ferdinand as far as the Austrians were concerned. The allies now began to take serious measures against the possibility of a French descent into the plains.

At this time (20 June) Bonaparte produced a second version of his plan for preparatory operations, no doubt at the request of the Representatives.[17] It was more detailed than the previous version, and somewhat ominously, it began with measures for internal security. Indeed, this was a time of great uncertainty in France, when Maximilien Robespierre was at the height of his power, and the guillotine was working overtime. No doubt the internal political situation made the French authorities hesitant about undertaking offensive military operations, and Bonaparte's new plan was not put into effect. The lack of French activity was noted by the Archduke Ferdinand, who in a letter of 4 July expressed surprise that they had done nothing in May and June.

Augustin Robespierre was no more satisfied with the lack of activity than Bonaparte, and when he left for Paris at about this time, he took with him another document prepared by the latter, which he undoubtedly intended to use as a basis for arguing in favour of offensive operations in Italy. It was dated 19 July, and was entitled 'Note on the Political and Military Position of our Armies in Piedmont and Spain'. It contains the following observations, which are revealing of Bonaparte's thinking about the conduct of the war:

> The general principle of our war is to defend our frontiers. Austria is our most determined enemy. It is necessary, therefore, as much as is possible, that the type of war of the different armies delivers direct or indirect blows at this power ... In systems of war, it is like sieges of fortresses. Concentrate one's fire on a single point. The breach made, the equilibrium is broken. All the rest becomes useless and the place is taken ... It is Germany that we must crush. Having done that, Spain and Italy will fall of themselves ... If we obtain great successes, we can in the next campaigns attack Germany via Lombardy, the Ticino, and the County of the Tyrol, while our armies on the Rhine attack the heart.[18]

Apart from expounding the ideas of concentration of forces, and of throwing the enemy off balance, which come from his studies of Du Teil and Bourcet, it is noteworthy that Bonaparte shows he is not just thinking of the short-term, but of the ultimate goal of the campaigning, and indeed of the war itself. Despite the fact that the French were still on the Riviera, he envisaged crossing the Ligurian mountains, the flood-plain of the Po, and launching into the Alps on the far side to invade the most southerly part of Austria (the Tyrol). This seemed fantastical to some, but to Bonaparte it was a natural progression, and there was hardly any point in doing the first part if one did not go on to do the rest. As we shall see, the idea of penetrating into the Tyrol became a constant in his plans, right until the latter stages of the 1796 campaign.

In the meantime, on 11 July, Bonaparte had left Nice to go to Genoa, ostensibly to negotiate and get provisions, but really to reconnoitre the place with the help of Marmont, Junot and a couple of others. His arrival caused immense interest, and on 17 July the Austrian minister there, Giovanni Girola, described him to Thugut as 'a young man of about 27 years, who is to be feared as a troublesome man, of ardent republican spirit, of vast knowledge in military things, great activity, and of great courage, recognised also in his plan which he himself executed in the recapture of Toulon'.

He also related how the young men had made rude jokes about the sedan chairs used by the senators and had not bothered to raise their hats when the Doge went past, 'something which irritated all those who saw such an insolent and churlish act. And if they continue on this footing, something unpleasant will happen to them ...'[19] Having thus outraged the locals with their behaviour, and no doubt gathered a lot of useful information, they left on 21 July.

At this point, there was a distinctly unpleasant hiatus in Bonaparte's career. On 27 July, Robespierre and his supporters were overthrown, and on the day afterwards went to the guillotine. Augustin shared his brother's fate. Being associated with powerful men, however distantly, had its dangers, and on 6 August, Saliceti and the other Representatives denounced what they oddly referred to as the '*liberticide*' plan of campaign 'of Robespierre *jeune* and Ricord, proposed by Bonaparte'.[20] Three days later, Bonaparte was placed under arrest – probably merely confined to his living quarters – while he was investigated. Innocence was never a guarantee of survival in those days, and although there was nothing incriminating in his papers, Bonaparte had to count himself lucky to be set free on 20 August. Officially, he was not reinstated as commander of the artillery of the Army of Italy, but he continued to carry out the functions. This little episode did not pass unnoticed in the enemy camp, and the Archduke Ferdinand made some interesting comments on it to General Colli: 'It is true that General Bonaparte, who was latterly sent to Paris [sic] in chains, returns with the command. He is a bold, enterprising Corsican, who will certainly want to risk an attack.'[21]

He was no doubt right that Bonaparte would have wanted to go onto the offensive, but while the latter had been under arrest, Carnot had ordered the Representatives with the Army of Italy to maintain the defensive and prepare for the next campaign. It was the allies, therefore, who took the first steps for an offensive operation, their plan being to attack the flank of the French positions around Loano. The movement was to be carried out by going up the valley of the Bormida di Spigno and advancing to Finale, then occupying Vado and Savona. However, allied secrecy proved to be insufficient, and the preparations for the offensive were noticed by the French in late August. Bonaparte gave Dumerbion his views on the dangers of the situation, and was told, 'Present me with a plan of the kind you know how to produce and I shall carry it out as well as I can.'[22] Bonaparte swiftly obeyed, and came up with a plan for an advance on Cairo Montenotte that may well have been influenced by a reading of the memoirs of de Maillebois, who had carried out an advance in this area in May 1745. It was duly accepted on 26 August.

The operation was to prove of immense value as a preparation for the initial phase of Bonaparte's 1796 campaign, some of which was to be fought over the same terrain, and it is therefore worth dwelling on it. On 5 September, Bonaparte left Nice with the staff, bound for Oneglia. The French began their approach march on 15 September, and the plan for the operation was issued on the 17th. Like previous plans by Bonaparte, its provisions were characterised by frequent use of the word 'if', a variety of scenarios being anticipated and planned for.[23] It also made use of turning movements combined with frontal attack. In his memoirs he remarked:

> Amongst mountains there are many positions to be found of great natural strength, which we must take care not to attack. The genius of this kind of warfare consists in occupying positions, either on the flanks or in the rear of those of the enemy, which leave him only the alternative of evacuating his position without fighting, or of coming out to attack you. In mountain warfare, he who attacks is always at a disadvantage; even in offensive war, the art consists in engaging only in defensive actions and obliging the enemy to attack.[24]

The initial attack, on San Giacomo, would seem to have been a classic example of this philosophy at work. In his own account of it, he states: 'By marches arranged with art and executed with much unison, we obliged the enemy to abandon the positions where he was entrenched, and which were very favourable to him.'[25] The enemy retired to Carcare, then, being threatened with another turning movement via Millesimo, to Dego. Bonaparte commented that the retreat was carried out in great order. The main action took place in the area of Dego, behind which was a formidable defensive position overlooking the Bormida valley. Bonaparte's own description of the engagement was as follows:

> About two o'clock in the afternoon, we discovered the enemy, from the village of Rocchetta. They had rested their left and their right on mountains which they esteemed to be very strong. Their centre was entrenched behind the Bormida, and supported by their artillery.
>
> Their Uhlans, who were all their cavalry, performed evolutions in the plain. They only tried to hinder us.

If we had thought that they wished to wait for us on the morrow, we would willingly have postponed the engagement. But, certain that they would flee during the night, we immediately made our preparations for an attack.

Six battalions and some pieces of mountain artillery marched over the mountains on the right and had orders to turn the enemy left, take up a position on the road from Dego to Spigno, and by that operation completely intercept the retreat of the enemy.

Two battalions were sent to drive the enemy from the position that safeguarded his right.

The rest of the army ranged itself in line of battle behind the village of Rocchetta, with the cavalry and the artillery.

All these dispositions could only be completed very late. The left attacked, and, after having charged four times, captured the height which the enemy had occupied.

The fire was very lively on the right, where the enemy had placed much of his strength. We drove them from part of their positions, but the very dark night did not permit us to advance any further and to arrive as far as Dego.

The centre attacked with great vivacity. The enemy retreated everywhere, and their cavalry, so brilliant in its evolutions, judged it prudent not to await the shock with our own.

Night separated us. We bivouacked on the field of battle. We placed our artillery in order to strike them down at the break of day, but the enemy did not judge that they should wait for us. They marched a night and a day without stopping … Thus, his designs on Savona have been thwarted for a long time.

The combat at Dego would have been decisive for the Emperor in his territories of Lombardy, if we had had three more hours of daylight.[26]

The allies did not view the result of the action in quite the same way, however. They asserted, and genuinely believed, that they had won a victory, and regarded the retreat as a move they had intended to carry out anyway.

To the disgust of many French military men, it was decided (probably by the Representatives) not to press the advance any further, although the most obvious thing to do would have been to make a drive for Ceva, which was now the most important defensive position between the French and the plains of Piedmont. The movement may not have been taken to its logical conclusion, but at least the French now held good positions roughly on the watershed between the coast and the inland plain. There were several entrenched strong-points at important locations on these ridges, generally where a route went over a high peak. Some of the most important were Monte Sotta and Monte Spinarda, between the valleys of the Tanaro and the Bormida di Millesimo; Monte Settepani, standing 4,550 feet high at the head of the valley of the Bormida di Pallare; and San Giacomo. Not only were these good defences, but they provided potential jumping-off points for an advance into Piedmont.

Even if the French operations had been concluded prematurely, there was no denying that they had been a success, and Dumerbion was gracious in his praise of those who had done most to achieve it. 'It is to the talents of the General of Artillery (Bonaparte) that I owe the clever arrangements which have secured our success,'[27] he wrote. He also singled out Massena, and the Swiss general La Harpe for special distinction. With a job well done, if incomplete in his view, Bonaparte left Cairo for Nice on 24 September.

On his way back, Bonaparte went via Colle di Cadibona, the lowest pass over the mountains on the Western Riviera. The choice of this route may have been influenced by the memoirs of de Maillebois, from which Bonaparte would have learned that the road from Madonna di Savona that went inland to Montezemolo, not far from Ceva, had been made practicable for artillery during the campaign of 1745. It had the significant name of 'chemin du cannon' – the road of the cannon. He must have realised immediately that this route, which connected Savona on the coast with Altare, Carcare, Millesimo, Montezemolo, Ceva and Mondovì, as well as Dego, was still potentially quite usable by an army. Not only that, but being the lowest pass, it had the advantage that it was usually the last to be closed by snow in winter, and the first to open in spring. Operations were therefore possible using this route when no other was available. From this point on, he seems to have been convinced that the road from Savona to Ceva would be a key element in a successful invasion of Piedmont.

He immediately incorporated this important information into his next plans, which precisely foreshadow those which he was to use in 1796. About a month after returning from Dego, he produced a plan proposing a penetration into Piedmont which exploited this route, but the Committee of Public Safety were unimpressed, and ordered the army to remain on the defensive. After this categoric refusal, nothing better could be found to occupy the army than the old idea of recapturing Corsica, which came up with some regularity, and never resulted in anything. It was duly exhumed, and Bonaparte was occupied for three months with planning the expedition.

Given his views on the importance of carrying the offensive to Austria, he cannot have been too pleased to see operations in Italy suspended, but there was little he could do to bring about a change of policy. In November, Dumerbion had been replaced as army commander by Schérer, and Bonaparte lost much of his influence. Schérer was a veteran of the Seven Years War who had also been an officer in the Austrian army, and he seems to have imbibed some of the grinding slowness and excessive caution that were typical of their methods. He showed no interest in the plans previously put forward by Bonaparte: indeed, he thought them mistaken. His own plans of January 1795 stated very clearly his belief that an attack on Piedmont would have to be launched over Colle di Tenda, because this was the only pass (apart from the Bocchetta) that was usable by an army taking its heavy artillery and supply wagons with it.[28] He seems, in short, to have envisaged the sort of lumbering behemoth of an army with mountains of baggage that had been typical of the Seven Years War. His view that the siege of the great fortress of Cuneo was the key to success made him consider it essential to encumber his forces with heavy equipment from the outset, in contrast to Bonaparte's preference for lightness and speed.

A further divergence from Bonaparte's views is revealed by Schérer's proposal to use the Bormida valley for an advance by his right wing, via

Carcare, Dego and Ceva, then Mondovì and Cuneo. This was intended
to give the initial impression that he planned to advance on Alessandria.
Such an extremely long 'right hook' would not have found favour with
Bonaparte because it isolated the right wing, and put it out of range of
support from the centre. Schérer, unlike Bonaparte, also felt that enormous reinforcements would be necessary before carrying out an offensive. Schérer believed that the Army of Italy would only be able to act
when it had reached an effective strength of 65,000 men – which, as
Jean Colin points out, was as good as saying never. That number of
troops was quite beyond the capability of the government to provide.
Rather, the army was shrinking rapidly due to outbreaks of typhus and
other diseases. The *Marchese* Carlo Guasco, who was in Alessandria at
the time, says:

> The letters which arrive from Genoa, Savona and the Riviera of
> the Ligurian Sea all agree in reporting that the French are dying
> like flies in the Genoese territory, and that they are burying 300
> to 400 a week.[29]

In February, the health problems became so acute that the French abandoned Savona and moved into the country.

Although there was a general lack of military action on the Italian
front at the beginning of 1795, there was a certain amount of diplomatic negotiation taking place behind the scenes, some of it between
France and Piedmont, and some with France's other enemies. Indeed,
two of the most important of the latter, Prussia and Spain, gave up the
war during the year, which considerably eased France's military position. French negotiations with Piedmont were not new, of course, and
as early as January 1793 they had put forward the suggestion of an
alliance. This was later expanded little by little, to include the cession
to Piedmont of Lombardy, and even Liguria. At the end of 1794,
secret negotiations were being conducted through intermediaries in
Switzerland. Undoubtedly, Piedmont's ability to resist was being
stretched to the limit, and the personal feelings of the King had to be
set against some harsh realities. In particular, the economic situation

of Piedmont was very bad, as may be judged from the fact that the King had pawned the crown jewels, placing them with Dutch bankers. Later on, the Austrians were also to open secret talks with the French, offering them Belgium if the French would agree not to oppose them expanding in Bavaria. The French reply was to suggest the cession of Lombardy to Piedmont in exchange for Savoy and Nice. Naturally, Austria rejected this out of hand. Against this background of diplomatic and financial uncertainty, there was a marked reluctance to embark on serious military action on the Italian front.

At the end of March, Bonaparte received the surprising news that he had been transferred to command the artillery of the Army of the West, which was involved in pacifying the rebellious Vendée region of France. It should be emphasised that he had consistently taken the view that Italy was the most important theatre of war, and that the most damage could be done to the allied war effort by a sustained and vigorous offensive there, so being sent home to engage in something like police work, where his talents would be wasted, was extremely unwelcome. He was reluctant to depart, and waited over a month, until he received a positive order to take up his new post.

While he was waiting, Prussia withdrew from the Coalition, signing a treaty with France at Basle on 4 April. The same month also saw planning conferences between the Piedmontese and Austrians, during which their usual disagreements prevented the early adoption of a unified plan. Spring was well advanced before the Austrians began to stir, but by that time their most dangerous opponent was no longer available to organise measures against them. On 7 May, Bonaparte received direct orders to join the Army of the West. The successes that have been described here may make his transfer to a less crucial theatre seem surprising, but Marmont observes:

> He had made his name by his actions, but these actions did not yet have enough brilliance to make his renown arrive beyond the circle of the army in which he had served. If his name was pronounced with esteem and consideration from Marseille to Genoa, he was unknown in Paris, and even in Lyon.[30]

Marmont ought to have returned to his unit in the Pyrenees but suggested that Bonaparte should visit his home at Châtillon on his way to Paris, and set off to precede him there. Bonaparte left Marseille on the 8th accompanied by Junot, and spent a few days in the country in the company of his friends. They arrived in Paris on 25 May, and Bonaparte went to see the Minister of War on the 26th. His hope and intention was to get himself sent back to the artillery of the Army of Italy. The minister, however, was in the process of weeding out politically suspect officers, and Bonaparte, with his (admittedly slight) links to the Robespierres, was deemed to be one of them. Bonaparte was removed from the list of artillery generals, on the grounds that the cadres were full, and he was the most junior. He was offered the command of a brigade of infantry with the Army of the West instead, but had no desire for such work. Either in sadness or anger, he asked for two months' sick leave, which he spent in Paris. Marmont paints a neat picture of their situation:

> So, there we were in Paris, all three: Bonaparte without a job, me without regular authorisation, and Junot attached as aide-de-camp to a general of whom they did not wish to make use, lodged at the Hôtel de la Liberté, rue des Fosses-Montmartre, passing our lives at the Palais-Royal and the shows, having very little money and no future.[31]

Bonaparte was still kicking his heels in Paris when news arrived on 15 July that the Army of Italy, now under Kellermann, had been defeated and forced to retreat along the coast of the Riviera. It was a considerable setback, and clearly required determined measures to stabilise the position. There was a new Minister of War by now, a youngish man named Doulcet de Pontécoulant, who discussed the situation with some of the Deputies who had been Representatives with the Army of Italy, and the name of Bonaparte soon emerged. According to Count de Vaublanc:

> Bonaparte ... presented to the Committee for War of the Convention, of which M. de Pontécoulant was a member, a

Memoir on the War in Italy. In it he promised to beat the Austro–Sardinian army by taking the positions he indicated, to separate the two armies, to force the Austrians to seek their safety beyond the Po, to turn then on the Piedmontese, and crush them and force them to make peace. Pontécoulant was charged with examining this memoir, and making a report on it to his committee. I got these details from him. He added that this writing contained many mistakes in French and spelling.[32]

This document is highly interesting in the context of Bonaparte's 1796 campaign, because it was to form the basis for the plans he was to use at that time. The main points of the Memoir were, first, that it was vital to retake the port of Vado, near Savona, to permit the grain trade with Genoa to be re-established. Secondly, Piedmont must be driven out of the war by taking the fighting into their lands, and making the Austrians abandon the positions where they dominated Piedmont. Both of these goals could be achieved by taking Ceva, which was easy to reach by going over the Apennines from Vado, using the route that Bonaparte had discovered in the autumn of 1794:

> From Vado to Ceva, the first frontier fortress of Sardinia on the Tanaro, it is eight leagues [about nineteen and a half miles], without ever rising more than 200 to 300 toises [roughly 1,300 to 1,900 feet] above sea level. These are therefore not mountains proper, but hills covered with plants, fruit trees and vines. The snows never block the passes. The heights are covered during the winter, but without there being a great quantity ... As soon as Vado has been taken, the Austrians will move in preference to those points which defend Lombardy. The Piedmontese will defend the exit into Piedmont. In the instructions, details will be given of the means to accelerate this separation ...

Bonaparte goes on to state his belief that it was important to make such an attack at the right time of the year, a belief that was based on his knowledge of what had happened in the wars of the 1730s and 40s:

Our armies in Italy have all perished due to the sicknesses caused by the great heat. The true moment to make war there and to strike great blows, once in the plain, is to act from the month of February until July ...

He also emphasises the material advantages of the advance, and proposes goals that were far beyond those which Kellermann had put forward in one of his own plans:

If, as is probable, peace has been made [with Piedmont], we may, before it is published, in agreement with Piedmont, from Ceva secure Alessandria, and go into Lombardy to win the indemnities which we shall give to the King of Sardinia for Nice and Savoy. The theatre of war will then be in a plentiful country, scattered with large towns, offering everywhere great resources for our transport, to remount our cavalry, and clothe our troops. If the campaign in February is successful, we shall find ourselves, in the first days of spring, masters of Mantua [the strongest fortress and main Austrian military base in Lombardy], ready to capture the gorges of Trento [in the Tyrol], and to carry the war, together with the Army of the Rhine, into Breisgau, up to the heart of the Hereditary Lands of the House of Austria.[33]

Another version, no doubt carefully prepared to be shown to the top men, since it was in Junot's legible hand, emphasises the need to separate the enemies, and adds some important details which are also relevant to the 1796 campaign:

The Austrians will retire on the positions which defend the road to Lombardy. They will occupy in preference the chain of mountains from Priero, Montenotte Superiore, and Montenotte Inferiore ... The Piedmontese will in preference occupy the positions which defend the entrance to Piedmont, that is to say the heights of San Giovanni, La Sotta, Biestro, and Montezemolo. One must in preference, and by a successive movement and without interrupting that which made us master of Vado, attack or oblige the enemy to evacuate, by a false march on Sassello, all the positions up to Montenotte Inferiore, and to retire on Acqui or even Alessandria. Then, via Cairo and Millesimo, capture the height of Montezemolo, which dominates Ceva. At the same time the division which remained for the defence of the Tanaro advances beyond Battifollo, invests Ceva on the side of Garessio, and effects its junction with the division which is at Montezemolo as close to Ceva as possible. During this time, the road from Madonna di Savona to Altare will be repaired, where the thirty-six cannon necessary for the siege of Ceva will pass.[34]

As we shall see, the movements that Bonaparte was to carry out when he made his own offensive in this area were very close to the ones described here.

There was nothing in Bonaparte's proposals that was radically different from what he had suggested before, but Pontécoulant had probably never seen anything like them before, and would seem to have been duly impressed. It probably helped that one of Pontécoulant's friends wrote to him around the same time, voicing the opinion that the Italian theatre was more important than Germany, which agreed with what Bonaparte believed.[35] Bonaparte clearly hoped that he would be sent back to the Italian front to assist in carrying out his ambitious plan, and on 30 July he wrote to his brother Joseph, telling him, 'The peace with Spain makes an offensive war in Piedmont certain. They are discussing my plan, which will certainly be adopted. If I come to Nice we shall see each other.'[36]

However, the Committee thought too much of his planning ability, and promptly gave him a job in the *Bureau Topographique*, which he took up on 30 or 31 July. Despite its name, this Topographical Bureau was in effect a staff headquarters where a lot of strategic planning was done. From this office Bonaparte was to supply a whole series of plans and instructions for the Committee to send to the Army of Italy. Initially, his Memoir was turned into an 'Instruction' for Kellermann, written out in Junot's hand once again, and containing many passages copied directly from the original. It also pointed out the need to advance into Piedmont out of economic necessity: 'The first principle that must drive us when directing the armies of the Republic is that they must supply themselves through war at the expense of the enemy countries. If the Army of Italy does not change its theatre of war as quickly as possible, it will become extremely onerous for the public treasury, as it cannot be maintained in a neutral country except with cash.'[37] An interesting minor detail is that measurements were given for bridging materials for crossing the Mincio, the river that flows from Lake Garda past Mantua. Once again, this shows how far ahead Bonaparte was thinking. It was a bit too far for Kellerman's taste, it would seem, and he proved somewhat resistant to Bonaparte's proposals, writing back to the Committee that 'the plan for the next campaign will depend on the reinforcements that the Committee sends. With 100,000 men available, we can drive the Austrians from Italy and capture Piedmont ...'[38] This number of troops they simply did not have.

Perhaps the reluctance to carry out his plans intensified the frustration Bonaparte was clearly feeling at this time. Despite the fact that he was working in an obviously key position (he was made head of the Topographical Bureau on 19 August), he was apparently suffering from a deep sense of dissatisfaction, and hatched the strange scheme of going to Turkey. On 20 August he told Joseph about it:

At the moment, I am attached to the Topographical Bureau of the Committee of Public Safety for the direction of the armies, in place of Carnot. If I request it, I would be able to go to Turkey to organise the artillery of the Great Seigneur ... The commission and the decree of the Committee of Public Safety that employed me to be responsible for the direction of the armies and plans of campaign being highly flattering to me, I fear they no longer wish to let me go to Turkey. We shall see. I have yet to see a campaign.[39]

That last sentence may hold the key to his mood at the time. He was a professional soldier, knew that he was very good at his job, there was a war going on round him, and had been for more than three years, and so far he had only been involved in limited operations lasting a couple of months at most. Now he was stuck in an office. What he wanted most of all was to be at the front, in the thick of a proper campaign. In short, he probably wanted to test his powers. Until he did, he could not be sure of his abilities, though he must have suspected that they were of a high order. But the proof he wanted could only come from the front line.

The decree attaching him to the military bureau of the Committee stated: 'You are placed under requisition with the Committee, to contribute by your zeal and knowledge to the work of plans of campaign and the operations of the land army.'[40] His zeal was much in evidence. On 25 August he wrote to Joseph, 'I am weighed down with work ...'[41] He found time to draft his request to go to Turkey, however, and sent it on 30 August. It was rejected. A member of the Committee, Jean Debry, saw it on 13 September, and wrote in the margin, 'I believe that ... the Committee of Public Safety must refuse to send away from the Republic, above all at this time, such a distinguished officer.'[42] For the time being, then, Bonaparte was kept in Paris. As things turned out, it was probably the best thing that could have happened to him.

Once again, it was internal political disorder that was to have a vital role in shaping Bonaparte's career. The problems were brought about by the introduction of yet another new constitution, and the election of a new Assembly. This took place against a background of continued Royalist activity, particularly in the west, but also in Paris. In the first few days of October trouble began to brew in the capital. Rebels were organising the violent overthrow of the government.

On 4 October, Bonaparte went to the theatre, and sensing that there was trouble in the air, he left to walk through the wind and rain to see what was happening at the National Convention. There he found that Paul Barras, one of the Representatives he had met at Toulon, had just been appointed to command the defence of the Tuileries, the seat of the government. Barras needed the support of an artilleryman, and asked Bonaparte if he would serve him. Bonaparte was no lover of anarchy and mob rule, and he wanted to see stability in France for a while, not another abrupt change of direction with the loss of everything gained by the Revolution. He agreed without hesitation.

He was quick and decisive as usual. Where were the guns? At Sablons, six miles away, he was told, with a rebel column already on its way to seize them. Someone would have to go and try to capture them. At this moment Joachim Murat, one of the most extraordinary figures of the Empire, walked into Bonaparte's life.

There is nothing one can say about Murat that has not already been said a thousand times before. The most unlikely candidate for the priesthood in the history of the Church, he was to blaze a multi-coloured trail through the Napoleonic Wars as the most over-dressed man in Europe and gain a reputation as one of the most spectacular battlefield cavalry leaders in history. Tall, handsome, flamboyant in the extreme and extravagantly brave, this hoarse-voiced Gascon was always in search of women to seduce when he was not thundering about on horseback looking for other kinds of action. He was an ideal man in this particular emergency, and galloped through the night with his men, scattered the rebel column just in time, and came back with the guns.

Meanwhile, curiosity had brought others to see what was happening. Paul Thiébault, a young subaltern who had been brought up in Prussia, was among those who went to the Convention that night to see what was happening. On arriving, he asked for General Menou, whom he took to be the commander.

'Menou?' they replied. 'Mercy of God! that traitor is no longer commanding us. Barras is our General-in-Chief and General Bonaparte is his second.' –

'Bonaparte?' I said to myself. 'Who the devil is that?'[43]

It seems a pretty fair indication of what was known of him by those who had not served in the Army of Italy.

Bonaparte set up the guns around the Tuileries, with care. Among other Republicans who lent help was a General Brune, who was also to serve in Italy, and later became a marshal. It was not until the afternoon of 5 October that the rebels came into view. It was not a polite demonstration – they were fully armed, and there were many thousands of them. The government had perhaps 8,000 men. But with the support of Bonaparte's artillery, placed in the narrow streets, they were not too badly off. When the rebels attacked they were subjected to what has memorably been called 'a whiff of grape-shot' – an expression that does little to communicate the effect of being flattened or eviscerated by a hail of small iron balls. By the evening it was over. The Revolution was safe, the Royalists went back into hiding, and Bonaparte had won himself a reputation.

His promotion was swift, and he soon found himself with considerable influence. By 9 October he was second-in-command of the Army of the Interior, under Barras. Bonaparte's friend, Chauvet, was nominated Chief Commissary at his request. On 16 October, Bonaparte was promoted General of Division. Ten days later the Convention was dissolved and the Directory was formed, with Barras one of the Directors. The day afterwards, Bonaparte was made commander-in-chief of the Army of the Interior. He asked for Marmont as his ADC, and the latter came back from Germany to find a situation that was very different from the one he had left:

> I found General Bonaparte established in the headquarters of the Army of the Interior, rue Neuve des-Capucines … He already had an extraordinary aplomb, an air of grandeur that was completely new to me, and the feeling of his importance which must have been growing continually.[44]

As so often, however, success in one field had been accompanied by success in another, so he was probably suffused with a double glow. Just after the revolt he had met Josephine, the fascinating widow of General de Beauharnais, and had fallen madly in love. And for once, that clichéd expression is appropriate, for at times his passion for her bordered on being unhinged. It was a passion that was to form a distracting background to the taxing times of his first campaign.

This new-found sense of satisfaction must have been increased by news of improved French fortunes in Italy, for Bonaparte never lost sight of, or interest in, what was happening on this front — the most important in his eyes. The arrival there of units released by the ending of the war in the Pyrenees had strengthened the army, and Schérer, who had returned with them, had taken over command from Kellermann. Schérer had received some prompting to take the offensive and at least win back some of the territory recently lost, particularly Vado, and eventually launched an attack in November. By the 15th, the French had advanced until on the coast they were only separated from the enemy by the valley between Borghetto and Loano. On 18 November the weather worsened, and a hurricane blew away all the tents and covered the mountains with snow. De Vins, either because he assumed that very little else was going to happen after this, or because he was genuinely ill (Costa says he was suffering from scurvy),[45] handed over command to General Wallis on the 22nd, and left the HQ. This was unfortunate timing, because on 23 November a major battle was fought at Loano. Joubert provides a description of some of the action, with a welcome touch of humour:

> I commanded the advance-guard of the centre, which attacked General Argenteau. We found before us two redoubts, defended by 1,200 men and seven cannon. I climbed up to them at the break of day with 600 grenadiers or chasseurs, and, in concert with General Pijon, who had a similar head of column, we fell on the redoubt without firing a shot, through the most terrible fire. My column entered first. I was thrown into the redoubt by two grenadiers. Forty of my men were there sabring away. A commander was disputing his sword with a chasseur. I placed my sabre on his chest saying: 'Surrender!' My grenadiers drew back from him immediately, but said to me: 'Kill him, General!' (I was in a soldier's coat and in gaiters). – 'What! Are you a general?' replied the officer, letting fall his weapon. Immediately twenty other officers surrounded me and demanded their lives. During this scene, which took a minute, the redoubt was so full that you could not move. It was like being in a square on a market day ...[46]

After a ferocious combat of many hours in terrible weather, the French drove the enemy from their defences. Argenteau, to whom much of the blame for the defeat was attributed, retired from Bardineto all the way to Ceva. Count Moretti says that the Austrian army 'had suffered much from the sicknesses of the summer, and many had died from the cold. In the retreat they did great damage wherever they passed, taking money and linen from the inhabitants.'[47]

This major battle brought the campaign season to a close, and, as usual, the belligerents settled down to use the period of bad weather to rebuild and prepare for the next one. Unbeknown to them, of course, they were preparing for the campaign in which Bonaparte was to make his début.

After their unpleasant defeat, the Austrians made considerable efforts to reinforce their army and renew its equipment. Troops were trans ferred from the Rhineland, others were sent down from the nearby Tyrol, and a battalion of Grenzers was even despatched from far-away Galicia. Moreover, recruits were sent to bring the much-depleted regi ments that were already in Italy back up to strength. The transport serv ices and the bridging train were also augmented. The Austrians also took the opportunity for a very necessary overhaul of their supply services, and dismissed their chief commissary for swindling. However, there was a limit to what could be done for the army in Italy, due to the need to keep considerable forces in Germany, where Austria was now France's only active opponent, following the withdrawal of the Prussians. The contribution of the English was limited to providing Austria with vast sums of money, and chasing French ships wherever they could be found.

As far as Piedmont was concerned, their major difficulty in preparing for a new campaign was financial. By 1796 their currency had lost 60 per cent of its value, and the public debt reached 244 million during the year. In addition to this, morale in the army was at a very low ebb. Costa, who was with Colli and the army at Ceva, states that the soldiers and officers almost all desired peace.

In fact, the Piedmontese government had entered into peace negoti ations with the French, but conducted themselves with their habitual ineptitude. On 10 January, their ambassador in Vienna was instructed by the King to inform Thugut of what they were doing, and that 'The outcome of our negotiations depends on the conduct that is adopted in Vienna ... it is only with the greatest repugnance that we shall make a separate peace with France if we are forced to it, that this eventuality will certainly not take place if we find our allies sincerely disposed to provide us with all the help that may assist in sheltering our states from the danger of invasion with which they are threatened.'[48] The Austrian reaction was predictable. Thugut commented on 17 January: 'There is hardly any doubt that the Piedmontese are busy with secret plots that could become very dangerous if we do not take precautions to forestall the effects.'[49] Victor Amadeus had probably never taken the negotiations seriously, and on 27 January he held a council meeting which decided to reject the proposals that the French had made, while not informing the French immediately. However, the damage to the alliance with Austria had already been done, with possibly fatal consequences for the 1796 campaign.

Meanwhile, on 13 January, the Directory had sent Schérer a letter[50] stating its intention to begin campaigning in Italy at an early date. There seems little reason to doubt that this was inspired by Bonaparte, who must have been working hard to convince the Directors that Italy was the key to winning the war. Schérer responded on the 25th with various objections:

> If, as you seem to desire, the campaign in Italy opens very early, the snow obstructs the exits from the Alps and half the Apennines until the month of prairal[51] [late May to early June]. It is evident that at the moment when I enter Piedmont I shall be obliged to fight the almost completely unified armies of the Austrians and Sardinians together. Then the Army of the Alps will not be able to be of any use to me, because it can only act towards the end of prairal. The snows themselves will oppose any kind of diversion.
>
> I must also observe that the end of pluviôse, which corresponds roughly to the middle of February, is not the time to open the campaign in Piedmont, which, in that season, is still largely covered by snow ...

Schérer related numerous other difficulties, and requested another 18,000 men and 8,000 transport animals to bring his forces up to the strength he believed necessary. He closed by saying:

> If I was not sustained by the true belief that you have considera-
> tion for my demands, my spirit would wither from discourage-
> ment, and I would say to you, Citizen Directors, if you find a
> man more capable than me through his energy, his courage, and
> his resources, of succouring and directing this army, send him at
> once and without hesitating entrust him with the burden of a
> command that I never sought.[52]

It seems likely that he is referring to Bonaparte, whom he suspected or knew to be the source of the plans the Directory was putting forward. Bonaparte had already produced another of them on 19 January, expressing all his irritation with the constant temporising, and setting out the strategy he had recommended so often before:

> If the Army of Italy lets the month of February go by without
> doing anything, as it has let the month of January go by, the
> campaign in Italy will be entirely lost. We must convince
> ourselves that we will only obtain great successes in Italy in
> winter. If we suppose that the Army of Italy begins its movement
> as soon as possible, it can march on Ceva, and carry the
> entrenched position there before the Austrians, who are at Acqui,
> have joined the Piedmontese. If, on seeing the preparations that
> the French make, the Austrians move along behind the Tanaro, to
> join the Piedmontese, our army must make two marches on
> Acqui, that is to say to Cairo and Spigno. We may be assured that
> then the Austrians will hasten to return and defend their commu-
> nications with the Milanese. The operation that we must carry
> out is simple: are the Piedmontese alone? March on them via
> Garessio, Bagnasco, La Sotta, Castelnuovo [di Ceva], Monteze-
> molo. Having beaten them and carried the entrenched position,
> conduct the siege of Ceva ... Have the Austrians had the wit to

go to Montezemolo to join the Piedmontese? It is necessary to separate them, and for that, march on Alessandria ... Masters of Ceva, we must not lose a moment in making the division that guards Tenda ... advance ... and march straight on Turin. The King of Sardinia then makes peace proposals. The General must then say that he does not have the right to make peace, that a courier must be sent to Paris, and during that time the King will be obliged to make proposals such that they cannot be refused ... In any case, as war in Italy depends entirely on the season, each month requires a different plan of campaign. The government must have complete faith in its general, leave him great latitude, and only give him the goal it wishes to achieve. It takes a month to get a reply to a despatch from Savona, and in that time every-thing can change.[53]

Some of these recommendations seem to have found their way into a letter which was sent to Schérer by a somewhat impatient Directory on 22 January. It was couched in the smooth and courteous language of the time, but its message was clear – get on with it. He was urged to capture Ceva, threaten Turin in order to convince the Piedmontese to join forces with France, then attack Acqui and Tortona, to open a route into Lombardy.[54]

Bonaparte's previously stated view that Italy was the most important front continued to receive independent support from prominent figures, including the diplomat François Cacault, who wrote on 26 January:

It seems to me that it is now for the Army of Italy to secure defin-itively the glory and the destiny of the Republic, and I cannot cease to be persuaded that its operations and its successes are much more important than those of our generals of the Rhine, where it will be more difficult to obtain decisive advantages than in Italy, and where our success will always afflict the Austrians less.[55]

Unfortunately, this view was not shared by the Directory. Their overall plan, mainly the work of Carnot, called for offensives on both fronts, but accorded primacy to the fighting in Germany. Interestingly, the Austrians also held the view that the most important theatre of operations was the Lower Rhine.[56] This meant that there was a certain amount of reluctance to dedicate too many precious resources to the southern theatre.

The Army of Italy, meanwhile, was suffering from every kind of deprivation. On 3 February, La Harpe wrote to Massena from Savona saying, 'We are absolutely without paper: the correspondence will suffer.'[57] Under these conditions, faced with the problem of mere survival, the stream of ideas flowing from Paris began to irritate those who were at the front in Italy. On the same day, the government commissioner with the army, Ritter, complained to Letourneur, a member of the Directory:

> I had said to you that eternal project-mongers surrounded the Government. I did not wish to name these individuals, gnawed by ambition and greedy for posts above their capacity. You had judged them at the time and on the spot. Why did you not oppose their chimerical and gigantesque plans? Will you suffer the Army of Italy, so deserving by its patience and its victories, to go to its destruction because some madmen are pleased to show you on the map of a country of which no correct map exists, how they could seize the moon with their teeth?[58]

Just to add to the annoyance, on 3 February Schérer was sent another letter in which there was a sudden change of scheme. Schérer was still enjoined to attack as soon as possible, but now he was told to make his main effort against the Austrians, not the Piedmontese, which meant that the siege of Ceva fell out of the calculations.[59] The main push of the offensive was now to be towards Acqui, then Gavi (the fortress which guarded the northern end of the Bocchetta Pass and therefore the main road between Genoa and Milan), and after that directly for the Milanese. This cannot have been one of Bonaparte's ideas, for it ran contrary to his view of how best to exploit both the political situation and the topography of the area. The abrupt change of objective suggests that there must have been something of a tussle taking place in Paris over how best to prosecute the war in Italy, and at this point at least, the pressure against Bonaparte's view had prevailed. Schérer, having been given this prodding from afar, was also given the glad news that Saliceti was on his way to light a fire under him, having been appointed government commissioner with the army.

On 4 February, Schérer replied to the Directory's letter of 22 January. With his letter he sent a memoir with his views on the plans of campaign he had received. The Directory could hardly ignore the tone of his communication:

> As far as I am concerned I will make every preparation to satisfy your wishes. But unfortunately these preparations will be limited to the organisation of the 19,000 or 20,000 infantry, all that I have at my disposal, and to saying to them 'March!' ... As for me, I beseech you, I implore you to send here a general of more resource and skill than I have, for I admit that I am incapable in the present conditions of sustaining the burden of command. In my letter of 5 pluviôse [25 January, asking for the services of Berthier] I asked you for a helper. I now request you as a special favour to send me a successor. My health has broken down due to bodily fatigues and the pains of the spirit, and my moral and physical means are too far below the needs that you demand of me.[60]

Interestingly, Schérer's plan of 4 February provided for an advance to Ceva, as Bonaparte had consistently suggested. However, it was to be carried out only when the army had reached a strength of 60,000 men, a quite impossible figure.[61] As if to emphasise that the campaigning season was not far off, the weather improved noticeably that day. This must have given Schérer a glimmer of optimism in his customary gloom, for he wrote to Massena on the 5th, 'Tell your soldiers that their sufferings are about to come to an end, and that the prize for victory will be the conquest of a country that will abundantly provide them with something to live on.'[62]

On the far side of the mountains there was still something of a struggle of wills between the so-called allies. The attitude of the Austrians may be judged by Gherardini's observation to Thugut that '... our army, while it defends Piedmont, can dictate law to the King of Sardinia and this country can only be regarded at present as a province of the house of Austria.'[63] The Archduke in Milan was also badly disposed towards Piedmont, and expressed the view that the Austrians should keep their army in the Milanese, instead of moving to support their allies.

It was not much of an atmosphere in which to discuss campaign plans, but in mid-February, Victor Amadeus officially designated General de La Tour, accompanied by the Marquis de Saint Marsan (who had been ADC to De Vins during the previous campaigns), to go to Vienna to discuss the bases for the plan of operations for the coming year. La Tour's mission was difficult because he not only had to work out a plan that was agreeable to both sides, but also judge to what extent the Austrians were likely to stick to it.

The King's instructions to La Tour stressed that 'it is absolutely in defending Piedmont that one is certain to defend Lombardy, and this defence of Piedmont is the most important for the common cause in every respect, just as it is the most pressing'.[64] La Tour was also to put forward the view 'that the essential point, above all at the opening of the campaign, is to secure the position of Ceva and of Mondovì against any attack threatened by the enemy, and absolutely to prevent the French from penetrating into the three provinces of Mondovì, the Langhe, and Acqui by the valleys of the Tanaro, the Belbo and the Bormida to establish themselves there, which would put all the rest of Piedmont in the greatest danger ...'[65] In other words, as far as strategy was concerned, the Piedmontese had much the same convictions as Bonaparte.

The latter's constant harping on precisely these subjects finally brought Schérer's exasperation to its height. On 19 February, he wrote bitterly to Massena (who now commanded the two divisions of the advance-guard):

I need the report from Aubernon [the commissary] to stop the mouths of some show-offs, who, from Paris, assert that we can do much better than we have done. You will have guessed of whom I am speaking: of Bonaparte, who is besieging the Directory and the Minister with ever more insane plans, and who sometimes has the art of getting himself listened to ... I know, my dear General, that some intriguers and incompetents have permitted themselves to spread the rumour in Paris that the Army of Italy, after its victory of 2 frimaire [23 November] ... could have captured Ceva and its camp, and even penetrated into Piedmont.[66]

Massena replied sympathetically, calling the men in Paris intriguers, while General Augereau, another divisional commander, called them imbeciles.[67]

Not long after this was written, on 22 February, Saliceti, whom some probably regarded as Bonaparte's advance-guard, arrived in Nice. On the following day, Saliceti had a discussion with Schérer, which he reported to Carnot, reiterating the ideas we have seen so often before:

Ritter and the commander-in-chief wish, before beginning, to be able to put their hands on everything they require. If that were possible no doubt it would be better, but in the impossibility of obtaining the things that are necessary in our own territory, would it not be more useful and more appropriate to go and get them from the enemy, and while providing for the needs of the first moment, to attack the Piedmontese between Ceva and Mondovì and try to gain a decisive victory over them, should they accept an action, or, if they retreat, to enter the country which they abandon and supply ourselves at their expense?'[68]

Such a plan was to be carried out, of course, but not by Schérer. Just six days later, Bonaparte wrote some letters concerning the movement of troops destined to reinforce the Army of Italy, and asked for the replies to be sent to him in Nice. Clearly, he knew by this time that he had got the command he really wanted.

The campaign instruction, which he no doubt helped to form, was issued on 2 March. This stated that the political situation in Italy dictated that the main effort would need to be directed against the Austrian army and possessions there. However, conducting an offensive against the Austrians demanded 'the defeat of the Piedmontese at the beginning of military operations' so that the French army would not be further troubled by them. It also stated that it left the details of the planning in the hands of Bonaparte 'in whom [the Directory] places its confidence'. Although it was intended that the major effort was to be made in the direction of Milan, it was conceded that this could not be achieved without capturing Ceva first, so Bonaparte was given permission to attack this point. However, 'The entry of the Republican army into Piedmont must only be considered as a preliminary disposition, which places us in a position to attack the Austrian forces with greater advantage ...' The penultimate paragraph stated, 'The Executive Directory reserving to itself the faculty to make peace, the General-in-Chief will not agree to any cease-fire, and will not slow his military operations in any way.'[69] They had yet to learn that the difficulty with Bonaparte was stopping him, not getting him to move.

On 2 March 1796, the Directory wrote to Schérer accepting his resignation, and issued a decree appointing Bonaparte in his place. He finally had his chance to prove himself. It was time to pass from planning to execution.

NOTES

1. Bergadani, R. *Vittorio Amedeo III (1726–1796)*. Turin, 1939, p. 243.

2. Ibid., p. 245.

3. Oliveri, L. *Battaglie napoleoniche in Val Bormida (1793–1796)*. Cairo Montenotte, 1996, p. 9.

4. Vivenot, A., Ritter von, and Zeissberg, H., Ritter von. *Quellen zur Geschichte der Deutschen Kaiserpolitik Oesterreichs während der Französischen Revolutionskriege. 1790–1801*. Vienna, 1873–85, IV, pp. 27–9.

5. Bergadani, op. cit., p. 265.

6. Ibid., pp. 249–50.

7. See ibid., pp. 252–3.

8. See Conterno, G. 'Una cronaca inedita di èta napoleonica in val Bormida.' *Atti e Memorie della Società Savonese di Storia Patria*, XIX (1985, p. 113.

9. Wilkinson, S. *The Rise of General Bonaparte*. Oxford, 1930, pp. 165–66.

10. See Colin, J. L. A. *L'éducation militaire de Napoléon*. Paris, 1900, pp. 405–13.

11. See Duval, C. 'La 19e demi-brigade à l'armée d'Italie (1793–1796) et le brigadier-général Dichat de Toisinge.' *Mémoires et documents publiés par la société savoisienne d'histoire et d'archéologie*, 36 (1897), p. 524.

12. Vivenot, A., Ritter von. *Vertrauliche Briefe des Freiherrn von Thugut*. Vienna, 1872, I, p. 90.

13. Bergadani, op. cit., p. 261.

14. See Marmont, A. F., de. *Mémoires du duc de Raguse de 1792 à 1832 imprimés sur le manuscrit original de l'auteur*. Paris, 1857, I, p. 50.

15. Bergadani, op. cit., p. 261.

16. Napoleon. *Correspondance de Napoléon Ier publiée par ordre de l'empereur Napoléon III*. Paris, 1858–69, no. 27.

17. See ibid., no. 30.

18. Colin, op. cit., p. 444.

19. Vivenot and Zeissberg. op. cit., IV, p. 340.

20. Garros, L. *Quel roman que ma vie! Itinéraire de Napoléon Bonaparte (1769-1821)*. Paris, 1947, p. 73.

21. Colin, op. cit., p. 310.

22. Garros, op. cit., p. 74.

23. See Colin, op. cit., p. 457.

24. Napoleon. *Mémoires pour servir à l'histoire de France, sous le regne de Napoléon, écrits sous sa dictée à Sainte-Hélène, par les généraux qui ont partagé sa captivité*. Paris, 1829, III, chap. V. Also Napoleon. *Maximes*. Paris, 1820, no. XIV.

25. Napoleon. 1858–69, op. cit., no. 37.

26. Ibid.

27. Colin, op. cit., p. 461.

28. See ibid., p. 467.

29. Raggi, A. M. 'La campagna franco-austro-sarda del 1795 nelle lettere di un patrizio alessandrino.' *Rassegna storica del Risorgimento*, XLI (1954), p. 55.

30. Marmont, A. F., de. op. cit., I, p. 60.

31. Ibid., I, p. 62.

32. Vaublanc, V. M. V., comte de. 'Bonaparte et Carnot (1796).' *Revue rétrospective*, XII, Jan–July (1890), pp. 400–1.

33. Napoleon. 1858–69, op. cit., no. 49.

34. Ibid., no. 50.

35. Six, G. 'Un document intéressant sur l'origine de la campagne d'Italie de 1796.' *Revue des études napoléoniennes*, 45 (1939), pp. 212–14

36. Napoleon. 1858–69, op. cit., no. 54.

37. Ibid., no. 53.

38. Massena, A. *Mémoires de Massena, rédigés d'après les documents qu'il a laissés et sur ceux du dépôt de la guerre et du dépôt des fortifications, par le général Koch.* Paris, 1848–50, I, p. 291.

39. Napoleon. 1858–69, op. cit., no. 56.

40. Derrécagaix, V. B. *Le maréchal Berthier.* Paris, 1904, p 62.

41. Napoleon. 1858–69, op. cit., no. 58.

42. Ibid., no. 61.

43. Thiébault, P. C. *Mémoires du général Baron Thiébault. Publiés sous les auspices de sa fille Mlle. Claire Thiébault d'après le manuscrit original par Fernand Calmettes.* Paris, 1895–96, I, p. 532. These memoirs, like so many that were written after the restoration of the Bourbons, are well known to be immensely unreliable, and it is wise to treat them with caution.

44. Marmont, A. F., de. op. cit., I, p. 86.

45. Costa de Beauregard, C. A, *Un homme d'autrefois: souvenirs recueillis par son arrière-petit-fils.* Paris, 1879, p. 297.

46. Chevrier, E. *Le général Joubert d'après sa correspondance.* Paris, 1884, p. 27.

47. Conterno, op. cit., pp. 118–19.

48. Fabry, J. G. A. *Histoire de l'armée d'Italie (1796-1797).* Paris, 1900–14, II, p. 39.

49. Vivenot, 1872, op. cit., I, p. 282.

50. See Fabry, op. cit., II, pp. 304–5.

51. One of the months of the Republican calendar, which was adopted in 1793. For a full explanation see Jones, C. *The Longman Companion to the French Revolution.* Harlow, 1988.

52. Fabry, op. cit., II, pp. 401–2.

53. Napoleon. 1858–69, op. cit., no. 83.

54. See Fabry, op. cit., II, pp. 418–19.

55. Cleyet-Michaud, R. 'Un diplomate de la Révolution: François Cacault et ses plans de conquête de l'Italie (1793-1796).' *Revue d'histoire diplomatique*, 86 (1972), p. 315.

56. See Vivenot, A., Ritter von. *Thugut, Clerfayt und Wurmser. Original-Documente aus dem k. k. Haus-, Hof-, und Staats-Archiv und dem k. k. Kriegs-Archiv in Wien vom Juli 1794–Feb 1797.* Vienna, 1869, p. 443.

57. Fabry, op. cit., III, p. 3.

58. Wilkinson, op. cit., p. 76.

59. See Fabry, op. cit., II, pp. 424–27.

60. Ibid., III, pp. 124–5.

61. See ibid., pp. 125–33.

62. Ibid., III, p. 36.

63. Ibid., IV, p. 72.

64. Ibid., IV, p. 88.

65. Ibid., IV, p. 89.

66. Derrécagaix, op. cit., p. 61.

67. See Fabry, op. cit., III, p. 152, and Derrécagaix, op. cit., p. 61.

68. Wilkinson, op. cit., pp. 76–7.

69. The date given in Fabry, op. cit., IV, §2, pp. 63–7, is 2 March. The Instruction is not given a date in Napoleon. *Correspondance inédite officielle et confidentielle de Napoléon Bonaparte: avec les cours étrangères, les princes, les ministres et les généraux français et étrangers, en Italie, en Allemagne, et en Egypte.* Paris, 1809, I, p. 12-23, but it appears below a covering note which is dated 6 March.

7

PREPARATIONS

Following his nomination, Bonaparte spent another nine days getting ready to depart. This was no doubt largely taken up with paperwork, arranging cash, supplies, troop movements, trying to get hold of subordinates he valued, and so forth. But some of his time must also have been taken up with reading, and he took the trouble to obtain a number of books on the geography and history of northern Italy. It was to become a normal feature of his working methods to read as much as he could about the campaign area when preparing for operations, so it is interesting to note that this practice was already established at the very start of his career.

Some of the books were collected from the Bibliothèque Nationale by Murat, who had managed to get himself onto Bonaparte's staff. According to the receipt, which he signed styling himself 'chef de brigade aide de camp', he borrowed the *Memoirs of de Catinat* (Paris, 1775); the *History of Prince Eugene* (Amsterdam, 1740); *the Campaigns of de Maillebois*; the *Battles of Prince Eugene* (1725); the *Theatre of Piedmont and Savoy* (1700); and *War in the Alps* by Saint-Simon.[1] Other sources add the *Campaigns of Vendôme* to this list, and a number of maps, including the all important map of Piedmont and Lombardy by Borgonio. This ancient and inaccurate piece of cartography was the only readily obtainable map of the area. It seems likely that Bonaparte also took a large number of other books to Italy, to judge from the comments of Thiébault quoted below. Bonaparte also asked for a telescope.[2]

One of the books was rather unusual in its usefulness. Apart from a history of the 1745–6 campaigns in Italy, the memoirs of de Maillebois had an invaluable geographical index with highly detailed descriptions of towns, villages, landscape, fortresses, river crossings and the like, often concentrating on the features of most interest to an army commander. It was rather like a tourist guide for a general, and gave him a fair degree of knowledge of strategically important places he had not seen. It did not stop at the places where the French had campaigned in the 1740s, but included descriptions of places far into Lombardy and beyond, such as the crossing over the River Mincio at Borghetto, which Bonaparte was to use in May. To Bonaparte, the book was no doubt a vital part of his campaign equipment, and although Nelson managed to capture one copy, there seems to have been another which Bonaparte kept until he reached Verona.[3]

While waiting to depart, Bonaparte sent Marmont off ahead of him to carry out inspections and make reports on the condition of the army. It cannot have been very good, as it had recently been through a deal of suffering. On the last day of February, a violent and heavy snowstorm had struck the Ligurian mountains and continued for more than a week, blocking the roads and passes, and making movement impossible for the armies. General Dellera reported that around Mondovì the snow was knee-deep.[4] For Bonaparte this was a piece of luck, because it meant the campaign could not open immediately, and it gave him time to arrive in Nice and effect the transfer of command of the army before the enemy could move against him. For the French soldiers in their miserable billets on the mountain slopes, it was an extension of the purgatory they had been enduring.

When Quartermaster-Corporal André Dupont-Ferrier wrote home on 3 March he painted a bleak picture. His spelling is quite inimitable (in another letter he spells 'Italy' two different ways in the space of six words – incorrectly both times) but an attempt has been made to give something of the flavour:

Dear brother.
I riplie to your letter which Marquin brawt me, soe he has arrived safely. He spennt 28 days on the rode. He dilivered me the handkerchief that my dear sister gave himm; I cood never do himm an equal service such as he didd me in thatt moment – though being a long way from my relashuns, when they still thinkk of me; I truly bileeved that nobody thawt of me; arfter having ritten sevral letters, not receiveing enny riplie! And he dilivered me the money that you gave him.
You asked me to note down a descripshun of this army. I coodnt doo it till now, when we ar billited. On 12 pluviôse [1

February], 12th, 13th, 14th, the locals were abliged to fead us. We had noe bread, noe meat. The transspots coodnt manage, because ther wer 5 feat of snowe. To get through the mountinns they neaded all the men to goe and owpen the rode.

Though the rodes ar owpen, menny of us ar withowt meat for much of the time. Vegetables we downt get at all.

During the munth the municipal officials was abliged to goe to the locals to rekwisition bread: 8 pounds here, 10 ther, to fead the troops. Menny of the locals ar abliged to buy grain. They still have to supplie us with it, like the others.

In the whole battalion, ther ar ownly 40 who have got a bed. Ther ar noe sheets and no blankets. We ar alsoe as black as colemen. Where we ar billited the houses downt have chimneys at all. For light they only burn wood. Theres a lot of cleanliness: the menn, the wimmin, the cowse, the donkies, the piggs, the gotes, the chickins, they all eat together; the sayme cookin iz for everybody.

I cant go on, becos I coodnt give you a descripshun, and perhaps you wood think I was having you on.

I can tell you we ar going to be re-brigaded. Out of eleven battalions they ar going to make only three. So thaire will be many soopernoomery offissers and NCOs. We still downt know what it will be like, but thaire will be menny changes. In thiss battalion they have taken the names of the offissers and NCOs and the time they became offissers, and so forth.

I downt know if I will rimane a quarter-master, or if I will have to take a muskit or perhaps they will dismiss me until ferther orders.

We ar to leeve during the munth to go to the fort of Sairé, where we came from. We wer within muskit-range of the fort of Sairé and it will be brigaded for us.

I conclude by embrasing with all my hart my mother, brother, sister and brother-in-law, and sister-in-law, withowt forgetting my sister Babet.

your brother.

FERRIER

You ort to be very happie, becos the poor peeple who ar on the frontier ar to be piteed. They leeve them nothing. They have to werk day and nite for the troops, for wood or to goe and look for our food.

As soon as we are brigaded, I will give you my news.[5]

It should not be thought that the officers lived in any greater luxury. One of them wrote that 'It is quite usual, when the soldiers are paid, to see the officers ask them to lend them a sol so that they can have themselves shaved.'[6]

These unspeakable conditions had calamitous effects on both health and morale. In early March, the Army of Italy had 38,119 men in hospital[7] – or what passed for a hospital in those desperate times. It is a staggering figure, and it underlines the fact that hunger and sickness were often the worst enemies of the ordinary soldier. Moreover, when we consider that the force which Bonaparte managed to collect in his four main combat divisions for his offensive in April totalled just under 38,000 men, the scale of the problem is underlined. Survival rates among the sick were not good either. The French historian Félix Bouvier tells us that 'in January 1796 in Savona, 600 men of the 21st demi-brigade had died in twenty days as the result of an epidemic'.[8] There were also numerous mutinies of greater or lesser seriousness, though none of them seems to have got completely out of control, which says something about the overall quality of leadership, though General Sérurier (one of the divisional commanders) complained that his officers were 'as drunk as his soldiers'.[9] Clearly, an improvement in conditions and supplies was urgently needed if more severe outbreaks were to be avoided.

The time for opening the campaign was now fast approaching, and on 5 March the Austrian troops in Lombardy began their movement from winter quarters.[10] There were also signs that the French were beginning their build-up. Such large movements could not go unnoticed, and the Tuscan consul at Nice, De Negri, kept his ambassador in Paris (Don Neri Corsini) very well informed of everything he saw and heard:

They are making substantial and pressing preparations here for an imminent attack, but the snows that have been falling on these mountains for the past six days can only delay it ... The [French] troops in general are discontented and hope for nothing but peace. Every day, detachments of 50 to 100 young conscripts arrive from the interior, and are immediately sent to the army, well guarded ... While the French army on the one side makes preparations to attack the Piedmontese and Austrians, these on their part also make considerable preparations, and it is said in order to be the aggressors. It is also said that, to this end, part of the army has already advanced to the borders of Genoese territory. This may well be, as for several days the courier from Nice to Genoa has not gone by land, but by sea, for fear of being arrested by the Austrians. It is confirmed that reinforcements have reached their army in Italy ...[11]

Although there was plenty of information circulating, the allies did not have accurate figures for the strength of the enemy forces. On 7 March, for example, General Wenckheim reported to his superiors that a deserting officer had told them that the French army amounted to 27,000 men. Piedmontese intelligence reports, some of which were very full and detailed, indicated a similar figure, which was about 5,000 less than the number of troops in the four main combat divisions along the Riviera.[12] Their actual numbers at the beginning of March were as follows: the two divisions of the advance-guard, under Massena, were positioned around Savona and Finale, and numbered 8,140 and 8,544 men under arms respectively. Augereau's division, with 8,576 men, was in the area of Albenga, and Sérurier was in the mountains at Garessio, Ormea and Ponte di Nava, with 7,202. Other divisions garrisoned the coastal defences and the County of Nice.[13]

The imprecision of allied intelligence regarding French numbers may well have been due to the fact that a total reorganisation of the demi-brigades was taking place at this time. Most of them had shrunk to battalion size, and the Directory had decreed that a new *amalgame* should be carried out, with several of the old units being combined to form new demi-brigades. The inspector-general responsible for this, Fontbonne, did very little of the work, then suddenly departed. The divisional commanders and their subordinates therefore got down to completing the work themselves, profiting from the temporary protection of the bad weather. This reorganisation occasioned considerable moving around of some of the units, in order that the scattered component battalions of the new demi-brigades could be brought near to one another, so there must have been quite an air of activity in the cantonments, which would have served to arouse the interest of spies, but made it more difficult to estimate unit strengths.

These movements were insignificant, however, compared to the one that Saliceti had begun to meditate. Since his arrival, he had been trying to persuade the Genoese government to make the army a substantial loan so that it could buy food and equipment, but had not made much progress. He wrote to the Directory on 8 March, saying that the Genoese had not yet made up their mind, but if they had not accepted in three days, he would try to intimidate them by having a French force move to Sampierdarena – under the walls of Genoa itself. This was a rather risky plan, which extended the French line (already some 80 miles from Nice to Savona) by another 28 miles, and left it vulnerable to being cut by an enemy force coming over the mountains to the coast. And yet Saliceti was to suggest an even deeper and more hazardous advance, as we shall see later.

The day after that letter was written, Bonaparte managed to fit a completely non-military piece of business into his crowded life by getting married to Josephine. He was two hours late for the ceremony, which was concluded with great rapidity. Among the witnesses were Barras, and Bonaparte's young ADC, Le Marois. It was only a brief interlude amid the frenetic work.

At this time, official notification that Bonaparte had been appointed to command the Army of Italy had still not reached Schérer. On the 9th, Adjutant-General Vignolle, the Deputy Chief of Staff, wrote a letter to Massena from Nice commenting that it was eight days since the last courier had arrived from Paris, which serves to explain the delay. However, rumours of Bonaparte's appointment had filtered through, and Vignolle remarked that 'many people still believe this news, and I am not far from giving it credence, knowing the ambition of this general'.[14] For many, the probability of his arrival was no source of rejoicing, though Schérer may have felt some sense of relief that his burden was about to be lifted. On 10 March, he gave further evidence that he had reached the end of his tether by writing to the Directory saying that if the loan from the Genoese did not materialise he would have to abandon the Riviera and retreat into French territory.[15] A Piedmontese intelligence report of the following day noted that the Senate of Genoa had rejected Saliceti's request for a loan, but had agreed to supply a large quantity of grain. Saliceti had already taken steps to put pressure on the Genoese, and on the 11th Schérer wrote advising him that he had received his request for 6,000 troops to advance towards Genoa, and had instructed Massena to hold them ready. He also noted that the new chief commissary, Chauvet, had not yet arrived in Nice.[16] Chauvet was known to be a friend of Bonaparte, and his appointment was no doubt seen as further evidence that the latter was likely to be made commander of the army.

Eventually, on Friday 11 March, the moment came for Bonaparte himself to set off and meet his destiny. Once again, Thiébault went along to see what was happening:

> Informed of the time at which General Bonaparte was to leave Paris, I went, at the time of his departure, to say my farewells to the commander who had been mine. His two carriages were being harnessed as I arrived, and his last effects were being carried to them, notably a great pile of books, all relative to the wars conducted in Italy, as I could see from those that I took down myself. These books, which he urged us to be careful with, were, with the exception of those that I always had with me, the first that I saw leaving for an army.[17]

Our hero kissed Josephine good-bye – probably several times, if his letters are an accurate reflection of his passions – and left for Nice. 'Finally, at ten o'clock in the evening, the General-in-Chief set out, accompanied by Murat, Junot, Duroc, and I believe, Le Marois.'[18] As he trundled over the roads in his carriage on his two-week journey we can only guess at his excitement, his head stuffed with dreams of Eugene of Savoy and Vendôme, not to say Hannibal and Alexander, intermixed with thoughts of orders, letters, manoeuvres and lines of attack. He was ambitious and confident and here at last was a chance to prove his worth.

His departure was a matter of some interest to the Tuscan ambassador in Paris, who, although he represented a neutral state, had good reason to be anxious about developments in Italy. His government was in a tricky position because its port at Livorno was being used by the British, which could easily be turned into a pretext for hostile action by the French. On the 12th, the ambassador wrote saying that he believed Bonaparte would be leaving soon, and went on to relay some other intriguing information:

> Only the weather has delayed the start of the campaign, which is to begin with the siege of Ceva, a place which the snows render almost inaccessible to an army and a train of artillery. All my information inclines me to believe that the peace between France and the King of Sardinia, which is now being negotiated in Paris, will be agreed either at the beginning of the campaign, or at the first reverse suffered by the Austrians. A negotiator with a passport from the Ambassador of Spain residing in Genoa or Turin has recently arrived.[19]

He was wrong about the peace talks, which were shortly to be broken off, but the rest of his message reveals that a great deal was known, or guessed, about French plans. He was not alone in believing that Ceva was the key to Bonaparte's strategy. Throughout March all the information received by the Piedmontese staff indicated that the French plan was to capture this fortress.[20] Their problem, as it turned out, was to convince the Austrians of this.

The day after Bonaparte left Paris, General Berthier, who was Kellermann's chief of staff with the Army of the Alps, received orders that he was being transferred to carry out the same functions with the Army of Italy. Berthier's reputation was such that he was often in demand to fulfil this role, and it is some measure of Bonaparte's leverage that he managed to obtain his services. Berthier, who had just recovered from a bad fall from his horse, was not entirely happy to go, as he got on well with Kellermann, but duly departed a couple of days later. Had he but known it, he was setting off to meet the man who would dominate the rest of his life.

Rumour continued to travel faster than official documents, and Vignolle wrote a further letter to Massena on 13 March, saying: 'General Schérer awaits his fate with impatience. Two newspapers speak of his replacement, and it is even said that Bonaparte has left Paris ... to come and take command ... I think, if this news turns out to be true, that the government has committed a great stupidity. I think that Bonaparte has military talents, but not enough, nor the experience to be commander-in-chief of an army.'[21] He was only one of many who would have to revise their opinion. Louis Suchet, *chef de bataillon* of the 18th demi-brigade, who was to be given his marshal's baton by Napoleon in 1811, commented: 'This Corsican has no other reputation than that of a good gun commander. As a general he is only known by the Parisians. This intriguer is supported by nothing.'[22]

On 14 March, the Genoese Secretary of State officially communicated the refusal of the loan to the French.[23] That day, Saliceti wrote to the Directory from Genoa, informing them of the decision, and of supposed enemy intentions to take the fortress of Gavi, Genoa's main defence against attack from the direction of Alessandria and Milan. Saliceti also wrote to Schérer, pointing out that the latter's instructions provided for the occupation of Gavi, stressed its importance, and invited Schérer to take the decision to move over the Bocchetta and seize it.[24] During the next few days, various letters skimmed back and forth between Saliceti, Massena and Schérer concerning this matter, as there seemed to be some doubt as to whether Saliceti or Schérer should give the definitive order to advance. It was probably fortunate for Bonaparte that the move was thus not carried out before he arrived, as it would have extended the French line to quite dangerous length.

On about 15 March, General Beaulieu, who had been in Pavia for two weeks as chief of staff to Wallis, was officially notified that he was to be the new commander of the Austrian army, with the rank of *Feldzeugmeister*. On the same day, Beaulieu and Colli, who were old friends, had a meeting in Pavia, during which they discussed various matters, including the latest reports of the enemy strength and, probably, plans of campaign. The day afterwards, Beaulieu officially took command of the Austrian army in Italy.

It was the culmination of a very long career. Jean-Pierre de Beaulieu was a gaunt, 70-year-old Belgian, who could boast some 53 years' service in the Imperial army. He was a native of Brabant, a province in the southern part of his country that contains a well-known place called Waterloo. As a young man, his bold and fiery character combined with his great energy and constant activity had made him well-suited to the military life. Soon after entering the infantry regiment of Prince Charles of Lorraine, he found himself caught up in the War of the Austrian Succession. He also fought through the Seven Years War as an infantry officer and then as ADC to Field Marshal Daun. He was present at some of the most important engagements of that war, notably at Kolin (where he suffered his first wound), Schweidnitz, Breslau, Leuthen, Olmütz, Gera, Hochkirch and Maxen. In 1760 he was awarded the Knight's Cross of the Order of Maria Theresa, and later he was also made a baron.

Far from being just a fighting man, he was enough of an artist to have designed embellishments for some of the Imperial palaces, and seen them approved and carried out, and he spent the years of peace on the staff in Belgium largely in retirement, collecting books and works of art. He also spent much time designing and laying out a formal garden at Broqui.

The revolt in Brabant in 1789 disturbed the quiet tenor of his life, bringing with it a return to active service, promotion to the rank of *General-Major*, and the death of his only son, who was killed while serving as his ADC. This was not the first time that war had brought family loss in its train, for one of Beaulieu's brothers had been killed at Breslau, and another at Hochkirch.

After playing a significant part in crushing the unrest in Belgium, he received promotion to *Feldmarschall-Lieutenant* on 2 October 1790. It was then but a short wait before the storm of war against the French broke over his native land and he found himself commanding a division under the Duke of Saxe-Teschen. In this role he was present at the defeat at Jemappes. In the meantime he had also been accorded the great distinction of being the first Belgian to be made *Inhaber* (colonel proprietor) of a Hungarian regiment, no. 31, which had belonged to Esterházy. He then became chief of staff to the Duke of York, and took part in the victory of Menin. His 'can-do' attitude made a good impression on Thugut, who commented to Count Colloredo in September 1793:

> I am delighted with the successes of Beaulieu, whom the Prince of Coburg and his clique try to annoy as much as they can ... I have known for a long time that all these slow-coaches at the headquarters detest Beaulieu uniquely, because he is a determined man, always of the opinion that one should attempt things, and whose opinions consequently contrast too much with those who find everything difficult and only take such wise measures that after ten years of warfare one finds oneself at nearly the same point one started from ...[25]

The energetic and enterprising side of Beaulieu was undoubtedly positive in a potential army commander, but the intense dislike of him on the part of those with whom he was supposed to co-operate sounds an ominous note for the future.

Despite the distrust with which he was viewed by Coburg, he commanded the main attack column at Fleurus and greatly contributed to the victory of the first day (16 June). At the second battle of Fleurus (26 June) he made great inroads into the enemy before being ordered to retreat by Coburg. Had Beaulieu but known it, he had been involved in the battle that had broken Austrian power in Belgium for ever, and was to exile him for the rest of his life. The conduct of this battle seems to have occasioned a violent disagreement, because Coburg then relieved Beaulieu of his command. However, the powers in Vienna seem to have been on his side. He was awarded the Grand Cross of the Order of Maria Theresa, and rapidly appointed to be Clerfayt's chief of staff. He held this position until the beginning of the following year (1795). His tenure of this post brought forth an illuminating assessment of him from one of Thugut's trusted confidants, Dietrichstein:

> M. de Beaulieu, who would be excellent as a *Feldzeugmeister* in the lines, or with a separate corps, apart from his decrepitude, is absolutely useless in his job as chief of staff, of which he cannot carry out the functions. It would be infinitely better if there was no chief of staff at all – he is worse than a fifth wheel, he is really a spoke in the wheel …[26]

It seems we must conclude from this that Beaulieu was an energetic fighting man, but not a good organiser or administrator. Despite this, Thugut continued to support Beaulieu and must have been instrumental in getting him sent to Italy. To sum up, we could do worse than quote what Carlo Botta says of him:

> Beaulieu, though already very advanced in years, was spirited, lively, and thus capable of facing up to that French fury which is easier to overcome by preventing it than by waiting for it … But though he had the qualities most necessary in a good captain he had no knowledge of the area, never having campaigned in Italy, nor led such large forces as he had been promised … Nor was Beaulieu such as could easily lead captains and peoples of different languages and different nations, being more of a warrior than a courtier, for which reason he was more feared than loved by his own people and by foreigners, and obeyed perforce rather than voluntarily. Nor did the Piedmontese nobles, who thought very highly of their own, approve of him.[27]

Since we are dealing with commanding officers, this would seem an appropriate moment to take a brief look at the other man who was to oppose Bonaparte at the beginning of his first campaign: General Colli.

His full name was Michelangelo Alessandro Colli-Marchi, and he had been born in Lombardy, though his family was of Piedmontese origins. He was described as being 'of medium height and very thin; an aquiline nose, a very small graceful mouth, and very lively, big blue eyes, gave him a very remarkable face. He joined to this much natural intelligence and great finesse.'[28]

He was 58 years old, and had been an infantry officer since the age of eighteen. His service during the Seven Years War had included Prague and Torgau, where he was wounded. The War of the Bavarian Succession had seen him commanding a battalion of IR Caprara, no. 48, with the main army, when he would have had a fine opportunity to observe the effectiveness of Field Marshal Lacy's supply arrangements. He also distinguished himself in the next war against the Turks at Esseg, the capture of Schabaz, and at Belgrade, where he was badly wounded. In 1787 he was promoted *General-Major* and rose to *Feldmarschall-Lieutenant* in 1793, when he was also seconded to the Piedmontese army. Something of his service and his frustrations on the Italian front have already been described in the previous chapter. His appointment to overall command of the Piedmontese army increased the pressures on him, and early in 1796 his chief of staff, Colonel Costa, wrote:

> Colli wants to resign. He feels the danger of his position, servant of two masters whose interests are opposed. It is almost impossible for him not to become suspect to one or the other of his masters, and it is to be feared that he will be to both. He believes that the army of the King is insufficient to defend the country alone, and he sees no way of soon giving it the strength to be independent. On the other hand, although he does not say it openly, he is so convinced of the lack of good faith of the Austrians that he does not expect anything from them.[29]

He continued to be unhappy about his situation, and even wrote to Beaulieu on 11 April, when the fighting had already started, asking to be given command of the Auxiliary Corps 'if ... I decide to retire from this army'.[30]

He was strongly appreciated by Costa, who drafted a letter to the Minister of the Interior, listing some of his general's qualities:

If M. Colli has weak points, he takes too little care to hide them … One cannot deny that he has a vivacity and a penetration that are very rare, joined to an acquired knowledge of his profession. Everyone grants him personal valour … the soldiers readily follow a chief who is covered with honourable scars. To this kind of courage he joins another which is more precious, and which everyone admits: it is steadiness and presence of mind at the most dangerous moments. He is then calm and master of himself. He possesses an agility and a vigour which at his age, in his rank, and in a war like this, must be placed among the most precious qualities.

This agility and extraordinary physical strength permit him to reconnoitre the most difficult sites himself and to show himself to the troops. He also knows perfectly the country and the army he commands. Although severe and hard, he has gained an influence over this army that is very remarkable … The General is perfectly disinterested and does not enter into any of those schemes of avidity of which some generals make so little mystery.[31]

Although Costa gives us a picture of a man of energy and activity, Colli's body had suffered an unusual amount of wear and tear over the years and the after-effects of his wounds meant that he sometimes had to have himself carried on a stretcher. None the less, his experience of campaigning in the area made him a precious potential asset to Beaulieu, if the latter could make use of him, and the long friendship that subsisted between them made Colli hopeful that better co-operation would be achieved. The fact that these hopes were not fulfilled was not entirely the fault of either commander.

The most intractable problem, of course, was the air of mistrust between their political masters, which was very clear from the secret instructions that Beaulieu had been sent on the 3rd, and which he now found himself reading. In particular, these warned him:

The general commanding the army of His Majesty must never lose sight of the fact that it is possible, not only that the Court of Turin will unexpectedly make a separate peace, but that it will even join the enemy either from weakness or from motives of perfidious politics. It is above all from the possibility of such an event that the need derives of never dividing the army of His Majesty so as to place the different corps out of range of assembling as quickly as possible in case of some unforeseen accident. For the same reason it would be essential to be able, under some plausible pretext, and without arousing the suspicious jealousy of Turin, to introduce into and to keep in some of the strong places, such as Alessandria and Tortona, a sufficient number of Austrian troops to facilitate or ensure their seizure by a *coup de main* in case an unexpected defection on the King's part or other circumstances should require it.[32]

It was an awful situation for Beaulieu to be in. In simple terms, he did not know exactly whom he would be fighting with or against, and he had to face a range of possibilities that included seeing the enemy nearly doubled in strength at the same time as his own force was halved. Whatever his personal feelings towards Colli, he was effectively precluded from discussing large areas of his plans with him, because they would have to include what to do if the Piedmontese defected. If some of Beaulieu's decisions seem questionable, we have to consider to what extent they were conditioned by having to allow for this eventuality. Indeed, it is possible to argue that the responsibility for Beaulieu's defeat lies squarely with the politicians, who, if they sincerely believed that the Piedmontese might defect, ought to have provided Beaulieu with an army that was sufficiently strong to oppose the combined forces of France and Piedmont. We can only wonder at his feelings when thinking of his old friend, Colli, and the hopes for co-operation he had so recently expressed in a personal letter to him.

The position of Piedmont was not the only problem he faced, however. Beaulieu pointedly outlined some of the others in his letter of acknowledgement to the Emperor of 17 March:

I have just received the greatest mark of confidence from Your Majesty, to which I can only reply with victories ... I received the command yesterday, according to the order that FZM Count Wallis received from the Hofkriegsrath. I am busy today in forming the order of battle, in relation to the different nominations of the generals. I am already awaiting some of them, who have to come from the armies of the Rhine, with impatience ... I have already informed General Colli, who has been to see me here, of this ... That which pains me extraordinarily, is the sickness and the mortality of our soldiers. Nine hundred and twenty-seven have died in our hospitals during the past month of February. The army is extremely weak ... [and] has no chasseurs [light infantry] and pioneers ...[33]

An army that had neither enough generals nor enough soldiers was hardly in a good condition. That it was weaker than the French is beyond doubt, although there is some uncertainty about the exact figures. That most meticulous of Austrian historians, Johann Baptist Schels, tells us that at the beginning of the year the total strength of the army was 28 battalions and ten squadrons, or 28,523 men, though about 6,000 of these were sick or otherwise unfit for service, leaving 21,976 combat-ready troops. In addition, there were four battalions and two squadrons on garrison duty in Lombardy. To these could be added thirteen weak squadrons of cavalry, which constituted Naples' only contribution to the war effort, amounting to about 1,500 men at the most.[34] According to the French historian Gabriel Fabry, Beaulieu had 25,000 men at his disposal at the beginning of March. This force consisted of: fourteen battalions south of the Po, mainly around Acqui, Tortona and Alessandria; nineteen battalions north of the Po, mainly in Pavia and Lodi; and twenty squadrons of cavalry, of the Erzherzog Joseph Hussars, the Erdödy Hussars and the Uhlans.[35] These numbers had swelled somewhat by the end of the month, but it has been pointed out that not all of them could be used due to the need to reserve a significant proportion for the possible task of taking Tortona and Alessandria.

The bulk of the Piedmontese army on the southern front was in crowded winter quarters around Savigliano, in the middle of the plain south of Turin, and at Ceva, Mondovì and the surrounding area. This force amounted to about 15,000 men. The Austrian Auxiliary Corps, under General Provera, had its troops near Savigliano, Alba and Fossano. It numbered eight battalions of infantry and four squadrons of cavalry, totalling about 5,000 men. Both Colli and Provera kept their HQ at Savigliano, within reach of the Piedmontese capital. Being somewhat nearer to the French than the Austrian main army was, they were kept in a state of semi-readiness in case the enemy made any unusual moves.

Although much has been made of the problems faced by Bonaparte when he took command of the Army of Italy, the picture of Beaulieu's situation that has been sketched above leads one to feel that in fact the latter had the much more difficult task. Indeed, he had been handed something of a poisoned chalice. He undoubtedly made mistakes – the most serious of which was probably underestimating his opponent – but the puzzle he had to solve was not easy. It also has to be said to his credit that he did not seem to lack willingness, unlike some other Austrian generals of the time.

He expressed his gratitude to Thugut on 17 March, saying: 'I will try to prove you right to have so much supported me by the good opinion that Your Excellency has given of me to the Monarch without my knowing it.'[36] He also gives an interesting hint that he had already taken to heart the idea that he was to mistrust their allies, saying that during their interview two days previously, Colli had shown Beaulieu a report from the Piedmontese outposts which spoke of '14,000 French ready to swoop on Piedmont when the good weather comes'. Beaulieu thought this was being used as a means of persuading the Austrians to move: 'You can easily see what such reports tend to. M. de Colli does not believe them himself ...'[37] From this point on, there was to be fairly consistent disagreement between the allies about French strength and intentions. On 15 March, for example, Costa reported that the French army on the Riviera amounted to 25,000 men with 10,000 reinforcements marching to join it. This document was transmitted to Beaulieu, but he estimated the French at 60,000, basing himself on other information, which was accurate as far as the sum total was concerned, but not for the active divisions.[38] None the less, the meeting between the two old friends must have been cordial, perhaps because Beaulieu rather exaggerated the help he was intending to give. After the meeting, Costa wrote: 'Colli arrived this morning from Pavia, gorged with promises … The enemy on the Riviera will not get forces sufficient to resist the fifty thousand Austrians who are to come …'[39] Unfortunately these promises turned out to be rather empty.

The meetings that the Piedmontese representatives had been attending in Vienna to discuss campaign plans had also been fruitless. The Austrians managed to get the Piedmontese to give them a written proposal containing their own views on what should be done, but would put nothing down on paper themselves, except a note which Thugut gave to the Piedmontese ambassador on 24 March, to be sent to Turin, 'summarising succinctly the various verbal explanations which, on the orders of His Majesty, he had had the honour to give to M. Lieutenant-General Baron de La Tour'. This was to the effect: 'His Majesty admitted the proposition to charge his army from the present with the defence of the country up to the right of the Tanaro, and that he would address orders in consequence to M. Baron de Beaulieu, unless, which he did not presume, this general found in the localities and in other circumstances unknown here, greater and insurmountable difficulties …'[40] From all the tricks and ruses they used, one gets the feeling that the Austrians were more interested in out-manoeuvring their allies on the diplomatic front than in actually arriving at an agreement that would result in the defeat of the French. They were to pay the price – though they would blame others for the failure of the campaign.

Bonaparte, meanwhile, was gradually getting nearer to his army, and on the 20th he passed through Marseille where he saw his family, and seems to have collected Leclerc, who was to be his favourite sister Pauline's husband.[41] Gaultier, the Chief of Staff, wrote to Massena the same day, saying: 'The General-in-Chief has not yet received an official letter touching his replacement. General Dujard received one yesterday evening from Bonaparte, which announced his nomination by the government to command the Army of Italy ... Chauvet ... left this morning by sea for Savona ... I have this moment received a despatch from General Berthier that he is coming to the Army of Italy to be employed in the quality of Chief of Staff ...'[42] On the 21st, Bonaparte arrived in Toulon.[43]

News of Bonaparte's impending arrival made Saliceti decide to delay the movement on Gavi, and on the 21st Massena informed Schérer that the decision on whether to carry it out had been put back to the following day.[44] Saliceti was not without support for his risky enterprise, and the new French envoy to Genoa, Faipoult, who had just arrived in Nice, wrote on the 22nd, '[his] plan is bold, but the position of the army is so unfortunate that it has to be adopted'.[45] In another letter he commented that the army's problems were entirely due to lack of money. His picture of them was succinct: 'The clothing supply does not suffer, at the moment there is wheat for four or five months, but there is no meat, no animal fodder, and no transport. All the cavalry is scattered the length of the Rhône.'[46] Schérer's long wait for official confirmation that his resignation had been accepted finally came to an end that day, and he replied to the Directory, noting that Bonaparte had already informed him of his arrival in Marseille.[47]

At that time, Beaulieu was occupied with arranging the initial movements of his troops. He had received an order from the Emperor on 21 March (dated 10 March) authorising him to move four battalions under General Rukavina towards Ceva if the Piedmontese fear of an irruption in those parts seemed justified.[48] He therefore wrote immediately to Victor Amadeus explaining that he was having four battalions march from Pavia towards Nizza and Acqui, to replace the four battalions that would move from there towards Ceva:

> As for me, at the same time I shall take my HQ to Alessandria, from where, after my dispositions for the security of that part of the states of His Majesty the King of Sardinia, I shall come to Turin to reassure His Majesty that I shall work with all my might not only for the defence of his states, but to re-conquer, with the

good harmony and the co-operation of his brave troops, the part of his states invaded until now. I shall begin these movements between the 26th and 27th ...[49]

The march of Rukavina's brigade was to be the prelude to a general movement ordered on 24 March.[50] With uncanny symmetry of timing, Saliceti issued an order to Massena on the 23rd to march on Voltri with 3,000 men, to arrive there on 25 March.[51] On the 24th, General Pijon therefore left Savona with his brigade, consisting of the 75th Line and part of the 51st. These demi-brigades had only been in existence for about two weeks, having been formed by the new *amalgame*. The regimental history of the 51st Line tells us:

> On 4 germinal, the demi-brigade, known then as the 99th, had its 3rd battalion at Savona and the 1st and 2nd before that town on the heights that extend up to Voltri. The three companies of grenadiers were detached, and formed, together with the other corps of the division, the advance-guard that occupied that village.[52]

A Piedmontese spy's report on this movement provides us with a fascinating insight into the condition of the army:

> The newly formed battalions which marched on Voltri had new silk colours with the number of the battalion and an inscription in gold letters. They were newly shod. The grenadiers also had new bearskin bonnets. On the eve of their departure they were paid the whole of their back-pay ... On the 24th the demi-brigade of General Meynier departed, newly clothed and shod, and paid in cash.[53]

Among various other measures taken to ensure the safety of the units near Voltri, a detailed instruction was issued to Pijon by General La Harpe, concerning an important defensive position above Savona called Monte Negino. We shall look at this in some detail later.

In the evening of the 24th, Bonaparte met Berthier in Antibes, and the two then spent the whole of the following day working together at the Hôtel Agarrat.[54] It was an important meeting. Berthier held a crucial position, for he was to be responsible for transmitting Bonaparte's orders and organising the movements of the army. In fact he became one of the most indispensable of Bonaparte's helpers, staying so close to his master (who was some fifteen years his junior) that he was nicknamed 'the Emperor's wife'. He became perhaps the most famous chief of staff in the history of war, and was later made Prince of Neuchâtel and Wagram. The scion of a military family, he had served in America under Rochambeau, and, until he became worn out by work later in life, he was of a jolly disposition. In the words of General Desaix he was 'short, stocky, always laughing, very busy'.[55] He was later described in unflattering terms by Junot's widow:

> Small, and badly made, without, however, being misshapen; having a head a little too large for his body, hair that was frizzy rather than curly, of a colour that was neither dark nor light ... hands that were naturally unsightly and which he made appalling by continually chewing his nails, to the point that his fingers were almost always bleeding; his feet were similar, except that he did not chew the nails.[56]

However, General Lejeune, who later became Berthier's ADC, looked at him with a soldier's eye: 'despite his average height, he had a very neat athletic form ... his abundant frizzy hair proclaimed his energy'.[57] He was, indeed, like Bonaparte, a tireless worker.

While they were occupied with their meeting, Beaulieu reached Alessandria, where he placed his HQ. Colli was in Turin, and at 9 p.m. he wrote to Beaulieu: 'At 5 in the afternoon I received Your Excellency's orders by the despatch-rider who left Pavia yesterday at 5 o'clock. Orders have been given to make way for the four Imperial battalions which are to be cantoned between the two Bormidas. I shall have the rest of the Piedmontese troops advance towards Mondovì and Ceva. I shall threaten the enemy via the valley of Loano ... and that of the

Bormida.' He also proposes to send two battalions 'to join the army corps that you will have advance on the Bocchetta if you plan to forestall the enemy there'.[58] From this it would appear that the allies were already concerned about French intentions in that area.

Austrian preparations in the Bormida valley had been discovered by the French, and the same day General Ménard told Massena: 'Two ovens for bread are being constructed near Dego: 800 sacks of flour for the subsistence of the advance-guard have been delivered there.'[59] Massena communicated this information to Schérer and also commented that the snows were melting fast.[60] Saliceti, having only just ordered the move on Voltri, decided to suspend operations again, now that Bonaparte was on the point of arriving.

The new commander finally reached Nice with Berthier on the 26th and lodged in the Maison Sauvaigo in the rue St-François-de-Paule. Vignolle hurriedly wrote a note to Massena, dated '7 in the evening', saying, 'Generals Bonaparte and Berthier have arrived at this moment' and that the latter had sent him his good wishes.[61]

The state in which Bonaparte found the army was not as bad as it had been. If it was almost ready to begin a campaign, this was largely thanks to the immense efforts of people like Saliceti, Chauvet, many of the generals commanding the divisions and brigades, some of the suppliers, and probably Schérer. Bonaparte recognised that a lot of good work had been done, as his letters over the next few days prove. Nevertheless, there were still inadequacies of food, clothing, equipment, finance, morale and discipline, as well as transport. Bonaparte did not waste any time in setting to work to sort out the army's problems, and many of his letters dwell on such practical issues as the supply of shoes, shirts, oats, mules and corn. He wrote to Chauvet on 27 March sending him a list of the cavalry regiments' movements, and informing him that the route from Menton to Finale was to be supplied with '40,000 hundredweight of oats', which gives an idea of the quantities involved in feeding an army. He also said he had '1,600 mules on the move for my artillery', and ended with an urgent appeal:

Come to Nice quickly, I need you. You should be on the road, after the letter I wrote you yesterday. Every day that you delay you take from my operations a chance of probability of success. There are measures which, in the present position, cannot be taken except from here. There is an initial movement that must be given from here, where my magazines and my artillery are. I wrote to Saliceti yesterday. The government expects great things from this army. They must be achieved, and the country pulled out of the crisis she finds herself in.[62]

Bonaparte was also concerned about the local political situation. Far from following Saliceti's line, he wrote to Faipoult in Genoa saying: 'The affairs that are being dealt with on your side disquiet me. I fear that we go too far, and that we may upset the essential military operations that we have to carry out. I pray you to inform me precisely of the way this affair is developing.' After calling the Genoese 'proud and brave', he adds, 'It is said that the Genoese offer three millions. My opinion is that we should take it without a murmur, and continue to live in peace and friendship with this republic, the enmity of which would be fatal to our commerce, our supplies, and would upset all our military calculations.'[63]

In the meantime, however, the advance on Voltri had aroused a great deal of interest. On 27 March, General Pittoni, one of the Austrian commanders, reported the arrival there on the 25th of 1,200 French with 55 beasts of burden carrying *matériel* and baggage. He observed that a French captain had said that in two weeks, 3,000 men would be arriving per day. There was other evidence of a French build-up in the area, including the arrival of provisions by ship, and the hiring of mills to grind corn. As Fabry comments, 'It is understandable that Beaulieu gave the greatest importance to this report.'[64] Indeed, it probably played a large part in convincing him that the French planned to advance over the Bocchetta Pass. He was right, in a way, because that was precisely what Saliceti had intended – but it was not what Bonaparte wanted at all. His plan was still to separate the enemy armies by advancing along the road from Savona towards Ceva. In other words, the French had quite unintentionally pulled off a successful diversion. Contrary to what Saliceti and Schérer had expected, Bonaparte quickly issued orders to suspend the movement on Voltri, instead of following it up. On 28 March, he wrote to Massena:

Citizen General: will you kindly return to the positions you occupied. You will leave only 3,000 men on the heights of Voltri if the Government Commissioner judges it necessary to his operations. You will take care to safeguard communications with Savona. As soon as the Government Commissioner judges that these troops are no longer useful to him, you will have them return to their first position. Have the soldiers rest. Guard yourself against doing anything to arouse the suspicions of the enemy and from doing anything that could make him think that we have hostile intentions.[65]

It seems from this that Bonaparte had not yet grasped that the force at Voltri was a useful decoy. A few days later the picture had changed, and it was Massena who was nervously asking to pull them back, and Bonaparte who was prepared to leave them there a little longer, despite the obvious danger to them.

For a commander of the inspirational sort, such as Bonaparte, it was important to be seen by the troops and try to motivate them. One of his first concerns, therefore, was to hold an inspection, which was also an excuse to deliver a pep-talk to the men. Lieutenant Desvernois of the 7th Hussars, one of the witnesses, thought Bonaparte had arrived on the 27th, which would place the inspection on the 28th:

On the day after his arrival, he assembled the troops of the garrison. At 9 o'clock in the morning he inspected them on Place de la République. Then, placing himself in the centre of the square, in the middle of the old generals and the subaltern officers that each corps had sent, he addressed to them that famous speech that recalls that of Hannibal on his crossing of the Alps ...[66]

Here, Desvernois inserts a slightly modified version of the 'proclamation' which was actually written decades later on Saint Helena, and published in Napoleon's memoirs.[67] There is no record of what was actually said at the time, but it would seem likely that Bonaparte praised the soldiers' courage in the face of their difficulties, and promised a victorious campaign. Whatever it was, it seemed to be effective, as Desvernois reports that it was greeted with wild enthusiasm. The inspection, of course, also gave Bonaparte the opportunity to form his own impression of the state of the army. His views may be judged from the letters he wrote to the Directory and to Carnot on the 28th. In the first he states:

> The administrative situation of the army is bad, but no longer desperate. I am compelled to threaten the agents who have stolen much and who have credit, and I take great advantage of it, in the end by caressing them. From now on the army will eat good bread and will have meat, and it has already had considerable advances on its back-pay. The stages on the road from the Rhône to the Var are provisioned, and my cavalry, transport and artillery have already been in movement for five days. Citizen Directors, your intentions will be fulfilled. I shall march in a short while ...

He goes on to reveal that he had dissolved a battalion that had mutinied in Nice, and acknowledges his predecessor's helpful reception of him:

> I was particularly satisfied with the frankness and honesty of General Schérer. By his loyal conduct and by his eagerness to give me all the information that could be useful to me, he has gained the right to my recognition. His health seems indeed a little impaired. He joins to a great facility for talking, moral and political knowledge that perhaps will render him useful to you in some essential employment ... In four days I shall transfer my HQ to Albenga.[68]

He begins his letter to Carnot by saying: 'I have been very well received by the army, which shows a confidence in me which obliges me to a lively recognition.' This was perhaps a little inaccurate, as there was not much of the army in Nice, and the most sorely tried part of it was eking out a precarious existence in the mountains or half-way to Genoa. He then complains that the engineers have not arrived, and of those who were on their way, 'there is only Chasseloup from the old corps. I do not have here, out of fifteen engineers, a single one out of Mézières [the school for engineer officers]. I beg you to send me two other good ones.' Considering that part of his plan was to besiege Ceva, this was a serious shortage. Money also presented a difficulty, and he remarked that it was going to be necessary to audit the army's treasury.

It is clear, however, as he implies, that much of the good work of preparing the army had already been done before he arrived, and it was nearly ready for the campaign.

There are great obstacles, but the greatest have been overcome ...
I shall get started soon, vigorously. I hope that before the end of the month there will be more than ten thousand spare hats among the enemy.

He closed by saying that he was trying to find jobs for some of those who had been displaced by the new *amalgame* 'in order to earn some bread for some old officers who have no other resources',[69] a creditable show of concern for those who had fallen on hard times, on the part of one who had himself been very poor. The same day he issued orders for the whole HQ to be transferred to Albenga, to arrive by 6 April.

Beaulieu had already moved his HQ forward to Alessandria, and it was here that he had a further meeting with Colli on 29 March, when the latter presented him with two plans of campaign. One was offensive, the other defensive.

The first was interesting in that it was almost a mirror-image of that which was to be used by Bonaparte. It suggested a vigorous thrust to the sea towards Savona and Finale to cut off part of the French army and defeat it in detail. Its preparation involved attracting the attention of the French towards Genoa. For the main movement, it stated: 'At least 16,000 men of Colli's army and an equal number of Beaulieu's must be employed in this expedition. The former will concentrate before Ceva and the others around Cairo.' On the day of the attack, feints were to be made on the heights of Voltri and Ormea, while the best troops would take Montenotte and Monte Negino. On the right, Settepani would be attacked, and the troops would then descend to the sea. Another force would similarly advance from the area of Garessio towards Loano. It is notable that this plan only really has one 'branch', and there is very little suggestion of what to do if things did not go according to plan. Indeed, it even states, 'As to the risks, the allied army … does not seem to run any',[70] which is nothing if not optimistic. As far as Beaulieu was concerned, a difficulty may have been that the Piedmontese army was assigned quite a prominent role, something his secret instructions probably made him keen to avoid.

The other plan prescribed concentrations of a kind that Costa had suggested in a report of 18 March, saying that it would upset French plans

> to find two armies united in mass; one before Ceva, the other before Acqui, both strong enough to support themselves, and at a distance to help each other at need. While one of these corps presents itself in front of the enemy, the other will always threaten to take him in the flank, by marching to his right or left. The allies must forestall the French everywhere, and it is not at all probable that the latter will dare to advance between their two armies to attempt to arrive at Alba or Asti. The enemy cannot attempt this movement without exposing his flank to us with all sorts of disadvantages.[71]

Fabry suggests that Costa probably drafted the offensive plan. If that is so, he may have been responsible for the other as well, though he makes no mention of them in a letter which alludes to the conference, and also expresses his concern at the delay in beginning operations:

> The General has left me at Ceva to go and confer with Beaulieu again. They will reach an agreement. I believe that the weather is the most beautiful in the world. And in the meantime the French are at the gates of Genoa, and we do not move to prevent them from entering. Alas! the arrogance and the haughtiness of the Austrians will always be the same.[72]

It was probably not so much arrogance as lack of trust that motivated Beaulieu to reject both of the Piedmontese plans, and it was no doubt fortunate for Bonaparte that he did, because the adoption of either of them would have made the French task much more difficult. As for the danger to Genoa, events were to prove that Beaulieu was just as concerned about it as Costa, though his answer to it was not what Costa might have hoped. In the meantime, there was some movement from the Austrians on the 29th, when, in accordance with the plan that Beaulieu had communicated to Victor Amadeus, Argenteau moved four of his battalions into the valley of the Eastern Bormida. The villages of Rocchetta Cairo, Giusvalla, Mioglia and Pareto were occupied by a battalion of Grenzers, while General Rukavina moved to Dego with two battalions. Provida, Santa Giulia and Monte Alto were also occupied by two companies.[73]

On the same day Bonaparte issued a number of orders relating to the distribution of commands in the rear areas, on the coast, the organisation of the cavalry, and ordered all the engineer officers to accompany the HQ when it moved. The instructions concerning the cavalry were particularly detailed, laying out the organisation into two divisions, and precisely regulating their movements. The first division was composed of: 1st Hussars; 10th, 22nd and 25th Chasseurs; and 5th and 20th Dragoons. The second was composed of: 7th Hussars, 13th and 24th Chasseurs, 8th and 15th Dragoons. The regiments were to move along the coast road, roughly one after another, the first destined for Giogo di Toirano, on the road to Calizzano, the others halting at various different places. General Saint-Hilaire was ordered to precede the 1st division to make sure there were enough stables for the horses. General Sérurier was to delegate a general to do the same thing for the 2nd division. Moreover, Berthier was commanded to 'recommend to these generals to be discreet in this inspection, and not to do anything that might discover our plan'.[74] Yet another order went to Massena:

> Beginning tomorrow, Citizen General, some brigades of draught animals of the artillery will march towards the right. They will be placed at Finale and Vado. There will be, before ten days are past,

more than 800. My intention is that they will be left, and that they will not be used under any pretext whatsoever. These animals are destined for a rigorous task and need to be rested. I pray you to give the most precise orders so that my intentions are known and executed.[75]

The transport of the artillery was indeed a very serious problem. In theory, the army had some 342 cannon at its disposal, although 146 of them were siege artillery, and another 171 were only 4pdrs or smaller. There were also 39 howitzers and 32 mortars of various calibres. However, the totals are rather academic, because this number of guns would have needed in the order of 14,130 transport animals, against the 1,528 that were actually available at the end of the month of March.[76]

Bonaparte also issued what seems to have been his first Order of the Day to the army. When compared to the well-known but fictitious 'proclamation', its opening is less stirring, but still confident in tone:

> The General-in-Chief Bonaparte has inspected the 100th and 165th demi-brigades, the battalion of Montferme [which all belonged to Macquard's division, and combined to form the 45th Line], the 7th regiment of Hussars and the artillery. He was satisfied with the bearing of the troops, with the feelings of devotion to the Republic and the strong resolve to conquer which they evinced. He has visited the most active divisions of the army; he has found everywhere soldiers accustomed to conquer and to suffer, and devoted as much to freedom as to discipline, which is the strength of an army. They will find in him a brother-in-arms, strong in the confidence of the Government, proud of the goodwill of patriots and determined to realise a destiny worthy of the Army of Italy.

If that left any doubts about the intentions of the commander, they may well have been dispelled by the remarkably businesslike instructions addressed to the staff:

Generals who do not have the number of aides-de-camp decreed by the law are ordered to choose them following the dispositions the law prescribes. Similarly, all adjutant-generals [*chefs de brigade* on the staff] who do not have assistants are ordered to propose without delay the officers they judge capable of carrying out these important functions. They must appreciate that no special considerations may influence their choice: talent, morality, and a pure and enlightened patriotism alone must determine it. On reception of the present order, the adjutant-generals will address to the Chief of Staff the name, rank, and seniority of service of each of their assistants. They will add notes on their knowledge. The adjutant-generals are informed that the Chief of Staff has very precise orders from the General-in-Chief to have the assistants undergo an examination, so that those who are not suitable to second the work with which their adjutant-generals are charged may be moved to the auxiliaries and replaced.[77]

The order was undoubtedly drafted by Berthier, but if it succeeded in giving the impression that the commander was not a man to be trifled with, it was certainly accurate. And Bonaparte had good reason to be demanding when it came to the staff. He was well aware that an army that was about to undertake a campaign demanding speed and precise co-ordination of movement required an active and resourceful staff above all things. It was essential to have the 'brain' and 'nervous system' of the army in perfect working order, or nothing else would work properly.

Berthier found time to dash off a letter of his own that day, telling Kellermann of his sorrow at having to leave him, and giving his first impressions of his new situation:

Everything was lacking here, but our condition has improved. Some money has arrived, and because of that, abundance will be reborn. It seemed to me that the army was fairly indifferent to the change of general ... we are going to move on Acqui and Ceva, a corps will hold the Austrians in check while we take the Piedmontese in the rear ... Bonaparte will inform you of the moment of his attack and of his plans. It is certain that in a fortnight we will have gone into action ... I am pleased with Bonaparte: he has ability and he works a lot ...[78]

Berthier's perception of a lack of enthusiasm at Bonaparte's arrival contrasts interestingly with the picture painted by the latter in his letters to the Directory. Certainly, the brief note that Massena wrote to his new commander from Savona on the 29th seems rather less than effusive, despite the positive remarks:

I received your letter yesterday. I send you my compliments with good heart on the command of the Army of Italy, which has been given to you. You have known for a long time of the justice I do to your military talents. I shall see to it that I merit your confidence, as I have gained it from all the generals who have commanded until now ...[79]

In fact, Massena was to prove himself the most talented of all the divisional commanders with the army. He was 37, and a former soldier who had risen to the rank of sergeant-major before the Revolution. He was expert at handling troops on the field of battle, but he was not a strategist, like Bonaparte. Nor was he a man to study a problem and meditate on it, and his generalship was of an instinctive kind. He was not an educated man and disliked reading, a characteristic that made him the opposite of his new commander. According to Bonaparte he 'possessed complete equilibrium only under fire: it came to him in the middle of danger'.[80] He was blessed with what the French called *coup d'oeil*, a good eye, or an ability to assess a situation, the terrain, the strength of an enemy, all in an instant. Ségur, who was later to be Bonaparte's ADC, gives us his portrait:

As for his appearance, he was of average height, a not very remarkable figure, manners and habits simple, perhaps even a little common, but of a wily and attentive physiognomy. His eyes, until his last day, sparkled like stars, twinkling with that sacred fire that makes heroes, and with all the shrewdness of the southerner.[81]

To this we may add some of Thiébault's observations of his chief:

> His figure was full of shrewdness and energy; his glance was that of an eagle; he had in the pose of his head, which was always raised and a little turned to the left, an imposing dignity and a provocative audacity; his gestures were imperious; his ardour, his activity inexpressible; his words, brief in the extreme, proved the lucidity of his thoughts; his least words were salient, and the rapidity as well as the justice of his comments proved that he could raise himself even further without exceeding his ability. In his character, he was a man made for authority and command; no-one was therefore more in his place than was Massena at the head of his troops.[82]

This paragon of the military virtues had, unfortunately, some rather human faults, for he had an uncontrollable lust for women and loot, and made millions out his astute plundering of Italy and any other country that he happened to serve in. He was, however, 'a good comrade, reliable in his dealings ... very rarely did he speak badly of others'.[83] Being a native of Nice, he had the useful ability to speak Italian.

The day after Massena had written his letter of welcome to Bonaparte, it was the turn of Augereau to send his compliments. These were also fairly concise. He wrote from Pietra Ligure:

> I have received your letter of the 8th of this month [germinal, i.e. 28 March], by which I learn that you arrive to take overall command of the army. I congratulate myself on being under your orders, knowing your civic sense and your military talents. I shall do what I can to carry out your intentions in all the orders that you give me: count on my zeal, my energy and my devotion to the public cause.[84]

Pierre Augereau, who was 39, was of humble origins, being the son of a Parisian servant. His hawk nose gave him an aggressive look, and there was an element of brutality in his nature. He tended towards pessimism – 'He had always had enough; he was fatigued and as if discouraged even by victory itself'.[85] The story of his life as told by his ADC, Marbot, is that of an adventurer and soldier of fortune who had served in more than one army, and travelled around Europe one step ahead of the authorities who were trying to arrest him. It is impossible to say how much of this was true, but his character was not that of a shrinking violet. Ségur described him as 'a kind of coarse and uncultured Ajax, intrepid and boastful, proud of his tall stature, of his martial figure and his valour'.[86] Marmont mentions some other characteristics, but did not agree that he was a brave man:

> [Augereau] took much care of his troops ... a good comrade and obliging; of mediocre bravery, disposing his troops well before combat, but directing them badly during the action, because he was habitually too far away from them. Rather a braggart, he believed himself to be of merit and capable of commanding a large army ... He loved money; but, being very generous, he had almost as much pleasure in giving it away as in getting it; despite his origins he was grand in his manners ...[87]

It has to be said that there is not much evidence of Augereau's supposed propensity for hanging back in battle, and it seems probable that the criticism is more due to some personal dislike on the part of Marmont.

The other divisional general who was to fight through the campaign was Jean-Mathieu-Philibert Sérurier, who, at 53, was the oldest of them all, and a veteran of the Seven Years War. His somewhat chequered career went back to 1755, when he had become a lieutenant in the militia at the age of thirteen. He had campaigned in Germany from 1758 to 1760, when he had had his jaw broken by a bullet at the battle of Warburg. He had got stuck in the rank of lieutenant for sixteen years, and had only risen to major just before the Revolution. Some said that in spirit and methods he remained a major. Of the senior generals mentioned here, he was the one who seems to have had least fire and initiative, which is probably why he was later given command of the siege at Mantua. Desaix's description of him tells us that he was 'big ... honest, upright, worthy by all accounts, passes for an aristocrat, but is supported by General Bonaparte, who esteems him'.[88] In accordance with that logic that distinguishes all armies when they come to post people, Sérurier, who was from Laon, not far from the Belgian border, had spent the whole of the present war serving in the Alps or on the Italian frontier.

Although these generals were older and much more experienced than Bonaparte, which might have led them to challenge his authority, they must have known that his connections in Paris gave him great political power. Just how much may be gathered from the submissive letter that Saliceti wrote to the Directory on the 30th, informing them of the suspension of operations on Genoa. 'I have written to General Bonaparte. The military movements are his responsibility. He will decide them himself. The powers that you have given me being those of seconding him, I shall not lose sight of the fact that I must limit myself to that.' He also passed on the unwelcome news that Chauvet was 'dangerously ill'.[89]

This was quite a blow to the new commander, who was heavily involved at this time in trying to sort out the supply and transport of food. He expressed a concern about the latter to Massena that was probably all the more lively because the two divisions of the advance-guard were likely to take the brunt of the early fighting, and needed to be in good condition:

> Your division has been without meat, pay, and often without bread, for two months. This painful situation affects me vividly. Already the left, the centre, and the coast have good bread, fresh meat five times every ten days, and have part of their pay. I have taken measures so that your division will have good bread, meat five times every ten days, and brandy whenever the circumstances require it. I am having some beef cattle march for your division ... I hope, Citizen General, that in a few days the fate

of your soldiers will improve. Tell them that, if they should suffer, it will be because it is physically impossible for them to be better.[90]

Berthier also received instructions that the troops were to alternate fresh meat one day, and salted the next, but Massena's men were still waiting for it on 4 April. The exchanges of letters between the commanders were constant and unremitting, and Massena wrote to Bonaparte more than once on the 30th:

> Nothing new with the advance-guard. The two divisions of the advance-guard occupy: the first from Monte Negino up to Toirano; the second from Seigno up to Melogno. The principal posts of the first are Monte Negino, Cadibona and Baraccone. Of the second, San Giacomo and Melogno, also called Settepani. The enemy having reinforced himself in the area of Dego, I have sent a reconnaissance in force, led by General of Brigade Ménard. All the outposts of the enemy were overthrown. They had ten men killed or wounded. We captured a corporal. On the French side, no dead or wounded.[91]

It seems he was beginning to expect an enemy attack, and also wrote requesting to keep a demi-brigade that was supposed to be going to Augereau's division:

> The snows melt rapidly, our line needs to be reinforced ... my two divisions of the advance-guard find themselves very weakened, counting in total only 13,000 men, and having to guard from Melogno up to Monte Negino and Madonna di Savona.[92]

In Sérurier's area, however, the snow was still thick. He wrote to Bonaparte from Ormea, informing him:

> It is ten to twelve days, General, since I have had any news from Piedmont ... The position of our advanced posts is very bad,

being placed in a valley bottom, the heights not being practicable except in passing.[93]

Considering the amount that had to be done, it was remarkable that Bonaparte found any time for anything but business, but he was not wholly bound up with his work. On the contrary, there were some little domestic difficulties that forced their way into his thoughts and inspired some of his most disjointed letters:

I have not passed a day without loving you, I have not passed a night without holding you in my arms, I have not taken a cup of tea without cursing the glory and the ambition that keep me far away from the soul of my life. In the middle of business, at the head of the troops, while going through the camps, my adorable Josephine is alone in my heart, occupies my spirit, absorbs my thoughts ... and meanwhile, in your letter of the 23rd, of the 26th ventôse [13th and 16th March], you address me with *vous* ... *Vous! vous!* Ah! what can have happened in two weeks? ... My soul is sad, my heart is a slave, and my imagination torments me ... Farewell, woman, torment, happiness, hope and soul of my life, whom I love, whom I fear, who inspires me with tender sentiments which call me to nature ... Farewell! Ah! if you love me less, you have never loved me. Then I should be to be pitied.

Bonaparte.

PS: The war, this year, is no longer recognisable. I have had given out meat, bread, animal feed, my cavalry will march soon, and my soldiers show a confidence in me that is inexpressible. Only you make me sad, only you, the pleasure and torment of my life. A kiss to your children, whom you do not speak of. By heaven! that would lengthen your letters by half. Visitors would not have the pleasure of seeing you at ten o'clock in the morning. *Woman!!!*[94]

With these things teeming in his head, perhaps it is remarkable that he did any work at all.

The effect of the work that was being done did not pass unnoticed by the enemy, however, and it was recorded in Costa's very long and detailed intelligence report on the state of the French army between 15 and 30 March. It was generally accurate in its estimation of numbers, and noted that the army had been in a very poor condition at the beginning of the fortnight. Indeed, there had been a mutiny in Savona on the 17th, 'But all of a sudden things have changed face' and 'as for the spirit which animates the troops, a very remarkable change has taken place in the past few days: from murmuring and despair they have passed to exaltation and confidence'. The report also gave a brief sketch of some of the new arrivals on the staff. Saliceti was described as being 'impervious to pleasures or money. His only passion is an unbridled ambition.' They were right about the ambition, but not about the money, as Saliceti was to prove one of the greatest looters with the army. Of Bonaparte, it said, '[He] is Corsican, like Saliceti, but it is believed that he is neither Jacobin, nor one of his friends … This general, a creature of Barras, is not, moreover, known for any brilliant act, but he is said to be a profound theoretician and a man of genius.' When discussing enemy plans, two possibilities were foreseen. 'One, where the French penetrate into the Milanese and Piedmont with a regular war, advancing step by step against the fortresses and the armies, or rather inundating the country by an irruption in the manner of the barbarians, masking the strongholds, avoiding pitched battles, and subsisting on contributions.' It was thought that they would need more men for the second type of war, but in any case it was thought that the French were intending to make an effort in the direction of Ceva.[95] As always, therefore, the Piedmontese appreciation was at variance with that of the Austrians.

At about this time Costa revealed some of his bafflement at the progress of affairs in a private letter, which ends on an unconsciously ironic note:

What is happening on the Riviera of Genoa? The French troops were in mutiny and went in rags, and now a captured courier informs us that, following a new order, they are clothed, newly shod, and their back wages are paid … They have announced the

arrival at the army of a new general-in-chief. He is named Bonaparte, Corsican in origin like Saliceti. He was an artillery officer
under the old regime, and consequently a gentleman, but not well-
known in the army, where he was only employed as an artilleryman
at the siege of Toulon. He is not believed to be a Jacobin. He is a
man of education and good company. He is said to be full of genius
and of wide views ... What will he do? I do not know yet. The
blows come less quickly than we had reason to fear. These two
weeks will be most interesting: our plan seems superb to me, and
it is a question of what we manage to make of it.[96]

Costa was not the only one asking himself what Bonaparte would do,
but for Beaulieu it was rather more pressing to come up with an answer.
The evidence provided by the French advance towards Genoa suggested
to him that the enemy was intending to attack the town, though this
was contradicted by the opinion of others. For example, Cossila, the
Piedmontese envoy in Genoa, seemed to believe that the danger to the
town was past, and that the French had given up their intentions against
it. Moreover, Beaulieu received 'a whole series of reports containing very
precise information and conceived in the same sense'.[97] One of these,
sent by an informant in Genoa, and dealing with the period from 25 to
31 March, said, 'It is presumed that the arrival of the [French] troops in
this country is only a feint before throwing themselves suddenly on
Piedmont where it is undoubted that they have views.' He also
remarked, 'I still believe that their demonstrations towards our town are
only made to frighten us and to attract the attention of the Austrians to
this side while they have plans elsewhere.'[98]

Beaulieu's attention was indeed sharply focused on Genoa by that
time, and despite the reports he had received, he formed the opinion
that Genoa was in danger of being attacked, and that the best method
of forestalling this was by advancing over the Bocchetta Pass. He was not
alone in his opinion. An operation to take the Bocchetta had been
discussed and approved at a council of war in Turin at which
d'Hauteville (the Foreign Minister), Gherardini, and the English diplomats Trevor and Drake had been present, so the idea was not lacking in

support. Indeed, Gherardini told Thugut on 30 March that he approved of the decision to move into Genoese territory, which he felt was 'of the highest importance and of the greatest use for the security of Italy', and added: 'It appears demonstrated that the enemy wished to possess himself of the riches which the occupation of the territory and the town of Genoa offered to his cupidity in order to invade Lombardy ...'[99]

Having made up his mind, Beaulieu began to make preparations for action on his left wing. It was only a few days since he had ordered four battalions to move towards the Piedmontese, but he now proceeded to withdraw them again. On 30 March he wrote to Colli ordering him to transfer part of the Auxiliary Corps to replace them, as they were moving out of the Bormida valley. Since he had no brigade commanders, Provera was to be sent with the replacements. He also added: 'It would be good, M. Lieutenant-General, if you placed your HQ nearer to this part, which, at the moment, is the only one of the extent entrusted to your care which will be in range of the enemy, seeing that the season and the snows do not permit the French to act on your centre or right at all.'[100]

As it turned out, the Austrian move was to have the gravest consequences, for by directing a major part of his forces over the Bocchetta Pass, Beaulieu was to place a mighty mountainous barrier, more than twelve miles wide and 3–4,000 feet high, between the right and left wings of his army, something he had been clearly instructed to guard against. Beaulieu could be excused if he found the picture confusing, but it has to be said that his decision to opt for *direct* defence of Genoa, rather than the more imaginative indirect defence proposed by the Piedmontese, was to be a major cause of his downfall.

NOTES

1. The receipt, dated 6 March 1796, is quoted in Lumbroso, A., ed. *Correspondance de Joachim Murat.* Turin, 1899, p. 15. See also Cronin, V. *Napoleon.* London, 1990, p. 110 (who gives the same list as Lumbroso) and p. 456

2.   See Bouvier, F. *Bonaparte en Italie, 1796.* Paris, 1899, p. 58. Bouvier does not give the source of his list of books and maps, but it probably comes from Pierron, E., Gen. *Comment s'est formé le génie militaire de Napoléon Ier?* Paris, 1889.
3.   See Wilkinson, S. *The Rise of General Bonaparte.* Oxford, 1930.
4.   See Fabry, J. G. A. *Histoire de l'armée d'Italie (1796–1797).* Paris, 1900–14, IV, §2, p. 1.
5.   Dupont-Ferrier, G. 'Trois lettres inédites d'un caporal-fourrier aux armées des Alpes et d'Italie (1795-1797). Un récit nouveau de la bataille de Rivoli.' *Annuaire-bulletin de la société de l'histoire de France,* (1929), p. 138. At the risk of labouring the point about spelling, it is noteworthy that some of the more 'difficult' words are spelt correctly, suggesting that Dupont-Ferrier asked a more literate colleague for help with them.
6.   Letter of Lieutenant Arnaud to the Directory, 29 January 1796, quoted in Gachot, E. *Histoire militaire de Massena. La première campagne d'Italie (1795–1798).* Paris, 1901, p. 49.
7.   Bouvier, op. cit., p. 3. The figure seems incredible, but Bouvier (who is both scholarly and thorough) states in his own footnotes that his figures are from the official returns (kept in the Archives de Guerre) of 5 March, and the weekly return for the period 1–10 March. While figures of this kind are never completely accurate even an error of twenty or thirty per cent would still give a frightening total.
8.   Bouvier, op. cit., p. 18.
9.   Delhorbe, C.-R. 'Retouches à la biographie d'Amédée Laharpe.' *Revue historique vaudoise,* (1959, 1964), pp. 105–56, 138.
10. See Schels, J. B. 'Die Gefechte in den Apenninen, bei Voltri, Montenotte, Millessimo, Cossaria und Dego, im April 1796.' *Oesterreichische Militärische Zeitschrift,* Bd. 2 (1822), p. 156.
11. Ciampini, R. 'Nuovi documenti sulla prima campagna d'Italia (marzo–giugno 1796).' *Rivista italiana di studi napoleonici,* (1970), p. 62.
12. See Fabry, op. cit., IV, §1, p. 194 and §2, pp. 1–20.
13. See ibid., III, p. 644–6.
14. There is some doubt about the date of this letter. Gachot gives 2 March, but there are various dubious datings in his work. Fabry makes it the 9th, which seems more likely from internal evidence. Not only does Vignolle say Schérer had been asking for a replacement for 'more than a month', but he says that Chauvet is expected 'from one day to the next',

while Schérer's letter of 11 March states that he has not yet arrived. See Gachot, op. cit., p. 85, and Fabry, op. cit., III, pp. 236–7 and pp. 291–2. There are also some cases when the dates given in the latter work do not agree with those in Napoleon. *Correspondance inédite officielle et confidentielle de Napoléon Bonaparte: avec les cours étrangères, les princes, les ministres et les généraux français et étrangers, en Italie, en Allemagne, et en Egypte.* Paris, 1809.

15. See Fabry, op. cit., III, pp. 289–90.
16. See ibid., III, pp. 291–2.
17. Thiébault, P. C. *Mémoires du général Baron Thiébault. Publiés sous les auspices de sa fille Mlle. Claire Thiébault d'après le manuscrit original par Fernand Calmettes.* Paris, 1895–96, II, p. 9.
18. Thiébault, op. cit., II, p. 9. The presence of Duroc is somewhat doubtful. Although he had met Bonaparte at Toulon, he did not become his ADC until October. He probably arrived in Italy in May, as ADC to General Lespinasse. Various other sources give different lists of companions, but this seems about the most likely, with the exception of Duroc.
19. Ciampini, op. cit., p. 63.
20. See Fabry, op. cit., IV, §1, p. 195 and §2, pp. 1–20.
21. Ibid., III, p. 324.
22. Pelleport, P. *Souvenirs militaires et intimes du général vicomte de Pelleport, de 1793 à 1853.* Paris and Bordeaux, 1857, I, p. 38.
23. See Fabry, op. cit., III, pp. 353–5.
24. See ibid., III, p. 358.
25. Vivenot, A., Ritter von. *Vertrauliche Briefe des Freiherrn von Thugut.* Vienna, 1872, no. LVI, p. 44.
26. Vivenot, A., Ritter von. *Thugut, Clerfayt und Wurmser Original Documente aus dem k. k. Haus-, Hof-, und Staats-Archiv und dem k. k. Kriegs-Archiv in Wien vom Juli 1794–Feb 1797.* Vienna, 1869, p. 121. Letter of 30 April 1795.
27. Botta, C. *Storia d'Italia dal 1789 al 1814.* unknown, 1824, I, pp. 331–2.
28. Costa de Beauregard, C. A. *Un homme d'autrefois: souvenirs recueillis par son arrière-petit-fils.* Paris, 1879, p. 300, fn.
29. Costa de Beauregard, op. cit., p. 297.
30. Fabry, op. cit., IV, §2, p. 35.
31. Costa de Beauregard, op. cit., pp. 298–9.

32. Fabry, op. cit., IV, §1, pp. 138–9 and §2, pp. 70–3.

33. Ibid., IV, §2, pp. 75–6.

34. Schels, op. cit., pp. 127–8.

35. Fabry, op. cit., IV, §1, p. 141.

36. Ibid., IV, §1, p. 131.

37. Ibid., IV, §1, p. 194.

38. See ibid., III, p. 469.

39. Costa de Beauregard, op. cit., p. 311.

40. Fabry, op. cit., IV, §1, pp. 112–13.

41. See Garros, L. *Quel roman que ma vie! Itinéraire de Napoléon Bonaparte (1769–1821)*. Paris, 1947, p. 87.

42. Fabry, op. cit., III, p. 352.

43. See Bouvier, op. cit., p. 201.

44. See Fabry, op. cit., III, pp. 401–2.

45. Bouvier, op. cit., p. 199, fn.

46. Fabry, op. cit., III, p. 413.

47. See ibid., III, p. 410.

48. See ibid., IV, §1, pp. 194–5.

49. Ibid., IV, §1, p. 196, fn.

50. See ibid., IV, §1, p. 198.

51. See ibid., III, p. 406.

52. Napoleon. *Mémoires pour servir à l'histoire de France, sous le regne de Napoléon, écrits sous sa dictée à Sainte-Hélène, par les généraux qui ont partagé sa captivité*. Paris, 1829, I, p. 379. The newly formed demi-brigades did not receive their new numbers until they drew lots for them at Soncino on 26 May. For the first weeks of the campaign they were known by the number of the most senior battalion or demi-brigade among those forming the new unit. For example, since the 32nd was formed from the 21st, 118th and 129th, it was temporarily known as the 21st. In the interests of consistency I have tried to use the new numbers, not the temporary ones. For those who are interested, Bouvier's appendices list all the old units that went to form the new demi-brigades.

53. Fabry, op. cit., IV, §2, p. 17.

54. See Gachot, op. cit., p. 86.

55. Desaix, L. C. *Journal de voyage du général Desaix, Suisse et Italie (1797)*. Paris, 1907, p. 74.

56. Abrantès, Duchess of. *Mémoires de Mme la duchesse d'Abrantès*. Paris, 1905–13, pp. 103–4.

57. Quoted in Bouvier, op. cit., p. 68.

58. Fabry, op. cit., IV, §2, p. 18.

59. Gachot, op. cit., p. 92.

60. See Fabry, op. cit., III, p. 428.

61. Various dates have been suggested for Bonaparte's arrival in Nice. Vignolle's note is contradicted by a letter of Berthier, dated 29 March, which says that they had arrived on the 27th. It seems impossible to reconcile these two versions. See Garros, op. cit., p. 88 and Fabry, op. cit., III, pp. 431–2 and IV, §2, p. 81.

62. Napoleon. *Correspondance de Napoléon Ier publiée par ordre de l'empereur Napoléon III*. Paris, 1858–69, no. 92.

63. Ibid., no. 93.

64. Fabry, op. cit., IV, §1, p. 202.

65. Gachot, op. cit., p. 89.

66. Desvernois, N. P. *Mémoires du général baron Desvernois ... d'après les manuscrits originaux, avec une introduction et des notes par A. Dufourcq. 1789–1815*. Paris, 1898, p. 39.

67. 'Soldiers, you are naked and badly fed. The government owes you much, and can give you nothing. Your patience, the courage which you show among these rocks are admirable. But they procure you no glory, no brilliance reflects on you. I wish to lead you into the most fertile plains in the world. Rich provinces and great towns will be in your power. You will find there honour, glory and riches. Soldiers of Italy! Will you lack courage or constancy?' Napoleon. 1858–69, op. cit., no. 91.

68. Ibid., no. 94.

69. Ibid., no. 95.

70. Fabry, op. cit., IV, §2, pp. 84–7.

71. Costa de Beauregard, op. cit., p. 316. See also Schels, op. cit., pp. 159–63.

72. Ibid., p. 314.

73. See Schels, op. cit., p. 157.

74. Napoleon. 1858–69, op. cit., no. 99.

75. Gachot, op. cit., pp. 90–1.

76. See Bouvier, op. cit., p. 702.

77. Napoleon. 1858-69, op. cit., no. 104.

78. Fabry, op. cit., IV. §2, p. 81.

79. Napoleon. 1809, op. cit., I, p. 23.

80. Las Cases, E. A. *Mémorial de Sainte-Hélène*. London, 1823, 4 and 5 December 1815.

81. Ségur, P. P., comte de. *Histoires et mémoires*. Paris, 1873, I, pp. 191–2.

82. Thiébault, op. cit., II, p. 29.

83. Marmont, A. F. V., de. *Mémoires du duc de Raguse de 1792 à 1832 imprimés sur le manuscrit original de l'auteur*. Paris, 1857, I, p. 147.

84. Napoleon. 1809, op. cit., I, p. 25.

85. Las Cases, op. cit., 6 November 1815.

86. Ségur, op. cit., I, p. 192.

87. Marmont, op. cit., I, p. 149.

88. Desaix, L. C. op. cit., pp. 69–70

89. Fabry, op. cit., IV, §2, p. 87.

90. Gachot, op. cit., pp. 91–2

91. Ibid., p. 90.

92. Napoleon. 1809, op. cit., I, p. 26.

93. Ibid., I, pp. 46–7.

94. Napoleon. *Lettres d'amour à Joséphine*. Paris, 1981, no. 5.

95. Fabry, op. cit., III, p. 474.

96. Costa de Beauregard, op. cit., pp. 312–13.

97. Fabry, op. cit., IV, §1, p. 208.

98. Ibid., IV, §1, pp. 208–9.

99. Ibid., IV, §1, pp. 189–90.

100. Ibid., IV, §1, p. 207.

8

OPENING MOVES

By the end of March, Colli had collected more than 20,000 men of the Piedmontese army and the 5,000 of the Auxiliary Corps in 'cramped cantonments' around Mondovì and Ceva. The Piedmontese advanced troops were positioned at Cairo, La Pedaggera, Montezemolo, Bagnasco, Battifollo and La Bicocca.[1] According to one source, the total Austrian force available towards the end of the month, including the Neapolitans, but not the Auxiliary Corps, numbered 35 battalions and 32 squadrons, or 32,000 infantry, 5,000 cavalry and 148 guns.[2] Beaulieu, however, claimed that his battalions were under-strength, so his manpower was considerably less.

The Austrian forces were at that time arranged as follows.

Division	Brigade	Regiment	Strength	Position
Argenteau	Rukavina	1st battn Carlstädter Grenzer	various coys	Rocchetta Cairo, Giusvalla, Mioglia, Pareto
		IR (Infantry Regiment) Preiss	6 coys	Dego
		IR Toscana	1 battn	Dego
		IR Brechainville	1 battn	Moncerchio, Carretto
	Lipthay	IR Pellegrini	1 battn	Spigno, Montaldo
		IR Alvinczy	2 battns	in and south of Acqui
		2nd battn Carlstädter Grenzer	various coys	in the area before Novi, Ovada
		Erdödy Hussars	2 sqdns?	Gamalero

Division	Brigade	Regiment	Strength	Position
Sebotten-dorf	Wetzel	IR Wenzel Colloredo	2 battns	Tortona
		Uhlans	2 sqdns	Voghera, Tortona
	Unknown	IR Terzi	2 battns	Alessandria
		IR Lattermann	1 battn	Alessandria
		IR Stein	1 battn	Alessandria
Kerpen		IR Erzherzog Anton	2 battns	Pavia
		IR Wilhelm Schröder	1 battn	Pavia
		IR Huff	2 battns	Pavia
Unattached	Nicoletti	IR Thurn	3 battns	around Lodi
		IR Wallis	1 battn	around Lodi
		IR Jordis	1 battn	around Lodi
	Roselmini	IR Deutsch-meister	1 battn	around Lodi
		IR Strassoldo	2 battns	around Lodi
Schübirz (cavalry)		Erzherzog Joseph Hussars	10 sqdns	Pavia
		Uhlans	unknown	around Lodi
Pittoni		IR Reisky	3 battns	see below
		IR Nádasdy	2 battns	see below
		IR Terzi	1 battn	see below
		IR Lattermann	1 battn	see below
		Szluiner Grenzer	1 battn	see below

The Neapolitan cavalry, which took relatively little part in the campaign, was around Lodi and even further to the rear.[3]

On 31 March, Argenteau reported to Beaulieu that his troops were occupying such extended lines and were so spread out in weak posts, that he had no reserves left. He also expressed the suspicion that the French would make their main attack in the area he was occupying, and that it would probably be directed at Dego.[4] His opponent in this area,

Massena, had himself expressed disquiet to Bonaparte about the first stirrings of the Austrians, but on the 31st his commander wrote back showing he was not unduly worried:

> The enemy movement is a natural and indispensable consequence of that which you have made. Keep on your guard, and do nothing that may force him to hurry. If the post at Voltri is useless for the diplomatic operations on Genoa, my intention is that you should have it return, and that everything should remain in the usual state.[5]

In another letter Bonaparte also informed Massena that six or seven ships loaded with artillery were to leave Nice in two days, to go to Vado. He instructed him that there was to be no communication between the ships and land, so that no one would know what they carried. There were, in fact, 36 guns of varying calibres, two howitzers and two mortars, which Bonaparte had collected by emptying the arsenals of Toulon and Antibes. Massena, for his part, wrote to Saliceti urging that the withdrawal of the troops at Voltri should be delayed 'as little as possible',[6] and also complained to Bonaparte that Saliceti would not give an adequate explanation of his reasons for wanting to keep them there.

At 10 a.m. on the same day, Colli replied to Beaulieu's orders to replace the battalions in the Bormida valley, saying that they would be carried out, and advised him that he was leaving Turin for Mondovì that day and expected to be in Ceva in the next two days 'to observe at close hand the enemy's movements on the Bormida and the Tanaro'. He also added his voice to those who did not think the threat to Genoa was serious: 'The enemy cannot attack it without artillery at the approach of the two armies. He could well change his plan and turn suddenly on Piedmont, which will then be supported by the army of Your Excellency, that of the King being too weak to support itself, if it is vigorously attacked via the valley of the Tanaro and Bormida.'[7] Nelson, who was sailing just off Genoa, was similarly unconvinced about French motives, and wrote to his wife:

> We are watching and expecting movements of the two armies. The French are advanced with 4,000 men to within nine miles of

Genoa and have talked of possessing themselves of the town but I fancy it had been more to endeavour to awe the Genoese into the loan of money demanded of them than from any real design ...[8]

Beaulieu, however, still clung to the other view, which he explained to the Emperor:

I am assured by the movements of the enemy, his concentration at Voltri, and the unanimous reports of spies that his intention is to capture Genoa in order to find new resources for the continuation of the war in Italy, given the bad economic situation of the French army, to cross the Bocchetta favoured by the powerful support of the mass of the Genoese population and to carry the war into the flat lands.[9]

For these reasons, he had decided to begin his operations by advancing against the French force at Voltri, and issued orders on the 31st to move into Genoese territory and cross the Bocchetta Pass. But at the same time, he decided not to bring up the troops on the other side of the Po yet. The initial moves were entrusted to General Pittoni, who received verbal instructions backed up by a letter, in which Beaulieu told him to threaten to bombard Novi if the Genoese refused to let him enter, but 'in no case' would he pass to the execution of this threat.[10] Operations were begun by gathering ten battalions and two squadrons around Pozzolo Formigaro. The snow was still thick on the northern slopes of the mountains, which impeded the march of the troops, who had to climb to at least 2,500 feet above sea-level, the height of the pass. On the way they occupied the most important towns that lay along the road.

In order to 'preserve secrecy', Beaulieu did not inform the Genoese of his intentions until the moment the troops entered their territory, when they were notified by his ADC, Maelcamp, who gave them a letter dated the previous day, in which Beaulieu maintained that he was being 'forced' to take the step of entering Genoese territory, but he would do so as a friend to protect them from 'the enemies of all social order'.[11]

Pittoni entered Novi with 2,800 men, where the local Genoese governor greeted the invasion with the usual ritual protests at the violation of neutral territory, while knowing that his government was quite powerless to do anything about it. From there, as Beaulieu later reported to the Emperor, his troops then passed through

> Gavi, by the town, which is at the foot of the fortress, Carrosio, and Voltaggio. The advance-guard of the battalion of Szluiner Grenzers arrived at the Bocchetta on the same day at 6 in the evening, and the rest of the battalion of Szluiner Grenzers commanded by Major Sillobod arrived there immediately. Lieutenant-Colonel Hubner, of IR Reisky, arrived there the same night with three companies, and three other companies of his battalion went to the right ... Two battalions of IR Reisky arrived in Voltaggio. Two battalions of IR Nádasdy, which were in Tortona, made a forced march via Serravalle and one remained at Carrosio and the other marched up to Mornese and Spezza ... A battalion of IR Terzi remained at Gavi ... A battalion of IR Lattermann remained at Novi, where I also had advance a squadron of Uhlans. I sent a 12pdr cannon, two 7pdr howitzers and a 6pdr to the Bocchetta as well.

Beaulieu added that the weather up at the pass 'was so cold it pierced me', and that the troops were forced to make camp without tents and with precious little firewood. He also remarked, 'I placed GM Pittoni at the head of this expedition, although he was indisposed. He took on this task with all the good will possible, although he was unwell.'[12]

Coincidentally, the French general opposing him, Pijon, was also ill, and wrote to La Harpe at 8 p.m. on the 31st, saying that it would be necessary to send someone to replace him. Happily for the French army, there was no shortage of generals, and he was soon substituted by General Cervoni. In the same letter, Pijon also reported that two men who had left Ovada at midday had told him that 600 Austrians had arrived there with a detachment of cavalry. On April Fool's Day, the Austrians actually occupied Ovada, which controlled the valley of the

Orba, and the nearby villages of Tagliolo, Lerma and Molare similarly passed into their hands. This move gave them a stepping-off point for an advance over the Turchino Pass, directly towards Voltri.[13]

Massena was not slow to inform Bonaparte of the Austrian moves, which did nothing to decrease his feelings of insecurity about the French positions near Genoa. He clearly wished to shut up shop and retire before they were cut off, and no doubt hoped to receive orders telling him to do so. But he would have to wait for the couriers to make the journey to Nice and back, which was likely to take two or three days. He also complained that the two divisions of the advance-guard were short of 2,000 muskets, and passed on the information that the snows were melting quickly, and that the roads to Piedmont were open. Some of these had been inspected by Marmont, who wrote to Bonaparte from Loano on the same day with a report on the condition of those which led towards Ceva from the area of Sérurier's division, and the time it would take to reach various places.

Bonaparte was keen to see Massena, no doubt both to get his impressions of the situation and to try to win him over to his side, and wrote him a rather warmer letter than the one he had been sent: 'I have received, my dear General, your letter of 10 germinal. I am leaving tomorrow for Albenga where we shall see each other. I shall be delighted to renew our old friendship, which I hope you will wish to rejuvenate. I pray you to believe that on my side I hold you in esteem and friendship.'[14] Massena, however, felt the situation was too precarious at the front for him to be able to leave his post, and showed no sign of budging.

At the HQ the main preoccupations continued to be those of supplies, organisation and intelligence. Bonaparte gave Berthier a breakdown of the composition of the divisions that were to guard the coast in the rear, and informed him that: 'General Stengel will command the cavalry of the army. General Kilmaine will command a division of cavalry of the army. General Dujard will command the artillery. Citizen Sugny, *chef de brigade* of artillery, will be Chief of Staff of that arm.'[15] This was easy enough, but supplies continued to be a real headache. In reply to a panicky letter from Commissary Sucy in Genoa about horse-fodder, Bonaparte soothingly pointed out that the rear areas were well supplied, and that the transport services were hurrying forward: '2,000 mules will be departing tomorrow. They are all going to Finale and Vado.' But perhaps the most striking thing is the large quantity of shoes that is mentioned:

> Citizen [Flosque], who is going to Genoa, has promised me 20,000 pairs of shoes, which will be paid for in Paris. I shall have 5,000 pairs despatched from here tomorrow; 12,000 pairs will be despatched from Marseille. You will deliver the letter here enclosed, in which Collot orders his firm to despatch 10,000 pairs of shoes and 800 hundredweight of hay. Hurry the despatch of the shoes that you have bought.[16]

The shoes were, in fact, desperately needed. When La Harpe heard a week later that they were to receive some, he exclaimed that it was 'the coming of the Messiah'.[17] Bonaparte closed his letter by saying that he was leaving for Bordighera on the following day and would be in Albenga on 4 April, that the HQ with all the agents of the supply services had just left, and that he wanted to see Sucy as soon as possible.

Bonaparte also wrote to Faipoult advising him of his intended move to Albenga, 'where I hope to have your news', and, unaware of the day's events, expressed the opinion that 'Gavi is a stronghold that should resist for several days. It could only be taken by treason ... But I do not think this is to be feared, Citizen Minister.' While the Austrians had not actually occupied the fort at Gavi, this had not stopped them from advancing past it, which might have affected Bonaparte's view of the situation, had he known. He continued with requests for frequent letters, 'so that I know your position and ideas well ... I pray you to send some spies into Piedmont who will keep me informed of the strength and movements of the enemy'. The letter ends on a charming personal note, showing that Bonaparte was never too busy to notice the people around him: 'Your wife is well, and your little niece is still very coquettish. She is courting my aide de camp, and she does not love anything about me apart from my fine coat.'[18] In accordance with his plan, at 8 o'clock in the morning on 2 April,

Bonaparte left Nice 'to the music of the bands'[19] and made his way along the tortuous road to Menton, some thirteen miles further up the coast, where he was to spend the night.

The Austrians, meanwhile, consolidated their position north of Genoa, and began to probe further forward to test the ground towards the city. Four battalions positioned themselves at the Bocchetta and sent patrols down through Campomorone as far as Sampierdarena, which was virtually a suburb on the western edge of Genoa.[20] Although his first move had caused no difficulty, Beaulieu was acutely aware of a number of problems which he emphasised in his report to the Emperor. 'The generals who have to come from the Rhine and Bohemia have not arrived. Only Lieutenant-General Sebottendorf has arrived. I can learn nothing of the others. Two of the generals here are ill: Lipthay and Humbourg. I fear that in a short time Pittoni will also announce he is ill.[21] The colonels who have recently been made generals remain in the rear to hand over their regiments.' He also begged for reinforcements, claiming to have only 21,000 troops available, and saying that 'every day the army shrinks, the country is unhealthy, and the bread very bad ... the soldiers have been lodged during the winter in large churches, dying of cold, and are already destroyed by fatigue ...'[22]

Not surprisingly, the French reacted to the Austrian moves with a little probing of their own. On 3 April a force of 2,000 men advanced from Voltri towards the outposts of the Austrian left wing, but took care to maintain a respectful distance from them. Four large patrols of about 150 men roamed the mountains to the north of Voltri in the vicinity of Campo Ligure, which was well beyond the Turchino Pass, no doubt wishing to discover what was 'on the other side of the hill'. On the same day several thousand French began to move towards the Austrian right wing, and two columns of 1,000 men each appeared at Montenotte. Only twelve Austrian companies were available to defend these positions, and the gaping holes that existed in the Austrian defensive line in this area made the French advance a most unwelcome development for Argenteau.

Knowing that the fight could not long be delayed, Bonaparte and his staff continued to make every effort to pull their army into shape. On 3 April a rather sharply worded Order of the Day was issued:

The General-in-Chief renews the order to the generals commanding the divisions to accelerate, as much as possible, the work relative to the new organisation. The generals of division will inspect the troops that are under their command and examine the state of the armament with care. They will replace the muskets that are unserviceable. The generals and adjutant-generals must not lose a single moment in providing the troops with the objects that may be necessary to them ... The adjutant-generals responsible for the administration of the divisions will send with the greatest exactitude to the Chief of Staff at Albenga the ten-day return giving the position and strength of the troops in the divisions. In their execution of their orders for the move-ment of the troops, several generals have forgotten to have detachments relieved. They are ordered to pay more attention to the dispositions that they make, so that no detachment remains isolated from a corps that receives orders to change destination.[23]

It provides a curious contrast with another kind of missive that Bona-parte was regularly producing during this period. If the orders that emanated from his HQ were spare and clear, the letters he wrote his wife were anything but:

I am at Porto Maurizio, near Oneglia. Tomorrow I shall be at Albenga. The two armies are on the move. We try to deceive each other. To the most able the victory. I am quite happy with Beaulieu: he manoeuvres well, he is better than his predecessor. I shall beat him, I hope, in style. Do not worry, love me like your eyes – but that is not enough – like yourself, more than yourself, than your thoughts, your spirit, your life, your everything. Sweet love, forgive me – I am delirious ... [24]

The following day saw Bonaparte continue his journey and arrive in Albenga exactly on schedule, having now covered two-thirds of the distance between Nice and Savona, where Massena had his HQ. He then wrote to Massena giving a strong hint of his intentions:

I have arrived in Albenga and have received your letters. At Porto Maurizio I had received the news of the continuation of the enemy movement on the Bocchetta. We have advanced on Voltri. They have advanced on their side. You moved out of your winter quarters. They have also moved out of theirs. This is normal.

We must not hasten, my dear general, to evacuate Voltri. But we must not indeed leave there anything of consequence. You must order the construction of new ovens at Voltri and announce that you need to have forces pass near Voltri.

Do not do anything that could make people think you wish to evacuate this position. It must still be kept for a while longer since we occupy it. Keep your eyes open on Montenotte, and always do that which an enemy who wishes to move forward and believes himself strongest would do. Watchfulness and boldness is the case. All common methods, in war, are always good and succeed.

I authorise you, when you think you can come here, to do so. Apart from the pleasure of embracing you, I wish to confer with you.[25]

From this letter, Bonaparte's thinking seems clear. He had perceived that the French force at Voltri could be a bait to bring the Austrians down on Genoa in force, which would place them so far out of reach of the troops in the Bormida valley that they would be quite helpless to stop Bonaparte's thrust from Savona towards Ceva. Massena was to give the appearance of intending to advance over the Bocchetta, but everything important was to be got out of the way so that a rapid withdrawal could be made. The injunction to keep a watch on Montenotte was important, as it lay on the flank of Bonaparte's intended line of advance, and it was also the most likely area from which an Austrian attack would be directed to cut off the French forces at Voltri. Partly to give the Austrians even further reason to think he was intending to attack Lombardy through the Bocchetta, and partly to bolster the slightly slender force at Voltri in case of attack, Bonaparte ordered the 1st battalion of the 51st demi-brigade (800 men) to move to Varazze. This brought the number of men near Voltri to over 5,000. Bonaparte did not neglect the area marked out for his own advance, and also had the valley of the Eastern Bormida reconnoitred as far as Cairo. During this operation an Austrian outpost was pushed back and several prisoners were taken.

Sérurier's men had also been involved in some minor actions with the Piedmontese during this period, and one (unauthorised) French attempt to take the positions on the ridge between the Tanaro and the Mongia must have looked to Colli suspiciously like a preparation to outflank Ceva and try to cut his line of retreat to Mondovì. This almost certainly helped to discourage the Piedmontese from moving forward into a position where they would be better placed to support the Austrians. But an even greater incentive to stay where they were was provided by Beaulieu himself, who, when he informed Colli of his advance on the Bocchetta, assigned Colli a largely defensive role, only asking him to 'watch the two valleys of the Bormida and Tanaro, and make demonstrations against the enemy by ably advancing his outposts'.[26] Given that Bonaparte was hoping to separate the armies of his two enemies so that he could fight each of them in turn, he could hardly have asked for more. Yet he was to be further assisted by the difficulties that Argenteau was facing. The latter had been instructed to provide the link between the two armies, and was to move his men as far forward as possible, a dual task that was impossible with the number of men he had. Indeed, he even sent a warning to Beaulieu that his forces were too spread out, and would be unable to support one another if they were attacked. This seems to have made no impression on Beaulieu.

The French, meanwhile, continued to be troubled mainly by problems of supply and transport, and once more Bonaparte issued orders concerning these subjects. The valley of Oneglia found itself obliged to find a contribution of 400 sacks of grain for the sustenance of the army, and a detailed instruction was sent to Berthier regarding the formation of convoys of mules. This seems to have been intended as a temporary measure, for the 350 mules were to be hired from local drivers 'for two ten-day periods',[27] to build up a considerable magazine of foodstuffs and ammunition in Ormea and Pieve di Teco. Since these two places were on the route from Oneglia to Ceva, it seems likely that Bonaparte was already stockpiling supplies against the projected siege of that place.

Next day, 5 April, he was still engaged with the same problems. This time it was the unfortunate town of Altare that was instructed to provide 200 sacks of corn, or 25 livres in cash for every sack they could not furnish. Since the farmers in that area had sold their grain to the Austrians during the winter, they found themselves obliged to pay the money. This soured the relationship between the French and the locals, who had previously been well-disposed and would now no longer act as guides.[28] Berthier was ordered to hire another 600 mules, this time to establish a magazine at Bardineto, near Garessio, and supply the positions around San Giacomo and beyond, as well as the area of Altare. Bonaparte concluded: 'As this operation is very urgent, the commissaries will make the agreements immediately, and the generals commanding the divisions will do everything to help them in their dealings with the Genoese governors. It is indispensable that this levy is executed by the day after tomorrow at the latest.'[29]

He was also extremely anxious to have the most accurate information possible about the strength of his own forces, and Berthier accordingly issued an order stating:

> The adjutant-generals responsible for the administration of the divisions are expressly ordered to send to the Chief of Staff at Albenga by the quickest way a return with the strength and position of the troops in their division. They must not forget to give the strength of the auxiliary company. The General-in-Chief has the most pressing need to know these states.[30]

Bonaparte's strategy, of course, depended on having the right number of troops in the right place at exactly the right time, so his urgency in demanding the most complete and precise information is not surprising. He could not plan his moves without it. The staff officers in the divisions, however, do not seem to have been used to providing such detailed and accurate reports, and did not immediately grasp the need for them. Acerbic comments about their lack of efficiency in this respect were still issuing from the army HQ some time later.

The Austrians were continuing their slow build-up. On their left wing, Beaulieu had moved his HQ to Silvano d'Orba just in the foothills four miles north of Ovada. Colonel Vukassovich pushed his advance-guard into the mountains several miles south of Ovada, to Campo Ligure. Here, he was placed on the northern side of the crest, on the road that led over the Turchino Pass to Voltri, and surrounded by 3,000-foot peaks, their slopes covered with snow. On the right, Argenteau's division was still awaiting reinforcements. It consisted of eleven battalions and two squadrons, of which three battalions were still to the rear at Acqui and Bosco (a few miles south of Alessandria). Two other battalions (of IR Erzherzog Anton) only arrived in Alessandria at about this time, and so could not be expected to take up their intended station in Sassello before 8 April.[31]

While these movements were taking place, one of Massena's most valuable spies, who had been missing for six days, suddenly turned up in Savona with a band of gypsies. He was a small man called Pico, who used many disguises in his travels, and spoke Italian, German and the local dialect. He had been given the rank of inspector *aux revues* under General Rusca, and received the substantial fixed pay of 4,000 livres per year. He was not a lone operator, but the head of a network of informers that he had built up in the area since 1794. There was nothing improvised about it, and his spies, who were mainly vagabonds and a few local people who were unsympathetic to the Austrians, were all identified by numbers, met him at fixed times, and communicated with him in code. He was also extremely useful in counter-espionage, and often alerted the French to 'leaks' of information within their ranks. Massena treated his information with a great deal of respect, and himself kept a register of his letters.[32] The one that he handed over at that moment is worth quoting as an example of the quality and detail of intelligence that was available to the French commanders:

> The regiment of Tortona, which was at Dego and Cairo, has gone to Millesimo. At Baraccone de Salvetto, there are 700 Austrians with two cannons. At Santa Giulia there are about 800 men, who

should have two cannons. At Cairo a company of Croats, a company of Chasseurs de Nice, a company of French [sic] chasseurs and four or five companies of militia ...[33]

Massena seems to have concluded from the information he was receiving that the Austrians were not yet ready for a major effort, and also felt reassured by Bonaparte's letter giving his intentions with regard to the force at Voltri, as he replied saying, 'I shall neglect nothing to second you in deceiving the enemy as to our operations.' He added that he hoped 'to have the pleasure of embracing you in three days at Albenga'.[34] Bonaparte was indeed still in Albenga, where he must have spent some time listening to Marmont's reports. The day closed with a dreadful shock that affected Bonaparte deeply. In the quiet of his room he took up his pen and wrote to his wife:

> It is an hour after midnight. They have brought me a letter. It is sad, my soul is affected. It is the death of Chauvet. He was the Chief Commissary of the army. You saw him at Barras's a few times. My love, I feel the need of being consoled. It is only in writing to you, the thought of whom can greatly influence my morale, to whom I have to open my pain. What is the future? What is the past? What will happen to us? What magic fluid surrounds us and hides from us the things that it is most important for us to know? ...

It was a terrible blow in both a professional and personal sense. A chief commissary who was both good at his job and honest was a treasure beyond price. Bonaparte knew his worth and must have realised that his chances of conducting a successful campaign had suddenly declined steeply with the loss of one man. Apart from that, Chauvet was an old friend, and the same age as he. A young man, in the prime of life and full of energy, he had been plucked from the earth with dreadful suddenness, in the space of a few days, by a mere fever. One minute he had been immersed in business, with a glorious campaign in prospect, the next he was dying in a lonely room in Genoa. It was a sobering thought to Bonaparte with his hopes of glory and his high ambitions. No wonder he was plunged into philosophical thoughts on the mysteries of destiny – and yet somehow or other his fatalism and self-belief brought him round to an almost triumphant tone:

> Chauvet is dead. He was attached to me. He would have rendered the country essential services. His last word was that he was coming to join me. But yes. I see his shade, it roams through the apartment, it whistles in the air; his soul is in the clouds; it will be in charge of my destiny ...

From there it was but a short step to the practical:

> I am very busy here. Beaulieu is moving his army. We are in each other's presence. I am a little tired. I ride every day. ... B.P.[35]

The last sentence alerts us to the fact that Bonaparte was not only concerned with office work, but was making tours, reconnaissances and inspections. One of the latter became an excuse for a little morale-boosting, and on 6 April Berthier issued an Order of the Day recounting it:

> Today the General-in-Chief inspected the 39th and 69th demi-brigades. He has pleasure in publishing, by means of this order, the satisfaction that he felt on seeing the state of the clothing and arms, as well as the discipline, the instruction, the good spirit and the ardour that animate the demi-brigades. He expressed his satisfaction to the assembled officers and NCOs that they belong to the troops they command. The General is persuaded that all the corps of the army merit the same praise.[36]

Bonaparte also wrote a businesslike report to his government that day, beginning by roundly condemning Saliceti's little strategic *faux pas*:

> The movement that I found begun against Genoa has brought the enemy from his winter quarters. He has crossed the Po and

has advanced his outposts to Dego, by following the Bormida, and to the Bocchetta, leaving Gavi in his rear ... I was very angry and displeased by this movement on Genoa, the more out of place because it compelled that Republic to adopt a hostile pose and awoke the enemy when I could have surprised him when he was at rest. These are more men that it will cost us ...

After then making some comments about the Piedmontese, and casually stating that he is intending to sell some marble statues that have been found in Oneglia, and are expected to fetch 30-40,000 livres (they actually belonged to the cathedral), he returns to the perennial question of supply and its consequences:

Flachat's company, which has the grain business, and Collot's company, which has the meat, are conducting themselves well. They give us very good grain, and the soldiers are beginning to get fresh meat. The army is in a frightening state of destitution. I still have some great obstacles to surmount, but they are surmountable. The poverty has authorised indiscipline, and without discipline, no glory. I hope that this will sort itself out promptly. Already everything is changing aspect ... Chauvet, the Chief Commissary has died in Genoa. This is a real loss for the army. He was active and enterprising. The army has shed a tear in his memory.

In other words, everything was under control, and even if mistakes had been made (by other people) there was nothing to worry about. It was, in this sense, a fairly transparent piece of propaganda.

The letter is also interesting in that it contains Bonaparte's estimate of the rival forces. He puts the Piedmontese army at 40,000 infantry and 5,000 cavalry, the Austrians at 34,000 infantry and 3,000 cavalry. Against this he claimed to have only 45,000 men available in total, and complained that they had kept back many troops from him in the rear and beyond the Rhône. Almost as an aside, he stated: 'In a few days we shall be in action.'[37]

Bonaparte was still doing his utmost to get the transport service and the supplies into some kind of order. Berthier received yet another letter ordering him to form more transport divisions of 200 mules each for the supply of Pieve di Teco, Ormea and Garessio, where Sérurier's division had been reduced to half rations. Lambert, the new Chief Commissary, was informed that the store-keeper of the fodder-magazine had been giving short measure. He was ordered to place the culprits under arrest and check the weight of all the bundles of fodder. 'It is important, Citizen Commissary, that no thief may escape. For a long time the soldiers and the interests of the country have been the prey of cupidity. An example is necessary at all times, and particularly at the opening of the campaign.'[38]

As usual he also found time to write Josephine a letter filled with his customary eccentric mixture of passion and practicalities, in which he demonstrated that it was not just the procurement of supplies for the army that had been receiving his attention:

> My brother [Joseph] is here ... He is sending you a box of sweets from Genoa as a present. You will receive some oranges, some perfumes and orange-flower water which I am sending you. Junot and Murat send you their respects. A kiss lower, lower *than the heart.*[39]

The meeting between the two brothers must have been both joyful and melancholy. They had not seen each other for some time, but Joseph's arrival in Albenga had been occasioned by the death of their mutual friend, Chauvet, whom Joseph had attended in his last hours. Yet time was pressing, and Bonaparte was no doubt soon pumping his brother for as much information as he could give him about affairs in Genoa, where Joseph had been living for some considerable time as a representative of the French government.

The intelligence services of friend, foe and neutral continued to relay whatever they could learn, often with a fair degree of accuracy. The Tuscan consul in Nice, who was some distance away from the centre of operations, sent his superior in Paris a wild overestimate of the strength of the French army (he put it at 80,000), but the rest of his report was much nearer the mark. After saying that the army's HQ, 'which had never moved from this city', had left on the 2nd for Albenga or Finale, he comments: 'while on one side the French make pressing preparations on the right wing, for an imminent attack, the Austrians on the other side seem to wish to forestall the operations of the former, because it is assured that a corps of Germans with much cavalry has already moved into Genoese territory'.[40] This would seem to prove that Austrian intentions were no great secret.

They were certainly no mystery to Massena. His intelligence service maintained an admirable level of efficiency. Pico wrote to him on the 7th, having finally left his band of gypsies. It was a letter of the utmost importance:

> The Austrian troops at the Bocchetta have increased, because out of the 5,000 which was the total that had arrived at Novi (where General Beaulieu is) up till now, they have left 300 Uhlans, and the others have come to position themselves at the Bocchetta and its environs.
>
> The English squadron will soon appear in the Gulf of Genoa and there is reason to believe that, on the invitation of the Genoese government, part of it will even enter the port.
>
> The allies try, by every means, to dislodge us from Voltri and to cut off all communication with Genoa, and it is said that they also have a plan to attack us in the area of Cairo and San Giacomo, to oblige us to retreat.
>
> At this moment a man has reached me from Sassello, who tells me that 3,000 Austrians have arrived in this village and that another 2,000 are expected, who should arrive tomorrow or the day after.[41]

This information was supported by another letter dated the same day and sent from Novi by a spy called Gabardi. It was a very detailed report stating that the Austrian concentration north of Genoa was definitive, and indicated Beaulieu's latest plans. It also spoke of the numbers of troops still expected from Austria, and gave information about the strength of the forces that were still on the right bank of the Po, and in the foothills of the mountains between Cuneo and Piacenza.[42]

The intentions of the Austrians were therefore made perfectly clear to Massena. The build-up in the area of the Bocchetta seemed to indicate that an attack could very well be imminent, but that had been expected for some time, and a frontal attack down the narrow coastal strip was something he could deal with. When he received the information, the day after it had been written, the news that concerned him most was the build-up at Sassello and the plan to attack from the area of Cairo to cut off the troops near Voltri. We shall see how he reacted to this in a moment.

On 8 April, Beaulieu finally felt his concentration was sufficient to make his dispositions for the attack on the force at Voltri, and sent out preparatory orders to the commanders on the other wing of his army. Colli was asked to devote much attention to the area around Cairo, while Provera was to defend the terrain between the two Bormidas. Beaulieu also instructed Argenteau to form strong patrols which he would send into the area of Montenotte until he was strong enough to occupy the position.

Beaulieu was undoubtedly somewhat premature in his actions, for his troops were not at all well positioned for the operations he had in mind. Vukassovich ended a report written the same day by observing that he could not link with General Argenteau, from whom he was separated by high mountains and a day's march, and that it was not much more easy to link with Pittoni without putting his position in danger. Pittoni, for his part, noted that from the Bocchetta it was impossible for him to support Vukassovich in a serious affair because it would take him six hours to reach Campo Ligure and Masone, and by roads so bad that he would lose half his men on them.[43] Similarly, Rukavina, who had just accomplished the march from Dego to Sassello, reported on the 8th that if Dego should be attacked it would take him eight hours to reach it because of the bad, narrow roads and numerous streams that he had to cross. This cautionary note did not seem to make a sufficient impression on Argenteau, who was later to make a bad miscalculation in this respect when Dego actually was attacked.

Between Rukavina and the Piedmontese army, the allied line was even weaker. Provera had arrived in the Bormida valley on 6 April with four battalions and two companies (probably only around 2,000 men) of his Auxiliary Corps. With these meagre resources he had proceeded to form a line of cantonments that stretched from the Austrian army on his left and ran through Dego, Santa Giulia, Monesiglio and Mombarcaro down to Ceva, where he linked with the Piedmontese on his right. It was about 22 miles of hills, valleys, woods, rivers and snow-covered mountains. Given the number of troops he had to man this line, a daisy-chain would have been stronger.

The Piedmontese army, for its part, remained on the defensive as ordered. Colli would probably have been reluctant to move much in any case, as he had become worried by French activity to the south of Ceva, which seemed to him to presage an attack on his positions. He informed Beaulieu of this, but of course the latter had already made up his own mind that Genoa was the goal of French ambitions. It probably did not help matters that at this critical time, Colli found himself incapacitated with a swollen leg, and was unable to move around much.

The tempo of operations was beginning to pick up. To the south-west, the French carried on sounding out the Piedmontese defences in the Tanaro valley, and Rusca pushed patrols of the 29th Light beyond Priola. Far to the right, La Harpe's troops continued to tease the Austrians in the area where they were expecting the main French attack, and on 8 April they once again advanced from Voltri into the hills, while the 75th demi-brigade, under its *chef,* Chambarlhac, moved up to Sampierdarena on the coast. Colonel Vukassovich had the force in the hills attacked by four companies of Carlstädter Grenzers, supported by two companies of IR Alvinczy. The French were driven from the heights and moved their defences to Acquasanta, a couple of miles north of Voltri, but these were stormed by the Grenzers, and the French were driven to the coast with a loss of 40 dead, 26 captured, and many wounded. The 75th, after having fought for six hours, had to withdraw to positions before Voltri, but counter-attacked in the evening.[44] La Harpe wrote to Massena saying that his troops were exhausted and they had run out of cartridges.

Bonaparte knew that the storm must break soon, and in a letter to the Directory largely dealing with the subject of royalist infiltration in the army and problems of finance, he adds the observation: 'as you read this we will already have fought'.[45] He had still not seen Massena, which he earnestly desired to do, so Berthier was instructed to write to him, asking him to meet Bonaparte in Garessio on the following evening.[46] By this time, however, Massena had received the reports from his spies. At 6 o'clock in the evening of 8 April he wrote an urgent letter to the officer commanding the troops at Madonna di Savona:

> My dear Rampon, tomorrow morning, before day, you will make a reconnaissance with 600 men in the area of Sassello making in the direction of Stella. This latter is occupied by our men. The word of the day is 'Friendship'. The good of the service requires that you make this reconnaissance yourself. The enemy seems to be gathering at Sassello. They could cut off the retreat of the troops who are at Voltri.[47]

The man entrusted with this vital operation was a *chef de brigade* who had found himself without a permanent command when his unit had been incorporated into the 32nd Line during the recent reorganisation. General Desaix, who wrote telegraphic descriptions of many of the prominent members of the Army of Italy, gave this picture of him: 'square figure   hat a little big, leans backwards, very dark skin'.[48] He was to make quite a name for himself in the next few days.

Rampon rapidly made his preparations. According to the report he gave later, he ordered 300 carabiniers of the 17th Light and 300 men of the 32nd Line to be gathered two hours before day on 9 April on the road to Cairo, near Montenotte. In the event he found himself with 800 men when he got to the rendez-vous. He obtained a local guide, and the party left at 2 o'clock in the morning in a fine, icy rain. The guide proved to be only partly reliable, and led them not to Sassello, but straight towards Stella, 'where we arrived at 7 in the morning, after having gone over impassable paths, covered in woods'.[49] Glimmerings of dawn came under lowering grey clouds that hid the peaks of the mountains. Rampon did not allow anyone to enter Stella, and let his wet, shivering soldiers rest for half an hour, while he questioned some locals, who assured him that there were only about twelve hundred Croats in Sassello. With that, the party staggered back to Montenotte without encountering any of the enemy. As Rampon admitted, the operation had not been a success, but at least it seemed that the threat to Savona was not imminent.

In fact, some of Argenteau's troops were already on the move on the 9th, although there was nothing immediately aggressive in this. Since the battalions that had been on their approach march to the division had finally arrived, Rukavina's brigade was ordered to move from Sassello back into the valley of the Bormida to Dego. The positions in and around Sassello were taken over by Lieutenant-Colonel Leczeny with four battalions. As this shunting around rippled down the line, so General Provera moved his four battalions and two companies closer to the Piedmontese, into the valley of the Western Bormida, and positioned himself on both sides of the river at Saliceto and Camerana.

Argenteau, with his forces still very spread out, had been extremely reluctant to make any move against Montenotte. This irritated Beaulieu, who reacted by sending him a strongly worded order:

> Since I am moving against Voltri and will attack this locality tomorrow at the break of day without considering your strength or your weakness, you will move forward from your position as much as it is possible for you, to maintain communications with Colonel Vukassovich ... [and] in order to facilitate his attacks by your movement.[50]

After receiving this stinging directive, Argenteau prepared to attack. Strangely, however, he never seems to have thought of informing Colli of what he was planning to do, nor of asking for his co-operation. There is no doubt that Colli remained in perfect ignorance of the attack until it was over. Argenteau himself says in his report:

> I could never have imagined that they would have placed such a small corps as mine in the centre of enemies without having

informed the Piedmontese army of it and without having given orders to General Baron Colli to move at least towards Cairo and Carcare. However the thing was such that the Piedmontese never knew a word of the movement that had been made, not a single man moved to support me.[51]

As Fabry points out, however, Argenteau had as much responsibility as anyone else to inform Colli of the impending advance of his division, and the reasons for it. It may therefore be that the failure to alert Colli was an oversight due to the fact that everyone thought everyone else had done it, or ought to do it. But it seems more likely that Beaulieu had been in too much haste, and had gone into action before he had formed a clear and detailed picture of how operations should develop. The Austrian soldier-historian, Johann Baptist Schels, summarises the situation by saying:

> In the allied armies, there was at that time still no general operational plan known to the commanders of the individual parts of the army, exactly indicating the employment of the assembled combat forces. The advance of the Austrian left wing towards Voltri appeared, however, to be a special undertaking directed against the division on the French right wing, because it was not combined with simultaneous powerful operations by all the remaining allied troops ... The corps of FML Provera and the Piedmontese army of FML Colli – apart from the written expression of a general invitation to active co-operation – received no firm orders on the ways and means that the offensive was to be carried out to the attainment of a common purpose. It was therefore left up to FML Colli to arrange separately the movements of his Piedmontese army and the Auxiliary Corps under FML Provera, which was allocated to him.[52]

On the front line, the 9th had passed with only localised fighting, a number of minor skirmishes taking place between the outposts of the armies. The Piedmontese occupied a redoubt near San Giovanni di Muramazzo, and exchanged a few shots with Rusca's men, while near

Voltri the 75th Line fought throughout the day. The French commanders were about as certain as they could be of what the enemy was preparing to do, but they could not be sure of the timing. Massena, however, had a pretty shrewd idea that things were just about to come to the boil, and when he received the letter inviting him to go to see his commander at Garessio, he refused point-blank to leave the front line at such a critical juncture. He wrote to Berthier from Savona:

> I do not think I should set out before the arrival of General La Harpe. Besides, I could only reach Garessio after two days' journey. I could not therefore meet the General-in-Chief there. As soon as General La Harpe has returned I shall set out, but I do not think I should do it before.[53]

Bonaparte had also come to the conclusion that something serious must be in the offing, and another letter was soon on its way to Sérurier in Garessio.

> I inform you, General, that unexpected movements oblige the General-in-Chief to go to Savona instead of coming to Garessio today, as he had first decided. You will receive further orders when he is able to come to the latter place.[54]

In fact he never got there. Nor did Augereau get to Bardinetto or Calizzano that day as he had planned, for he encountered Bonaparte on the road, and went away with some detailed instructions for his division. Some of the soldiers also found their arrangements overwhelmed in the sudden surge of events that occurred in the next few days. Sergeant Vigo-Roussillon, a volunteer of 1793 who was with part of the 32nd demi-brigade at Quiliano wrote:

> We received orders to leave our cantonments during the night of 20 germinal Year IV [9 April 1796]. We had seen no unusual preparations, and no order had been communicated to us, and

we believed it was a simple reconnaissance. We were all far from thinking that this unexpected march was going to be the first step towards the conquest of that Italy which until then had been seen only from the summit of the Alps and in the mist of the horizon. Our error on this point was such that, convinced that we would soon return to our cantonments, we left there the few effects that we possessed, judging it pointless to pack our knapsacks.[55]

Nelson was to be less surprised, though rather more disappointed. That day he wrote to his wife from Genoa:

I anchored here yesterday ... We are here in expectation every moment of the campaign commencing. Probably the grand attack will be in two or three days, perhaps sooner ... I trust we shall do better this campaign than the last.[56]

NOTES

1. Schels, J. B. 'Die Gefechte in den Apenninen, bei Voltri, Montenotte, Millessimo, Cossaria und Dego, im April 1796.' *Oesterreichische Militärische Zeitschrift*, Bd. 2 (1822), p. 157.
2. Ibid., p. 154.
3. See Fabry, J. G. A. *Histoire de l'armée d'Italie (1796 1797)*. Paris, 1900–14, IV, §1, pp. 204–6.
4. Schels, op. cit., p. 158.
5. Gachot, E. *Histoire militaire de Massena. La première campagne d'Italie (1795–1798)*. Paris, 1901, p. 94.
6. Fabry, op. cit., IV, §2, p. 91.
7. Ibid., IV, §2, p. 20.
8. Naish, G. P. B., ed. *Nelson's Letters to his Wife, and other Documents, 1785–1831*. London, 1958?, p. 287.
9. Fabry, op. cit., IV, §1, pp. 203–4.
10. Ibid., IV, §1, p. 209.
11. Ibid., IV, §1, pp. 187–8.
12. Ibid., IV, §2, pp. 108–9.

13. See Schels, op. cit., pp. 163–4.
14. Gachot, op. cit., p. 96.
15. Napoleon. *Correspondance de Napoléon Ier publiée par ordre de l'empereur Napoléon III*. Paris, 1858–69, no. 110.
16. Ibid., no. 112.
17. Napoleon. *Correspondance inédite officielle et confidentielle de Napoléon Bonaparte: avec les cours étrangères, les princes, les ministres et les généraux français et étrangers, en Italie, en Allemagne, et en Egypte*. Paris, 1809, p. 40.
18. Napoleon. 1858–69, op. cit., no. 113.
19. Bouvier, F. *Bonaparte en Italie, 1796*. Paris, 1899, p. 205.
20. See Schels, op. cit., p. 163.
21. Colli also complained that some of his generals were ill.
22. Fabry, op. cit., IV, §2, pp. 108–10.
23. Napoleon. 1858–69, op. cit., no. 115.
24. Napoleon. *Lettres d'amour à Joséphine*. Paris, 1981, no. 6.
25. Gachot, op. cit., pp. 96–7.
26. Fabry, op. cit., IV, § 1, p. 217.
27. Napoleon. 1858–69, op. cit., no. 116.
28. See Gachot, op. cit., p. 98.
29. Napoleon. 1858–69, op. cit., no. 118.
30. Ibid., no. 120.
31. See Schels, op. cit., p. 167.
32. See Gachot, op. cit., pp. 70–1.
33. Ibid., pp. 76–7.
34. Fabry, op. cit., IV, §2, p. 123.
35. Napoleon. 1981, op. cit., no. 7.
36. The two demi-brigades were the *old* 39th and 69th, which were to become part of the 4th and 18th Line respectively. Napoleon. 1858–69, op. cit., no. 123.
37. Ibid., no. 121.
38. Ibid., no. 125.
39. Napoleon. 1981, op. cit., no. 8. The words in italics were underlined three times in the original.
40. Ciampini, R. 'Nuovi documenti sulla prima campagna d'Italia (marzo–giugno 1796).' *Rivista italiana di studi napoleonici*, (1970), p. 64.

41. Gachot, op. cit., p. 77.
42. See ibid., p. 78. Gachot also states that when Massena gave this written information to Bonaparte on 11 April, the latter did not believe it, but he offers no supporting evidence.
43. See Fabry, op. cit., p. IV, §1, pp. 228–9.
44. See Schels, op. cit., pp. 169–72, Martinel and Bouvier, op. cit., pp. 223–4.
45. Napoleon. 1858–69, op. cit., no. 126.
46. See Gachot, op. cit., p. 88.
47. Ibid., pp. 103–4.
48. Desaix, L. C. *Journal de voyage du général Desaix, Suisse et Italie (1797)*. Paris, 1907, p. 138.
49. Fabry, op. cit., IV, §2, p. 154.
50. Ibid., IV, §1, pp. 229–30.
51. Ibid., IV, §1, p. 241.
52. Schels, op. cit., p. 173.
53. Gachot, op. cit., p. 88.
54. Napoleon. 1858–69, op. cit., no. 128.
55. Vigo-Roussillon, F. *Journal de campagne (1793–1837)*. Paris, 1981, p. 28.
56. Naish, op. cit., p. 288.

9

THE AUSTRIAN OFFENSIVE

Sunday, 10 April 1796, was the day that General Beaulieu had chosen for the offensive with which he expected to drive the French from before Genoa, and cut off their advance-guard in the vicinity of Savona. To judge from the arrangements that had been made for this attack, he seems to have committed the cardinal sin of underestimating his opponent. The attack was badly organised, poorly co-ordinated, and used a surprisingly small number of troops.

The attack on the French force lying near Voltri was to be undertaken by two main columns totalling ten battalions and four squadrons. The first column was under the command of GM Pittoni, and consisted of the following units:

> 1 battalion Szluiner Grenzer
> 1 battalion IR Terzi
> 1 battalion IR Nádasdy
> 2 battalions IR Reisky
> 4 squadrons Uhlans

This gave a total of 3,350 infantry and 624 cavalry. The second column was led by FML Sebottendorf, consisting of:

> 1 battalion Carlstädter Grenzer (2nd)
> 1 battalion IR Alvinczy
> 2 battalions IR Wenzel Colloredo
> 1 battalion IR Lattermann

These five battalions totalled 3,200 men.[1] In other words, Beaulieu was proposing to undertake this part of his attack with only about 7,000 men.

It is true that rather more were theoretically available for the 'right hook' that was to be carried out by Argenteau. Under his command were eleven battalions and two squadrons, which initially amounted to roughly 9,000 infantry and 340 cavalry, but they could not all be used in the attack due to the way they were positioned. On 10 April the units and their positions were:

1st Carlstädter Grenz battalion, which held the outposts before Sassello in the mountains, and the routes leading there from Savona, Albisola, Stella, Voltri, etc.

1 battalion IR Preiss, 1 battalion IR Toscana and 1 battalion IR Brechainville, which were in the camp behind Sassello, resting on the right of the Erro.

2 battalions IR Erzherzog Anton, which were at Mioglia and Squanero, and had detachments in Giuovalla and Piana Potte.

1 battalion IR Terzi, which was scattered about in Malvicino, Ponzone and Murbello.

1 battalion IR Terzi, which was still in Acqui.

1 battalion IR Alvinczy, which was at Pareto.

1 battalion IR Stein, which was at Dego, of which 2 companies were detached at Rocchetta Cairo.

1 battalion IR Pellegrini was at Cairo.

2 squadrons of Erdödy Hussars were at Cantalupo, Borgoratto, Gamalero and Rocchetta Cairo.[2]

From this it can be seen that the troops were still widely scattered. The distance between the most widely separated of them was about 20 miles as the crow flies, but considerably more by road, and those roads were shockingly bad. To effect a concentration for an attack would take some time.

According to the return for 9 April, the forces opposing the allies were:

| Advance-guard (Massena) | La Harpe | 17th Light, 22nd Light, 32nd Line, 75th Line | 8,614 men |
| | Meynier | 11th Light, 25th Line, 51st Line, 27th Light, old 51st, 55th Line | 9,526 men |

Battle divisions	Augereau	4th Light, 29th Light, 4th Line, 18th Line, 14th Line	10,117 men
	Sérurier	69th Line, 39th Line, 85th Line	9,448 men

Various other small divisions guarding Nice and the coast brought the overall total to about 56,000, not counting the cavalry and artillery. The former only amounted to about 3,500 men. Hidden among the lists were many names that would later be famous, including, for example, Reille and Mouton, who would both command army corps at Waterloo.[3]

The strength of the brigade positioned at Voltri under the command of General Cervoni was over 5,000 men. It consisted of the 75th demi-brigade (3,181 men), a unit that was to become one of the most famous in the army, two battalions of the 51st (about 2,000 men) and three companies of grenadiers.[4] The farthest outposts were just beyond Pegli, almost exactly half-way between Voltri and Genoa, and extending into the hills above the coast. To the north of Voltri was an outpost on Bric (Mount) Ghigermasso, a 1,800-foot peak that over-looked the road leading from the Turchino Pass. The distance between these two wings of the French lines was roughly eight miles. A few skir-mishers or vedettes ranged well beyond the Turchino Pass, while to the rear there was a weak reserve on the coast at Arenzano, three and a half miles from Voltri.

The Austrian movement against these forces was initiated by their left-most column, which was to use the road from the Bocchetta and reach the coast just on the western edge of Genoa. It did not start out until a surpris-ingly late hour, a factor that turned out to be detrimental to the Austrian operations because they were to run out of daylight before they had really achieved everything they ought to have done. At 8 o'clock in the morning, General Pittoni sent his ADC, Lieutenant Lilienberg, with 250 volunteers to advance via Madonna della Guardia, an enormous monastery perched high in the mountains overlooking the road from the Bocchetta. He was to cover Pittoni's right flank, and make for the area of the coast between Sestri di Ponente and Pegli, two or three miles west of Genoa.

At 11 o'clock Pittoni left Campomorone, a pretty little town in a cleft in the mountains, and moved off with his whole column and some artillery 'with flying standards and ringing music'. It was a straightforward march along the best road in the whole area, through a valley where the very first shoots would have been appearing on the trees. The route went via Rivarolo, to Sampierdarena on the coast, then across the *Torrente* Polcevera, and along the shore to Cornigliano and Sestri di Ponente. It was not a rapid advance, and it took the column several hours to pick its way down to the coast.

Sebottendorf's column, which was accompanied by Beaulieu, also made satisfying progress. In the vanguard was Colonel Vukassovich, who attacked the enemy pickets at Masone at about 2 o'clock in the afternoon, before crossing the Turchino Pass and descending on the seaward side of the Apennines, making in the direction of Voltri. As soon as firing was heard, General Cervoni moved to Bric Ghigermasso to supervise the French defence. The Austrians did not make for this position, but bore to their left instead, evidently to draw nearer to Pittoni's column. A couple of miles away from the coast, in the hills above Voltri, were some French entrenchments, and the Austrians made for these. Vukassovich detached three companies of Croats to attack Acquasanta on his left, and three others to his right towards Monte Cornoli. Each of these detachments was supported by a company of IR Alvinczy, marching behind them in reserve.

The French outposts that had been pushed back by the Austrians consisted of three companies of grenadiers of the 51st, commanded by a *chasseur chef de brigade* named Jean Lannes. As yet he was little more than a phenomenally brave fighting man, but he was to develop into one of Bonaparte's most trusted subordinates, a Marshal of the Empire, and a close friend. It was his 27th birthday[5] so he was called on to celebrate in fairly rough fashion. He seems to have done little to oppose the enemy advance, however, for the entire loss sustained by the 51st during the day only amounted to two killed, six wounded and two prisoners.[6] This strongly suggests that the entire brigade had orders to put up only token resistance, and to draw the enemy after them as they fell back, luring them onto the coast where they would have no hope of maintaining a link with Argenteau's division or the Piedmontese.

Down on the coast, the 75th came under serious attack at 3 o'clock in the afternoon. The advance-guard of Pittoni's column, which was composed of the four companies of the Szluiner Grenzers, led by Beaulieu's ADC (who was also his son-in-law), Captain Baron Maelcamp, attacked Pegli, while Lieutenant Lilienberg carried the heights on the right of Pegli with his volunteers. They then fell on the French left flank with the bayonet, and drove them away from two hills they were defending. The officer who made the first local studies of this campaign, Martinel, notes that the Austrians even employed some cannon on the coastal road, and that several years later one could 'still see the effects of the shot on the wall of a reservoir placed at the foot of Castelluccio which the French employed for a time like an entrenchment'.[7]

Vukassovich's Croats made short work of capturing the defences above Voltri, from where they observed the advance-guard of Pittoni's column on the coast, where it was in action with the enemy. As a result of the attack by the Croats, the French troops north of Voltri had moved back to the redoubt at Pian del Mele. It was now about 5 o'clock, and the fighting near Pegli seemed to intensify. The French resisted for about an hour longer, but perceiving the danger of being outflanked they withdrew from the heights behind Pegli.

The 75th, although it had spent some hours exposed to heavy fire, retired in good order along the coast. Four of its companies were temporarily cut off by the enemy at Campo dei Preti, but fought their way out at bayonet point, and managed to effect a retreat via Monte dei Cappuccini. Captain Nicolas Gruardet, who was to become a general in 1811, held off 200 Austrians with 45 men by using an improvised entrenchment. The day was dying, and this made it more difficult for the pursuing Austrians. By about 7 o'clock[8] the 75th had broken contact with the enemy and was gaining safety.

Vukassovich, a willing workhorse and a man of great energy, seems to have been sent off in the intervening time to command on Sebottendorf's right. Here he drove away the enemy outposts from Rocca del Dente, and made to go round the left flank of the enemy. Cervoni could see that it was approaching the time when he would have to retreat and ordered the small redoubt of Pian del Mele to be abandoned.

By twilight the second Austrian column had reached Voltri. By 8.30 it was almost completely dark. Despite the French stratagem of leaving camp-fires burning, the Austrians soon saw they were retreating and the rearmost troops were subjected to some harassment. The 1st battalion of the 51st, commanded by Menzweig, formed the rearguard, but the 3rd company of grenadiers of the 75th somehow managed to find itself even further behind. Placed at the Cappuccini, it was still being attacked there at 10 o'clock in the evening.

Voltri turned out to be empty, apart from two French officers and some men who were found hiding in the houses. However, the Austrians had captured some weapons and a magazine of 200 sacks of flour during their advance. Pittoni occupied Voltri himself with three of his battalions and the four squadrons of cavalry. The other two battalions were placed at Sestri. Beaulieu himself entered Voltri around midnight, apparently with good reason to be satisfied with the day's achievements and seemingly eager to pursue the French in the morning.[9]

It was time to count the cost. On the Austrian side the losses were fairly light, and have been estimated at about 50 in total.[10] Schels, who is normally very informative on these matters, limits himself to saying that 'there were some killed and wounded on both sides' but gives us the precise figure of nine wounded for the Carlstädter Grenz battalion.[11]

French losses were far worse. According to the historian of the 75th, they lost one officer killed and seven others wounded or captured. Among the other ranks there were sixteen dead, 45 wounded and 148 prisoners. Of the latter, however, it is claimed that many escaped during the night. The large number of prisoners was attributable to some of the outposts not having time to fall back and being cut off. The losses of the 51st were claimed to be very light, as we have noted, due to the fact that only their grenadiers were much involved in the fighting. Bouvier is not inclined to take the French figures at face value, and thinks that a total loss of 250 is more likely.[12]

Bonaparte, who had arrived in Savona during the day,[13] seems to have been completely unconcerned by these events, as Ségur recalled in his memoirs:

[The person] who took him the news of the first of these attacks
on 10 April told me that Napoleon, whatever the responsibility
that weighed on him, received it smilingly and with a calm air,
and replied to him: 'that everything had been foreseen, that the
enemy attack on the following day would be much more serious,
but that he knew how to make them regret it!'[14]

In fact, the attack that took place on the 11th was probably not as
serious as he had expected. He may well have overestimated his enemy,
who was not able to concentrate nearly as strong a force as he himself
would have used for such an important operation. Argenteau was
faced with great difficulties in collecting his scattered troops, and
despite being undisturbed by the enemy while Pittoni and Sebottendorf were edging down to the coast, was not able to scrape together a
large total. He was not helped by the fact that none of his battalions
were up to full strength.

With the need to keep some troops in reserve, some to occupy
important positions, and a number who were in Acqui and simply too
far away to arrive in time, Argenteau ended up with an attack column
that was no bigger than those that had advanced on Voltri. With this he
was supposed to take the road through Montenotte and attack Savona
from the north-west. It was a tall order for such a small force, and once
again it seems to betray a severe underestimation of enemy capabilities
on the part of the Austrian supreme commander.

Seemingly untroubled by any sense of urgency, Argenteau reconnoitred Montenotte on 10 April, finding it unoccupied by the French.
Massena himself had been there three days before, and had decided
against placing any men there as it would extend his forces too much.
Argenteau then went to Dego to confer with Rukavina. It was typical
Austrian practice to hold a council of war before an important operation, which allowed everyone to state their point of view, but it did tend
to slow things down. When he returned to his HQ in Pareto at 8.30 in
the evening he received Beaulieu's blunt order to support his attack on
Voltri. As Argenteau observed later, there were some strange omissions
in the order. 'He did not communicate anything to me either of the

dispositions of the centre nor of those of the left wing of the army nor of the intentions of the General-in-Chief. I did not know moreover if FMLs Colli and Provera had received some orders in relation to my march. I hoped that it had the mission to make a movement against Cairo to cover my right flank and my rear and support my small corps which advanced in front of its line.' Argenteau was aware that he stood in some danger.

> My worries were not small ... there were only two routes for me: I had to expose the troops to danger or pass for a coward. I decided to follow the first hoping that immediately after the eight battalions had captured Voltri, they would turn their march to the right along the sea, and that the division of the centre and the left wing would similarly advance along the Riviera. Moreover, I counted on FMLs Colli and Provera defending my right flank and my back as they had been ordered to.[15]

Hoping for the best, Argenteau ordered the troops positioned in Pareto, Mioglia, Cairo and Dego to assemble one and a half miles from Montenotte Superiore before dawn on the 11th. The units in question were:

> 2 battalions IR Erzherzog Anton
> 1 battalion IR Alvinczy
> 1 battalion IR Stein
> 1 battalion IR Pellegrini
> 3 companies Frei-Corps Gyulay

These amounted to something over 3,000 men: indeed, Martinel spoke to an inhabitant of Giusvalla who claimed that Argenteau himself had told him he had 3,700 men.[16]

The place that had been chosen as the assembly point was an isolated farmhouse called Cascina Garbazzo (now abandoned and rather dilapidated), the property of a certain Signor Obix. Although it was in the middle of an area of thick woodland, it was immediately surrounded by a number of fields that gave ample space to assemble the infantry. It was also sufficiently distant from the French outposts to make it likely that the assembly would be unobserved and undisturbed.

Argenteau set off from Pareto at 3 o'clock in the morning of the 11th with the battalion of IR Alvinczy, and collected the two battalions of IR Erzherzog Anton in Mioglia. This column was therefore composed wholly of Hungarian troops. Rukavina left Dego independently with the battalion of IR Stein, and was joined by the three companies of Croats of Frei-Corps Gyulay and the battalion of IR Pellegrini. As often happened to the Austrians, the marches were not well timed and co-ordinated, and Rukavina arrived at Cascina Garbazzo well before Argenteau. There does not seem to be any record of what Signor Obix and his family thought when a couple of thousand Croat and German-speaking soldiers suddenly began to gather outside their windows in the grey light of dawn, stamping their feet in the cold, but they had every right to be terrified.

It was also Rukavina who engaged the enemy first, and it seems to have been entirely in character for him to do so. Mathias Rukavina was one of those fighting generals from the Borders who seem to have been happiest leading from the front. A native of Croatia and the son of an officer, he was 59, and had seen distinguished service in a Hungarian infantry regiment during the Seven Years War. He then spent many years in Grenz regiments, and was twice badly wounded while fighting the Turks. In 1794 he took two of the four Carlstädter Grenz battalions to Italy. Commanding these wild men was not a job for a staid and retiring personality, and it probably says something about Rukavina that he remained among Grenzers for so long. He was promoted general in May 1795, managed to get himself wounded again in June, and particularly distinguished himself at Loano.

As Cascina Garbazzo was slightly above the floor of the valley that ran parallel with the valley of Montenotte, the troops had to make their way down through the woods, cross a stream, climb up the other side, still in thick woods, and then go over the crest and down into the valley of Montenotte, using whatever paths they could find. The crest, which reached the respectable height of 2,800 feet, had two high points, one of which was topped by substantial earthworks (still largely intact) with the planform of a trapezium. The longest side of this was about 40 yards at its base. It had not been garrisoned by the French as it was too far from their main defensive positions. This peak is now known as Bric del Tesoro, but at that time went by the name of Monte Castellazzo or Bric Castlas. It was to figure quite prominently in the events of the following day. Half a mile north-east of Monte Castellazzo was a farmhouse called Cascinassa. After crossing the crest in the vicinity of this, the Austrians were intending to move southwards along the valley towards Montenotte Superiore, then turn to follow the road that led south-eastwards along a prominent ridge or chain of peaks that met the sea just north of Savona. Its significance is not immediately obvious, but Martinel said that it 'must number among the most important positions on the Western Riviera'.[17] Since this ridge was the scene of some of the most famous events of the campaign, both on this and the following day, it is necessary to describe it in greater detail.

It was highest at its north-western end, where it overlooked Montenotte Superiore, then the peaks gradually stepped down in height, each a little lower than its neighbour. The first three are the only ones that need concern us here. They were: Monte San Giorgio (2,785 feet), Monte Pra (2,680 feet) and Monte Negino (2,329 feet). Monte San Giorgio was the point where the ridge met the main crest of the Apennines, which separated the streams flowing inland to the Po from those flowing the short distance to the sea. In fact, the ridge stood between two of the latter. On its southern side was a stream called the Letimbro, which went to Savona, and on the north another called the Sansobbia went to Albisola.

It was quite common in this area for ridges of this kind to carry roads or paths, which were often more usable than those in the valleys when the rivers were in spate, and the road along this ridge was the key to Austrian, and French, interest in it. Martinel, who examined it only a few years after the campaign, stated:

A very practicable road for carriages from Savona leaves that maritime town, follows the Letimbro up to the sanctuary

[Madonna di Savona], from there becomes very bad, climbs, passing Ca' dei Barbieri, by the western slope of Monte Negino up to the col of Montenotte and goes to Cairo.[18]

In contrast to this, there was a whole area shaped like a triangle, with its point near the col of Montenotte, and its base running roughly from Altare to Madonna di Savona, where the going was very difficult. Rapid streams dropping over rock ledges, thick undergrowth, trees, lung-bursting slopes and narrow paths all meant that large bodies of troops needed to go round the area rather than through it.

The importance of the ridge in the local communications network is self-evident, hence the need to defend it. Fortunately for the French it was well-suited to defence. This depended partly on the fact that its sides were very steep and broken, and the lower slopes were wooded, which meant it was easier to walk along the crest than to climb up to it. But moving along the crest was not always easy either. In particular, to reach Monte Negino from its neighbour to the north-west, Monte Pra, one had to walk along a ridge that might be compared to a stone tight-rope. The sides to this part of the ridge, while not meriting the word 'precipice', were extremely steep, and might only have been clambered over with difficulty. To add to this, Monte Negino itself was a small enough 'pimple' of a peak for the whole of its summit to be turned into a redoubt. This had been done by the Austrians the year before, a little piece of construction work that they were to regret. Very few traces of it remain, so once again it is to Martinel that we have to turn for a contemporary description:

The principal redoubt, situated most to the north, at 710 metres [2,329 feet] above sea-level, is constructed at the source of the small streams of Pocapaglia, Rezzo and delle Sliggie. It is a pentagon of 50 paces in circumference, very irregular, with bastion and without ditches to the south. The avenues to it are almost inaccessible, if one excepts the very sharp crest by which one arrives and on which it is impossible in very many places for four men to approach abreast. It presents itself to the view of the enemy absolutely like the salient of a demi-lune … [there is a] ditch which surrounds it on three sides, which gives two ranks of fire … One might easily take advantage of the two spurs that appear to follow the construction of the redoubt, by ranging men in their shelter … They would thus flank the work of which we have just spoken, but it does not seem that anything was done to destine them for this use. More to the south, at a distance of more than 200 metres [218 yards], is another small closed redoubt, 45 paces in circumference, and 684 metres [2,244 feet] above sea-level. It was destined to prevent the enemy from advancing too far from the principal redoubt. It was surrounded by ditches …

This latter redoubt was very accessible from the south because of a rock that covered the approaches to it up to pistol range. The large one, on the contrary, was unapproachable from the south and it was this one that provided the great strength of the small one. It had a sally-port in the centre of the southern face. The troops were camped between the two redoubts. All the slopes are very steep. They become more broken still lower down, near Rian d'Acqua Bona …

Martinel also says that there was a redan lying in front of the largest redoubt, and that:

the two redoubts … were not even in a defensive state, and were without artillery. These three works were moreover only capable of receiving 400 men if one did not want to crowd them uselessly against one another.

To conclude, he adds:

There are some sparse and very inconsiderable bushes of heather on the slopes of Monte Pra. They seem never to have been more bushy. The road, which seems to go round the redoubt to the west would have served to attack it. But the enemy was so exposed there that he would only have been able to fire badly-aimed shots from there. Before this position, 1,900 metres [2,077 yards] more to the north ... was a *flèche* disposed in such a manner that proved that the French had constructed it to place an advance-guard there.[19]

This useful defensive complex was to go down in history – with the incorrect name of Monte Legino – as the scene of one of the first grand gestures to be incorporated into Napoleonic legend: the swearing of an oath to fight to the death. How much truth there is behind the legend is something we shall examine in a moment.

The French commanders had recently devoted great attention to defensive arrangements for the area. Apart from Bonaparte's recommendations to Massena, which we have already mentioned, and which had brought him out to make a detailed reconnaissance on 7 April, General La Harpe had issued most minute instructions to General Pijon on 24 March:

If the position of Monte Negino is attacked, the troops at Madonna and San Bernardo [half a mile east of Madonna] will set out. Those of Madonna will take the road that leads from Madonna to Monte Negino and those of San Bernardo will go by the road that leads to the heights to the right and behind Madonna. These troops, when they have arrived on the heights, will take up positions on the hill and in front of the entrenchments already established. Small detachments will be sent to the flank of the entrenchments who will spread out as skirmishers to trouble the enemy and halt his march. If the enemy succeeds in forcing some of the advanced posts, the troops will retire, also under the redoubt and in order, where they will resist vigorously. Should the enemy in much superior numbers force them to evacuate the redoubt, the troops will retire, still in good order, along the crest of the mountain, from hilltop to hilltop, defending the terrain from the enemy ... The troops and the officers are warned that under no circumstances may the retreat take place except when the majority of the troops are on the field of battle, and it has been ordered by the General, the troops from Savona having reinforced the rear.[20]

There could be no clearer indication of the importance that the French attached to the position, nor greater proof that they considered an enemy attack on it to be of the highest probability. In accordance with this they placed some of their best troops and commanders in the area. Massena's memoirs tell us that on 11 April:

> *Chef de brigade* Fornésy had been occupying the large redoubt with two battalions of the 17th Light for some days. The third was in reserve half-way up the slope on the side of Madonna di Savona. One battalion of the 32nd [Line] held Palazzo Doria, at the bottom of the peak. The two others were camped at Cadibona, two and a half miles further away.[21]

The demi-brigades of light infantry were considered to be an élite in the French army and the 17th was to prove to be one of the best of them. It later saw distinguished service at Rivoli and Austerlitz. Like all the demi-brigades of the army, it had only just been formed, and it was at that time probably only around a thousand strong.[22] Its commander was a 45-year-old Swiss from the area of Lake Geneva, named Fornésy. He had served in the French army since 1763, and, in the year of Bonaparte's birth, had actually been serving in Corsica. Desaix described him simply with the words 'small, round figure'.[23] As the Austrians were to find out, he was also a soldier of considerable skill and determination. As for the 32nd, that became one of the most celebrated demi-brigades of all, one of the units that Massena was constantly leading to where the action was hottest. Its second battalion was 1,192 strong, according to the return of 4 April.[24] The commander at Madonna di Savona was Rampon, whom we have already met.

It was towards these troops and defences that Rukavina was wending his way. The first couple of miles proved easy enough. First contact was made with 'a patrol of the 2nd battalion of the 32nd'[25] in the area of Cascinassa, which was conducting one of the sorties that La Harpe had ordered to be made at regular intervals. It prudently conducted a with-drawal, but without offering much resistance.[26] By about 10 o'clock in the morning the French had retired from Traversine, near the col of Montenotte, onto the steep road that led to Monte San Giorgio. By this time, Rampon, who was at the inn at Madonna di Savona, had been alerted to the enemy attack, and 'immediately went to the scene with the 3rd battalion of the 17th Light, but he was pushed back by a more numerous corps towards the redoubts of Monte Negino'.[27]

The activities and whereabouts of Bonaparte, Massena and La Harpe during the critical days of 10 and 11 April are something of a mystery, but some sources say that it was precisely to the vicinity of Madonna di Savona that Bonaparte took himself on the morning of the 11th, in the company of one of his ADCs and Captain Marchand, one of the junior officers on La Harpe's divisional staff. This seems to have been after the fighting started, because according to Martinel, Bonaparte 'gave orders to the custodian of the sanctuary to take in the wounded, and the Chapel of San Bernardo was set aside for them'.[28] After having made these arrangements and studied the terrain around Madonna di Savona, where he also encountered La Harpe, Bonaparte led the party back to Savona, to the HQ installed in the bishop's palace.[29]

Bonaparte's motive for going to Madonna di Savona may not have been purely to gain an idea of the seriousness of the fighting, but also to remind himself of the lie of the land that he had not seen for eighteen months and to inspect the state of some of the roads he was intending to use for his imminent advance. Martinel reminds us that apart from the road via Montenotte to Cairo, there was also a road that had been constructed for artillery by the Piedmontese, and was used by carriages to go from Madonna di Savona to Cadibona.[30] It was in a very bad state, but it was another important part of the network that would be used to move the thousands of French troops to the most inconvenient place for the Austrians.

On the road to Monte Negino, the Austrians now disposed of their whole force, because by 11 o'clock Argenteau's column had been able to go into action. This was no doubt to some extent counter-balanced by the arrival of the rest of the 2nd battalion of the 32nd, who would have had to toil up the steep, twisting road from Palazzo Doria to Naso di Gatto, having been attracted by the firing. According to Martinel, Argenteau's column made slower progress than the other, but his description of events is not at all clear. Nevertheless, it seems that by about midday, the French had retired to Ca' di Ferrè, on the southern slopes of Monte San Giorgio, and were steadily retiring towards their redoubts. By the early afternoon the Austrians had driven them from Monte Pra back to Monte Negino. At this point the tactical withdrawal was over, the French had reached their main defensive position, and the real fighting began.

The Austrian units deployed themselves for the attack in the following positions.

The battalion of IR Alvinczy, split into 4 groups, was on brics Gaglione, Variolassa, Cianasso and Monte San Giorgio. This formed a sort of reserve during the attack, partly on the ridge leading to Monte Negino and partly on the crest of the Apennines.

The two battalions of IR Erzherzog Anton were at Naso di Gatto and on Monte Pra. The battalion of IR Stein was before Bric del Pogetto. The battalion of IR Pellegrini was below Monte Pra, near the main road to Montenotte. These three corps were those which actually carried out the major attacks on the position.

The three companies of Croats, meanwhile, were spread out as skirmishers before Monte Negino.

Two cannon were available, and one was placed at Naso di Gatto, with the other below Monte Pra. In Martinel's opinion, they should have been much further forward.[31]

The Austrians made relatively short work of capturing the small redan which was the first obstacle, but the redoubts proved an entirely different matter. The regiment IR Erzherzog Anton immediately attacked the first of them, but was repulsed by a triple volley. The Austrians returned to the attack three times, but the inaccessibility of the redoubts was an insurmountable difficulty. From their positions on the slopes of Monte Pra, the attacking troops were obliged to funnel onto the narrow ridge 'not a metre wide',[32] cover perhaps 100 yards, then fan out and clamber 150 feet up a steep incline towards the pale stonework of the defences, standing proudly above them.

From their magnificent vantage point on the top of the peak, the French had an uninterrupted view of all the slopes before them, including both sides of the ridge. On either side of them they could look over the rolling ocean of rounded peaks with their covering of stunted, leafless beech and chestnut trees for a distance of ten to fifteen miles. If the weather stayed clear, hardly a man could move on the slopes to their front and sides without them seeing him. Any attempt by a usefully large number of men to outflank the redoubt by picking their way over the difficult gradient on the side of the ridge would have taken at least an hour or two, and would have been in plain view of the enemy for the whole of that time. With insufficient forces, or time, to make a wider encircling movement, the Austrians were compelled to try to dislodge the French by frontal attacks.

The battle became as much psychological as physical. The Austrian commanders had to persuade their men to undertake the perilous advance along the narrow part of the crest nearly in single file, almost certainly into the teeth of every sharpshooter the French could find, then probably wait until enough men could be assembled to make a rush for the redoubt. It says something for their courage that they did this three times.

The French, on the other hand, had to keep their nerve and prevent their men from wilting in the face of undoubtedly superior forces, knowing that their position was isolated, and being well able to see that there was no reinforcement on its way. Despite wavering on at least one occasion, the morale was sufficiently high to hold the men together. Various individuals gave an example for others to follow. Sergeant Jérôme Moreau of the 3rd battalion of the 17th Light led a few men on a sortie and got into an entrenchment at the point of the bayonet, killing two of the enemy himself. He was later to win a musket of honour under the Consulate. According to Thiébault, who joined the army at a later date, Fornésy even drafted his regimental craftsmen into the fight, and 'under the orders of the master-tailor, they performed prodigies'.[33] François Vigo-Roussillon,

who was then a sergeant with the 3rd battalion of the 32nd (and
therefore not actually present at the time), also recalled a story of
personal bravery in his memoirs:

> We were told that at a critical moment, when the soldiers were
> abandoning the parapet, a corporal named Rouach, born in
> Toulouse, climbed onto the top and cried to his neighbours:
> 'Cowards! I'll show you how a good soldier should die!' and he
> continued firing from there, out in the open. The soldiers returned
> to their places and the enemy was repulsed another time.[34]

The exact role played by Rampon in this stubborn defence has been
questioned by some, particularly Bouvier, who looks upon him as an
able self-publicist who exaggerated his actions. The editor of Massena's
memoirs, General Koch, also says that 'nothing proves that he did more
than others here'. But there seems no escaping from the fact that he took
overall command of the defence of the redoubt, and that he was entitled
to do so as the designated commander of Madonna di Savona, who,
moreover, had the special trust of Massena. His most famous action
during this defence was to call upon his soldiers to swear an oath to fight
to the death, though Koch, once again, is sceptical about this,
commenting that 'the officers and soldiers had other things to do'. Yet
at least one person who was actually there, an officer of the 32nd named
François Roguet, who later became a general of the Grenadiers of the
Imperial Guard, says that '... from the height of the platform, a colour
in his hand, he swore, and we all swore with him, to: *conquer or die.*'[35]
This story is slightly spoilt by Koch, who points out that light infantry
did not have colours, and the 2nd battalion of the 32nd was unlikely to
have had the regimental colours with it. Vigo-Roussillon limits himself
to the slightly equivocal words, 'It was said that Rampon made the
soldiers of the 2nd battalion of the 32nd Line swear to defend themselves to the death.'[36]

On balance, it seems likely that something of this kind did happen,
but that it was not quite the theatrical performance of the sort
depicted in the highly romanticised paintings that were turned out in

the period of greatest Napoleonic myth-making during the heyday of the Empire. It is worth noting that of the *Historiques* of the 17th Light and 32nd, which are the most nearly contemporary accounts we have, the former says nothing of an oath, and the latter tells us simply and soberly that 'Rampon encouraged the soldiers with his words: "It is here, my friends", he said, "that we must conquer or die."'[37]

While these events were unfolding, Cervoni's brigade had been making its weary way back towards Savona. It was not a simple walk along the sea-shore. Believing that the coastal road was too exposed to the attentions of Nelson's ships, Cervoni climbed into the hills above Varazze, where he received support from two battalions of La Harpe's sent from Savona.[38] After snaking over the awful mountain paths towards Stella, he was able to turn in the direction of the coast again and descend to Albisola.

Beaulieu soon decided against pursuing Cervoni. He had achieved his objective of cutting the French off from Genoa and forestalling their supposed advance over the Bocchetta. He now thought it best to turn his attention to the Austrian right wing, though quite what he intended to do with it is not clear. One can only surmise that he planned to follow up Argenteau's attack in some strength, because 'he had several battalions march from Lombardy to Acqui and hastened to go there himself in order to be in the right place to take the necessary measures for the advance that had been arranged'.[39] The units that had taken part in the advance on Voltri were also mostly transferred to the right, as he explained in a letter to the Emperor:

> Four battalions are marching at once to Faiallo, and I am leaving two battalions here [Voltri], and all the rest will march at once towards my right, and, to arrive there, all have to return to Acqui, which is very inconvenient, but we cannot go through the mountains by crossing the valleys.[40]

In the last sentence Beaulieu innocently reveals the fundamental flaw in his strategic arrangements. It was a very long way from Voltri to Acqui, and a very long way from there to Argenteau's right wing. But, happy with his progress so far, he set off for the Bocchetta Pass, and at 2 o'clock in the afternoon most of the Austrian troops began to pull back over the roads they had used to advance.[41] Vukassovich, however, went in the other direction (with three battalions, not four) by the shortest, but most arduous route to Sassello, over the Faiallo Pass, four and a half miles north-west of Voltri.

Just about the time that the Austrians were marching away from Voltri, Massena arrived back in Savona having been away carrying out inspections. Bonaparte now conferred with his generals in the bishop's palace, where he received intelligence reports, listened to the latest information from his subordinates, and made arrangements for the following day's operations.[42]

They must have been made to the sound of distant gunfire, for Argenteau's men were still trying to take Monte Negino. The last two desperate attempts to capture the redoubts were made by volunteers, a number of whom were hard-fighting Croats of Frei-Corps Gyulay. Schels says that these attacks were beaten back 'with great losses to the attackers'.[43] An Austrian report of 14 April also tells us 'most of the officers who led them were killed or wounded in these attacks on the redoubts'.[44] The casualties included the intrepid Rukavina, who was wounded in the shoulder, and Lieutenant-Colonel Habbein of IR Pellegrini. The French, many of them protected by the defence works, exploited the advantage of firing down on their attackers, and inflicted more casualties than they suffered. The last of these efforts was over by about 4 o'clock.[45] Argenteau decided that he could not continue with full-scale attacks because the troops were exhausted (they had been either marching or fighting for over twelve hours). Any further serious attempts would have to be deferred till the morrow, when he hoped to receive some reinforcements, and the troops would be rested. Rukavina seems to have had some doubts about the wisdom of waiting. According to Count Moretti: 'He said ... to Rolando Beltrame, who served him as a guide, and who sympathised with him, "I do not regret my wound, but I regret that I fear that my colleague will let himself be deceived."'[46] Despite the suspension of full-blooded assaults, the sniping continued for some time.

At half-past five, when the lull in the fighting gave him some time for other things, Rampon scribbled a note to Massena, which, miraculously, still exists. It was to the point:

General

Send us five barrels of cartridges, some bread and brandy –

You promised us two 3-pdr cannons. If we had had them I believe we would have flushed them out. Have them sent up to us this evening and even a 4-pdr if it is possible. It is urgent for a thousand or twelve hundred men to advance on the side of Palazzo Doria, and then we can make a vigorous sortie.

We have just made one in which several brave men distinguished themselves, among others Sergeant Moreau and Carabinier Olliviere of the 17th Light ½ bde, Citizens Bataili and Cabaux, and Sergeant-Major Houssai of the 32nd ½ bde. Citizen Fornésy lost his horse in front of the entrenchments.

Up to the present we have not seen anyone from the staff. The firing is still going on.

Salut et fraternité

Rampon

NB: Citizen Sergeant Belin of the 32nd ½ bde is of the number of those who have distinguished themselves.[47]

Unusually for a commander serving under Napoleon Bonaparte, Rampon was going to receive rather more reinforcements than he had asked for. But that was part of a much larger plan. The fighting meanwhile carried on at a much reduced level until darkness finally brought it to an end. The Austrians moved back and their commander 'disposed them in several lines, one behind the other, on Monte Pra, where they spent the night under arms'.[48]

It had been a less expensive day than one might think from some of the rather dramatic accounts of the fighting. The *Historique* of the 17th Light tells us that five officers were wounded, one mortally. Of the other ranks, three men were killed, 25 wounded and twelve captured. The battalion of the 32nd Line had two men killed and ten wounded.[49] Not a significant percentage of the 2,000 men engaged for several hours. The Austrians were not so lucky, and their losses were estimated at about 100,[50] the Croats having suffered particularly. General Rukavina was also temporarily incapable of exercising his command. Although the number of casualties looks quite low, Vigo-Roussillon, who saw the position the day after the combat, was struck by its appearance:

> When ... we rejoined the 2nd battalion we were astonished by the immense number of Austrian bodies that lay on the ground on the glacis and even in the trenches of the redoubt.[51]

This impression may have been influenced by the powers of suggestion – amply contributed to by Bonaparte's propaganda skills over the next few days[52] – or the excitement of the moment. Rampon himself estimated the enemy casualties at two or three hundred, and there was a general tendency to 'talk up' the engagement into a famous victory – excusable, perhaps, if you consider that Bonaparte was trying to build the morale of his own army while undermining that of his opponents.

From about 4 o'clock onwards, Cervoni's exhausted soldiers had been trailing into Savona, and Bonaparte was careful to spend some time with them. The 75th Line arrived at 5 p.m. and was inspected by Bonaparte, who no doubt gathered the troops around him and congratulated them on their performance, as he habitually did on such occasions. The demi-brigade then bivouacked until midnight in the streets of the town, the soldiers trying to gain a little rest before they had to haul themselves to their feet and stumble off again. It was a short respite, for Bonaparte's own plan was about to swing into action.

NOTES

1. All figures from Schels, J. B. 'Die Gefechte in den Apenninen, bei Voltri, Montenotte, Millessimo, Cossaria und Dego, im April 1796.' *Oesterreichische Militärische Zeitschrift*, Bd. 2 (1822), pp. 174–5.
2. Figures from ibid., p. 170.

3. See Bouvier, F. *Bonaparte en Italie, 1796*. Paris, 1899, pp. 704–6.

4. Ibid., pp. 202, 224 and 704–5. Schels believes there were only 3,000 French. See Schels, op. cit., p. 175.

5. At least, it was according to some sources. Others give 11 April 1769 as his date of birth. Opinion seems to be fairly evenly divided over the two dates.

6. *Historique* of the 51st Line, in Napoleon. *Mémoires pour servir à l'histoire de France, sous le regne de Napoléon, écrits sous sa dictée à Sainte-Hélène, par les généraux qui ont partagé sa captivité*. Paris, 1829, I, p. 380.

7. Fabry, J. G. A. *Mémoires sur la campagne de 1796 en Italie*. Paris, 1905, p. 15.

8. The *Historique* of the 75th says that the combat lasted from 3 to 7 p.m. See Bouvier, op. cit., p. 224.

9. Schels, op. cit., pp. 175–6; Fabry, 1905, op. cit., p. 16.

10. Bouvier, op. cit., p. 226.

11. Schels, op. cit., p. 176.

12. Bouvier, op. cit., p. 226, and fn.

13. This is proved by a letter to Faipoult (if the date is not incorrect) which is dated Savona, 10 April. It seems to have been written before Bonaparte had any news of the Austrian attack. Napoleon. *Correspondance de Napoléon Ier publiée par ordre de l'empereur Napoléon III*. Paris, 1858–69, no. 129.

14. Ségur, P. P., comte de. *Histoires et mémoires*. Paris, 1873, p. 200.

15. Fabry, J. G. A. *Histoire de l'armée d'Italie (1796–1797)*. Paris, 1900–14, IV, §1, p. 235.

16. Schels, op. cit., p. 177, and Fabry, 1905, op. cit., p. 17.

17. Fabry, 1905, op. cit., p. 6.

18. Ibid., pp. 6–7.

19. Ibid., pp. 7–8. The author examined the site in June 1995 and again in April 1996. The fact that anything was visible at all was entirely due to the efforts of a group of volunteers from Savona who, on the second occasion, were engaged in cutting down the trees that had sprouted all over the peak. The fortifications have gone, but the site is impressive none the less.

20. Wilkinson, S. *The Rise of General Bonaparte*. Oxford, 1930, pp. 171–2 and Fabry, 1900–14, op. cit., III, p. 416.

21. Massena, A. *Mémoires de Massena, rédigés d'après les documents qu'il a laissés et sur ceux du dépôt de la guerre et du dépôt des fortifications, par le*

général Koch. Paris, 1848–50, II, pp. 22–3. See also p. 430, where we are informed that the components that were to form the 17th Light were ordered to Madonna di Savona on 9 April, to effect the new *amalgame.* This was completed by the evening of the 10th.

22. Inevitably, perhaps, these figures are open to debate. Bouvier does not seem to be able to make up his mind whether or not the whole unit was present. If it was, it numbered 1,136 men. If the 3rd battalion was absent, it counted only 924. See Bouvier, op. cit., pp. 229–32. On balance, it seems likely that all three battalions were present, but the difference is slight.

23. Desaix, L. C. *Journal de voyage du général Desaix, Suisse et Italie (1797).* Paris, 1907, p. 166.

24. Bouvier, op. cit., p. 232.

25. Massena, op. cit., II, pp. 22 3

26. See the *Historique* of the 32nd, quoted in Massena, op. cit., II, p. 431.

27. Massena, op. cit., II, pp. 22–3.

28. Fabry, 1905, op. cit., p. 19.

29. Krebs, V. L., and Moris, H. *Campagnes dans les Alpes pendant la Révolution, d'après les archives des Etats-majors français et austro-sarde.* Paris, 1891–95, p. 384.

30. Fabry, 1905, op. cit., pp. 6–7.

31. Ibid., p. 17.

32. Ibid., p. 2.

33. Thiébault, P. C. *Mémoires du général Baron Thiébault. Publiés sous les auspices de sa fille Mlle. Claire Thiébault d'après le manuscrit original par Fernand Calmettes.* Paris, 1895–96, II, p. 42.

34. Vigo-Roussillon, F. *Journal de campagne (1793–1837).* Paris, 1981, p. 29.

35. Roguet, F. *Mémoires militaires du lieutenant général comte Roguet (François), colonel en second des grenadiers à pied de la Vieille Garde, pair de France.* Paris, 1862, p. 221.

36. Vigo-Roussillon, op. cit., p. 29.

37. Massena, op. cit., II, p. 431.

38. Schels, op. cit., pp. 176–7 and Fabry, 1905, op. cit., pp. 16–17.

39. Schels, op. cit., p. 177.

40. Wilkinson, op. cit., p. 95.

41. Fabry, 1905, op. cit., p. 16.

42. Gachot, E. *Histoire militaire de Massena. La première campagne d'Italie (1795–1798)*. Paris, 1901, p. 99.
43. Schels, op. cit., p. 178.
44. Fabry, 1905, op. cit., pp. 31–2.
45. Fabry, 1905, op. cit., p. 17.
46. Conterno, G. 'Una cronaca inedita di èta napoleonica in val Bormida.' *Atti e Memorie della Società Savonese di Storia Patria*, XIX (1985), p. 121.
47. Reproduced in: Di Renzo, L., and Salmoiraghi, A. *Aprile 1796*. Cairo Montenotte, 1996, p. 89. The spelling of some of the names is uncertain.
48. Fabry, 1905, op. cit., p. 32.
49. Bouvier, op. cit., p. 240.
50. Ibid., p. 240.
51. Vigo-Roussillon, op. cit., p. 29.
52. Bonaparte asked for the names of the defenders of Monte Negino to be sent to their native *départements*, an accepted way of advertising their patriotism to their fellow-citizens. (Note of Berthier of 17 April). Bouvier, op. cit., p. 241.

10

BONAPARTE'S REPLY

The scene was now set for the manoeuvre that really launched Bonaparte's career as an independent commander: the outflanking and dispersal of Argenteau's force at Montenotte. This action has been called a 'battle', though it was really only a minor engagement that formed a necessary preliminary to the execution of a larger strategic plan. Although we have no detailed written statement of the objectives and means of attaining them – Bonaparte did not need to write it down for anyone else this time – he was clearly executing the strategy he had outlined in July 1795, and more recently on 19 January. What he was proposing to do was very much in line with Bourcet.

He was intending to exploit the fact that the communications network allowed him rapidly to concentrate three of his divisions in the Bormida valley, centred roughly on Carcare. Two (those of Massena) would come from the east and one (Augereau) from the south. This would give him 20–30,000 troops massed in a fairly small area, right in the place where the two enemy armies linked. The position would permit him to move north, south, east or west at need. Sérurier was still isolated in the Tanaro valley, but Bonaparte's intention was that he should move to Ceva to join the bulk of the army as it moved west.

The fact that Beaulieu had been induced to manoeuvre the left of his army into a place from where it could not possibly reach the area of Carcare until after Bonaparte had effected the first phase of his concentration made the task easier. Moreover, Beaulieu had encouraged his ally, Colli, to stay on the defensive, so that he was also further from the initial point of concentration than Bonaparte was. The only enemy forces within range of the area of concentration were Argenteau's unevenly distributed 9,000 men, and Provera's Auxiliary Corps, which was woefully under-strength, and numbered only 2,000. They were hardly likely to be able to do much to resist two or three times their number, and risked being annihilated before help could reach them. This was precisely what Bonaparte intended, and in the case of Argenteau, his first victim, he achieved it very quickly.

During the late afternoon of the 11th, while Argenteau's attack on Monte Negino was petering out, there must have been some hurried scribbling going on in Savona and Albenga, and some fast riding by the couriers. The HQ with its staff was unfortunately still located in the latter city, so the orders were all issued from there, though Bonaparte himself remained in Savona.

There was quite a stream of letters, each of them concise, lucid and confident. First there were warning orders, then more detailed instructions. Every part in the machine of Bonaparte's organisation received its directions, detailing where it was to move, when it was to depart and arrive, what it was to take with it and, where necessary, what other units of the army would be doing. That which was issued to General La Harpe will serve as an example of their style and the great precision of the commands, but also of the amount of latitude allowed to the commander in tactical matters:

General of Division La Harpe is ordered to depart tomorrow, 23 germinal, to be at the position of Monte Negino one hour before day, where he will join the troops that are already there, and will attack the enemy, following the dispositions which I have agreed with him and General Massena.

He will immediately have the troops of the 15th demi-brigade that are at Stella fall back to Monte Negino.

He will have care to place a battalion in reserve at Madonna di Savona to be in a position to go to the redoubt of Monte Cucco in case the troops of General Massena should be obliged to retire, and to prevent the enemy from advancing between Altare and Monte Negino, with the plan of cutting off the right of General Massena. This plan is not probable, but it is prudent to forestall it.

Following the movements that he observes on his left, he will push back the enemy and make all the dispositions that he judges suitable to put him to flight and link his operations with those of the troops on his left.

He will leave a few auxiliaries at Savona to guard our magazines.

From the moment that he judges that the enemy can undertake nothing on the right of General Massena, he will join to his troops the battalion which he left in reserve at Madonna di Savona, or that he has pushed to Monte Cucco, according to circumstances.

He will have distributed 80 cartridges per man; 40 in their cartridge pouches, and 40 in their haversacks. He will have care to have bread or biscuit taken for the 23rd and 24th [germinal]. He will give orders and make all the dispositions so that the ammunition, brandy, food and everything appertaining to the ambulances follows the movements of the troops.[1]

This, of course, is a single order, but what is striking when reading them all is the co-ordination of a number of units, all working to a common end. Massena is ordered to send Ménard's troops (4,000 men) from Baraccone to Cadibona, Quiliano and Altare. While La Harpe is attacking the enemy to the front with 7,000 men, Massena must 'try to cut off the enemy between Carcare, Altare and Montenotte'. General Dommartin was to be on the heights of Montefreddo before midnight, then depart in the small hours for Carcare, where he was to arrive before 8 o'clock in the morning. General Joubert was instructed to go to Altare 'by the shortest route', and arrive there before 7 o'clock in the evening. The last two brigades amounted to about 5,000 men. Augereau was to go to Mallare with 6,000 men, once again 'by the shortest route' (unlike Beaulieu, when Bonaparte moved he cared not whether there were mountains and valleys in the way) and arrive before midnight. He would collect a reserve of artillery from there and set out again at 5 o'clock in the morning for Cairo. When he arrived there he was to occupy the mountains on his left and send reconnaissances towards Dego. Since he was to guard against arousing the enemy, he was to forbid the lighting of fires on the heights. Rusca was to hold La Sotta and Monte Spinarda. Finally, Sérurier, who was not directly involved in the first phase of operations, was clearly informed of everything that was happening, and asked to 'make demonstrations that may trouble the enemy without exposing your troops'.[2]

By early evening on 11 April, Argenteau had suspended his attack on the redoubt of Monte Negino, and pulled back his troops to rest until morning. According to a report that may have been written by him, he had had no news at all of the outcome of the attack on Voltri, nor any from Lieutenant-Colonel Leczeny in Sassello. A messenger was sent to Leczeny to ask him to send one battalion, or if possible two, as reinforcements. A battalion of IR Preiss duly arrived during the night, but was positioned so far back that it took no part in the following day's fighting. The 3rd battalion of IR Terzi, which was in Squaneto, was also ordered to move up in support. Having set out at 8 p.m., it marched through the night, and finally reached its allotted place at 5 in the morning.

Argenteau was clearly concerned about the possibility of an enemy force approaching him by way of Altare, and had instructed this battalion of IR Terzi to take up a position on Monte Castellazzo where it could block such a move. As a further 'flank guard', a company of IR Erzherzog Anton and two of Frei-Corps Gyulay were placed on and near Bric Menau, astride the road from Altare, about half a mile south-west of the col of Montenotte. It is possible that a detachment of IR Stein was placed even further along the road to Altare, but this is very uncertain.

In order to link the forces covering the road to Altare with the rest of his troops, there were two companies of IR Stein about half-way between Bric Menau and Montenotte Superiore, and another two companies of the same regiment on Bric Porassine, between the col of Montenotte and Monte San Giorgio.

Most of the rest of the troops remained opposite Monte Negino, in position to renew the attack in the morning. Two battalions of IR Erzherzog Anton seem to have been furthest forward, at Naso di Gatto and on Monte Pra. Somewhere near these were two guns, probably at Naso di Gatto. To the right of Monte Pra was a battalion of IR Pellegrini, with a division of IR Stein. To the rear of all these was the battalion of IR Alvinczy on Monte San Giorgio. Just to increase the discomfort of the troops on the mountainside, and make it more difficult to see what might be going on, a thick fog came down at 10 p.m., deadening sound and cutting off any sign of bivouac fires.

In the meantime, the execution of Bonaparte's manoeuvre was not going perfectly smoothly. Augereau wrote to him at 9 p.m., saying he had just received his orders and would try to reach Mallare by midnight, but added as a postscript: 'At the moment of sealing the letter they have announced the arrival of 3,500 pairs of shoes, which will delay my march a little.' Later, he wrote to General Victor with more than a hint of anxiety: 'I pray you, General, to hasten the distribution to the troops. It is midnight, I should already be at San Giacomo. I know that the order arrived late, but I could make the expedition fail ...' He also informed Bonaparte that he had tried to carry out his orders immediately, but 'the distribution of food and ammunition has delayed me beyond what I hoped. I shall only be able to leave Pietra at 4 o'clock in the morning.'[3] He added that he had at least a thousand men without weapons.

Bonaparte, Berthier, Saliceti, Massena and some of the troops seem to have left Savona at 1 or 2 a.m. (Bonaparte and Saliceti give different times) and headed in the direction of Altare. On foot, it was a two-and a-half-hour climb to reach the village of Cadibona, and another hour to reach Altare, on the other side of the col. As the troops were toiling up the steep, winding paths their misery was increased when the skies opened at about 3 a.m. In these unhelpful conditions Massena was to effect the concentration of the troops at Quiliano under General Ménard (the 18th Line and part of the 75th Line) and those at Cadibona (1st and 3rd battalions of the 32nd Line). Afterwards, Massena's route lay north-east from Altare towards the col of Montenotte. The French engineer who researched his movements and inspected this road in 1805 tells us that 'General Massena left Cadibona with some infantry, some dragoons, and two cannons. He followed the road which in part runs along the border of Piedmont and the State of Genoa ... there are more climbs than descents. The road is good in many places. In others ... it is narrow and stony. I do not know how they managed to get cannons through there.'[4] He says that although most of the country was wooded at that time, the road was in the open apart from the last stretch, from Ca' dell'Uomo Morto to a point beyond Pian del Melo, almost on top of the first Austrian positions on this flank. After stumbling through the rain and the darkness, the troops halted short of the far edge of the wood to rest and prepare for the attack.

Cervoni states that La Harpe's division left Savona for Madonna di Savona at 2 a.m., though the letter to Massena mentioned above says 1 a.m., and so does the memoir of Sergeant Rattier of the 51st Line. It is not clear what troops he had with him, even Cervoni saying that he did not know. The letter that Bonaparte sent to Sérurier informing him of their movements that evening said that La Harpe would have about 7,000 men in total, so this may be assumed to be somewhere near the mark. A proportion of these were Cervoni's troops, the 1st battalion of the 75th Line, and the grenadiers and 1st and 2nd battalions of the 51st Line. It is also said elsewhere that Rampon received a reinforcement of 700 men and four guns during the night. Sergeant Rattier said the troops marched towards the redoubt of Monte Negino 'in very heavy rain, exhausted, but encouraged however by the desire to bring help to those who guarded it'.[5]

The weather was not much better in the morning, and an official Austrian report tells us that: 'At the break of day the fog was still so thick that it was absolutely impossible for our men to see the enemy positions. The sun appeared between eight and nine o'clock in the morning. It permitted us to see the enemy on Monte Negino, numbering about 4,000 men.' This force, however, posed the least of their problems:

The Austrian commander, having observed that the enemy carried some cannons onto the height, immediately ordered his advanced posts to retreat, as they had become exposed to the enemy cannons. But the retreat had hardly begun when we were warned by the commander of the division of IR Stein, which was very far to the rear of us, that the enemy was marching in great numbers against our right wing. Other similar reports came at the same time as this news. The enemy, five or six thousand in number, came from Cadibona towards Carcare and had already made much progress. All this I verified with my own eyes. FML Argenteau then ordered the retreat to avoid being surrounded. The battalions were disposed in the following order: IR Stein and IR Pellegrini, which could not be the first to be attacked, received orders to occupy the heights situated on the right of Monte Pra, with a division and a half battalion, with the sole aim that there would always be a corps formed in order of battle to support and receive the troops who were retiring from position to position. Another corps of three battalions [two of IR Erzherzog Anton and one of IR Alvinczy] was disposed in the same way on Monte Pra. It was hoped thus to be able to gain Monte Castellazzo. The irruption of the enemy began soon after. The last division of IR Stein, which was in front of the 3rd battalion of IR Terzi, was attacked by an excessive number of the enemy.[6]

The sequence of events that morning is not completely clear, but Cervoni said that the French assault began at about the same time everywhere. On the French left, Massena had advanced to the edge of the wood, then burst out of cover to attack the outposts at Bric Menau and nearby. These stood no chance against his vastly superior numbers, and fell back towards Monte Castellazzo, hotly pursued by the French. The latter seem to have formed three columns, the first of which followed two footpaths in the valley that led behind Monte Castellazzo. The second and strongest column marched towards Montenotte, while the third and least strong moved in two groups directly against Monte Castellazzo.

On the French right, La Harpe began to advance towards the bulk of Argenteau's troops, on Monte Pra, detaching a small force to try to make its way round the enemy left flank. La Harpe's advance was much slower than that of Massena because he was facing greater numbers of the enemy, whose resistance was much more ordered. As they withdrew, they attempted to move their units back alternately, leapfrogging from position to position. The Austrian report tells us that after Massena began his advance:

> The other divisions which were on the slopes of Monte Pra were not slow to be attacked in their turn. The troops made every effort to resist the enemy. We must admire, at such a critical moment, the courage and presence of mind of Lieutenant-Colonel Nesslinger, who commanded them. Despite all this, the division of IR Stein, drowned by the number of its attackers, was forced to retire.[7]

The division of IR Stein on Bric Porassine, which numbered only about 300 men, was said in Martinel's report to have 'performed prodigiously'[8] before falling back. The battalion of IR Pellegrini also resisted bravely.

The critical point was to the rear of the Austrian right, however, as Argenteau well knew, and he had not wasted any time in seizing the rearmost unit to go and shore up his crumbling defences:

> At the first volley of the enemy on his rearguard, FML Argenteau went there at the head of the battalion of IR Alvinczy, through the streams and bushes of the valley of Montenotte and of Monte Pra to gain Castellazzo, support the battalion of IR Terzi and, if the circumstances lent themselves, attack the enemy during his movement.[9]

While Argenteau was thus occupied with trying to disengage his right wing, the two battalions of IR Erzherzog Anton were attempting to retire from Monte Pra in the direction of the valley of Montenotte and Monte Castellazzo, followed by the badly battered remnants of IR Stein and IR Pellegrini under Colonel Nesslinger, who desperately fought to hold off La Harpe.

French reports say that Massena's attack proceeded with great speed – much too quickly for Argenteau. Massena's advance-guard, commanded by Rondeau, moved forward with his carabiniers as skirmishers, and his grenadiers in formal order 'under the cover of bushy woods hardly suffering fire. It threw back the battalion of IR Terzi with such rapidity that the 4th Light did not arrive in time to cut off its retreat.'[10] The Austrian version adds:

> The enemy ... attacked the 3rd battalion of IR Terzi at Castellazzo, and with such superior numbers that the battalion was almost destroyed.[11]

The 4th Light, despite having failed to cut off IR Terzi, continued its flanking movement on the extreme left. Having previously penetrated through the valley of Ferriera over difficult paths to the source of the Erro, it made rapidly down the side of the valley, opposite Cascina Garbazzo, in the direction of Montenotte Inferiore. Taking this hamlet would have completely cut off Argenteau's retreat to Dego or Pontinvrea. As for Massena's centre, it turned its attention to Argenteau:

> Before the arrival of the battalion of IR Alvinczy, the battalion of IR Terzi had already had to give ground, and the enemy, who had already made great progress, attacked the battalion of IR Alvinczy, killed many men, and forced it to retreat and join the rest of the column which was retiring in the midst of the fire which troubled it on all sides. It was in vain that one tried to halt the enemy by opposing them with various troops.[12]

The battalions of IR Erzherzog Anton and IR Alvinczy were now faced with the task of saving themselves by making their way down the valley of Montenotte, closely attended by the French who harassed them all the way. There was a need to go at some speed in order not to be cut off at Montenotte Inferiore, but it was also important to retain order. The battalion of IR Alvinczy, which was already seriously weakened, formed the rearguard of this little group, and received a further mauling. In particular, it found an enemy force across its line of retreat at a bridge over the stream of Montenotte, and had to fight its way over, losing many men in the process, as well as its colour, which was taken by Grenadier Antoine Boiron of the 75th Line. None the less, the conduct of Colonel Adorian, the commander of IR Alvinczy, was so distinguished that it received special mention in official reports. His companion, Colonel Nesslinger, who had stayed behind on Monte Pra the longest, was only able to bring away a small proportion of his men by displaying 'the greatest composure and determination'.[13] A small detachment of 200 men which had earlier been placed down the valley of Montenotte at Ca' dell'Isola was also captured. The first skirmishers of the French outflanking force arrived in Montenotte Inferiore at about the same time as the Austrians were leaving, and after the exchange of a few musket shots, the Austrian column continued its march.

The conclusive phase of the action seems to have taken little more than an hour. At 9.30, Massena wrote to Bonaparte saying 'We have just driven the enemy from the positions of Montenotte ... I have sent a senior officer with a hundred men to discover where La Harpe is ...'[14] He added that the enemy loss had been great, perhaps four hundred, while he had only lost five or six killed and twenty wounded. He also complained that his men had received no bread.

The timing is confirmed by Padre Piuma, a chaplain accompanying the Austrian army, who was somewhat taken aback to find that by mid-morning the French were in total control:

About 10 in the morning I had gone in the direction of Montenotte. I saw a crowd of country-people who said to me in fear: 'Go and see them with your own eyes. All Montenotte is covered with French. As soon as the Austrians saw them ... they ran away faster than us.'[15]

While the action had been taking place, Bonaparte had been watching from a distant vantage-point. From Altare, he had been guided by the mayor to a spot on the hills north-east of the town, a hundred yards south of a house called Casa Bianca. We are told:

The General (Bonaparte) was on the butte early. He was on foot, without gloves, a telescope in his hand, decorated with all the attributes of his rank, and accompanied by 18 to 20 officers. Citizen Saliceti, commissioner of the government, was with him, in an olive-green coat.[16]

Four miles away, against the sky, he could see the gently undulating line of the crest of the ridge and the dip of the col of Montenotte. The early movements of the troops would have been marked by the smoke of the muskets, and he would have seen the action disappear from view into the valley of Montenotte. Probably at this point he tried to make his way to the field of battle, as he is known to have gone a mile or so along the road towards it. However, the group lost its way and a Dominican monk warned them they were on a bad road. The arrival of an orderly also informed Bonaparte of the success of the action, so he decided to return to Altare, where he and several of his companions ate a meal at the house of the mayor, whose family was part of the local clan of master glass-makers. Coincidentally, the surname of the mayor was Lodi – also the name of a town in Lombardy that was to see an important action in just a month's time.

Bonaparte must have been well satisfied with the morning's activity. Reports indicated that the enemy had been thrown back with heavy losses and in great disorder, while his own troops had only suffered light casualties. Indeed, official figures available later showed that for the French this had been more an action of chase and harass than a killing match. The 32nd Line had suffered three dead and seven wounded; the 51st Line had three dead and five wounded; the 75th Line had eight dead, thirteen wounded and six prisoners; and the 17th Light had fifteen wounded and four prisoners.[17] The figures for the other units must have been similar.

More importantly, perhaps, the French were in control of the battle-field and the surrounding country, and they could now move on to the next phase in Bonaparte's plan, which entailed achieving the total separation of the enemy armies, and completing the concentration of his own. These objectives required the capture of the positions at Monteze-molo and Dego. The former was the highest point on the road from Savona to Ceva, and provided an important line of defence that would have to be overcome before the fortress could be reached. Dego was a crucial defensive position on the road between Acqui and Carcare. This road had recently been much improved and was a vital communications link for the Piedmontese and Austrian armies. Taking Dego would almost completely sever the link between them, forcing them to use poor routes through the mountains, or make excessive detours.

Before turning to these objectives, however, it was necessary to ensure that the Austrians would not return to the attack at Montenotte. La Harpe was told to 'take the positions that you think the most advantageous for having the appearance of threatening the enemy at Sassello' and to send a patrol to discover the enemy's movements and hasten his evacuation of that place. 'Augereau, Dommartin and Joubert, who are in the plains, will move to Montezemolo tomorrow to beat the Piedmontese, unless the report you give me this evening makes me change arrangements.'[18] Massena was ordered to make for Dego as soon as he was sure that Argenteau had retreated, while Augereau was supposed to make for Millesimo, though because he was behind time he actually ended up spending the night before Carcare.

As the French busied themselves with these arrangements, the remnant of Argenteau's unhappy band eventually trailed into Mioglia and Pareto 'broken with fatigue',[19] having, over the previous forty hours, spent fourteen of them marching, another eighteen in combat, and the rest under arms in rain and fog. According to official returns, the losses sustained by Argenteau's division during the actions of the 11th and 12th amounted to four officers and 162 men killed, six officers and 108 men wounded, and seven officers and 409 men missing.[20]

On arriving in Pareto, Argenteau sent Beaulieu an account of his misfortunes: 'I was extremely unlucky today. Yesterday I beat the enemy and today I was almost completely destroyed … my losses are extremely great, Dego in the greatest danger. Cosseria on my left flank did not help me. The Piedmontese did not move. I am therefore sending the remains of IR Stein and IR Pellegrini towards Dego and if it is necessary I shall follow with IR Erzherzog Anton.'[21] In Dego, where he had returned the previous evening, Rukavina learned of the surprising events at Montenotte at around midday and realised what the consequences must be. Not long after Argenteau had written his report, he received an urgent appeal from his colleague: 'In the name of God, come immediately with your troops, the enemy has not yet arrived. I have sent some Piedmontese ahead as a deception and I have also written to General Colli in order that he should make a movement from there. There are two battalions of Piedmontese here and a division of IR Stein. I have ordered them to hold.'[22]

Rukavina was in a precarious situation. The garrison of Dego totalled only two battalions of Piedmontese and two Austrian with a division of IR Stein. However, Argenteau was not much better off, and by the time he transmitted Rukavina's letter to Beaulieu, he had decided that it would be impracticable to march on Dego. He commented to Beaulieu that the four battalions that had arrived in Pareto with him only totalled 700 men, and were so completely exhausted and disorganised that he felt it was unrealistic to expect to be able to do anything with them. He therefore believed it advisable to limit himself to covering Acqui, though he warned that 'Dego is very weakly occupied, and the great amount of Imperial artillery which is there merits consideration.'[23] Instead of doing something, however, Argenteau said he would await orders.

The mood in the French camp was naturally rather different. La Harpe announced to Bonaparte at 5.30 p.m. that they had achieved a brilliant success during the day, but his letter also revealed the worrying discovery that some of the troops had been issued with cartridges made with sand, some of which he sent for Bonaparte's inspection. Massena, meanwhile, had accomplished a rapid advance to a position near Cairo, though he arrived with only 1,200 men. Carcare was reached during the afternoon by the 11th Light, under *chef de bataillon* Giuseppi, and the French HQ was moved there when it was clear that the village was in no danger from the enemy. From here Bonaparte issued an order of the day, giving the army news of their success. It was full of inaccuracies, stating that Beaulieu had been at Montenotte in person with 13,000 men, and that the enemy had lost 3,000 killed or wounded, but it was no doubt good for morale, and anyway, there was no denying that the day had been victorious.

Bonaparte also took the opportunity to communicate his good wishes to some of the men in person. Those of the 32nd Line were trying to make themselves as comfortable as they could that evening when they were paid a surprise visit:

> Towards the end of the action, coming back from the pursuit, we prepared to spend the night on the field of battle by lighting some fires, because it was cold on this high plateau, when General Bonaparte arrived. He expressed his satisfaction to General Massena, and placing himself in the middle of the 32nd, he congratulated it on its fine conduct. He was not yet known, and when it was repeated from mouth to mouth that this was the General-in-Chief, I myself had some difficulty in believing it. His appearance, his costume, and his manner, were not captivating. Here is how he seemed to me then: small, thin, very pale, with big black eyes and hollow cheeks, long hair falling from his temples to his shoulders, and forming, as they were called, dog's ears. He was dressed in a blue coat, and wore over it a hazel-coloured overcoat. He was mounted on a big, light chestnut horse, thin and with its tail cocked up. He was accompanied by a solitary servant, who happened to be my compatriot, who had served with me in the 1st battalion of the Hérault. He was called Bouscarène. He followed his general on a mule of fairly sorrowful appearance, belonging to the transport of the army, and carrying on one side a leather canteen, and on the other a small barrel of brandy which was distributed to the soldiers ...

Vigo-Roussillon, the author of this description, comments that the Representatives had had a habit of selecting generals on their physical qualities, being the only thing they could appreciate, and Bonaparte did not fit what the troops were used to:

> Some of the soldiers believed that they could conclude from this that he had no military talents. Massena had gained the victory, they said, because General Bonaparte had only appeared on the field of

battle when the action was over ... In a few days the continual successes did not take long to demonstrate to everyone the superiority of a chief who thinks, over the troops who carry out.[24]

News of the French offensive had reached the Piedmontese during the afternoon, but Colli was remarkably untroubled by it. He issued an order to the combined grenadier battalion under Colonel Del Carretto, consisting of two companies each of the regiments Monferrato, La Marina and Susa, to advance to Cosseria and occupy the heights there at daybreak, and instructed them to 'defend to the last extremity'. However, he also wrote to Provera at ten in the evening saying, 'I do not think ,,, that [the enemy] will advance very far along the Bormidas.'[25] Nevertheless, he promised him more reinforcements if necessary and said that he would try to turn the enemy's attention to the south. Later on the 12th he left for Montezemolo himself with four battalions of grenadiers to await the next French move.

Bonaparte's intentions for 13 April are very clear from the letter he sent to Massena outlining the movements of the divisions:

General Massena will advance with the 32nd Line demi-brigade beyond Dego ... These movements must be begun at the very break of day ... General La Harpe, departing at the break of day, will advance as far as the heights of Cairo at nine o'clock in the morning ... General Augereau will advance at the break of day with his two demi-brigades and his artillery, via Millesimo, Roccavignale and Montezemolo. General Joubert will move at the break of day, via Castelnuovo [di Ceva], and will try to occupy the troops that are at San Giovanni. Master of Montezemolo, he must capture all the positions that approach Ceva ...[26]

To Sérurier, who was still waiting in Garessio, he wrote: 'Your division's turn is arriving. Today I shall attack Montezemolo. Make your dispositions so that one of your columns throws itself into the town of Ceva as soon as I am master of Montezemolo.'[27] To Meynier, he expressed the intention for Augereau to attack Montezemolo 'today, or tomorrow at the latest'.[28]

This eagerness to take Montezemolo was not merely dictated by a desire to get to grips with the Piedmontese and start the siege of Ceva which had occupied his thoughts for so long. As he pointed out to La Harpe:

> It is important to occupy Montezemolo today, in order to effect, during the night, or as soon as possible, our junction with General Sérurier, and to be able to draw our food from the magazines of Bardinetto and Garessio, and be able, tomorrow, to set in movement the troops of General Sérurier, who amount to more than 14,000 men.[29]

The anxiety to be able to use another source of food was caused by the fact that the army had been suffering from a very poor supply service, and many of the troops were hungry. Berthier administered a sharp reproof to the commissaries at Vado, Savona and Finale, telling them:

> The General-in-Chief orders me to repeat to you that the success of our armies depends on their subsistence, and that he places on you the responsibility for the lack of bread and brandy. It is in the name of our country that he demands from you the greatest activity in the preparation and the transport [of the bread].[30]

It was doubly unfortunate that the French army now suffered serious delays in its attempts to secure both Montezemolo and Dego. Early in the morning of 13 April, the decision was taken that it would be unwise to attack Dego that day as it was reported (falsely, in fact) to be strongly held, and the French had not yet assembled sufficient forces. Massena was not at full strength because Joubert had been detached to Augereau, and Dommartin had not yet arrived, while La Harpe's division was also still on its way from the area of Montenotte. In order to profit from the time, however, it was decided to conduct a thorough reconnaissance of the enemy positions at Dego.

The other check to the French advance was caused by unexpected resistance on the way to Montezemolo. At daybreak, Augereau had turned aside from the Eastern Bormida near Carcare, to march due east through the narrow valley that led to Millesimo, beyond which lay the road to Montezemolo. About three-quarters of the way down this valley lay Cosseria, and its ancient ruined castle, perched on a looming bluff high above the valley floor. Spread hopefully, and rather thinly, over some of the heights nearby were the puny forces of General Provera. These were promptly attacked by vastly superior numbers of French. A column which the Austrians estimated at roughly 5,000 infantry and 300 cavalry moved over the crests on the side of the valley, another 2,000 came down the valley itself, a third column of 1,500 made for the grenadier division of IR Strassoldo, while the fourth, of 2,000 men, engaged IR Belgioioso. These numbers were probably something of an overestimate, but it is certain that Provera was opposed by nine battalions, including the 4th Light under Ménard, the 4th Line under Beyrand, and other troops under Banel and Joubert. There was nothing that Provera could do against these odds, except retreat. But he did so in the direction of the castle.

In the meantime, the Piedmontese grenadier battalion under Del Carretto had been approaching from Montezemolo, taking no precautions, as it was believed that the enemy was nowhere near. A short distance from Millesimo, this illusion was rudely shattered, when the 548 grenadiers and 21 officers found themselves within sight of the advance-guard of a division of several thousand French. Observing that some Austrian troops were retiring towards the castle, the proud and spirited Del Carretto ordered the two companies of Monferrato to close on the enemy with the bayonet, while his other troops moved in echelon towards the slopes leading to the castle. This manoeuvre was carried out calmly and in good order. The grenadiers reached the castle not long before the French accomplished the encirclement of it.

It was now about 8 o'clock in the morning. The various detachments that Provera had placed on heights supporting the castle were all driven off, and he and Del Carretto were left with the stark choice of trying to break out before the encirclement became too complete, or attempting to defend a dilapidated medieval ruin until help could arrive. Provera had only been able to manoeuvre a small number of Frei-Corps Gyulay towards the castle, and with the Piedmontese grenadiers there were now

892 men in total. The castle had no supplies of any kind, there was no water, and the troops were short of ammunition. Nevertheless, the decision was taken to defend the castle. By about 8.20 the French had completely surrounded it.

The Austrian general and the Piedmontese colonel did not have much time to converse before a French officer appeared, at about 9 o'clock, to summon them to surrender. According to Carlo Birago, who was then a second lieutenant in the first company of La Marina, Del Carretto told Provera rather emphatically that he was 'resolved to defend himself', and Provera, a little confused, handed over command to him. For a high-ranking officer in an army as status-conscious as the Austrian to step down for a junior seems highly improbable, but it may well be that the elderly Provera felt it best to entrust the active leadership of the defence to the younger and fitter man. Provera, a veteran of the battle of Kolin, was 60 years old. In any case, Del Carretto sent the French emissary away with a courtly rebuff, uttering words that have become famous. 'Know', he said, 'that you are dealing with grenadiers, and that Piedmontese grenadiers never surrender.'[31]

With that, the small band of allies set about trying to create something like defences, piling up rocks and stones that would serve both as shelter and as missiles to drop on assailants. While these preparations were being made, the French advanced to just beyond musket-range. There was not much about the situation of the defenders that was positive, but at least they had the advantage of knowing the direction from which attacks would come. The castle was on the end of a spur or bluff, and was not round, but had a ground plan that was almost like a flattened triangle. On one side of this was a steep drop to the valley below. On the other there was a series of grassy terraces and walls, and some entrenchments that had been constructed during the course of the war. The French could only come from this side, up a fair slope. Their strength lay in numbers, as there were about 6,000 of them placed round the castle.

There are differing accounts of the course of events over the next few hours, but it seems likely that there were at least three distinct

French attacks. Bonaparte had arrived to see what was going on, and had inspected the castle from La Monta, about 600 paces away. According to Pelleport, who was then a lieutenant with the 18th Line, Bonaparte gave the order to try to capture the place. At about 10 a.m. General Banel duly advanced with the 18th Line in three columns, in the words of Birago 'at the *pas de charge*, without firing a shot'.[32] The defenders had been told to husband their ammunition, and waited until the storming-parties were only twenty paces away before opening fire. The action lasted only about twenty minutes before the attackers drew off.

Another attack seems to have been carried out at about 11 a.m., but the attackers only found it wise to remain in front of the entrenchments for about five minutes. Then Provera received a letter signed by Bonaparte at 11 a.m., couched in the ritual formula: 'You are surrounded on all sides. Your resistance would only cause the spilling of blood without gaining any advantage. If in a quarter of an hour you do not all give yourselves up as prisoners, I shall show mercy to no one.'[33] This attempt at intimidation bore no fruit. Provera treated it with the contempt it deserved, and chose to make the French wait for several hours before giving a reply.

During this interval, some troops that Colli had ordered to move up in support of Dego ran into the French at Cengio, and a small skirmish began. The sound of firing attracted Bonaparte, who decided to go and investigate, leaving Augereau in charge of affairs at Cosseria. Colli remained at Montezemolo and limited himself to observing events at Cosseria from a distance. Continually concerned about his southern flank, and having too few troops nearby, he could do little to help Provera at that time.

During the afternoon, the French continued to make unsatisfactory progress against Cosseria. Three small-calibre guns (4pdrs) had been brought up and placed only a hundred yards from the defences, but they had to fire uphill, and had almost no effect. At 2 p.m., Provera finally delivered his answer to the previous summons, reiterating that he intended to defend to the last extremity, unless he was given free passage for his troops. There was then a pause, during which much firing was probably heard in the distance, as Massena was carrying out his reconnaissance of Dego.

At about the time this concluded, around 4 p.m., the next attack was made on the castle at Cosseria. Three columns were involved, advancing from different directions. One, under Joubert, came straight for the middle of the defences. Banel made up the steep slope from Braida, in the east, with the old 51st and a battalion of the 4th Line. Adjutant-General Quenin came from the west with the 18th Line, in the direction of the castle gate. The defenders waited until the enemy was within pistol-range, then opened fire. However, as ammunition began to run out, so the fire slackened, and some of the enemy closed and began to get into the defences.

Del Carretto gave the example to his men by climbing onto a stone and despatching a couple of the attackers with his sword, but was killed by a shot in the chest from very close range. With ammunition running short, the Croats and grenadiers used desperate measures to defend themselves. The historian of the 11th Light tells us:

> The walls were of such a height that they could not be climbed, and the enemy let rain on the assailants a hail of enormous stones, which made numerous victims. Citizen Carrère, a captain, was hit on the head by a stone. The brave General Joubert also got one at the foot of the wall, which knocked him down between Citizen Carrère, the captain, and Malerat, the lieutenant. The latter, a moment before, said to the General, who was showing the intention of penetrating into the redoubt by an opening made in the wall: 'It is not for you to enter first, there are officers here who know how to sacrifice themselves when it is time.' Among the last to retire, he received a number of bullets through his hat. Most of those who tried to climb the walls perished for their efforts. The enterprise was abandoned when General Joubert was seen to be out of action.[34]

He was not the only one. Quenin was hit in the chest and killed, while Banel was wounded in the head and taken away to a nearby house, where he died. The commander of the 18th was also among the dead, and his place was taken by Suchet. Joubert's own description of the attack was graphic:

> Nothing more terrible than the attack during which I was wounded while passing through an embrasure. My carabiniers held me in the air – with one hand I gripped the wall, I parried the rocks with my sabre, my whole body was the aiming mark for two entrenchments dominating the position at ten paces. I had parried two rocks and had only received one bullet through my jacket, and I was knocked down the moment I got in. My column, amazed by this new kind of attack, was shaken. I had to be ready to sacrifice myself, once again remembering I had been a grenadier. An officer helped me to get up. My whole column, believing I was dead, had gone back thirty paces. The attack did not succeed ... I elaborate on this affair because there is nothing more terrible. Pannetier [Joubert's ADC] was with me. I was consoled for my wound on hearing my chasseurs cry 'Vive notre général!'[35]

The French fell back, and another emissary was sent with the usual demands, which were rejected. However, at 7.30 Provera put forward his own proposal to evacuate the castle on the condition that all the garrison could leave with its arms and baggage and return to their own lines, where they would not serve against France until an appointed time. There was no immediate reply to this offer, but with the fall of twilight the enemies arranged a cease-fire so that the wounded could be collected, the Austro–Sardinian casualties being taken into French care because of the lack of facilities for them in the castle. Birago says:

> This act of humanity was carried out with the greatest diligence, and I must add that the Republican army showed itself to be most generous on this terrible day, because many of their soldiers, knowing our complete destitution of everything, profited from the period occupied by the negotiations and the

cease-fire to send us some chestnuts or some pieces of biscuit and bottles of water.[36]

Since many of the troops had not eaten for one and a half days, this must have been most welcome.

The total number of casualties suffered by the French does not seem to be recorded, though Sergeant Petitbon of the 4th Line notes that they had twelve men killed, three officers and seventeen men wounded.[37] The 11th Light suffered much more, losing four officers killed, and estimated that they had 150 men killed and wounded.[38] The 18th Line, however, during its many efforts, had built up the frightening total of 107 men killed, and nine officers and 206 men wounded.[39] Provera put forward a total of 600 French killed and wounded in the report he wrote on 16 April, but others have suggested a figure of 1,000. It had certainly been a ferocious fight – Marmont later wrote to his father about the affair, saying 'in my life I have never seen fire like it'[40] – and the losses must have been proportionately large. The defenders had also suffered during the day. Apart from Del Carretto, they had lost Captain Rubin, a captain of Croats, and Baron Martonitz had been wounded. About 150 men had been killed or wounded.

The effects on the French were not merely physical. One of the local people, a lawyer from Millesimo, named Fassino, gives an intriguing picture of the mood of the man who was responsible for reducing the castle:

> The commanding general, Augereau, who was lodging in the house of the author of this account … holding his hands on his forehead, and his elbows resting on the table, repeated these literal words several times, 'This blasted castle will force us to turn back to the Riviera.'[41]

After dark, the French went to work to block the access roads to the castle with barrels, carts and other sorts of obstacles to prevent a sortie. The commanders of the defending troops held a council of war, and decided against making any such attempt to break out, but a corporal volunteered to try to slip through the French lines and ask Colli for help. He was captured and interrogated, giving the information that the Piedmontese numbered 400 and the Croats 1,200, and that there was very little ammunition left.

It was precisely for this reason that Bonaparte believed the resistance would not last long. That evening, he told Massena: 'Tomorrow, I hope, they will surrender because of lack of ammunition.'[42] He therefore made arrangements for subsequent operations, including the attack on Dego. On the other wing of the army, General Rusca was ordered to send out patrols towards Murialdo during the night of 13/14 April. He was to light big fires to make the enemy think that a large part of Sérurier's forces were there, then at daybreak he was to depart with all his forces and go to San Giovanni di Murialdo. Sérurier was ordered to attack Montezemolo. In the middle of all this work, Berthier somehow found time to write to his friend, General Clarke. 'I am very tired,' he admitted, but added, 'Another day or two, and we can be certain of having a decisive advantage for the campaign.'[43]

Far away in Acqui, the unfortunate Beaulieu was making efforts to recover the situation. Argenteau had written to him at 8 a.m., 'painting a pathetic picture of his division'[44] and saying the troops would need a further day's rest before they could move. In his immediate area he had the remains of the battalions of IR Pellegrini and IR Stein at Dego, two battalions of IR Erzherzog Anton at Mioglia, one battalion of IR Alvinczy at Pareto, and the remains of the 3rd battalion of IR Terzi at Malvicino. There was also a battalion of IR Terzi still in the rear at Acqui, and two squadrons of hussars were distributed at Cantalupo, Borgoratto, Gamalero and Rocchetta Cairo.

Beaulieu replied that 'Dego must still be held for two or three days, then [he] would arrive there with his whole force, in order to remedy the previous reverses'.[45] Argenteau knew that Dego was very weakly held, with only two battalions of the Piedmontese regiment La Marina and some companies of Frei-Corps Gyulay in addition to the badly beaten battalions that had come from Montenotte. At 9 p.m. on the 13th, Argenteau ordered the two battalions of IR Deutschmeister that were cantoned in Spigno, and the two Piedmontese battalions of

Monferrato, to advance over Monte Alto in order to support Dego, if the enemy should turn against this point. They began their march to Monte Alto at 3 o'clock in the morning of the 14th.

Beaulieu also made an appeal to Colli, saying that if the latter did not attack the enemy in the flank, Dego would be lost. Beaulieu himself was assembling his forces to strike the enemy frontally and hoped that Colli would take him in the flank and rear, a movement which he believed would reverse the situation in his favour. He begged Colli to hurry, saying, 'It is the moment of the safety or the loss of Beaulieu. Hurry, do not hesitate, it is no longer time.'[46]

Colli for his part wrote to Beaulieu at 8 p.m., saying that the latter would already have learned of the movements towards the enemy that he had made, but he expressed concern, once again, that the enemy had appeared in force in the Tanaro valley. He stated that he had recently learned of Argenteau's reverse, and noted that he had been ignorant that the move on Montenotte had been made. Colli yet again expressed the view that the enemy would not advance in the Bormida valley.

During the night, at 1 a.m., evidently feeling that Dego was still inadequately defended, Argenteau sent an order to Colonel Vukassovich to march to Pontinvrea, but added: 'if Dego is threatened by the enemy, the colonel will create a diversion towards Dego tomorrow morning'.[47] There seems little doubt that Argenteau was thinking of the morning of the 14th, but it was physically impossible for Vukassovich to get there in time. A few days previously it had taken Rukavina eight hours to cover the distance from Sassello, where Vukassovich was, to Dego. Vukassovich received the order at 6 a.m., and at best could have reached Dego some time in the afternoon, but must have logically concluded from the dating that Argenteau had meant the morning of the 15th.

If Vukassovich did not hurry, it is understandable. His column had led a nomadic existence over the previous few days and had been sampling the roads and tracks in the area between Voltri and Sassello in search of the enemy, of whom they had found no trace. According to one estimate, they had been up hill and down dale over narrow mountain paths covered with drifting snow for three days in succession, and had marched a distance of over 25 miles to make their rendezvous with

Leczeny in Sassello. Since there did not seem to be too much urgency, Vukassovich sent Argenteau a reply with some proposals of his own, and waited for an answer, which also gave his men a few hours to rest and cook some food.

At about the same time that Vukassovich received his orders, Augereau told Provera that he was refusing the request the latter had made the previous evening. After more negotiations, Provera finally signed a capitulation at 8.15 a.m., having obtained the honours of war, and permission for the officers and a sergeant from each company to return to their lines, promising not to serve against France until exchanged against a similar number of French prisoners. The rest of the garrison was to remain prisoner. As soon as the capitulation had been signed, a signal fire was lit to communicate the news, and Augereau also wrote to Bonaparte, informing him. The garrison eventually marched out after midday, leaving behind the much-admired Del Carretto in a grave that Birago says was 'crowned by us with roses'.[48]

It was the end of an episode that had been remarkably costly for the French, perhaps even pointless, and many have wondered why the French did not throw a cordon around the castle and by-pass it. Since this was basically what Bonaparte did at Ceva a few days later, it may well be that the affair at Cosseria had some effect on his approach to the problem posed by the larger fortress. Certainly, the gallant, even desperate, resistance at Cosseria first angered, then deeply impressed Bonaparte. When he was crowned King of Italy some years later, he made enquiries after Del Carretto's widow and accorded her a pension. He also arranged for his son's education, and on meeting Birago gave him a post in his army.[49]

With the surrender of Cosseria, there was nothing to distract the French from the task of attacking Dego. The reconnaissance of the previous day had told them much about its defences, and had allowed the troops to get a useful look at the lie of the land, which some of them must have remembered from their visit in 1794. As on that occasion, they had approached Dego from Cairo, along the Bormida valley. This is quite narrow until just before Rocchetta Cairo, where it widens again, becoming pleasant, open countryside, with sloping hills forming the sides of the valley. Both Rocchetta and Dego lie on the right, or eastern bank of the river. About a mile from Dego is a low ridge, called Il Colletto, which extends towards the river from the east, and from which one has a good view towards the north.

Just short of Dego, a stream called the Grillero flows into the Bormida from the east, through a steep-sided cutting, forming a protective line in front of the village, which boasted 300 houses. At Dego the valley suddenly narrows again, and the river bends very sharply to the west. Dominating the outside of this bend, from a considerable bluff, is the castle. The latter is overlooked from behind by an even higher line of hills. This ridge is rather like a blunt arrow-head that points south, the tip being half a mile north-east of the castle. The whole ridge is about two miles in length. Running from east to west, its highest points are Brics Rosso, Casan, Magliani (the tip of the arrow-head), del Groppo, del Poggio and Sella. The road that led to Spigno climbed out of the valley at the foot of the castle, taking several hair-pin bends, passed the hamlet of Costa, ran along the front of Bric Magliani, and passed between Bric del Groppo and Bric del Poggio, before turning northwards.

The Austrians had fortified Brics Casan, Magliani, del Groppo, del Poggio and Sella. On Bric Casan, there was a small, elevated redoubt made of stone, and surrounded by ditches. Bric Magliani was similarly fortified. On Bric del Poggio there were some entrenchments, to defend the main road to Spigno and Acqui. Below those of Groppo and Magliani, there were others which covered the same road. The southern slopes were planted with vines, and the north-facing ones with woods, but they had been cut down for a distance of 100 yards around the defences.[50]

These were well provided with artillery. There were eighteen guns altogether. Three were on Bric Casan, to the west of the redoubt on a small platform. They were intended to defend the sweep of flat ground lying between the ridge and the river. Two guns were on Bric Magliani, covering Santa Lucia, a prominent hill about 500 yards south of Dego. Another two were on Bric Groppo, one covering the road to Spigno, the other turned towards the hamlet of Costa. Single guns were placed on

Bric del Poggio and Bric Sella, providing crossfire on the road to Dego from Girini, a village lying to the east, beyond which was Giusvalla.

There were also guns positioned lower down the slopes. Two were below Magliani on the grass to the left of the turn in the road from the village of Costa. One was placed above Costa, covering a spur on which a house called Casa Pilotti stood. There were three others in front of Cascinazza (about half-way between the castle and Costa), defending Santa Lucia and the flat ground before the Pollovero, a stream which flowed into the Bormida half-way between Dego and Il Colletto. Another two were below Magliani, turned towards the road to Girini. One small gun stood at the crossing over the Pollovero.

These were the positions that Massena was busy sounding out during the afternoon of 13 April, while Augereau was involved in trying to reduce the castle of Cosseria. At 2 p.m., the French arrived at Rocchetta, and separated into three columns. On the right were 3,000 men under Rondeau, who went into the valley of the Pollovero and in the direction of Girini. The centre went along the main road to Dego, and stopped at Il Colletto, where Massena ordered a cannon shot to be fired with the purpose of getting the enemy artillery to reply, and reveal its strength and position. A thousand men went forward over the flat land to the mouth of the Pollovero, while some skirmishers (of the 32nd Line) pushed on to the summit of Santa Lucia. They were followed by some staff officers with telescopes, who proceeded to inspect the enemy positions.

The left column, of the 75th Line, under Cervoni, had gone along the Bormida to find a good site to cross it, and had arrived at Verme-nano, near Dego village, where they tried to ford the river. Cannon-fire, brought on by Massena's decoy shot, forced it to pull back to the bridge at Rocchetta, where it crossed to the left bank of the river. It then advanced to near Supervia, a locality on the low hills opposite Dego. The defenders, no doubt thinking they were in some danger, put up a lively fire, which showed the weak points in the line. After two hours of firing, the French pulled back to Rocchetta.

According to an anonymous officer who was sent from the Pied-montese army to Dego during the night of 13/14 April, Rukavina was in some pain from his wound, and departed for Acqui on the morning of the 14th, leaving the defence of this important position in the hands of Colonel Avogadro, the commander of La Marina, 'who had only arrived the day before, and who, as he told me himself, had absolutely no knowledge either of the environs, or almost even of the position that had been entrusted to him'.[51] This officer also tells us that Avogadro had under his command about 3,000 men, and that he was expecting reinforcements under Argenteau to arrive from Spigno.

They heard a few shots at about 9 or 10 a.m., and around 11 a.m. 'we saw a great column of smoke rise about a mile from the position, on the heights, which, I believe, are above Cairo. This smoke was repeated by another column of smoke which rose on the right of the French army.'[52] The firing soon became heavier, and more French appeared in the plain. While this was going on, a strong French column was seen advancing in front, coming from the heights on which the first smoke had been seen. Another four large columns also appeared, making to turn the allied left. Avogadro expressed the opinion that they would never reach him, because Argenteau would be able to block their way.

The attack they were observing was a variation on the method that had worked so well at Montenotte, namely a distracting frontal assault accompanied by turning movements. Massena had split Meynier's division in two, his right-hand force being under La Salcette, while he kept the rest under his own command. Massena's column had advanced down the main road with 2,600 men of the 32nd line and the 14th provisional. La Salcette, with 1,800 men, including the 17th Light and another battalion of light infantry, followed the hill crests on the right, parallel with the road. It was this force that Avogadro assumed would be intercepted by Argenteau. Massena halted his formation at the line of low hills before the River Grillero, allowing only his sharpshooters to cross to the far side and gall the enemy with their fire.

On the far side of the Bormida, La Harpe had occupied the ground on the inside of the river bend opposite Dego, placing six of his guns in suitable positions to support the crossing he intended to make. According to the anonymous officer, these movements were perceived by the defenders at about 3 p.m., but were viewed with indifference, because the frontal attack which was just developing was thought to be more important. Indeed, at about that time, Massena, seeing the progress of La Salcette's turning movement, crossed the Grillero and attacked the hills beyond it. The troops gained ground in open order, using the broken terrain to advantage, and hiding from the cannon-fire.

The commotion had not gone unnoticed by Argenteau, who heard the firing in the distance, and set out from Pareto at about the time Massena initiated his frontal attack. He took with him the battalion of IR Alvinczy and that of IR Terzi, and sent orders to IR Erzherzog Anton to march from Mioglia. It was rather too late, because it was a four-hour march to Dego. Meanwhile, La Salcette's advance-guard was in the process of by-passing the defensive positions on the ridge on the left, making progress over hill-tops near 'frightening precipices',[53] to try to cut the road to Spigno to the rear of the defences.

On the other flank, La Harpe now crossed the Bormida, having split his force into three small columns. The 1st battalion of the 75th Line was held in reserve, while the 3rd battalion provided the left-hand column. The 2nd battalion was in the centre with Cervoni, and the right consisted of two battalions of the 51st, under Causse. On the extreme left were 400 men of the 22nd Chasseurs à Cheval and the 5th Dragoons, under Stengel. These columns forded the Bormida in water up to the soldiers' waists, to the flat land inside the loop of the river to the north of Dego. Having paused on the bank to allow everyone to arrive, the attackers then climbed the steep slopes towards the defences.

Over the next couple of hours, the defenders were placed under intense pressure from all sides, and were gradually squeezed from one position to the next. Eventually, an hour before sunset, Massena's men managed to capture the castle, which was defended partly by Croats who had got drunk on wine looted from nearby houses. Some of the French were quick to follow their example, and also began pillaging the houses, but ransacked the church as well. On the French right, La Salcette had by now gone round the end of the ridge, and advanced to a position about half a mile to its rear, almost cutting the road to Spigno. Argenteau arrived in view of the battlefield just about in time to see the battalion of IR Deutschmeister, which was still on the march to

Dego, come into contact with La Salcette's men. The latter, having climbed to the top of Bric del Caret, collided with the Austrian battalion, which had been climbing up the other side. The Austrians were driven back, and in the chaos the two Piedmontese battalions of Monferrato, which were following, were also thrown into disorder. Men of the 17th Light captured two colours.[54] Argenteau tried to stem the tide by attacking with his two battalions, but the French had now overcome the defences through sheer weight of numbers, and with darkness falling they drove the allies back everywhere, sending in their cavalry to harass the withdrawal.

The allied casualties are not precisely known, but may have been as many as 400 dead. Likewise, there is uncertainty about the number of prisoners, and estimates vary from 1,500 to the improbably large total of 4,373 given in a report by Berthier.[55] Nevertheless, the disorder into which the allies had been thrown meant that their forces in the immediate area had practically ceased to exist. At least sixteen of the guns had been lost, together with 24 ammunition wagons. The French had also collected a number of trophies – at least four colours. The French losses were relatively light, including about 200 dead, most of them having fallen before the redoubt on Bric Casan.[56] Massena commented that the morale of the enemy troops must have been low, for 'a sort of panic made them fly before they had even been seriously attacked',[57] an assertion that would seem to be debatable. However, the capture of Dego had been much easier than Bonaparte had any right to expect, considering the inherent strength of the position, and went a long way towards compensating for the delay suffered at Cosseria.

Affairs had also been going well on the other wing of his army, though at the time of the capture of Dego he did not know the extent of the success. While Massena's division had been in action, Sérurier had been carrying out his orders and had moved along the Tanaro in the direction of Ceva. This unspectacular advance, which did not result in heavy fighting, is easy to overlook, yet in strategic terms it was very important. It was yet another example of an outflanking movement of the kind that was intended to oblige the enemy to abandon his position or risk being cut off. It was eminently successful. As the brigades of

Guieu and Fiorella advanced on either side of the Tanaro, the Pied-montese were driven back, and by 6 p.m. Sérurier had placed his HQ at Bagnasco, about six miles south of Ceva. The news of this must have been even more unwelcome to Colli than that of the fall of Cosseria. There was now a substantial enemy force to the right rear of Monteze-molo, and about as close to Ceva as he was. This made the position at Montezemolo untenable, and with no sign that the Austrians would be able to assist him, Colli took the decision to pull back to Ceva. This was accomplished during the night of 14/15 April, under the cover of dark-ness and a thick fog.

Unaware of the fact that Colli had made this decision, Bonaparte consulted his generals at Cairo at 10 p.m. on the 14th, and made his plans for the following day. He must have been convinced that the Austrians were no longer in a position to cause him any trouble, and his arrangements were mostly concerned with the attack on Montezemolo. Bonaparte ordered La Harpe to move back to Cairo, then bear west to Saliceto, to arrive north of Montezemolo, join Augereau, and fall on Colli. Joubert received a letter from his commander-in-chief ordering him to leave Biestro at 7.30 a.m. on the 15th to go to Montezemolo. Bonaparte must already have been impressed with Joubert's enthusiasm, because he also wrote to him saying that he imagined that Joubert would reproach him for not having called him to Dego, 'but you were too far to the left. Tomorrow you will have the advance-guard.'[58] Massena was to stay where he was and reconnoitre as far as possible towards Acqui.

Despite appearances, however, the French were not yet finished with the Austrians. There may have been considerable disorder on the side of the defeated at Dego, but it was almost matched among the victors. Disci-pline completely broke down, and the soldiers went on a rampage of looting. The confusion produced by the pursuit, the darkness, the broken terrain, and the splitting and mixing of various units, had favoured a fatal loss of control. Moreover, generals, officers and soldiers were all exhausted by the rapid marches and the constant fighting of the previous few days, and few of them had had much to eat. According to La Salcette, 'the lack of regularity in the food supply produced many marauders'.[59]

For all these reasons, there was a disintegration and abandonment of duty which officers and generals were unable to do much about, always supposing they wished to make the effort, and not all of them did. The local priest went to one officer to seek to prevent the looting of the church, and was roughly turned away, though another managed to get some of the soldiers to give back the things they had taken, and advised the priest to hide them. A further factor in slackening professional vigilance was that the night was cold as well as dark, and torrential rain began to fall, which did little to encourage the looters to leave the shelter of the houses where many of them had gone.

It was at this juncture that Vukassovich wrote his name in the history books by giving some of the unwary French the surprise of their lives. He had waited at Sassello on the 14th until he had received a second order from Argenteau, at about midday, and then set off for Dego with five battalions: 2 Carlstädter Grenz, 1 IR Alvinczy, 1 IR Nádasdy and 1 IR Preiss, totalling roughly 3,000 men. By a great effort of mind and body, they arrived an hour short of Dego at daybreak, having captured a French picket in Mioglia, and picked up numerous stragglers during their march. These all confirmed that Dego had been taken, and an enemy officer assured Vukassovich that there were 20,000 French in that area. Despite this, Vukassovich decided to find out the enemy strength for himself. He therefore ordered Leczeny to attack the last hills before Dego on the road to Spigno with the Carlstädter Grenz battalions. They arrived like a bolt from the blue. Vigo-Roussillon remembered:

On 26 germinal [15 April], the rain, which had not stopped falling all night, persisted in the morning. Towards 7 o'clock, the light infantry was attacked by an enemy corps, the strength of which it could not judge because of a thick fog. This infantry fell back on the 32nd and took position with us on the height of Dego. The enemy, whose strength increased every minute, attacked us with vigour. Our weapons, having been soaked by the rain for a long time, could no longer fire, and we had to give ground. We retreated in disorder. Two companies of the demi-brigade, which could not be helped in time, were made prisoner.[60]

Dupuy, the commander of the 32nd, and Rondeau managed to rally 2–3,000 men, while Vukassovich and Leczeny, encouraged by their success, pressed their attack, taking the various redoubts and the village of Magliani. Before long, both Dupuy and Rondeau were seriously wounded. This temporarily broke French morale and at about 10 a.m. there was a precipitate retreat. Hundreds were taken prisoner, while others rapidly de-camped towards the south. In the chaos, La Salcette shut himself in the castle with a handful of men, just as the Croats had done the day before. By 11 a.m. Vukassovich was almost completely master of the position, and having taken many guns, pressed his grenadiers into service as artillerymen, and began to use them against the French. In Dego only the castle was still in French hands, but the Austrians surrounded it and La Salcette, at the head of some men, mostly of the 17th Light, fought his way out and headed south, rallying some distance from Dego.

Massena, who was at Cairo, some two miles distant, had heard the sound of firing and arrived at the gallop at Rocchetta at about 11 a.m., with Monnier, one of his staff. The Austrian attack was now four hours old, and it might legitimately be asked why it had taken Massena so long to go and see what was happening. Some have suggested that he was with a woman, and others that he was engaged in looting, but neither of these really explains a delay of four hours. Massena was both a womaniser and a rapacious plunderer, but he was also a first-class general at the peak of his powers, and too much of a soldier not to run to the sound of a serious fight. A more likely explanation is that the seriousness of the Austrian attack was underestimated by everyone at first. After all, as we have heard, there was little enough firing to begin with, and the fog would have blanketed sound as well as making it difficult to see what was happening any distance away. The final French collapse was fairly sudden when it came at about 10 a.m., and it may be that Massena only became aware that a major attack was in progress, rather than skirmishes, a short time before he arrived from Cairo. An even simpler explanation is that he may have been elsewhere on one of his habitual reconnaissances or inspections. Whatever the reason for his absence, Massena did not delay in trying to rectify matters. He saw that it would be impossible to rally the troops close to the enemy and ordered the officers to guide the troops to Il Colletto. Having rallied them, he assembled them where they had formed for their attack just 24 hours earlier. They were back to square one.

At about midday the weather got better, and the rain stopped. Massena had been able to gather about 3–4,000 men, and according to the historian of the 32nd Line, proceeded to give them a sharp piece of his mind, before leading them back into the attack. Bonaparte had also appeared on the scene having already ordered La Harpe to retrace his steps because the size of the attacking force at Dego was not known, and it seemed to be very determined. Vukassovich's situation now began to deteriorate. The wave of the Austrian attack, having reached its highest point, was about to flow back again as ever greater numbers of French were fed into the battle. The first elements of La Harpe's division appeared – the 51st under General Causse, Victor with the 18th, the 4th Light, and 400 cavalry of Stengel's. The soldiers of the 4th Light must have been particularly disgruntled, because they had had a frustrating 24 hours, during which they had been obliged to wander back and forth between Cosseria and Cairo. They had finally got back to their bivouac at Cairo at 10 a.m. after a tiring and dangerous night march during which the guides had lost their way and 30 men had fallen down ravines. The soldiers were cleaning their weapons and looking forward to a meal when, at midday, the drums beat assembly and they quickly had to march to Dego.

The new French attack was basically like that of the previous day, but on a smaller scale and without the wide turning movement on the right. Massena advanced frontally on Dego, but encountered great difficulties around the hamlet of Costa, above the castle. On the left, Causse forded the Bormida as on the day before, and made a somewhat reckless attack, during which he was mortally wounded. Victor's troops spread out as skirmishers and gave support, but a counter-attack by Leczeny pushed back the 51st and their *chef* was captured, only to be rescued again shortly afterwards. At about 4 p.m. the 4th Light, under Ménard, mounted a turning movement on the right. They rapidly proved their usefulness, and 200 men under their *chef,* Destaing, were able to mount a counter-attack from the flank at a moment when Massena's troops were being pushed back.

The Austrians, facing ever greater numbers of the enemy, and fearing they would be enveloped, withdrew along the crests of the heights to Bric del Caret, which was then attacked by La Salcette's men and the 51st under Lannes. Adjutant-General Lanusse had to rescue Destaing, who became isolated in front of his troops and was nearly taken. Massena was also in the thick of the action, leaping from his horse to lead forward the 32nd. Vukassovich's forces were slowly eroded, and eventually, after ten hours of combat during which there was no sign of the support he had requested from Beaulieu, he only managed to extricate a small number of his troops, which he took via Spigno to Terzo, near Acqui. Vukassovich's attack, though undoubtedly gallant, had little effect apart from gaining him notoriety as almost the only Austrian commander to make an impression on the French during the first phase of the campaign. It did, however, make Bonaparte more circumspect for a while, and he made sure that the Austrians had really drawn back before he gave himself fully to affairs on his left wing.

Their recent experiences were far from making the ordinary French soldiers wary: cold, starving and exhausted, they began another orgy of looting, roaming the houses and stealing whatever they could find. In some cases this was motivated by desperation, as the supply services had proved inadequate to the task of feeding the troops. The carabiniers of the 4th Light, for example, had been on detachment with Rondeau for three days, and had not received a single issue of rations during the period. However, there were numerous examples of sheer vandalism, and greedy profiteering. The church was completely wrecked and might have been burned down if it had not been turned into a hospital. Monnier, who went to lodge in the house of the unfortunate priest, found that he had lost everything, and had to provide him with food.[61] La Harpe, scandalised by the behaviour of Adjutant-General Galeazzini, a Corsican crony of Saliceti's who had tried to spirit away the enemy draught horses and mules to sell, promptly put him under arrest. Eventually exhaustion took over and things quietened down during the night.

The mishaps had caused tempers to become frayed among the commanders, however. Matteo Fontana, with whom one of them was lodging, recalled: 'In the evening, General Cervoni returned beside himself with anger. In the room where there were eleven of his aides and other officers he roared, "Here's disorder! That [blank] General Massena! I told him to leave the army at Dego, and he brought it back to Cairo! We've lost a brigade and a half. If I was the commander-in-chief I'd have him shot immediately!"'[62] Bonaparte does not seem to have been of the same opinion, but he can have been in no doubt that the discipline of his army was balanced on the edge, and that faulty supplies were doing great damage to morale and order. This provided an even greater spur, if one were needed, to hasten the invasion of Piedmont and move the army onto the plains, where it ought to be easier to feed.

NOTES

1.   Napoleon. *Correspondance de Napoléon Ier publiée par ordre de l'empereur Napoléon III*. Paris, 1858–69, no. 135.

2.   See ibid., nos. 130–6.

3.   Fabry, J. G. A. *Histoire de l'armée d'Italie (1796–1797)*. Paris, 1900–14, IV, §2, pp. 165–6.

4.   Fabry, J. G. A. *Mémoires sur la campagne de 1796 en Italie*. Paris, 1905, pp. 179–80. Having walked from Altare to Castellazzo and beyond, the author can say with some feeling that it seems like a long way if you are not very fit, though the modern road makes the going easier.

5.   Rattier, J.-H. 'Campagne d'Italie (1796): notes d'un sergent-major.' *Revue rétrospective*, XX (1894), pp. 219–20.

6.   Fabry, 1905, op. cit., pp. 32–3.

7.   Ibid., p. 33.

8.   Ibid., p. 25.

9.   Ibid., p. 33.

10. Fabry, 1900–14, op. cit., IV, §1, p. 245.

11. Fabry, 1905, op. cit., p. 33.

12. Ibid., p. 33.

13. Schels, J. B. 'Die Gefechte in den Apenninen, bei Voltri, Montenotte, Millessimo, Cossaria und Dego, im April 1796.' *Oesterreichische Militärische Zeitschrift*, Bd. 2 (1822), p. 183.

14. Fabry, 1900–14, op. cit., IV, §2, p. 173.

15. Piuma, Padre. *Récit historique de la campagne de Buonaparté en Italie, dans les années 1796 et 1797. Par un témoin oculaire.* London, 1808, pp. 10–12. Much of this work is of extremely doubtful historical value.

16. Anon. 'Bonaparte au combat de Montenotte (12 avril 1796), suivi des instructions de Martinel à Bagetti pour les aquarelles de Montenotte et Monte Legino.' *Le carnet de la sabretache*, 7 (1899), p. 371.

17. Thiry, J, *Bonaparte en Italie 1796–97*. Paris, 1973, p. 35 and Napoleon. *Mémoires pour servir à l'histoire de France, sous le regne de Napoléon, écrits sous sa dictée à Sainte-Hélène, par les généraux qui ont partagé sa captivité.* Paris, 1829, I, p. 381.

18. Napoleon. 1858–69, op. cit., no. 137.

19. Fabry, 1905, op. cit., p. 33.

20. Schels, op. cit., p. 183.

21. Fabry, 1900–14, op. cit., IV, § 1, p. 245.

22. Ibid., IV, § 1, pp. 245–6.

23. Schels, op. cit., p. 186.

24. Vigo-Roussillon, F. *Journal de campagne (1793-1837)*. Paris, 1981, pp. 29–30.

25. Fabry, 1900–14, op. cit., IV, §2, p. 36.

26. Napoleon. 1858–69, op. cit., no. 144.

27. Ibid., no. 143.

28. Ibid., no. 142.

29. Ibid., no. 145.

30. Ibid., no. 140.

31. Birago, C., Gen. 'La difesa di Cosseria.' *Antologia italiana, Giornale di scienze lettere ed arti*, 2 (1847), p. 636.

32. Ibid., p. 636.

33. Schels, op. cit., p. 195.

34 Napoleon. *Mémoires pour servir à l'histoire de France, sous le regne de Napoléon, écrits sous sa dictée à Sainte-Hélène, par les généraux qui ont partagé sa captivité.* Paris, 1829, II, pp. 439–40.

35. Chevrier, E. *Le général Joubert d'après sa correspondance.* Paris, 1884, p. 33.

36. Birago, op. cit., pp. 638–9.

37. Godechot, J. 'Le carnet de route du sergent Petitbon sur la campagne d'Italie de 1796–1797.' *Rivista italiana di studi napoleonici,* 15 (1978), p. 37

38. Napoleon. *Mémoires pour servir à l'histoire de France, sous le regne de Napoléon, écrits sous sa dictée à Sainte-Hélène, par les généraux qui ont partagé sa captivité.* Paris, 1829, II, p. 441.

39. Bouvier, F. *Bonaparte en Italie, 1796.* Paris, 1899, p. 281.

40. Marmont, A. F. V., de. *Mémoires du duc de Raguse de 1792 à 1832 imprimés sur le manuscrit original de l'auteur.* Paris, 1857, I, p. 315.

41. Oliveri, L. 'Napoleone in Valbormida: la battaglia di Cosseria (13-14 aprile 1796).' *Alta Val Bormida,* July (1989), p. 19. At least, that seems to be the sense of the phrase. Fassino reports it as 'Ce vilain chateau il ne fut rebancé sur la rivièr.'

42. Fabry, 1900–14, op. cit., IV, §2, p. 199.

43. Ibid., IV, §2, p. 203.

44. Schels, op. cit., p. 200.

45. Ibid., p. 201.

46. Fabry, 1900–14, op. cit., IV, §2, p. 36.

47. Schels, op. cit., p. 203.

48. Birago, op. cit., p. 638.

49. Birago also tells us that the defenders of Cosseria dined with Bonaparte on the evening of their capitulation. In a conversation between the two of them it transpired that Birago's brother had been badly wounded at Dego. Bonaparte immediately gave him one of his ADCs to help look for him.

50. The site seems to be much as it was in 1796, though it is difficult to discern any sign of fortifications. A local farmer told the author that when he was young it was still possible to find small cannon-balls on the slopes, and that once he even found the remains of a sword under a juniper bush.

51. Fabry, 1900–14, op. cit., IV, §2, p. 201.

52. Ibid., IV, §2, p. 201.

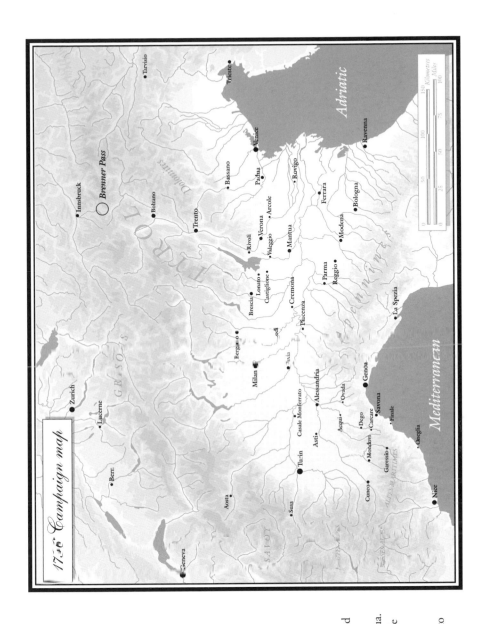

1796 Campaign map

April 1796–April 1797

Phase 1: French advance from
Savona to Mantua via
Mondovi, Piacenza, Lodi and
Valeggio.

Phase 2: French besiege Mantua.
Battles of Castiglione, Arcole
and Rivoli. Mantua falls to
French.

Aftermath: French advance into
Austria via Tarvisio.

1792–96

1792: French take Nice, Piedmontese retreat to Saorgio.

1793: French attack on Saorgio fails. Piedmontese counter also fails.

1794: French take Oneglia, Saorgio and Tenda. Later, they push along the Bormida beyond Cairo. Bonaparte inspects road from Carcare to Savona.

1795: Austrians drive the French back behind Finale. In November, French defeat allies at Loano.

1796: In April, Austrians advance over Bocchetta to Genoa and Voltri. Bonaparte counters by moving westwards from Savona to Carcare, Ceva, and Mondovi, then north to Cherasco.

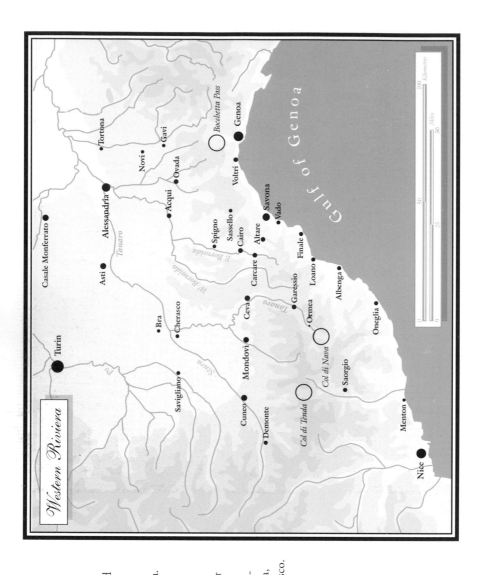

Western Riviera

Gulf of Genoa

Bocchetta Pass
Genoa
Tortona
Gavi
Novi
Ovada
Voltri
Alessandria
Acqui
Savona
Vado
Casale Monferrato
Spigno
Sassello
Altare
Cairo
Finale
Tanaro
Asti
Carcare
Loano
E. Bormida
Garessio
Albenga
W. Bormida
Bra
Cherasco
Ceva
Ormea
TANARO
Oneglia
Stura
Mondovi
Col di Nava
Pò
Turin
Savigliano
Saorgio
Cuneo
Col di Tenda
Demonte
Menton
Nice

Kilometres
Miles

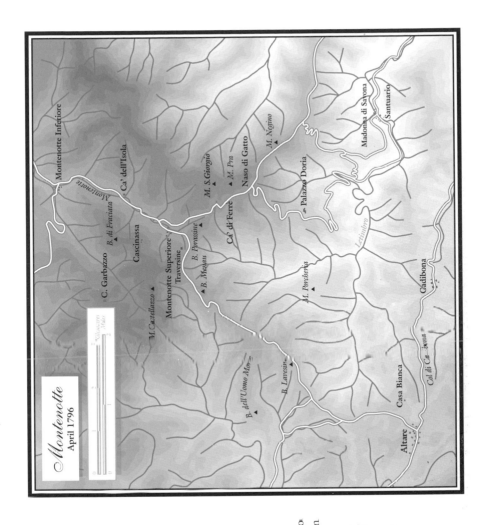

Montenotte
April 1796

Kilometres
Miles

Montenotte Inferiore
Ca' dell'Isola
Montenotte
C. Garbazzo
B. di Fracata
Cascinassa
M. Castellazzo
Montenotte Superiore
Traversine
B. Porassine
B. Menu
B. dell'Uomo Mor
B. Lavesin
Altare
Casa Bianca
Col di Ca... ivona
Cadibona
M. S. Giorgio
Ca' di Ferre
M. Pra
Naso di Gatto
M. Porcheria
M. Negino
Palazzo Doria
Lettimbro
Madonna di Savona
Santuario

11–12 April 1796

11 Apr: Austrians advance via C. Garbazz ,
Cascinassa, Montenotte Superiore to M. Neg o
11/12 Apr (night): Austrians hold positi ns fr m
M. Pra to M. Castellazzo. Massena ad ance
via Altare, B. Lavesino, to near B. Me au. L
Harpe advances via Madonna di Savor a to l
Negino.
12 Apr: Massena advances via M. Castella o an
Montenotte Superiore towards Montenc tte
Inferiore. La Harpe advances towards
Montenotte Inferiore via M. S. Giorgio.
Austrians retreat northwards in disorder.

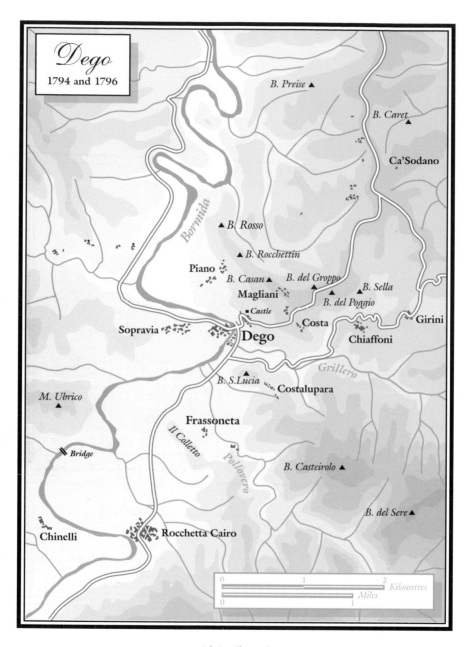

Dego
1794 and 1796

B. Preise ▲

B. Caret ▲

Ca'Sodano

Bormida

▲ B. Rosso

▲ B. Rocchettin

Piano

B. Casan ▲   B. del Groppo
               ▲ B. Sella
Magliani
               B. del Poggio
■ Castle
                              ▲ Girini
Sopravia   Costa
            Dego   Chiaffoni

                    Grillero

B. S.Lucia ▲
              Costalupara

M. Ubrico
▲   Frassoneta

            Il Colletto   *Pollovero*

⫫ Bridge

                    B. Casteirolo ▲

                              B. del Sere ▲

Chinelli   Rocchetta Cairo

0   1   2
                         Kilometres
0   1
              Miles

14 April 1796
Massena attacks frontally from Il Colletto towards Magliani.
La Salcette makes flanking movement via Girini towards Bric Caret.
La Harpe crosses river near Sopravia, making for Piano and Bric Casan.

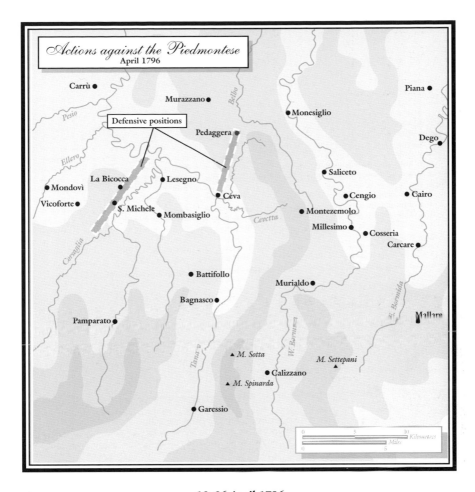

Actions against the Piedmontese
April 1796

Defensive positions

Carrù
Murazzano
Piana
Monesiglio
Pesio
Ellero
Pedaggera
Dego
La Bicocca
Saliceto
Mondovì
Lesegno
Cengio
Cairo
Vicoforte
Ceva
S. Michele
Montezemolo
Mombasiglio
Cevetta
Millesimo
Cosseria
Carcare
Corsaglia
Battifollo
Murialdo
Bagnasco
B. Bormida
Mallare
Pamparato
W. Bormida
Tanaro
▲ M. Sotta
M. Settepani ▲
Calizzano
▲ M. Spinarda
Garessio

0   5   10   Kilometres
0   5   Miles

13–26 April 1796

13 Apr: Augereau delayed at Cosseria by Provera and Del Carretto.
14 Apr: Sérurier moves from Garessio towards Ceva.
14/15 Apr (night): Colli abandons Montezemolo
16 Apr: Augereau reaches Montezemolo, then attacks La Pedaggera. Sérurier advances to within sight of Ceva. Colli withdraws to La Bicocca.
19 Apr: French attack La Bicocca/San Michele. They are repulsed.
21 Apr: Piedmontese withdraw, but caught at Vicoforte and routed. Mondovì surrenders.
22–26 Apr: Piedmontese continue withdrawal northwards.

Crossing the Po / Battle of Lodi
May 1796

28 Apr–10 May 1796

1. Austrians retire NE via Valenza.

2. French advance via Casteggio and Castel S. Giovanni to Piacenza, then cross the Po.

3. Austrians retire to Lodi, and cross the Adda.

4. French catch Austrian rearguard at Lodi and force crossing of the Adda.

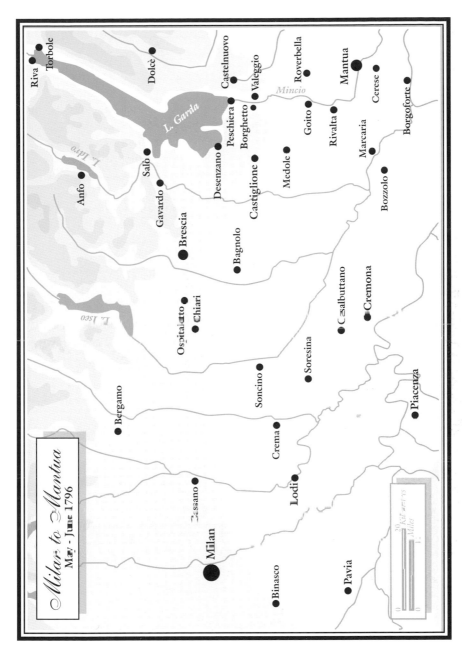

Milan to Mantua
May - June 1796

21–31 May 1796

1. French advance towards Mincio via Cassano and Lodi.
2. Rebellions in Milan, Binasco and Pavia.
3. French take Brescia (feint to north).
4. Rapid French advance to Valeggio and crossing of Mincio.
5. Austrian main force retreats towards Dolcè.

Map labels: Riva, Torbole, Dolcè, Castelnuovo, Roverbella, Mantua, Valeggio, Peschiera, Cerese, Mincio, Borghetto, Goito, Rivalta, Marcaria, Borgoforte, L. Garda, Salò, Desenzano, Medole, Bozzolo, Anfo, Gavardo, L. Idro, Castiglione, Brescia, Bagnolo, L. Iseo, Cremona, Ospitaletto, Chiari, Casalbuttano, Soresina, Soncino, Piacenza, Bergamo, Crema, Lodi, Cassano, Milan, Binasco, Pavia

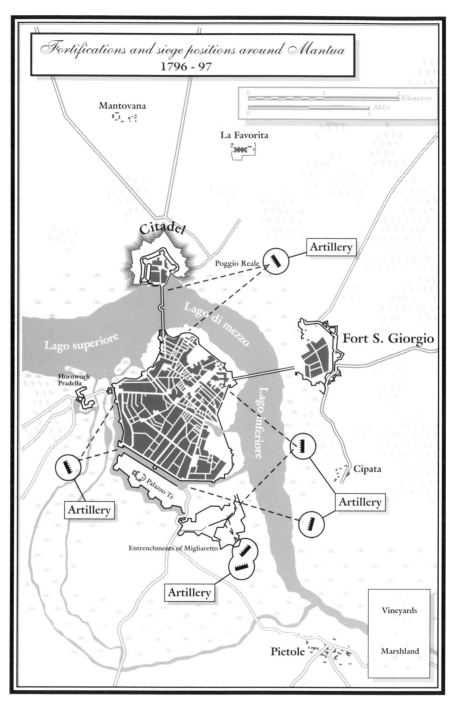

Fortifications and siege positions around Mantua
1796 - 97

Mantovana

La Favorita

Citadel

Artillery

Poggio Reale

Lago di mezzo

Lago superiore

Fort S. Giorgio

Hornwork
Pradella

Lago inferiore

Cipata

Artillery

Palazzo Tè

Artillery

Entrenchments of Migliaretto

Artillery

Vineyards

Marshland

Pietole

Main battery positions shown for period June–July 1796.
The French had no siege artillery from August 1796 to February 1797.

Battles of Lonato/Castiglione
July – August 1796

31 July–5 August 1796

31 Jul: Ott takes Lonato. Sauret advances N from Desenzano. Despinoy recaptures Lonato, Ott retires to P. S. Marco, and is pursued by the French.

3 Aug: Ocskay moves from Desenzano to Lonato, but is then driven back. Augereau attacks Lipthay at Castiglione. Lipthay retires slowly towards Solferino, where he receives support from Wurmser.

5 Aug: Fiorella begins to arrive in Austrian rear from Guidizzolo. French right drives Austrians from redoubt into hills. Austrian centre is also dislodged and whole force retires to Valeggio.

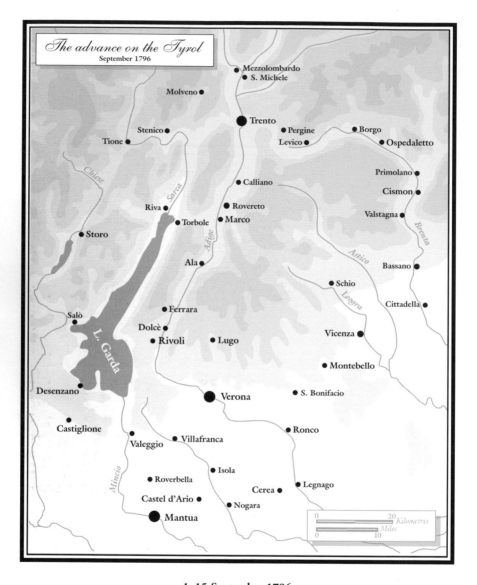

The advance on the Tyrol
September 1796

Mezzolombardo
S. Michele
Molveno
Stenico
Tione
Trento
Pergine
Borgo
Levico
Ospedaletto
Primolano
Cismon
Calliano
Rovereto
Valstagna
Riva
Marco
Torbole
Storo
Ala
Bassano
Schio
Cittadella
Ferrara
Salò
Dolcè
Rivoli
Lugo
Vicenza
Desenzano
L. Garda
Montebello
Verona
S. Bonifacio
Castiglione
Ronco
Villafranca
Valeggio
Isola
Roverbella
Legnago
Cerea
Castel d'Ario
Nogara
Mantua

Chiese · Sarca · Adige · Astico · Brenta · Leogra · Mincio

0   20 Kilometres
0   10 Miles

1–15 September 1796

1. Austrian main force moves from Trento along Brenta valley towards Bassano
while French advance via Chiese and Adige valleys towards Trento.

2. Austrian covering force is driven northwards beyond Trento.

3. French pursue Austrian main force and defeat it at Primolano and Bassano.

4. Remnants of Austrian main force reach Mantua via Legnago.

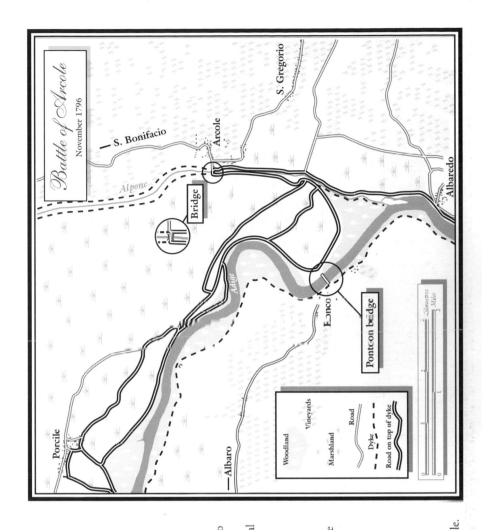

Battle of Arcole
November 1796

S. Bonifacio

Alpone

Arcole

S. Gregorio

Bridge

Adige

Albaredo

Fonco

Pontoon bridge

Porcile

Albaro

Woodland
Marshland
Vineyards
Road
Dyke
Road on top of dyke

Kilometres
Miles

14–17 November 1796

14/15 Nov (night): French build bridge at Fonco and cross Adige.

15 Nov: French attempts to cross Arcole bridge all fail. Crossing at Albaredo successful. Arcole taken.

15/16 Nov (night): Arcole abandoned, French prepare to march away westward.

16 Nov: Austrian attacks from Porcile and Arcole both halted. French attacks on Arcole bridge renewed, but unsuccessful. Attempt to ford Alpone fails.

16/17 Nov (night): French build bridge over Alpone near confluence with Adige.

17 Nov: French attacks on Arcole and its bridge along both banks of Alpone. Austrian counter almost successful. French eventually take Arcole.

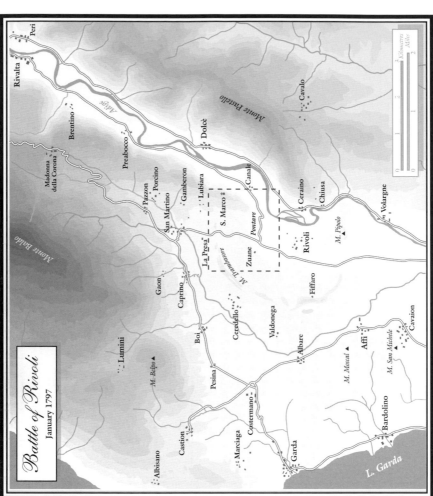

Battle of Rivoli
January 1797

Peri
Rivalta
Brentino
Preabocco
Madonna della Corona
Pazzon
Porcino
San Martino
Gamberon
Lubiara
S. Marco
Pontare
La Presa
Zuane
M. Trambasore
Gaon
Caprino
Ceredello
Valdonega
Fiffaro
Rivoli
M. Pipolo
Ceraino
Chiusa
Canale
Volargne
Dolcè
Monte Pastelo
Adige
Cavalo
Monte Baldo
Lumini
M. Belpo
Boi
Pesina
Albare
Affi
M. Moscal
M. San Michele
Cavaion
Castion
Marciaga
Costermano
Garda
Bardolino
Albisano
L. Garda

Kilometre
Miles

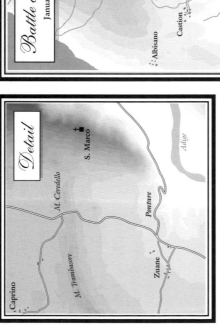

Detail

Caprino
M. Ceredello
S. Marco
M. Trambasore
Pontare
Zuane
Adige

11–14 January 1797

1. Austrians advance via Lumini, Madonna della Corona and Adige valley, driving Joubert back to Rivoli

2. Bonaparte supervises defence of S. Marco, M. Trambasore and the Pontare with divisions of Joubert and Massena. A panic seizes the Austrian troops at the point of victory. They retreat northwards.

53. *Historique* of the 17th Light, quoted in Bouvier, op. cit., p. 294.

54. *Historique* of the 17th Light.

55. Bouvier, op. cit., p. 299.

56. Ibid., p. 298.

57. Massena, A. *Mémoires de Massena, rédigés d'après les documents qu'il a laissés et sur ceux du dépôt de la guerre et du dépôt des fortifications, par le général Koch.* Paris, 1848–50, II, p. 33.

58. Napoleon. 1858–69, op. cit., no. 154.

59. Bouvier, op. cit., p. 300.

60. Vigo-Roussillon, op. cit., p. 31.

61. Fabry, 1900–14, op. cit., IV, §2, pp. 197–8.

62. Oliveri, L. 'Una comunità nella tempesta: la val Bormida durante l'invasione napoleonica 1792–1800.' *Bollettino della Società per gli Studi Storici, Archeologici ed Artistici della Provincia di Cuneo,* 82 (1980), p. 135.

11

DEFEATING PIEDMONT

April 16th dawned with the French in a much more satisfactory position than the allies. After four days, the Austrian and Piedmontese armies had been prised apart, and there was little they could do to support each other. Bonaparte knew that provided the Austrians did not quickly return to the attack with large forces (which did not seem likely) he would be able to hold them back with a small proportion of his army, and switch the rest against the Piedmontese. However, after the surprise of the previous day, Bonaparte was not in too great a hurry to carry out this switch.

On the French right, the 16th was devoted to regrouping and reconnaissance to make sure that no substantial Austrian force was within striking distance. La Harpe was ordered to use some of his men to patrol the Erro valley and search Sassello. He was also authorised to exact contributions in food and drink from the local authorities. As he continued his search in the direction of Mioglia during the day, it became clear that the Austrians had withdrawn and broken contact. Massena remained at Dego and dedicated the time to getting his soldiers' shoes repaired. On the French left, Sérurier was poised to continue his advance towards Ceva on the morning of the 16th, having managed to link with the left of Augereau's division on the previous day.

In the French centre, Augereau's troops, who had not pressed their attack on the Piedmontese on the 15th because of the incidents at Dego, marched off in the early hours of the 16th, and toiled up the steep, winding road to Montezemolo. The view they had of Piedmont from this vantage-point was magical, and moved Bonaparte to describe it in a suitably poetical manner:

> On the horizon a white girdle of snow and ice of prodigious height encircled this rich basin of the promised land ... These gigantic barriers which seemed the limits of another world, and

which it had pleased nature to make so formidable, had fallen as if by enchantment.[1]

The first obstacle to an advance into Piedmont – the mountains – had been overcome. There now remained the man-made one of Ceva. This fortress, and the defences to the north of it, could be approached by two roads from Montezemolo. One of them went down the winding valley of the Cevetta towards the town of Ceva, which stood at the confluence with the Tanaro. The other went more northwards, over the crests flanking the River Belbo, to La Pedaggera, Murazzano, Dogliani, Cherasco and, ultimately, Turin.

It was in order to try to block both these routes into the heart of Piedmont that a formidable network of defences had been constructed between the two. At the southern end was Ceva itself, the siege of which Bonaparte had advocated for so long. Bonaparte knew from the pages of de Maillebois's memoirs that the fortress of Ceva stood several hundred feet up on a cliff overlooking the walled town, which had 450 houses, and that 'with twenty guns and twelve mortars well served, one could take it in twelve days'.[2] However, the precise details of the considerable entrenched position that lay to the north of the fortress were unknown to him. He would no doubt have found them impressive, as Martinel said of them, 'Few military sites offer positions more fortunate.'[3] The fortress of Ceva was perched on the southern end of a ridge that went almost due north for about four miles, climbing gently all the way, to La Pedaggera. The front of this ridge, which was planted with vines, woods, copses and undergrowth, sloped down to a stream called the Bovina, which ran all the way down to the Tanaro. The valley of the Bovina, although not steep-sided, is about 450 feet deep from the stream to the crest of the ridge. It has a wide, open aspect, being more than one and a half miles from side to side.

As usual, the highest points on the crest of the ridge had been garnished with redoubts and supplementary earthworks. From south to north, they were at Baione, Testanera, Belvedere, Mondoni, Sanguinetti, Bastia, Govone, La Pedaggera and Giorgini. They were varied in form, size and construction, some of the supporting flèches only being capable of taking twenty men, while the major redoubts were big enough for 200. With a sufficiently large, determined force in occupation of it, and enough artillery, the line was an obstacle that would not be easily over-come. Nevertheless, Martinel was moved to comment that the defences, being the combined work of two men, an Austrian (Martonitz) and a Piedmontese, 'completely lacked unity',[4] and had a gap in the centre.

On the 16th, Colli was not at Ceva himself, because he had become anxious at the possibility that the whole army might find itself cut off from Turin by an enemy flanking movement — a fear that was quite justified given his experience of the methods Bonaparte had used in 1794. He had gone to Mondovì, and that afternoon he revealed in a letter to Beaulieu: 'All reports announce a general attack for today on Mondovì. At midnight I marched to the position of La Bicocca [an important defensive line four miles east of Mondovì] with eight battal-ions.' Unaware that the French were already probing his defences by that time, he also commented: 'The position of Ceva and La Pedaggera is quiet, however, [the enemy's] design seems to be to attack us. I shall be embarrassed if he tries to turn me by Mombarcaro [just north of La Pedaggera]: he will fall on Cherasco, which will force me to quit Ceva.'[5] The attack on Mondovì did not materialise, of course, but Colli's other fears were to be proved well-founded.

The troops he had left occupying the position at Ceva were divided into three groups. General Baron Brempt commanded the left, General Vital the centre, and General Count di Tornaforte was governor of the fortress of Ceva. The exact number of troops is not known, but Schels suggests there were roughly 13,000, though it is not clear whether this is supposed to include the eight battalions which Colli had drawn off during the night. However, we do know that the individual units were arranged as follows:

Commander	Regiment	Position
Brempt	Croats (2 coys)	on far left in skirmish order
	Light Infantry (Colonel Colli-Ricci)	behind the Croats

Commander	Regiment	Position
	Genevois	redoubt of Pedaggera
	Royal Grenadiers	between Pedaggera
	(1 battn, with 2 guns)	and Govone
	Royal Allemand	between Pedaggera
	(Brempt's regiment)	and Govone
	Acqui (1 battn, no artillery)	redoubt of Govone
	IR Belgioioso (Austrian)	near Govone, in the open
Vital	Foot Chasseurs	in front of the
	(a small number)	positions
	Savoy (1 battn)	redoubt of Bric Mondoni
	Stettler (1 battn and	between Mondoni and
	some artillery)	Belvedere
	Royal Grenadiers	redoubt of Belvedere
	(1 battn, under de Bellegarde)	
	Sappers (3 coys, who had been working on the defences)	north of Testanera
	Oneglia (2 battns, and	in and around
	some artillery)	Testanera
	Piedmontese Free Corps	in and around Testanera
	Mondovì (1 battn,	between Testanera and
	under Pallavicino)	Baione
	Artillery park	between Testanera and Baione
	Stettler (2 battns)	Baione
Tornaforte	Mondovì, Acqui, Tortona	around and mostly
	(1 battn each),	inside the fortress of
	1 coy artillery, 66 recruits	Ceva

Having admired the view from Montezemolo, Augereau now took the road along the crest towards La Pedaggera. When in sight of the position, a number of attack columns were formed, two of which were commanded by Beyrand and Joubert. Opinions vary as to the seriousness of the fighting that followed. The French were inclined to minimise its importance, and their accounts of it are noticeably thin. The historian of the 11th Light, for example, calls it a reconnaissance, and says almost nothing about it. The Piedmontese saw the action as a far more serious affair, though their reports on it are lacking in detail. In Brempt's account he states that the attack began at midday, in considerable force, on three points. The first was on the redoubt of Govone, which resisted well. The second attack was made on the front of the positions held by Royal Allemand and the Royal Grenadiers. The last of the attacks was made on the left of the line. All his troops, he says, fought with the greatest valour and were successful in beating back the French. General Vital states that the enemy was in several columns but that only three went into action, two on La Pedaggera and one on Mondoni. This resulted in his communications with La Pedaggera being cut for some hours, before the enemy was forced to fall back. He therefore feared that they might be cut completely the following day. Martinel tells us that the cannon of Mondoni and Belvedere fired without stopping, and when the French pulled back after suffering withering close-range fire from the redoubts, some of the Piedmontese soldiers pursued them down the slopes in their enthusiasm, only stopping at the stream. It was two hours before sunset, and the French attack had either failed or been deliberately suspended.

Some idea of the seriousness of the fighting may be gleaned from the casualty figures. The 4th Line counted among its dead four officers, including their *chef*, and 25 men, while the wounded numbered three officers and 57 men, which sounds a little too many for a mere reconnaissance. On the other hand, the 11th Light only reports losing one officer and 'some chasseurs' wounded and captured, which is certainly not the kind of loss one would expect from a wholehearted attack on a heavily defended position. Total losses are not known, though Brempt reported that he had lost a considerable number of men, probably about 150.[6]

Whether the French had been defeated or had merely pulled back, the Piedmontese did not feel confident about continuing their defence. Morale among the senior officers of the army was extremely low, and it showed. In his report to Colli, Brempt expressed concern that he might be cut off, and said that if the enemy attacked again on the following day, he would need help. Indeed, there was an additional threat to his line of retreat by now, as during the afternoon Sérurier had advanced to within sight of Ceva, where he camped.

That night, Colli went to Lesegno, a village near La Bicocca, and stopped at the house of the *Marchese* Del Carretto (a distant relative of the defender of Cosseria). He was conversing with General De La Chiusa when he received the reports from the commanders at Ceva, who suggested it would be wise for them to retire. He was also told that Mombarcaro had been turned. Colli's hostess wrote in her journal that 'the dejection could be seen on the faces of the generals, and disorder in their deliberations ... Fear and indecision were the result of the council of war. Finally, the General-in-Chief took a pen, said not another word, and wrote the fatal order to abandon Ceva.'[7] The troops were instructed to pull back, some to the position of La Bicocca and some to Cherasco. The withdrawal was carried out under cover of darkness, leaving a small garrison in the citadel to delay the French. Ironically, Beaulieu had already written to Colli that day to recommend him to concentrate his troops as much as possible, a piece of advice he might have taken himself at the outset of the campaign. He had evidently partly realised its value by this time, because he also informed Colli that he was intending to pull back to Alessandria and Tortona to gather his own troops. This bombshell, when he received it, was to alarm Colli considerably, because such a withdrawal would further separate the allied armies.

That same night, one of the French staff, Adjutant-General Franceschi, told Bonaparte that they could find no trace of the enemy in the whole area where the Austrian army had retired towards Acqui. This left Bonaparte largely free to concentrate on the operations of the left wing, though La Harpe remained in the area of Dego and Montenotte to keep a watch on the enemy. He was still experiencing great difficulty in keeping his troops under control, as he lamented to Bonaparte:

> Despite all my severity, I see that I am unable to repress pillaging. I send you my resignation, preferring to work the soil to live,

rather than find myself at the head of men who are worse than the Vandals were in the past.[8]

Perhaps the threat to resign was not entirely serious (La Harpe remained at his post) but the breakdown in discipline certainly was, and the situation was to get worse, though it was not La Harpe's troops who were responsible.

As for the divisions on the French left, Augereau established his men in the entrenched position at Ceva on the 17th, while Sérurier's advance-guard marched up to the town. The governor of the fortress was invited to surrender, but although Tornaforte was elderly he was still fiery, and not about to give up easily. He refused. However, he could do nothing to prevent the French entering the town, and in the evening it was occupied by Fiorella's brigade. Meanwhile, the HQ of the army, under the direction of Adjutant-General Vial, was moved to Millesimo, and then on the evening of the 17th to Saliceto.

The following morning, while awaiting developments, Joubert found time to write his father a jubilant letter 'from the bivouac above Ceva', announcing their recent successes:

Complete victory! We have been fighting for eight days – eight regiments taken, colours, artillery, and I got off with a blow on the head from a stone which I received during the attack on a castle-fort where we took an enemy lieutenant-general and 1,300 of the best Sardinian and Austrian troops. At the present we surround Ceva, and in an hour it will be summoned to surrender … The siege of Ceva will give us some rest. Pannetier has had his jacket pierced while carrying my orders. My wound bothers me a little, but does not impede even the most active service. We must finish it after all, and I promise you we are going like mad.[9]

Joubert was to be disappointed in his hope of rest, for there was no siege. On the 18th, Augereau again asked the garrison of the citadel to surrender, but Tornaforte replied that he had been ordered to hold out for as long as possible, and he intended to obey. Bonaparte reacted to this by deciding simply to by-pass the fortress. Whether this was because he was reluctant to slow his advance and wait for his artillery, or merely because he realised there was no danger in leaving the fortress to his rear is impossible to say. However, taking this decision showed remarkable flexibility, for Bonaparte had been saying for some time that the siege of Ceva was a vital operation, but now that he had been presented with the opportunity to carry it out, he abandoned the plan without embarrassment when he realised the situation called for other measures. Instead, he left Rusca, who was of Italian origins and spoke the language, to manage affairs in the town and negotiate with Tornaforte. The army then moved on to engage the Piedmontese in their new position at San Michele, or La Bicocca.

This defensive line was yet another formidable position on the crest of a line of hills, and was protected by the River Corsaglia running along its front. Martinel describes it simply as 'one of the finest defensive positions that Nature could present'.[10] It extended roughly from the Tanaro at its north-eastern end, to the village of San Michele at its southwestern. The three principal defensive points on the ridge (from south to north), Buon Gesù, La Bicocca and Madonna delle Casette, were rather different in their characteristics. The first had slopes so steep and broken that it had been considered pointless to add entrenchments to its eastern side. La Bicocca, on the contrary, was gently sloping, though it was the highest point on the ridge. But in its vicinity the bank of the Corsaglia was in many places cut vertically and quite impossible to climb. Moreover, fording the river was out of the question at that time, because the rapidly flowing waters were much increased by the recent rains and melting snow. The heights of Madonna delle Casette defended the crossing over the Corsaglia from the village of Lesegno, and had plenty of space for three or four ranks of fire in all directions. Colli appointed General Dichat to command the line, which was defended by about 8,000 men and fifteen guns.

During the night of 18/19 April, Bonaparte gave orders to force the position. Sérurier was to attack on the French left, and Augereau on the right near the confluence of the Tanaro and the Corsaglia, making from the direction of Castellino. Massena was to take positions that would support the attack, having by this time moved via Mombarcaro to a position north of Ceva in the valley of the Belbo, where he was well placed to cut the Piedmontese off from Turin. Stengel had sent the available cavalry from Cairo and Carcare to Priero to support Sérurier.

Early in the morning, Sérurier's division set off in two columns, each 3,000 strong, under Fiorella and Guieu. Sérurier himself commanded the reserve. The Piedmontese had been at readiness since dawn, and a couple of hours after sunrise they observed the French columns as they came down from the hills opposite their position, and moved in the direction of the bridge to San Michele. They were met by heavy fire from the defending batteries, and made contact with the outposts on the right bank of the Corsaglia at about 8 a.m., just as the Piedmontese were preparing to eat. The pickets managed to slow down the French advance, but were gradually driven in. The Piedmontese advance-guard then exchanged a volley with the French, before retiring towards the bridge at San Michele, having been ordered by Dichat to take up a position on the other side. Guieu continued to advance, but as he closed on the bridge he began to suffer terrible casualties from the artillery on the heights beyond it. By midday, both Guieu and Fiorella found themselves under heavy fire and could make no progress. A few brave soldiers who had tried to ford the river had been swept away by the current.

On the right flank, Augereau was similarly in trouble. All attempts to find a place where it was possible to ford the Tanaro were defeated both by the fire of five guns, and the fullness and rapidity of the river. The *Marchesa* who had been Colli's hostess so recently now found that she had French guests, as the windows of her house provided a useful observation-post from which to view the action on that flank. Augereau also received a visit from Bonaparte to press for action, but his troops could not walk on the water any more than he could, and he had to accept that there was nothing that could be done. Joubert tried to get his men to attempt a crossing by riding his horse into the river, despite the fire from the opposite bank, but no one offered to follow him and he returned saying 'You are right, it is impossible to get across.'[11]

With the attack completely stalled on the right, the French were very fortunate to achieve a breakthrough on the left. A few of Guieu's skirmishers had followed a small group of enemy pickets who had not been able to reach the bridge of San Michele with the rest of their comrades. They were seen to cross the Corsaglia over a small aqueduct[12] which was not guarded, nor did the retreating troops make any attempt to destroy it. The French soldiers slipped across without loss and made for the shelter of the houses on the other side of the river, from where they opened a flanking fire on the Piedmontese. This toe-hold on the opposite bank was immediately exploited by Guieu's brigade, which rushed into the attack, crossing the river and driving back the enemy, who rapidly broke, fleeing in all directions. Guieu now took the nearby battery in the rear and attacked San Michele itself from the south.

At the news that the French had crossed the river in force there was near panic among the Piedmontese, some of whom abandoned positions, guns and equipment. In the confusion, a young officer tried to destroy the powder magazine in San Michele, but it tragically exploded before everyone had got clear, adding to the chaos and causing a number of casualties. Fiorella took advantage of this turmoil to cross the bridge to San Michele. By 1.30 p.m. the French had taken the village, nearly capturing Colli and Colonel Costa in the process, while Dichat actually was made prisoner, but managed to buy his freedom from the man who had captured him.

This little commercial transaction conducted in the midst of battle is indicative of the attitudes of the French soldiery, who were rapidly losing their sense of duty. Excited by their victory, desperate for food, and greedy for plunder, they now became completely uncontrollable, and 'there was more disorder than at Dego'.[13] Sérurier's men had not been there, of course, and had not learned that particular lesson, but they were about to get one all for themselves. Unbeknown to them, 75 grenadiers of a Swiss regiment had managed to hide in a garden when the French overran their positions.[14] Captain Schreiber, their commander, decided that rather than surrender they should slip out and try to make it back to the positions on La Bicocca, which were still in Piedmontese hands. Having left the garden without being noticed, the Swiss realised that the

French were wide open to attack, being engaged in eating, drinking and looting. In a vigorous assault the Swiss massacred the French pillagers, set free numerous prisoners, and recaptured a cannon, which they turned on the enemy. It was now the turn of Sérurier's men to scatter in panic.

In the meantime, Colli had reached La Bicocca himself at about 2 p.m., and re-organised for a counter-attack. This unexpectedly found the French already in disorder as a result both of the break-down in discipline and the irruption of the Swiss. The French were easily driven back from all points, many being taken prisoner, while others fell into the river in their attempt to escape. Guieu's brigade was lucky to hold on to the bridge over the Corsaglia at Torre, a little upstream from San Michele, thus keeping a link with the far bank, but Fiorella's brigade was driven back to its positions of the morning. The French therefore ended the day with almost nothing to show for their efforts. Moreover, their attacks, which had been made without the support of artillery, had been costly. The 39th and 85th demi-brigades had lost particularly heavily, while the historian of the 69th speaks of 72 dead and 50 prisoners, though it is not clear if this includes the actions of the next few days.[15] In total, the French had probably lost about 600 men, the Piedmontese half this number.

Bonaparte had suffered a distinct check, largely due to poor discipline, and it must have been clear to him that there was now some danger of the army disintegrating into a rabble. The lack of food was at the bottom of most of the trouble, for the area they had moved through was mountainous and incapable of supporting a large population. An army had as many people as a medium-sized town, and could strip an area of food in a very short time. The speed of the French advance had been too much for their meagre and inefficient supply service and the magazines were now many miles away, reachable only by poor mountain roads. 'Pillage was therefore the only means of living.'[16] Not only had this contributed to the incident at San Michele through the sudden break-down of cohesion among the troops, but there was a certain continual diminution in the number of soldiers with their colours as more and more of them dispersed to look for food and loot.

It was not just Bonaparte's plans that were being compromised by these disorders. For the civilian population, the effect was catastrophic, as thousands of violent intruders ransacked their homes and farms, murdering those who dared to try and defend themselves. Many local people turned to the Del Carretto family for help, and when Bonaparte arrived at their house in Lesegno at 3 a.m., the *Marchesa* hurried to see him and made a personal plea to him to stop the pillaging. He had had a bad day, and it was a moment when his mood was unreceptive. 'He replied coldly, without looking at her: "Have they done you some wrong?"'[17] Nevertheless, he held a meeting of his generals in Ceva, which resulted in orders being issued that anyone, whether officer or soldier, who either encouraged or participated in looting, would immediately be shot in front of the troops. Such a measure, however, could only have an effect if the supply situation improved, and the soldiers were able to live without stealing. 'If you don't want us to pillage, we must be fed, paid and clothed!'[18] they said. But there were enormous practical difficulties that would have taxed an efficient and honest administration and supply service. It had been raining continually for days, and the snow was begin-ning to melt in the mountains, swelling the rivers and reducing the roads to a terrible state. Supplies of food, equipment and munitions had almost stopped on the road from Savona, so it was fortunate that the penetration of the French advance now meant that they were able to straighten and shorten their line of communication by using the Tanaro valley instead of the coast road and the Cadibona Pass, which ought to have helped to speed up supplies.

At the meeting in Ceva it was also decided that it was essential to overcome the defences of San Michele as soon as possible, but it seems likely that the state of the army was such that time had to be taken in restoring discipline, and resting the troops after their recent efforts. In any case, the whole of 20 April passed only in preparations, and moving up extra troops.

As for Colli, his problems were of a different kind. He had won something of a victory at San Michele, but his troops were few and tired, his communications with Turin were threatened, and Beaulieu's army was now a long way out of reach. Beaulieu had in fact gone back on his decision to withdraw, and had written to Colli to inform him that he was going to advance between the Belbo and the Bormida, but this news would not immediately reach Colli, who was obliged to act as if there would be no support from the Austrians. Colli informed Beaulieu that he had successfully repulsed the enemy, but said that if he was attacked again and beaten, he would be left with very few troops. Although defending the terrain between La Bicocca and Turin was important, it was clearly even more important to try to prevent the destruction of his army, without which nothing could be done. In other words, Colli felt it was more wise to manoeuvre than to stand and fight. This view was supported by a council of war of the senior Piedmontese officers, and it was decided to retire to a position behind the Ellero or the Stura. After discussions, it was agreed that the army would move first to Mondovì, where there were large magazines and useful defensive positions, then to Cuneo. Although moving towards the latter meant leaving the direct route to Turin uncovered, it would permit the army to gather reinforcements from the area of Tenda and Cuneo. Colli duly ordered the army to retreat in two columns through Briaglia and Vicoforte.

On the 20th, Colli had the bridges over the Corsaglia destroyed, and sent the baggage to Mondovì, ordering the magazines there to be emptied. During the night of the 20th/21st, the army pulled back under the cover of darkness, taking the usual precaution of leaving camp-fires burning, which permitted them to march off unnoticed. As Bonaparte magnanimously remarked to some Piedmontese officers a few days later, 'You escaped from my clutches very adroitly.'[19] The escape was not complete, however. At midnight on the 20th, Bonaparte arrived in Lesegno, and had the bridge at San Michele reconnoitred. On being informed that it had been demolished, he ordered some scouts to cross the river. These managed to find a ford and came back with the news that the enemy camp-fires were burning, but the army had gone. The French immediately set off in pursuit, and at about 10 a.m. caught up with the Piedmontese at Vicoforte, where they were attempting to take up a defensive position. It seems unlikely that Colli was intending to do more than use it as a temporary holding-point until the magazines at Mondovì had been emptied, and that he hoped to be able to retire to a better position before the French overtook him. He certainly cannot have thought the terrain very suitable for defence, as it was too cramped, had no place where a tactical reserve could be held, and was completely without entrenchments or other defensive works. Moreover, the position had the defect that it could be outflanked. This danger must have been obvious to Colli, because although he had exhorted the troops to hold as long as they could, he also told the commanders not to let themselves be surrounded. Unfortunately for the Piedmontese, the French overhauled them even before it had been possible to deploy the troops properly, and the positioning of them left much to be desired, with gaps in some parts of the line, and too many men in others.

The rearguard, around Buon Gesù, was soon driven in by Guieu and Fiorella, and fell back on Vicoforte, where its arrival did nothing to help the organisation of the defensive line. The troops in this area seem to have been rather jittery, and at the first cannonade from the French, a number of units gave way. There was a period of chaotic house-to-house fighting, as a result of which Fiorella and Dommartin took one part of Vicoforte, while Guieu took the Sanctuary, Fiamenga, and the other side of Vicoforte. The only point that was not affected by the disorder was the height where Dichat was in command, but he was killed and his troops were forced back. Within a fairly short time, the whole army was retreating in disorder beyond the Ellero, some of the soldiers profiting from the confusion to pillage the houses of their countrymen. The main road to Mondovì was choked with fugitives.

The day was not completely satisfactory for the French, however, and the weakness of their cavalry was exposed by a small incident that had larger consequences. Stengel had spent the entire day in the saddle with 200 dragoons, and had worked his way round onto the far bank of the Ellero to try to harry the Piedmontese retreat. There he was charged by 125 Piedmontese dragoons under Colonel Chaffardon, who scored a notable success, driving the French back and taking more than twenty prisoners.[20] Even worse for the French, General Stengel was mortally wounded and died five days later, depriving the army of a man who knew his job and was to prove very difficult to replace.

At about the same time as this skirmish took place, the French arrived before Mondovì, and suffered a check of an unusual sort. The governor, General Dellera, saw more profit in talking than fighting, and having been summoned to surrender, he bought time for the rest of the army to retreat by engaging in lengthy discussions of the precise terms for the capitulation. This dragged on for a couple of hours before Bonaparte became impatient and had a few shells lobbed into the town. Under pressure from the citizens, who were more interested in safety than in martial glory, Dellera brought the negotiations to a more rapid conclusion. It was about 6 p.m.

There followed one of those rituals that had become enshrined in custom over the centuries, when the victorious general was met by a delegation from the surrendering town. In this case it included the mayor of Mondovì and prominent members of the clergy, who offered Bonaparte the keys of the town, and asked him to respect religion and property, which Bonaparte conceded, as hundreds of conquerors had done before him. Accompanied by Saliceti, Bonaparte then made what was to be the first of many triumphal entries into a captured town – it was 7 p.m. on 21 April 1796. After this, he returned to his HQ in Lesegno, leaving his men in occupation. These were welcomed somewhat nervously, but 'with festive cries'.[21] It was no doubt in the citizens' interests to appear friendly and co-operative, as the devastation that had been visited on the surrounding countryside might easily be extended to the town. As it turned out, discipline was maintained, but the French did levy quite large official contributions to feed the troops, which at least reduced the likelihood of any illegal search for food by individuals. Sérurier's division was to receive 8,000 rations of bread, 3,000 of biscuit, 8,000 of meat and 4,000 bottles of wine, with a similar amount to be provided before 10 a.m. on the following day. In addition, 30,000 rations of biscuit were to be sent to Lesegno, and 1,500 rations of everything to Joubert's troops at La Bicocca. All arms and munitions were also seized.

The engagement before Mondovì does not seem to have been costly in terms of lives, and Martinel suggests there may have been as few as a hundred killed in total, but the disorder in which the Piedmontese had stampeded from the field meant that their situation was almost as bad as if they had suffered great casualties. Collecting sufficient forces seriously to oppose the French if they made another rapid attack would be immensely difficult. During the night, however, the Piedmontese continued their retreat without further disturbance, moving in two directions: towards Cuneo and Fossano.

That same evening, King Victor Amadeus held a meeting of the Council of Ministers in Turin to discuss the now desperate situation. The King's sons, supported by the English and Austrian ambassadors, pressed for a continuation of the war. The Cardinal Archbishop of Turin, Costa, was eloquent for peace. Even more eloquent was the state of the treasury, whose superintendent estimated that the war had so far cost the equivalent of fifteen years' revenue.[22] There were also reports of revolutionary rumblings among the populace, which, if they were true, could mean that the invading French would receive decisive support from the people. In the face of these difficulties, with the army crumbling by the day, and the French almost in sight of Turin, the King decided that there was no alternative but to open peace negotiations. On 22 April, therefore, Piedmontese plenipotentiaries were despatched to Genoa to meet the French envoy there. A letter was also sent to Colli informing him of the decision, and inviting him to open negotiations with Bonaparte for an armistice.

The French troops passed the day in rest and preparation, as there were a number of things to organise before the army ventured into the plains. The artillery park and the transport, such as they were, had lagged well behind, and there were also prisoners to be sent to the rear areas. Bonaparte also took the opportunity to make a minor adjustment to the organisation of the army by dissolving Meynier's division, and attaching that general to the HQ. On the same day, Marmont snatched a few moments to dash off a letter to his father describing the furious pace he was now expected to live at: 'The other day, I spent twenty-four hours on horseback without getting off, and after three hours rest, I was back on again for fifteen hours.'[23]

Joubert also wrote to his father, passing rapidly over another lucky escape to make known his feelings about the problems of discipline. 'I have had another spent ball hit me on the right breast. The wealth of the country brings back our army's love of pillage, and I curse and rage to the General-in-Chief to have some of the guilty shot. Because I foresee great troubles if this continues.'[24] Bonaparte was of much the same opinion, and issued a lengthy order of the day on the subject, with strict instructions for the divisional generals to submit reports on the conduct of the generals under them, and so on down the scale.[25] From the way the order is set out, one may conclude that as far as Bonaparte was concerned, discipline was something that worked from the top downwards. If the generals and officers did not behave, there was no hope that the troops would. Regrettably, of course, some of the worst looters in the army were Massena and Augereau, and there was a limit to what Bonaparte could or would do to restrain their activities. However distasteful their propensity for theft, they were also difficult to replace, and could not be lightly dismissed. None the less, this order was clearly a 'shot across the bows' that must have discouraged the less hardened criminals, and large-scale disorders of the kind that had compromised the successes of Dego and San Michele did not recur.

On the morning of 23 April, Bonaparte received a letter from Colli:

> Having learned that His Majesty the King of Sardinia has just sent plenipotentiaries to Genoa to negotiate for peace, under the mediation of the Spanish Court, I believe, General, that humanity requires, while these negotiations last, that hostilities be suspended by both sides ...[26]

Bonaparte had foreseen such a situation a long time ago, and he now did what he had once advised others to do: he continued his movements and did not reply until the evening. He then stated that only the Directory could negotiate peace, but that if two of the three fortresses of Cuneo, Alessandria and Tortona were placed in his hands, he would be prepared to suspend hostilities. This reply was taken by Murat to Colli at his HQ in Fossano on the 24th, and it was sent on to Turin for approval. Colli's position was now almost hopeless, as he only had about 10,000 men to cover Turin and also maintain a link with Cuneo.

The Piedmontese peace negotiators had arrived in Genoa on the morning of the 23rd, and were able to make contact with Faipoult through the offices of the Spanish ambassador. By the time they met,

Faipoult had been informed by Bonaparte of Colli's overtures and also told the plenipotentiaries that they would have to deal with the Directory. Having come up against this impasse, the negotiators left Genoa empty-handed on the morning of the 25th, but passed through Acqui to see Beaulieu. The latter gave vent to all his disapproval of their betrayal of the alliance, and threatened to seize Alessandria, Tortona and Valenza to prevent them from falling into French hands. Beaulieu must have been feeling very vulnerable by this time, and had in the past few days asked for a pontoon bridge to be built over the Po at Valenza, to facilitate his retreat into Lombardy should it become necessary.

In the meantime, Bonaparte had continued his march northwards. On 24 April, Sérurier moved to Trinità with the 22nd Chasseurs à Cheval, while Massena took Bene Vagienna and pushed his advance-guard towards Cherasco. Augereau was also moving towards Cherasco, but on the right bank of the Tanaro, sending reconnaissances as far as La Morra. Colli judged Cherasco too weakly manned to hold against an attack by these two divisions, and therefore had the place evacuated, apart from a skeleton holding force. La Harpe remained in the valley of the Belbo, in a position where he could cover any sudden appearance by the Austrians. The weather continued to be bad, and got worse in the next few days. At 11 a.m. on the 25th the French entered Cherasco, the small garrison left by Colli having decamped with speed at the sight of numerous French troops approaching that morning. These also managed to prevent the Piedmontese from totally destroying the pontoon bridge over the Stura, and it was soon repaired.

With the first phase of his campaign almost at an end, Bonaparte decided to despatch his brother Joseph and Junot to Paris to announce the army's successes in person. Joseph was the bearer of a letter to the Directors, communicating the Piedmontese request for an armistice, while Junot was to present them with 21 captured colours, both Austrian and Piedmontese. The two messengers left on 25 April.

On the same day, Colli decided to continue his retreat as far as Carmagnola, twelve miles south of Turin, to prevent himself from being cut off from the capital. The retreat was carried out during the night, and was a miserable affair:

Only the cavalry, which was covering the movement, and a division of infantry could follow the main road ... The other divisions, which had to take the more westerly route, wandered all night in the mud, by rutted paths, going over fields, through the middle of vineyards, in rain mixed with snow. Some got lost and came out at Bra where Brempt's cavalry covered the retreat ... The rest, scattered, chilled to the bone and exhausted, dragged themselves to Carmagnola where they arrived in groups during the morning of the 26th, leaving behind them lines of stragglers whose sad procession lasted all day.[27]

There was not much left to play for by this time, but Colli and Beaulieu both hoped it would be possible to extricate the much-reduced Austrian Auxiliary Corps from the shambles of the Piedmontese defeat, and preserve it for the inevitable moment when the French would turn their full force on Beaulieu. On the 26th, Schübirz took command of what was left of the Corps, to try to manoeuvre it back towards the Austrian army.

Bonaparte was showing no inclination to lessen the pressure on the Piedmontese, and preparations were made to cross to the north of the Stura and pursue them in their retreat. There was not much sign of him lessening the pressure on himself and his own army either, and orders kept streaming from the HQ, with arrangements to make contact with the troops at Colle di Tenda, payment for spies to bring information for the continuation of operations against the Austrians, and much more. In particular, he issued a proclamation to the army, both lauding its achievements and pointing out its defects:

Soldiers, in fifteen days you have gained six victories, taken twenty-one colours, fifty-five guns, many strong-points, and conquered the richest part of Piedmont. You have taken fifteen thousand prisoners, and killed or wounded more than ten thousand men ... You have won battles without cannons, crossed rivers without bridges, made forced marches without shoes, and bivouacked without brandy and often without bread ... But, soldiers, you have done nothing, because there is still work to do. Neither Turin nor Milan are ours ...[28]

The figures were fantastic, of course, but as usual they were good for morale – which was in any case one of the primary reasons for issuing the proclamation. However, it did go on to say at some length that pillaging would have to stop, and that there would be grave punishments for those who transgressed the order. As if to show that this was not an empty threat, there were a few executions. A certain Sapper Latouche was shot during the day for looting, and two soldiers called Urgel and Lefort followed the day after.

Late on the 26th Bonaparte learned from La Harpe that Beaulieu was in the process of moving towards him, but saw no great danger in this. He had, in any case, written to La Harpe earlier in the day, indicating that he was already preparing to turn on the Austrians. 'It is time to think seriously about entering Acqui ...' he said. 'If you think that, by means of a junction with Victor, you have enough men to make a movement on Acqui, I authorise you to do it. Only you must do it on your left, so that I can have you supported by Augereau, who is at Alba.'[29]

Alba was one of the towns where it was known that there were strong Republican sympathies. Before his departure from Paris Bonaparte had had meetings with proscribed Piedmontese radicals, some of whom had also followed and co-operated with the French army. Bonaparte did not nurture any great respect for these people, but he felt obliged to tolerate them. The French entry into Alba at midday on the 26th, with Bonaparte at the head of the 4th Line, was triumphal, and was followed by the establishment of a new town council which had a Tree of Liberty planted in the main square of the town a few days later. While Bonaparte was hopeful that the movement might spread, and that other towns in Piedmont might follow suit, he did not want the French to appear to push the Piedmontese too much in this direction. 'Public spirit must be nurtured, both by our good conduct and by religious respect for property,'[30] he wrote to La Harpe on the 27th, but there was to be no direct French pressure on the Piedmontese to start their own revolution.

Turin by now was in tumult, expecting the arrival of the French from one moment to the next, and some of the ordinary populace was thought to be in a revolutionary frame of mind. The danger of an explosion of popular unrest had induced those who had most to lose by it to make their own preparations, either by shipping what they could out of the city, or getting it ready for a rapid departure. The mood was not helped when late in the evening of the 26th the plenipotentiaries returned from Genoa to report their failure, and the artillery park and the baggage of the army entered the town, causing rumours of all kinds.

A few hours later, at 2 a.m. on the 27th, one of Colli's ADCs went to Bonaparte's HQ to offer Cuneo instead of Tortona as the price of the armistice, but the answer was negative. Bonaparte wanted Cuneo and either Tortona or Alessandria, as well as the surrender of Ceva. To keep up the pressure he ordered his nearest troops to cross the Stura, which they did in pouring rain. In other places there was a heavy snowfall. In these dismal conditions, Colli moved his HQ back to la Loggia, only five miles from Turin, and sent his ADC to get the King's decision on the terms of the armistice. In the afternoon, Colli informed Beaulieu that he was writing to the King to tell him that he was going to retire. His health was ruined, he said, and he no longer had the strength to walk, he was so worn out by the fatigues of the campaign.

The French, meanwhile, were making efforts to get ready for the next clash with the Austrians. At daybreak on the 27th, Fiorella sent a patrol to Colle di Tenda to link with the forces under Generals Garnier and Macquard, and order them to join the rest of the army. Apart from bringing in reinforcements, the opening of this link was important because the Colle di Tenda provided a more direct line of communications, straight to Nice, which ought to alleviate some of the immediate problems of supply, provided that the weather was not too bad. During the day, Bonaparte also called Massena, Augereau and Sérurier to receive their instructions for the next phase of the campaign. The object of their interest, Beaulieu, had by then conceded that he could do nothing to help the Piedmontese, and on the 27th he turned back towards Alessandria and Tortona. He was aware that the French wanted possession of these as the price of a suspension of hostilities, and had every intention of trying to seize them before the enemy could occupy them.

It was 2 p.m. on the 27th when an ADC arrived at Colli's HQ bringing the King's final decision to agree to Bonaparte's terms. Representatives of the Piedmontese government then went, escorted by a picket of dragoons, to the French commander to agree terms. They were General Sallier de La Tour and Colli's Chief of Staff, Colonel Costa. The latter described their mournful journey and humiliating task:

> The French advance-guard extended as far as the village of Sanfrè; its fires lit the plain and the hills. It was by their light that the commissioners advanced to Bra. They were courteously received by Massena and spent three quarters of an hour with him preparing the escort of hussars to be added to the dragoons sent from Carmagnola.[31]

They then continued to Cherasco. It was 10.30 on a rainy evening when they finally reached Bonaparte's HQ at the house of Count de Salmatoris:

> No guard defended the approach to the house, which was almost unlit. Only a few soldiers sleeping on the threshold and on the steps could be seen. No horses, no wagons, nor mules for transport, no servants. Silence and calm appeared to reign in the rest of the town.[32]

They descended from their carriage, and 'after some enquiries and a few moments delay, a young man attached to the staff appeared' who took them into a room 'where a large fire was burning'. Berthier appeared and then went to inform Bonaparte who was resting in the next room, remaining with him nearly half an hour:

> Bonaparte finally appeared. He was in the uniform of a commanding general, and booted, but without his sword, hat or sash. His demeanour was grave and cold ... His smooth chestnut hair was tied in a queue. It was not powdered, and hung very low

over his forehead and down the sides of his face. His eyes were red
and tired. He had that wan and even complexion that the physi-
ologists attribute to the melancholy temperament, and, according
to them, bespeaks the greatest faculties of the soul. In conclusion,
as we have already said, he totally lacked affability and grace.[33]

When General de La Tour opened discussions, and made some slight
complaint about the conditions being hard, Bonaparte cut him off
short and pointed out that he had taken Cherasco, Fossano and Alba
since he had made that offer. 'You should find me very moderate,' [34]
he commented.

Bonaparte continued to be cold, polite and laconic, but at 1 a.m. his
patience ran out, and pulling out his watch he said, 'Gentlemen, I warn
you that a general attack has been ordered for 2 o'clock, and if I am not
certain that Cuneo will be delivered into my hands before the end of the
day, the attack will not be delayed a moment … It may happen that I
shall lose battles, but I shall never lose minutes through idle talk or
sloth.'[35] This was no doubt one of Bonaparte's habitual pieces of theatre
designed to bring psychological pressure on the negotiators, as there is
no trace of any order concerning such an attack. Having thrown this
firecracker into the gathering Bonaparte then left Berthier to do the
talking, and paced up and down and from side to side of the room in
silence. By 2 a.m. the 'amnesty', as Bonaparte frequently called it in his
Corsican French, had been signed. A Piedmontese ADC left immediately to inform the King and obtain an order for Cuneo and Tortona to
be placed in French hands, while the negotiators began to relax:

General de La Tour having asked for some coffee, Bonaparte gave
an order to look for some in the town. He himself pulled two
porcelain cups from a small overnight bag which was on a sofa
with his sword, but having no coffee spoons they had to use
yellow-metal spoons like the soldiers used for eating. After the
signing of the articles, Murat, Marmont, General Despinoy and
two or three staff-officers appeared. The company went into the
dining-room, where a sort of *médianoche* was laid on a table

covered with a multitude of candlesticks. The dish in the middle was a bowl of clear soup. There were also two or three dishes of coarse meat, some very mediocre sweets and ammunition bread. The most conspicuous dish was a pyramid of *gimblettes* that the clergy of Cherasco had offered to the conqueror on his arrival. Numerous bottles of wine from the region of Asti filled the large empty spaces on the table.[36]

It was a meal that was entirely in character with the army whose commander was offering it — cut down to the bare essentials. The aristocratic Piedmontese representatives must have been astounded at the frugality of the enemy HQ. After the meal, which was quickly over, Bonaparte became more relaxed and spoke more freely:

He spoke of the events of the preceding days in a very open manner. He blamed himself for the pointless and murderous attack on the castle of Cosseria, and blamed the mistake on his impatience to separate the Piedmontese and Austrian armies from each other.[37]

He spoke of discipline, saying that a soldier found guilty of violence towards a woman had been shot the previous day. Bonaparte also made some unfavourable comments on councils of war, saying that nothing would ever be decided by that method in any army under his command. 'A council of war is never called except when it is a question of taking a cowardly decision and to attenuate the blame by sharing it among several individuals.'[38]

As if to underline the poverty of the meal they had just eaten, which was evidence enough of how little transport the French used, he criticised the Austrian habit of overloading their armies with baggage, and took Costa into the nearby room to see 'the slender portmanteau, which, together with the overnight bag, was all his luggage'. Bonaparte then leant on the balcony of a window to watch the day break, and continued to talk with Costa for over an hour. He seemed completely sure of the outcome of the campaign. 'M. de Beaulieu will not be able to stop me before the walls of Mantua: he will have to expect to have my victorious army always on his flanks.'[39] He also gave Costa his thoughts on the subject of leadership: 'It is almost indispensable to be young to command an army. For this job you need much luck, audacity and pride!'[40] Costa, however, was too much dispirited by his country's recent failure fully to enjoy the company of this remarkable man: 'The impression that one had near this young man was of a painful admiration; the intellect was dazzled by the superiority of his talents, but the heart remained oppressed.'[41]

Piedmont had been fighting France since 1792. Twelve days of fighting against General Bonaparte had seen its army completely defeated, and another five days had brought peace, in fact, if not yet signed and sealed. It must have seemed like a miracle. Joubert had no doubt about the significance of what he had become involved in:

> We have just done great service, and we are destined for great things. Cuneo and Alessandria are in our hands … We have done our work well: in fifteen days we have destroyed two armies and forced a king to ask for peace. I feel the effects of the general good fortune. I have eight horses, and a collection of sugar and coffee that I will send to you, goods taken from the enemy staff … I lodge only with counts and marquises who call us heroes and who still find in us the likeable character of the French. We do not speak of politics. We do not get ourselves mixed up in their government … I am finally going to take a rest. For fifteen days, sixteen hours on horseback every day, without counting the journeys on foot. I am also like a skeleton and black as a moor. Do not forget me in the family, above all Charlotte. My brother embraces you.[42]

The first phase of the campaign was over, and it was about as convincing a demonstration of Bonaparte's superiority as a strategist as he could have wished for. Years later he made some remarks that could almost be a commentary on the errors committed by his opponent at the very outset of the campaign:

To act upon lines far removed from each other, and without communications, is to commit a fault which always gives birth to a second. The detached column has only its orders for the first day. Its operations on the following day depend upon what may have happened to the main body. Thus the column either loses time upon emergency, in waiting for orders, or acts without them and at hazard. Let it therefore be held as a principle that an army should always keep its columns so united as to prevent the enemy from passing between them with impunity ...[43]

The principles were applicable not just to the disastrous separation between Beaulieu and Argenteau, but also to that between the Austrian and Piedmontese armies. If the Austrians had chosen to concentrate closer to the Piedmontese positions, as Colli had wanted, it would have been less easy for Bonaparte to effect their separation. The defeat of the Piedmontese became almost inevitable from the moment Bonaparte managed to drive a wedge between the allies and obliged the Piedmontese to draw ever further from their only source of help by threatening to outflank them. It would be easy to heap the blame for this on Beaulieu, but as we have said before, he was given a difficult hand to play, and if he came off second best in a contest with one of the greatest strategists in the history of war, it is not surprising.

NOTES

1. Napoleon, *Campagnes d'Italie*, quoted in Bouvier, F. *Bonaparte en Italie, 1796*. Paris, 1899, p. 334.
2. Pezay, A. F., marquis de. *Histoire des campagnes de M. le Maréchal de Maillebois en Italie pendant les années 1745 et 1746*. Paris, 1775, II, p. xxiii.
3. Fabry, J. G. A. *Mémoires sur la campagne de 1796 en Italie*. Paris, 1905, p. 50.
4. Ibid., p. 56.
5. Fabry, 1905, op. cit., p. 43.
6. See Bouvier, op. cit., p. 336 and Fabry, J. G. A. *Histoire de l'armée d'Italie (1796–1797)*. Paris, 1900–14, IV, §2, p. 218. Bouvier gives a

second figure for the 4th Line, which indicates a total loss of 182 officers and men.

7. Argan, G. C. 'Bonaparte in Italia. Dal Diario inedito della Marchesa Del Carretto. "Journal de ce qui est arrivé à Lesegno à l'occasion de l'invasion des François en Piemont. (Extrait des Mémoires écrites chaque jour par la Marquise Carret elle même)". *La Cultura*, Jan–Mar (1932), p. 18.

8. Napoleon. *Correspondance inédite officielle et confidentielle de Napoléon Bonaparte: avec les cours étrangères, les princes, les ministres et les généraux français et étrangers, en Italie, en Allemagne, et en Egypte.* Paris, 1809, I, p. 79.

9. Chevrier, E. *Le général Joubert d'après sa correspondance.* Paris, 1884, p. 33.

10. Fabry, 1905, op. cit., p. 74.

11. Ibid., p. 94.

12. This is according to Martinel. Bouvier calls it a small footbridge.

13. Bouvier, op. cit., p. 356.

14. It is also said that they had been captured, were badly guarded, and were able to use German to discuss secretly how to overpower their captors. See Bouvier, op. cit., p. 356 and Duval, C. 'La 19e demi-brigade à l'armée d'Italie (1793–1796) et le brigadier-général Dichat de Toisinge.' *Mémoires et documents publiés par la société savoisienne d'histoire et d'archéologie*, n36 (1897), pp. 528–9.

15. Duval, op. cit., p. 537.

16. Krebs, V. L., and Moris, H. *Campagnes dans les Alpes pendant la Révolution, d'après les archives des Etats-majors français et austro-sarde.* Paris, 1891–95, p. 418.

17. Argan, op. cit., p. 22.

18. Massena, A. *Mémoires de Massena, rédigés d'après les documents qu'il a laissés et sur ceux du dépôt de la guerre et du dépôt des fortifications, par le général Koch.* Paris, 1848–50, II, p. 43.

19. Bouvier, op. cit., p. 367.

20. Lerda, A. 'Con il generale Stengel sulla piana di Cassanio il 21 aprile 1796.' *Bollettino della Società per gli Studi Storici, Archeologici ed Artistici della Provincia di Cuneo*, (1980), p. 127.

21. Pinelli, F. A. *Storia militare del Piemonte.* Turin, 1854–55, p. 665.

22. Ibid., p. 411.

23. Marmont, A. F., de. *Mémoires du duc de Raguse de 1792 à 1832 imprimés sur le manuscrit original de l'auteur.* Paris, 1857, II, p. 314.

24. Chevrier, op. cit., p. 34.

25. Napoleon. *Correspondance de Napoléon Ier publiée par ordre de l'empereur Napoléon III.* Paris, 1858–69, no. 214.

26. Bouvier, op. cit., p. 412.

27. Ibid., p. 422.

28. Napoleon. 1858–69, op. cit., no. 234.

29. Ibid., no. 237.

30. Bouvier, op. cit., p. 428.

31. Costa de Beauregard, C. A. *Un homme d'autrefois: souvenirs recueillis par son arrière-petit-fils.* Paris, 1879, p. 332.

32. Ibid., p. 332.

33. Ibid., pp. 333 and 341

34. Ibid., p. 334.

35. Ibid., p. 334.

36. Ibid., p. 335.

37. Ibid., p. 336.

38. Ibid., p. 336.

39. Ibid., p. 337.

40. Ibid., p. 340.

41. Ibid., p. 339.

42. Chevrier, op. cit., pp. 34–5.

43. Napoleon. *Maximes.* Paris, 1820, no. XI.

12

CROSSING THE PO

'Tomorrow I shall march against Beaulieu, I shall force him to recross the Po, I shall cross it immediately afterwards, I shall take the whole of Lombardy, and before a month is over, I hope to be in the mountains of the Tyrol, meet the Army of the Rhine and in co-operation, take the war into Bavaria.'[1] This was the intention that Bonaparte expressed to the Directory on 28 April. It did not happen quite like that, but the next month was still pretty remarkable.

Beaulieu, on the 28th, was already preparing to retreat behind the Po. The previous evening he had reached Oviglio, a few miles short of Alessandria, with thirteen battalions and twenty squadrons. His rearguard, of three battalions and two squadrons under Vukassovich, had remained at Castelnuovo Belbo, three miles from Nizza. On the 28th, Lipthay pulled back behind Acqui, and detachments were sent to secure the crossing over the Po at Valenza. Schübirz had begun extricating the remnant of the Auxiliary Corps, taking a somewhat round-about route towards Asti through Carmagnola, Poirino and Villanova. Bonaparte had tried to get this Corps included in the terms of the armistice, thereby neutralising it, but Colli had replied that it did not belong to his army, and that he had no jurisdiction over it.

After the cease-fire was signed, Murat was despatched to Paris to deliver the text to the Directors. Bonaparte also rapidly sent off letters to La Harpe and Augereau informing them of the agreement, and ordering La Harpe to go to Acqui immediately, and Augereau to Nizza. Sérurier was to go to Cherasco on the following day, and await orders, while Massena was ordered to Alba. Bonaparte also informed General de La Tour of the arrangements he had made for the hand-over of Cuneo, and requested him to speed the order to surrender Alessandria or Tortona, saying that one of his divisions had already moved in that direction. At 6 p.m. on the 28th, Cuneo was consigned to Despinoy, who garrisoned it with men from Fiorella's brigade.

Beaulieu was not yet prepared to abandon hope of inconveniencing the French advance, and on the 29th he took up a position that would permit him to seize Alessandria or Tortona if the opportunity should arise. He placed his HQ in Marengo – which in 1800 was to lend its name to one of Bonaparte's most famous battles – and his main force of nine battalions and ten squadrons moved into position there, under Sebottendorf. The town of Tortona was also occupied by two battalions. An invitation to the garrisons of the citadels of Alessandria and Tortona to hand them over to the Imperial troops was met with a decided negative, so the Austrians decided to sit and wait until the bridge at Valenza was completed. Oviglio was the site of Vukassovich's rearguard, while Schübirz was at Felizzano, half-way between Asti and Alessandria with the Auxiliary Corps and four squadrons of Uhlans. Finally, Lipthay was at Cassine, eight miles to the north of Acqui.

The process of turning the French army back towards Alessandria and Tortona proceeded without delay, but not in haste, and on the 29th and 30th the various divisions carried out carefully planned moves in that direction by different routes. On the 30th, Bonaparte wrote to Faipoult saying, 'Beaulieu flees so fast we cannot catch him', a misleading statement, in view of the fact that Beaulieu had been stock-still near Alessandria since the day they had started to move in his direction. The rest of the letter is a characteristic example of Bonaparte's boundless desire to know about an area in which he was to be campaigning:

> Send me notes on the geography, history, politics and topography of the Imperial fiefs which border Genoa, so that I can take as much advantage of them as I can. Send me notes on the dukes of Parma, Piacenza and Modena: the forces that they have in being, the strongholds they have, and what the wealth of their country consists in. Above all, send me a list of the paintings, statues, collections and curiosities there are in Milan, Parma, Piacenza, Modena and Bologna.[2]

Bonaparte was not planning a cultural tour, of course. What he wanted was a list of the best items to remove and ship off to Paris as a kind of 'official plunder'. In a second letter to Faipoult he expresses his view of the political state of the country, saying: 'There is not the first idea of a revolution in Piedmont, and France would not wish, I think, to make one at its expense.'[3]

There are many curious transitions of subject among Bonaparte's letters, which sometimes pass from matters of international diplomacy or politics to the most homely concerns, testifying to the extraordinary range of business he had to deal with. Nestling among the other letters written that day is one to Commissary Lambert that gives abundant proof that an army 'marches on its stomach':

> Bread will no longer be baked at any bakery on the Riviera of Genoa, except for the garrisons. It will no longer be baked at Cuneo or Mondovì, nor at Ceva, nor at Ponte Derlin, except for the garrisons. It will be baked at Cherasco for the division of General Sérurier, and at Acqui for the other divisions of the army. You will keep a magazine of a thousand sacks of flour at Cairo, which you will supply from Savona.[4]

The bridge over the Po at Valenza was completed that day, and Beaulieu began to draw back his troops to make the crossing. His own HQ was moved to Valenza, along with Sebottendorf's troops. Lipthay halted temporarily at Cantalupo in the morning, and at midday passed through Alessandria and over the Tanaro, stopping a mile or so before Valenza. Vukassovich took up a position at Solario, two and a half miles west of Alessandria. On the left wing, Roselmini moved to Tortona, leaving a rearguard to observe the Orba. His orders were to go through Tortona, bear to the east, and move to Voghera, in order to make a crossing further down the Po.

The French were similarly preparing for a river crossing. At 5 a.m. on the 2nd, Massena started out for Castellazzo, about four miles south of Alessandria, where he had been instructed to seize all the boats he could find nearby on the rivers Bormida and Orba, for the purpose of building a bridge. La Harpe had been ordered to take the right wing to Tortona that day, and Augereau was to move to Bosco, in the centre.

Augereau and Beaumont, who was now commanding part of the cavalry, both sent out mounted patrols to search for the enemy, a change of procedure made advisable by the change of terrain. The army was now moving out of the mountains onto the broad, flat plain of the Po, which gave more scope for the use of mounted troops, and presented the French with something of a problem. In a letter to the Directory of the 29th Bonaparte had remarked that: 'If I have some risks to run in Lombardy, it is because of the enemy cavalry.'[5] He knew that his own was in a poor state.

Sebottendorf crossed the Po on the morning of the 2nd, and took up a position twelve miles north-east of Valenza behind a stream called the Erbognone, between Valeggio and Ottobiano, where the HQ was also established. Lipthay followed, and placed himself a few miles closer to Valenza, at Lomello, on the Agogna. Here he was joined by Schübirz. The last to cross at Valenza was Vukassovich, who had the bridge demolished, then formed a cordon along the river from a point opposite Valenza to the confluence of the Agogna. Roselmini, still on the other bank, continued his march and went via Casteggio, which is on the edge of the foothills opposite Pavia, to Casatisma, a couple of miles closer to the Po.

At this point in operations, Bonaparte effected a quite significant change in the organisation of his army. On 3 May he issued orders to form an élite advance-guard consisting of combined grenadier and carabinier battalions and a small detachment of cavalry. There were four battalions of grenadiers, and two of carabiniers, amounting to about 3,500 men, with 1,500 cavalry. Orders were given for the units to be ready in two days. The commander was General Dallemagne. It is probably not stretching things too far to see in this small band of hardened fighters the forerunners of the Imperial Guard – the best men selected to do the toughest jobs.

The overall organisation of the army had also changed, because instead of having the advance-guard of two divisions under Massena and the 'Battle Divisions' of Augereau and Sérurier, there now stood four divisions of equal status, La Harpe having emerged from the shadow of Massena, the latter taking the division of Meynier, who had been relegated to duties in the second line. With the death of Stengel, the command of the cavalry had passed to Kilmaine.

Various deficiencies had emerged in the previous two weeks, and Bonaparte used the lull in the campaigning to remedy whatever he could. The cavalry was in a particularly bad condition, being under-strength and hampered by a lack of good horses, defects that could not be cured in a short time. Its discipline also left much to be desired, which was indicative of poor leadership at many levels. Once again, it took time for more effective commanders to appear and take charge.

The artillery was a problem, being weaker than Bonaparte desired, and he was not at all happy with its commander, Dujard. The latter had once been Bonaparte's own commander, and he was reluctant to dismiss him, keeping him on until his faults could no longer be tolerated. The move out of the mountains was also likely to bring the artillery into greater prominence, and Bonaparte could not afford it to be anything less than efficient.

The divisional staffs did not meet with Bonaparte's approval, either. Only Adjutant-General Boyer of Augereau's division sent in the proper returns and journals of march. Adjutant-General Monnier of Massena's division sometimes provided them, but the others were negligent. This was something that those supreme organisers, Bonaparte and Berthier, were likely to find particularly trying, and no doubt the guilty found themselves on the receiving end of some sharp complaints.

The administration was also chaotic, or corrupt, causing the army to 'die of starvation in the midst of plenty'.[6] This accentuated the problem of pillaging, which still went on at an unacceptable rate. The 25th demi-brigade, which had long given trouble, according to Massena, was particularly disorderly, and so was the cavalry. Saliceti even had his seal stolen, which added to the confusion because of the issue of forgeries in his name, so an order of the day of 5 May stated that papers with his seals were not valid. Joubert, who was a great disciplinarian, complained:

> Everything would go very well if the soldiers did not abandon
> themselves to pillage: not a day passes without some pillagers

being shot. Despite this severity the mania does not stop: the country people are arming themselves. In the meantime discipline is beginning to get better: the soldiers see that they will be murdered if they stay behind, and this consideration stops them more than the examples that we make. In the meantime these are frequent.[7]

On 3 May there was a rush of highly significant activity. La Harpe was sent instructions to enter Tortona immediately, while Augereau was ordered to send Rusca via Castelnuovo Scrivia to the banks of the Po during the day. He was to establish a battery of guns there and gather as many of the boats navigating the Po as he could. These were to be held at the place where the battery was positioned. Massena was similarly ordered to send an advance-guard to the Po via Sale, whose commander was to do exactly the same as Rusca. He was also to send a guard to Bassignana, four miles east of Valenza, to seize the boats there. Moreover, both divisions were ordered to move closer to the Po. Yet another order instructed both the commander of the engineers and the head of the bridging service, Andréossy, to go to Bosco immediately. All this clearly presaged an attempt to cross the river. Sérurier, who was some distance behind in Alba, was ordered to move to Asti on the following day.

It was not all work though. Massena and Joubert seem to have been among the first French to arrive in Alessandria, and caused a great deal of interest among the inhabitants. Joubert describes how they sent a message to the governor:

We told him that we were not coming with hostile intentions, and without waiting we entered with forty dragoons. It was raining heavily. All the windows were filled with heads, and all the streets crowded with curious people. The parade ground filled up in an instant, and we were obliged to make our way through an enormous crowd that had come to see its conquerors. The people were neither happy nor sad. One could only perceive gestures of curiosity, and the tranquillity that the armistice had brought. We went down to Government House. *Il cavaliere Solaro*, decorated with the insignia of all the grand orders, arrived from the citadel. He invited us to dinner, made Massena and I get into his carriage, and had our officers accompanied by some colonels. When I saw myself in the citadel, separated from our troops, before the armistice was officially recognised, I feared that we would be held for exchange with general officers taken from the Piedmontese. I communicated my fears to Massena, who was also less than tranquil because he is from the County of Nice, though he has always served in France. We were repaid for our fear. We dined with three generals and four colonels. Nothing could have been more merry.[8]

Bonaparte arrived in Tortona in the afternoon of the 3rd, no doubt to a similar kind of reception. On the 4th he had an interview with Faipoult during which he most probably subjected him to a searching interrogation on every detail of the subjects he had mentioned in his letter of the 30th.

By 4 May, the Austrians had most of their troops concentrated at Lomello, Ottobiano and Sommo, Roselmini having crossed the Po just south of Pavia that day. In front of them was a long cordon observing the River Po from the confluence of the Sesia, a little west of Valenza, to that of the Olona, which was just beyond Pavia. Beaulieu's main objective was now to prevent the French from reaching Milan, and the floodplain of the Po did not offer much in the way of defensive positions to help him to achieve this. About the only obstacles were an abundance of water-courses, the most significant of which were the Po and the Ticino. There was little else that the Austrians could use to slow down a French advance towards Milan, so every effort had to be made to prevent the French from crossing these rivers. Naturally, the larger of them, the Po, provided the most effective barrier, and Beaulieu must have pinned much of his hopes on keeping the French on the far side of it until reinforcements could reach his depleted army from Austria.

For Bonaparte, the goal was to destroy Beaulieu's army, or drive it out of Lombardy completely, something that could most easily be achieved before his opponent could be much reinforced. But in order to do this he had to get across the Po. The way he achieved this provided his contemporaries with another piece of evidence of his superiority as a general. It has come to be considered, as David Chandler says, 'a classic'[9] of the military art, and an object lesson in how to carry out the crossing of a stretch of water in the vicinity of a large enemy force. Indeed, it must have provided inspiration to military men faced with similar problems right down to the Normandy landings in 1944, if not beyond. As so often in Bonaparte's style of war, the success was due to a combination of thoughtful planning, deceiving the enemy about his intentions, and speed of movement. His approach was once again based on Bourcet, and Du Teil, but with a river instead of mountains as the obstacle.

As Bonaparte knew, if Beaulieu could oppose his crossing with a large number of troops and artillery, he might be able to prevent it, or at least cause the French prohibitive casualties. But opposing the crossing required two things: knowing, or guessing, where it would take place, and being able to move enough troops to that point in time to oppose it. Bonaparte's problem was the reverse of this. If he could lead the enemy to believe he was intending to cross in one place, and then move his troops to another crossing-point quickly enough, he ought to be able to cross without difficulty.

The calculations that had to be made were complicated. First of all, would the enemy be deceived, and form the view that the French were going to cross at Valenza, which was the most obvious place for them to do so? If so, how long would that deception last before the truth was realised? Always supposing the deception was successful, it was necessary to choose the crossing-place with some care. It had to be suitable for building a bridge, or embarking and disembarking large numbers of men from boats, and it had to be the right distance away. The 'correct' distance was no easy thing to work out, because it depended on how long the deception lasted, and how fast both armies could march. Too close, and there was a risk of the enemy arriving before the crossing could be completed. Too far, and the enemy was bound to realise what was going on and would have plenty of time to arrange counter-measures.

Related to the choice of crossing-place was the question of what Bonaparte intended to do once he was on the other side of the river. Here again, Bonaparte's appreciation of the geography of the area, and what that signified when related to the Austrian line of communications, was fundamental to his strategic planning. The direct approach was pointless as far as he was concerned. Why cross at Valenza, which was the most heavily guarded crossing-point, and be faced, if he got across, with a frontal battle to try to smash through to Milan? Far better to do as he had done before, and skirt round the side to threaten to cut the Austrians off, thus forcing them to abandon their positions and retreat. If he could force them to fight a battle in a position that was disadvantageous to them, so much the better. It was probably only after careful calculation of speeds and distances and an attentive reading of de Maillebois' memoirs, with its descriptions of campaigning in the area in 1745–6, that Piacenza was chosen as the most likely crossing-point.[10]

The arrangements for the operation continued on 4 May, with various instructions for movement being issued. In addition, very obvious preparations for a crossing were made on the stretch of the Po near Valenza. Massena was ordered to move all the boats on the Tanaro and at Bassignana to a position opposite Sale – in other words very close to the confluence of the Tanaro and the Po. Both he and Augereau were instructed to stop all crossings of the Po, and all navigation on it, in the hope of making it more difficult for the enemy to find out what was happening on the opposite bank of the river. Rusca, meanwhile, was ordered to go along the Po from the Scrivia as far as the Coppa (opposite Pavia), and collect all the boats he could.

Bonaparte's deception does not seem to have been wholly effective, because Beaulieu received a report on 4 May that French troops were moving east. This raised the likelihood that the defensive line on the Agogna would be by-passed, so Beaulieu decided to move behind the Ticino. General Lipthay therefore set off the same day, and marched via Pavia to Belgioioso, five miles to its east, where he arrived on the morning of 5 May. He proceeded to form a cordon from the confluence of the Olona as far as that of the Lambro. Beaulieu kept the rest of his forces in their old positions on the 5th, which meant he was now covering a much greater stretch of the river, so his troops were spread more thinly. On the same day he took the precaution of ordering the castle of Milan and the fortress of Mantua to be put into a defensive state. In the case of the latter, this was vitally important, as it was the greatest stronghold in the Po valley, and the key to Austrian domination of Lombardy. Should the army be forced to retreat, there could be nothing more crucial than holding on to Mantua.

For the French, 5 May passed in carrying out the prescribed movement eastwards. La Harpe advanced from Tortona to Voghera, and Augereau took up a position on La Harpe's left. The cavalry also moved to Voghera. Massena began the work of constructing bridges, very ostentatiously, in the area of Sale, while Joubert moved to Casei Gerola, just west of Voghera. Sérurier left Asti and moved to Alessandria. All day there was a coming and going on the plain south of the Po. In the evening, a squadron of cavalry was sent nine miles beyond Casteggio, to Stradella, to requisition 15,000 rations of bread for the following day. Jean Lannes had evidently attracted the attention of his commander-in-chief, because he was sent a special order to go to Casteggio immediately and take command of three battalions of grenadiers. A mile from Casteggio was Montebello, the scene of the battle that was to give Lannes his ducal title under the Empire. Dallemagne, the overall commander of the new advance-guard, inspected his men and had cartridges and shoes issued.

At 6 a.m. on 6 May, the race began, with the advance-guard in the lead. By the evening it had reached Castel San Giovanni, half-way to Piacenza, having marched seventeen and a half miles in a day. La Harpe and the cavalry under Kilmaine followed, stopping for the night at Stradella, with Augereau a little behind them. Bonaparte himself hung on at Tortona till late, then galloped off to join the advance-guard at Castel San Giovanni, having sent a most revealing letter to the Directory sketching his plans:

This river [the Po] is very wide and very difficult to cross. My intention is to cross it as close to Milan as possible, so that I have no obstacle before arriving in that capital. By this measure I shall turn the three lines of defence that Beaulieu has arranged along the Agogna, the Terdoppio and the Ticino. I shall march today on Piacenza. Pavia has been turned, and if the enemy persists in defending this town, I shall be between him and his magazines. Boats and rafts are being constructed on all sides ... When will we cross the Po? Where will we cross? I do not know. If my movement on Piacenza decides Beaulieu to evacuate the Lomellina, I shall cross easily at Valenza. If Beaulieu remains ignorant of our march to Piacenza for forty-eight hours, and there are boats at that town, or materials to make rafts, I shall cross during the night.[11]

On the same day, Lipthay positioned himself at Porto Morone, exactly opposite Castel San Giovanni, and reported to Beaulieu that 'on the stretch of the river from the mouth of the Ticino as far as Piacenza, there are seven ferries or flying bridges, which would permit the crossing of several thousand French in a few hours if the river is not quickly occupied with troops'.[12] All reports received by Beaulieu on the movements of the French concurred in saying that the greater part of their army was moving towards Piacenza. Their left wing, however, remained in the area of Valenza, and it would be necessary to maintain a force to oppose it, if it should cross the Po at Valenza or nearby. Beaulieu now pulled back his main force about eight miles, in two columns under Sebottendorf and Pittoni, to Gropello. Vukassovich also withdrew from the banks of the Po, to a position behind the Agogna, at Valeggio, and somewhat further north at Cergnago.

The next day the French intended to cross the Trebbia into the lands of the Duke of Parma, who was technically at war with France, so there was no bowing and scraping. Instead, Bonaparte issued an extraordinarily peremptory summons to the governor of Piacenza: 'Having to confer with you, Sir, on subjects of the greatest importance, will you kindly come immediately to Castel San Giovanni. It will be necessary to be here before 2 a.m., since I have to be in the saddle at that time.'[13] It was not actually for a conference that the governor was thus courteously invited. 'My intention is to hold him as a hostage in order to be master of the dispositions in the town with regard to us,'[14] he informed Lanusse. The same letter also instructed Lanusse to depart immediately with Andréossy and 100 cavalry for Piacenza. They would send out patrols between the town and the Po, seize the ferry, and any boats they could find. They would also send for the mayor, and have him accompany them everywhere. They were to organise rations, and lodgings for the HQ.

The unfortunate governor of Piacenza arrived at the French HQ as bidden, and not only found himself a prisoner, but was led to believe that the French were intending to march on Parma to punish it for its hostility to France, unless the Duke would agree to certain conditions. Hours later, the French launched themselves over the border. At 4 a.m. on the 7th, Dallemagne left Castel San Giovanni with the advance-guard. Bonaparte and Kilmaine accompanied him, while the cavalry left Stradella an hour later. These two forces moved to Piacenza. La Harpe followed, but instead of crossing the Trebbia, he bore left towards the Po. The advance-guard reached Piacenza at 9 a.m., having covered nearly 30 miles in 27 hours.

Beaulieu was travelling in rather more leisurely fashion, and began by falling back to Pavia with his main force on the 7th. Lipthay was also instructed to move further down the Po, and occupy the stretch of the river between the Lambro and the Adda – right opposite Piacenza. Lipthay was also to send two battalions and two squadrons with some guns to Casalmaggiore to guard the crossing over the Po there, and to secure the army's link with Mantua through Pizzighet-tone (where there was a bridge over the Adda) and Cremona. Lipthay therefore moved over the Lambro towards Piacenza in the morning with eight battalions and eight squadrons. He was supported by Colonel Wetzel, who moved to Corteolona and Santa Cristina (oppo-site Stradella) with three battalions and two squadrons from the main force. Beaulieu seems to have believed that these precautions would be enough to prevent the French from crossing the Po at Piacenza or Cremona, and that he would have plenty of time to move up in support of Lipthay. In this he was no doubt influenced by the knowl-edge that the French had no bridging train, which led him to assume that it would take them a long time to arrange a crossing. Once again, he had underestimated his opponent, who was not prepared to let rivers stand in his way any more than mountains.

Having arrived at Piacenza, Bonaparte no doubt immediately went to inspect the river. It was about a quarter of a mile wide, and flowed very rapidly over sand-banks and islets. It was bordered by a wide, flat plain of alluvial land, with low banks covered in clumps of bushes and small trees. A crossing-place was chosen a little upriver from the town, towards the confluence of the Trebbia. On the other side of the Po some 150 enemy hussars were observed. The commander of these must have been more than a little disturbed to find large numbers of the enemy on the far bank, and rapidly sent off a rider with a message. By midday, Lipthay knew that the French were preparing to cross the river, and at this alarming news hastened his march to intercept them. Bonaparte also sent urgent messages to Augereau and Massena: 'The General-in-Chief has decided to cross the Po with the advance-guard of grenadiers and the 1,800 cavalry which follow them. The division of General La Harpe will follow the advance-guard, and will cross during the night.'[15] Augereau and Massena were ordered to move to Piacenza by forced marches.

This urgency contrasts noticeably with the unhurried progress of Beaulieu, who admittedly was not yet aware of the danger to him, and took a three-hour rest in Pavia. Afterwards, he continued his march to Belgioioso, taking only Pittoni and Schübirz with seven battalions and twelve squadrons. Sebottendorf remained behind the Ticino at Pavia with six battalions and six squadrons, guarding the magazines. He was told that if an enemy advance made it necessary to abandon Pavia, the stone bridge over the river was to be demolished. The upper Ticino was covered by Colli, who had now returned to the Austrian service, with a small force of two battalions and two squadrons. Vukassovich was acting as rearguard with two battalions and two squadrons along the Terdoppio, parallel with the Ticino, in front of Pavia. Roselmini covered the Po from Pavia to the Olona with two battalions, and positioned another two battalions and four squadrons behind them in support. It was all very professional, and totally useless.

At about 2 p.m., the French advance-guard crossed the Po, with Lannes and his troops in the lead. There was a ferry available that could carry 500 men or 50 horses, but it took half an hour to reach the other side, so to save time, Lannes seized a boat. Having arrived on the far side, a brief exchange of fire was enough to scatter the enemy hussars. The rest of the advance-guard rapidly crossed in his train and began to establish themselves. Now that the far bank was in French hands, Andréossy was ordered to finish the 'flying bridge' he had already begun, then build a normal bridge. La Harpe's division and the cavalry began to cross, making what use they could of the ferry, boats and rafts. The crossing carried on all afternoon.

On the far side, Lipthay, with his 4,000 infantry and 1,000 cavalry, had hurried towards the crossing-point during the afternoon, but only got as far as Guardamiglio, five miles from the Po, when he ran into the French outposts. These he attacked and drove back, but he was forced to break off the action when darkness fell. In the face of superior forces, who moreover were increasing with the passing of every hour, he moved back to the village of Fombio to await the reinforcements he had requested from Beaulieu.

Unfortunately for the Austrians, it was not the only bridgehead they had to contend with. Augereau had begun his march towards Castel San Giovanni at 6 a.m. on the 7th, and had arrived there at 5.30 p.m. He had then sent out a reconnaissance along the Po to find a crossing-place, and four and a half miles beyond Castel San Giovanni found a ferry with a light Austrian defence on the far bank. It was not as good as the place where La Harpe was crossing, but Augereau felt it had the advantage of giving protection to the left flank of the army and suggested crossing there. Bonaparte agreed. Augereau's men found some barges carrying salt, but had no means of unloading them. Nevertheless, they were able to use them to cross the river, and by nightfall his first echelons were on the far side of the river, moving towards La Harpe's division.

The latter continued to move its troops to the northern bank during the night using 48 large torches to illuminate the crossing. Boats continued to criss-cross the water as first Franceschi, then Vial, stood on the southern side to organise and hasten the crossing, placing the cavalry on the ferry, and the infantry in the smaller boats. Before midnight, Chasseloup was on the far side with his engineers and sappers, rapidly constructing entrenchments to defend the bridgehead. La Harpe's divisional HQ was established between the river and Lipthay's position at Fombio.

By first light on 8 May, the French were well established on the left bank of the Po. The advance-guard was all across, with 3,500 infantry and 1,500 cavalry. La Harpe's division, consisting of the 3rd Light, the old 14th Line, the 51st and 75th Line, totalling about 6,500 men, was either wholly or mostly on the northern side of the river. Augereau, whose crossing-place was more difficult, was feeding his troops over more slowly. His division consisted of the 27th Light, 29th Light, 4th Line and 18th Line, for a total of 7,000 men. Although the precise strength of the Austrian army would not have been known to Bonaparte, it was clearly essential to concentrate his troops as quickly as possible in case he was attacked by a large part of it. A slight worry, therefore, was that the army was still split, with Massena and Sérurier yet to effect the crossing. However, they were approaching, though Sérurier did not receive his orders until late, and only arrived in Voghera during the day instead of Casteggio. Massena managed to reach Castel San Giovanni, so he was at least within striking distance of the crossing. The artillery was way behind, despite Bonaparte's constant efforts to extract more speed and activity from Dujard.

It was perhaps fortunate for Bonaparte, therefore, that the Austrian army was not well positioned to oppose the French. Although returns show that Beaulieu had a total of 36 battalions and 44 squadrons at his disposal on 7 May, totalling 20,691 infantry and 5,441 cavalry, with roughly 70 battalion guns and an artillery reserve of 53 guns and sixteen howitzers, these were spread over such a wide area in an attempt to cover as much of Lombardy as possible, that they could not rapidly be brought to oppose the French crossing. This was amply proved by the events of 8 May. Beaulieu had intended to spend that morning in Belgioioso letting his troops cook and eat, then at midday move to cross the Olona and march to Santa Cristina, four miles to the east, which would serve as a central point from which to support both Sebottendorf and Lipthay. This plan was abandoned when, during the course of the morning, he received Lipthay's startling news that the French were across the Po at Piacenza, and he duly set off towards him with nine battalions and twelve squadrons. Lipthay was more than eighteen miles away, however, and by 5 p.m. Beaulieu had only reached Chignolo, still a good ten miles short.

This inability to get supporting troops to the French bridgehead meant that Lipthay was faced with an almost hopeless task, though he defended as long as he could. During the morning of the 8th the French took the village of Guardamiglio 'without resistance',[16] but Fombio was more difficult as it was defended by three or four cannon, and the Austrians had used the night to improve its defences. The attack on it was launched about midday. As usual, the French tried to exploit their rapidity of movement and cut the Austrians off. Although the landscape of this flat river-plain could not be farther removed from the mountains of the first ten days of the campaign, it was still terrain that favoured the French. The countryside on the banks of the Po was marked by numerous rice fields, irrigation channels, and dikes with roads or pathways running along the top. This made it difficult to move in large formations, because of the need to keep to the paths and cross so many water-courses.

According to Bonaparte's report to the Directory, the advance-guard went forward in three columns, each of two battalions, Lannes on the left, Lanusse on the main road in the centre, and Dallemagne on the right. La Harpe followed in support. The intention seems to have been for Lannes to make for Somaglia, about a mile west of Fombio, to try to cut off Lipthay from any reinforcements arriving from that direction. Dallemagne was to make for San Floriano, which was a mile to the east of Fombio, and try to reach Codogno, in its rear. The details of the combat are unclear, but according to the history of the 4th Line, serious losses were sustained during the attack on the village.

Although the Austrian hussars succeeded in driving the French away on at least one occasion, and Lipthay was managing to hold Fombio, it was clear to him that he had been cut off from the main army, and that the French were trying to encircle him. He therefore decided to retire via Codogno to Pizzighettone and try to keep the road to Cremona and Mantua open for the main army. In this he was ably assisted by the Austrian and Neapolitan cavalry, and reached Codogno in good order. The French, however, attacked them again and carabiniers of the 17th Light took a number of prisoners. At that point Lipthay, who had sent a detachment of Uhlans to Pizzighettone in the morning, received a message from them to the effect that there were no enemy in Pizzighettone itself, but the road to it was already overrun with French troops. There was no time to lose, and Lipthay rapidly moved to fight his way through. Not all of his troops succeeded in this, and three battalions, of IR Thurn, IR Nádasdy and IR Alvinczy, were cut off, and had to turn towards Lodi, fourteen miles north-west, where there was another bridge over the Adda. It was evening by the time Lipthay arrived in Pizzighettone with most of his troops, harried all the way by the French cavalry. Lieutenant Desvernois of the 7th Hussars claimed in his memoirs that he was so close on the heels of the Austrians that 'the drawbridge was raised under the hooves of my horse'.[17]

Lipthay immediately sent his own cavalry over the Adda, while the ramparts of Pizzighettone were manned and provided with cannon. A little gunfire encouraged the pursuing French to pull back to a more respectful distance. During the evening Lipthay also sent Colonel Count Sola to Casalmaggiore, with three battalions and five squadrons, retaining only two battalions and three squadrons at Pizzighettone. In the fighting of these two days, Lipthay had lost ten officers, 558 men and 79 horses.[18]

Since the defences of Pizzighettone were not in a good state, Lipthay did what he could to make temporary repairs, while La Harpe took up positions around Codogno watching the roads to Lodi and Pavia. Bonaparte went to reconnoitre Pizzighettone (in a very bad mood, according to Desvernois) and was greeted with more cannon-fire. Having told La Harpe to be most vigilant, particularly along the road to Casalpusterlengo to the north-west, he returned to Piacenza for the night.

Beaulieu, as we have seen, had reached Chignolo by 5 p.m., and he continued his march from there via Orio to Ospedaletto, where he placed three battalions and his cavalry. He was now about four miles from Fombio, but as he did not know where the enemy was, and could not confidently direct his forces on a single point, he ordered a number of other battalions to fan out to his left and front: one at Senna, one at Somaglia, two towards Fombio and two towards Codogno. A much-delayed message from Lipthay finally reached him in the evening, reporting that he was still in Fombio, and had beaten back the enemy. This was no longer true, of course, and the battalions that were ordered to move in his direction could only find large numbers of the enemy. Later in the evening they were able to confirm that Lipthay had been driven back by superior numbers, and that Fombio and Codogno were in the hands of the French. Beaulieu was therefore cut off from Lipthay, and from the road through Pizzighettone. In these circumstances, he decided that he would have to try to force a way through to Lipthay by capturing Codogno as soon as it was light.

The force that he had already sent in that direction was under the command of Schübirz, and consisted of two battalions of IR Reisky (about 1,000 men) and four squadrons of Uhlans (580 men). Schübirz, who had gone ahead with his cavalry, arrived at Casalpusterlengo without problems and pushed on towards Codogno in total darkness. Despite having no orders to do so, Schübirz decided to attempt to capture the town by a surprise attack. At getting on for 10 p.m. he approached Codogno, overran the pickets, and clashed with the outposts. The entry of the Austrians into the town was made simpler by the fact that the French had only barricaded the access road to it with overturned wagons. Captain Count Czernin made his way forward with a company of IR Reisky, and was soon followed by two more and some Uhlans. Soon, much of the town had been captured, and a number of prisoners taken.

At the time, La Harpe was dining with his staff in the house of Count Lamberti, and when they were informed of the enemy action, the French officers immediately mounted and dashed to the centre of the town to discover what was going on. The group reached the main square just after the 51st Line, which was marching through from Fombio, and had not the least idea of any danger. As the 51st reached the square, a fusillade of bullets struck them, killing and wounding a number of men, and in panic and surprise the French infantrymen blasted off volleys into the blackness of the square. La Harpe, not believing that there could be enemy troops in the town, made his way forward to see what the trouble was. After chaotic moments and sporadic firing, torches of burning straw were lit, to reveal a large square with 300 Austrians on the one hand, hugging the side of the church, and on the other the 51st lined up against the shops. After a short fight the Austrians were made prisoner, and La Harpe's staff had the leisure to realise that he was no longer with them. A frantic search revealed him lying dead on the ground, hit by a single bullet. Sergeant Rattier, of the 51st, commented: 'I will not say, like many others, that he was killed by our troops, observing that the enemy was firing, just like us, on the same street. Moreover, such a dark night could not permit anyone to make a just judgement on the matter.'[19] In his report to the Directory of 9 May, Bonaparte wrote that the army had lost one of its best generals.

The panic and confusion among the French was not diminished by the loss of the guiding hand of the divisional commander, and the Austrians, having penetrated Codogno in various places, began a mortal game of hide-and-seek, and shooting at shadows. Berthier was informed of La Harpe's death at 4 a.m., and of the chaos at Codogno, and went to take things in hand. He was joined by the 75th, which arrived from Fombio with General Ménard, followed by the 17th Light. In the inky darkness the fighting went on, the occasional flashes of musket shots revealing the position of a combatant, but not his nationality. Anything that moved or made a noise became a target. Eventually, however, the odds started to tilt in favour of the French, and Schübirz began to feel sure that he was facing far superior forces. Around daybreak on the 9th, having received no support from Beaulieu, and knowing that Lipthay, whom he had been sent to help, was no longer in reach, he ordered his troops to pull back to Casalpusterlengo. With daylight, Berthier could do more to establish order, but the loss of La Harpe was a blow, and made organisation more difficult. Only the advance-guard of his division, led by the 75th, followed the Austrian column towards Casalpusterlengo, where it arrived at about 10 a.m.

The lack of French pressure at this moment, occasioned both by Schübirz's attack and the fact that the French were still bringing men across the Po, proved to be something of a let-off for Beaulieu. He had, by this time, reflected on his situation, and countermanded his previous orders. He realised that there was no hope of extricating all his troops by marching them across the face of the French army towards Pizzighettone, added to which he did not know for certain that the latter was still in Austrian hands. Moreover, if the French had also managed to cross the Po between the Adda and Mantua, he would undoubtedly be forced to retreat northwards into the Tyrol. All this meant that the only sensible course open to him was to try to cross the Adda at Lodi. He therefore issued orders during the night for a retreat on this point, struck camp early in the morning of the 9th, and hastened to make his way there via Casalpusterlengo. He arrived at Lodi at midday, and in the absence of any news of Lipthay, feared that he was now in great danger of being cut off not only from Mantua but also from the Adige valley. This would have been disastrous, as his main supply route and line of retreat lay along this valley, where the Tyrol reached its most southerly point near Belluno Veronese, about fifteen miles from the northern edge of the flood-plain of the Po.

At about the same time, Colli received orders to retire to Milan, where he was to place a small garrison in the citadel. He duly carried out his march during the afternoon and evening. By the time his men arrived, the Archduke Ferdinand, who had spent 25 years as governor of Lombardy, had decided that the French were getting much too close, and had fled towards Bergamo. Beaulieu was apparently not yet ready to give up, because at 4 p.m. he wrote to Vienna saying he had decided to march on Mantua. Two hours later he learnt that Lipthay was still in Pizzighettone, which convinced him that the French were not in a position to reach Cremona before he could. He therefore issued orders to march there with all speed so as to gain the most direct road to Mantua. Lipthay was ordered to leave a weak garrison behind and withdraw to Cremona. If Pizzighettone held for a short time, the army would be able to concentrate at Cremona and put itself in order. Sebottendorf, in the meantime, had moved off from Pavia late in the afternoon, and was carrying out a forced march towards Lodi. Beaulieu, leaving four battalions and four squadrons under General Schübirz to wait for Sebottendorf, crossed the Adda at 10 p.m. and made for Crema.

Part of Bonaparte's time on the morning of the 9th had to be spent in diplomacy. The Duke of Modena advised that he was sending plenipotentiaries to meet the French, while representatives of the Duke of Parma had already arrived and were deep in discussions. These representatives displayed great eagerness on the part of their master to be left in peace and avoid the prolonged presence of a French army on his territory. Luckily for him and his subjects, the territory was of little strategic interest to the French, who merely deprived him of a substantial cash contribution and a number of valuable paintings, including a Correggio. The cease-fire agreement was signed during the morning.

As far as military matters were concerned, the army was still split by the Po, though during the 9th most of it was brought to the northern side. The exception was Sérurier's division, which was still at Tortona, being obliged to make a forced march the following day to reach the crossing. Massena's division, which had marched 50 miles in the most dilapidated state, with its footwear in appalling condition, reached the crossing on the morning of the 9th, its numbers reduced by exhausted soldiers falling behind. By the evening, it was mostly on the northern side of the Po. Augereau's division also continued to cross during the day, and by the evening it was all on the left bank, though his troops were exhausted and disorderly, carrying out much looting. 'I contain my division, but will I be able to for long?'[20] he warned. Bonaparte was well aware of the problems. In a letter to Carnot written that day, he commented that 'we often have to shoot men, because some are incorrigible, and cannot control themselves'.[21] In preparation for his next moves, Bonaparte carried out some more minor retouches to his organisation, placing the advance-guard under Massena's supreme tutelage, while also leaving him the command of his division. He detached most of the cavalry accompanying the infantry divisions and placed it directly under Kilmaine.

By the end of the day, the operation to cross the Po had been largely completed. La Harpe's division, temporarily under the command of

Ménard, now formed the right of the army, watching the Adda and Pizzighettone. The advance-guard was a short way beyond Casalpusterlengo, observing the road towards Lodi. Behind it, at Casalpusterlengo itself, was Massena's division with the cavalry. Augereau was on the left, and during the day had moved from Ospedaletto to Borghetto Lodigiano, sending patrols towards Lodi and along the Lambro towards the Po. It was now time for the army to move out of the rather restricted area around the bridgehead, and into Lombardy.

NOTES

1. Napoleon. *Correspondance de Napoléon Ier publiée par ordre de l'empereur Napoléon III.* Paris, 1858-69, no. 257.
2. Ibid., no. 280.
3. Ibid., no. 281.
4. Ibid., no. 288.
5. Ibid., no. 266.
6. Bouvier, F. *Bonaparte en Italie, 1796.* Paris, 1899, p. 465.
7. Chevrier, E. *Le général Joubert d'après sa correspondance.* Paris, 1884, p. 36.
8. Ibid., p. 35.
9. Chandler, D. G. *The Campaigns of Napoleon.* London, 1966, p. 81.
10. Interestingly, Piacenza is now the home of the Italian army bridging school. In the words of the hotelier the author stayed with, 'Every now and then, when they don't know what to do, they build a bridge.'
11. Napoleon. 1858–69, op. cit., no. 337.
12. Schels, J. B. 'Die Kriegsereignisse in Italien vom 15 April bis 16 Mai 1796, mit dem Gefechte bei Lodi.' *Oesterreichische Militärische Zeitschrift,* Bd. 2; Bd. 4 (1825), p. 215.
13. Napoleon. 1858–69, op. cit., no. 347.
14. Ibid., no. 349.
15. Ibid., no. 350.
16. La Harpe to Bonaparte, Bouvier, op. cit., p. 494.
17. Desvernois, N. P. *Mémoires du général baron Desvernois ... d'après les manuscrits originaux, avec une introduction et des notes par A. Dufourcq. 1789–1815.* Paris, 1898, p. 43.

18. Schels, op. cit., p. 225.

19. Rattier, J.-H. 'Campagne d'Italie (1796): notes d'un sergent-major."
Revue rétrospective, XX (1894), pp. 225–6. As Rattier indicates, there is
more than one version of La Harpe's death. His own is supported by
Landrieux, who was there, and the *Historique* of the 51st, which was
written about a year after the event. Bouvier dedicates a part of his
appendices to a discussion of the various versions of the tragic death of
the Swiss general. The truth, of course, will never be known. Landrieux,
in his memoirs, says the Austrians were bridging troops, who would
have been easily recognisable as such because of their blue uniforms.

20. Bouvier, op. cit., p. 505.

21. Napoleon. 1858–69, op. cit., no. 366.

13

LODI

During the night of 9/10 May, reports reaching Bonaparte indicated the Austrians were everywhere in hasty retreat, but it was difficult to estimate their overall strength and the direction in which their main force was marching. Bonaparte left Piacenza at 1 a.m. and reached Casalpusterlengo at 3 a.m. on the 10th, where he found Massena and Kilmaine. Augereau had reported that he thought Beaulieu was making for Lodi, but since he did not know if any Austrian troops remained between Pavia and Lodi and along the Lambro, Augereau proposed to carry out a reconnaissance in the morning towards Belgioioso. Nobody wanted a repeat of the surprise at Dego. Bonaparte agreed, but Kilmaine was sent with 500 cavalry to reconnoitre towards Pavia, while Augereau was told to reconnoitre from Borghetto towards Lodi, to bring him into proximity with Massena and the bulk of the cavalry. He was told to follow the enemy 'as closely as possible'[1] without compromising himself. Massena, with the advance-guard in front, was to throw out patrols to within three or four miles of Lodi. Sérurier, still on the far bank of the Po, was hurrying towards the crossing, and was to cross during the afternoon or evening. Marmont reconnoitred Pizzighettone, but though it seemed in a poor state it was not possible to take it easily, so Ménard remained there with La Harpe's division, covering the flank and rear of the French army from any attack by the Austrians through Pizzighettone.

Sebottendorf, meanwhile, had been making for Lodi as fast as he could. His troops had carried out an exhausting forced march which had continued all night, and they began to trail into the town during the morning, overcome with fatigue. According to an account written by a local, as soon as they reached the massive town square, they fell down and went to sleep there and could hardly be roused from their slumbers by the sticks of the corporals.[2] By 9 a.m. the last battalion was clearing Sant'Angelo Lodigiano, still twelve and a half miles south-west of Lodi.

Since there had never been any intention to hold Lodi, as soon as the first of Sebottendorf's men had arrived, General Schübirz began to withdraw his four battalions and four squadrons, and took the road towards Crema, in the wake of Beaulieu, who had spent the night there, but was now marching south towards Pizzighettone. While awaiting the last of his troops, Sebottendorf detached General Nicoletti with one battalion of IR Toscana, two battalions of IR Strassoldo and two squadrons of Erdödy Hussars (1,958 men in total) to Corte Palasio, about an hour's march southwards along the left bank of the Adda. He also positioned his eight squadrons of Neapolitan cavalry (1,092 men) half an hour's march beyond Lodi at Fontana.

As a result of these detachments, the force that Sebottendorf had in Lodi – or would have when it all arrived – amounted to 6,577 men. These included:

Regiment	Strength
IR Terzi	3 battns
IR Belgioioso	1 battn
Carlstädter Grenzers	2 battns
Warasdiner Grenzers	1 battn
IR Thurn	1 battn
IR Nádasdy	1 battn
IR Alvinczy	some coys
Erzherzog Joseph Hussars	4 sqdns
Uhlans	2 sqdns

Some of the infantry battalions were very weak indeed. That of IR Belgioioso, for example, numbered only 311 men. The strongest was that of the Warasdiner Grenzers, which had 1,262 men. The battalion of IR Nádasdy (623 men) and two squadrons of Uhlans (286 men) were placed before the town of Lodi, under Roselmini, to receive the last troops as they arrived. On the other bank of the Adda, Sebottendorf placed the three battalions of Croats, supported by eight guns from the reserve, and their own six battalion guns. These were arranged to enfilade the bridge. The remaining five battalions and six squadrons were placed several hundred paces behind the Croats.[3]

It was at about 9 a.m. that the French advance-guard had come upon the Austrian rearguard consisting of two battalions of Carlstädter Grenzers under the orders of Vukassovich. These were attacked, and a skirmish developed, during which the Croats moved back towards Lodi, which they reached without suffering serious losses. At 11.30 a.m., Dallemagne attacked Roselmini's screening force, which was unable to resist for long before having to pull back into the town. The gates were then closed. Finding this, 'The French then deviated towards Colombiana Alta, not forgetting to pay a visit to the inn called "Due Chiavi", just outside the gate, taking everything they required ...'[4] Others continued the tour of the walls, looking for a way into the town.

The walls of Lodi presented no great obstacle to Dallemagne's grenadiers. Not only were they in great disrepair, but they were only about ten feet high. The history of the 32nd Line recounts that five of its men, Sulpice, Cabrol, Galthier, Brachenet and Léon Aune, managed to climb over the walls and open the gate. The last of these men had already distinguished himself at Dego, and was to become something of a legend, earning from Bonaparte the appreciative words, 'after Bennezet, you were the bravest grenadier in the Army of Italy'.[5] Having found a way into the town, the grenadiers pursued the Austrians in their withdrawal towards the bridge, which the latter rapidly crossed.

The bridge, which was to become so famous, was situated a short distance from the city walls, which were bordered by a stretch of water acting as a moat. Just inside the walls was an open space, or square, with the town gate on one side of it. The gate was flanked by a guard tower and a toll-house on the northern side, and a short distance away on the southern side, outside the gate, was a small church. The road did not lead straight from the gate to the bridge, but had a slight 's' bend, the bridge being a little upriver from the gate. Between the walls and the bank of the river there were several houses, so that the gate was not plainly visible from the opposite side of the river, except from a position a few yards upriver. On the northern side of the road, between the walls and the bridge, was a small building housing a famous majolica factory. Completing this collection of obstacles was a row of trees lining the bank to the south of the bridge, another in front of the majolica factory, and a statue of St John of Nepomuk, which had been erected at the end of the bridge by a devout Austrian colonel.

The bridge itself was a very simple structure, based on wooden piles driven vertically into the river bed every four or five yards. The gaps were spanned with wooden beams laid horizontally, over the top of which was spread a layer of gravel, which was periodically renewed. The bridge was about 200 yards long and 20–25 feet wide. About 60 yards before reaching the side the Austrians were defending, the bridge passed over a sand-bank or island some 35 yards wide, beyond which was another stretch of water. When the water was at its normal level, the roadway on the bridge stood about ten feet above it.[6]

The end of the bridge on the 'Austrian' side of the river was surrounded by disused fortifications that had been intended to prevent access to the bridge from the direction of Crema. There were also some farmhouses nearby, and on the banks were numerous very vigorous trees. In terms of its defensive possibilities, this bank of the river suffered from the great disadvantage of being lower than that on which Lodi was built.

According to most sources, none of the Austrian commanders had made any arrangements to destroy the bridge and thereby prevent the French from chasing them any further. However, one witness, Vigo-Roussillon of the 32nd Line, says that when they got to the bridge there were men working on it, and that some light artillery was brought up to fire on them and drive them away.[7] If it is true that no preparations had been made to destroy the bridge – an easy task because it could simply be burnt – it was a surprising omission. However, the French now found the bridge intact, providing a clear opportunity to force a crossing and press the pursuit of the much-harassed enemy, giving him no time to settle and recuperate. The only disincentive was that the bridge was heavily enfiladed, and the attacking troops would be completely exposed to the defensive fire for its entire length.

The opposing forces now took up positions facing each other. The battalion of IR Nádasdy was placed nearest the bridge, with the three Croat battalions, to cover the eight cannon of the artillery reserve.

Sebottendorf's other soldiers, who had been cooking a meal, soon joined the action. Having appraised the situation, Sebottendorf decided that it was not advisable to retire in daylight, and opted to fight on until darkness fell, when he had more hope of effecting a successful retreat.

Bonaparte initially had only the advance-guard and some cavalry at his disposition, neither Massena's nor Augereau's division having arrived. It would be necessary to wait for support before attacking, but in the meantime Bonaparte placed two light guns aiming down the bridge to prevent any attempt to destroy it. The Austrians, on their side, raised a barricade at the end of the bridge under the fire of the French sharpshooters who had found positions on the roofs, parapets, and at the windows of the buildings at the edge of the town. Bonaparte also climbed the bell-tower of the church of San Francesco with some staff-officers to observe the enemy positions. At some point, Bonaparte ordered Beaumont to look for a ford and try to cross the river above the bridge with his cavalry in order to outflank the defenders. This was a very difficult task, as the banks upriver were thickly wooded, making it hard to approach the water.

As the afternoon wore on, the French moved up some more artillery, and a violent cannonade began, which continued for several hours. During this, some of the Austrian guns were obliged to fall back, thereby reducing their effectiveness. Eventually, elements of Massena's division began to arrive, and the troops were given time to rest and consume the food and wine that had been requisitioned for them in the town. The cavalry had found a ford half a mile upstream from the bridge,[8] but was experiencing great difficulty in its attempts to get across. Late in the afternoon, Bonaparte began to prepare for the attack by gathering his best men in the square near the gate leading to the bridge. Dupas, the commander of the 2nd carabinier battalion, composed of men of the 27th Light and 29th Light, mostly from Savoy, asked for his men to be given the honour of leading the column, which was agreed. At about 6 p.m., after inciting the men for some time, Bonaparte ordered the attack.

The artillery increased its rate of fire. The gate was opened, and the carabiniers charged out in close formation, sheltered partly by the houses and the trees, and made for the bridge, with the red-haired, six-foot-four-inch Dupas in the lead. The rest of the advance-guard followed. According to Vigo-Roussillon, the enemy artillery only had time for one discharge of grape, but it was extremely deadly. Part of the way across, the head of the column hesitated, and stopped. At that point, one of the most remarkable collections of officers ever to lead a storming-party threw themselves forward, shouting, cajoling, and inciting the men back into the attack. Among them were Massena, Berthier, Lannes, Cervoni, Dallemagne and Dupas. The carabiniers rushed forward again, no doubt in looser formation, and reached the opposite bank. Behind them, others had perceived that they could clamber down the piles onto the sand-bank, where they quickly spread out as skirmishers, sniping, hiding in the bushes, and wading up to their thighs through the last stretch of water before the bank.

The first line of the Austrian defence, the battalions of Croats and of IR Nádasdy, had been watching the attempts of the French cavalry to ford the river with some apprehension, fearing they would be cut off. They had also been unsettled by the continual enemy cannon-fire. Now they were subjected at close quarters to the attentions of the French skirmishers, and presented with a horde of charging carabiniers, closely followed by the rest of the élite of the French army. They broke.

With this precipitate retreat, the cannon were abandoned, and Sebottendorf's second line found itself attacked by the French advance-guard. His three battalions of IR Terzi, one battalion of IR Belgioioso and one battalion of IR Thurn amounted to only 2,145 men, and were facing about 3,000 élite troops, behind which many more of Massena's division were hurrying to the bridge, to be followed by Augereau, Rusca and Beyrand. As usual, the French supporting troops spread out to try to outflank the enemy. The only thing possible for Sebottendorf was to try to carry out an orderly retreat, and pray for nightfall. The battalions of IR Belgioioso and IR Thurn set off first, with IR Terzi bringing up the rear with its 1,212 men and some cannon. The commander of IR Terzi, Colonel Count Attems, did all he could to slow down the enemy advance, losing two horses in the process, then being wounded, and a few minutes later, killed.

Despite his loss, and despite being nearly cut off, the regiment succeeded in carrying out its withdrawal.

Six squadrons of Hussars and Uhlans covered the retreat to the village of Fontana, where the eight Neapolitan squadrons were added to the screening force, and General Nicoletti rejoined with his three battalions and two squadrons. Having collected his men, Sebottendorf proceeded to carry out an orderly withdrawal, which was not much troubled by the French, as Vigo-Roussillon confirms. In part this was because Beaumont and his cavalry had found so much difficulty in fording the river, and partly because the French infantry was tired out by its own rapid marches. After being subjected to a few counter-attacks by the allied cavalry, the French finally gave up the pursuit in the area of Tormo and Crespiatica, about four miles from Lodi, leaving the Austrians free to continue to Crema. It had been a costly experience for Sebottendorf. His losses during the day amounted to 21 officers, 2,015 men and 235 horses. Of these, fifteen officers and 1,686 men were missing or prisoners. In addition, he had lost twelve cannon, two howitzers and 30 ammunition wagons.[9] French losses are not known exactly, but have been estimated at about 500.[10]

The reports that Bonaparte received from Adjutant-General Franceschi the same evening indicated that the opposing force had numbered 10,000 enemy infantry and 1,500 cavalry. They also mentioned the presence of Sebottendorf, Vukassovich and Rukavina (perhaps in error for Roselmini), and gave the erroneous information that the first two had both been killed. The order of the day that Bonaparte issued on the evening of the 10th (perhaps before he had received Franceschi's report) informed the army that 'This battle was one of the most lively of the campaign', and considerably exaggerated the strength of the enemy forces, either from ignorance, or more probably for effect. It stated that Beaulieu himself had assembled 14,000 infantry and 4,000 cavalry at Lodi, and had drawn back over the river to a position defended by 20 guns. This position had been attacked, and the enemy had lost 3,000 men and all the artillery.[11]

News of the action reached Beaulieu during the night of 10/11 May, after which he sent Sebottendorf and Schübirz (who was already four miles south of Crema by that time) orders to join the main army in the area between Pizzighettone and Cremona on the 12th. The line of retreat from Pizzighettone to Mantua had already been secured by Lipthay, who had sent troops to Cremona, Casalmaggiore and Bozzolo, and had himself received support from Beaulieu. The last element of the Austrian army, the small force under Colli, was some 25 miles to the north of the area of concentration, having crossed the Adda at Cassano, and arrived in Treviglio on the 10th.

On the morning of 11 May, Beaulieu continued his march with Pittoni to Acquanegra, a village half-way between Pizzighettone and Cremona. His place near Pizzighettone was taken by Schübirz. Lipthay had already departed (leaving Colonel Adorian in Pizzighettone with 1,300 men) to go via Casalmaggiore to Borgoforte, about eight miles south of Mantua. Adorian was ordered to depart from Pizzighettone himself that evening, leaving only five officers, 200 men and four guns to prevent the French from crossing the Adda there. Sebottendorf's much depleted force marched off from Crema at daybreak, and bearing south-east in the direction of Cremona, went via Soresina to Casalbuttano.

Bonaparte knew that he had failed to cut off any part of the Austrian army, but had no intention of letting them escape undisturbed. He wrote to Carnot saying: 'You may count in your calculations as if I was in Milan. I shall not go there tomorrow, because I want to pursue Beaulieu, and try to profit from his disorder to beat him again.'[12] He also sent the town councillors of Lodi a letter asking them to procure him 'in the shortest possible time, an accurate map, and the best that you can find, of the States of Venice and of Mantua',[13] which indicates where he was expecting to go. However, with the troops very tired after the hard marching of the previous few days the pursuit could not be pressed immediately, and the day passed rather quietly in rest and recuperation. This must have been very welcome in many quarters. Joubert told his father: 'It is an extraordinary thing how we pursue the Austrians so vigorously. I have never felt such lassitude, and it stops me from sleeping.'[14]

Nevertheless, the success of the previous day was skilfully exploited by Bonaparte in another way. He was never slow to seize an opportunity to convince the Directory he was doing a good job (probably rightly, as it happened, because he soon had to fight very hard to persuade them not to curb his freedom of action) and the report he wrote them on 11 May painted a brilliant picture: 'I thought that the crossing of the Po would be the most audacious operation of the campaign …,' he began, 'but I have to tell you of the battle of Lodi.' He is not specific about the numbers of enemy infantry at Lodi, but he considerably inflates the strength of their artillery. (He must have discovered the true figure at some time during the day, because he had Ménard informed that the enemy had had 'fifteen pieces'.[15]) He states: 'Beaulieu, with the whole of his army was ranged in battle. Thirty pieces of heavy artillery defended the crossing of the bridge.' The Austrian losses were slightly adjusted to '2 to 3,000', while Bonaparte estimated his own losses at 150 dead and wounded. In addition, he gave considerable praise to a number of individuals, and said: 'If I was to name all the men who distinguished themselves on this extraordinary day, I should be obliged to name all the carabiniers and grenadiers of the advance-guard, and almost all the officers of the staff.' To round off the impression that this was a most extraordinary feat of arms, he said: 'Although we have had some very hot actions since the beginning of the campaign … none has approached the terrible crossing of the bridge of Lodi.'[16] This was nothing if not showing the army in a good light.

However, a quite different assessment of the action comes through another source. At 9 a.m. on the 11th, Bonaparte received a visit from the Bishop of Lodi, Monsignor Count Beretta. Having made the usual requests that the practice of religion should not be interfered with, and having found Bonaparte accommodating, the Bishop asked him to do him the favour of dining with him. Bonaparte accepted, and in the late afternoon arrived at the Bishop's Palace with a large number of officers. The event was recorded by the Bishop's secretary, Lampugnani, who had also taken a great interest in watching the previous day's fighting from a small tower on the palace, until a couple of chimney-pots were knocked down by cannon-fire. Bonaparte seems to have found the 75-year-old Bishop congenial, and seeing a painting showing a view of Lodi and its bridge, he used it to give the prelate a brief account of the action, concluding with the words, 'However, it wasn't a big thing.'[17] The difference between the public and the private voice is striking.[18]

In the meantime, many of the French troops had settled down to camp near Lodi. A local priest noted them 'on the other side of the bridge in the nearby fields and woods, making huts for themselves with branches and cutting down the trees to make fires'.[19] Some of the officers seem to have found themselves other comforts, and Bonaparte felt compelled to issue an order forbidding officers 'of whatever rank'[20] to have women with them. More important, as it affected the mobility of the army, was an order prohibiting carriages to follow the columns.

There was no rest for the advance-guard cavalry, on the other hand, and it continued to trail the enemy, causing a great deal of trouble to the local civilians as it went, despite the fact that it had moved into neutral territory (the border between Milanese and Venetian territory being half-way between Lodi and Crema). The parish priest of Ombriano, a village not far from Crema, was aware that the French were not far off, as he had seen many Austrian wounded passing during the evening and throughout the night of 10/11 May. 'In the morning, at about 12,[21] the French advance-guard reached Ombriano,' he recounted. 'The troops ... broken with fatigue, hungry, despoiled all the houses, the parishioners having fled to other villages and into the marshes ... I was with Sig Francesco Donati, and was assailed by a picket of twelve French hussars, who robbed us of everything, with sabres and with muskets at our chests.' But to the priest, what happened to his church was even worse:

> All the women of my parish had retired inside the church with their belongings at the arrival of the French, and locked themselves inside. The soldiers were angry at not being able to knock down the door, and entered my house, went through the sacristy, and having found that the door from the sacristy to the church was very strong, fired musket shots at the lock to break and open it, but they could not ... Therefore these soldiers went above to my bedroom, and from its small window three soldiers entered the church and opened the door.

(The fear of the women cannot be described.) They also brought two horses into the church.[22]

The desecration was completed by the theft of all the church vestments and sacred vessels, and the women also had their possessions taken.

The swarm of human locusts moved steadily towards Crema, where the announcement of their arrival was witnessed by an engineer called Massari:

> We had only just entered the Ombriano Gate [of Crema] when we saw the country people come running panting into the town from the nearby villages, saying that the few Germans [sic] who were retiring had begun to steal, at first only at isolated farm-houses, and then in some of the villages, and the first small groups of French who pursued them had begun to do the same as well. At the very same instant that this news spread through the town, with the addition that the French themselves were arriving at any moment, you could see all the houses and shops and also even the gate of the town shut with precipitate speed, so that it seemed that the end of the world had come.

Eventually, the French themselves arrived:

> Suddenly, towards evening, a thick pall of dust was seen to rise on the road around the town, in the midst of which one could with great difficulty glimpse a confused movement of horses, in front of which but at very great distance there was a man on a horse who seemed to be shouting at the Germans whom he encountered while advancing towards us.[23]

This turned out to be Beaumont, who halted his men before the gate, and asked for food for his men and horses. Massari, who plainly states he was not anti-French, takes some pains to emphasise that the French troops drawn up outside the gate behaved impeccably, which was perhaps to be expected from those who were disciplined enough to remain in the ranks, under the gaze of their general, instead of going off to pillage the district.

It was not just churches and unfortunate individuals who suffered from the arrival of the French. Indeed, the whole economy was put under enormous strain. This happened not only on a small level, when the French soldiers tried to pay for things with *assignats* (French paper money, which had hardly any value in France, let alone anywhere else), but also on a large scale, where the demands for supplies to feed the army became a grave threat to the mere survival of the local population. The Austrians had already made great demands on the local supplies of basic foodstuffs when they had passed through Lodi, and the town authorities had then been ordered by the French to supply 40,000 rations of bread and wine on the 10th, and the same amount for the 11th and 12th. For a town of 10–12,000 souls, this was a staggering figure, and threatened to make a huge dent in the reserves of flour and grain that were intended to take them through to the next harvest – which was many months away. Not only that, but the number of bakers in the town was insufficient, even working through the night, to prepare and bake the required amount of bread. It was clearly beyond the capacities of the town to provide such an amount of food, and they were lucky to receive considerable assistance from the authorities in Milan.

The Milanese, for their part, had not been slow to realise that a French occupation of their own city was inevitable, and had taken steps both to organise for it, and to enter into negotiations with the French in order to minimise its impact. A delegation of two[24] was sent to meet Bonaparte and arrange further meetings with representatives from the city. One of them was a certain Francesco Melzi d'Eril, a widely travelled minor noble, whose elegant command of French it was hoped would make a favourable impression. Melzi recounts in his memoirs that they reached Lodi while Bonaparte was dining with the Bishop. When Bonaparte arrived to receive them he asked various questions about the militia that had been recently formed in Milan. Melzi assured Bonaparte that it was only intended for maintaining internal order, and underlined its unmilitary character by commenting that if it rained they would probably not find enough men to furnish the minimum number of patrols and sentries. Bonaparte seemed satisfied with this, asked a few questions about the garrison of the castle, and of Mantua, then demanded to know what the Milanese people wanted. 'Peace and quiet,'[25] he was told, which was, perhaps, asking rather a lot under the circumstances. With the interview over, the delegation left that night to prepare for the arrival of the French army.

In the meantime, Bonaparte must have concluded that there was little point in pursuing the Austrians closely, and chose instead to give his troops a few days rest while he consolidated his hold on the occupied part of Lombardy. Beaulieu used this period of respite to gather his forces at Cremona, then retire towards Mantua. While the Austrians were slowly withdrawing, Bonaparte found himself with much to occupy his mind. May 13th must have been a day of mixed and confusing emotions for Bonaparte. On the one hand, it seems to have brought some personal news that filled him with excitement and disquiet. He had been hoping that Josephine would travel from Paris to join him, but this expectation was dashed by a letter from Paris:

> So it is true that you are pregnant. Murat writes to tell me this, but he says that it makes you ill, and that he does not think it prudent for you to undertake such a long journey. I shall therefore again be deprived of the happiness of holding you in my arms ... Is it possible that I shall not have the happiness of seeing you with your little belly? It must make you interesting! You write to me that you are much changed. Your letter is short, sad, and the writing is shaky. What is wrong with you, my sweetheart? ... Alas! the idea that you are ill makes me so sad.[26]

Of course, Josephine was no more pregnant than Bonaparte was, but it provided a useful excuse to put off going to see her over-eager husband.

It was probably also on 13 May that Bonaparte received a letter from the Directory that helped to change his views about himself and the politicians he was serving. The letter was a response to Bonaparte's despatch of 28 April, in which he had spoken of joining the Rhine armies in Bavaria after advancing through the Tyrol. The Directory was, of course, considerably out of touch with events, and when their reply was written, on 7 May, they evidently assumed that Bonaparte was still camped near Alessandria, and believed that Tortona had not yet been given up to the French. By the time their letter reached Bonaparte it was totally out of date, and the situation on which it based many of its assumptions no longer existed. It stated that Bonaparte's plan presented 'difficulties which are, so to speak, insurmountable ... [The Republic] must limit itself to a less extended circle than that which you propose to travel ...' Having raised the reasonable objection that Bonaparte might be cut off, and that he had too few troops to occupy the conquered territories, and would be in danger if Piedmont re-entered hostilities, it put forward its own plan.

Bonaparte was ordered to take the Milanese, and drive the enemy to the edge of the Tyrol. Then he was to divide the army (enlarged by the incorporation of the Army of the Alps) into two and leave the weaker part to hold the Milanese, supported by the Piedmontese – if they accepted the offensive and defensive alliance that was to be proposed to them. This smaller part of the army was to be handed over to General Kellermann, and the control of the movement of the troops was to be vested in the commissioners Saliceti and Garrau. The larger part of the army, which was to be as strong as possible, was to go first to Livorno, then threaten Rome and Naples. Since France was not at war with Tuscany, the entry into their territory was to be properly announced. Once in Livorno, the French were to seize the ships and other effects belonging to enemy nations (in other words, the English). There were also instructions about how to treat various other Italian powers, and, 'If Rome makes advances, the first thing to require is that the Pope immediately order public prayers for the prosperity and the success of the French Republic.' However, 'Some of his fine monuments, his statues, his medals, his libraries, his bronzes, his silver Madonnas, and even his bells would compensate us for the expenses that this visit to him would cost us.'[27]

On St Helena, a few months before his death, Bonaparte described to General Bertrand the effect this letter had on him:

The moment when I felt the difference that there was between me and other men, and when I foresaw that I was called to finish the affairs of France, was a few days after the battle of Lodi ... I had just received the Directory's orders to march with a part of the army on Naples and leave the command of Italy to General Kellermann. I reflected on this letter, saw the Army of Italy lost by this stupid measure, and drafted the letter which is in my correspondence, where it is said that one bad general is worth more than two good ones. I was in a room near a fire, near the hearth, which was in the corner of the room, although the weather was already hot ... I was absorbed in my reflections, when Melzi was announced. The opinion that I formed of my superiority must be related to that moment. I felt that I was worth much more, that I was stronger than the government that gave such an order, more capable than them of governing, that there was in this government an incapacity, and a lack of judgement on subjects so important that must ruin France, and that I was destined to save her. From that moment, I glimpsed the goal and I marched towards it.[28]

The letter from his correspondence to which Bonaparte refers was dated 14 May. He began it by informing the Directory of his latest victories, saying: 'Beaulieu is at Mantua with his army. He has flooded all the surrounding country. He will find death there, because it is the most unhealthy in Italy.' He then continued:

I believe it very impolitic to divide the Army of Italy in two. It is also contrary to the interests of the Republic to have two different generals. The expedition on Livorno, Rome and Naples is a small thing. It must be carried out by divisions in echelon, so that, by a counter-march, we can meet the Austrians in force and threaten to envelop them at the least movement they make. It is necessary for this not only to have a single general, but also that nothing hampers him in his marches and his operations. I have conducted the campaign without consulting anyone. I could not have done anything good if I had had to win over the views of another. I have gained some advantages over superior forces, and in complete destitution of everything, because, persuaded that your confidence rested on me, my marches have been as prompt as my thoughts. If you impose hindrances of every sort on me, if I have to refer all my steps to the commissioners of the government, if they have the right to alter my movements, to hold back or to send me troops, do not expect anything good any longer. If you weaken your means by dividing your forces, if you break the unity of military thought in Italy, I tell you with sorrow, you will have lost the finest opportunity to impose your dictates on Italy. In the position of the Republic's affairs in Italy, it is indispensable that you have one general who has your entire confidence. If it is not me, I should not complain ... Everyone has his own way of making war. General Kellermann has more experience, and will do it better than I, but the two of us together will do it very badly.[29]

Support for Bonaparte came from both Saliceti and Berthier. The latter wrote to General Clarke on the same day, saying: 'The genius of Bonaparte, the precision and clarity of his ideas, his character, which is as audacious and as enterprising as it is cool in the execution, has given us the means to second him and to conduct one of the finest campaigns of which history has ever provided the example.'[30]

There was, of course, a considerable lag in correspondence, and the Directory received a number of announcements of Bonaparte's successes before these letters reached them. Just how far behind the times they were may be judged by the fact that on 15 May Carnot wrote to Bonaparte saying the Directory had received his news of the occupation of Tortona, 'which has given it a new degree of confidence in the success of your dispositions for the crossing of the Po'. He added, rather superfluously: 'It puts you in a position to take the Austrian line of defence in the rear ... if they persist in holding the banks of the river in the area of Valenza.'[31] Carnot would no doubt have been somewhat startled to know the French were already in Milan.

These continued successes and the forceful statements in Bonaparte's letter were partially successful in getting what he wanted. The Directors were reluctant to give up the scheme of an advance into the south of Italy, and Bonaparte was still putting forward objections to it at the beginning of June. However, the Directory accepted that it would have to wait until Beaulieu was completely defeated, and that Bonaparte should make this his first objective. Most importantly, on 21 May Carnot replied to Bonaparte's letter of the 14th saying: 'You seem, Citizen General, desirous to continue to conduct the whole series of military operations of the present campaign in Italy. The Directory has reflected deeply on this proposition, *and the confidence that it has in your talents and your zeal, have decided the question in favour of the affirmative.* General Kellermann will remain in Chambéry …'[32]

While awaiting this reply, Bonaparte was not idle, and by the time it arrived he was already busy with another phase of operations.

NOTES

1. Napoleon. *Correspondance de Napoléon Ier publiée par ordre de l'empereur Napoléon III*. Paris, 1858–69, no. 378.
2. Agnelli, G. 'La battaglia al ponte di Lodi e l'inizio della settimana napoleonica lodigiana.' *Archivio storico lombardo*, 60 (1933), p. 12.
3. Schels, J. B. 'Die Kriegsereignisse in Italien vom 15 April bis 16 Mai 1796, mit dem Gefechte bei Lodi.' *Oesterreichische Militärische Zeitschrift*, Bd. 2, Bd. 4 (1825), pp. 267–8.
4. Agnelli, op. cit., p. 11.
5. Cottreau, G. 'Léon Aune, deuxième grenadier de France.' *Le carnet de la sabretache*, 3 (1895): 156–65, p. 158.
6. Agnelli, op. cit., p. 14–16
7. Vigo-Roussillon, F. *Journal de campagne (1793–1837)*. Paris, 1981, p. 34.
8. Agnelli, op. cit., p. 30.
9. Schels, op. cit., p. 280.
10. Bouvier, F. *Bonaparte en Italie, 1796*. Paris, 1899, p. 527.
11. Napoleon. 1858–69, op. cit., no. 381.

12. Ibid., no. 383.

13. Agnelli, op. cit., p. 41.

14. Chevrier, E. *Le général Joubert d'après sa correspondance*. Paris, 1884, p. 38.

15. Napoleon. 1858–69, op. cit., no. 398. It is also worth noting that Joubert was fairly accurate in telling his father that the enemy had 7,000 men and sixteen guns, while Vigo-Roussillon talks of fifteen guns.

16. Napoleon. 1858–69, op. cit., no. 382.

17. Agnelli, op. cit., p. 56.

18. Lest it be thought that Bonaparte was the only one who was capable of doctoring reports for political or morale purposes, it should be pointed out that the Duke of Wellington did the same thing, and so did the British government during the Second World War.

19. Agnelli, op. cit., p. 43.

20. Napoleon. 1858–69, op. cit., no. 400.

21. It should be pointed out that the Italian system of telling the time in the 18th century was to count the 24 hours from sunset to sunset. 'Twelve' therefore corresponds to something like 8 or 9 a.m.

22. Benvenuti, M. 'Curioso documento.' *Archivio storico lombardo*, 9 (1882), p. 147.

23. Agnelli, op. cit., p. 58–9.

24. Gallavresi, G., and Laurani, F. 'L'invasione francese in Milano (1796). Da memorie inedite di Don Francesco Nava.' *Archivio storico lombardo*, s. 3, v. 18 (1902), p. 113. Other sources indicate four delegates, though this may be due to a confusion with later meetings.

25. Agnelli, op. cit., p. 69.

26. Napoleon. *Lettres d'amour à Joséphine*. Paris, 1981, no. 8.

27. Napoleon. *Correspondance inédite officielle et confidentielle de Napoléon Bonaparte: avec les cours étrangères, les princes, les ministres et les généraux français et étrangers, en Italie, en Allemagne, et en Egypte*. Paris, 1809, I, p. 153.

28. Bertrand, H. G., Gen. *Cahiers de Sainte-Hélène. Journal 1816–1817*. Paris, 1951, III, p. 78. Vincent Cronin, in his excellent biography

of Napoleon, seems inclined to doubt the authenticity of this story, but it does not seem inconsistent with Napoleon's extremely ambitious nature.

29. Napoleon. 1809, op. cit., I, pp. 161–2.
30. Bouvier, op. cit., p. 555.
31. Napoleon. 1809, op. cit., I, p. 171.
32. Ibid., I, pp. 201–2.

14

LOMBARDY

At about 11 o'clock in the morning of Saturday 14 May, Massena arrived before the gates of Milan, and was greeted by a delegation which presented him with the keys to the city, thereby symbolising their willingness to co-operate with the occupying forces. Later, Massena and Joubert entered the city accompanied by the 17th Light, the 10th and 25th Chasseurs à Cheval, and two guns of the horse artillery. Other units drew up outside to await the triumphal entry programmed for Sunday.

The Milanese must have been stunned by the band of skeletal scare-crows that shambled up to their gates, dirty and unshaven, with sunken cheeks and haunted eyes. Vigo-Roussillon commented:

> I have never seen a more striking contrast than the luxury of the Milanese and the grotesque attire of the army. Our clothes, worn out during the long wars in the mountains, had been replaced with anything that came to the soldiers' hands. Only our weapons were in a good state. In place of our ruined cartridge pouches we wore belts of goatskin that contained our cartridges. Our heads were covered by bonnets of sheepskin, cat or rabbit. Fox-furs with their tails hanging down behind were a great luxury.[1]

The advance-guard of this rag-tag mob immediately set up positions from which they could observe the castle of Milan, which was occupied by the small garrison that Beaulieu had ordered to be left there to prevent its artillery and magazines from falling into French hands. They were quite a prize, totalling 112 cannon, 40 mortars and 3,000 cwt of powder, as well as foodstuffs. They would certainly not have been left behind but for the fact that there was no means of transporting them, and Beaulieu no doubt hoped to be able to return to Milan before the

French could capture them. Ample supplies had been left to feed the garrison for two months, and it was fully expected to be able to hold out for at least two weeks after formal siege works were begun. The defending troops were 1,300 men of Frei-Corps Gyulay, eight companies of the 1st Garrison Regiment, 136 artillerymen and two engineer officers, though about 200 of the men were sick, leaving roughly 1,800 fit for duty. The commander of the garrison, Lieutenant-Colonel de l'Ami[2] of the Engineers, had blocked the castle gate and raised the draw-bridge, but having too few men to occupy the outer works, he was obliged to limit himself to the defence of the main walls.[3]

It was not the only fortress whose defence had to be hurriedly arranged because of the rapid French advance. Their unexpected progress during the first half of May had raised the alarming prospect for the Austrians that Mantua might come under threat, and might even have to be left to defend itself for a time. This mighty citadel, one of the most formidable strongholds in Italy, if not in Europe, was of crucial importance for Austrian power in northern Italy, as it provided a convenient point at which to collect the supplies and reinforcements that came down the main line of communications from Austria. This ran from Innsbruck, over the Brenner Pass, and down the Adige valley via Trento and Rovereto. Without Mantua, the Austrians would have no large base closer than Trento, in the mountains of the Tyrol, which would greatly increase the logistic difficulties of their operations. A determined defence of Mantua, should it come to that, was also important because it would pin down the French for as long as the fortress could be maintained. While it had been possible for Bonaparte to by-pass Ceva and leave a few men to blockade it, the same could not be done with Mantua if it were fully garrisoned. On a war footing, it was supposed to hold 14,000 men to defend it, and if a force that size were to break out and attack him, Bonaparte would need most of his army to be sure of beating it. If he managed to reach Mantua, therefore, he would have no alternative but to halt his advance and lay siege to the fortress. This was no small undertaking. Although Mantua was most famous as the birthplace of the Latin poet Virgil, the city had also been the seat of the powerful Gonzaga family, and it had long been known for its defences. As far back as the 14th century it had been described by another poet, Dante, as being 'strong because of the marshes that it had on all sides'.[4] Apart from these, it was also surrounded on three sides by a lake formed by the broadening of the River Mincio, and had fortifications that had been steadily enlarged and improved over several centuries.

The Austrian commander of the fortress, the 65-year-old General Count Canto d'Irles, who had been a soldier since the age of fourteen, seeing service during the Seven Years War as well as the Turkish wars, had made hasty preparations for a siege. However, the lack of time had not made it possible to bring them to a level that permitted him to face the arrival of a large enemy force with equanimity. He had had the walls repaired and cannon placed on them, but successful defence required more than this. Mantua was a very large fortress, with proportionately large needs in terms of garrison and supplies, and it was here that Canto d'Irles had most worries.

On the same day that Massena entered Milan, Canto d'Irles presented a report to Beaulieu that painted a disquieting picture of Mantua's state of preparation. The number of troops in the city only amounted to 2,154 men, and there were serious shortages of engineer officers, boats (for use on the lake), transport, various military officials and bakers. The magazines for provisions were poorly stocked, and there was not enough money available to buy supplies or pay the soldiers over a long period. In addition to this, not even a third of the necessary beds for the barracks and hospitals were available. Large numbers of artillerymen were also lacking, though the artillery's supplies of shot, powder and equipment of all kinds, including cannon, were complete. In terms of heavy-calibre artillery there were 179 cannon and 76 mortars or howitzers. The smaller-calibre weapons numbered 60, giving a total of 315 guns. (By 10 June, 214 of these were actually in use on the defence works.) Apart from the muskets already issued to the troops, the arsenals in the city held 11,540 firearms of various calibres. The magazines contained 6,288 cwt of powder, and 560,000 ready-made musket cartridges.[5]

It was imperative for Beaulieu to do something to improve the defensive state of Mantua in case he failed in his intention of maintaining his army behind the line of the River Mincio (a significant natural barrier that ran due south from Lake Garda via Mantua to the Po) until he received enough reinforcements to be able to return to the offensive. If he was driven back from the Mincio and into the Tyrol, Mantua would need to be in a condition to sustain a siege for as long as it took to rebuild the army and advance to relieve the city. In other words, it needed to be capable of holding out for some months.

On the same morning that he received Canto d'Irles's report, Beaulieu issued various orders relating to the defence of the city. He confirmed Canto d'Irles as commander and ordered the garrison to be brought up to 12,000 men immediately. Signals were arranged, by which the garrison could communicate with the army, and Canto d'Irles was ordered to find men who would act as secret messengers. All foreigners were instructed to leave the city. Supplies for the garrison were to be obtained as soon as possible, while the townspeople were ordered to submit lists of their own stocks of food, and the merchants of all their wares. These were to be ready within 24 hours. It was forbidden to send money, goods or any kind of food out of the city. The sluices were to be opened on the following day to flood the ditches around the city. It was also to be formally prohibited for any person even to talk of surrendering the fortress, except in the direst necessity.[6] On the same day, Beaulieu moved the bulk of his forces to Rivalta, about ten miles west of Mantua, ready to cross the Mincio there.

On the 15th, the French went about the pleasant task of entering Milan in as much style as their unwashed and threadbare condition would allow. It was, after all, a remarkable occasion. It was the first time that Bonaparte was to enter a capital city as a conquering general, and the first triumphal entry to such a place that the unfortunates of the Army of Italy were to make, after four years of squatting in the mountains. There was some competition for places of honour:

> Among the demi-brigades composing the division of General Massena, only the 32nd had a band, and what a band! … Massena wished to place it at the head of the division for the solemn entry, separating it from the demi-brigade, because the

units were to march in the order of their numbers, but the soldiers opposed this, and they had to place the 32nd at the head of Massena's division ...[7]

The city dignitaries had come some way outside the gates to meet Bonaparte, and were resting inside a house when the French commander, always in a hurry, shot past with his escort, and had to turn back to receive their welcome. He was presented with the keys, and made the usual promises to protect property, religion, and so forth. He then entered the city with Saliceti and Kilmaine at his side, followed by an escort of dragoons. He already seems to have learned how to make himself noticeable, because for this moment he chose to ride a white horse. This creature, described as 'small and worn out', was called 'Bijou', and accompanied him for most of the campaign.[8] Joubert wrote to his father a couple of days later saying that the entry of the French was received with great acclamation by 'a whole people'.[9]

War provides endless contrasts of situations and emotions, and while the Milanese were enthusiastically greeting the arrival of the French, others were apprehensively observing the withdrawal of the Austrians. In the hills not far from Lake Garda a young priest, Giovanni Battista Alberghini, saw worrying signs of the gathering storm that was shortly to make life a misery for the people of his quiet valley:

> The borders of the Tyrol, crossing the Venetian state and crossing the Adige near Rivole [Rivoli] were the predetermined limits of [the Austrian] retreat. Hence, without delay and with speed, the 15th day of May 1796, day of the Pentecost, a bridge of boats was made over the above-mentioned river in the area called La Perarola, over which passed the troops and baggage wagons, among which there were a large number of Milanese, Cremonese and Mantuan wagons loaded with the riches of Lombardy. The retreat was so precipitate that, doubting that a single bridge was enough, a few days later another was built not far away from the first, but the second was shortly taken down since the other was enough.[10]

While the money and valuables were hastily being shipped to safety, Beaulieu continued making arrangements for the defence of Mantua and the line of the Mincio, as well as the preservation of his line of communications with Austria. On the 15th, the right wing of his outpost line, under Schübirz, pulled back behind the Chiese, a smallish river that ran parallel with the Mincio about twelve to thirteen miles to its west. Vukassovich was given command of the outposts along the Po and the Oglio, south-west of Mantua. In the evening of the 16th, Beaulieu drew his main force, consisting of twelve and two-thirds battalions and 29 squadrons under Sebottendorf and Colli, behind the Mincio, and positioned it around Roverbella, some seven miles north of Mantua. This meant he was well placed to cover the southernmost two-thirds of the river between Lake Garda and Mantua. In addition, this movement towards the north brought him a little nearer to his line of retreat through the Adige valley. To the right of the main force was General Lipthay with two and a half battalions and six squadrons, also stationed behind the Mincio, between Castelnuovo del Garda and Peschiera, watching the crossing-point over the river at the latter place. To cover the extreme right flank, Major Maelcamp was positioned at the northern end of Lake Garda, in Torbole and Riva, with four companies and one squadron. He kept watch on the lake, and the area north of Salò on its western shore.

On the same day, Beaulieu had also allocated 23 battalions under Roselmini, Rukavina and Vukassovich to the garrison of Mantua, which would bring the total number of troops there to 24 battalions and three squadrons, or 12,799 combatants. Unfortunately, it was not to remain at this figure for long. The men who had been on the Riviera only four weeks previously were absolutely exhausted by forced marches, fighting, lack of food and sleep, and in the next fourteen days a thousand of them had to be hospitalised. The troops allocated to Mantua were split into two groups, half of which manned outposts in various places outside the fortress, while the other half carried out guard duty (which required 751 men), laboured to get the fortress into a decent defensive state, and got in provisions. The extra manpower provided by transferring men to the fortress was useful in forwarding the preparations for a siege, but had one drawback. The small stock of food was rapidly diminished by the mass of hungry workers, exacerbating an already difficult situation.[11]

On 16 May the commander of the Austrian garrison in the castle of Milan received the usual summons to surrender. He therefore gave the usual refusal, but also proposed that, in order to spare the town, if the French would refrain from making reconnaissances or attacks on the side of the castle facing the town, he would also refrain from using the cannon on that side. This civilised initiative was agreed to by Bonaparte a couple of days later.[12] In the meantime, he gave orders to prepare for a siege, including instructing Dujard to organise a train of 40 guns in Tortona and have them transported to Milan without delay. Dujard's inability to do anything with speed or efficiency had been trying Bonaparte's patience, and his performance over the next week cannot have been any better, because at the end of it he was quite suddenly replaced and sent to the rear areas.

Bonaparte was also taking an interest in the political situation locally, and on the 16th he sent the Directory a report commenting that Milan already had a political club with 800 members, and was ripe for liberty. 'If this people asks to organise a republic, may we allow them to?' he asked. 'This country is much more patriotic than Piedmont: it is closer to liberty.' This was somewhat ironic, considering that Pavia was the scene of much anti-French or anti-Jacobin unrest during the day, the tragic sequel to which we shall see later. From Bonaparte's appraisal it would appear that he had little or no inkling that trouble was brewing, and possibly his contacts with a liberal, pro-French set of people in Milan led him to underestimate the strength of anti-French feeling in other parts of Lombardy. Yet he blithely says in the same letter: 'We shall obtain 20 millions in contributions from this country. It is one of the richest in the universe, but entirely exhausted after five years of war.'[13]

Such a considerable levy, coming at a difficult time, can hardly have been expected to increase the benevolence of the Lombards towards the French, and the proclamation that was issued a few days later attempting to justify it can have done little to help. This called the levy 'a very small contribution for countries so fertile',[14] and presented it as a fair price to pay for liberation from the Austrians. Yet Pietro Verri, who was involved in the administration of the province, commented that the sum was the equivalent to four years of direct taxation, and that it would take many years, 'perhaps even a generation',[15] to recover from the effects. Moreover, the heavy-handed way in which the French commissaries and officers put forward their demands for supplies of all kinds, often to be delivered 'in 24 hours', led to a good deal of ill feeling, and gained General Despinoy, the French commander of Milan, the nickname 'General 24 hours'.

However, the instruction that Bonaparte had been given at the opening of the campaign had stipulated that he was to exact large contributions from conquered enemy territory, so his actions were in line with this. Moreover, the fact that he was able to send large quantities of money and treasure to Paris, and even to help the finances of the struggling armies on the Rhine, undoubtedly increased his political leverage, and he must have been aware that every franc he could raise would help him to get agreement for his plans. The Duke of Modena was also made to pay a high price for being left alone, and in an armistice signed on the 17th he agreed to pay seven and a half million francs in cash, supply foodstuffs and ammunition for the army worth two and a half millions, and deliver twenty paintings from his galleries.[16]

Bonaparte was not avaricious, though, and merely regarded the money as a means to an end. He was far more interested in the next phase of the campaign, which he felt should be pressed as quickly as possible, since Lallement, the French minister in Venice, had sent him reports indicating that Beaulieu had received 6,000 reinforcements, and that another 10,000 were on the way. Bonaparte wrote to Lallement that day, asking for 'an accurate and very detailed map of the States of Venice'. He also thanked him for his reports on the enemy positions and urged him to 'send spies to Trento, Mantua, and on the road to the Tyrol … make sure that your letters are frequent and instructive. I rely on you for news. Fix a price for the couriers, so that if they arrive early, they receive a bonus.'[17]

The following day Bonaparte sent the Directory an extraordinary list of art works that had been selected to be sent to Paris. These included paintings by Leonardo, Raphael, Giorgione, Titian, Rubens, Correggio,

Caracci, Guercino, Van Eyck, manuscripts, and various other items. It was not just the government that was benefiting from this 'official plunder', however. He also issued orders on the 18th to pay the army, which was something of a novelty. A lieutenant of the 18th Line, Pelleport, wrote: 'Pay was regulated according to the scale of the law of 2 thermidor, Year II, but reduced by half. For my part I received 65 francs 50 per month, instead of the 4 sous promised, but never paid, by the Directory.'[18] Similarly, Roguet, who was then a captain in the 32nd demi-brigade wrote, 'for the first time since 1793, we received cash'.[19] The effect was miraculous. Vigo-Roussillon tells us:

> Nothing could have been more comical than seeing the French walk around Milan a couple of days after our entry. A uniform coat hurriedly made was the only military note of our costume. We were shaven and our hair was dressed with powder and pomade. For a hat, anything we had been able to procure. With the coat, waistcoats of red, or embroidered with flowers of all colours ... trousers of green, yellow or blue silk. For footwear, boots or shoes, whatever we had found. The officers did not know what to do with the money they had been given. As they did not have portmanteaux, canteens, nor any form of transport, they bought jewellery. The watchmakers and jewellers saw their shops emptied in twenty-four hours, and everyone strutted around with two watches decorated with chains and ornaments that fell half-way down their thighs, just as the fashion was in Paris at that time. We transformed ourselves into *Incroyables*![20]

Bonaparte shared the mood, and wrote to Josephine that day:

> I don't know why, since this morning I am more content. I have a presentiment that you have left to come here. This idea fills me with joy ... You will come to Milan, where you will be very happy, the country being very beautiful. As for me, it will make me so happy that I will be mad. I am dying to see how you carry a child.[21]

As far as his wife was concerned, there seemed to be no end to his ability to delude himself.

On 19 May, Bonaparte issued orders for the army to recommence its pursuit of the Austrians. Joubert was to set off the following day, while most of the other troops were to begin their march on the 21st. In a rather odd arrangement, Massena's division was to go from Milan to Lodi, while Augereau was to cross behind him and go through Milan to Cassano. This manoeuvre has always slightly puzzled historians, who have struggled to find a convincing military reason for it. However, it is at least possible that it was part of a plan to keep the enemy guessing about his intentions. Sérurier was to take a southerly route via Pizzighettone towards Cremona.

On 20 May Bonaparte signalled the beginning of a new series of operations by issuing a proclamation 'to his brothers in arms':

> Soldiers! You have descended like a torrent from the summit of the Apennines; you have overthrown, dispersed, and scattered everything that opposed your march. Piedmont, delivered from Austrian tyranny, has yielded to its natural inclination for peace and friendship with France. Milan is yours, and the Republican standard flies over the whole of Lombardy ... Yes, Soldiers! you have done much, but is there no more to be done? Shall it be said of us that we knew how to conquer, but that we did not know how to profit from victory? ... But I already see you run to arms; a cowardly repose fatigues you; days lost for glory are also lost for your fortune. Very well, let us go! We still have forced marches to make, enemies to conquer, laurels to gather, injuries to avenge ... To restore the Capitol, to replace there with honour the statues of heroes who have rendered it immortal, to arouse the Roman people deadened by many centuries of slavery – such will be the fruit of your victories. They will form an epoch in history. You will have the immortal glory of having changed the face of the most beautiful part of Europe. The French people, free and respected by the whole world, will give to Europe a glorious peace, which will indemnify her for the sacrifices of every kind

she has made for the last six years. Then you will return to your homes, and your fellow citizens will say as they point you out: HE BELONGED TO THE ARMY OF ITALY![22]

The following day, the divisions moved off. There were now, technically, only three of them, though the advance-guard had been reinforced and was actually stronger than Augereau's division. According to the returns for 30 May, it numbered 6,262 men, and it was now commanded by Kilmaine. Augereau had 6,089, Massena 9,481 and Sérurier 9,075. The blockading force for the castle in Milan took 5,278 men, and there were another 5,500 in various garrisons.[23] During the day, Bonaparte received the good news that the Peace Treaty with the Piedmontese had been signed in Paris. On the 22nd, the French movement eastwards continued without incident.

It was a different story on the 23rd, but the trouble that broke out was not in front of the French, it was behind them, and its focal point was Pavia. This town, which was the seat of one of the oldest universities in Europe, had already seen a deal of trouble a week before, when a group of local Jacobins, or revolutionaries, had managed to get Augereau to agree to their pulling down an ancient bronze equestrian statue of a Roman Emperor. This monument, which was known as the 'Regisole' and was something of a symbol of the town, was popular with the townspeople, to whom it was a familiar and inoffensive landmark. It was not inoffensive to the Jacobins, however, who took the view that the effigy of a 'tyrant' ought not to share the same square as their newly erected Tree of Liberty. The act of destruction duly took place, despite the presence of a throng of angry protesters, who could do little to oppose the act of vandalism with the French in strong occupation of the town and its environs. Nevertheless, there were ugly scenes during which Augereau, who disapproved the destruction, according to a local diarist,[24] and Rusca (a former student of the university) had to draw their swords to make their way through the crowds. Despite appeals for calm on the part of the Bishop and the Council of Pavia, the following days had seen gatherings in the nearby villages of anything up to 100 men armed with agricultural implements, and there was plenty of evidence to suggest that there would be trouble when the bulk of the French forces moved on.[25]

At about 8 a.m. on the 23rd, people began to gather in the square in Pavia near the Tree of Liberty. A local notable called Fenini saw among them a monk named Agostino, and a number of people 'of humble origins' who seem to have been known to him for some reason. He named them as Fortunato Vaga, Francesco Antonio Bullani, Giacomo Pedrazzi, Francesco Valli, and a certain Pietro Mussi, who rejoiced in the eloquent dialect nickname of *el Pisson* – the drunk.[26] In no time the tree was cut down. The commander of the garrison, who had 450 men at his disposal, was warned of what was going on, and took a patrol to the square, but not being able to discover who had been responsible for felling the tree, he decided to return to the castle.[27]

The tumult increased. The tocsin was rung from the Town Hall and the church of Santa Maria del Carmine, and people began to flood in from the nearest villages, armed with any weapons they could find – sticks, pitchforks, scythes and sometimes guns. The French picket guarding the bridge across the Ticino was taken prisoner, as were the guards at the city gates. Their weapons were taken by the rebels. To identify themselves, the latter stuck sprigs of leaves in their hats, like the Austrian soldiers. There were cries of 'Long live the House of Austria!' By 10 a.m., the number of people in the town had grown considerably, and continued to grow. According to some witnesses the country people, who probably suffered more from the depredations of looters, were more angry and violent than the townspeople. A hunt for Jacobins was begun and a number of genuine or presumed supporters of the French were beaten up, imprisoned, and had their houses broken into and ransacked. The Jacobin club was stormed by the mob and yet more people were incarcerated.[28]

At about 11 o'clock, into this maelstrom rode the man who was on his way to take command of Milan, General Haquin. He later reported that when he had been approaching Pavia with some other officers they had heard sounds of a disturbance, but carried on into the town because they thought that Augereau's division must still be there. 'On arriving at the town square, we found a great number of people, armed with muskets, pistols, sabres, etc, and many country people, with weapons or implements of every kind. A considerable platoon of volunteers, who were on the steps of the town hall, shouted to us that all the guards had been disarmed, and that they wanted to kill them.'

Haquin tried to overawe the mob by riding forward boldly, but was forced to dismount. He was able to get into the Town Hall, and instructed the commander of the garrison to send out large patrols to restore calm, but the order could not be carried out. The mob now demanded that the garrison be disarmed, but for two hours Haquin denied their requests:

> In the end, the furious people forced their way into the Town Hall, and entering the room where I was, hauled me out. The municipal officials whom I had around me covered me with their bodies, and not being able to prevent me from being dragged into the square, they attached themselves to me, and made every effort to contain the people, some of whom threw themselves at me, others aimed at me, and, to conclude, thanks to their care, I got away with a bayonet thrust between the shoulders … which did not go far in.[29]

Eventually, Haquin found shelter in the house of a magistrate, Valsecchi. In the meantime there were some exchanges of fire between the garrison of the castle and the rebels outside, during which a few men were wounded. The rebels had also tried to equip themselves with artillery and had brought four small cannon which had been used as ornaments along the façade of the Prince's palace in Belgioioso. However, they were totally useless, as there were no cannon-balls for them. With the fall of night, the town became more quiet, as the country people returned to their villages.

Surprisingly, perhaps, no news of this uprising reached Bonaparte, and very early in the morning of the 24th he left Milan for Lodi, escorted some of the way by Despinoy. He had not long gone when it was the turn of Milan to suffer some disturbances. Roguet, who had remained in the city with his battalion tells us: 'About 9 in the morning,

I was going back to our quarters with the order of the day. Near the Cathedral, I saw some mysterious comings and goings. I carried on to the Cathedral Square. At that moment a large crowd of people was coming from the opposite side, uttering the most hostile cries against the French. This was warning enough. I went with all haste to the monastery … where the 1st battalion of the 32nd was.' Having returned to the square at the run with his men, he formed them up. 'At that moment, numerous rebels were tearing down the Tree of Liberty. Our appearance and the dispositions I made put them to flight.'[30] Another group of rioters at the gate on the road to Pavia was also dispersed by the soldiers. Elsewhere in the city, it was remarkably quiet. Captain Laugier, of the 27th Light, recalled in his memoirs: 'That same day I took a quiet walk in a part of the town, and I did not learn until my return to the camp that there had been a riot in one of the quarters, which had been dissipated as soon as it had formed.'[31] Despinoy returned at about midday, and on learning of the troubles immediately sent a courier to Bonaparte. News also began to filter through of what was happening outside Milan.

In Pavia, the disturbances had continued, but with even greater numbers of people arriving in the town. Indeed the situation was taking on the aspect of an invasion by the country people, who demanded 'contributions' of food, like a proper army. Many townspeople began to shut themselves indoors, not daring to go out, and fearing to be taken for Jacobins, while others began to try to leave to escape the noise and the violence and to avoid whatever unpleasant scenes might ensue. Some of the rebels opposed this, unless the fugitives were prepared to pay, and the gates began to be guarded by bands of men who obviously intended to make the most of the situation. Further attempts were made to get the garrison to surrender by forcing Haquin to negotiate, but without success.

When Despinoy's courier reached Bonaparte in Lodi, the latter immediately left Berthier to supervise the army's movements, issued orders for a small force of grenadiers, cavalry and artillery to retrace its steps, and returned to Milan. He arrived in the afternoon, to find the city quiet. A meeting was held with the municipal authorities, the Archbishop, and various other clergy and nobles, during which Bonaparte angrily told them they had not done enough to pacify the protesters. Bonaparte then asked Monsignor Visconti, the Archbishop of Milan, to publish a pastoral letter to be printed and posted immediately, calling for calm and asking the clergy in particular to encourage submission to the French. Despinoy was ordered to form a court-martial of five officers to hear the case against those who had been arrested with weapons in their hands during the day, 'and to have shot those who are convicted of having taken part directly or indirectly in the insurrection'.[32] Instructions were also given for the arrest of hostages.

Having taken whatever measures he could in Milan, Bonaparte now left for Pavia. He had been preceded, it would seem, by what he called a 'mobile column', commanded by Lannes, no doubt mostly consisting of the 6th battalion of grenadiers. As this approached the village of Binasco, about half-way to Pavia, it came into contact with a large rebel force. Bonaparte later reported that the village was held by about 7–800 of them, with various kinds of weapons, and that they seemed determined to defend themselves. However, the rebels, neither well-armed nor properly trained in war, could not hope to withstand an attack by Lannes's grenadiers. In the ensuing fight, 100 rebels were killed and the rest put to flight, after which the soldiers sacked the village, and, on Bonaparte's orders, set the houses on fire.[33]

For some reason, perhaps because it was too late to continue to Pavia, Bonaparte then returned to Milan, and at 2 a.m. wrote to Berthier:

A vast conspiracy was being hatched against us. At Milan, Pavia and Como they rebelled at the same hour. Measures of all kinds have been taken in Milan, which is absolutely tranquil. I have come back from half-way to Pavia. We encountered a thousand peasants at Binasco and beat them. After having killed a hundred of them, we burned the village, a terrible example, which will be effective. In an hour we march on Pavia, where they say our men are still holding out. I desire that you advance as little as possible tomorrow, in order to have more considerable forces the day after tomorrow to attack the enemy. However, I believe there will be no risk in executing the movement on Brescia.[34]

He also issued a proclamation to the people of Lombardy, giving the rebels 24 hours to lay down their arms, and threatening that after that time their villages would be burnt like Binasco if they had not complied. This proclamation he gave to the Archbishop of Milan, and sent him to Pavia with it to try to get the rebels there to give up their futile insurrection.

The rebels, however, had achieved a notable success that morning. At 6 a.m. they had once again summoned the castle to surrender, followed by the same request six hours later. The French officers had called a council of war, and decided that, since they had no food apart from some sacks of maize, no artillery, no ammunition, a third of the troops were without weapons, and there were twelve wounded who had received no medical attention, they would surrender. The capitulation was drafted in the castle together with representatives of the Town Council, and stipulated that the latter would take responsibility for the safety of the troops. The last article stated: 'The garrison can only praise the zeal, the pains, and the care that the Council of Pavia has taken to bring the parties to agreement on the capitulation, that it has treated and treats the troops of the French Republic as friends and brothers, and that it only desires peace. The Council for its part, renders justice to the conduct of the French troops.'[35] The French troops then filed out 'and an honest citizen having placed himself beside each one, they were accompanied without the least disturbance, partly to the large seminary, and partly to the former College of Santa Clara, where a large meal was sent them by the Council, of which they had great need'. According to the *Marchese* Belcredi, who gives us the preceding description, the rebels were as delighted as if they had conquered an empire, and began a bacchanalian celebration on the streets.

At this point, Archbishop Visconti and his companions arrived at the Bishop's Palace. 'The eloquent and learned Monsignor Rosales went onto the balcony giving onto the square to harangue the crowd to bring them to obedience, but there were some who heckled him and called him a Jacobin. The murmuring increased, and his speech was made useless because it could no longer be heard, and he retired in desolation.' Having failed in this attempt, the clergymen went to the Town Hall, and had Bonaparte's proclamation read from the balcony by the secretary, but this only made matters worse. 'It was conceived in terms felt to be threatening and insulting to the courage of this insignificant handful of men, so instead of calming that irrational rabble, fuming with wine and presumption, it irritated them the more.'[36]

The clergymen had been in Pavia only a couple of hours when the French approached, Lannes's grenadiers marching down the main road, accompanied by troopers of the 5th and 15th Dragoons, and the 24th Chasseurs. Further detachments swept the fields to the sides. On arriving before the town, Dommartin's artillery was positioned at half musket range, and essayed a few shots. Bonaparte then sent a messenger to summon the town to surrender, but the historian of the 5th Dragoons states that he was fired on before being able to reach the gates.[37] 'General Dommartin immediately had the 6th battalion of grenadiers placed in close column, axes in their hands, with two 8-pdrs at their head. The gates were smashed down ...'[38] The resistance was almost non-existent, and 'in the blink of an eye'[39] the streets and squares emptied of rebels, who either hid in the empty houses or took flight, escaping through the gates on the far side of the town, as dragoons galloped through the streets, sabring those they found. In the mêlée, Monsignor Rosales, who had unwisely gone to find news of his sister, was killed, his body not being discovered until some time later. In total, contemporaries estimated that about 80 rebels were killed. The Frenchmen then began to sack the town, though care seems to have been taken to protect some of the most illustrious inhabitants, such as Alessandro Volta, one of the greatest pioneers of the study of electricity, who taught at the university.

It is impossible to establish exactly what happened in the next few hours, but it would seem that the damage done was not as bad as might have been expected, and that it was above all the jewellers and shops selling clothing that suffered.[40] A contemporary account noted that no women were molested, 'which, on the part of the French,

above all French soldiers, may pass for a wonder'.[41] In his own version
of events, Bonaparte wrote that the damage was rumoured to be
greater than it actually was, which was useful in discouraging similar
rebellions.[42] Interestingly, Bonaparte seems to have been keen to give
the impression that he had been very rigorous, because he reported to
the Directory on 1 June that he had had the Town Council shot,
which was quite untrue.[43] He also later stated that the commander of
the town was shot for surrendering the castle, but no evidence of this
has ever been found.[44]

Bonaparte stayed in Pavia during the night, and on the 26th, wrote
to Despinoy: 'By now, I think you will have had shot those who were
taken with weapons in their hands. It is indispensable that during the
day you have sent to Pavia under a good escort, to be transferred to
Tortona, all the Prisoners of State who have been arrested.' He also
speaks of taking two hundred hostages from Milan, who will be transported in large *Berlines*. Ever precise over details, he instructs that 'One
servant per man may follow them, but only in a few days'. To emphasise the gravity of the situation he tells Despinoy, 'You must not give
yourself rest' until all his instructions have been carried out.[45] The
hostages, mostly from prominent and wealthy families, were destined to
spend several unpleasant months in prison.

The court-martial had gone to work fairly quickly in Milan, and
on the same day, Don Domenico Pomi, Ignazio Dancardi, Giuseppe
Grugni (who had been captured while armed with an Austrian
musket), Antonio Maria Storta and a Pole called Osip Volenski (an
escaped prisoner) were all shot outside the walls of the city. In Pavia,
their fate was shared that day by Natale Barbieri, one of the most
violent of the agitators. Over the next ten days about a score of others
were shot, including several priests, the most prominent of whom was
Don Giuseppe Pacciarini of the cathedral chapter of Milan, a known
Austrian spy. Various others appeared before the courts, which
continued their sittings for weeks, but as time wore on there was less
and less desire for rigour, and having made a few examples the courts
were inclined to be lenient. On 21 June, seven men who had been
wounded were none the less acquitted, one of them being recognised

as having saved a French officer, and a number of others with much to fear were to escape lightly.

By 26 May, Berthier was becoming somewhat restive at his commander's prolonged absence, and wrote to him noting that they had not received news from him for over 24 hours.[46] The French had occupied the neutral Venetian town of Brescia on the previous day, and with the army edging closer to the Austrians, Berthier felt that the master's guiding hand was needed. After all, Bonaparte was the only one who knew precisely what his plans were. By that time, however, Bonaparte was already on his way back to the army to carry out the operation that had been interrupted by the rebellion.

His intention was to cross the Mincio, though as usual he tried to give his enemy the impression that he might have other views. Deception was made easier by the fact that Beaulieu was obliged to cover a great extent of country which lent itself to various lines of attack. One possibility was that Bonaparte might go via Brescia along the western side of Lake Garda, then turn east to cut the route to the Tyrol near Rovereto. From the southern to the northern end of the lake was 30 miles as the crow flies, so the small force that Beaulieu had placed in the north to cover that area was very isolated, and Beaulieu knew that it would take time to move to its support should it be attacked.

The line of the Mincio was also fairly long, being about nineteen miles from Mantua to the lake. The river was much less of an obstacle than the Po, as it was only about 40 yards wide at the most, but it was still virtually impossible to ford at that time of the year, and had only four bridges. Running from south to north, these were at Rivalta, Goito, Borghetto and Peschiera. They were roughly equidistant from one another, about six or seven miles apart. Such a small number of potential attack points theoretically made the line easier to defend, but Bonaparte hoped to be able to induce his opponent to move his forces to defend one when he was intending to use another, and then exploit speed of movement to arrive at his chosen crossing-place and force a way over before the enemy could switch back and oppose him.

As in the operation on the Po, it was important to choose the right crossing-point. Those at the ends of the line were not really suitable,

Rivalta because it was much too close to Mantua to be safe, while Peschiera was defended by a Venetian fortress entirely surrounded by water, and might prove difficult to carry. This left Borghetto and Goito. Borghetto was closer to the area where Bonaparte was gathering his main attack force, and in any case the terrain nearby was more favourable. Between the southern end of the lake and a point roughly half-way between Borghetto and Goito, the country is very hilly. This terrain has something of the look of gigantic mounds of bulldozed rubble, a characteristic that testifies to its morainic origins. In such country it was easier to conceal movement than it was farther south, where the land was a completely flat plain. The route that Bonaparte was considering for his advance on Borghetto skirted the line of these hills, and then for the last six miles before the bridge it went through them. This would give the French an opportunity to exploit the greater agility of their troops in broken terrain in the area that was likely to be best defended.

A further advantage was that while Goito was protected by entrenchments, the bridge at Borghetto had no special defences, save those offered by the surrounding terrain. These consisted of the hamlet of Borghetto itself, which had twelve houses, and lay in the bottom of the valley, which was quite deep at this point. On the far side of the river, the valley side was steep, and the road up it led to the village of Valeggio, perched on the top, and its nearby ruined castle, which looked right down on the bridge. The latter was an extraordinary construction in stone and brick, dating from the 14th century, which had a very wide roadway. However, its centre section had been destroyed in a previous war, and replaced with a narrower wooden structure. Bonaparte had never seen it, of course, but knew about it from the detailed description in de Maillebois's memoirs. All in all, Borghetto seemed the best candidate for a crossing, if Beaulieu could be persuaded that the main danger lay elsewhere.

Of course, the length of Beaulieu's line not only gave Bonaparte the advantage of easier deception, but put Beaulieu in danger of committing the same mistakes that others had made nearly a century before in a similar situation, as described in de Maillebois's memoirs:

Prince Eugene, in 1701, had a bridge thrown across the Adige between Castelbaldo and Villabona. Chevalier Folard informs us that this famous general was able, by his stratagems, to get M. de Catinat to extend himself too far along the river, to oppose its crossing, which made him weak everywhere. He held some twelve leagues [29 miles], and was beaten. On the same river, M. de Vendôme fell into the same error five years later. The enemy crossed as it had the first time, opposite the very position of the General.[47]

The French occupation of Brescia had two effects, one negative for Bonaparte, and the other exactly in line with what he hoped. The violation of Venetian neutrality gave Beaulieu the excuse he needed to seize the fortress of Peschiera, which was carried out by Lipthay's men on the morning of the 26th. However, Beaulieu was also clearly made uneasy about his extreme right flank, as was reported by Colonel Thomas Graham (later to be Wellington's second-in-command in Spain), who had arrived only a few days before to be the official observer for the British government. 'The possession of Peschiera effectively protects the Right of the army,' he said, 'provided the French do not find their way round the north of the Lake by Riva, which I don't think the General [Beaulieu] is without apprehensions of their attempting, tho' it is reckon'd a very impracticable Road.'[48]

The attention of the Austrians had undoubtedly been attracted to their right, and the occupation of Peschiera by Lipthay's troops was only part of a general shuffling in that direction. In the afternoon of the 26th, General Melas, a 61-year-old native of Transylvania, who had now arrived to take command of the troops forming the right wing, moved the brigades of Colonel von Beust and General Gummer ten miles north, from Roverbella to Oliosi, a position almost equidistant from Valeggio and Peschiera, where they were to form a reserve. The other elements of the main force echoed this movement, and Sebottendorf placed Nicoletti's brigade at Campagnola (one mile south-west of Valeggio) and that of Pittoni as well as the Neapolitan cavalry of the Prince di Cuto behind Valeggio itself.

This meant that the link with Mantua, which was maintained by Colli from Goito, had become rather tenuous.

On the 27th, Bonaparte passed through Soncino on his way back to the army, and reached Brescia. On the 28th, the French continued their movement towards the Chiese: Massena reached Montichiari, Augereau reached Ponte San Marco, and Sérurier arrived at Ghedi, to the right rear of Massena. Bonaparte's report to the Directory of 1 June states:

> The HQ arrived at Brescia on the 9th [prairal: 28 May]. I ordered General Kilmaine to go to Desenzano with 1,500 cavalry and six battalions of grenadiers. I ordered General Rusca to go to Salò with a demi-brigade of light infantry. It was a question of making General Beaulieu believe that I wanted to turn him by the top of the lake, to cut him off from the road to the Tyrol, by passing through Riva. I kept all the divisions of the army to the rear, so that the right, with which I really wanted to attack, was a day-and-a-half's march from the enemy. I placed it behind the Chiese, where it had the air of being on the defensive, while General Kilmaine went to the gates of Peschiera, and had skirmishes with the enemy outposts every day ...[49]

When he arrived in Salò, Rusca was told to collect as many boats as he could, which would give the impression that the French were preparing to cross to the north-east shore of the lake. That Beaulieu continued to be apprehensive about his right seems to be confirmed by the fact that he ordered Lipthay to send five companies and two cannon to Riva, though circumstances prevented this from being carried out. However, a battalion of IR Keuhl and two cannon, which arrived in Torbole from the Tyrol during the night of 28/29 May, provided a useful reinforcement of this area. The rest of the Austrian positions on 29 May are detailed below.

The right wing, which had now been handed over to Lipthay, was covering a lot of ground and was split into numerous small groups scattered over thirteen miles of country from Garda to Salionze (half-way between Valeggio and Peschiera). It consisted of:

Regiment	Battns	Sqdns	Men
IR Lattermann	2		1,015
IR Reisky	2⅓		1,351
IR Keuhl	1		683
Croats	2 coys		unknown
Erdödy Hussars		1	125
Erzherzog Joseph Hussars		2	264
Principe di Napoli		4	390

These totalled over 3,049 infantry and 779 cavalry. Peschiera was garrisoned by two battalions, one company, and two squadrons with six cannon.

The centre, which now consisted of the troops of Melas and Sebottendorf, held various positions extending from about three miles north of Valeggio to a similar distance south of it, but at least half of the troops were placed as reserve midway between Valeggio and Peschiera:

Regiment	Position	Battns	Sqdns	Men
IR Huff	Salionze	1⅔		1,246
IR Brechainville	Salionze	1		538
IR Alvinczy	1 mile SW of Salionze	2		1,203
IR Wallis	1 mile SW of Salionze	1		878
IR Wenzel Colloredo	Oliosi (1 mile E of Salionze)	1		1,320
Colloredo	Valeggio and outposts	1		
Uhlans	Valeggio and outposts		4	519
Regina di Napoli	Valeggio and outposts		4	437
Erzherzog Joseph Hussars	Valeggio and outposts		2	263
IR Toscana	Campagnola and outposts	1		628
IR Thurn	Campagnola and outposts	1		675
Napoli Dragoons	Campagnola and outposts		4	419
Erzherzog Joseph Hussars	Campagnola and outposts		3	448
IR Jordis	1 mile NE of Valeggio	1		761

Regiment	Position	Battns	Sqdns	Men
IR Strassoldo	Borghetto	1 ⎫		920
IR Strassoldo	Pozzolo	1 ⎭		

Total: 8,169 infantry, 2,086 cavalry.

On the Austrian left, apart from the 2,583 infantry and 80 cavalry under Rukavina, which belonged to the garrison of Mantua, Colli had four squadrons of Uhlans (518 men) and four of Re di Napoli Dragoons (377 men). This force was positioned in the area of Goito. Colli had been instructed that if he had to withdraw to join the rest of the army, he was to send Rukavina's men back to Mantua.

The army's outposts were close to the Mincio in the north, at Ponti, Monzambano and Volta, but further south they were placed forward, at Ceresara and Gazoldo. Patrols pushed a little further on, and watched the roads from the west.[50]

Kilmaine's feints towards Peschiera seemed to have had the desired effect of making the Austrians suspect that the French would attempt a crossing in that area. They may even have feared that Bonaparte would throw a bridge across the river as he had done to cross the Po, and some poorly organised attempts were made to form a cordon along the Mincio between Valeggio and Peschiera. Various contradictory orders relating to these arrangements were issued during the day, which caused a great deal of confusion. This was partly due to the fact that Beaulieu had been taken ill, and orders were being sent from his HQ near Valeggio without his knowledge. Some of them only arrived during the night of the 29/30th, which meant that attempts to carry them out had to be left until the morning.

Bonaparte issued orders for the advance on the Mincio at 11 p.m. on the 29th, and the divisions set off at 2 a.m. on the 30th. Kilmaine's élite troops began a rapid march of eleven miles from Castiglione to Borghetto, via Solferino and Cavriana. Massena left at the same time for Cavriana, from where he was to support the advance-guard, while Andréossy set off for the same place with the bridging equipment. Augereau was to make for Castellaro, to the left of Kilmaine, and Sérurier for Guidizzolo, on Kilmaine's right.

At 7 a.m. Kilmaine attacked the Austrian outposts of three squadrons of hussars, which fell back towards Borghetto. Over the next two hours, the French pushed forward steadily, until they reached the bridge. This was only lightly defended, by one battalion of IR Strassoldo, because the other units of the Austrian centre were still in the process of trying to sort out the orders they had received the previous day and during the night, and were busy forming the cordon along the river up to Peschiera. The commander of the battalion of IR Strassoldo, which was roughly one-tenth the strength of Kilmaine's advance-guard, described the arrangements he had made for the defence of the bridge:

> I had the gardens and houses of Borghetto occupied by 1 officer, 2 corporals and 50 men, in order to cover the retreat of the cavalry, which could recross the Mincio. After the retreat, the supports of the bridge were to be thrown into the water. One officer, 50 men and 4 carpenters should have sufficed for this work. Three companies with a cannon, under the command of Captain Ertel, placed along the river, were to halt the enemy, cannonade and destroy the three supports of the bridge. The fourth company, under the orders of Captain Buch-mayer, stayed at the foot of the hill, in order to cover my left wing. A fifth company, of Captain Cronise, and a cannon, formed the reserve.[51]

By 9 a.m., the retreating Austrian advanced troops were piling up at the bridge, the crossing of which greatly slowed their withdrawal. Some hussars, in a hurry to reach safety, took advantage of the fact that the water was unusually low at the time and forded the river, thus revealing to the French that they could do the same. At about the same time, the part of Borghetto on the right bank was abandoned by the Austrians, but the defensive arrangements were enough to delay the French main force and its artillery from advancing over the bridge. Bonaparte later reported to the Directory: 'The enemy hastened to cross the bridge and to cut an arch. The Light Artillery immediately began a cannonade. The bridge was being repaired with difficulty under the fire of the enemy batteries, when about fifty grenadiers, who became impatient, threw themselves in the water ...'[52] These men, commanded by Gardanne, forded the stream in water up to their armpits, supported by artillery fire and musketry, and reached the bank near the position of one of the companies of IR Strassoldo. Pittoni, who had arrived to take control of the defence, sent another company in support, but the two of them were unable to maintain their position, and had to toil up the valley side to reach four companies of IR Jordis, which had earlier joined the fight in the valley but had then retired to the castle. Pittoni received no reinforcements from the reserve, and gradually the Austrian defence began to weaken. Some of the guns were put out of action, and at about midday the Austrians began to run short of ammunition. In Bonaparte's words, 'The bridge was then repaired with ease ...'[53] The rest of the advance-guard soon crossed and tried to outflank the Austrians on their left. The latter retired to Valeggio, pursued by the French, who engaged them in the streets of the village, and drove them out. However, the French were driven back in their turn by enemy cavalry when they tried to advance beyond Valeggio, and a short pause ensued until more French cavalry could arrive.

While this desperate and uneven fight to defend Borghetto had been going on, the rest of the Austrian forces had spent the morning variously occupied. Colli had been calmly awaiting orders far to the south, at Goito, while Sebottendorf's attention had been devoted to driving off some French troops who had been trying to ford the river near Campagnola. The reserve, meanwhile, had left only one battalion of IR Wenzel Colloredo in Oliosi, and had taken up positions along the river to the north of Borghetto, where it became involved in some sporadic firing over the river with French patrols that appeared on the other bank. It was not until about midday that any of these Austrian forces was presented with evidence of the seriousness of what was happening at Borghetto, and not until early afternoon in the case of Colli.

Their reactions were varied. Colli immediately marched for Valeggio with all his men to attack the French on their right, in the belief that they would be fully engaged by Melas and Sebottendorf. The latter, on the other hand, initially only sent a squadron of hussars to investigate the truth of the report he had received, which stated that part of the French army had managed to cross the river. Things were a little more dramatic for the battalion of IR Wenzel Colloredo, which first got an inkling that something might be wrong when the whole artillery park, ammunition train, and the HQ's baggage suddenly appeared on the road from Valeggio in great disorder and full flight. These were soon followed by swarms of troops of all arms and units, who announced that the enemy was not far behind them. Things might have deteriorated further had the situation not been taken in hand by General Prince Hohenzollern, who turned up fortuitously, having been on a reconnaissance to Peschiera. He managed to stem the chaotic retreat, and even gathered enough troops to stage a counter-attack on Valeggio in the afternoon. While this had been going on, Beaulieu had issued an order for the army to retire to the Adige. Under the cover of Hohenzollern's attack, Melas was able to gather his recently scattered units from their positions along the Mincio and withdraw to Oliosi. From there he observed that Hohenzollern was being driven back from Valeggio by Kilmaine and Murat, and therefore moved off towards Castelnuovo. When Hohenzollern got back to Oliosi, he found it had been evacuated, and consequently continued his withdrawal in the same direction.

In the meantime, the French had established their HQ in Valeggio, and Massena had moved up to Borghetto, where his men occupied themselves with cooking. With the Austrians apparently in full retreat, there did not seem to be any danger to the HQ, but this illusion was shattered when at some point in the afternoon Sebottendorf's reconnoitring hussars arrived in Valeggio. According to an account he gave many years later, on St Helena, Bonaparte had been suffering from a severe headache, which he was trying to cure with a foot bath, and he was forced to flee with only one boot.[54] The alarm was of short duration, though it startled Massena's troops enough to interrupt them in their meal, and caused them to pack up and advance across the bridge. A longer-term effect was that it persuaded Bonaparte to create a protective force for the HQ, initially consisting of two battalions of grenadiers and 50 cavalry. That same day he issued an order for Lannes to take command of this guard. The officer of chasseurs who was to lead the cavalry was Jean-Baptiste Bessières, later to become a marshal, and one of Bonaparte's intimates. This was effectively the origin of that most prestigious regiment, the Chasseurs à Cheval of the Imperial Guard.

Having learned that the enemy was in Valeggio, Sebottendorf collected his battalions of IR Strassoldo, IR Toscana and IR Thurn, and tried to fight his way through to join the rest of the army on the other side, but without success. At about 5 p.m. he gave up, and after rallying his men he continued his march by inclining to the right, and reached Villafranca safely, where he halted for two hours. At some time during the afternoon, Colli also discovered he had been cut off, and sent his infantry back to Mantua before turning in the direction of Villafranca.

Bonaparte was less concerned with pursuing these fragments of the enemy army than with tracking the main force, and at 5 p.m. he issued orders to Kilmaine to gather his troops as soon as possible and march on Castelnuovo. At the same time, Augereau was ordered to advance along the left bank of the Mincio, and invest Peschiera. Such a move had been foreseen by Beaulieu, and about an hour earlier Lipthay had received an order to abandon the place when the enemy appeared in force, as the army was falling back to the Tyrol.

Sergeant Petitbon of the 4th Line tells us that his demi-brigade got separated from the rest of Augereau's division due to the speed of its march, and rashly fell on Lipthay's rearguard near Peschiera. Pushing too far ahead, the leading companies were engaged by cavalry, and severely mauled. Schels claims that Austrian losses were only nine men, while Petitbon says his demi-brigade lost three officers, and 97 men killed, wounded or captured.[55] After this, Lipthay reached Castelnuovo at about 6 p.m. in good order. Melas had already gone by this time, but Hohenzollern arrived between 6 and 7 p.m., and according to Schels there was fighting at Castelnuovo until nightfall.

Shortly before this time, Sebottendorf had moved on from Villafranca, and gone via Sona towards the Adige. He crossed the river at Bussolengo at about 11 p.m., at which time Lipthay and Hohenzollern also continued their retreat from Castelnuovo towards the Adige.

A little to their rear was Colli, who had gone via Villafranca, and arrived in Castelnuovo at midnight. By mid-morning on the 31st, all these troops had arrived at Dolcè in the Adige valley, where they were almost safe from serious attack.

The losses sustained by the Austrians during these engagements (including a small number of men over the next two days) amounted to eleven officers and 561 men, killed, wounded or captured.[56] The commander of the Neapolitan cavalry, the Prince di Cuto, was also captured. Precise French losses for the same period do not seem to be known, but they cannot have been slight, if the experience of the 4th Line was typical. Nevertheless, at the conclusion of these operations, the French were masters of Lombardy, with the exception of Mantua, to which they now turned their attention.

NOTES

1. Vigo-Roussillon, F. *Journal de campagne (1793–1837)*. Paris, 1981, pp. 34–5.
2. The name is also spelt Lamy or Lami.
3. Schels, J. B. 'Das Treffen am Mincio am 30 Mai, und die übrigen Kriegsereignisse in Italien, von der Mitte des Mai bis zu Anfang des Juli 1796.' *Oesterreichische Militärische Zeitschrift*, Bd. 3; Bd. 4 (1827), p. 75.
4. Dante Alighieri, *Inferno*, XX, pp. 89–90.
5. These figures are from Schels, J. B. 'Die Vertheidigung von Mantua im Juni und Juli 1796." *Oesterreichische Militärische Zeitschrift*, Bd. 1 (1830), pp. 87–8.
6. Ibid., pp. 86–7.
7. Vigo-Roussillon, op. cit., p. 35.
8. Melzi d'Eril, F. *Memorie, documenti, e lettere inedite di Napoleone I e di Beauharnais.* Milan, 1865, I, p. 144, and Bouvier, F. *Bonaparte en Italie, 1796.* Paris, 1899.
9. Chevrier, E. *Le général Joubert d'après sa correspondance.* Paris, 1884, p. 37.
10. Alberghini, G. B., don. *Gli austro-galli in val di Caprino (1796–1801) memoria storica.* Verona, 1880, p. 19.
11. Schels, J. B. 'Die Kriegsereignisse in Italien vom 15 April bis 16 Mai

1796, mit dem Gefechte bei Lodi.' *Oesterreichische Militärische Zeitschrift,* Bd. 2; Bd. 4 (1825), pp. 295–6, and Schels, 1830, op. cit., pp. 87–8.

12. Schels, 1827, op. cit., p. 76, and Napoleon. *Correspondance de Napoléon Ier publiée par ordre de l'empereur Napoléon III.* Paris, 1858–69, no. 448.

13. Napoleon. 1858–69, op. cit., no. 437.

14. Ibid., no. 453.

15. Verri, P. *Lettere e scritti inediti di Pietro e Alessandro Verri.* Milan, 1881, IV, p. 215.

16. Napoleon. 1858–69, op. cit., no. 439.

17. Ibid., no. 441.

18. Pelleport, P. *Souvenirs militaires et intimes du général vicomte de Pelleport, de 1793 à 1853.* Paris and Bordeaux, 1857, pp. 43–4.

19. Roguet, F. *Mémoires militaires du lieutenant général comte Roguet (Français), colonel en second des grenadiers à pied de la Vieille Garde, pair de France.* Paris, 1862, p. 244.

20. Vigo-Roussillon, op. cit., pp. 34–5.

21. Napoleon. *Lettres d'amour à Joséphine.* Paris, 1981, no. 12.

22. Napoleon. 1858–69, op. cit., no. 461.

23. Bouvier, 1899, op. cit., p. 629.

24. The *Marchese* Belcredi. See Capra, C. *L'età rivoluzionaria e napoleonica in Italia, 1796–1815.* Turin, 1978, p. 110.

25. See Bouvier, F. 'La révolte de Pavie (23-26 mai 1796).' *Revue historique de la Révolution française,* 2; 3 (1911–12): 519–39; 72–89, 257–75, 424–46.

26. Ibid.

27. According to Bouvier, the commander was Augereau's ADC, Captain Latrille, but this is open to doubt. His signature does not seem to appear on the act of capitulation of the garrison, as one might expect.

28. Magenta, C. 'L'insurrezione di Pavia nel 1796.' *Rivista storica italiana,* 1 (1884), pp 273–93

29. Napoleon. *Correspondance inédite officielle et confidentielle de Napoléon Bonaparte: avec les cours étrangères, les princes, les ministres et les généraux français et étrangers, en Italie, en Allemagne, et en Egypte.* Paris, 1809, I, pp. 207–9.

30. Roguet, op. cit., pp. 246–7.

31. Laugier, J.-R. *Les cahiers du capitaine Laugier. – De la guerre et de l'anarchie, ou Mémoires historiques des campagnes et aventures d'un capitaine du 27me régiment d'infanterie légère par Jérome-Roland Laugier. Publiés d'après le manuscrit original par Léon G. Pélissier.* Aix, 1893, p. 88.

32. Napoleon. 1858–69, op. cit., no. 494.

33. Many historians have placed the sack of Binasco on the same day as that of Pavia, but the letter quoted below would seem to contradict this, and so does the History of the 5th Dragoons.

34. Napoleon. *Lettres inédites de Napoléon Ier. Collationées sur les textes et publiées par Léonce de Brotonne.* Paris, 1898, p. 5.

35. Magenta, C. 'L'insurrezione di Pavia nel 1796.' *Rivista storica italiana*, 1 (1884), p. 284.

36. Capra, op. cit., p. 112.

37. Napoleon. *Mémoires pour servir à l'histoire de France, sous le regne de Napoléon, écrits sous sa dictée à Sainte-Hélène, par les généraux qui ont partagé sa captivité.* Paris, 1829, I, p. 452.

38. Napoleon. 1858–69, op. cit., no. 536.

39. Capra, op. cit., p. 113.

40. Manfredi, S. *L'insurrezione e il sacco di Pavia nel maggio, 1796: monografia storica documentata.* Pavia, 1900, pp. 138–9.

41. Bouvier, 1911–12, op. cit., p. 426.

42. Napoleon, *Campagnes d'Italie*, vol XXIX.

43. Napoleon. 1858–69, op. cit., no. 537.

44. Napoleon, *Campagnes d'Italie*, vol XXIX.

45. Napoleon. 1858–69, op. cit., no. 496.

46. Napoleon. 1809, op. cit., I, p. 212.

47. Pezay, A.-F.-J. M., marquis de. *Histoire des campagnes de M. le Maréchal de Maillebois en Italie pendant les années 1745 et 1746.* Paris, 1775, II, pp. 2–3.

48. Holland Rose, J. 'Despatches of Colonel Thomas Graham on the Italian Campaign of 1796–1797.' *The English Historical Review*, 14 (1899), p. 115.

49. Napoleon. 1858–69, op. cit., no. 537.

50. Schels, 1827, op. cit., p. 177.

51. Gachot, E. *Histoire militaire de Massena. La première campagne d'Italie (1795-1798).* Paris, 1901, pp. 150–1.

52. Napoleon. 1858–69, op. cit., no. 537.

53. Ibid., no. 537.

54. Interestingly, the editor of Massena's memoirs, General Koch, comments that he had asked many officers attached to the staff about Bonaparte's near-capture at Valeggio, and none of them could remember it. See Massena, A. *Mémoires de Massena, rédigés d'après les documents qu'il a laissés et sur ceux du dépôt de la guerre et du dépôt des fortifications, par le général Koch*. Paris, 1848–50, II, p. 439.

55. Godechot, J. 'Le carnet de route du sergent Petitbon sur la campagne d'Italie de 1796–1797.' *Rivista italiana di studi napoleonici*, 15 (1978), p. 40.

56. Schels, 1827, op. cit., p. 305.

15

MANTUA TO CASTIGLIONE

On 31 May, the Austrians continued their withdrawal northwards via Peri and Ala to Rovereto and Calliano, leaving Lipthay with a rearguard of 5,600 men near the pontoon bridge at Dolcè. He was not left undisturbed for long, and at about 4 p.m. men of Augereau's division arrived near Rivoli, and made their way down the steep road into the Adige valley. A skirmish ensued, the Austrians drew back, breaking up the bridge, and the two sides then had to limit themselves to exchanging artillery fire across the river until dark.

On the following morning, Massena marched from Villafranca and occupied Verona (until late April the place of exile of the future King Louis XVIII); then part of his division advanced up the left bank of the Adige towards Volargne and the Chiusa, a small fort blocking the valley near Rivoli. On 2 June, Lipthay's troops found themselves heavily involved in skirmishes with Massena's division, which was gradually taking control of the heights overlooking the Adige. Anxious that he might be cut off by these superior forces, Lipthay pulled back towards Ala, and was promptly relieved of his command by Beaulieu, who disapproved of his actions. He was replaced by Colli.

Beaulieu was not the subject of much approval himself, and Thomas Graham commented:

> The General from personal intrepidity seems to expect too much from troops in the state of mind his are in, and his Language (publickly) is not conciliatory or encouraging either to officers or soldiers. His temper, naturally warm, seems irritated by disappointment and he is anxious to vindicate his own plans by throwing the whole Blame on the execution: on the other hand, if I may judge from the very improper language held unreservedly by the officers I have conversed with, the army has no confidence in him. – But as there is much of party intrigue in the Austrian

army, I don't know that this sentiment is at all general, but almost all I have met are *Frondeurs* & hope that he will be removed from the command – a younger man more capable of *bodily* exertion would be desirable in such a war as this.[1]

Not surprisingly, the Austrian high command had been unable to ignore the catastrophic series of reverses that Beaulieu had suffered in such a short time, and a replacement had already been appointed a few days before, though, as we shall see, he was not the young man that Graham wanted.

Also on the way to Italy were considerable reinforcements, partly marching from the Rhine army under General Bajalich, amounting to 24 battalions, five Jäger companies, eighteen squadrons of hussars, two pioneer companies, and a whole artillery reserve. In an attempt to redress the problems of command that Beaulieu had complained about, three *Feldmarschall-Lieutenants* and four *General-Majors* were also being sent. Of the three senior generals, two of them (Davidovich and Mészáros) had been born in Hungary, and were 59 years old, while the third (Quosdanovich) had been born in Croatia, and was 58. All of them had careers going back to the Seven Years War, and had distinguished themselves either in the War of the Bavarian Succession or the Turkish wars. More recently, Davidovich had served in the Netherlands, where he had been decorated, while Quosdanovich had been in Germany, and made a particularly good showing at Handschuhsheim in October 1795, for which he had also won a decoration. Mészáros was the *Inhaber* of the Uhlans, and had served under Wurmser in Germany, twice winning decorations, and earning recent promotion.

On 2 June, the first French troops had reached Mantua. Augereau had pushed forward clouds of skirmishers, under the cover of which he had approached the northern walls, and spent more than fifteen minutes inspecting them.[2] Had the antagonists known it, a new phase of the campaign was about to open: one characterised largely by many months of siege, in which Mantua became a kind of Holy Grail for both armies.

The city, which had passed to the Austrians in 1714 with the Peace of Rastadt, had some 2,650 houses, nineteen churches and about

25,000 inhabitants. It was surrounded by a wall in which there were a number of main gates, those of Mulina, San Giorgio, Cerese, Pusterla, Pradella and Catena. There were also seven sally-ports. Various outworks had been built since 1714, but had been neglected in the previous half-century of peace, and had had to be hastily repaired. To the west was the hornwork outside Porta Pradella, to the south the crownwork of Palazzo del Tè, before Porta Pusterla, and to the south-east the entrenchments of Migliaretto, before Porta Cerese. To the north and east, the city was protected by the lake.

On the other side of the lake to the north was the citadel, which had five bastions. To the east was the suburb of San Giorgio, which only had a weak earth wall around it. The citadel was connected to the city by the causeway called Ponte Mulina, and there was another similar causeway from San Giorgio to the city. They were strongly built and had draw-bridges, and divided the lake into three parts, known as the Upper, Middle and Lower Lakes. Ponte Mulina dammed the upper lake about eight feet higher than normal, and the waters served to drive twelve mills, called the Apostles. The moats between the city and the outer works of Pradella, Tè and Migliaretto could be filled by raising the sluices that separated them from the lake. Much of the surrounding area consisted of swamps and marshes, which kept the enemy at a distance, and made any entrenching work difficult.

The area around Mantua was also known to be extremely unhealthy, particularly in summer. With such an abundance of water, it was, of course, a paradise for mosquitoes, though their contribution to sickness was not understood at the time. Indeed, the bad health was attributed to bad air, which is what '*mal aria*' means in Italian. Bonaparte had been keen to see this part of the campaign concluded before the onset of the great heat in high summer, but this had not happened. A few days later, he wrote to Carnot observing that the heat was increasing, and commented: 'The campaign in Italy began two months too late. We find ourselves obliged to remain in the most unhealthy place in Italy.'[3] He was well aware that illness and heat exhaustion would badly affect the fighting capabilities of his army, and used these as another argument for postponing the Directory's favourite project of an advance to Naples.

He would no doubt have been supported by Joubert, who complained to his father: 'I am not ill, but I am so tired that I can't describe it. All day on horseback in excessive heat.'[4]

In the meantime, the Austrians had been making preparations for what was to be the twelfth siege in the history of Mantua. One of the members of the city council, a Cremonese called Baldassare Scorza, who was in daily contact with the commander, left a very full description of the events. Like other civilians he must have been alarmed when 'the 1st of June dawned with the frightening blocking of all the streets of the city with cannons, mortars, howitzers, *petriere* and swivel guns, with their ammunition, hurriedly transported from the park at Gradaro and from the arsenals to the bulwarks and other fortifications'.[5] They were, in fact, a motley collection of weapons, of thirteen different calibres, and supplying them with the correct ammunition was not the simplest of tasks.

The ability of the fortress to resist also depended greatly on supplies, however, and reports indicated that the military magazines had sufficient quantities of bread, flour, and so forth, for 71 days, oats for 124 days, hay for 22 days and wood for 54 days. To these could be added not inconsiderable quantities of maize, rice and corn in the civilian magazines. However, other things, such as meat, wine and fodder for the animals, were lacking.[6] The shortage of wine was not perceived as a problem because of the undoubtedly prodigious drinking capacity of the Austrian soldiery – no army of the time could lay much claim to sobriety among its troops – but had more to do with the supposed medicinal qualities of wine. Various measures were taken to regulate consumption among the civilian population, and a list of prices for all comestibles was published. Scorza also tells us:

We published the prohibition, during the blockade, to ring the bells, keep open the windows of the houses towards the country, to climb onto the observatories, towers and belfries out of curiosity, to send dogs out of the houses without collars, to keep wood ... and other masses of combustible materials in the tops of houses, to walk, singing, playing or making noise in any way through the quarters after 8 in the evening, to make gatherings or meetings of greater than three people, to spread news, distasteful or alarming writings, to throw into the street rubbish or other infected things capable of increasing the unhealthiness of the air, and we ordered the roofs of the houses and buildings to be covered with at least an ell thickness of stable manure, to make the explosions less destructive in case of a siege.[7]

On 3 June, the French duly closed in on the fortress, and Vukassovich pulled his men back from the Serraglio, the area to the south of the city. The garrison was distributed in the following manner. General Roselmini was in the citadel with:

Regiment	Battns	Men
IR Nádasdy	2	1,332
IR Thurn	2	1,264
Warasdiner Grenzers	1	1,070
	5	3,666

General Vukassovich was at the gate and in the hornwork of Pradella with:

Regiment	Battns	Men
Carlstädter Grenzers	1	1,018
IR Erzherzog Anton	2	1,431
	3	2,449

Colonel Salisch was in the crownwork of Palazzo Tè with:

Regiment	Battns	Men
IR Belgioioso	3	837
IR Pellegrini	1	147
IR Preiss	1	247
IR Stein	1	195
1st Garrison Regiment		63
	6	1,489

General Rukavina was in the entrenchments of Migliaretto with:

Regiment	Battns	Men
Carlstädter Grenzers	1	838
2nd Garrison Regiment	1	622
IR Terzi	3	983
	5	2,443

Colonel Sturioni occupied San Giorgio and the bastion in the town behind it, on the other side of the causeway, and the shore of the lake from Porta Mulina downwards, with:

Regiment	Battns	Men
2nd Garrison Regiment	1⅓	871
Frei-Corps Gyulay	1	1,194
Mantuan militia	⅙	233
	2½	2,298

The infantry therefore numbered 20½ battalions, totalling 12,345 men. The cavalry consisted of:

Regiment	sqdns	men
Stabsdragoner	2	177
Erzherzog Joseph Hussars	1	168
Mészáros Uhlans	½	89
	3½	434

There were also 96 officers and men belonging to the engineers, sappers and miners, as well as 701 officers and men of the artillery. The lakes had eight ferries, seven flat-bottomed boats and one cannon-armed shallop, with crews of two officers and 64 men. Counting the 111 staff (including the generals), the garrison arrived at a grand total of 13,753 men. In addition to these, there were 81 men belonging to the Transport service, with 235 horses and 755 cavalry horses.[8]

The other half of the army was, by now, in the Tyrol, with the HQ at Calliano. Colli had the advance-guard, numbering 5,852 infantry and 508 cavalry, at Santa Margherita in the Adige valley, with his outposts under Hohenzollern at Ala. General Henrici was camped near Rovereto with 3,923 infantry and 386 cavalry. Sebottendorf was in the same area with 4,102 infantry and 580 cavalry, while Melas was at Borgo in the Brenta valley with 2,052 infantry and 732 cavalry. The Neapolitan cavalry, numbering 1,583 men, was sent to the rear beyond Trento, as was the artillery reserve. Maelcamp remained on the Sarca (flowing into Lake Garda from the north) with 676 infantry and 104 cavalry, while Loudon with 842 infantry and 110 cavalry was looking after the border with Grisons. The grand total for this army on 4 June was 24⅓ battalions (19,822 men) and 37 squadrons (4,236 men), supported by some units of Tyrolean militia, which had already mobilised for the defence of their home territory.

As for the French, no sooner had the army crossed the Mincio than some radical changes to its organisation had been put into effect, partly in preparation for the operations that the Directory wished Bonaparte to undertake towards the south of Italy, and partly to incorporate reinforcements from the Army of the Alps, which included a few generals that Bonaparte was to wish he had not received. The advance-guard under Kilmaine was dissolved and the components sent back to their divisions, but three battalions of grenadiers, amounting to 2,100 men, were kept under Dallemagne, as a special reserve for the HQ. Lannes and Dupas, who had been so prominent in the action at Lodi, were specifically included among the personnel. Massena's division was greatly increased in size, to 13,600 men, and took up a position on the right bank of the Adige near Rivoli and Madonna della Corona, to watch the Austrian army in the Tyrol. This positioning incidentally gave Massena and Joubert their first opportunity to get to know an area that was to be most important to them in January 1797. Also under Massena's command was General Sauret, previously in charge of some of the occupying troops in Piedmont, who was ordered to Peschiera to command a separate division of 4,460 men. He was also to guard the western side of the lake. On 4 June, Augereau positioned his division, now consisting of only 4,820 men, near Cerese, three miles south of Mantua. Sérurier was near La Favorita, which lay half an hour's march north of the city, with a division of 4,700 men. Another new division, of 5,500 men under the newly arrived General Vaubois, was also created for the expedition to the south. Kilmaine retained command of the cavalry arm.[9]

In Mantua, the city council had been dissolved, and a politico-military commission formed, with Scorza dealing with economics and accounts. On 4 June, he wrote: 'The case is decided. If it is not tomorrow it will be the day after, and not later, that Mantua is completely invested ... so everyone hurries to bundle up and escape from the city. We employed four secretaries to write out passports. Few nobles and few rich people remain by now.'[10] He also tells us that the military arrangements included a well-equipped observation post:

> For several days, on the tower of the Gabbia, opposite Casa Guer-rieri, conveniently close to the house of the commander, some subalterns of the engineers have been placed to observe the movements of the enemy ... by use of excellent telescopes and an exquisite English catadioptric telescope, graciously provided by the mathematician *Abate* Mari, with which they could see the country up to the face of the public clock in Verona ... They were to occupy themselves with these observations, write a journal, and report anything notable to the commander immediately, using acoustic trumpets ...[11]

That day, the defenders were also subjected to a lively attack in the direction of San Giorgio, which nearly caught them napping: 'Luckily, our commander was walking with various officers in the vicinity. He immediately ran at great risk to the gate, and the ordering and executing of the raising of the drawbridge, bringing back the boats, and firing the cannons of the ravelin against the attackers was but a moment, the blink of an eye.'[12] In fact the attack was a feint that had been ordered by Bonaparte to cover a reconnaissance around San Giorgio which he made with Andréossy, and another from La Favorita by Chasseloup. As a result of his inspection, Bonaparte issued orders to Andréossy to collect boats, and give the impression that the lake might be crossed at any moment, while Chasseloup was ordered to secure the shores of the lake and block the roads from the fortress to the surrounding country.[13]

There was little else that could be done for a while, for two reasons. One was that the French had no siege artillery available. Some of it had been captured by Nelson on 30 May while it was being transported from Toulon to Genoa, and some was needed in Milan. Moreover, as Bonaparte explained to the Directory a couple of days later: '[Mantua] is unapproachable at the moment because of the overflowing rivers and the rising waters caused by the melting snows ... The overflowing of the Po, which is greater than it has been for 20 years, because it has flooded 10 leagues around, makes any attack impossible at the moment. All the streams are large rivers in this season: the snow is melting fast.'[14] Having done what he could, Bonaparte left for Milan on 5 June to deal with other affairs, placing Sérurier in charge of operations around Mantua: 'The General-in-Chief leaves him master to make all the dispositions that he believes suitable, with the troops under his orders, having for his aim to make us master of the shores of the lake and the exits from the fortress.'[15] This was soon done, and three days later Canto d'Irles gave the signal that had been arranged with Beaulieu (six cannon-shots at two-minute intervals) to communicate that the fortress was now completely blockaded.[16]

Among the other affairs that occupied Bonaparte's attention at the time, the most important had a bearing on the projected expedition to the south. On 5 June, Bonaparte had signed an armistice with Naples,[17] which must have been a matter of great satisfaction to him, because if it led to a peace agreement there could be no question of having to under-take the long march down the peninsula. Bonaparte was already preparing to march to Livorno, perhaps even Rome, but he continued to argue against a deeper penetration. Indeed, on 7 June he did precisely that in a letter to the Directory: 'Can we and should we go to Naples?' he asked, rather rhetorically, and after suggesting that the army had too few men for such a venture, he added, 'but, if we had 20,000 men, it would not be advisable for us to carry out a twenty-five day march, in the months of July and August, to find sickness and death'. He also expressed the opinion that Rome was likely to cave in as soon as the French entered their territory south of the Po, and it seems clear that he wished to convince the Directory that it would be unnecessary to go as far as Rome itself:

> By means of this armistice with Naples, we are in a position to dictate to Rome all the conditions we like … From the conversation that I had this morning with M. d'Azara, minister of Spain, sent by the Pope, it seemed to me that he had orders to offer us contributions. Soon I shall be in Bologna [in the Papal States]. Do you wish me to accept then, in order to agree an armistice with the Pope, 25,000,000 in contributions in silver, 5,000,000 in food, 300 paintings, statues and manuscripts in proportion, and that I have put at liberty all the patriots arrested for acts of Revolution?[18]

There could be little doubt of the Directory's answer.

The beginning of June had also seen the ending of an armistice – that between the French and Austrian armies on the Rhine – and hostilities there were due to reopen. This must have been a relief to Bonaparte, because it meant that the Austrians would have less scope for sending reinforcements to Italy. On 11 June he wrote to General Moreau, who was commanding the Army of the Rhine, telling him he had sent his comrades in the north a million francs.[19] It was generosity with a pragmatic side, because any success of Moreau would undoubtedly make life easier for the Army of Italy. Furthermore, it was essential for the Army of the Rhine to advance if Bonaparte's original plan of making a junction between the two armies were to be carried out.

In the meantime, the impossibility of beginning the siege of Mantua meant that Bonaparte had time and resources to devote to other military operations. First, he had to put down another revolt. The rebellion in Pavia had not been the end of the French army's troubles with the civilian population, and there had been considerable unrest in the Imperial fiefs near Genoa. Various detachments of French soldiers had been attacked, and the rebellion had culminated with the troops in Arquata (a few miles east of Gavi) being besieged. In the second week of June, therefore, a punitive expedition was made to the area. Bonaparte himself went as far as Tortona, but left the active command in the hands of Lannes, who had already proved himself at Pavia. In his report to the Directory of 15 June, he states: 'The Imperial fiefs ... gave themselves up to every excess. *Chef de brigade* Lannes marched there with 1,200 men. He burnt the houses of the rebels, and captured the principals, who have been shot.'[20] Regrettably, it was not to be the last such incident.

The second operation was, of course, the expedition to the south, which Bonaparte wished to conclude as rapidly as possible. Reports indicated that the Austrians were receiving large reinforcements, and while Bonaparte was away he tried to keep track of their state of readiness, particularly asking the French envoy in Venice to send spies to Trento and Rovereto. Bonaparte was fortunate both that Austrian preparations for a return to Mantua were not completed during his excursion south of the Po, and that he found almost no obstacles during the operation.

The expedition began on 15 June, when Augereau departed for Bologna, and Vaubois for Reggio, in the Duchy of Modena. Four days later, the divisions arrived at their respective destinations. On that day, Bonaparte passed through Modena and arrived in Bologna at midnight. Fort Urban, a castle situated at Castelfranco Emilia, on the border between Modena and Bologna, surrendered without a fight. This capture yielded a very useful quantity of artillery, as the fort had 50 guns. Bonaparte also had the Cardinal Legate in Bologna made prisoner, but sent him off to Rome to make known the French demands. Preparations for a further advance were made, with Murat being given command of the advance-guard of Vaubois' division, with Lannes under his orders. In the meantime the French also took Ferrara, capturing a further 114 guns which were in the castle, and another Cardinal Legate. Bonaparte must have been highly satisfied with affairs, and reported to the Directory: 'The artillery that we have found in Modena, Fort Urban, and in the castle of Ferrara forms a siege train that will permit us to besiege Mantua.'[21] Even better news was to come on 23 June, when a cease-fire was signed with the Pope, virtually liberating Bonaparte from any further need to worry about a long march southwards.

There was, however, still the matter of Livorno, which had been a haven for the English and a constant thorn in the side of the French, but this too was very quickly dealt with. The French entered Tuscan territory on 26 June, despite the alarm and protests of the Grand Duke, and rapidly advanced to Livorno, arriving on the following day shortly after numerous English vessels had left the port. All goods belonging to enemy nations were sequestered by the French, and the governor was arrested on the grounds that he had favoured the enemy instead of behaving as a neutral. He was sent off to Florence with the suggestion that the Grand Duke might want to punish him severely, and Vaubois and his division were installed in Livorno as garrison. With the military expedition thus successfully concluded with the minimum of fuss, Bonaparte departed for Florence on 29 June, travelling through San Miniato. Here he met Canon Filippo Buonaparte, a distant relative, who thoroughly amused Bonaparte by trying to enlist his help in having one of their ancient forbears, who had been beatified, 'promoted' to the status of sainthood. In Florence, Bonaparte was received by the Grand Duke, and dined with him on 1 July. Unexpectedly, the Republican general and the brother of the Emperor seem to have got on very well. The following day Bonaparte was in Bologna, and by the 4th he was with his main army again, at Roverbella.

Relatively little fighting apart from some skirmishes had taken place in his absence, but the Austrians had been taking steps to rebuild their forces. On 21 June, Graham had written:

General Alvinski one of the members of the *Conseil de Guerre* [Hofkriegsrath] having been sent to hasten the preparations & examine into the state of the army, arrived here yesterday, after being some days in the Tyrol – General Beaulieu still retains the command as General ... Melas [who was to be interim commander] is not sufficiently recovered from the Bruises he received by being overturned down a precipice. General Colli who was second in command seems to be very glad to retire on a pension. Lieutenant Generals Sepottendorf & Henrizi with major Gen[ls] Liptaye, Gurner, Hoenzollern, Lassdon & Shurbirstz are the only Generals now wth the army: I don't know what is become of all the rest …[22]

To the implicit criticism of the Austrian generals contained in the last phrase may be added the report that Graham made of 'the almost incredible fact that about 400 different officers … were found in Trent, having, like the Croats, abandoned their corps during the preceding part of the campaign'.[23] Not surprisingly, the army in the Tyrol was in poor condition, and greatly in need of replacements and reinforcements. On 22 June it could only find 15,927 infantry and 2,804 cavalry fit for combat (there were large numbers of sick), though there were about 3,000 militia available purely for the defence of the local territory. There were 48 battalion guns with the infantry and 64 field pieces with the park, while a further 77 guns were placed in prepared defensive positions in the mountains.[24]

On the 30th, Graham reported that Melas was taking command temporarily, that Beaulieu had departed, and that Field Marshal Wurmser was in the Tyrol and was expected to take command. Once again the Austrians had chosen to give their army to an officer with long experience – or, to put it another way, an old man. Count Dagobert-Sigismond de Wurmser was 72 years of age, and a native of Strasbourg, on the Franco–German border. He had first served in the French army, and made his first campaign in Bohemia in 1742. A specialist in the use of light troops, he had served under Soubise during the Seven Years War, then passed to the Austrian army in 1762. During the Revolutionary war, he had spent the years since 1792 in Germany, and had made a favourable impression on Thugut by his energy – a quality he shared with Beaulieu, and which Thugut seemed to prize.

Wurmser would certainly have found plenty of work to do when he arrived in the Tyrol, as organising an operation to relieve Mantua was now a matter of some urgency. The same urgency was felt by Bonaparte, and over the next month there was to be something of a race to see whether he could capture the fortress before Wurmser could complete his preparations and attack him. Fortunately for Bonaparte the castle of Milan had been obliged to surrender on 29 June after a 48-hour bombardment, thus providing him with yet more guns to use on Mantua. However, evidence of increasing enemy activity in the north was not reassuring: 'The storm is beginning to gather,'[25] he wrote on 2 July. On the 5th, he reported to Paris that the Austrians had increased by 25,000 men, and wrote twice to Despinoy to hasten the despatch of the artillery from Milan, but also found space to make a sly reference to the effect that the delights of that city had had on the habitual bachelor, Berthier: 'Do not write letters that may turn the head of our poor chief of staff, because since you spoke to him of a beautiful actress who awaits him in Milan, he is dying with impatience to go there.'[26] Bonaparte was probably more than a little excited at the prospect of female company himself, as Josephine had finally been induced to leave Paris (in floods of tears) and join her husband in Milan, where she eventually arrived in the middle of the month.

On the 6th, in a letter to the Directory, Bonaparte enlarged on his reasons for wanting to take Mantua quickly: 'Sérurier's division, which besieges Mantua, and is 7,000 strong, is beginning to suffer 50 sick every day … I hope that we shall soon have the town, otherwise we shall have many sick. Wurmser is beginning to make movements to try and relieve Mantua.' This was, in fact, a little premature, as Wurmser had hardly had time to get his bearings. The same letter is also rather inaccurate in estimating the Austrian forces at 67,000. It is no doubt more precise about the French army, which it puts at 44,000 (in five divisions, under Massena, Sauret, Augereau, Sérurier and Despinoy, but not including the garrisons in various places).[27] Another letter, written to Despinoy on 9 July, is also revealing of Bonaparte's impatience to begin the siege: 'I am in an abominable temper with everyone in Milan. Nothing is arriving, neither siege artillery, nor officers nor gunners … I am sending you an ADC post to speed the despatch. In the circumstances in which we find ourselves, days are centuries.'[28]

The need to hurry was brought home by indications that the Austrians had used the Brenta valley, which provided an easterly route from the Tyrol to the Po valley, to send a force estimated at 8,000 to

Bassano, from where they could advance over the plain to Mantua. This may well have convinced Bonaparte that time was running out, and inspired an attempt to capture Mantua by a quicker method than a siege. In a letter to the Directory of 12 July he says he is contemplating a *coup de main* against Mantua on the 16th, for which he has boats and Austrian uniforms ready.[29] Orders for the surprise attack were issued to Murat, Sérurier and Dallemagne on the 16th, but the attempt was frustrated by the garrison making a sortie on the same day. This was one of a number they had made since the blockade began, either to gather fodder, or to hinder the progress of the siege works. The losses sustained by the Austrians indicate just how serious the fighting was. Rukavina's ADC, another officer and 68 men were killed, ten officers and 320 men were wounded, and one officer and 63 men were captured.[30]

Undeterred at being pre-empted, Bonaparte wished to go ahead with the *coup de main* on the following day. In his report to the Directory, he says that 800 grenadiers under Murat and Vignolle were to be shipped across the lake, and an officer and 50 men dressed as Austrians were to try to surprise one of the gates. However, the water had gone down three feet in 24 hours, making the attempt impossible.[31] Interestingly, Scorza tells us that a captured officer who was exchanged on the 17th 'reported he had heard that an attack with boats towards Cerese was arranged for the 19th',[32] which does not say a lot for the secrecy of French preparations. He also reported rapid work on the trenches, that the army round about was 10,000 strong, with another 8,000 in the vicinity, and that General Fiorella had told him the bombardment would begin on the 19th.

Fear of this inevitable development had already had its effect on the unfortunate population of the city, as Scorza noted:

> Whoever has a house with no cellars, and whoever has a house exposed to the batteries of the enemy raves and runs desperately around the city seeking places to make himself safe. The Ducal palace, which as you know has abundant cellars, is already stuffed

full of people of every condition, and seems like a hospital for lunatics and obsessives.

Scorza also humorously commented that the prohibition on discussing news and spreading rumours had rebounded on them, and that 'now everybody talks. We, who prohibited it, talk. The military men, who should be silent and encourage us, talk ...'[33] and that their prohibition had intensified the very thing they had wanted to suppress.

Reliable information about what was happening in the Tyrol was no doubt rather scarce in the blockaded fortress, but Bonaparte was, if anything, even more keen to obtain news of Wurmser's activity, and he was prepared to use unconventional methods at times. This included giving Massena specific orders that when the Neapolitan cavalry came down from the mountains on 18 July (to be held until a full peace agreement was signed) the officers were to be treated to a grand banquet. French officers were to play the solicitous host, and pump their guests for as much information as they could get.

In the meantime, the batteries around Mantua had been completed. They were ten in number, many of which had smaller-calibre weapons, and were intended for defence against sorties. A few emplacements boasted very heavy-calibre siege weapons. Scorza saw them later, and provided a quite detailed description of some of them: 'The first is placed on the heights at Belfiore, covered in front with gabions and fascines, and inside with sacks full of sand. The internal floor is four feet lower than the level of the terrain ... It is armed on the right with two pieces of 24 cannon for 24-pdr shot, and on the left with six 67-pdr bomb-throwing mortars (Vienna weight).'[34] The second was outside the citadel, near Poggio Reale. It had four guns turned towards the citadel and four towards the causeway. They were a mixture of 26 and 36pdrs. The third was outside San Giorgio, on the heights of Cipata. It had the form of a saw with four teeth. There were six 24pdr guns on the left, three 25pdrs on the right, and ten mortars of between 64 and 70lb in the middle. The fourth was at Frassine, having four guns that took Migliaretto in the flank. Batteries five to eight had smaller-calibre guns, while the ninth had four 75pdr mortars, and was behind a height near the lower lake. Scorza claimed it did little damage. The tenth battery, once again, had lighter weaponry. Altogether, there were 33 cannon, 20 mortars and two howitzers, according to Scorza's count.[35]

They went into action on 18 July. 'At 10 in the evening we had just left the theatre, where, by chance, our actors had performed the play of Charles XII ... when the French raised the curtain again to perform, with a rapid shift from fiction to reality, the opening of the siege of Mantua.' After a false attack on the hornwork of Pradella, 'they began from the batteries of Belfiore and Cipata to bombard the city with a downpour of shells, bombs, and red-hot balls which criss-crossed each other ...'[36] There was also an infantry attack on the palisades, and at midnight Chasseloup had opened a trench 350 paces from the glacis of Migliaretto. One of Canto d'Irles's aides was shot in the thigh, and during treatment of the wound, the 'bullet' was discovered to be a button. The shelling lasted until 6 a.m., then for two hours the mortars and howitzers were silent, and only the field guns fired. It was estimated that 500 rounds had been fired at the town, and perhaps double the number fired back. In Scorza's words, 'many houses had been damaged',[37] and some had been set on fire and destroyed.

Thus began an almost nightly bombardment, sometimes varying in intensity, occasionally in its timing and duration, under the cover of which the French sappers continually extended their trenches, and occasional infantry attacks were launched. The house in which Canto d'Irles was lodging was soon hit, and he decided to move. On the 20th, he was summoned to surrender, but replied that 'the law of honour and duty demanded him to defend the place entrusted to him to the last extremity'.[38] The French trenching operations continued with speed, and during the night of 20/21 July, a second parallel was begun before Migliaretto. An agreement was also made between the antagonists to safeguard the hospitals in the town, which were to fly a black flag.

In the afternoon of 23 July, Canto d'Irles received a letter from Wurmser in Rovereto dated 20 July, saying that the army would move southwards imminently, and that the relief of Mantua would be effected by 2 August. Yet all was not well in the army. On 25 July, Graham wrote pessimistically:

Had the confidence of the army been gained (the only means left to recover the broken spirit of the soldiers and the Disgust of the Officers by the Choice of an efficient & able commander) there would be more probability of great things being done. The zeal of this good old man [Wurmser] is not enough, & there is nothing else. He is undecided, either from being perplexed by the contradictory opinions of those around him or from no one chusing to take the lead and the responsibility attached to it, I believe this last to be the case ... Many of the officers comfort themselves with thinking that defeat must force peace, & others express themselves in terms of despair ...[39]

At the same time, the pounding of Mantua was continuing as the French made every effort to breach the walls before a relieving force could appear. On 25 July the firing began at 10 p.m. and lasted till 4 a.m. 'It is calculated that in these 6 hours of public suffering, 400 bombs and double the number of round-shot have fallen. Imagine the damage that has occurred. There is hardly any house or public building that has been respected by the cannon-shots or fire in the last few days.'[40] The tired and unhappy people were willing to see any sign as possible evidence of help at hand, and when between 8 and 9 in the evening of 26 July a number of rockets were seen in the air towards Verona, there was soon a rumour that the Austrian army was only 30 miles away. Unexpectedly, too, 'The night of the 26th to 27th was very quiet, without even a musket-shot. It is as well to believe that the enemy needed rest. We certainly did.'[41] The following night was equally peaceful, and so was the whole day of the 28th.

By this time Bonaparte must have believed an Austrian offensive could not long be delayed, because that day he ordered Massena to hurry the defensive works around Rivoli, particularly the bridgehead on the Adige, saying the men were to work 'day and night'.[42] He added that they would be on the Adige in 24 hours, and instructed the drawbridges of the Chiusa to be repaired as well. At that time the French forces destined to oppose the Austrian attack were disposed as follows:[43]

Division	Brigades	Position	Men
Sauret (under Massena)	Guieu, Rusca	Salò and exit from Chiese valley	4,462
Massena	Joubert, Valette, Rampon, Victor, Pijon, Guillaume	Rivoli to Verona	15,391
Despinoy	Bertin	Peschiera and Zevio	4,772
Sérurier	Pelletier, Charton, Serviez, Dallemagne	Around Mantua	10,521
Augereau	Beyrand, Robert, Gardanne	Legnago, Ronco	5,368
Kilmaine (cavalry)	Beaumont	Valeggio	1,535
	Total		42,049

In fact, Wurmser had fixed the start of his relief operation for 29 July, and the first of his troops moved to their initial points on the 26th. On the 28th his forces were assembled and ready to march. The attack was to be made by four main columns, numbered from west to east (or right to left):

Column	Commander	Brigades	Infantry	Cavalry	Howitzers Guns	
I	Quosdanovich	Colonels Klenau and Lusignan (advance-guards), Generals Ott, Ocskay, Spork, and Prince Reuss	15,272	2,349	16	8
II	Melas	Generals Gummer, Bajalich, Nicoletti, and Pittoni (the last two under Sebottendorf)	13,676	727	16	8
III	Davidovich	Generals Mittrovsky,	8,274	1,618	32	8

Column Commander	Brigades	Infantry	Cavalry	Howitzers Guns
	Lipthay, and an unknown staff officer			
IV Mészáros	Generals Hohenzollern and Minkwitz	3,949	1,072 8	2
Total		41,171	5,766 72	26

The whole army advancing from the Tyrol came to 46,937 men in total, while the garrison in Mantua had 10,724 men fit for service on 31 July, giving the Austrians a superiority over the French of about 15,000 men. The battalion guns with the army, if they were complete, would have amounted to 94 pieces, in addition to the 98 listed here.[44]

Wurmser's troops began their offensive in the early hours of 29 July. Before daybreak, Quosdanovich set off with I column, making through the mountains down the western side of Lake Garda in the direction of Salò and Brescia. The principal objective of this column was to capture the latter city on the 30th. This was an important part of the Austrian plan, as the road through Brescia provided the most direct link between Verona and Milan. If Brescia was taken, Massena's troops would be obliged to make a long detour south in case of retreat.

Melas and Sebottendorf began their advance down the eastern side of Lake Garda with their respective elements of II column at 3 a.m. Melas, with the right wing, took the rocky paths over the 7,000-foot peaks of Monte Baldo, while Sebottendorf took the slightly easier, but better defended route on the left, through Ferrara and Madonna della Corona. Their objective was to capture Rivoli, which lay at the foot of the mountains and was a position of great importance. This was due to the fact that the western wall of the Adige valley, which was a sheer rocky cliff hundreds of feet high in this area, dropped to nothing between Rivoli and Canale. This had permitted a road to be built, which the locals called the Pontare (meaning 'hill') which climbed out of the valley to the much higher land between the river and Lake Garda. Since the road Sebottendorf was taking was unsuitable for cavalry and field artillery, the only way to get them to that area without making a considerable detour was via the Pontare.

Davidovich marched along the left bank of the Adige towards Dolcè with the main part of III column, while some of his troops also threatened Verona by moving over the mountains to his left. However, his main objective was to support II column by cannon-fire over the river, then throw a pontoon bridge across the river at Dolcè, and climb the Pontare to Rivoli with the majority of his men and his artillery. When II and III columns had united at Rivoli, they were to advance under Wurmser's command to the relief of Mantua via Valeggio and Goito. The last of the four columns, under Mészáros, left Vicenza for Montebello at 4 a.m. His role was to distract the enemy's attention from the main area of the attack, then move to link with the left of III column.

Captain Laugier of the 27th Light, which was in the area of Salò, tells us: 'Rusca was warned of the approach of the enemy during the night of 10/11 [thermidor] by a village curate, but did not trust the information. In the morning, the carabiniers who were moving on reconnaissance were attacked on the road to Lake Idro, and thrown back ...'[45] Their assailants were troops belonging to Ott, to the right of whom Ocskay had descended on Gavardo, on the River Chiese. Under pressure from these forces, Sauret moved southwards into the hills towards Desenzano. General Guieu, however, was cut off in Salò, but managed to blockade himself inside a large house (Palazzo Martinengo) with 400 men, of whom Laugier was one. By afternoon, Ott was otherwise in control of Salò, having captured 27 officers, 476 men and two guns. There were many dead and wounded on both sides, Rusca being among the latter. Ocskay arrived in Salò in the evening, and was ordered by Quosdanovich to take over blockading Guieu. At 7 p.m., Quosdanovich sent a message to Wurmser saying that his columns would march on Brescia in the morning.

In the centre, progress had been similarly satisfactory for the Austrians. The French had been driven from the positions at Madonna della Corona, and Sebottendorf had captured Brentino after a hard fight. A French demi-brigade, the 11th Light, was cut off in the Adige valley, and its *chef* and 900 men were taken, with four guns. During these actions, III column had given support as intended, by firing across the river. Davidovich advanced to Dolcè without difficulty, and a pontoon bridge was rapidly built there. Most importantly, Sebottendorf's men successfully drove away Massena's troops from the rocky outcrops that overlooked the Pontare. This permitted Davidovich's troops and artillery to move from the valley and join Sebottendorf by evening. Soon afterwards, Melas's sadvance-guard came down from Monte Baldo to complete the junction, though the difficulties of his advance over the mountains had been so great that his last squad only arrived at about midday on the 30th. Wurmser, from the HQ in Dolcè, ordered positions to be taken before Rivoli, with the left wing at Cavaion, and the right at Campara. Mittrovsky also took possession of the Chiusa. In the meantime, Massena moved Pijon and Victor to Piovezzano, two and a half miles south of Cavaion, and prepared to defend the terrain between the Adige and Lake Garda.

Bonaparte had arrived in Montichiari (a crossing-point over the River Chiese) from Brescia early in the morning, where he received reports from Massena about the early successes of the Austrians. Apparently unmoved by them, he wrote back: 'The fate of arms changes from day to day, my dear general. We shall recover, tomorrow or afterwards, what you have lost today ... Nothing is lost while courage remains.'[46] He immediately gave orders to Augereau to move north towards Montebello to threaten to outflank the columns advancing to Rivoli, and Kilmaine and Despinoy were ordered to Castelnuovo, to lend support to Massena.

At some point, however, Bonaparte received news that another Austrian column (that of Quosdanovich) had advanced via Anfo in the direction of Brescia. This immediately raised the prospect of the French being cut off from Milan, and he rapidly altered his dispositions, ordering Augereau to move westwards to Roverbella instead, going by way of Castel d'Ario (nine miles north-east of Mantua), where he would receive fresh orders if the situation had changed. Bonaparte's appreciation of the state of affairs is revealed in a letter to General Gaultier, saying, 'The circumstances are fairly critical.'[47] He also wrote to Sérurier that Massena's reverse 'obliges me to take serious precautions for a retreat' and ordered him to move non-essential equipment to the rear.[48] Over the next few hours, the situation for the French rapidly worsened.

By the evening of the 29th, Colonel Klenau had moved to a position only five hours' march from Brescia, and had decided to attempt a surprise attack if the opportunity presented itself. Finally, after midnight, a report arrived that Brescia was negligently guarded. Klenau therefore set off with his two squadrons of Wurmser Hussars, one battalion of IR De Vins and one company of Mahony Jägers. Their march was covered by a thick morning mist. At about 10 a.m., some volunteers burst into the town without finding much resistance, and were rapidly followed by the rest of Klenau's troops. Surprise was total, and the haul of prisoners proportionately large. Murat and Lannes were both captured, but the former, being sick, was released on parole. Another celebrity prisoner was General Kellermann's son, the future cavalry general. Also captured were more than 30 other officers, and 6–700 men, as well as 2,000 sick in the main French hospital. Quosdanovich soon moved up, and entered Brescia with Spork's brigade after midday, followed by Reuss.

His initial objective having been achieved with some ease, Quosdanovich now turned his attention to the task of making a junction with the rest of the army, which should have been moving south towards Mantua, though he had no news of its progress. At about midnight, therefore, after a few hours' rest, Quosdanovich continued his march south-eastwards, in the direction of Mantua, intending to cross the Chiese at Montichiari. Ott, who was covering his left, was not able to reach his objective of Lonato because his troops were exhausted and lacking food. He therefore stopped at Ponte San Marco, another crossing over the Chiese. While these movements were being made, Ocskay continued to blockade Guieu in Salò.

These movements left the Austrians largely in control of the terrain around the south-western quarter of Lake Garda, an area where there are notable contrasts of terrain. Between Brescia and Salò there are mountains over 3,000 feet high, cut through with winding gorges, while between Brescia and Castiglione the landscape is about as flat as it could be. From Salò, there is a crescent of morainic hills that curves away southwards via Lonato, Castiglione and Solferino to Volta, just south of the crossing of the Mincio near Valeggio. These hills are not high, but are very broken, with small steep-sided valleys, and are covered in vineyards, orchards and olive-groves. The difficulty of this terrain, where it is not always possible to see very far, contributed to the often confused nature of the subsequent fighting, which was also exacerbated by the continual movements of the troops, who sometimes found themselves seeking an enemy who had, in turn, gone looking for them somewhere else.

On the other Austrian wing there had been no action on the 30th, and Mészáros had remained at Montebello, awaiting orders. In the centre, however, II and III columns had moved southwards from Rivoli. It had been intended for Sebottendorf to go towards Peschiera, while Melas and Davidovich went via Sandrà to camp at Castelnuovo. Mittrowsky was to patrol towards Verona. During the late afternoon, Massena was driven back from before Piovezzano, retiring to Castelnuovo, but on their right the Austrians could only get as far as Lazise, due to French resistance. After dark, the flashes of their musketry were seen by Laugier from the other side of the lake. Eventually, Melas camped at Calmasino. The Austrians had therefore only covered about half the intended distance, although General Spiegel had managed to enter Verona. During the night, Massena retired to Peschiera.

Bonaparte had spent some time in both Desenzano and Castelnuovo during the day, and had been informed of the capture of Brescia. He sent a summary of the situation to Augereau, commenting, 'You can see that our communications with Milan and Verona have been cut.' Augereau was ordered to retreat to Roverbella without delay since 'moments are precious'.[49] Augereau's unfortunate soldiers had about an hour's rest at Roverbella, when the order was countermanded, 'circumstances having changed',[50] and the division was told to go back to Castel d'Ario. According to Petitbon, one of its sergeants, the division then marched from there back to Goito on the Mincio, and arrived at 8 a.m. on the 31st 'crushed with fatigue',[51] having covered 60 miles in 55 hours. Other demi-brigades were to have similar experiences of almost continuous marching over the next few days, leaving hordes of exhausted stragglers by the wayside.

It was no doubt on the 30th that Bonaparte took the decision to put all his efforts into defeating Quosdanovich first. He explained his reasoning a few days later in a report to the Directory:

> If my army was too weak to face the two enemy divisions, it could beat each of them separately, and by my position I found myself between them. It was therefore possible for me, by retreating rapidly, to envelop the enemy division that had descended on Brescia, take it prisoner, or beat it completely, and from there turn back to the Mincio to attack Wurmser and force him to go back to the Tyrol. But, to carry out this plan, the siege of Mantua, which was on the point of being taken, had to be raised in 24 hours, and it was necessary to abandon the 40 pieces of cannon which were in the batteries, because there was no means of delaying six hours.[52]

Early on the 31st, Bonaparte therefore issued orders to Sérurier to transfer Pelletier's brigade to Augereau, and Dallemagne's to Massena. He was to raise the siege, and retire to Marcaria to guard the route to the west. 'As for the siege artillery, you will bury everything that cannot be transported to Borgoforte. You will have the shot thrown into the marshes, destroy the other ammunition, and throw the equipment into the river and the marshes.'[53] He was told that the rest of the army was marching to Montichiari. As for Massena, he was told:

> General Augereau, with the troops of his division, part of those which were at the siege of Mantua and those under the orders of Rampon and Cervoni, forming a total of 12,000 men, with the necessary cavalry and artillery, are going to Montichiari, where the advance-guard will have arrived at 4 in the morning. There, in concert with Generals Sauret and Despinoy, they will attack Brescia and overwhelm the divisions of the enemy ... You will leave with your troops to arrive between Lonato and Castiglione and be able to co-operate with the planned attack ... Arrange it so that with your troops, and those of Generals Sauret and

Despinoy, you will be in a position to attack Ponte San Marco, Lonato, and even to cross the Chiese at the highest point ... Whatever happens, and however much it costs, we must sleep in Brescia tomorrow.[54]

The French divisions duly set out for Brescia very early on the 31st, precautions having been taken to delay an enemy crossing of the Mincio by leaving a garrison under Guillaume in Peschiera, and a rearguard under Valette watching the bridges further south. At about the same time, Quosdanovich was moving in the opposite direction, and arrived in Montichiari with the bulk of his column at 9 a.m. Here, having marched through the early hours, he appears to have rested for most of the day. By contrast, Ott attacked Lonato first thing in the morning, and succeeded in driving the French out of the town and into the nearby hills, where they were closely pursued by his hussars. However, the latter immediately ran into the division of Despinoy, and were forced to turn back. According to Bonaparte's report to the Directory, he immediately ordered Dallemagne to retake Lonato, and 'A most stubborn combat was engaged, which was for a long time undecided, but I was calm: the brave 32nd demi-brigade was there.'[55] These words became something of a battle-honour for the 32nd, who had them inscribed on their colour, but they brought forth an angry protest from Despinoy, who later wrote to Bonaparte. 'Is this the combat of Lonato, and of the 4,000 men who took part in it with me?'[56] Indeed, it seems quite likely that Bonaparte was not actually there,[57] and in any case it was largely weight of numbers and the threat of encirclement that finally forced Ott to give way and retreat to Ponte San Marco, which he did after a good four hours of resistance.[58]

While this sharp little action, (often known as the first battle of Lonato) had been going on, Sauret had advanced from Desenzano round the shore of the lake to Salò, fallen on Ocskay at dawn, and forced him back after several hours of fighting. Having thus liberated Guieu, Sauret chose to abandon the town again almost immediately as he felt he had too few troops nearby. The two left in the afternoon and marched to Lonato, where they joined Despinoy and Massena.

Having discussed the situation, the four generals planned to march on Ponte San Marco.

Towards evening, Quosdanovich arrived in Ponte San Marco himself, as three strong French columns approached the town. Quosdanovich made plans for Ott to retake Lonato on the following day, while he himself advanced to Goito, but he then received news at about 9 p.m. that Ocskay had lost control of Salò. This meant there was a very real danger of the whole right wing of the army being cut off from the road to the Tyrol, and Quosdanovich hurriedly changed his plans to give priority to recapturing Salò in order to secure his line of communications. At 10 p.m., therefore, Reuss and Spork set off for Gavardo, leaving Ott to follow in the morning, while Klenau remained at Montichiari.

The day had been much quieter for the centre of the Austrian army. On the morning of the 31st, the bulk of II and III columns had advanced to Castelnuovo, while Bajalich approached Peschiera. Wurmser had no news of his right wing, but from the hills it could be seen that I column was in action with the enemy. This did not seem particularly noteworthy to Wurmser, who had received reports indicating that the siege of Mantua was still in place, and that Bonaparte was at Roverbella. He therefore believed that the main force of the French army was still around Roverbella and Mantua, and that he would need to take measures to cover this force as he advanced to Valeggio, where he planned to secure the crossing of the Mincio, and permit a junction with I column. At 4 p.m., he marched towards Valeggio. It was only later in the night that information arrived indicating the enemy army had, in fact, crossed the Mincio.

In Mantua, there was some bombardment during the night of 31 July/1 August, but it had soon stopped:

Now that it is early morning, we have been for some hours in a perfect and mysterious quiet. Only, for some time, in the trenches and the enemy batteries can be heard noises of wagons and great tramping of men and horses … What can it be? Perhaps the abandonment of the siege?[59]

Eventually, patrols were sent out, and brought back the best possible news. The effect was electric:

> The siege ended, we no longer have suffering painted on our faces, but laughing and jocund hilarity. The jubilant sound of the bells, which have been silent for two months, announced to the poor citizens a kind of resurrection ... The shops being reopened after being closed and abandoned for thirteen days, the city was converted from an empty desert to the most flourishing market.[60]

At 7 a.m., General Alvinczy entered Mantua to take stock of the situation of the fortress and its garrison and report to Wurmser. He found that the siege had cost the defenders seventeen officers and 974 men killed and wounded, and that there were now 3,275 officers and men sick. To the civilian inhabitants, the cost in lives does not seem to have been as great as one might expect, and Scorza mentions very few casualties, but the material damage must have been enormous, not to mention the psychological effects on those who had lived through the trauma of nightly bombardment.

Measures were swiftly taken to send out patrols in pursuit of the retreating French, and to establish contact with the relieving army. Efforts were also made to collect the immense amount of equipment left behind by the French, who had not had time to carry out Bonaparte's orders for its destruction. It included a total of 179 guns of various calibres, among them 32 siege mortars, some of which came from the park at Borgoforte, which was captured by patrols before it could be got away. There were also 29,341 round-shot, 3,390 bombs and 3,758 shells, not to mention great quantities of lead and other military supplies. The roaming squads of Austrian cavalry also rounded up some 775 French officers and men in the vicinity of the fortress.[61]

Having achieved the major goal of his operations by relieving Mantua, Wurmser now showed no great hurry to pass on to the next phase. He realised that Quosdanovich was threatened with attack by almost the whole French army, and on 1 August he informed Canto d'Irles of his intention to cross the Mincio to assist his right wing. But for some reason, although he had originally intended to cross at Valeggio, he decided to use Goito instead, which considerably lengthened his march. To the east, meanwhile, the rather forlorn column of Mészáros crossed the Adige at Legnago during the morning, so distant from the action that it can hardly have seen a single Frenchman. It was now left to Bonaparte to try to exploit the yawning separation between the Austrian right wing and the rest of the army, much as he had done at Montenotte.

By the time the Austrians discovered that the siege of Mantua had been lifted, Quosdanovich's column must already have been under attack. On the French left, Klenau had been attacked around daybreak on the 1st by Augereau, part of whose division tried to go past his flank, towards Brescia. At 8 a.m., faced with overwhelming numbers, Klenau retired to Brescia, where he arrived at 11 a.m. He only got there a short while before Bonaparte, with Augereau's division, which was soon joined by those of Massena and Despinoy. Klenau had no hope of resisting the united forces of most of the French army, and had to leave very rapidly to avoid being destroyed, moving through the mountains to the north-east towards Gavardo.

In the meantime, Quosdanovich had been informed during the morning that the French had abandoned Salò. He therefore halted at Gavardo, and contemplated attacking Desenzano, but then at about midday received the news that the French were in Brescia. Once again, this raised the possibility that the French would turn him to the north and cut his line of communication along the western side of the lake. Since Quosdanovich had no idea where Wurmser was, nor what his intentions were, it was essential to secure these communications in case a retreat became necessary, so detachments had to be sent into the mountains to occupy important positions. At the same time, Quosdanovich arranged his defences to the south by placing the brigades of Ott and Ocskay to form a screen running from the mountains to the lake, roughly half-way between Salò and Ponte San Marco.

Although the rapid movements of the French had enabled them to assemble a powerful force to oppose Quosdanovich, it had been at the cost of great suffering for men and animals, who had marched in searing heat with no rest and little to eat. Laugier tells us that when a coffee-shop was opened by its proprietor,

> a crowd of starving officers devoured drinks and food. I arrived soon enough to buy three dozen small biscuits and a glass of lemonade, which I shared with a friend. This small repast having refreshed me a little, I rested on the pavé of cobbles between the piles of arms. My sleep was often interrupted by the continual movement of the horse artillery and the patrols of cavalry which came and went.[62]

The weariness was shared by Bonaparte, who was working under immense pressure. On the 2nd, he wrote to Saliceti saying: 'We are extraordinarily tired here. Five of my horses have collapsed from fatigue.'[63] He also told him that now he had the whole army together, he would give battle at the first opportunity.

According to some sources, notably a report which has been attributed to Augereau,[64] the decision to fight was only taken after a council of war held on the 1st, during which Augereau argued strongly for aggressive action. Knowing Bonaparte's aversion to such meetings, there must be some doubt about this, though it seems unlikely that there was never any discussion of what course to adopt. Whatever the truth, some hasty measures were taken to prepare the army for a battle, with an instant restructuring of the divisions being ordered on the 2nd, giving each of them roughly the same number of demi-brigades, which was clearly more appropriate when they all had much the same role to perform. A garrison was ordered to remain in Brescia, then arrangements were made to manoeuvre the army so that it lay between Quosdanovich and the rest of the Austrian forces. At 3 a.m. on 2 August, Bonaparte marched from Brescia with Massena and Augereau, the former to a position before Ponte San Marco, while the latter placed himself at Montichiari during the afternoon. Despinoy took up a position at Rezzato, between Massena and Brescia. Because Sauret had been injured, his division was now commanded by Guieu, who positioned himself before Lonato.

Laugier says that Bonaparte passed in front of his demi-brigade, which formed part of this division, in the afternoon:

> The soldiers said to him 'General, we have no food.' 'I know,' he said, 'and you will not find any, because you have not retaken Salò. You have no other resources than the magazines of the enemy.' Such was the confidence in the General, that his reply, repeated among the ranks, contented our spirits and we said 'We are going to retake Salò.'[65]

Quosdanovich, meanwhile, had spent the whole morning of 2 August in his previous positions, awaiting news or orders. About midday, at which time Klenau also arrived in Gavardo, he finally received a letter saying that Wurmser would cross the Mincio that same day. In these circumstances, Quosdanovich decided to do what he could to support Wurmser, and issued orders for his brigades to move forward. His plan was for Ocskay to go south to Desenzano, then turn west and meet Ott at Ponte San Marco in the morning, after which the two would march on Brescia. The bulk of Quosdanovich's column would move south to Montichiari, where it would await Wurmser.

This slightly complicated movement, which provided for one brigade crossing from the extreme left wing to the extreme right, went wrong from the very beginning. At nearly midnight, Quosdanovich received a report from Ott that during the late afternoon an enemy force estimated at 4,000 men had moved towards Salò from Lonato, and had not been opposed. It was, in fact, Sauret's division, which Laugier says had begun its march at about 4 p.m. By one of those extraordinary chances that sometimes occur in war, it had taken a little-used road over the hills, and had therefore marched straight past Ocskay, who had set off in the opposite direction, without either of them having the least idea of the other's presence. This accident meant that Salò was now open to the French, who had camped about four miles short of their destination, so in the early hours Quosdanovich had to divert Reuss to try to intercept them.

The centre of the Austrian army had also spent the day in movement, but not with quite the same sense of urgency displayed by the

French. At 3 a.m., the centre had begun its march towards Goito, though only Lipthay and Schübirz actually crossed the Mincio there during the day. At 11 a.m., Rukavina went to Valeggio with a report on the siege for Wurmser, and a despatch was sent back saying that the latter had decided to visit Mantua personally. Wurmser also called for reinforcements from Mantua, but only 2,000 men under Vukassovich could be spared, and these only moved to Goito on the following day. An order was also sent to Mészáros, far away to the east, to pursue Sérurier. Lipthay's advance-guard, meanwhile, made its crossing, and moved in the direction of Castiglione, which was occupied by 1,800 men under General Valette. In a show of unsteadiness rare among French commanders during this campaign, Valette bolted with half his men, and arrived in Montichiari spreading alarm at the enemy advance. The other half of his men shamed him by conducting a fighting withdrawal. Bonaparte was not pleased, particularly as Valette had shown signs of unreliability a few days before, and removed him from his command.

A sharp contrast is provided by the hero's welcome that Wurmser received in Mantua. He arrived at Porta Mulina at 6 p.m. to be received by the notables in 'gala dress'. 'We accompanied him, to the festive and majestic sound of all the bells, the firing of 72 guns, and to the most triumphant acclamations of the populace, to the quarters of our commander.'[66] After a brief visit he returned to his HQ.

The following day, 3 August, was one of heavy fighting, there being a number of quite distinct actions involving different elements of the opposing armies, from Salò all the way down to Castiglione. Bonaparte's main goal was to defeat Quosdanovich, and to this end he had ordered the divisions of Sauret and Despinoy, linked by the brigade of Dallemagne, to advance towards Salò and Gavardo. However, Bonaparte also had to hold back the advance of the main Austrian force so that it did not take him in the rear. For this purpose, he ordered Augereau to attack Wurmser's advance-guard at Castiglione. Massena was to move from Ponte San Marco to Lonato, where he was within striking distance of Castiglione, but could also move towards Quosdanovich if necessary.

These divisions met with varying degrees of success, the most unfortunate being that of General Despinoy, on the extreme French left. This ran into Ott's troops half an hour's march before Gavardo, where they had concentrated that morning. According to Captain Blandin of the 5th Line:

> After 12 hours' march, of which 8 by night, exhausted by fatigues and hunger, we came on the enemy unexpectedly. The General should have had us halt to catch our breath, assemble us, take positions, reconnoitre those of the enemy. None of all this. As soon as 800 men had arrived, he had us beat the charge and go for the enemy flank![67]

Not surprisingly, the French were beaten off in some disorder by Ott's men, and eventually fell back to their previous positions before Brescia.

In the meantime, Guieu, of whom Reuss had found no trace during the night, had moved forward with his advance-guard and taken Salò, which was unoccupied. Without waiting for support, this force inclined left towards Gavardo, where Quosdanovich had his HQ. Not far from this, the French came across the artillery park, which was lightly guarded, captured it, and turned the guns on the enemy. The commotion to his rear alerted Quosdanovich, who hurried back with superior forces of Spork's brigade, recaptured the park, and drove the French back to Salò. At the same time as Guieu had been mounting this attack, Dallemagne had engaged Ott, and even managed to go round his flank and reach Gavardo, but was then forced to retire and prepare another effort.

Quosdanovich, having cleared Guieu from the road along the Chiese valley, took up a position on the heights towards Salò, and waited for news of Ocskay and Reuss, who had not been heard of since midnight. In the meantime, he took the precaution of sending the park and most of the cavalry up the Chiese into the mountains, and also sent Klenau to reinforce Ott. Dallemagne had meanwhile returned to the attack and managed to take Gavardo again, severing the link between Ott and Quosdanovich. However, a counter from Ott finally drove Dallemagne off, and he retired in the direction of Brescia, where illness forced him to take to his bed.

Although the successes of the French on this wing were somewhat limited, they had at least prevented Quosdanovich from moving forward to support either Wurmser or Ocskay, and the latter in particular was to suffer greatly because of his isolated position. In the early hours of the morning, he had advanced from Desenzano to Lonato and vigorously attacked the French occupying force under Pijon, which was driven back, its commander being captured in the process. Before long, however, Bonaparte arrived at Lonato with part of Massena's division, and set about retaking the town. The 32nd was a little behind, but was committed to the fire as soon as it arrived. Roguet says that Bonaparte

> formed us in columns of platoons, the band at our head. 'March like that,' he said, 'on the main road, straight to Lonato. Do not fire a single shot. Enter the town without heeding the skirmishers that the enemy has thrown forward. With the bayonet only. Drummers, beat the charge. Musicians, a patriotic march ...'[68]

This small incident alerts us to the fact that some of the French units had modified their tactics. Vigo-Roussillon, who only returned to the 32nd later, having been ill, says:

> I found my comrades very proud of having manoeuvred at the battle of Castiglione [sic]. They had marched in columns of platoons. As I have said, we had not, until then, any theoretical or practical instruction. We only knew how to place ourselves in line in two or three ranks. When we were within reach of the enemy, the charge was beaten, the order was given to charge, then it was a case of who could reach the enemy first. The most difficult thing for the unit commanders was to rally their troops after the combat. But we were no longer in the mountains. The plains of Lombardy lent themselves ... to manoeuvres and evolutions. We then felt the need to work. It was M. Roguet, adjutant NCO of the 32nd demi-brigade, who had served before

the Revolution in a regiment of the royal army, who taught the NCOs the principles of our trade.[69]

As it moved forward in its new-found order, the 32nd almost immediately lost both battalion commanders present, but pressed its attack, supported by the 18th. Ocskay had deployed in line, but had extended it further in an attempt to envelop his attackers, thereby making it too weak to resist the impact of the French columns. He was forced back and overwhelmed by the greatly superior forces, making a hurried withdrawal towards Desenzano. Unfortunately for the Austrians, Junot had been sent ahead with the cavalry company forming Bonaparte's escort, supported by other units, to cut them off. This ploy succeeded, and though Junot was seriously wounded, receiving six sword-cuts, Ocskay was encircled and forced to surrender with most of his brigade.

While Ocskay had been thus embroiled with superior French forces, Prince Reuss had failed to find any at all on the road between Salò and Desenzano, and was approaching the latter when he heard firing, then began to come across the debris of Ocskay's brigade in full retreat. He rapidly attacked Desenzano, captured it, and held it for over an hour, but was then faced with the sight of Bonaparte appearing with Massena's victorious division. Reuss only had 1,800 men, and was not in a position to resist so many enemies. He therefore retired the way he had come, but was continually harried, losing many men. Some of them were saved by Maelcamp, who put in to the shore with some boats from the Austrian flotilla that cruised on the lake, and took them off to Sirmione. It was Maelcamp's report of these events, which reached him during the night of 4/5 August, that gave Wurmser his first information about the fighting.

Quosdanovich remained ignorant of the disaster that had overtaken his left wing for several hours, but during the afternoon he received a report that one of his detachments in the mountains above Gavardo had been dislodged, which made it ever more important to ensure that there could be no impediment to a retreat along the Chiese. Ott was therefore ordered to leave rearguards behind him and move the rest of his troops to join Quosdanovich and Spork on the heights near Salò. Ott received this order at about 6 p.m., and after making the necessary arrangements, hurried on ahead of his troops. It was around 11 p.m. that he discovered that Quosdanovich was intending to attack Salò yet again, and he and Spork both argued strongly against it, on the grounds that the troops had little food or ammunition and were worn out. Instead, they favoured a retreat along the Chiese. Quosdanovich insisted, as he felt it was important to maintain their position, and by their resistance give the French sufficient trouble to make Wurmser's advance easier. However, Prince Reuss arrived in the night with news of Ocskay's capture, which changed the complexion of affairs.

A council of war was held, and various points considered. No news had been received from Wurmser since his letter of 1 August, and nothing had been heard of any movements on his part. It therefore seemed likely that he had not crossed the Mincio on 2 August, as he had hoped. The fact that I column had been engaged by almost the whole French army seemed to confirm that Wurmser was not within striking distance of them. Quosdanovich's own force had now withered from 17,621 to less than 10,000, and numbers of these were already employed in guarding the line of retreat. The council therefore came to the conclusion that I column could not risk being attacked by the main enemy force, or encircled and cut off, and that saving the division required a retreat behind Anfo. Orders were therefore issued to begin the withdrawal on the morning of 4 August, with the intention of joining Wurmser by going right round the northern end of the lake.

In fact, Wurmser's force *had* attempted to move towards Quosdanovich during the day. Orders had been issued for Sebottendorf and Davidovich to leave Goito for Guidizzolo at 3 a.m., while Schübirz was to go to the hills of Castiglione, and Lipthay to Montichiari. However, these arrangements were impeded by the intervention of Augereau, whose actions over the next few days caused him to be given the title of Duke of Castiglione under the Empire. Augereau had planned his attack on Lipthay in the following manner: Beyrand would make for the hills to the south-east of Castiglione, occupied by the Austrian left wing, while Verdier would attack the castle of Castiglione, and Pelletier would carry out a demonstration against Lipthay's right wing. General Robert, with the 51st, had been ordered to move round the Austrian left flank during the night and place himself in ambush to their rear. Augereau would support the attack with the 45th Line, one battalion of the 69th and the 22nd Chasseurs. The French forces probably stood at about 11,000 men, Lipthay's less than 4,000.

Nevertheless, Lipthay received the attack, which came at daybreak, with impressive resoluteness. Sergeant Rattier of the 51st tells us: 'The ground was disputed with great tenacity. We advanced, we retreated, we took and gave up the same positions three times.'[70] Despite his desire to resist, Lipthay saw that he could be outflanked on both sides, and withdrew a short distance. He then halted, and waited for another attack. This duly occurred, and enemy superiority forced Lipthay to retreat again. When the Austrians came within range, Robert sprang his ambush, causing some disorder. Augereau then joined the attack, and Lipthay abandoned Castiglione to take a good position further down the line of hills.

While the fighting had been going on, General Schübirz, who had been at Pozzolengo, had begun to march to the sound of the guns. Davidovich was also on the move, and some of his troops soon began to appear to the south-east around Guidizzolo. Davidovich shook his men into battle order, and sent a detachment forward to occupy a hill near the road, about half-way between Solferino and Medole. At 8 a.m., Davidovich reported to Wurmser that Lipthay was in action, and seemed to be surrounded. Although his situation was precarious, Lipthay continued to fight hard all morning in his second position, and the French sustained heavy casualties. General Beyrand as well as several *chefs de brigade* were killed, and General Robert was among the wounded. As the combat continued, Kilmaine arrived with the cavalry, and positioned himself in support, while on the Austrian side Davidovich drew nearer, permitting Lipthay to essay a counter-attack. Schübirz also reached the battlefield, launching a violent assault on the French left, which had managed to advance as far as the last hill before Solferino, and drove them back.

Lipthay's gallant defence had won precious time for Wurmser to arrive, and as the day wore on, his divisions marched up and took battle positions on the heights of Solferino, facing towards Castiglione. The Austrian force that assembled there eventually amounted to not quite 20,000 men, but the troops were very tired after a hard march in unbearable heat, so Wurmser took no offensive action. The fighting therefore petered out, great losses having been suffered by both sides. Rattier said: 'Our demi-brigade had 500 men put out of action, and the 4th at least as many again.'[71] The Imperial troops lost about 1,000 during the day, including General Nicoletti wounded.

Augereau wrote Bonaparte two quite distinct reports on the day's events. The first spoke of the enemy being 'completely beaten', but the second was written after an early-evening visit by some enemy cavalry had sown alarm in Castiglione, and tells a different story. Augereau says the enemy is estimated at 20,000 men, and: 'I shall be attacked tomorrow morning by fresh troops in much superior numbers. If you do not send me troops, it will be impossible for me to resist ... I pray you to tell me what I am to do in case I am obliged to retreat ...'[72] However, Augereau had bargained without the unhurried style of Wurmser, and was in less danger than he thought. In the evening, Wurmser wrote to Quosdanovich from Goito saying that 'he had advanced to Castiglione today because he believed the right wing was in Brescia and awaited support from the centre. In the morning (of 4 August) the centre would still not be able to attack the enemy because the troops had suffered too much. He had, however, to expect to be attacked by the French. If this took place, Quosdanovich was to support him with all his strength ...'[73] The decision not to force an engagement on 4 August was to give a precious breathing space to the French.

Bonaparte arrived in Castiglione in the evening, and issued orders for Despinoy, Guieu and Saint-Hilaire to make new attacks on Quosdanovich in the morning, to try to drive him right back into the mountains. These proved to be unnecessary, as Quosdanovich had already prepared his troops to march off at 2 a.m. on the 4th. His withdrawal was not achieved without incident, and some of the troops found themselves cut off. Their commander decided to try to reach Wurmser instead, and had the misfortune to arrive at Lonato at about 5 a.m., shortly before Bonaparte turned up there with a force of only 1,200 men. Bonaparte could easily have been taken prisoner, but calmly told the Austrians they were surrounded, and got them to surrender instead.

This incident, and the reports he received from Guieu, indicated that he now had nothing to fear from Quosdanovich, who seemed to have broken contact and withdrawn. Bonaparte therefore made plans to throw all his weight against Wurmser. At 8 a.m. on the 4th an order was sent to Sérurier (who had been taken ill, and was replaced by Fiorella) to march from the south against the left flank of Wurmser's position. Arrangements were also made for Massena and Despinoy to move to Castiglione by night marches, thus avoiding the heat of the day.

Wurmser, for his part, had received the report of Quosdanovich's withdrawal from Maelcamp, and realised that the plan of joining forces with him and striking a great blow against the French could not now be effected. However, positioned as he was, it was impossible to retreat without fighting. Moreover, it was important to gain time for Canto d'Irles to prepare Mantua for another blockade by obtaining provisions and demolishing the enemy siege works, as it was conceivable that the army would be obliged to retreat again. Wurmser did what little he could to prepare for the inevitable battle by calling up a detachment commanded by Colonel Weidenfeld, which was watching Peschiera, and ordering Mészáros to move to cover Sérurier. The rest of the day passed in small movements and skirmishes between Castiglione and Solferino, as both armies sought to adjust their positions in readiness for the clash that promised to take place on the day after, and would come to be known as the battle of Castiglione.

The line of battle taken up by the Austrians ran roughly north-east to south-west. The right wing lay at Solferino, in the hills, where the road from Montichiari to Valeggio passed. The line then descended to the plain and stretched over the flat land to the small, isolated hill standing by the road from Montichiari to Guidizzolo. On this hill, a strong redoubt had been built. In total, the Austrian forces consisted of nineteen and a third battalions, four companies, and ten and a half squadrons, amounting to just less than 20,000 men.

While the divisions of Massena, Despinoy and Sérurier were marching towards the army, Bonaparte issued his last instructions verbally. Joubert, who had been about to take to his sick-bed in Brescia when a letter from Berthier had peremptorily ordered him to the army 'ill or well', says that 'the General-in-Chief spoke to us all night about the dispositions to take'.[74] Before dawn, Augereau's division, which numbered about 10,000 men, was positioned in two lines in front of Castiglione, its left on the hills, and its right on the plain opposite the redoubt. Massena's division had been reduced by detachments and losses in combat, and now counted about the same as Augereau's. It formed the left wing, partly deployed in line, part in column. The cavalry reserve is estimated to have numbered 1,200 men, and it was positioned on Augereau's right wing, echelonned across the road to Brescia. Of the other two divisions, that of Despinoy had been rein-forced by Cervoni, and now had 7,500 men, while Sérurier's, under Fiorella, numbered about 5,000. When the whole French army was assembled, therefore, it would amount to about 33,700 men, giving it a significant advantage over the Austrian army. By daybreak, however, the last two divisions had still not arrived, and even Massena's was probably not complete.

Bonaparte now decided to make a small backward movement with the object of enticing the Austrians from their positions, and buying time for Sérurier to arrive. It also had the merit of moving the army slightly in the direction from which Despinoy was marching. As Bona-parte reported to the Directory, this manoeuvre only partly succeeded in its principal aim.[75] However, Joubert commented that the enemy followed them 'step for step', and in particular abandoned a very good position on one of the hills in the centre. More seriously, they extended their right wing, apparently in an attempt to outflank Massena on his left, towards Castel Venzago.

In the meantime, Despinoy's and Sérurier's divisions were approaching the battlefield from opposite directions. Wurmser had intended that Sérurier's division should be covered by Mészáros and part of the garrison of Mantua, but Canto d'Irles had not been able to detach troops because of his own needs, and Fiorella's early start had made it possible for him to evade Mészáros. Fiorella therefore approached Guidizzolo without hindrance.

Joubert tells us: 'At 9 o'clock, we heard musketry and cannons on our right. Bonaparte came running to me: "See Sérurier, who is attacking on his arrival? You should already be engaged. Go with your chasseurs and drive in the enemy centre."'[76] A similar order was given to Verdier, who reported that the attack 'began at two points: on the left with the 17th Light [under Joubert], supported by the 51st, and, on the right, by the 4th, the light artillery [fifteen guns, under Marmont], and the cavalry under the orders of General Beaumont'.[77] With almost perfect timing, troops of Despinoy's division marched onto the field of battle just before the French swung into the attack.

By 10 a.m., the 4th Line, under Verdier, was in range of the redoubt on the hill, and coming under severe fire, which caused serious casualties. However, the counter-fire from the light artillery proved highly effective. Half an hour later, the other attackers, under Joubert, had taken the village of Solferino. By the time a further hour had elapsed, the fire from the Austrian redoubt was slackening, and the 4th captured it with the support of some cavalry, as well as some of Despinoy's troops. On the other wing, Wurmser had stopped the attempted advance round Massena's flank when it became clear that his own left rear was threatened by Sérurier's division moving through Guidizzolo, and the Austrian right was now engaged with Massena's troops. The fighting was fierce along the whole front, and the Austrians had the misfortune to lose Lipthay, who was severely wounded, while Davidovich lost two horses.

According to Verdier, the Austrian troops that had been driven from the redoubt withdrew to the hills, where they rallied around a tower, and were attacked again by the left of Augereau's division. At the same time, the 4th made off to try to cut the Austrian line of retreat to La Volta, though this proved to be too much of a detour. However, this was not the only threat to the Austrian rear, as Fiorella was now moving from Guidizzolo in the direction of Cavriana. The Austrian army had resisted for several hours, but if it kept its position for much longer, it risked being cut off from the crossings over the Mincio, and perhaps even trapped in the corner formed by that river and Lake Garda. Wurmser therefore ordered a retreat along the road to Borghetto and Valeggio.

On the right wing, this became somewhat hurried when the castle of Solferino was captured, putting the Austrian right in peril of being cut off. Indeed, Massena tried to outflank them, but was resisted by Schübirz and Mittrovsky, who had the good fortune to receive timely assistance from Weidenfeld. The latter appeared in the nick of time with his whole force of four battalions and one squadron, and subjected Massena to such an emphatic attack in the left flank, that he was obliged to discontinue his advance. The Austrian right wing was therefore able to regain composure, and continue its march towards the Mincio in good order. The left wing also managed to reach the river despite the attentions of the pursuing French, who harried them until nightfall. The last men to cross the bridge at Borghetto were three squadrons of hussars, under Schübirz, who had the bridge knocked down immediately afterwards.

The total exhaustion of the French troops had not permitted much of a pursuit, but Bonaparte had no intention of allowing Wurmser to rest on the other side of the Mincio and improve the defences of Mantua at his leisure. On 6 August, therefore, Augereau began to make preparations to cross the Mincio at Borghetto. However, this was only a ploy to keep Wurmser's attention concentrated in that area while Massena rapidly marched on Peschiera. He arrived at about 8.30 a.m., roughly at the same time that Mittrovsky reached Cavalcaselle, to cover Peschiera. Despite this reinforcement, Massena had twice the number of men available to Bajalich and Mittrovsky, who were predictably beaten back. Once again, the Austrian position had been turned, and their army was in danger of being cut off. In the evening of the 6th, Wurmser therefore ordered the abandonment of the line on the Mincio, and on the following morning, Mantua was left to fend for itself again, as the army began its retreat into the Tyrol.

This effectively brought to a close one of the most critical periods of the whole 1796 campaign, which had seen success and failure for both sides. The Austrians had succeeded in relieving Mantua and capturing the French siege artillery, but Bonaparte had managed, if only narrowly, to keep his army intact, and by a brilliant piece of active defence, had not lost an inch of ground. The cost for both sides had been enormous.

The Austrians finally calculated that they had lost about 12,500 men, while in his memoirs Bonaparte admitted to a loss of 7,000, though it is impossible to say how accurate this is.[78] It was two thoroughly exhausted and severely weakened armies that now tried to recuperate before the next phase of operations.

NOTES

1.   Holland Rose, J. 'Despatches of Colonel Thomas Graham on the Italian Campaign of 1796–1797.' *The English Historical Review*, 14 (1899), p. 116.
2.   Napoleon. *Correspondance inédite officielle et confidentielle de Napoléon Bonaparte: avec les cours étrangères, les princes, les ministres et les généraux français et étrangers, en Italie, en Allemagne, et en Egypte.* Paris, 1809, I, p. 253.
3.   Napoleon. *Correspondance de Napoléon Ier publiée par ordre de l'empereur Napoléon III.* Paris, 1858–69, no. 590.
4.   Chevrier, E. *Le général Joubert d'après sa correspondance.* Paris, 1884, p. 39.
5.   Scorza, B. *Cronaca vissuta del duplice assedio di Mantova degli anni 1796 e 1797: le vicende di Mantova nel 1796.* Mantua, 1975, p. 69.
6.   Schels, J. B. 'Die Operationen des FM Grafen Wurmser am Ende Juli und Anfang August 1796, zum Ensatz von Mantua; mit der Schlacht bei Castiglione.' *Oesterreichische Militärische Zeitschrift*, Bd. 1; Bd. 2 (1830), p. 89.
7.   Scorza, op. cit., p. 76.
8.   Schels, op. cit., pp. 91–3.
9.   Napoleon. 1858–69, op. cit., no. 540.
10. Scorza, op. cit., p. 72.
11. Ibid., p. 74.
12. Ibid., p. 71.
13. Napoleon. 1858–69, op. cit., nos. 575 and 577.
14. Ibid., no. 587.
15. Ibid., no. 579.
16. Schels, op. cit., p. 115.
17. Napoleon. 1858–69, op. cit., no. 570.
18. Napoleon. 1809, op. cit., I, p. 230.

19. Napoleon. 1858–69, op. cit., no. 613.

20. Ibid., no. 639.

21. Ibid., no. 633.

22. Graham understandably has trouble with the names here: only Colli seems to get his spelt correctly. Holland Rose, op. cit., pp. 117–18.

23. Delavoye, A. M. *Life of Thomas Graham, Lord Lynedoch*. London, 1880, p. 120.

24. Schels, op. cit., p. 257.

25. Napoleon. 1858–69, op. cit., no. 710.

26. Ibid., no. 721.

27. Ibid., no. 725.

28. Ibid., no. 739.

29. Ibid., no. 755.

30. Schels, op. cit., p. 130.

31. Napoleon. 1858–69, op. cit., no. 783

32. Scorza, op. cit., p. 85.

33. Ibid., p. 83.

34. Ibid., p. 107.

35. Ibid., pp. 107–9. Schels, op. cit., p. 120, gives the slightly different total of eleven batteries with 54 cannon and 22 mortars, but his account is from official reports, whereas Scorza gives the distinct impression that he is describing what he has seen himself. In any case, the number of guns in use varied during the siege, and some of the batteries were added after the bombardment had begun.

36. Scorza, op. cit., p. 86.

37. Ibid., p. 87.

38. Schels, op. cit., p. 139.

39. Holland Rose, op. cit., p. 118.

40. Scorza, op. cit., p. 96.

41. Ibid., p. 97.

42. Napoleon. 1858–69, op. cit., no. 793.

43. Jomini, A.-H., baron. *Histoire critique et militaire des guerres de la Révolution*. Paris, 1820–24, VIII, p. 305.

44. Schels, op. cit., pp. 268–70.

45. Laugier, J.-R. *Les cahiers du capitaine Laugier. – De la guerre et de l'anarchie, ou Mémoires historiques des campagnes et aventures d'un capitaine du 27me régiment d'infanterie légère par Jérome-Roland*

Laugier. Publiés d'après le manuscrit original par Léon G. Pélissier. Aix, 1893, p. 91.

46. Napoleon. 1858–69, op. cit., no. 797.
47. Ibid., no. 804.
48. Ibid., no. 805.
49. Ibid., no. 806.
50. Ibid., no. 811.
51. Godechot, J. 'Le carnet de route du sergent Petitbon sur la campagne d'Italie de 1796–1797.' *Rivista italiana di studi napoleonici,* 15 (1978), p. 43.
52. Napoleon. 1858-69, op. cit., no. 842.
53. Ibid., no. 813.
54. Ibid., no. 815.
55. Ibid., no. 842.
56. Massena, A. *Mémoires de Massena, rédigés d'après les documents qu'il a laissés et sur ceux du dépôt de la guerre et du dépôt des fortifications, par le général Koch.* Paris, 1848–50, II, p. 484.
57. This seems to be proved by the report that Despinoy sent him on 1 August saying, 'The combat of Lonato was terrible, and I can assure you that the enemy has been well beaten, in such a manner that he will remember it …' Napoleon. 1809, op. cit., I, p. 420. The *Historique* of the 5th Line confirms that Despinoy was in command.
58. Napoleon. *Mémoires pour servir à l'histoire de France, sous le regne de Napoléon, écrits sous sa dictée à Sainte-Hélène, par les généraux qui ont partagé sa captivité.* Paris, 1829, p. 414.
59. Scorza, op. cit., p. 103.
60. Ibid., p. 104.
61. Schels, op. cit., p. 152.
62. Laugier, op. cit., p. 97.
63. Napoleon. 1858–69, op. cit., no. 820.
64. Massena, op. cit., II, p. 458.
65. Laugier, op. cit., pp. 97–8.
66. Scorza, op. cit., p. 110.
67. Carnot, Capt. 'La bataille de Lonato racontée par un témoin.' *Le carnet de la sabretache,* s. 2, v. 5 (1906), p. 559.
68. Roguet, F. *Mémoires militaires du lieutenant général comte Roguet*

(*François), colonel en second des grenadiers à pied de la Vieille Garde, pair de France.* Paris, 1862, pp. 260–61.

69. Vigo-Roussillon, F. *Journal de campagne (1793-1837).* Paris, 1981, p. 37.

70. Rattier, J.-H. 'Campagne d'Italie (1796): notes d'un sergent-major.' *Revue rétrospective,* XX (1894), p. 234.

71. Ibid., p. 235

72. Napoleon. 1809, op. cit., I, pp. 424–5.

73. Schels, op. cit., p. 81.

74. Chevrier, op. cit., p. 47.

75. Napoleon. 1858–69, op. cit., no. 842.

76. Chevrier, op. cit., p. 47.

77. Massena, op. cit., II, p. 482.

78. Schels, op. cit., pp. 158–9.

16

INTO THE TYROL

Even before Wurmser's battered army had begun to wend its way back into the mountains of the Tyrol, hurried efforts were being made to prepare Mantua for another blockade.

On the morning of 6 August, FZM Alvinczy arrived in the fortress to investigate its state of readiness. He found there were 10,788 men, of whom only 7,455 were fit for service, there being some 2,500 suffering from the fevers that were blamed on Mantua's 'death-breathing marshes'. Canto d'Irles asked for the garrison to be brought to 13,000 if the army stayed on the Mincio, and 20,000 if it retreated into the Tyrol. As before, supplies were short. For the smaller number of troops there would be bread for 22 days, but wood only for eight. There was sufficient animal fodder for 90 days, and hay for 25. Naturally, if the garrison were increased to the higher number of troops, the supplies would last for a shorter period. There was also a lack of money, so Alvinczy authorised Canto d'Irles to borrow cash from the townspeople in order to purchase supplies and pay the troops.

Towards evening, a letter arrived from Wurmser with the unpleasant news 'that the army is moving back to the Tyrol: that the fortress therefore must expect a second attack; that the Field Marshal, however, as soon as FML Quosdanovich moved to him, would do everything to liberate the fortress'.[1] Alvinczy was instructed to provision the fortress as soon as possible, the aim being to provide enough to last for two months, while an engineer, General Lauer, was to repair the fortress works. At nightfall, Generals Spiegel and Minkwitz arrived with seven battalions and one squadron for the reinforcement of the garrison.

After the commander had divided the troops into brigades during the next few days, their strength was as follows:

Brigades	Regiments	Battns	Sqdns
GM Baron Minkwitz	Carlstädter Grenzers	1	
	2nd Garrison Regiment	1	

Brigades	Regiments	Battns	Sqdns
	IR Wenzel Colloredo	2	
	IR Stein	2	
GM Count Spiegel	Carlstädter Grenzers	1	
	IR Gemmingen	1	
	IR Strassoldo	2	
Colonel Sola	IR Thurn	2	
	Banal Grenzers	1	
Colonel Sturioni	2nd Garrison Regiment	1	
	IR Brechainville	1	
	Warasdiner Grenzers	1	
	Frei-Corps Gyulay	1	
	Stabsdragoner		2
	Erzherzog Joseph Hussars		2
General Brentano	IR Belgioioso	3	
	IR Pellegrini	1	
	IR Preiss	1	
	IR Terzi	1	
	Total	23	4

These came to 16,423 men, though the number fit for combat, including the 680 artillerymen and sappers, and 242 cavalrymen, was only 12,224 men.[2]

During the night of 6/7 August, the main Austrian army drew back, some elements via Monte Baldo and Canale, but mostly through Verona. Alvinczy also passed through the city, where he had discussions with the Venetian authorities, and got them to agree to supply some provisions for Mantua. The last Austrians left Verona at about 9 p.m. on the 7th, most of the troops having moved through the mountains to the north, except for Mészáros, who turned aside to Vicenza. On 8 August, Wurmser moved his HQ to Ala.

The decision to move back inspired some pointed criticism from Thomas Graham regarding the deficiencies of the Austrian commanders:

I should still entertain hopes if we were under a proper system – But all will depend on that – It is not only an able & efficient head of the army that is wanted but a stricter discipline – The Generals don't think it necessary to stay by their columns – of course in many reg^{ts} the officers are inattentive, & on every march, pursuit or retreat the men are scattered about in a most unsoldierlike manner. – But they are undoubtedly brave fine troops and an able chief w^d put all that to rights in a little time.[3]

Bonaparte, in reporting to his own government on the 8th, typically painted a very positive picture: 'So, here we are back in our old positions. The enemy flies far into the Tyrol. The help that you told me was coming from the Army of the Coasts of the Ocean is beginning to arrive, and everything here is in the most satisfactory situation. The Austrian army, which for six weeks threatened to invade Italy, has disappeared like a dream.'[4]

There was of course, another side to the picture, and Massena wrote to his chief the following day saying: 'The food supplies are still very bad: no bread, no fodder. The generals are murmuring like the officers and the soldiers. My promises have no effect, and pillaging is at its height: the troops are committing every excess. I tremble at it, and I can do nothing to remedy it. I ask you as a favour, Citizen General, for a successor. The state of my health no longer permits me to make war ...'[5] Evidence suggests that this was not an isolated case, and instances of looting, sickness and lack of supplies were widespread. A number of generals were ill, but Massena seems to have stayed at his post.

The authorities in Mantua had their own problems of supply. Efforts to get in provisions continued, and Scorza tells us that the surrounding areas had been carefully divided into four districts, and representatives sent out into each with powers to obtain what they could. Unfortunately, one of them deserted to the French, meaning that a quarter of the area's resources remained untapped. The others did not bring in much, 'having found the province already stripped because of the campaign fought in it over the previous two months. They could only just ensure the modest quantity of 35,000 sacks of wheat, 28,000 of maize, 6,000 of rice, a little wine, and less wood.'[6]

On 8 August, Fiorella advanced to Marmirolo to recommence the blockade of Mantua, but he too fell ill on the following day, General Sahuguet being ordered from Milan on the 10th to replace him. For a while, the Austrian garrison remained in control of the Serraglio, as the French only had 2,700 men at hand, and were forced to observe the fortress from a distance. Indeed, Austrian patrols saw little or nothing of them, but on the 10th, the drawbridge of the Citadel was raised. That day, Canto d'Irles reported to Wurmser that all French equipment had been moved into the fortress, their siege works had been levelled, and that the quantity of provisions in the city now sufficed for a month. On the following day, the garrison saw more of the enemy, with large numbers of French appearing near Marmirolo, though this was not the main cause of interest for the inhabitants. Scorza noted: 'Today is a more than usually noteworthy day. We had, after dinner, the hanging on the gallows of a French spy, caught yesterday disguised as a hen-keeper, and in the buttons of whose coat were found two bulletins in cipher, which no one could interpret, nor would he confess, though bitterly tortured, to whom they were addressed.'[7]

The 11th also saw fighting in the mountains, as the French sought to make their line more secure. The Austrian positions on the heights around Lake Idro and on Monte Baldo gave them too much scope to repeat their advance on Brescia and Rivoli, so Bonaparte had decided to drive them further back. Massena duly captured Madonna della Corona and Canale, while Augereau moved through the Monti Lessini, north of Verona, in a feigned move that threatened Ala and also the road to Rovereto and Trento. Simultaneously, Sauret was moving towards Anfo, to attack the positions there, which he carried a day later.

Apart from improving French defences, these moves also provided better positions from which to begin the next phase of operations that Bonaparte had suggested, and would shortly begin. On 12 August, the Directory wrote to him (though the letter would not arrive for some days) approving his proposal to advance to Innsbruck, and informing him that they had ordered General Moreau to occupy the line from Ingolstadt to Innsbruck, so that the two armies linked.[8] In fact, Moreau was already on the advance, and during the previous few days, the Austrian forces on the eastern edge of Lake Constance had been obliged to retreat south-east into the Vorarlberg. By 12 August most of them had moved as far back as Reutte, about 40 miles north-west of Innsbruck. On 15 August, the Directory sent a further letter to Bonaparte, saying that it had ordered General Moreau to send 15,000 men towards Innsbruck, and even to Bressanone. Bonaparte was instructed to second this movement, it being pointed out to him that if Wurmser was not pressed, he could send troops to oppose Moreau.[9]

On 13 August, Bonaparte, who had more direct sources of information about the fighting in the north, wrote to Massena saying: 'Our affairs are going perfectly well with the Army of the Rhine and Moselle. The enemy seems to want to retire behind the Lech, where we will pursue him. General Moreau counts on pushing the troops to Füssen [50 miles north-west of Innsbruck] and Schongau, which will cut one of the routes from Bavaria to the Tyrol.'[10] Bonaparte was already taking measures to prepare for new operations, for on the same day he also wrote to Augereau, and told him: 'The intention of the General-in-Chief is to concentrate, as much as possible, the troops of each division, to rest the soldiers, and to make them ready to march on the enemy again.'[11]

However, it was not just the advance to the north that had been occupying his thoughts. In fact, Bonaparte's fertile mind was already thinking that it might be possible to by-pass Mantua, which could probably not be captured quickly, now that the siege artillery had been lost. A simple blockade might take a long time to reduce the garrison to starvation, and there were good reasons for not beginning it immediately, as Bonaparte indicated to the Directory in a letter of 14 August, which also gave his thoughts on a quicker way to conclude the campaign:

The enemy has 4,000 sick in Mantua. During this month the environs of this place are pestilential, and I limit myself to placing some camps for observation there, to keep the garrison within limits.

If a division of the Army of the Rhine can come and take a position at Innsbruck and throw the enemy on the right, I shall move to Trieste, I shall blow up the port and sack the town. If the Army of the Sambre and Meuse arrives on the Danube, and that of the Rhine can be at Innsbruck in force, I shall march on Vienna, by the Trieste road, and then we shall have the time to move back the immense resources that place contains.

The first plan can be carried out immediately. For the second, it will take a good battle to scatter Prince Charles, like I scattered Wurmser, and immediately march on Vienna.[12]

Once again, it took a little time for an exchange of letters, the Directory replying on 23 August that it found the boldness of the scheme praiseworthy, 'but the favourable moment does not seem to us to have arrived yet'.[13] Bonaparte was therefore instructed to link with Moreau, and leave the expedition to Trieste until after the successful completion of that operation.

In the meantime, over the next couple of days, Reuss retired from Anfo, and the Austrians also withdrew along the Adige valley. On 14 August, Reuss arrived in Trento, where Wurmser also established his HQ the same day. Wurmser had hardly arrived in the Tyrol when he received the alarming news of the French advance from Lake Constance. The danger of invasion from the north was soon countered by reinforcements sent there by Archduke Charles, but Wurmser also took measures for the defence of the Tyrol by allocating some artillery to the fortress of Kufstein, and increasing the numbers of Tyrolean militia. By the end of August, these numbered over 5,500 men. However, it was still a worrying period, when the losses to the army seemed much higher, due to the fact that many stragglers were still on the road, and Thomas Graham reported to his government:

The total Loss of the army (exceeding 15,000 men in killed, wounded Prisoners & missing & 60 pieces of cannon) has so completely destroyed the spirit and confidence of all Ranks that I cannot flatter myself with the hopes of being able to send your Lordship any favourable intelligence.[14]

Two days later he added that the loss of the army was infinitely greater than he had imagined, and that if he had not lost his cipher with his baggage he would have been able to relate the excesses committed by the Austrian troops in their retreat. He concluded: 'PS: From Generals to Subalterns the universal language of the army is *qu'il faut faire la paix, car nous ne savons pas faire la guerre.*'[15]

In Bonaparte's view, some of his subordinates were in the same position. On 14 August, he wrote an illuminating assessment of them:

I believe it useful, Citizen Directors, to give you my opinion of the generals who are employed with this army. You will see that there are very few of them who can be of use to me.

BERTHIER: talents, activity, courage, character, everything for him.

AUGEREAU: much character, courage, steadiness, activity; is used to war, liked by the soldiers, lucky in his operations.

MASSENA: active, indefatigable, has audacity, coup d'oeil and is quick to decide.

SÉRURIER: fights like a soldier, takes nothing on himself, steady, does not have a good enough opinion of his troops, is ill.

DESPINOY: sluggish, without activity, without audacity, is not the right age for war, is not liked by the soldiers, does not fight at their head; besides, he has loftiness, intelligence, and healthy political principles; good for a command in the interior.

SAURET: good, very good soldier; not enlightened enough to be a general; not very lucky.

ABBATUCCI: not fit to command fifty men.

GARNIER, MEYNIER, CASABIANCA: incapable; not fit to command a battalion in a war as active and serious as this one.

MACQUARD: brave man, no talent, lively.

GAULTIER: good for an office; has never made war.

Vaubois and Sahuguet were employed in the fortresses. I have
had them come to the army. I shall learn how to appreciate them.
They have acquitted themselves very well in everything I have
given them up to now: but the example of General Despinoy,
who was very good in his office in Milan, and very bad at the
head of his division, bids me to judge men by their actions.[16]

A fascinating counterpoint to these comments is provided by the reflections on the state of the Austrian army contained in a letter written by
Thomas Graham just four days later:

> Could any means be found to restore the *spirit* of such a force (for
> notwithstanding the very general disgust among the officers,
> there can be no doubt but that the troops behaved with signal
> bravery till after the 3rd) to *reconcile* the officers to their duty by
> extraordinary means, & to obtain the confidence of the army for
> their generals, much might still be done by a bold and offensive
> plan. – I say Generals, for it is not only the Comm^r in Chief but
> the greatest number of the other Genl Officers that require to be
> replaced being objects of contempt & ridicule in the army …
> When the wonderful activity, energy & attention that prevail in
> the French service from the Comm^r in Chief downwards are
> compared to the indecision, indifference & indolence universal
> here, the success of their rash but skilful manoeuvres is not
> surprising. In action I saw officers sent on urgent messages going
> a foot's pace – they say their horses are half starved & that they
> cannot afford to kill them.[17]

A few days later, Graham passed on some information about the
French commander which gives us a rare insight into the enemy's
impressions of him:

> From General Kellermann's son and some other officers of Rank
> who were here some days, we understood that Buonaparte who is
> a man of 28 has the character of ability especially in every thing

concerning the supplying of his Army. He lives intimately with Berthier at the head of the état major & is supposed to have orders from the Directory to take his advice. He is silent and reserv'd with his officers, but talks a great deal with the soldiers.[18]

The comment about supply is more than a little ironic. If Bonaparte had some complaints to make about his generals, he must have been at his wit's end over the supply service. Their chronic inefficiency was at least partly to blame for the shocking indiscipline that still affected the army, which in some areas was bringing the people dangerously close to another armed insurrection. Alberghini, a priest who lived near Rivoli tells us:

> The passing of the days brought no respite from the robberies and invasions of the houses by the soldiers, because, with the pretext of searching for food, there was no piece of furniture or small animal that was safe from their hands. Thus the villagers, tired and angry at seeing themselves slowly stripped of their possessions, decided to put up a violent defence, and having got together in their respective *contrade* they put their resolute resistance to the test, even at the peril of their lives.

On 20 August, a serious skirmish occurred in one of the villages and 48 plundering cavalrymen were put to flight. Realising that things were getting out of hand, the villagers appealed to Rampon for help: 'And he promised that he would stop them, adding that if the villagers were disturbed in the future by marauding soldiers, they should defend themselves with stones, poles, and other similar weapons, but they should not use muskets.'[19] Fortunately, Rampon took serious measures, placing a picket in the largest village and sending out regular patrols, which finally brought order back to the area. However, Laugier tells us that Sauret tended to behave quite differently, setting free arrested looters, which only exacerbated the problem. Laugier noted with great satisfaction that he had been replaced by Vaubois at about this time.

Bonaparte's own concern about supplies is demonstrated by the letter he sent the Chief Commissary on 18 August saying:

In four or five days ... a new campaign will open for the invincible Army of Italy. The barriers of the Tyrol will be forced, and the theatre of war will end in Germany.

The army is partly naked, and the nights are very cold. The mountains require that the soldiers have shoes, and many of them are bare-foot. We need a great quantity of biscuit ... Get together all our means and let me know what we can count on for all those objects of first necessity. Do we have any overcoats? Ultimately, what can I tell the divisional generals?

The object of this letter is very important. The march of the Army of the Rhine and Moselle which is moving on Innsbruck does not leave us the time to delay our attack. It is in four or five days that we must concentrate all our means on the points of Brescia, Peschiera and Verona: food, transport, ambulances, clothing, because part of the army is naked.[20]

He cannot have received a very favourable reply, because it was much more than five days before the new operations began. It is true, however, that before the army could move, Mantua had to be properly blockaded, and since many of its troops were still outside the walls of the city, an attack was necessary to force them back inside, after which the French would have to position themselves much closer to the walls. On 20 August, Bonaparte ordered Sahuguet to carry out this attack after Dallemagne had reached him with reinforcements. He was ordered to make his preparations to attack on the night of 23/24 August. Thus, in the early hours of the 24th, several columns approached Mantua, Dallemagne attacking Borgoforte, which he captured at 7 a.m., while Sahuguet took Governolo. After the garrison moved back, the French began to work at redoubts and other defences to prevent the Austrians from making sorties, though still at some distance from the fortress.

These preparations for an offensive were soon to be matched by those of the Austrians. On 26 August, the Emperor's ADC, Lieutenant-Colonel Baron Vincent, arrived in Trento with an order dated 19 August, which instructed Wurmser to advance and liberate Mantua. It had been decided that, as each day spent in the Tyrol increased the diffi-

culty of feeding the army, and any delay permitted the further reinforcement of the French army in Italy, a rapid advance would have to be
carried out. The order nominated FML Baron Lauer as chief of staff,
and Wurmser was instructed to draft the operational plan with him, and
to pass to its execution without the least delay.

Lauer presented his plan that very day. In it he made some assumptions that were perfectly reasonable, namely that the French army had
suffered badly during the recent combats, and had not properly recovered, nor received significant reinforcements. However, he drew some
dangerous conclusions from this, stating: 'The enemy is unable to
consider an offensive operation, and will either await reinforcements or
further events on the Lech.' While it was admitted that the Imperial
army had also not recovered, it seemed that a positive result from operations depended on acting before the enemy did. As for the details of
the operation, FML Lauer held that it was especially necessary

> to occupy the passes from Ponte di Legno [30 miles west-north-
> west of Trento] to the Vallarsa [leading south-east from
> Rovereto] in such a way that there should be no further concern
> for the Tyrol from that side. Therefore 3,000 men should be
> used at Ponte di Legno, 9,000 men in the passes lying left and
> right of Ala, and a reserve of 5,000 men should be positioned at
> Trento. The remaining troops – about 26,000 men – would
> advance to the attack through the Val Sugana [the Brenta
> valley], the only one left open by the French, and a very easy
> road. This operational army would seek to avoid a major battle,
> and manoeuvre until it reached the bridge of Legnago. Mean-
> while, the 17,000 men distributed in the passes would occupy
> the enemy, but without advancing, until the favourable
> moment occurred, or until the enemy himself moved back.

It was calculated that if the Austrian army were able to cross the Adige
at Legnago, the enemy would have to gather his forces to attack it, or
move towards the Mincio and perhaps even recross that river. If the
enemy decided to attack, the rest of the troops in the Tyrol were to

advance and take the enemy in the rear, while the main Austrian army avoided battle, moved to Mantua and combined with the garrison, then turned on the enemy if he had decided to halt and give battle. The plan foresaw that, with the land between the Adige and the Mincio cleared of the enemy, it would also be possible, by crossing the Po and advancing up the right bank towards Tortona, to force him to abandon Lombardy.[21]

These plans were almost immediately thrown into flux by the news that arrived on 28 August that Moreau had made a further advance, and that the troops opposing him might have to fall back over the Inn. After consideration, it was decided to go ahead, in the hope that the successes of the Archduke Charles would force the French to retreat again. The council of war felt that the possibility that the enemy army in Italy would attempt to link with Moreau by advancing in the Adige valley seemed highly unlikely. It was believed that Bonaparte's army was too weak to force a way through the defending troops who were to be left behind, and that Davidovich, their commander, would only need to retire slowly in order for the Austrian troops in the Brenta valley to have time to make their way to Verona, and fall on the enemy in the rear. Having concluded these discussions, Wurmser ordered the army to be set in movement immediately, so that his troops would be assembled in Bassano on 7 September.

At about the same time, Wurmser received a letter from Canto d'Irles saying that the blockading force around Mantua had been much reinforced. Wurmser replied the same day that he hoped that the link with the fortress would be re-established soon, and asked Canto d'Irles 'to put a siege train in readiness, which the army could immediately make use of in their advance. Also, as FML Count Canto d'Irles received knowledge of the approach of the Imperial and Royal operational army, he should attack the enemy positioned before Mantua with a considerable part of the garrison, in order to make the army's operations easier.'[22]

The army under Wurmser was divided into two parts for the forth-coming operations. One consisted of the corps under FML Davidovich for the defence of the borders of the Tyrol:

Brigades	Battns	Sqdns	Infantry	Cavalry
General Graffen in the Vorarlberg	4²/₃		3,451	
General Loudon towards Grisons and the Valtellina	2	4	1,841	568
General Prince Reuss on the right bank of the Adige at Trento and in the passes leading there	6⁵/₆	2	5,011	218
Generals Vukassovich and Spork in the camp at Rovereto	12³/₆	4	7,840	626
Total	25²/₃	10	18,143	1,412
				19,555

If the 5,640 Tyrolean Schützen who were positioned on the borders were added to the defensive force, it amounted to 25,195 men in total.

The other part was the operational army under the command of FM Count Wurmser himself.

Divisions	Battns	Coys	Sqdns	Infantry	Cavalry	Men
Mészáros, at Bassano	10	3	23	7,365	3,308	10,673
Sebottendorf	6¹/₃	5	2	3,787	299	4,086
Quosdanovich	6¹/₆		6	3,742	847	4,589
Total	22¹/₂	8	31	14,894	4,454	19,348

To these could be added the brigade of General Schübirz, who had on 16 August marched with two battalions of IR Deutschmeister and two squadrons of Erdödy Hussars, through the Val Pusteria and Carinthia to Pontebba, in order to occupy this important position on the road that led from the Veneto to Tarvisio and Klagenfurt. Schübirz had hardly arrived, after a fourteen-day march, when he was ordered to go directly to Bassano, a journey that he estimated would take him another fifteen days.

At that time, the Austrian commanders seem to have reckoned that the usable combat force in Mantua was 24½ battalions, numbering 11,844 men, and four squadrons numbering 413 men, making a total of 12,257. (In fact this was slightly optimistic, and on 31 August it was recorded that out of 17,259 men in the fortress, there were 6,988 men unfit for duty, leaving only 10,271.) The whole combat force available to the Austrians was therefore reckoned at 52,665 men.[23] However, the only troops placed so that they could participate in operations from the beginning would be:

	Infantry	Cavalry	Total
The divisions at Bassano	14,894	4,454	19,348
The brigades of Prince Reuss,			
Vukassovich, and Spork	12,851	844	13,695
Total	27,745	5,298	33,043

At the end of August, the French forces ranged against them were in the following positions and numbers:

Division	Men
Vaubois (replacing Sauret on 25 August), forming the left wing on the western shore of Lake Garda, at Storo, Salò, etc	11,000
In the centre, Massena, at Rivoli, on Monte Baldo, etc	13,000
The right wing, commanded by Augereau, at Verona	9,000
Total	33,000

In addition, there were:

Division	Men
The blockading corps of Sahuguet, observing Mantua	10,000
Kilmaine, commanding roughly 1,500 cavalry, and 2 battalions of infantry, defending Verona and the lower Adige	3,500
Total	13,500

The whole French force in the immediate area of operations therefore came to 46,500 men.[24]

In the last couple of days of August, final preparations were made on both sides. Bonaparte wrote a proclamation to the people of the Tyrol, which included the usual appeal for them to co-operate with the invading forces, coupled with threats of awful retribution for civilians who put up armed resistance. On the 30th, he issued a detailed order to the commissary, Denniée, to

> load on boats at Peschiera tomorrow, 120,000 rations of biscuit, 240,000 rations of brandy, oats to feed 2,000 horses for ten days, and 3,000 pairs of shoes ... The commissary is also required to have loaded on boats on the Adige 60,000 rations of biscuit, 120,000 rations of brandy, 60,000 rations of flour, and oats for 4,000 horses for ten days. This loading will be carried out on the 1st, and on the morning of the 2nd the boats will go up the Adige to the pontoon bridge at Polo ...[25]

On the 30th, Guillaume was also ordered to have boats collected to transport 3,500 men from Salò across the lake on 1 September. Bonaparte also wrote to Moreau on 31 August, saying:

> On 2 September, the Army of Italy will march on Trento, where it will arrive on the 4th or 5th. General Wurmser seems to want to cover Trieste, and has in consequence taken a position on the Brenta with one of the divisions of his army. It is possible that the division which is at Trento will retire on Bressanone, and from there on the road to Lienz. This movement will be the only one possible for him if you advance on Innsbruck in force. I shall try to divine your progress from the enemy's manoeuvres, but it is indispensable for me to have news from you.[26]

Before Bonaparte had moved, however, the Austrian army had already set off in a quite different direction: over the mountains to the east of Trento and into the Brenta valley. As Lauer had said, the road down this valley to Bassano was an easy one, but once taken, there was very little alternative but to follow it to its end. In many places the river was closely hemmed by towering rocky cliffs, and there were relatively few places where there was a route out of the valley to the crags above. Even fewer led anywhere except higher into the mountains. There was also precious little flat land in the bottom of the valley where it was possible to deploy troops. Only when one reached Bassano, where the mountains ended quite abruptly, was it feasible to position many troops in a conventional manner. These factors were to prove important in the ensuing operations.

The Austrian move from Trento to Bassano was planned to take six days. Normally, the distance was divided into four increasingly long stages: the first from Trento to Pergine (about eight miles), the second from Pergine to Borgo (thirteen miles), the third from there to Primolano (fourteen miles), and the last to Bassano (eighteen and a half miles). It was possible to combine the first two, and thereby arrive in Bassano on the third day, but the Austrian plan opted for a slower movement, which would see the troops assembled there on 7 September. The first unit, that of Sebottendorf, therefore had Pergine as its goal when it began its march on the morning of 1 September. On the following day, Sebottendorf continued his march only as far as Levico, while Quosdanovich moved to Pergine, and the artillery and bridging train followed. The HQ brought up the rear, though Wurmser himself stayed in Trento.

To the south, the French advance that the Austrians had thought so unlikely also began. Bonaparte's aim was to move his three divisions to within supporting distance of one another, then attack the Austrian positions at Ala and Rovereto. It is noteworthy that this procedure was the opposite of that which the Austrians habitually adopted during the 1796 campaign, of splitting their forces and making multi-pronged attacks. The arrangements went ahead despite Massena telling Berthier:

> Two thirds of my division, at least, lack coats, waistcoats, trousers, shirts, etc, and are absolutely in bare feet … I inform you, general, that if the movement of the General-in-Chief takes

place, the soldiers that I command will not in any way be able to set out. It is physically impossible, unless we want to leave half of them on the road.[27]

Under protest, therefore, Massena's division crossed to the left bank of the Adige at Polo on 2 September, and took the road in the direction of Ala. To Massena's right, Augereau, who had to leave behind the 29th Light because the state of its equipment was so bad, advanced from Verona through the Monti Lessini to Lugo. Vaubois shadowed these movements on the far side of Lake Garda, setting out at dawn and making for the north. Laugier noted that after climbing for some time on a stony road:

> We bivouacked beyond the village of Tena, in the middle of vast grasslands which form an irregular plain, dominated by the Tridentine Alps which offer on their highest summits the white-ness of permanent snow. The physicists are right when they say that a league of height above the horizon causes more change in the temperature than a hundred leagues to the north on the same level. I perceived it during the night, because, thinking to sleep as I normally did, on the grass, I could not resist, and was obliged to draw near to the fires that had been lit by the companies.[28]

On 3 September, they made their way down from the mountains at the northern end of Lake Garda, and Saint-Hilaire, with the advance-guard, drove back the outposts of Prince Reuss from Torbole and Nago. Guieu landed in the evening, having sailed over the lake from Salò, thus completing the concentration of the division just west of the Adige valley.

In the valley itself, Massena had arrived in Ala at 2 p.m. His advance-guard, particularly the cavalry, had immediately engaged the enemy outposts there under Vukassovich. The latter only had 1,500 men posi-tioned near the road, as another 1,200 were placed in the mountains to the left, and not being able to resist at Ala, he moved back to Serravalle. He had repeatedly sent messages to Rovereto to inform Davidovich that he would not be able to halt the enemy, but Davidovich was not there, having been summoned to Trento to discuss details of the plans for forthcoming operations with Wurmser. This meant that the rest of Davidovich's troops stayed where they were for the time being.

Eventually, the French advance became known in Trento, and in the afternoon Wurmser ordered Davidovich and Prince Reuss to attack the enemy advance-guard at dawn on the 4th, and throw it back. Wurmser also repeated the order that had been contained in the operational plan, for Mészáros to advance on Verona on the 4th, with the intention of taking the French in the rear. Prince Reuss received his orders at 7 p.m., and he in turn ordered Lieutenant-Colonel Seulen to attack in the morning, but told Wurmser that he could not divide his main force as it was too weak, and would therefore not be able to carry out the instructions he had received.

In the evening of the 3rd, Pijon informed Bonaparte that the enemy was holding Serravalle in force, and was ordered to attack. Vukassovich strongly defended the village, but evacuated it after a heated action, withdrawing to spend the night at Marco. This was a strong position standing exactly opposite Mori, on the other side of the Adige, two and a half miles south of Rovereto. During the night Vukassovich was badly hurt in a fall (the cause of which is not clear), though he refused to relinquish his command for a couple of days longer.

While these various actions were taking place, Augereau's division had spent the day toiling through the mountains to the south-east, where Rattier says the troops suffered badly from the lack of water. 'We drank that which they collect in sluices, when it rains, for the numerous herds which pass in the summer, and although it tasted of mud, and a little of urine, we were very glad to find it.'[29]

Augereau was given orders to leave his camping place at dawn on the 4th and march to Rovereto, covering the right of Massena as much as possible during his advance. Massena himself was ordered to depart from his position at Ala and Santa Margherita at 3 a.m., and to be at Rovereto at 8 or 9 a.m. To complete the concentration of the French divisions, Vaubois was also to go to Rovereto, but was instructed to send a detachment to Serravalle. Laugier recounted that this division began its march by way of Nago and passed a long defile between two mountains having a small lake on the left. The column stopped for a moment in this pass. We perceived on the summit of the mountains an infinity of people in movement. We could not see if they were the enemy. We continued on our way when we knew that they were some of the inhabitants who had fled from fear.[30]

On the far side of the Adige, Davidovich reached Marco at about daybreak with Spork, who took up a supporting position to the rear with IR Nádasdy. Bonaparte reported to the Directory:

At daybreak we found ourselves in the presence of the enemy. One division guarded the impregnable defiles of Marco, another, on the far side of the Adige, guarded the entrenched camp of Mori. General Pijon, with part of the light infantry gained the heights on the left of Marco. Adjutant-General Sornet, at the head of the 18th Light, attacked the enemy in skirmish order. General Victor, at the head of the 18th Line, in close column by battalion, penetrated by the main road. The enemy's resistance was for a long time tenacious. At the same time, General Vaubois attacked the entrenched camp of Mori. After two hours of very lively combat, the enemy gave way everywhere.[31]

As usual, it was the threat of being turned – by Pijon this time – that decided the Austrians to pull back, which they did by moving along the road to where IR Nádasdy awaited them. They then continued their march towards Rovereto, closely pursued by Massena, who pressed them on all sides, with the result that many of the troops were scattered or cut off. Some of these finally managed to get to Rovereto, while others could only escape by going over the mountains to the east, and eventually made their way into the Brenta valley.

Vukassovich resisted in Rovereto till midday, but was gradually worn down to 500 men. Facing ten times his number, he was ordered back to Calliano, the main position of the division. Davidovich tried to take some of the pressure off Vukassovich by positioning IR Preiss (1,700 men) on the heights behind Rovereto, where they were to receive the remains of the retreating brigade, then form the rearguard. During his withdrawal, Vukassovich had yet more losses inflicted by Victor, and by Rampon with the 32nd Line. By 1 p.m., Rovereto was clear of the Austrians, while on the other side of the Adige, Vaubois had also been successful, and had taken Mori.

Bonaparte was now faced with the problem of overcoming the defences before Calliano, which were thought to be almost impregnable. He described them thus: 'The Adige almost touches sheer mountains, and forms a gorge which is not 85 yards wide, closed by a village, a raised castle, and a good wall, which joins the Adige to the mountains, and where they had placed all their artillery.'[32] Colonel Weidenfeld was to defend this narrow pass with IR Preiss alone, since Spork and Vukassovich had continued towards Calliano, trusting to the natural strength of the position to hold up the French for some time. However, IR Preiss had suffered many casualties during the retreat and was much weakened. Hardly had it reached the village, which was called La Pietra, than it was attacked again, having no time to organise its defence. Dommartin cannonaded the village with eight guns, while Pijon advanced on the French right, and 300 skirmishers scattered over the river bank. On the main road, three demi-brigades moved through the gorge in battalion columns. Thoroughly demoralised, and once again facing enormous odds, the Austrian soldiers did not maintain their position for long. The French entered the village without much difficulty, and IR Preiss retreated on the road to Calliano.

In the camp at Calliano were Spork's brigade and the remnant of Vukassovich's, which together came to about 4,800 men. The Austrian commanders were evidently very far from thinking that the French would launch an immediate and successful attack on La Pietra, as they permitted the soldiers to disperse, making preparations for cooking. The cannon-fire from La Pietra was, according to later reports, not heard at all, and not a single fugitive from IR Preiss arrived to give any warning. At 4 p.m., Massena's men suddenly drove into the camp. There was no time to organise resistance, and soon the road to Trento was jammed with cannon, baggage and powder wagons, and disordered crowds of soldiers. The French cavalry went forward to round up prisoners, but this pursuit was stopped after the commander of the 1st Hussars and a number of other officers were shot from the saddle. Among those singled out for praise by Bonaparte in his report on the day's fighting were his ADC, Le Marois, who was wounded, and the captain commanding his cavalry escort, Jean-Baptiste Bessières.

Wurmser was just departing from Trento for Bassano at 5.30 p.m. when the first news of the capture of Calliano reached him. By this time, of course, the other Austrian divisions had already advanced some distance towards their destinations. In fact, Sebottendorf arrived in Ospedaletto that day, and Quosdanovich in Borgo, while Mészáros set out from Bassano for Vicenza. There was therefore no hope of them returning to Trento before the French could get there, but on the other hand, there seemed to be little that the French could do to stop the Austrians relieving Mantua. Wurmser decided to leave the defence of the Tyrol to Davidovich's troops, and continue his offensive movement. He immediately ordered Prince Reuss to move his troops to Trento and also repeated the order for Schübirz to advance to Bassano through the Veneto. As he also suspected that the French would advance directly over the mountains from Calliano to Levico, in order to cut the link between Davidovich and the divisions in the Brenta Valley, he also had Quosdanovich place a battalion of IR Thurn and a half squadron of Wurmser hussars at Levico to observe French movements. Quite a number of troops from Vukassovich's brigade who had been cut off also turned up in Levico.

Towards evening, Davidovich arrived in Trento. While the Austrian commanders were making efforts to collect the stragglers from their disorganised formations, Davidovich informed Colonel Zach of the staff that his men were so scattered that he would be unable to defend the city, and he did not yet know where he might be able to take up a defensive position. At 8 p.m., Davidovich ordered Prince Reuss to hurry his march, and follow the division to Lavis. Vukassovich, who by this time had nothing much remaining to command, left the army to seek treatment for his injuries in Bolzano.

In the earliest hours of the 5th, Davidovich abandoned Trento and moved back towards San Michele. He now had only about 5,000 men left. Vukassovich had lost about 1,000 during the desperate defence of the previous few days, and Spork's brigade had lost three-quarters of its men, most of whom had been scattered by the attack on Calliano. Davidovich decided, despite the weakened and disordered condition of his division, to stop at Lavis and form an outpost chain there. He was not to remain in this position undisturbed for very long.

To the south of him, Vaubois crossed the Adige at Serravalle during the night of 4/5 September, and moved northwards, slightly behind Massena, who arrived in Trento at 8 a.m. Vaubois joined him about four hours later. Bonaparte had also arrived, and after interrogating prisoners and inhabitants, seems to have learned for the first time that the French advance had only been opposed by Davidovich, and that Wurmser had gone towards Bassano with the rest of the army. In the light of this discovery, Bonaparte had to change his plans completely, which he did with an ease and speed that suggest he had already considered the possibility of an Austrian advance down the Brenta and made some allowance for it. However, the change was bound to have extensive repercussions, as it also influenced the whole strategic plan involving the armies in Germany, and inevitably delayed any move to link with Moreau. Bonaparte gave his views on the situation in a letter written the following day. He begins rather abruptly:

> There is nothing else to be done, Citizen Directors, if we wish to profit from our present position, except march on Trieste. We will be in Bolzano as soon as the Army of the Rhine advances on Innsbruck. But this plan that we adopted and which was good in the month of June, is no longer worth anything at the end of September. The snows will soon re-establish the barriers of Nature: the cold already begins to be sharp. The enemy, who is aware of this, has thrown himself on the Brenta to cover Trieste. I shall march today along the Brenta to attack the enemy at Bassano, or to cut his rear if he makes a move on Verona. You will appreciate that it is impossible for me to penetrate into the

mountains of the Tyrol while the whole enemy army is at Bassano and threatens my flank and rear ... on the 22nd [fructidor, i.e., 8 September] I shall be at Bassano. If the enemy waits for me, there will be a battle which will decide the fate of this whole country. If the enemy retires further on Trieste, I shall do what the military circumstances suggest to me is most suitable, but I shall await your orders to know if I should move to Trieste or not.[33]

It is noteworthy that Bonaparte had misinterpreted the principal intention of the Austrian advance, though he foresaw that they might move west rather than east. However, it seems unlikely that he would have followed a different plan even if he had realised that the Austrian goal was the relief of Mantua. Either way, it was in his interests to exploit the wide separation of the two wings of the Austrian army, which had given him a wonderful opportunity to beat each of them in turn, just as he had done a month before. After that débâcle, Thomas Graham had acidly commented:

> We seem to have *separated* only for the purpose of *uniting* again & in every manoeuvre laid ourselves open to the attacks of an active, enterprizing and skilful adversary. I doubt if B. Parte had had the direction of the Austrian Forces he could have contrived it better for his own purpos [*sic*].[34]

He could have said much the same of the situation that Bonaparte found on 5 September, and the master strategist did not take long to make the most of it.

Before he could turn all his strength on Wurmser, he knew it would be necessary to ensure that Davidovich would be unable to assist Wurmser by attacking the French in the rear. It was therefore essential to drive him further into the Tyrol, and establish a good defensive position where a single French division would be able to hold him back. Vaubois was given the job of doing this, and in the afternoon of 5 September his division advanced towards Lavis. At the same time, Augereau, who had not yet reached Trento and could take a short cut, was sent to begin the pursuit of the other wing of the Austrian army. He was instructed to turn aside three miles south of the city, and take the shortest route to Levico, a road that led due east over the ridge that separated the Adige and the Brenta valleys.

Bonaparte accompanied the advance-guard of Vaubois's division, and at 6 p.m. they found Davidovich's men positioned behind a stream, which had to be crossed by a well-defended bridge that had been partly demolished. A first attack was driven off, but when the rest of the division arrived, Bonaparte had the position attacked by as many troops as the terrain would allow. Some men of the 27th Light eventually managed to cross the bridge, while Murat forded the stream with some cavalry, after which the Austrians evacuated Lavis, moving back to San Michele. This was not the limit of Davidovich's withdrawal, however, and when he reported to Alvinczy at 10 p.m. that he had pulled back, he stated that he would be obliged to make a further retreat to Egna at dawn. The separation between the two wings of the Austrian army was therefore increasing by the hour, because Sebottendorf and Quosdanovich had continued their march all day, the first reaching Primolano and the second Ospedaletto. Mészáros had also continued to move towards Vicenza. Wurmser, for his part, arrived in Bassano during the day.

On 6 September, Davidovich continued his retreat to Salorno, and Vaubois took up a position at Lavis to observe him. Far away to the south, Mészáros's advance-guard had now pushed as far as Montebello, while his main force had advanced via Vicenza to Olmo. Behind him, Sebottendorf arrived in Bassano in the morning, where he joined Wurmser. Quosdanovich's was the last of the Austrian divisions, and he was to spend the night of 6/7 September in Primolano. The small Austrian rearguard at Levico, which was now a long way from any supporting troops, was attacked during the 6th by Augereau's division and driven unceremoniously along the valley. The French advance was no leisurely affair in the Austrian style, and by evening Augereau had progressed beyond Borgo, with Massena now close behind him. Bonaparte himself spent the night in Borgo.

On the morning of 7 September, the French pressed forward with their customary rapidity. At midday, Augereau's advance-guard, commanded by General Lanusse, approached Primolano. By this time, Quosdanovich had moved on, leaving behind a rearguard at Primolano, and had already arrived in Bassano with the artillery reserve, bridging train and baggage, his division much weakened by detachments. In fact, he only had IR Wilhelm Schröder (1,617 men), and five squadrons of Erdödy Hussars (700 men). Primolano was occupied by Lieutenant-Colonel Gavasini with one battalion of IR Michael Wallis (1,108 men), four companies of IR Erbach (561 men), one company of Mahony Jägers (100), three platoons of Erdödy Hussars (90 men) and a half company of pioneers. The detachment under Colonel Stentsch which had been at Levico was also there, which gave a force of about 2,800 men in total.

Sulkowski, a Polish officer who was shortly to be appointed Bonaparte's ADC, says that the Austrians had taken a position where a bend in the river protected their front. Rattier recounts that the road was blocked by an entrenchment, and that 'the mountains, between which there were only the road and the river [were] of an immense height and almost perpendicular'. Some of Augereau's men crossed the river in water up to their waists, and a number of skirmishers climbed up the rocky outcrops to turn the Austrian left. Having succeeded in this, they had to cross the river again on a small bridge, where the enemy naturally concentrated his fire. In Rattier's words:

> After a heavy fusillade and cannonade, which made all the gorges tremble, the 5th Light demi-brigade drove on them with such bravery, at the moment when we [the 4th Line] formed close column, that they were obliged to give up their entrenchments.[35]

Gavasini moved his men back, through what Sulkowski described as 'frightful gorges, where no more than 100 men could deploy in line'[36] to the fort of Covelo. This was in a hollow in the rocks, and stood nearly 200 feet above the river. It could, however, be outflanked by infantry on both sides, and the French soon exploited this weakness.

Under heavy, rolling fire, the 5th Light went left of the fort, while 300 men of the 4th Line waded through the Brenta, climbed the dominating rock heights right and in the rear of the Austrians, and fired from there on the garrison of the fort. After an hour's resistance, the Austrians evacuated the position, and tried to retreat, but *chef de brigade* Milhaud, who was to command a cavalry corps at Waterloo, cut them off with the 5th Dragoons and a squad of chasseurs. Most of the Austrians, including their wounded leader, Gavasini, were captured. After this, the French advanced to Cismon, where they camped for the night. In reflecting on the day's events, Sulkowski made the interesting observation that the Austrian troops only knew how to fight in conventional formations, and that 'even their tight clothing, which stiffened them, never permitted them to climb over the rocks'.[37]

News that the French had forced their way through Primolano reached Wurmser at about 4 p.m. This did not change his determination to march to Mantua, and it was decided to set out for Vicenza and join Mészáros the following morning. However, preparations were made both to march and to receive an attack by the French. The army spent the whole night under arms, horses saddled, artillery and baggage on the road, in a position where it could take the direction of Vicenza or Padua at need.

On 8 September, Bonaparte set off from Cismon at 2 a.m. with the divisions of Augereau and Massena. As the advance-guard approached the exit from the valley they ran into the Austrian rearguard under Quosdanovich and Bajalich, which numbered 3,800 men at most.

The combat began at 7 a.m. The history of the 5th Dragoons states that 'Augereau had his light infantry march along the left bank of the Brenta, and the brave 4th Line, commanded by the intrepid Lannes, was to attack and take all the positions on the right bank, where the enemy had his élite troops.'[38] Massena had also crossed the river and was behind Lannes. The narrowness of the valley meant that the French could not fully exploit their superior numbers, but they were able to spread over the flanking heights in the way that had troubled the Austrians before. Repeated attacks weakened the rearguard, which gave way under the pressure, being harried as it retired by Murat's cavalry. During this phase of the fighting, Bajalich was captured and Colonel Mahony, the commander of the Jäger regiment, was killed.

On reaching the town of Bassano, Augereau entered on the left, while Lannes and Massena rapidly crossed the bridge from the other side of the river. The arrival of the French caused panic and disorder in the town, and the Austrians hastily began to retreat. The chaos was increased when the artillery and baggage, which had received an order to turn back and take a different road, ran into the retiring troops, and the whole mass became jammed solid in the narrow streets. Bonaparte reported that as a result they had captured '35 pieces of cannon, completely harnessed, with their ammunition wagons, two bridging trains of 32 pontoons, completely harnessed, and more that 200 wagons, also harnessed ...'[39] He also speaks of 5,000 prisoners, which was an exaggeration, but the Austrians undoubtedly lost many men as stragglers in the rout. Those who got out of the town took whichever direction seemed to offer hopes of escape, and the various roads were dotted with fugitives. By chance, most of Sebottendorf's shattered division went in the direction of Fontaniva and Cittadella, where the HQ also ended up. Wurmser then took the troops that assembled in Cittadella and made for Vicenza, intending to join Mészáros. Operations were now to turn into a race to see if Wurmser could reach Mantua before the French could cut him off.

Wurmser arrived in Montebello before dawn on the 9th and, being concerned to secure the crossing at Legnago, the shortest route to Mantua now that he had no bridging train, a detachment was sent to occupy it. Few of Quosdanovich's soldiers had arrived in Montebello, so it was assumed the majority must have taken the road towards Treviso. Wurmser therefore ordered Quosdanovich to go via Venice and Trieste to Gorizia, in order to collect the scattered troops and assemble the reinforcements that might arrive from that direction. He was to cover the approaches to Austria on that side and be ready to advance to assist in further operations. Over the next 24 hours, Wurmser managed to reach Legnago and cross the Adige, while Massena pursued at some distance, passing through Montebello on his way to Vicenza. Wurmser had no intention of doubling back towards Trieste, but in case it should have occurred to him, Augereau had been sent to Padua to cut that route.

Wurmser let his troops rest in Legnago, intending to march on Mantua on the 11th. It was a somewhat depleted force that he had at his disposal, numbering about 12,000 men, of which 3,000 were cavalry. Sebottendorf's 'division' was reduced to only one and a third battalions, four and a half companies, and two squadrons. In this condition, Wurmser's only hope of saving his men was to reach Mantua, because another engagement would surely mean destruction at the hands of an enemy who by now had vastly superior forces. Bonaparte, on the other hand, was doing everything to forestall him, knowing that he could destroy him if he caught him, and that if he were allowed to reach Mantua the garrison would be much strengthened. In an attempt to overhaul Wurmser, he had Massena take a different route to avoid the long diversion south to Legnago. Instead, Massena marched from Montebello to Ronco, near Arcole,[40] where he was to cross the Adige. The country east of Mantua was much cut up by water-courses, and Bonaparte hoped it would be possible to halt the Austrians at one of these, giving the pursuers time to catch up. To this end, Sahuguet was ordered to send a brigade from the blockading force at Mantua to Castel d'Ario and destroy the nearby bridges. Sahuguet himself, with most of his division, was to take a position near Governolo. In the evening, Massena made his crossing at Ronco, while Augereau marched towards Legnago during the night of 10/11 September to press Wurmser from the rear.

On the morning of the 11th, Massena marched towards Sanguinetto, hoping to arrive there before Wurmser. Unfortunately for him, there were two roads leading from Ronco, one of which took a rather winding route along the river. By chance, Massena's leading troops chose this longer route, which negated much of the advantage they had gained. At about the same time, Wurmser had Ott march off, also to Sanguinetto, with most of his brigade. Wurmser was to follow, leaving a garrison of 1,621 men and 22 guns in Legnago under Major Iuch to hold off Augereau.

On his way, Ott had reports of enemy troops moving towards him from the north, and thought it advisable not to get too far ahead of the main army. He therefore stopped at Cerea, but was forced to quit the village by Pijon, supported by Murat's cavalry. Knowing the importance of keeping the route open, Ott countered, and retook the village. The French attacked again at about 2 p.m., when Victor arrived in support, but the Hungarians of IR Alvinczy kept their hold, and Wurmser's troops eventually drove the French back along the road towards Ronco. The Austrians captured 736 men and seven guns, and Bonaparte had to abandon his hope of cutting off Wurmser from Mantua. In fact, Wurmser reached Nogara late in the night of the 11th, where he rested for some hours. Far to the east, Augereau's advance-guard approached Legnago at twilight.

Wurmser began his march again at midnight. Reports indicated that Castel d'Ario was strongly held by the French, and Wurmser had already ordered this position to be stormed, when a local man appeared and offered to lead the Austrians along a route to Mantua where there were no French. He duly took them to Villimpenta, where Sahuguet had omitted to have the bridge over the Tione destroyed, then over the Molinella. A few French who were guarding these crossings fled towards Castel d'Ario with news of the Austrian advance, but too late to prevent the main Austrian force from reaching Mantua without disturbance, Massena having been unable to catch up, despite marching hard all day.

On arrival, Wurmser's troops formed a line that stretched from forward of the citadel and ran in front of San Giorgio, with the extreme left resting on the road northwards, and the extreme right on the road to Legnago. The palace of La Favorita, a little forward of the line, was also occupied. By this time, the number of men Wurmser had fit for combat amounted to only 10,367 infantry and 2,856 cavalry. Nevertheless, he can have had no wish to move them inside the fortress unless he had to, because if he could keep them outside it would be easier to collect supplies for them from the surrounding countryside. Bonaparte appreciated this, and also knew that if he could drive Wurmser into Mantua he would need fewer troops to observe him, as the nature of the fortress made a break-out very difficult. For these reasons, Bonaparte decided to give Wurmser no respite, and attack him as soon as he could.

An initial surprise attack by Massena on 14 September failed to have much effect, but the surrender of Legnago had released Augereau's division, and Bonaparte planned a much more serious effort for 15 September. Sahuguet was to take the left wing with 10,000 men, Massena in the centre with 9,000, and Augereau's division, of 6,500 men, was to advance along the Mincio and try to outflank the Austrian position. (Augereau was suffering from haemorrhoids and severe rheumatic pains, so he had passed his command to General Bon.)

At 8 a.m. on the 15th, the Austrian outposts reported that the enemy was approaching. Sahuguet was the first to engage, at about midday, eventually forcing Ott's men back towards La Favorita. Thus began a contest on this wing that ebbed and flowed all day with neither side being able to gain a decisive advantage. On the other wing, Augereau's division eventually approached San Giorgio at about 2 p.m., having carried out its projected advance along the river. Wurmser moved some of his troops towards the right to counter this, and was promptly attacked in the left centre by Massena. There was now heavy fighting along the whole line, but it was particularly fierce around San Giorgio, which was eventually captured by the French. In the end, Wurmser had to give ground, and the right wing and centre were forced to retreat to the safety of the citadel, though some cavalry and Grenzers were cut off and surrendered. Ott resisted for a while longer, then also moved into the citadel in the late evening. The cost of the day to the Austrians was 2,452 men and 442 horses. The French gave their loss as about 1,000.

The second attempt to relieve Mantua had therefore come to a rather sorry conclusion for the Austrians. Their army commander had managed to get himself shut inside the very place he was trying to liberate, losing more than 11,000 men in the process. The French had failed to make the link between their armies in Italy and Germany, and Bonaparte was, in a sense, back to square one, still faced with the problem of reducing Mantua, which now had a much more powerful garrison. It was to be several months before that nut was cracked.

NOTES

1. Schels, J. B. 'Die Operationen des FM Grafen Wurmser am Ende Juli

und Anfang August 1796, zum Ensatz von Mantua; mit der Schlacht bei Castiglione.' *Oesterreichische Militärische Zeitschrift*, Bd. 1; Bd. 2 (1830): 254–97; 41–81, 129–59, p. 149.

2. Schels, J. B. 'Die zweite Einschließung Mantuas, im August 1796, und gleichzeitige Ereignisse bei dem k. k. Heere unter dem FM Grafen Wurmser in Tirol und Vorarlberg.' *Oesterreichische Militärische Zeitschrift*, Bd. 4 (1831), pp. 256–57.

3. Holland Rose, J. 'Despatches of Colonel Thomas Graham on the Italian Campaign of 1796–1797.' *The English Historical Review*, 14 (1899), p. 122.

4. Napoleon. *Correspondance de Napoléon Ier publiée par ordre de l'empereur Napoléon III*. Paris, 1858–69, no. 852.

5. Massena, A. *Mémoires de Massena, rédigés d'après les documents qu'il a laissés et sur ceux du dépôt de la guerre et du dépôt des fortifications, par le général Koch*. Paris, 1848–50, II, p. 496.

6. Scorza, B. *Cronaca vissuta del duplice assedio di Mantova degli anni 1796 e 1797: le vicende di Mantova nel 1796*. Mantua, 1975, p. 121.

7. Ibid., pp. 121–2.

8. Napoleon. *Correspondance inédite officielle et confidentielle de Napoléon Bonaparte: avec les cours étrangères, les princes, les ministres et les généraux français et étrangers, en Italie, en Allemagne, et en Egypte*. Paris, 1809, I, p. 409.

9. Ibid., I, pp. 455–6.

10. Napoleon. 1858–69, op. cit., no. 883.

11. Ibid., no. 886.

12. Ibid., no. 889.

13. Napoleon. 1809, op. cit., I, p. 459.

14. Holland Rose, op. cit., p. 122.

15. Ibid., p. 122.

16. Napoleon. 1858–69, op. cit., no. 890.

17. Holland Rose, op. cit., pp. 123–4.

18. Brett-James, E. A. *General Graham, Lord Lynedoch*. London, 1959, p. 67.

19. Alberghini, G. B., don. *Gli austro-galli in val di Caprino (1796–1801) memoria storica*. Verona, 1880, pp. 39 and 42.

20. Napoleon. 1858–69, op. cit., no. 906.

21. Schels, 1831, op. cit., pp. 280–2.

22. Ibid., p. 285.

23. Ibid., pp. 282–6.

24. Ibid., p. 292.

25. Napoleon. 1858–69, op. cit., no. 940.

26. Ibid., no. 945.

27. Napoleon. 1809, op. cit., II, p. 18.

28. Laugier, J.-R. *Les cahiers du capitaine Laugier. – De la guerre et de l'anarchie, ou Mémoires historiques des campagnes et aventures d'un capitaine du 27me régiment d'infanterie légère par Jérome-Roland Laugier. Publiés d'après le manuscrit original par Léon G. Pélissier.* Aix, 1893, p. 103.

29. Rattier, J.-H. 'Campagne d'Italie (1796): notes d'un sergent-major.' *Revue rétrospective,* XX (1894), p. 242.

30. Laugier, op. cit., 1893, p. 104.

31. Napoleon. 1858–69, op. cit., no. 967.

32. Ibid., no. 967.

33. Ibid., no. 968.

34. Brett-James, op. cit., p. 67.

35. Rattier, op. cit., p. 243.

36. Reinhard, M. *Avec Bonaparte en Italie; d'après les lettres inédites de son aide de camp Joseph Sulkowski.* Paris, 1946, p. 116.

37. Ibid., p. 117.

38. Napoleon. *Mémoires pour servir à l'histoire de France, sous le regne de Napoléon, écrits sous sa dictée à Sainte-Hélène, par les généraux qui ont partagé sa captivité.* Paris, 1829, I, p. 467.

39. Napoleon. 1858–69, op. cit., no. 978.

40. For some reason best known to themselves, English-speakers have acquired a habit of referring to this place as 'Arcola'. This is probably the result of ignorance leading to the assumption that Arcole is a gallicism, in the same way that Verone is of Verona. Nothing could be further from the truth. Arcole is the correct spelling, and the pronunciation, roughly speaking, is AR-coll-eh, with the stress on the first syllable.

17

ARCOLE

The citizens of Mantua had no doubt about the gravity of the situation facing them and their garrison in the middle of September. It had been obvious from the very moment when Wurmser and his generals had arrived. Scorza recounts: 'the people, who believed them to be covered with laurels had run to meet them and applaud them, but at the first cheer refused to continue, perceiving that they were crowned not with laurels, but with cypress.'[1] The defeat of the army under the very walls of the city could only confirm this, and the fortress soon filled up with the dispirited remains of the force that should have set the inhabitants free.

Most of the soldiery made camp inside the crownwork of Palazzo Tè, and the entrenchments of Migliaretto, but many of them bivouacked in the streets and squares of the town. This sudden influx had roughly doubled the number of soldiers in the fortress, bringing them to 29,676 men. However, the total was destined to diminish rapidly, and during the following six weeks, nearly 4,000 of them died from wounds or disease. Even more were temporarily incapacitated. Sulkowski provides us with an interesting glimpse of life in the fortress at this time:

> The General-in-Chief sent me to Mantua as a negotiator. It was about the subject of exchanging prisoners. Wurmser's reply was entirely obliging: one is very agreeable when one is surrounded. His aide de camp, who was dealing with me, invited me to refresh myself in the town, and I entered with my eyes blindfolded. Nevertheless, I saw only long faces at the cafe. Out of 100 officers whom I caught sight of, there were at least 60 who were sick, and, as they did not know that I understood German, I had the leisure of listening to their conversation, which resembled fairly well the discussions of the patients of the Hôtel Dieu ... The reports of our prisoners agree in saying that the enemy actually has 7,000 soldiers sick ...[2]

In addition to disease, there was the problem of food, and as on previous occasions the Austrian commanders had made it their main priority to establish how much was available in the city. On 16 September, Wurmser called the generals, colonels, civil and military officials to a meeting for this purpose. It revealed that there was enough flour for 21 days, and 3,000 sacks of wheat, which would give flour for another sixteen days when milled. There was only enough oats for eight days, but the civilian authorities could provide 15,000 sacks of maize to be made into fodder for the horses. It was calculated that this would last for 35 days. There was also a supply of hay sufficient for ten days, but wood for only six days. No precise information was available regarding quantities of meat, but there was a great shortage of wine, which was a source of some worry as it was considered a valuable medicine. However, since the harvest was imminent, it was hoped that large quantities could soon be obtained from the surrounding area.[3]

Fortunately for the Austrians, the French had not yet been able to blockade the fortress closely, being obliged to position troops to watch the roads from the east. Wurmser therefore found himself with an opportunity to exploit the resources in the immediate vicinity of Mantua until such time as the French closed in. There was no time to lose, and the old Field Marshal ordered foraging parties to go into the Serraglio on the following day to collect rough provender. These brought back nearly 200 wagon-loads of hay and captured two French wagons laden with bread, and one ambulance wagon containing bandages. Excursions were also made on the nights of the 18th, 19th and 21st, bringing in another 200 wagon-loads of hay, and 55 of wine. A much more aggressive sortie was made on 23 September, in an attempt to capture the lightly occupied position at Governolo, which, it was hoped, would make the gathering of supplies easier. The sortie was undertaken by Ott and Minkwitz, but was a costly failure, resulting in Austrian losses of over 1,000 men. Nevertheless, the Austrians were able to continue collecting supplies for a few days longer, as the French did not immediately alter their positions.

On 24 September, an important change was made in the Austrian high command. Since Wurmser had managed to entrap himself in

Mantua, it was necessary to appoint someone to get him out, and the Emperor's choice fell on Alvinczy. *Feldzeugmeister* Jószef Baron Alvinczy Borberecky was an ethnic Hungarian who had been born in Transylvania, which is now part of Romania. Portraits of him show a rather portly, round-faced man, but at 61 years old[4] he was much younger than his predecessors. Nevertheless, he had also seen service during the Seven Years War, as a grenadier captain. He was the last of his family, and perhaps it was partly because of this that he was, as Wurzbach states, 'a father to his soldiers'.[5] He may have been something of a father figure to his Emperor as well, for he had been Francis's military tutor and had taught him tactics. He was to prove a worthy, if slightly unlucky opponent, and gave Bonaparte some of the sternest tests of his first campaign.

Alvinczy's orders were to relieve Mantua as soon as possible, and within days of receiving them he held a council of war in Bolzano to make plans for this operation. They were drafted jointly with Davidovich, and with the help of Spork and a certain Major Weyrother of the general staff. The last name should sound a knell in the mind of anyone familiar with Napoleon's campaigns, for it was Weyrother who was responsible for the Austro-Russian plan at Austerlitz in 1805, which led to one of the most shattering defeats ever suffered by an army in battle. It is tempting to surmise that his contribution to the plans produced in Bolzano must have been limited, as they came quite close to being successful, despite making use of a pincer movement, a strategy that had failed dismally against Bonaparte on every previous occasion.

The overall strategy that was laid out was for Davidovich to push southwards with the Tyrol Corps while Quosdanovich should advance westwards from Friuli to Bassano, and offer battle to the French near Verona. Davidovich was to effect a link with the Friuli Corps as soon as he possibly could, using whichever route seemed most suitable at the time. Wurmser, for his part, was requested to make a sortie from Mantua, drive off the blockading corps, and take the French main army in the rear. However, it was stipulated that before all this could be attempted, the Friuli Corps must be brought to a strength of 20,000 men. The recent battering that the army had suffered meant that this would take time, even though some replacements were already on the march towards Italy. It would therefore be several weeks before an offensive could be undertaken.

Fortunately for the Austrians, they were able to carry out their work of rebuilding the army without disturbance, despite the fact that the Directory had originally been eager to see a follow-up to the French successes of early September. They had sent Bonaparte a letter on the 20th, instructing him to write to the Emperor threatening to sack Trieste. Bonaparte was then to march on the town after the message had been despatched, and was also told to open communications with Moreau. However, five days later the Directory sent Bonaparte another letter explaining that operations were going badly in Germany, and that the expedition to Trieste should be deferred.

While these orders were on their way to Bonaparte, the latter had made arrangements to blockade Mantua more closely. Kilmaine had been given overall command of the force dedicated to this task, with Sahuguet and Dallemagne under him, while the resourceful Chasseloup was in charge of the engineers. On 29 September the latter informed Bonaparte that the blockading of Mantua had been achieved without incident, and the French then settled down to observe the enemy, which was all they could do at that moment. As Bonaparte told the Directory on 1 October: 'It is impossible to think of besieging Mantua at the moment because of the rains: it will only be feasible in January.' He also made a pressing request for reinforcements. After giving a table showing the strength of the divisions, he commented:

I therefore have 18,900 men with the army of observation, and 9,000 men with the besieging army. I leave you to consider, if I do not receive help, whether this winter I will be able to resist the Emperor, who will have 50,000 men in six weeks ... I need another 15,000 men ... I also need 20,000 muskets. But it is necessary that the things that you send me arrive, and that they are not like everything which is announced for this army, where nothing arrives. We have a great quantity of muskets, but they are Austrian, and weigh too much. Our soldiers cannot use them.[6]

Bonaparte might have been less concerned if he had known the kind of army that the Austrians were putting together. It was true that it would approach 50,000 men in total, but the fighting in Germany was taking up precious resources, and this was the third time that Austria had had to rebuild its army in Italy. The majority of the reinforcements consisted of fifteen newly raised Grenz battalions, most of which travelled to the Alps in wagons. This gruelling method of transport was injurious to the soldiers, who often arrived stiff and bruised, and damaged many of the muskets with the jarring and shaking they received. Moreover, although most of the new battalions had the respectable strength of 1,200 men or more, the majority had no idea of how to use their weapons, and were still unused to military discipline and drill. To compound these problems, hardly a third of the necessary officers had been found. When the 5th battalion of Banal Grenzers arrived it had 1,167 men, but only one officer, a lieutenant. It also had field equipment for only two companies, instead of six. The 4th Banal battalion was slightly better off, having a major and three other officers in charge of its 1,358 men. By mid-October, there were fourteen battalions making up the right wing of the army with only 171 officers instead of 366. There were also serious shortages of clothing, especially coats, trousers, overcoats, shoes and much equipment, including cooking utensils, field ovens and transport.[7]

Not surprisingly, there was a lengthy pause while the opposing sides tried to prepare themselves for the next struggle, though on 2 October Bonaparte did write to the Emperor, politely telling him he had orders to destroy Trieste if the Austrians did not begin peace negotiations. However: 'Until now I have been held back from the execution of this plan by the hope of not increasing the number of innocent victims of this war.'[8] It hardly seems likely that the Austrians would have taken this at face value, and they must have suspected at the very least that the French were weaker than they would have wished.

On the same day, it was reported to Wurmser that the garrison in Mantua was now down to a supply of wood and bread-making materials for eight days, beef cattle for six days, and hay for two days. Some supplies were obtained from the civilian authorities, but Wurmser ordered a foraging sortie for 7 October, which was to be combined with an attempt to level the enemy siege works. On 4 October, Alvinczy went from Bolzano to Gorizia to supervise the preparations for a new offensive. A letter he had sent Wurmser from Bolzano on 1 October reached its goal on the 5th, and informed the beleaguered Field Marshal that he would soon come to his rescue. This was an incentive, if any were needed, to make sure the fortress could hold out for longer, but the sortie during the night of 6/7 October was something of a fiasco, and although 100 wagon-loads of hay were brought in, most of the oxen that were used as draught animals were lost to enemy action. A couple of days later, Alvinczy began to draw the left wing of the Friuli Corps together, moving the troops into a camp at Gorizia, and at about this time command of the right wing was given to Provera.

Bonaparte was fairly sure that there would be an offensive soon, and continued to prod the Directory on the subject of reinforcements. On 11 October he reported:

Numerous of the Emperor's corps are marching in the Tyrol. The autumn rains continue to cause us many sick. There is not much to be hoped from a reinforcement by the men who are in hospital, because it is presumable that great blows will be struck here in a month … I have so many generals of brigade wounded or sick that, despite all those which you make every day, I still lack them. It is true that some are sent to me who are so inept that I cannot employ them with the active army.[9]

His appraisal of the likely delay was quite accurate. On 12 October, Alvinczy sent a letter to Wurmser from Gorizia saying that: 'he would soon advance to his relief, but must still await the arrival of several columns of reinforcements. Hence, it could still easily be fourteen days before Alvinczy was in a position to move the army.'[10] To this and other messages, Wurmser replied with continual requests for aid, pointing out that the stock of medicines had already been almost completely exhausted by the middle of September, and that food was very short. Despite, or perhaps because of, the obvious desperation of the garrison, the French soldiers around Mantua did not disturb small Austrian parties in their work of gathering grass and reeds, and when the foragers ventured near the French positions, some even helped to collect the hay and bind it up.

On 16 October, Bonaparte wrote to Wurmser asking him to give up the fortress in exchange for a free passage for himself and his troops. Wurmser's reply is not recorded, but the old man was an extremely determined character, and must certainly have refused, despite the seriousness of the situation facing him. Its gravity may be judged by the fact that Wurmser received a suggestion on 20 October to start slaughtering the horses that were not needed in order to save the maize that was used to feed them, and give both horse-meat and maize to the troops. Wurmser did not make a decision immediately, no doubt hoping that he would soon receive better news from Alvinczy.

In fact, help was almost on its way. On 21 October, Alvinczy decided to commence his new offensive. His plan was to leave Gorizia on the 22nd, reach the Tagliamento on the 24th, rest two days, cross the river, and join Provera at Pordenone. The whole force would then cross the Piave, and Bassano would be attacked on 3 November, while the Tyrol Corps attacked Trento on the same day.

At this time the Friuli Corps was under the command of Quosdanovich, who was operating under the direct supervision of Alvinczy himself. The corps was split into several sub-units:

	Battns	Sqdns	Men
Advance-guard, General Prince Hohenzollern	$4^2/6$	7	4,397
Main corps, under FML Provera.			
First part, Generals Roselmini and Lipthay	8	2	9,380
Second part, Generals Schübirz and Brabeck	8	$1^1/2$	8,279
Reserve, General Pittoni	4	1	4,376
Total	$24^2/6$	$11^1/2$	26,432

At that time, the Tyrol Corps numbered 19½ battalions, and 11¼ squadrons, totalling 16,815 men. This gave a total for the whole army of 43,247 men, though this was to increase slightly as reinforcements continued to arrive. The army was not as well provided with artillery as before, the Friuli Corps having 54 line guns and 20 reserve, while the Tyrol Corps had 40 line and 20 reserve.[11]

The left wing of the Friuli Corps marched off on 22 October in fine autumn weather, which did not last very long. In the evening of the 23rd there was torrential rain, and the rivers began to rise alarmingly. In particular, the Tagliamento was much swollen, so the march was hastened in order to cross it before it became too difficult. On the 25th, it was discovered that the river was now too wide for a pontoon bridge to reach over it, but the troops managed to wade through the water to the other side. The advance was soon perceived by the French, and on the same day Bonaparte wrote to the Directory:

> We are in movement: the enemy seems to wish to cross the Piave and establish himself on the Brenta. I shall let him advance. The rains, the bad roads, and the streams will give me a good account ... Snow is falling, but this does not prevent them from fighting in the Tyrol. It is not impossible that I shall evacuate Trento. I should be displeased to do it ... Wurmser is at the last extremity: he lacks wine, meat and fodder. He is eating his horses, and has 15,000 sick ... I believe that we shall soon be in action here. In fifty days, Mantua will be taken or given up.[12]

A few days later, Joubert, who was convalescing as commander of Legnago, recounted that Bonaparte had told him to expect to be besieged, and asked him to hold the town for twenty days before surrendering.[13] It seems one must conclude from this that Bonaparte was already considering the possibility that he would have to retreat beyond the Adige, though as he suggests in the letter above, this would force the Friuli Corps to extend its lines of supply, and would lead to it suffering losses through some of the troops being unable to keep up with the march.

On the 26th, Bonaparte readied his staff for the coming fight by appointing three new ADCs. They were Sulkowski, the multi-lingual

Pole, Muiron, who had been wounded at Toulon, and the artilleryman, Duroc. A couple of months later, the first made a succinct summary of his new job: 'The service of aides de camp with a general as indefatigable as Bonaparte is nothing but continual work.'[14] The other two aides were to become famous in Napoleonic legend, Muiron dying gloriously at Arcole, and Duroc becoming Bonaparte's closest friend, and Grand Marshal of the Imperial Palace. His death in action near Bautzen in 1813 so profoundly affected his master that the latter spent the rest of the day sitting alone, quite unable to issue any orders.

Wurmser also surmised that the Friuli Corps was in movement, having received on 25 October a letter from Alvinczy dated the 18th, saying that he would start his march soon. This decided Wurmser against slaughtering any of the horses, and he also took the decision to organise a large sortie to draw French attention towards Mantua and away from Alvinczy. It was planned for the early hours of 28 October, and was to be a fairly elaborate affair involving four columns, the first of which was to cross the lake on boats and capture San Giorgio. The operation went wrong from the very beginning, as the French pickets discovered the first column as soon as it landed, and attacked it fiercely. The other three columns never left their starting-points. Fortunately for Alvinczy, this miserable failure had no immediate effect on his operations, as he had not yet made proper contact with the enemy. Indeed, it was only on the 28th that the concentration of the Friuli Corps became complete, when Provera moved to join Quosdanovich within reach of the Piave. Here the Austrians paused because it was impossible to throw a bridge over the river, which was still greatly swollen by the rains. The state of the rain-soaked roads, the rivers in spate and the stormy Adriatic Sea were also causing problems of supply for the Friuli Corps, much as Bonaparte had expected.

At about this time, Laugier, who was in the Tyrol, noted that the guards were doubled: 'I realised that it would not be long before we should run new dangers, and the season, which was advancing, offered us further miseries.'[15] He was right, and Davidovich attacked the French outposts in the Tyrol on 27 October, despite the heavy snow that had fallen in the mountains. During the night of 29 October, he attacked the castle of Segonzano, and there was heavy fighting in the area on the 30th. Ironically, Berthier wrote to Vaubois that day, saying:

> The General-in-Chief tells me to inform you, Citizen General, that it seems that the enemy is considerably weakened before you, and has moved into Friuli. You must have noticed that the deserters that came to you from different regiments are no longer arriving. The intention of the General-in-Chief is to remove 3,000 men from your division to reinforce those of Generals Massena and Augereau, but he desires, first of all, that you attack the enemy and push him as far as Egna and Caltern …[16]

Pushing the Tyrol Corps further back into the mountains so that he would have the freedom to deal with the Friuli Corps undisturbed was, of course, similar to the strategy that he had used before Castiglione. This time the execution of the plan was far from perfect, and for various reasons. One was that Bonaparte's appraisal of the weakness of the Tyrol Corps was completely inaccurate, as Vaubois was to discover. In fact, it had been reinforced, and by 1 November it heavily outnumbered Vaubois' division. It was disposed in six columns for its advance:[17]

Column	Commander	Battns	Comps	Sqdns	Infantry	Cavalry
I	Loudon	3	2	4	3,915	362
II	Ocskay	4	4	4¼	4,200	463
III	Spork	1	7		2,560	
IV	Vukassovich	4	5	¼	3,772	30
V	Vukassovich (sic)	2	5	1	2,958	120
VI	Seulen	1	2	½	1,022	74
Total		15	25	10	18,427	1,049

Mittrovsky's brigade was still positioned in the Brenta valley as a linking force, but was no longer assigned to the Tyrol Corps, having been placed at the disposition of FML Quosdanovich and the Friuli Corps. The latter had been reinforced in the last week, and now totalled 28,699 men. This corps therefore had a simple numerical superiority over the French divisions immediately facing it of nearly 6,500 men, but the poor state of many of the Austrian units largely nullified this advantage. On 31 October the number of troops in Mantua was reported as 12,420 fit out of a total of 23,708 men.

Towards the end of October the French army was deployed in the following manner:[18]

Division and Position	Men
Vaubois, at Trento and on the stream of Lavis	10,500
Augereau, on the Adige	8,340
Massena, at Bassano and Treviso	9,540
Macquard (infantry reserve) at Villafranca	2,750
Dumas (cavalry reserve) in Verona	1,600
Kilmaine, at Mantua	8,830
Total	41,560

The task of observing the advance of the Friuli Corps fell to Massena's division, which made no serious attempt to oppose its progress. This was rather slow, as the roads were a quagmire, and the troops were suffering a great deal from the frequent heavy rain. However, during the night of 30 October, the rain stopped and the level of the rivers fell a great deal, promising somewhat easier conditions for the rest of the advance. Towards evening on 1 November, the Austrians built a bridge of boats over the Piave near Campana, and the advance-guard immediately crossed under the watchful eye of French patrols. By this time, Massena had assembled most of his division around Bassano.

The advance had come not a moment too soon as far as Wurmser was concerned. On 30 October it had been reported to him that there were no beef cattle left in Mantua, so the distribution of horse-meat began on 1 November. During the afternoon of 2 November, Alvinczy himself crossed the Piave not far from Conegliano, but the main activity of the day actually took place in the Tyrol. At 3 a.m., Vaubois attacked the Austrian positions at San Michele, Cembra and Segonzano, resulting in several hours of heavy fighting. Eventually, Vaubois returned to his former positions, but not before suffering significant casualties. According to Bonaparte's report of 13 November, the French lost 650 men, and it would appear that the 85th Line had the worst of its encounter with IR Alvinczy, losing ten officers and 270 men, an experience that seems to have gravely shaken its morale, to judge from its conduct a few days later. The Austrians also took a battering, reporting losses of 20 officers and 1,096 men in total.

On 3 November, Davidovich advanced again, threatening to outflank Vaubois, who decided to move back to Calliano. That day, Louis Bonaparte observed in a letter to his brother that the enemy seemed very strong, was constantly on the move, and that 'His troops fight as they have never done before now. It is not simple bravery, it is ferocity, a rage which has something of desperation.' He added: 'What consequences our defeat will have! The officers, in general, are tired. There were some of them, who, under fire, spoke only of retiring to their homes.'[19] In the flood-plain of the Po, the day passed more quietly, Massena pulling back his outposts as Alvinczy advanced to a point halfway between Bassano and Treviso. During the day, Alvinczy issued orders to march to the Brenta on the 4th. Hohenzollern and Mittrovsky were to form the right wing, and advance to Bassano. On the left, Lipthay and Brabeck were to take the road directly towards Vicenza, which led to the crossing at Fontaniva. If possible, they were to pass onto the right bank there.

On 4 November, the two jaws of the Austrian pincer continued to close. In the mountains, Vaubois gave ground towards Calliano, while on the plain, Massena evacuated Bassano at 5 a.m. and moved towards Vicenza. He was shadowed at some distance by Hohenzollern, who entered Bassano the same day. Farther south, Lipthay managed to cross the Brenta at Fontaniva, and took up a position on the right bank with two battalions of IR Splény. Provera, who was now in overall command of the left wing of the corps, had a bridge built opposite Fontaniva, at a place where there was an island in the river.

At this point, one of the major inconveniences of the wide separation between the Austrian corps began to influence their operations, as it was to do constantly in the next two weeks. It was not easy to maintain communications between the two parts of the army, and as Alvinczy had no news of Davidovich's progress, he decided he would have to pause until he could be sure of what was going on in the Tyrol. He may also have been influenced by the condition of the Friuli Corps, which was far from good. On 4 November, he wrote a report describing the lack of organisation and the complete ignorance of military service of the majority of his troops, the shortage of officers, and the lack of much essential equipment. He added that with each step forward the difficulties of supply increased, and that because the many newly raised battalions were composed of recruits who were not used to marching, the roads were covered with stragglers.[20]

Although Alvinczy did not know it, affairs were continuing to go well for the Austrians in the Tyrol. On the night of 4/5 November, Vaubois moved behind Trento, which Davidovich entered during the day. Vaubois then took up a position at Calliano, and the two sides made preparations for its attack and defence. By 5 November, Bonaparte had become sufficiently concerned about the train of events to the north to pull Joubert from Legnago and send him to Vaubois 'to assist him in his retreat, and on the means to take the position of Madonna della Corona ...' Joubert, of course, was very familiar with the terrain near Rivoli, which Vaubois was not. Joubert's orders also told him that if Vaubois were forced to pull back from Lavis, 'the most important object is that Vaubois's division forestalls the enemy at the position of Madonna della Corona and holds there as long as possible'.[21]

Bonaparte, for his part, arrived in Vicenza with Augereau, and wrote back to Berthier in Verona to hurry the despatch of the bridging pontoons, saying that he would cross the Brenta during the night if they arrived. Fighting was limited to an attack on Lipthay in the afternoon, which caused him to move most of his men back over the river, though he did not feel insecure enough to take down the pontoon bridge in front of him. In Bassano, the Austrians were left completely undisturbed, still waiting for news of Davidovich.

On the morning of 6 November, Alvinczy decided to move forward again, and Hohenzollern crossed the Brenta at Bassano with the advance-guard, to be followed by the main part of the division.

While this movement was taking place, the French also advanced, Massena going the shorter distance towards Fontaniva, while Augereau took the longer road from Vicenza towards Bassano. It was therefore the Austrian left wing that received the enemy first, and at 7 a.m. smoke columns were seen to rise from the French positions, indicating the order to attack. Lipthay sensibly dismantled the pontoon bridge in front of him, but still found himself faced with an attempted crossing by most of Massena's division. The latter, however, encountered a heroic resistance by Lipthay's four battalions, particularly on the part of IR Splény. Between 7 a.m. and 6 p.m., Massena made ten attacks on the position, but could not carry it, despite inflicting severe casualties on the enemy. Lipthay himself had a foot injured when his wounded horse fell on him, but refused to leave his post. At about 3 p.m., Provera became convinced that there would be no serious attack further along the river, and withdrew some troops from Schübirz and Brabeck to support Lipthay. IR Deutschmeister therefore took over from the much battered IR Splény, which pulled back to count its losses. Both battalion commanders were seriously wounded, and the regiment as a whole, which had started the morning with about 2,200 men, had lost nine officers and 657 men, only eight of the latter as prisoners. Firing continued until late at night, after which Lipthay was able to calculate that his brigade had lost a total of 21 officers and 1,167 men during the day.

On the other wing of the army, there had been a similarly fierce engagement. The Austrians had begun to take a position before Bassano, between the hills and the river, blocking the road from Vicenza. They were facing the villages of Marostica, Nove and Marchesane, their right wing on Monte Grado, and their left on the Brenta. Cannon-fire could be heard from the direction of Fontaniva, leaving no doubt that fighting had already started there. Rattier, who was with the 51st Line in Augereau's division, says, 'We arrived in the presence of the enemy towards 9 or 10 in the morning',[22] while Sulkowski, who was with Augereau's advance-guard, noted that they met the enemy outposts at about midday. He also commented that Nature seemed to have given the area an abundance of obstacles: 'it was no more than a labyrinth of dikes, ditches, hedges and houses, and one could only advance a hundred paces in battle order before one had to break ranks and present one's flank to the enemy …'[23] Battle was joined in the early afternoon, before all of the Austrian right wing was across the river, and there was much fighting around and in the village of Nove, which changed hands several times. The battalion of IR Samuel Gyulay managed to hold it, but had nine of its ten officers wounded, and lost 381 men — approaching half its effectives. The fighting lasted until 10 p.m., according to Petitbon, and the French were obliged to leave the Austrians in their positions. Bonaparte's report on the day's fighting was nothing if not imaginative, as he told the Directory that the Austrians had been forced to recross the Brenta, and the field had been left in French hands.[24] Quosdanovich's division had certainly suffered heavily, losing 26 officers and 1,607 men, but Alvinczy was sufficiently satisfied with the outcome to write to Davidovich in the evening with news of a success. Moreover, during the night of 6/7 November Alvinczy issued orders for both wings to attack in the morning.[25]

In the Tyrol, meanwhile, progress for the Austrians had not been as good as heretofore, and although Davidovich had attacked Calliano, Vaubois had managed to remain in occupation. Austrian losses were serious, amounting to eight officers and 745 men. However, the difficulties of communication between the Tyrol and the plains were troubling the French as well as their opponents, and partly as a consequence, Vaubois had failed to take sufficient measures to hold Madonna della Corona and Rivoli. He wrote to Bonaparte from Rovereto, saying:

> Your order, general, arrived too late. I was ignorant of your plan and the importance of moving such large forces on the side of the Adige … I was not made aware of the importance of retiring by the other side and of holding it with my greatest forces. There was still time this morning. I would willingly have done it, if I had known your ideas, but I should have been beaten at La Pietra [Calliano] …[26]

The failure to secure the positions between the Adige and Lake Garda was a serious error, as it led to the possibility of an Austrian advance to Peschiera, which would almost certainly have necessitated a French withdrawal over the Mincio. During the next few days, the situation on this wing of the army rapidly worsened. At dawn on 7 November, Davidovich attacked Calliano, which had been weakened by Vaubois sending detachments to Mori and towards Rivoli in an attempt to remedy the earlier mistake. Calliano was taken and retaken several times, then at 4 p.m. the French troops were gripped by a panic and fled when some Croats appeared to their rear. Rovereto was then also abandoned in haste and confusion. Laugier, who was caught up in the rout, remarked:

> It is strange that this panic was general. When our battalion was in order on the road to Rovereto why did no general or senior officer come to us to stop the terrified soldiers? Why did the officers of our regiment and even those of our battalion disappear? … Why did the demi-brigade that was supposed to help us at Nago leave Mori when we arrived? Because Vaubois did not have the confidence of the generals, nor that of the soldiers.

Laugier adds:

> It was 10 o'clock in the evening when I left [Rovereto] … and on the following morning at 9 o'clock I was under the fort of Chiusa on the plateau of Rivoli. I had done 40 [actually about 22] miles without eating or drinking … It took the whole day of the 18th [8 November] to reunite the debris of the division, which was not at all harassed in its rout.[27]

The lack of pursuit may be partly attributable to the fact that the Austrians had suffered greatly in the encounter as well, losing sixteen officers and 1,507 men at Calliano. Their total losses for the 6th and 7th were 47 officers and 3,520 men – almost a fifth of Davidovich's initial strength. It is perhaps understandable that he was not in a great hurry to attack the Rivoli position, the capture of which would have been a very serious blow to Bonaparte. The latter made his discontent with

Vaubois's division, and particularly two of its demi-brigades, very public in a proclamation issued on the 7th:

> Soldiers! I am not pleased with you. You have shown neither discipline, nor steadfastness, nor bravery. No position could rally you. You abandoned yourselves to panic. You let yourselves be chased from positions where a handful of brave men should have stopped an army. Soldiers of the 39th and 85th, you are not French soldiers. General, Chief of Staff, have written on their colours: *They no longer belong to the Army of Italy.*[28]

With the defences on his northern flank having crumbled, it was fortunate for Bonaparte that he was able to slip away from Alvinczy unnoticed during the night of 6/7 November, and pull back towards a more central position where he would be within supporting distance of Vaubois. In the morning it was reported by all the Austrian outposts that the French were nowhere to be seen, and Hohenzollern began to follow towards Vicenza with the advance-guard. Provera was delayed in joining the movement because the pontoon bridge opposite Lipthay's position had to be rebuilt. This was finished at 1 p.m., and the crossing was then begun. At 9 p.m., Provera camped a short distance away, at San Pietro in Gu, while in the late evening Quosdanovich stopped for the night at Scaldaferro. The French army had already abandoned Vicenza and continued its retreat the whole night on a road covered in mud. In Mantua, Wurmser received a letter from Alvinczy dated 29 October, which informed him that the evening before crossing the Adige the army would give a signal consisting of three salvos at five-minute intervals, fired by eight 12pdr cannon. Wurmser was asked to support the move in every way possible, something that he signally failed to do.

In the morning of the 8th, Augereau, Massena and the reserve arrived in Verona. Here, Bonaparte issued an order to Vaubois stating that 'the little knowledge that you have of the terrain which your division now occupies absolutely requires that General Massena take command of all the troops between the Adige and Lake Garda, and that you temporarily remain under his command.'[29] The subsequent turn of events rendered this purely theoretical, but it does serve to illustrate how seriously Bonaparte took the position. Luckily for him, neither of the wings of the Austrian army was pressing forward very hard, the Friuli Corps only reaching Vicenza that day, while Davidovich took his HQ to Rovereto during the afternoon. The letter that Alvinczy had written him on the evening of the 6th with news of the action on the Brenta reached Davidovich at about this time. It also commanded him to hasten his advance as it was clear that the French were not in great strength in the Adige valley. However, the limit of the Austrian advance was Brentonico, which was occupied by Ocskay. Although heavy snow made occupation of the mountains difficult, Vaubois had by the evening taken up positions at Ferrara, Madonna della Corona and Rivoli.

There was a further exchange of news between the Austrian commanders on the morning of the 9th, Alvinczy learning of the capture of Calliano, while Davidovich received Alvinczy's report of the action of 7 November. This also reiterated the order to hasten the advance on Verona, an instruction that was repeated several times in the next few days. However, during this period the problems of communication contributed to a fatal lack of co-ordination between the two corps. At some time on the 9th, a report reached Alvinczy inaccurately stating that Massena had moved to Rivoli with his whole division, and Alvinczy wrote to Davidovich informing him of this. The letter did not reach Davidovich until the evening of the 11th, but he had already heard the rumour independently on the 9th or 10th, and instead of speeding his march, had taken the decision to delay it. During the 10th, Alvinczy wrote another letter confirming the report, and ordered Davidovich 'to occupy well every ravine, pass, and entrance, and moreover to defend and maintain his position to the utmost'.[30] Once again, this letter would not arrive until later, but on the 10th Davidovich had already taken defensive measures, and had spread out most of his troops in a cordon, from where it was to take some time to collect them again. The 10th therefore passed quietly both in the mountains and on the plain, where Alvinczy's outposts stood around Villanova, and those of the French a short distance away at San Martino, before Verona.

The calm was broken on the 11th, when Hohenzollern, who had reported that the French were evacuating Verona, moved forward to reconnoitre. As Hohenzollern approached during the afternoon, Bonaparte ordered the divisions of Augereau and Massena, which had in fact been camped on the far side of the city, to march through it and attack him. A heavy skirmish ensued, in the course of which Hohenzollern withdrew behind the bridge at Vago, losing four officers and 400 men, but certain in the knowledge that the French were not yet on the run.

This action was a prelude to a much bigger encounter the following day, when the French attempted to drive Hohenzollern from the position he had taken on the ridge that ran north from Caldiero. At dawn, the two French divisions, probably numbering about twice Hohenzollern's strength, advanced towards him, Massena against his right, Augereau against his left. Sulkowski tells us:

> The previous evening, the sky had been clear, but during the night the storms built up, and on the day itself, a terrifying tempest, accompanied by frequent showers and deluges of hail chilled our soldiers. This tempest blew straight in their faces, a heavy rain hid the enemy, who crushed them with their fire, from their view. Finally, the wind at every moment blew away their priming, while their naked feet slipped on the clay embankments, denying them support.[31]

These atrocious conditions not only blunted the French assault, but also caused enormous difficulties for the rest of the Friuli Corps which was already moving up to join Hohenzollern. The continual French attacks had no great success until about midday, when Dupuy established himself on the heights on the Austrian right. However, Hohenzollern held out until Brabeck arrived at about 3 p.m., to be joined by Schübirz soon after. The French were being pushed back on their left wing when Provera also arrived on the scene, and Augereau found himself similarly threatened with being cut off from Verona. The French situation was precarious, with both their wings pushed back, but night and darkness ended the battle before they could suffer serious harm, and they then retreated to Verona. Austrian losses were reported as 21 officers and 1,223 men. French losses are not precisely known, but must have reached a similar total, if not more. This time, the report that Bonaparte sent to the Directory was anything but rosy:

I must inform you of the operations that have taken place since the 12th of the month [2 November]. If they are not satisfactory, you will not give the blame to the army. Its inferiority and the exhaustion of the bravest men make me fear the worst. We may be on the eve of losing Italy. None of the expected help has arrived ... I do my duty, and so does the army. My spirit is lacerated, but my conscience is clear ... The wounded are the élite of the army. All our senior officers and all our élite generals are out of action. All those who arrive are inept and do not have the confidence of the soldiers. The Army of Italy, reduced to a handful of men, is worn out. The heroes of Lodi, Millesimo, Castiglione and Bassano have died for their country or are in the hospitals. The corps have nothing left but their reputation and their pride. Joubert, Lannes, Lanusse, Victor, Murat, Chabot, Dupuy, Rampon, Pijon, Chabran and Saint-Hilaire are wounded, and so is General Ménard. We are abandoned in the depths of Italy ... I have lost few men in this war, but they were all men of the élite, who are impossible to replace. Those brave men who remain see death as inevitable in the midst of such continual risks and with such slender forces. Perhaps the hour of the brave Augereau, the intrepid Massena, of Berthier, or me is ready to sound. Then what would happen to these brave people? This idea makes me circumspect: I no longer dare to face death, which will be the cause of discouragement and of hardship for those who are the object of my care. In a few days we shall make a final effort ...[32]

Bonaparte's ability to dramatise is well to the fore in this report, but one could hardly deny that the situation for the French was grave. They had sustained significant losses, and stood the very real danger of being squeezed between substantial enemy formations. Estimates of the forces available to both sides at this stage of operations are both confusing and contradictory, and any figures given can only be approximate. Quosdanovich and Provera now had a little less than 20,000 men, but Mittrovsky, whose brigade numbered roughly 3,000, was not far to their rear, having moved out of the mountains. Davidovich's corps, despite its losses, probably had more than 14,000, though Loudon's brigade was detached to guard the country north of Lake Garda. Mantua still had just under 13,000 men fit. By this time, Massena had 7,937 men, Augereau had about 6,000, and the reserve around 2,600, giving a total with the cavalry of about 18,000 men. There were another 3,000 in Verona. The blockading corps, somewhat weakened by detachments to Vaubois, Augereau and the garrison of Verona, was down to 6,626. Vaubois had been hastily reinforced, and seems to have had about 8,000.[33]

Both sides spent 13 November resting and making preparations. The French divisions were camped before Verona, with the Friuli Corps a short distance away at Vago and Gombion. Alvinczy now planned to throw a bridge over the Adige below Verona and hoped to cross in the direction of Mantua during the night of the 14th/15th. However, he desired Davidovich's co-operation and support for this manoeuvre, and on the 13th sent him three letters ordering him to make for Verona.

Davidovich issued orders for an advance on Rivoli to begin on the 14th, and in the morning his troops duly set off. In the meantime, Alvinczy continued his preparations for a crossing. These took much longer than had been intended, as the chosen crossing-point, at Zevio, was not very suitable for the purpose. The left bank of the river was very marshy there, and it proved to be necessary to work on the road leading up to the place where the bridge was to be constructed, in order to make it practicable for the army. This looked likely to take a couple of days, so Alvinczy postponed the crossing to the night of 15/16 November, a possible advantage of which would be that the Tyrol Corps should be nearer, and better able to lend support. Unfortunately for him, the Tyrol Corps was also experiencing delays. Ocskay, who was given the daunting task of making his way over Monte Baldo, encountered great difficulties because of the fresh snow which covered its rocky paths, and at 4 p.m. on the 14th, Davidovich wrote to Alvinczy from Peri explaining that he had no news of Ocskay, so he did not know if he would be able to continue his advance in the morning.

These delays were all that Bonaparte needed. Having failed to stop the Austrians by attacking them directly, he now found himself with an opportunity to turn to indirect defence, and set out to scotch Alvinczy's plans by conducting a manoeuvre that was almost a miniature version of the operation to cross the Po. On the 14th, Augereau and Massena were moved back through Verona and over the Adige. The city's garrison was left to protect Bonaparte from pursuit by Alvinczy, while Vaubois was ordered to hold Rivoli with the greatest determination. Bonaparte, with the divisions of Augereau and Massena, then marched along the southern bank of the Adige during the night of 14/15 November, intending to recross the river at Ronco.

This crossing-point was well known to the French, who had used it going in the opposite direction when they were pursuing Wurmser in September, and had left a pontoon bridge there until 9 November, when Bonaparte had ordered it to be taken down, and the boats made safe.[34] Foreseeing that the crossing would be useful, or that the enemy might try to use it himself, he had also posted a guard there on the 9th.

The crossing lay to the left rear of the position of the Friuli Corps, and Bonaparte hoped that if he could reach the other bank of the Adige undetected, he would be able to break out of the bridgehead and cut Alvinczy's natural line of retreat along the road to Vicenza. If this could be achieved, Alvinczy would probably be forced to retire northwards through the Monti Lessini to the Tyrol. It was also likely that his artillery and baggage, being to his rear, would be captured.

However, the intended bridgehead opposite Ronco was in an area from where it was difficult to move northwards to the main road, because of the nature of the terrain. Near Zevio, the Adige and the main road were about two and a half miles apart, and ran roughly parallel in an east–west direction. The Adige then curved away, so that about one and a quarter miles south-east of Ronco it was running in a southerly direction. At this point, the Adige was joined by a tributary called the

Alpone, which flowed north–south from Villanova, on the main road. Between the Alpone and the Adige was a wide stretch of marsh in a vaguely triangular shape, which was quite impassable. The only roads were those which ran along the tops of the large dikes that edged both rivers, and prevented their waters from further swamping the plain. The dikes along the Adige loomed above the nearby houses, and followed its course for a distance of 20 miles. Those along the Alpone were smaller, as it was only about 20 yards wide and 5 feet deep, but were still 26 feet high, and had very steep faces.[35] From Ronco, the only way to reach the main road (about seven miles away) was to cross the Adige, skirt the marsh on the dike, and go north beside the Alpone for about one and a half miles, until one reached a wooden bridge set on three stone piles, over which the road led to the small village of Arcole, on the left or eastern bank. From Arcole, one proceeded along the eastern bank on the road to San Bonifacio, which was just south of the main road itself. From the direction of Caldiero, Ronco could only be reached by a couple of dikes or causeways that went via the oddly named hamlet of Belfiore di Porcile (which might be translated as 'lovely flower of the pig-sty'). Apart from these causeways, only a few footpaths wriggled through the marshes to isolated buildings.

The lie of the land naturally posed a problem for Bonaparte, in that the rapid advance to cut off Alvinczy could only be made along one narrow road that presented at least one bottleneck – the bridge at Arcole – which might prove difficult to get past if well defended. On the other hand, the terrain offered corresponding advantages for defence, in that the difficulties of access meant that the Austrians would be unable to deploy large numbers of troops to attack the bridgehead if or when they realised what was happening.

Alvinczy was not blind to the danger to his left and rear, and had detailed Mittrovsky and Colonel Brigido to cover this area and observe the lower Adige. Mittrovsky had been ordered to go to Cologna with three battalions, while Brigido, with four battalions, occupied San Bonifacio and Arcole, where Prince Eugene of Savoy had briefly had his HQ some 90 years before. Brigido also placed pickets along the Alpone, while a squadron of hussars patrolled the causeway on its right bank, going right round the marsh and along the left bank of the Adige towards Belfiore. However, despite these precautions, Bonaparte's night march and the arrival of French troops in the area of Ronco went unnoticed, and Andréossy was able to build his pontoon bridge without being discovered.

The sequence and timings of the events which followed on 15 November, not to mention the 16th and 17th, are difficult to establish with any precision, as the various accounts of the engagement are frequently inconsistent. However, the day seems to have begun with a small exploratory force being sent across the Adige to gain a toe-hold, much as had been done at Piacenza. Rattier, of the 51st, recounted:

> Our battalion, which had been guarding the ... crossing since midnight on the 19th [9 November], crossed the river on a boat at daybreak [about 6.45], the bridge not having been finished, and scouted the attack divisions' route. The bridge having been finished towards 7 in the morning, the divisions advanced ...[36]

Augereau's men crossed first, headed by General Bon with the 5th Light, who moved in the direction of Arcole. Massena's division also crossed, but then inclined to the left, towards Belfiore di Porcile, to fulfil the largely defensive role of preventing the Austrians from reaching the bridge at Ronco. The 75th was left as rearguard in the copse to the right of the bridge, while the 12th Light guarded the bridge itself, and the cavalry remained in reserve at Ronco.

Bon did not have very far to go before he encountered the enemy. According to Augereau, the first clash occurred while it was still dark, which made it difficult to organise a proper attack.[37] Nevertheless, Bon drove back the outposts on the dike, but as he went further he was met by a ferocious fire. For the last one and a half miles up to the bridge of Arcole, he had to march directly beside the Alpone, silhouetted against a largely empty skyline, and with hardly a shred of cover. The other bank of the Alpone was well within pistol-range, and the massed ranks of marching soldiers made an excellent target. The houses in Arcole had been well barricaded and loopholed, and there were entrenchments from which the defenders, two Croat battalions and two guns, could rake the causeway with their fire. Sulkowski commented that the last 200 yards before the bridge were sure to be absolutely lethal.

A few miles away from this critical point, Alvinczy, who that morning had completed his own preparations for crossing the Adige, was quietly waiting for dusk before commencing the operation, when at about 9 a.m. cannon-fire was heard from the direction of Ronco. This aroused a certain disquiet, as there had been no previous indication of any French activity in that area. An hour later, just after Alvinczy had despatched a letter expressing amazement that Davidovich had not yet attacked Rivoli, and positively ordering him to carry out the attack with all speed, a report arrived from Colonel Brigido with the surprising news that 'the enemy had moved over the Adige during the previous night, and was advancing with a strong column towards Arcole. He had already driven back the posts at Ponte Zerpan on the way. A second column was moving on the causeway along the left bank of the Adige in the direction of Bionde, Belfiore di Porcile and Gombion.'[38] At first, this whole French operation was assumed to be a feint, but in no time at all opinions were revised and measures taken for defence. The artillery reserve and baggage were immediately ordered to move from Villanova to Montebello. At 11 a.m., Lieutenant-Colonel Gavasini's brigade advanced towards Belfiore di Porcile, and at midday Brabeck received orders to follow. Mittrovsky, who was already marching from Montebello, was ordered to go via San Bonifacio to Arcole.

While these orders were being sent from the Austrian HQ, the French had been making continued attempts to take Arcole. Bon's attack had been stopped in its tracks some way short of the bridge, and Augereau had then sent forward Verdier with the 4th Line, whose reception was described by Petitbon: 'Having arrived close to the village, we found the 5th Light thrown back on the right side of the causeway by a terrible musket fire. We advanced, and experienced the same fate.'[39] Sulkowski was with Verdier, and recounted how the men tried to shelter from the fire by sliding down the slope of the dike. Augereau ordered the rest of the division to move up in support, but this took time, and the enemy also sent up reinforcements, Sulkowski commenting, 'we saw them arrive at the double, towing their cannons behind them'.[40]

By now it was probably late morning, or even midday, and these new Austrian troops may well have been the first of Mittrovsky's men, who are reported to have arrived at 12.30. They placed two howitzers on the dike itself, which now became even more deadly than before. Augereau and Lannes, who had turned up that morning having just recovered from a wound, then essayed an attack with the two battalions of the 51st which were present, but they got no closer than 80 paces from the bridge, where Lannes was hit in the leg. The historian of the 51st did not seek to hide the men's reaction:

> Taken aback by the greatness of the danger, and influenced by the disastrous example of the other demi-brigades, the rest of the battalions suddenly fell back onto the slope of the causeway, and were soon mixed up with the rest of the division. Some enemy sharpshooters overlooked this slope and killed many of our men. We stayed there without taking a step forwards or backwards, getting ourselves killed to no purpose. Nothing was capable of making the troops make a new attempt and advance on the enemy again ...[41]

Augereau tried again with Verne and the 40th, but with no better success. Augereau was untouched during the fighting, but Bon, Verdier and Verne were all wounded while trying to lead their men forward.

While the attack had thus stalled on the French right, Massena was involved in a struggle to hold off the Austrians on the left. From the earliest, they had made attempts to find a way round Massena's flank, Brabeck detaching four companies with two 3pdrs to make their way along the Adige and create a diversion. Gavasini, who had been at the head of his troops with IR Splény, was ordered by Alvinczy to go through Belfiore di Porcile and drive the French back to Ronco. The regiment moved forward by the most direct causeway, and ran into the head of Massena's division at the hamlet of Bionde, a little more than half-way to Ronco. IR Splény threw back the French, captured two guns, and continued their advance. This movement had been shadowed by a battalion of Croats that Brabeck had sent along the other dike, which ran close to the Adige, and went through a wood where there was a sharp bend in the river. The Croats became confused by the nature of the terrain, and seeing the fighting between IR Splény and the French on the dike leading from Bionde, opened fire, thinking they were shooting across the river. IR Splény, which did not know of the Croats' advance, believed they were being attacked from the rear, and retreated in confusion, leaving behind three guns. Massena soon took advantage of this, and advanced easily to Bionde, then to Belfiore di Porcile.

Back on the French right wing, Bonaparte had decided that the continued lack of success of the attacks on Arcole demanded a different approach, and had ordered Guieu to take the 18th and 25th Line along the right bank of the Adige to a point beyond the confluence of the Alpone, and ferry across to Albaredo. If he was successful in this, he could march along the left bank of the Alpone and attack Arcole directly, thus avoiding the deadly causeway that led up to the bridge. It is difficult to say when Bonaparte issued these orders, but it may have been before midday, as the 18th Line seems to have been detached from Massena's division as early as 11 a.m.[42] It would have taken time for Guieu to collect his troops and march two miles to the ferry, so something may also be deduced from the fact that he began his crossing at 2 p.m. (his own estimate), and had collected his men at Albaredo at 4 p.m. (according to other sources).[43] During this part of the afternoon, at 3 p.m., the bulk of Mittrovsky's troops began to arrive in San Bonifacio after a forced march.

It was also at some time in the mid-afternoon that the 3rd battalion of the 51st, commanded by Soulès, received orders to cross the Alpone by boat near the confluence, and approach Arcole along the left bank. We are told by André Estienne, a drummer with the 51st's grenadiers, that at the same time as this attack was being made (probably around 4 p.m.) Augereau tried to incite his men to move along the right bank and make a supporting assault on the bridge. He took a colour, and advancing fifteen paces beyond his skirmishers, stood in the open on the road leading to the bridge, and shouted 'Grenadiers! Come and seek your colour.'[44] This produced no great effect, but Bonaparte decided to try the same thing. Sulkowski recounts:

> We suddenly saw him appear on the dike, surrounded by his staff and followed by his *guides* [cavalry escort], he dismounted, drew his sabre, took a colour and sprang towards the bridge in the midst of a rain of fire.

Estienne related that Bonaparte took the colour ten paces beyond where Augereau had been, to a distance about 55 paces from the bridge.[45] Sulkowski continued:

> The soldiers saw him, and none of them imitated him. I was witness to this extraordinary cowardice, and I cannot conceive it. Was it for the victors of Lodi to cover themselves with infamy? The moment was short, but it was catastrophic for all those who surrounded Bonaparte: his ADC, Muiron, General Vignolle, the lieutenant of the *guides*, and Belliard's two assistants fell at his side. I myself was struck right on the chest by a grape-shot, but my rolled cloak, which I was wearing bandolier fashion, saved my life.

Sulkowski was then knocked out by the explosion of a shell, so the rest of his story is second-hand. 'The General-in-Chief, as they told me later, seeing that his efforts were useless, retired, and this time the grenadiers hastened to follow his example.'[46]

Soulès's men, having got quite close to the village, were also forced back by a vigorous counter, and had to recross the Alpone. There was great disorder among Augereau's troops, as those at the front tried to fall back, but because of the narrowness of the dike were prevented by those behind. Some soldiers fell in the marsh while trying to escape as the Austrians launched an attack over the bridge. Bonaparte's horse also lost its footing, slid down the bank, and the two of them tumbled into the marsh, from where they were rescued, covered in mud, by a number of men. These included several from the 4th Line, one of whom, Sergeant Boudet, was killed in the process.[47] The division soon rallied at a safe distance, but made no other serious attacks since it was now almost night.

Guieu, however, met with much greater success when he finally reached Arcole after dark. His first attack, at about 6 or 7 p.m., was beaten back, but he later managed to enter the village, which was naturally much less easy to defend against a force on the same side of the river, and Brigido was obliged to evacuate his men and move back to San Bonifacio. The fighting eventually came to an end at about 11 p.m. It had taken all day, but the French had at last opened the route to the north, which, to the inexpert observer, seemed to promise that they could simply pass on to the execution of the next stage of their plan the following day. However, Bonaparte's own view was rather broader, and, as he explained in his memoirs:

> The advantage gained by the French on the first day was indeed very considerable, but still not sufficient for the army to advance into the plain and establish their link with Verona there. It was also to be feared that during the first day of battle at Arcole, Davidovich would already have advanced via Rivoli to Castelnuovo. If this had actually occurred, the French army would, without delay, have to march the whole night via Castel-nuovo and Villafranca, in order to unite with Vaubois, beat Davidovich, and maintain the blockade of Mantua undisturbed, and then, if possible, turn back before Alvinczy had crossed the Adige.[48]

For these reasons, and perhaps also because Guieu was rather out on a limb in Arcole, Bonaparte decided to abandon the village which had cost so much blood to win, and even send most of his men back over the Adige, in readiness to march and join Vaubois. The withdrawal was begun towards midnight, but the history of the 51st, and Roguet's memoirs, suggest that quite large numbers of men remained in the bridgehead on the left bank of the Adige. These included the 12th Light, 75th Line and some guns, which had the task of covering the bridge at Ronco. During the night, Provera took advantage of the withdrawal to position some men at Belfiore di Porcile, pushing his outposts to Bionde, within a few yards of Massena's pickets, while Mittrovsky placed himself between San Bonifacio and Santo Stefano, and had Arcole reoccupied. Marmont commented years later:

> The evacuation of Arcole on the evening of the first day was, for the army, a subject of great astonishment, and, afterwards, the occasion of great controversy, but incorrectly. This disposition is worthy of admiration. It was necessary to be superior as a general thus to renounce apparent successes in order to obtain real ones later.[49]

Bonaparte's fears that Davidovich might have defeated Vaubois were eventually allayed when he received news at 4 a.m. that the latter had not been attacked at Rivoli. It was just as well, because by that time 'the whole night' consisted of barely three hours of darkness, and it seems unlikely that Bonaparte could have joined Vaubois, defeated Davidovich, and then got back to the Adige before Alvinczy had crossed it. On receiving this good news, Bonaparte immediately ordered those troops that had already made the crossing to the southern bank of the Adige to move back again.

Alvinczy was similarly concerned about affairs on the other wing of his army, and at 5 a.m. he sent Davidovich a letter informing him of the events of the 15th, and repeated the order for him to press his attack. This was now doubly important because Alvinczy had decided that instead of trying to escape from the French, he would accept battle. Hohenzollern was ordered to stay and observe Verona, while Provera carried out an attack through Belfiore di Porcile with two brigades counting only six battalions and two squadrons. Mittrovsky, who was supported by Colonel Sticker and Schübirz, took command of the forces which were to attack through Arcole. These totalled fourteen battalions and two squadrons. The two columns were to attack at daybreak, drive the French back to Ronco, and effect a junction there. If the enemy was thrown back over the Adige, Alvinczy would immediately make his own crossing at Zevio, separating the two wings of the French army.

By about 5 a.m. on 16 November, Provera's advance-guard was already on the move, roughly at the same time as the French were advancing along the dikes to attack. Similarly, Mittrovsky had begun to file most of his troops through Arcole, while two battalions under Major Miloradovics went down the left bank of the Alpone to Albaredo to guard this crossing. It was not long before a heavy fight was under way between the opposing forces on the two causeways, which in Massena's case, after an early setback, turned completely his way. First he was able to halt the Austrian advance, and then his skirmishers spread into the bushes on the bank of the river and began to pepper the enemy columns. Just like Augereau's men the day before, the Austrians found themselves badly exposed on the top of the dike, and unable to deploy because of the marshes which hemmed them on either side. There was increasing disorder in their ranks, as individuals sought to take a shot at the half-hidden enemy who was galling them, and the foremost troops of the column moved down the bank of the dike to seek shelter from the fire. Some courageous artillerymen remained on the dike and held back Massena's men with canister, but resistance was broken when General Brabeck was killed, which completed the confusion. The troops in the front of the Austrian column tried to fall back, and carried away the hindmost battalions, which had managed to maintain their order. There was a general crush of bodies, and a disordered flight as far as Caldiero with Massena in pursuit. Five guns were lost in the retreat.

At the same time as this was going on, Mittrovsky had moved forward and pushed Augereau almost as far as the Adige in a lively combat. When Provera was beaten back, however, Mittrovsky's men, who could see what was happening on the other causeway, lost confidence and began to crumble. Augereau moved forward again and took two guns, but the 4th Warasdiner Grenz battalion slipped along and behind the dike on the left bank of the Alpone, and opened a devastating fire on the flank of the advancing French, so that they broke and fell back, leaving behind one of their guns. Mittrovsky rallied his troops at Arcole at midday, and deployed his men to meet the inevitable French attack. He placed Sticker with four battalions and one squadron of hussars on the dike leading to Ronco. Miloradovics had also lined the left bank of the Alpone up to the confluence with the Adige, enabling him to enfilade any troops moving towards the bridge at Arcole. Brigido, with four battalions and half a squadron of hussars, took up a position on the dike towards Albaredo. Because of lack of room on the dikes, four battalions (two from each brigade) were placed in Arcole as reserve, while another battalion had been left at San Bonifacio as rearguard.

Augereau's attempts to advance along the dike were all thwarted, and since day was drawing on, Bonaparte decided once again to try the indirect approach. A small detachment of the 5th Light was sent to Albaredo in a boat, but the Austrian artillery which defended the village prevented a landing. Bonaparte then ordered an attempt to bridge the Alpone near the confluence by using fascines, so that Vial could cross with two battalions of the 51st and the grenadiers of the 40th. The assault was overseen by Bonaparte himself, the chosen point being by a copse, from where French skirmishers were keeping up a lively exchange of fire with the Austrians on the other bank. The fascines were probably made by stripping the trees in the copse, which is perhaps where Chasseloup saw one of Bonaparte's aides, the young Elliot, hacking branches from the willows with his sabre.[50] Rattier, no doubt speaking of the same area, describes 'a very thick wood of young poplars, which the bullets, grape, shells and round-shot had totally ravaged, and where you could not see a single straight branch'.[51]

According to André Estienne, the plan was for each soldier to carry a fascine on his bayonet, and throw it into the water. This did not work very well, and Marmont tells us that after half-an-hour's intense shooting, a column raced forward and dumped its fascines in the Alpone, where they were promptly swept away by the current. 'Then,' Estienne wrote, 'Bonaparte, who was there present, ordered the canal [sic] to be crossed by swimming, seeing that it was not very deep. As he finished these words, one of his aides de camp [Elliot] was killed at his side.'[52] Lieutenant Ramand of the 51st plunged into the chilly water before anyone else, but only about 30 chose to follow his example. There were many officers, including Vial, and the 19-year-old drummer, Estienne, who carried his instrument on his head. As soon as he got out of the water, he began to beat the charge, but this inspiring sound failed to encourage his comrades to cross. The adventurous group sustained several casualties and was forced to swim back again. As night fell, the situation was still effectively a stalemate.

During the evening, Bonaparte, who seems to have concluded that continuing to direct his main effort against the bridge at Arcole would be pointless, began to organise a more co-ordinated attempt to outflank this obstacle. At 10 p.m., he informed Augereau that during the night a bridge would be built over the Alpone near the confluence, and instructed him immediately to send a battalion of the 40th to Legnago with 50 cavalry. A column was to be ordered to advance from there up the left bank of the Adige to support the troops who would cross the new bridge over the Alpone. The Austrians who had been positioned near the intended bridging-point withdrew during the night, and the French were able to bring four pontoons from the Adige to the Alpone without hindrance. Great efforts were also made to improvise paths over ditches, the intention being to make it possible for the whole of Augereau's division to cross, while Massena's division would both hold back the Austrians on the left, and attack the bridge at Arcole on the right. Part of the 51st was detailed to guard the bridge over the Alpone, and a redoubt was hurriedly constructed to defend the new bridgehead.

As on the previous night, some of the army was withdrawn to the southern side of the Adige, though it is not clear how much of it. An official history suggests that Massena's division first bivouacked near Belfiore di Porcile, then at 1 a.m. moved back half-way to the bridge at Ronco, but no further movement is mentioned. It also records that part of Augereau's division remained on the left bank of the Adige, and part crossed to Ronco. The likelihood, therefore, is that a substantial force was left to ensure that the two bridgeheads were not threatened, and the rest withdrew to camp in a rather less exposed position.

Alvinczy, however, was not planning any surprises for Bonaparte that night. Instead, he was rather concerned that he had heard nothing from Davidovich during the day, which suggested that the latter might have met with difficulties in his operations against Vaubois. Alvinczy therefore took the precaution of ordering Hohenzollern to fall back to Caldiero, where he was less well placed to link with Davidovich, but better able to support Alvinczy, should it be necessary. As it later tran-spired, there was no report from Davidovich because he had not yet made a serious attack, despite the fact that he was facing an enemy roughly half his strength. In fact, there had only been a minor skirmish at Rivoli that day, but Davidovich did write to Alvinczy saying that he would attack on the morning of the 17th.

This lack of co-operation from Davidovich was undoubtedly delete-rious to Alvinczy's operations, but the poor link between the two corps was bound to make co-ordination problematic. However, it is more difficult to understand the lack of activity on the part of the garrison of Mantua, which had now spent two days sitting listening to heavy gunfire, which clearly indicated a major engagement taking place not far away from them. Although the French had begun a bombardment of the city to cover the weakness of the blockading force, the Austrian observers on the towers had immediately noted that some of the camps around them seemed to be empty, suggesting that a proportion of the troops had been drawn off to join the combat on the Adige. Despite this, Wurmser made no offensive movement while the battle at Arcole was in course.

Alvinczy, no doubt, would have welcomed any help at all. He wrote to Davidovich at 8 a.m. on the 17th, in the belief that the attack on the Rivoli position had already been carried out on the 16th, stating that he counted on Davidovich to appear to the rear of the French main force that day. Alvinczy said he hoped to be able to maintain his position between Cologna and Albaredo, but would only be able to effect a crossing of the Adige if Davidovich came in force, and he appealed to Davidovich to do everything in his power to hasten the junction of the two corps. As this letter was being written, Davidovich was in fact finally rumbling into action. Ocskay launched his attack at daybreak by advancing from Monte Baldo, then at 7 a.m. Vukassovich began his movement to climb out of the Adige valley by way of the Pontare. The outnumbered French were forced back, and pursued from hill to hill as far as Affi. Then, at about 2 p.m., they were overcome, the 85th once again breaking under pressure, and the division retreated in disorder until it came to rest later in the after-noon at Piovezzano. Fiorella and Valette were captured, together with roughly 1,000 of their men, a fate which Vaubois himself only narrowly escaped. The Austrians lost a total of fourteen officers and 457 men. It was at about 2 p.m. that Davidovich pencilled a note to Alvinczy with news of his victory, which, if it had come two days earlier, might have had very grave repercussions for Bonaparte.

As it was, he had had very little to worry about to his rear, and had been able to devote all his attention to the problem of advancing past Arcole. On the 17th, as on the previous two days, this task remained his priority. According to the official history, Augereau's division began its movement towards the right at daybreak, while Massena's troops took responsibility for both the left wing and the centre. The latter was entrusted to General Robert, who took the causeway towards the bridge at Arcole with the 5th Light and the 75th Line. The column from Legnago, consisting of a battalion of the 40th, the 9th Dragoons and two guns, was in the meantime making its way towards Albaredo. The enemy also made a movement, sending some troops against the French right.

By the time it was light, the 51st had all crossed the Alpone, and attacked the enemy, which they drove from their first position. With the benefit of daylight, the Austrians perceived how the French had reached their side of the Alpone, and in the words of the history of the 51st, 'Soon afterwards ... directing a battery of three guns from Albaredo at the bridge, which they were able to see via the mouth of the canal, they managed to break it, and disquiet our troops.'[53] It would appear that while the bridge was being repaired, the 51st continued its movement towards Arcole. When they approached the second Austrian position, they were driven back by the musketry, and took the rest of the column with them, as they fell back to the bridge over the Alpone. They were troubled during their retreat by enemy forces which advanced on both sides of the Alpone, but were soon supported by the 4th. Petitbon tells us:

> At 8 in the morning, General Augereau marched at the head of the demi-brigade. After having crossed the Adige, we turned right and crossed a bridge which had been built in haste over a canal which flows into that river. We suffered a great deal from a battery that

defended this crossing. The bridge having been crossed, we encountered a large body of the enemy which had just repulsed the 51st demi-brigade. Our presence halted them, and we in our turn forced them to retire on the village of Arcole. Another body of the enemy, concealed behind the walls and in the ditches around the village, prevented us from pursuing them.[54]

After the Austrian assault had been turned back, the historian of the 51st noted that 'their artillery in Albaredo had just fallen silent, and their skirmishers stopped troubling us. We conjectured that they were evacuating. Indeed, part of our troops went there, and only had the time to take a few prisoners.'[55]

Arcole, however, was being reinforced, and towards midday, a battalion of Carlstädter Grenzers and another of IR Deutschmeister arrived there from Caldiero. The former took a position on the right, the other on the left bank of the Alpone, but Mittrovsky still felt uneasy enough to make an appeal to Alvinczy to attack the French left flank, as he feared to be crushed by superior numbers. The history of the 51st tells us: 'All the forces on both sides were piled up on the two dikes of the canal, from Arcole up to the Adige. The combat was stubborn and bloody. During the action, the different corps of the division had mixed up, and the terrain did not permit us to deploy. The bravest were the only ones who went forward.'[56] It was a see-saw engagement, and Petitbon speaks of the armies advancing and retreating four times altogether during the day, while Rattler speaks of three times. Mittrovsky's problems were compounded by the arrival of more French: at about 2.30 p.m., he sent another message stating that 'an enemy column from Legnago was marching on his left flank, and the enemy was pushing forward everywhere in great force'.[57] He repeated his request for a diversion to be made on the enemy left, but by this time it was no longer possible. At much the same time as the request was being made, the advance-guard and Provera's division were beginning to retreat from Caldiero to Villanova, an earlier attack on Massena's division having been beaten off. Alvinczy had also taken the decision to move to San Bonifacio, in order to be nearer the critical point.

The battle was now approaching its climax, and the French were making an attack on Arcole from both sides, Robert towards the bridge, and Augereau's men towards the village. At about 3 p.m., Robert had almost reached the bridge, and on the other side the French were on the point of entering the village when, in Sulkowski's words, 'We saw a column of more than 4,000 enemies come out of it, rush onto the fatal dike, and capture our cannons. Its shock was so violent that part of our troops were repulsed as far as the bridge [of Ronco].'[58] Augereau's men, on the other side of the Alpone, were unnerved at seeing their flank uncovered and fell back in disorder to the bridge over the Alpone. André Estienne commented that 'the first regiment of hussars ... in retreating, wanted to cross the little bridge among the infantry, and knocked many of the infantrymen into the canal ...'[59] Some of them managed to hold the bridgehead over the Alpone until 4 p.m., when force of numbers obliged them to retire over the bridge.

Roguet recalled that 'in the evening, the enemy gained the upper hand, and it was a question of nothing less than throwing us into the Adige ... towards 4 p.m., our situation seemed desperate'.[60] By this time, however, Massena's division was faced with very little opposition, and some of his men, including Roguet's battalion, were rapidly marched off to plug the gap that had been opened on the other wing. 'We met Bonaparte at the fork in the road to the bridge [over the Adige],' recalled Roguet. 'The soldiers greeted him with cries of "*Vive la République!*" – "Thirty-Second, I am pleased to see you," the General-in-Chief replied.'[61] It was not a sentiment shared by the Croats whom they ran into shortly afterwards. Taken by surprise, they mostly surrendered or fled towards Arcole, but, Roguet continued:

A strong column of Hungarian grenadiers, with two pieces of cannon, came from the bridge towards us. It made us uncertain in our march. We concealed ourselves on the right in terrain covered with willows. We took the enemy in the flank and halted them. During this time, Massena was following with our other two battalions. Then General Gardanne appeared alone on the causeway, his sword in his hand, and raised his hat as high as he could. He cried 'Forward!', and immediately fell grievously wounded. The charge was beaten, and we climbed onto the road, we ran to the pieces ... and captured them.[62]

The Austrians were simultaneously attacked by other units, and driven back towards Arcole. With the French pressing forward, Augereau was able to cross the Alpone again, and the attack continued on both sides of the river. Evening was already approaching as the last attack on Arcole began on all sides. At about 5 p.m., Massena finally made his way over the bridge to Arcole, while Augereau arrived in the village on the other side. He was aided by a diversion arranged by Bonaparte, who sent Lieutenant Hercule of his *guides* with 25 men to go right round the Austrian left, and then charge the enemy sounding several trumpets in order to give the impression of being a much larger force. In the semi-darkness, this stratagem sowed sufficient doubt in the minds of the Austrians to facilitate the attack by the infantry. Mittrovsky pulled back towards San Bonifacio in twilight, pursued by the French, who almost got to the main road to cut off the retreat of Provera's division, but Alvinczy himself led Schübirz's troops in a counter-attack and drove them back towards Arcole. Mittrovsky's troops then took up a position near San Bonifacio, while the right wing reached Villanova late in the evening.

Alvinczy was no longer in a defensible position, and was obliged to continue his retreat towards Montebello before daybreak. It was there, at 3 a.m., that he received Davidovich's letter saying that he would attack Rivoli on the 17th and approach Verona on the 18th. Many a lesser man might already have given up hope by this time, but Alvinczy was nothing if not a fighter, and was not yet ready to concede. He replied to Davidovich at 5 a.m., describing the position of the Friuli Corps and added that 'if Bonaparte turned against the Tyrol Corps with his main force, he would certainly try to the utmost of his power to help him'.[63] He also commented that if Bonaparte pursued the Friuli Corps, he believed Davidovich ought not to find it difficult to relieve Mantua.

In fact, news of Vaubois's defeat had reached Bonaparte the previous evening, and this had decided him to march against Davidovich immediately. Before daybreak on the 18th, therefore, Bonaparte turned back, leaving some cavalry to observe Alvinczy. Bonaparte himself went with Massena's division via Ronco to Villafranca to attempt to link with Vaubois, who had decided to retire to Peschiera. At the same time as Massena's division was marching to prevent Davidovich from nearing Mantua, Augereau's division was sent north to go through Val Pantena towards Dolcè, to try to cut Davidovich's line of retreat.

During the evening of the 18th, Alvinczy was able to take up a position at Olmo without disturbance, and at 5 p.m. called a council of war. The members were told that the council would reconvene in the morning, and that in the meantime they were to consider whether or not the Friuli Corps should continue its retreat, or return to the offensive. No one could have been surprised if they had opted for the retreat, because the corps was hardly in good condition. Over the three days of fighting at Arcole it had sustained losses of 6,211 officers and men, and was now reduced by nearly half its original strength. It now counted 13,266 men, in addition to which there were probably another 3,000 men under Miloradovics nearby. However, the question of numbers was not the only difficulty, and the commanders had to contend with problems of exhaustion, hunger and adversely affected morale. Notwithstanding these many difficulties, when the generals met again at 9 a.m. on the 19th, they soon agreed that the Tyrol Corps could not be left to face the enemy alone. They voted unanimously for a return to the offensive, and Alvinczy immediately wrote to Davidovich to say he would advance again on the 20th.

This letter naturally took time to reach Davidovich, and in the meantime, at midday on the 19th, he received news that Alvinczy had retired from Arcole and that Bonaparte was now manoeuvring to attack the Tyrol Corps. Towards evening he received further information that a French column was moving in the direction of Dolcè to cut him off. In these uncertain circumstances, he also called a council of war, which met at Piovezzano, and unanimously decided that if more favourable news were not received from the Friuli Corps during the night, the Tyrol Corps should pull back to the hills before Rivoli. In fact, the only message that arrived was not encouraging, and as reconnaissances confirmed the continued advance of the French, Davidovich duly withdrew on the 20th. Ironically, Alvinczy, who began his new advance at 10 a.m. on the same day, made better progress than expected, and was able to bring his HQ to Villanova by 7 p.m. However, he was too far away to be able to help Davidovich, who was rapidly being closed by large French forces.

Davidovich had originally intended to defend the position before Rivoli, but as the French advanced between the Adige and Lake Garda on the morning of the 21st, he issued orders for a retreat. Then, at 9 a.m., he received Alvinczy's letter from Olmo, and hastily ordered his men to turn back and take up their former positions. This caused such confusion and disorder in the columns that Davidovich changed his mind again, and ordered a retreat once more. However, by that time Lieutenant-Colonel Leczeny with the rearguard had gone back far enough to become entangled with the enemy, and it became necessary to involve other troops in the combat to support him. A running battle soon developed in the area between Cavaion and Rivoli as the Austrians attempted to extricate themselves, and the French constantly sought to cut them off. By some miracle, most of Davidovich's men managed to escape down the Pontare and reach Ala, while Ocskay retired to Madonna della Corona.

Alvinczy managed to advance as far as Caldiero on the 21st, but decided to go no further than this because the intelligence he received indicated that there were sufficiently large French forces in the area of Verona, Ronco and Legnago to make it inadvisable to attempt to cross the Adige and approach Mantua. It was a further irony that on the following day a messenger turned up in Mantua with news that Davidovich was at Castelnuovo, so Wurmser decided, with impeccable timing, to make a powerful sortie on the 23rd with 8,000 men. This was begun at daybreak, and was a qualified success. Some earthworks were destroyed and over 200 prisoners taken, but at a cost of 789 officers and men. From the prisoners, Wurmser learned that he was too late, and that the relief columns had turned back. Although Alvinczy was still at Caldiero on the 23rd, news reached him during the morning of Davidovich's retreat from Rivoli, which was confirmed at midday, and he realised he now had no alternative but to withdraw. During the night, the Friuli Corps retired to Montebello, and eventually took up positions behind the Brenta.

For both sides, the cost of the fighting had been enormous. The Austrians later calculated that during November they had lost 17,832 men,[64] though a number of them must have been stragglers, some of whom would later have returned to the colours. The figures for the French are more obscure (their Chief Commissary once complained that even he could not get accurate returns) but Schels estimated them at 19,507 men,[65] a not improbable total. Once again, it seems likely that there were more than a few stragglers. These figures emphasise that the margin of victory for Bonaparte had been very narrow this time – a month later he admitted, 'It took luck … to beat Alvinczy'[66] – but he had none the less managed to turn back the Austrians and maintain the blockade of Mantua. It was now a question of whether Mantua could be reduced before another attempt was mounted to relieve it.

NOTES

1. Scorza, B. *Cronaca vissuta del duplice assedio di Mantova degli anni 1796 e 1797: le vicende di Mantova nel 1796.* Mantua, 1975, p. 130.

2. Reinhard, M. *Avec Bonaparte en Italie; d'après les lettres inédites de son aide de camp Joseph Sulkowski.* Paris, 1946, pp. 124–25.

3. See Schels, J. B. 'Die Begebenheiten in und um Mantua vom 16 September 1796 bis 4 Februar 1797; nebst der Schlacht von Rivoli.' *Oesterreichische Militärische Zeitschrift,* Bd. 2; Bd. 3; Bd. 4 (1832), pp. 162–6.

4. Some sources state that he was born in 1726, but both Wurzbach and *Magyar életrajzi Lexikon* give 1 February 1735 as his date of birth.

5. Wurzbach, C., von. *Biographisches Lexikon des Kaiserthums Oesterreich.* Vienna, 1856–91, vol I, p. 22.

6. Napoleon. *Correspondance de Napoléon Ier publiée par ordre de l'empereur Napoléon III.* Paris, 1858–69, no. 1055.

7. See Schels, J. B. 'Das Treffen an der Brenta, bei Bassano und Fontaniva,

am 6 November 1796.' *Oesterreichische Militärische Zeitschrift*, Bd. 3 (1828), pp. 275–78.

8. Napoleon. 1858–69, op. cit., no. 1061.

9. Ibid., no. 1086.

10. Schels, 1832, op. cit., p. 177.

11. Schels, 1828, op. cit., pp. 279–80.

12. Napoleon. 1858–69, op. cit., no. 1109.

13. Chevrier, E. *Le général Joubert d'après sa correspondance*. Paris, 1884, p. 59.

14. Reinhard, op. cit., p. 160.

15. Laugier, J.-R. *Les cahiers du capitaine Laugier. – De la guerre et de l'anarchie, ou Mémoires historiques des campagnes et aventures d'un capitaine du 27me régiment d'infanterie légère par Jérome-Roland Laugier. Publiés d'après le manuscrit original par Léon G. Pélissier.* Aix, 1893, p. 111.

16. Napoleon. 1858–69, op. cit., no. 1127.

17. Schels, J. B. 'Die Gefechte im tirolischen Etschtale, Anfangs November 1796.' *Oesterreichische Militärische Zeitschrift*, Bd. 1 (1829), p. 124.

18. Schels, 1828, op. cit., p. 271.

19. Napoleon. *Correspondance inédite officielle et confidentielle de Napoléon Bonaparte: avec les cours étrangères, les princes, les ministres et les généraux français et étrangers, en Italie, en Allemagne, et en Egypte.* Paris, 1809, II, pp. 262–3.

20. Schels, 1828, op. cit., pp. 272–8.

21. Napoleon. 1858–69, op. cit., no. 1168.

22. Rattier, J.-H. 'Campagne d'Italie (1796): notes d'un sergent-major.' *Revue rétrospective*, XX (1894), p. 250.

23. Reinhard, op. cit., p. 164.

24. Napoleon. 1858–69, op. cit., no. 1182.

25. Schels, 1828, op. cit., pp. 300–4.

26. Napoleon. 1809, op. cit., II, pp. 274–5.

27. Laugier, op. cit., pp. 115–16.

28. Napoleon. 1858–69, op. cit., no. 1170.

29. Ibid., no. 1171.

30. Schels, 'Die Gefechte …' 1829, op. cit., p. 151.

31. Reinhard, op. cit., p. 167.

32. Napoleon. 1858–69, op. cit., no. 1182.

33. See Schels, J. B. 'Die Schlacht bei Arcole, am 15, 16 und 17 November 1796.' *Oesterreichische Militärische Zeitschrift*, no. Bd. 2 (1829), pp.

49–52; Napoleon. *Mémoires pour servir à l'histoire de France, sous le regne de Napoléon, écrits sous sa dictée à Sainte-Hélène, par les généraux qui ont partagé sa captivité*. Paris, 1829, III, p. 394, and Reinhard, op. cit., p. 175.

34. Napoleon. 1858–69, op. cit., no. 1176.
35. Reinhard, op. cit., p. 179.
36. Rattier, op. cit., p. 252.
37. Kryn, J. *Le petit tambour d'Arcole*. Cadenet, 1987, p. 223.
38. Schels, J. B. 'Die Schlacht bei Arcole …' 1829, op. cit., pp. 57–8.
39. Godechot, J. 'Le carnet de route du sergent Petitbon sur la campagne d'Italie de 1796-1797.' *Rivista italiana di studi napoleonici*, 15 (1978), p. 53.
40. Reinhard, op. cit., p. 177.
41. Napoleon. 1829, op. cit., II, p. 404.
42. Massena, A. *Mémoires de Massena, rédigés d'après les documents qu'il a laissés et sur ceux du dépôt de la guerre et du dépôt des fortifications, par le général Koch*. Paris, 1848–50, II, p. 513.
43. Kryn, op. cit., p. 229, and Schels, J. B. 'Die Schlacht bei Arcole …' 1829, op. cit., p. 67.
44. Kryn, op. cit., p. 228.
45. The Directory later had two colours made to present to Augereau and Bonaparte to commemorate their actions. Bonaparte passed his on to Lannes. Kryn, op. cit., pp. 227 and 233.
46. Reinhard, op. cit., pp. 178–79.
47. About half-a-dozen of them received awards for their actions, some of them many years later.
48. Napoleon. 1829, op. cit., IV, p. 343.
49. Marmont, A.-F. V., de. *Mémoires du duc de Raguse de 1792 à 1832 imprimés sur le manuscrit original de l'auteur*. Paris, 1857, II, p. 244.
50. Reinhard, op. cit., p. 186.
51. Rattier, op. cit., p. 256.
52. Kryn, op. cit., p. 238.
53. Napoleon. 1829, op. cit., II, p. 406.
54. Godechot, op. cit., p. 54.
55. Napoleon. 1829, op. cit., II, p. 407.
56. Ibid., II, p. 407.
57. Schels, J. B. 'Die Schlacht bei Arcole …' 1829, op. cit., p. 97.

58. Reinhard, op. cit., p. 181.

59. Kryn, op. cit., p. 250.

60. Roguet, F. *Mémoires militaires du lieutenant général comte Roguet (François), colonel en second des grenadiers à pied de la Vieille Garde, pair de France.* Paris, 1862, p. 296.

61. Ibid., p. 297.

62. Ibid., pp. 297–8.

63. Schels, J. B. 'Die Treffen bei Rivoli am 17 und 21 November 1796.' *Oesterreichische Militärische Zeitschrift,* Bd. 2 (1829), p. 160.

64. Ibid., p. 190.

65. Ibid., p. 188.

66. Napoleon. 1858–69, op. cit., no. 1319.

18

RIVOLI

The battles in November had found the French army much less resilient than Bonaparte had come to expect, and he began taking measures to improve its fighting capabilities even before the Austrians had been completely repulsed. Only two days after Alvinczy had first been pushed back from Arcole, and while Davidovich was still at Rivoli, letters were speeding from the French HQ, reporting the successes and failures to the Directors, proposing promotions, sackings, and expressing indignation at the state of the army's finances.

His letter to Carnot contained the surprising declaration: 'before ten days are out, I hope to write to you from the HQ of Mantua', but it is difficult to judge whether this was merely propaganda or misplaced optimism. Elsewhere in the letter he makes no secret of the problems he has faced, commenting: 'Never has a field of battle been as disputed as that of Arcole. I have hardly any generals left.' Unusually, he is also less than complimentary about his soldiers, saying: 'You know the character of the French – a little inconstant. Our good demi-brigades, weakened moreover by so many victories, are no longer more than ordinary troops.'[1] To the Directory itself he wrote:

> I must not conceal from you that I did not find among the soldiers
> my phalanxes of Lodi, Millesimo and Castiglione. Fatigue and the
> absence of brave men deprived them of that impetuosity with which
> I had the right to hope to take Alvinczy and most of his army.[2]

This negative assessment of the conduct of some of the troops was echoed by others, including Marmont and Joubert, but the latter was also ready to give the enemy his due: 'Never have we fought so badly,' he wrote, 'never have the Austrians fought so well.'[3]

There was nothing that Bonaparte could do to change the soldiers, but he could change the commanders, and he removed the least satisfactory of them before operations were even concluded. 'General Vaubois has no character, nor the habit of commanding large divisions,'[4] he told the Directory, and transferred him to the backwater of Livorno. His choice of replacement was highly significant. 'The General-in-Chief orders General of Brigade Joubert to fulfil the functions of General of Division, which rank he is about to ask for him from the Executive Directory,'[5] he wrote on 21 November, the day that Davidovich was driven back from Rivoli. Bonaparte had nominated other generals of division before, including Dallemagne, and just a couple of days previously, Guieu. But it is noteworthy that among these, Joubert was the one to whom the most important command was given: the division guarding Rivoli. Just how critical this command could be had been shown in the previous two weeks, when it was more by luck than judgement that the French had not been driven from Rivoli earlier, and forced to retire over the Mincio. This, and his experiences with Sauret, had no doubt made Bonaparte cautious, so this time he went for a known quantity, rather than having to rely on a reputation, the value of which he could not judge. He had seen Joubert in action since Cosseria, and it was quite a mark of Bonaparte's respect for Joubert's ability that he gave him this command.

Joubert was from the area of Bourg-en-Bresse and was a matter of four months older than Bonaparte. However, he had not been a career officer before the Revolution. Like Bonaparte, he had a lawyer for a father, and apart from an escapade in 1785, when he had run away to La Fère in Picardy to join the artillery, he had studied the law. He had only become a soldier again after the Revolution began, when his courage and his size (he was nearly six feet two inches tall) soon got him made a grenadier. As we have seen, he tended to lead from the front, and possessed the kind of appetite for work without which he would not have met with Bonaparte's approval. Joubert himself was unsure about his promotion. On 22 November, he replied to Bonaparte's letter:

> I shall do what I can, General, to respond to your views fittingly for the moment. But I pray you will observe that the command of my brigade is already more than I should have, and that I await a

general of division with impatience. There are enough of them without making new ones. Moreover, events are growing too many for you, General. To execute suitably everything which you order, one must not be a novice. I cannot repeat too often, General, that a division of 9,000 men is, for me, a burden that weighs me down. A brigade is my measure, and, while bowing to the General-in-Chief, I cannot prevent myself from representing this to him.[6]

This modesty and seriousness were typical of Joubert, who rather underestimated his abilities. But Bonaparte was skilled in getting the best out of men, and he knew how to deal with Joubert. A few days afterwards, the latter wrote wonderingly to his father:

Here I am with a division, despite two refusals. The General-in-Chief always writes to me as 'General of Division' ... He said, in speaking of me: 'I count on him as I count on myself.' With these fine words, here I am with 8,000 men today, and with ten tomorrow, reduced to a quarter ration of bread ...[7]

The last sentence hints at the fact that the first trial for Joubert was not to be combat, but supply. 'They are making us die of hunger,' he complained to Bonaparte shortly afterwards:

My ovens are ready, but there is no flour ... I daren't go out. People cry out to me 'bread!' ... I wanted to go out, the most gloomy silence reigned in the camps, and I saw some soldiers searching for food in the bushes. I am not the man ever to despair over anything, but I would be deceiving you if I hid my circumstances from you.[8]

The conditions provoked a mutiny among the grenadiers of the 33rd Line, but Joubert dealt with it firmly, having all three companies thrown into prison in Peschiera. Two of the ringleaders were shot, but much of the blame was attributed to the unsatisfactory conduct of the demi-brigade's officers.

Indeed, it was not only new generals that were necessary. On 24 November, Bonaparte had told the Directory, 'my demi-brigades have no officers',[9] but he seems to have been determined that he would not allow the most important positions simply to be taken by whoever was next in seniority. On the 23rd, a request had been made to the generals of division for the names of those suitable to be made *chefs de brigade* and *chefs de bataillon*, 'specifying those who have most distinguished themselves in the last battles'.[10] This was backed up by another on 8 December, when Bonaparte reminded his divisional generals: 'It is indispensable that the different corps are commanded by men of proven courage and intelligence.'[11] With some care being taken over the selections, it was not until just before Christmas that the work of reorganisation was complete.

Bonaparte did not neglect his own arm, the artillery, and its commander, Lespinasse, found himself receiving a number of very detailed instructions about how the guns were to be allocated. In addition, Bonaparte devised a system of signals using cannon that permitted the divisional commanders to inform him if they had been attacked, forced to retire, or the enemy had retired. A final touch to all the arrangements was the creation in early December of a fourth, reserve division, commanded by General Rey.

As the problems experienced by Joubert demonstrate, the administration and supply of the army had not really improved at all since the opening of the campaign. Bonaparte had to carry on a never-ending struggle to prevent his troops from starving, and, in contrast with his successes against the enemy, it was a struggle he showed little sign of winning. Immediately after Arcole, he addressed an angry letter to the commissioner, Garrau:

> The army is without shoes, pay, clothes, the hospitals lack everything, our wounded are lying on the floors, and in the most horrible state of destitution. All this is caused by the lack of money, and this at a time when we have just acquired 4,000,000 francs in Livorno ... Modena also owes us 1,800,000 francs, and Ferrara contributions as considerable. But there is neither order

nor unity in the field of the contributions, which you are specially charged with. The evil is so great that a remedy is necessary. I pray you to reply to me during the day whether you can provide for the needs of the army. If not, I pray you to order Citizen Haller, a thief who has only come to this country to steal, and who has set himself up as steward of finances for the conquered countries, to render his accounts to the Chief Commissary ...[12]

Unfortunately, swindling was such an intrinsic part of the administration that it could not be eradicated despite the most extraordinary vigilance on the part of the commander-in-chief. In December he even ordered the commanding officer of Casalmaggiore to be replaced and sent to Milan 'to give an account of the reasons that made him sell seventeen oxen belonging to the Republic'.[13] A number of officials were dismissed, including the Chief Commissary, and in the end, Bonaparte asked for three officials to be court-martialled and executed as being guilty of having 'stolen, and compromised the army and the most important operations of the war',[14] thereby indirectly causing the deaths of French soldiers. Although improvements were made, the problem could not wholly be solved, and the troops were sometimes reduced to plundering to live, with disastrous effects on the civilian population. Alberghini, one of the local priests near Rivoli, recounted that 'the damage caused by the ... troops round about the *contrada* where they were camped was great, leaving almost total desolation. Moreover, where the soldiers did not find wood, they burnt floors, the beams, and the door and window-frames of the houses that were not inhabited, in some of them even taking off the roof.'[15]

Alvinczy, like Bonaparte, left hardly a pause between the end of one operation, and beginning to prepare for the next. He immediately sent Wurmser a message, which arrived in Mantua on 4 December, assuring him that he would 'summon up all his strength in order to attempt the relief of the fortress again'.[16] He must have been acutely aware that it would be the last chance the Austrians would get to save the city. Four days later, Alvinczy received a letter from Wurmser describing how sickness and deprivation were leading to an appalling death-rate among the soldiery, and begging to know how soon another attempt at rescue could be made. There was no doubt that the situation was becoming critical, as we can gather from a letter written by Thomas Graham, who managed to slip out of the fortress at the end of December to join the new offensive.

> I hope to God they will succeed, but they failed before; and it *must* be soon. I should *then* see Mantua again with pleasure, the only circumstance that could make me wish to revisit the scene of such misery as cannot be forgotten.

However, it has to be said that this misery was not very equally shared, as Graham unconsciously reveals to us when he continues:

> For my own part I never had better health anywhere. I took a deal of exercise on horseback, and shooting ducks and snipe, and ate and drank more than usual. In short, if I could have been hardened to the distress of the soldiers, and my sense of duty had not disturbed my mind, I should not have wished to quit the very pleasant society in which I lived. We felt little of the hardships of the blockade, and only ate horseflesh by way of example. I left a fat cow alive there, having reprieved her from day to day on account of getting a little milk for breakfast; and I hope to hear that I have made a great deal of money by her, as I paid a price for her which afforded conversation to the inhabitants for some days.[17]

It was in the second week of December when Alvinczy received an Imperial order instructing him to relieve Mantua, and commanding Wurmser to hold to the last extremity. In addition, Wurmser was told that if it became impossible for him to resist any longer, he was to break through the blockading forces with the garrison and make for the Papal States. Alvinczy despatched copies of these orders to Wurmser on 11 and 15 December, but neither of them reached their destination.

Alvinczy's first step on receiving his orders was to ask his generals to submit written plans for a relief operation. These agreed that it was impracticable at that moment, citing the weather (four feet of snow had fallen in the mountains, making Monte Baldo impassable), and the lack of organisation and equipment as the greatest obstacles. Alvinczy wrote a report on the army's condition on 12 December, pointing out that the previous shortage of officers and experienced soldiers had been exacerbated by the casualties suffered during the fighting in November, and that the majority of the reinforcements consisted of raw recruits. Moreover, the strenuous marching and bad weather of the previous month had been too much for the army's clothing and shoes, which were now worn out. Lastly, there were no pontoons, and there was a lack of draught animals.

An immense effort was put into supplying these needs, which serves to underline how desperate the Austrians were to save Mantua. At the end of November, 6,081 Hungarian and German reinforcements set off for Italy, and in the following month numbers of recruits for the regular and Grenz battalions were despatched there in wagons. The regiment of Vienna Volunteers, 1,085 strong, also marched off to defend the Fatherland, and the reserve squadrons of the German cavalry regiments were pressed into active service. From 30 November to the beginning of January, the army increased by 14,249 men. Vast quantities of clothing and equipment were also delivered to the army, including 86,000 pairs of shoes, and 55,000 shirts. A weapons depot was set up at Klagenfurt with 13,000 muskets, while 21 pontoons arrived in the Tyrol and another 30 in Friuli.

The difficulties of getting messengers through the French blockading forces and into Mantua meant that news of what was happening to the army arrived only sporadically, which increased the sense of suspense among the inhabitants. Worse was to follow, however, when one of the messengers carrying a copy of the orders from Vienna was captured. On Christmas Day, General Dumas, who was temporarily in command of the blockade, reported to Bonaparte that three men had been stopped trying to cross the lake, and that he had paid particular attention to one who seemed to be more intelligent than the others. Dumas felt sure that the man had a written message but could not find it. 'I finally said to him that the despatches were in his belly. I threatened to have him shot if he persisted in denying it. The air of assurance with which I spoke to him disconcerted him, he stammered, I pressed him, and he admitted it.'[18] The prisoner was closely watched, and 24 hours later produced a small cylinder of wax, inside which was a letter. Not only did this inform the French that Wurmser was likely to try to break out to the south if he ran out of food, but there was a comment by Alvinczy that 'the situation and needs of the army at that time did not permit new operations to be attempted before three weeks or a month'.[19] Armed with this, the French had a clear indication that the next Austrian offensive could be expected in early to mid January.

The idea of a break-out to the south did not worry Bonaparte unduly, but it was an extra motive for taking an interest in developments in that area. In fact, during the month, the citizens of Modena, Reggio, Bologna and Ferrara had decided to band together and form the Cispadane Republic. This had not gone down well with the Pope, who moreover had been very reluctant to fulfil the terms of his armistice with the French, and a Papal army corps of more than 6,000 men was now gathering around Faenza. On 28 December, Bonaparte wrote to the Directory: 'As this very much frightens the Bolognese, and could assist Wurmser's escape from Mantua, I shall disperse this gathering, and march on Ancona, in conformity with one of the articles of the armistice.'[20] By 31 December, French troops were already crossing the Po to carry out this punitive expedition.

From the timing, it seems that Bonaparte must have assumed that a new Austrian offensive was unlikely to begin for a couple of weeks longer, perhaps more. He may have been influenced in this by the fact that an arrangement was made for a meeting in Vicenza on 2 January between General Clarke and the Emperor's ADC, Baron Vincent, to discuss a temporary cease-fire between the two powers. Bonaparte totally opposed such an arrangement, believing that it would effectively snatch Mantua from his grasp just as it was about to fall, because no matter what steps were taken to maintain the status quo in the fortress, the Austrians were bound to re-provision and reinforce the garrison in secret. However, he need not have worried on that score, because the negotiators could not even find a mutually agreeable starting-point. The result of this was that the meetings fell apart on the first day, instead of lasting for days or weeks, as might otherwise have been the case.

Whatever Bonaparte's reasons for arranging his expedition south-wards at this juncture, the new Austrian offensive was closer to starting than he expected. In the last days of December, a letter from Alvinczy dated the 22nd had reached Wurmser, informing him that 'considerable reinforcements had reached the army ... and that the army would soon advance to relieve him'. To this, Wurmser replied on 30 December that 'as long as a horse, a dog, a cat, a bit of bread is available in Mantua, there could be no talk of capitulation, and no hardship could force him to it'.[21] He added, however, that the condition of the garrison would not allow him to do much to support the advance. Indeed, by this time, his forces had been reduced to 18,493 men, of whom only 9,800 were fit for service. It is sobering to record that in the four months from September to December, 8,897 men had died in Mantua's hospitals.[22] It was perhaps unfortunate for the troops that on 2 January a commission appointed to inspect all the houses for reserves of food reported to Wurmser that there was enough to last until the 17th.

While waiting for the army to get back into condition to act, the Austrian commanders had considered how best to achieve their goal of liberating Mantua with their somewhat rickety army. Broadly speaking, they had two options: another advance over the plain from the east, or to come down through the mountains as Davidovich had done. Going over Monte Baldo to Rivoli was a daunting prospect at that time of year (though necessary, as we shall see later) but the advantage was that once the excellent defensive position at Rivoli had been forced, it became increasingly difficult for the defenders to stop an advance, because the terrain to the south became progressively flatter. It was also true that the Austrian positions in the Tyrol and on Monte Baldo meant that there would be no real approach march, and that overcoming resistance on Monte Baldo and at Rivoli, as had been done twice before, would be a useful boost to morale, and give the troops greater confidence for the rest of the operation.

An advance over the plain presented fewer physical obstacles, but brought with it the certainty that the army would have to face the French in the open field. It was felt that it was important to avoid this, as the state of the training of the recruits was so poor that it was unlikely that they would be capable of carrying out with any reliability the tactical manoeuvres required for combat. Any sort of muddle might have disastrous consequences, particularly as there were still insufficient numbers of officers to control the troops. Moreover, the proven superiority in marching of the French could easily lead to the army being out-manoeuvred and forced to fight on disadvantageous ground, as it had been on previous occasions.

Whatever the disadvantages, therefore, it was decided that the best course was to make the main thrust from the Tyrol, while a smaller diversionary force would advance over the plain. It was hoped that it would be possible to deceive the enemy as to the direction of the main thrust, and induce him to move some of his forces to the east, which would make it more likely that the defences at Rivoli could be overcome before help could arrive there. The plan was duly drawn up by Weyrother, and on 4 January, Alvinczy assembled all the generals and column commanders for a council of war in Bassano. No one present can have been in any doubt that the operation had to succeed if Mantua were to be saved. Each commander received written orders and any necessary explanations were given personally.

The diversionary force was to consist of two columns under Provera and Bajalich, who were to begin their advance on 7 January from Padua and Bassano respectively. The first of these forces was to advance to Legnago, and cross the Adige there, while the other would move in the direction of Verona. Once Provera had made his crossing, he was to drive towards Mantua at the same time as Bajalich attacked Verona. It was hoped that these feints would be sufficient to induce the French to switch the bulk of their forces to this area, in the belief that the Austrians were repeating the strategy they had adopted in November. The occupation of the Val Sugana, which provided the link with the Tyrol, was left in the hands of Mittrovsky. The forces allocated to each column were:

Commander	Position	Battns	Sqdns	Infantry	Cavalry	Total
Provera	Padua	10	6½	8,379	718	9,097
Bajalich	Bassano	6	1	6,081	160	6,241
Mittrovsky	Val Sugana	4	½	3,497	73	3,570
Total		20	8	17,957	951	18,908

In addition, a very small force of ten companies and half a squadron, totalling 875 men, was left at Tione under Loudon to guard the Tyrol.

The main army was divided into six columns, under the overall supervision of Alvinczy, and consisted of:

Column	Commander	Battns	Lt Coys	Sqdns	Infantry	Cavalry	Total
I	Lusignan	4	12		4,556		4,556
II	Lipthay	4	6		5,065		5,065
III	Köblös	5	6		4,138		4,138
IV	Ocskay	4		8	2,692	829	3,521
V	Prince Reuss	9		5½	6,986	885	7,871
VI	Vukassovich	3	5	½	2,795	76	2,871
Total		29	29	14	26,232	1,790	28,022

Each column was accompanied by one officer with 20 pioneers.[23]

The task allotted to this wing of the army was hardly easy, if only because of the nature of the terrain it had to advance over. A very brief description of some of the geography of the area has already been given in a previous chapter, but the lie of the land is such an essential factor in the succeeding chain of events that it is important to enlarge on that description here.

The Adige valley has always been the most important route southwards from the Tyrol, providing, as it does, a narrow corridor of flat land through a jumble of mountain peaks. However, in the vicinity of Rivoli, just before the mountains end and the river reaches the flood-plain of the Po, there is a difficult bottleneck. To the north of it, as we have noted before, the valley is lined with almost vertical, rocky cliffs, as much as 2,000 feet high, but the valley bottom is fairly wide. Near

Rivoli, it suddenly narrows, and there is a tight 's' bend where the river is constricted between imposing precipices. Here, the road on the left, or eastern bank of the river, is closely hemmed by the cliffs and the river, and passes the small fort of La Chiusa. With a determined garrison, it was capable of stopping an army. On the right bank there is simply no road at all round the 's', because the cliffs drop sheer into the water. However, just before the bend, the western wall of the valley lowers quite abruptly, almost to nothing, where a couple of small tributaries flow into the Adige. At this point, the road on the right bank is able to climb out of the valley up the steep incline called the 'Pontare', onto what is effectively a wide plateau, though it does not appear to be such when viewed from its surface because the deeply sunken groove of the valley is invisible unless one stands near the edge of the cliffs. The route out of the valley has been called a 'gorge', which is perhaps something of an exaggeration, but there is no denying that it is steep, and dominated on both sides by rocky bluffs, the one to the north being much the higher. From the top of the Pontare, the road continues southwards, past the village of Rivoli itself, towards Verona or Peschiera.

At first sight, it would appear that from the point of view of an army marching southwards, there is not much to choose between taking the left bank of the Adige, which is blocked by the Chiusa, or the right bank, which is blocked by the defences overlooking the Pontare. However, the latter did have a weakness in that they could be attacked from the plateau behind them. The only difficulty consisted in getting an adequate attacking force to the plateau, which involved a very arduous march over the high ground lying to the north of it. This was the task facing the first three columns of the main army, which, it will be noted, had a large allocation of light infantry, but no cavalry, because this could not cope with the terrain. Nor was it possible to take the battalion guns, which had to be left in the Adige valley to await further orders. A number of light mountain guns that could be carried on mules were taken instead. The columns were to start their advance on 11 and 12 January, and would carry the French positions at Ferrara di Monte Baldo and Madonna della Corona on the 12th. After this, they would take parallel routes southwards to Rivoli. In the meantime, the other columns were to advance along the Adige valley, Ocskay and Prince Reuss on the right bank, and Vukassovich on the left. On the 13th, Ocskay, who together with Prince Reuss formed Quosdanovich's command, was to carry out an assault from the bottom of the Pontare while the first three columns were attacking the top. At the same time, Vukassovich was to support Ocskay with cannon-fire aimed across the river. On the 14th, the whole army would assemble at Rivoli, and would proceed south towards Mantua on the following day.

When these orders were issued to the Austrian commanders, they were also instructed to maintain the strictest secrecy. Schels tells us: 'These orders were so precisely carried out that all the columns of the main army arrived at the places from which they were to advance to the attack without the slightest knowledge of their forthcoming use, and without knowing whether they themselves were being led on an offensive undertaking, or were only to oppose an expected enemy attack.'[24] Alvinczy also attempted to deceive the enemy as to where his main thrust would start from by appearing in Padua with his whole retinue, and carrying out inspections of the troops assembled there. While these efforts were laudable, and largely successful, their influence on the eventual outcome of the operations was not decisive.

The French forces ranged against the Austrians at the time are summarised in the following table.[25]

Division	Brigades	Position	Strength
Augereau	Guieu, Point, Walther, Verdier	From Verona to Legnago	8,665
Massena	Monnier, Brune, Leclerc	From Bussolengo to San Michele	8,851
Joubert	Vial, Lebley, Sandos	Rivoli and Monte Baldo	10,250
Rey	Baraguey d'Hilliers, Veaux, Murat	Brescia, Peschiera, and Salò	4,156
Infantry reserve	Victor	Goito, Castelnuovo	1,800
Cavalry reserve	Dugua	Villafranca	658
Total			34,380

Division	Brigades	Position	Strength
Blockading corps (Dumas & Dallemagne)	Davin, Miollis, Monteau, Serviez	Marmirolo and Pradella	10,230
Mobile column	Lannes	South of the Po	2,000
Grand total			46,610

In simple numerical terms, if the fit men in Mantua were included, the Austrians had a superiority of 10,000 men. However, as in November, some of the troops were of doubtful value, and they were also spread over a wide area. As both sides knew, what was really needed was overwhelming superiority in the local area where the main combat was to take place, and achieving this required secrecy and speed of movement. The Austrians believed they had achieved the first, but it remained to be seen whether they could achieve the second.

On 7 January, the same day that Bonaparte left Milan for Bologna to deal with the Papal forces, the troops under the command of Provera and Bajalich began the offensive by setting out from Padua and Bassano. The state of the roads was appalling, which meant that only a short distance was covered, and the bridging train was unable to move at all. This, coupled with determined resistance by Augereau, meant that Provera made unsatisfactory progress over the next few days, and was unable to cross the Adige. Alvinczy ordered Provera to hurry the crossing, but like Davidovich in November, he showed very little sense of urgency. In the meantime, Augereau concentrated most of his division at Zevio, Ronco and Legnago.

News of the Austrian advance reached Bonaparte in Bologna on the 10th, and he immediately ordered Lannes to march back via Ferrara and Rovigo to reinforce Augereau. The troops set off at 4 a.m. on the 11th and hastened through the night at the fastest possible pace. Laugier, who was with the 27th Light, tells us that 'hardly an hour before day there was only half the demi-brigade left'.[26] Later in the day, Bonaparte concluded some diplomatic business in Bologna by signing a convention with Tuscany, and hurried off to his army. Such rapidity of decision provides a stark contrast with Provera, who simply could not make up his mind what to do. On the 11th, he decided to order a bridge to be built over the Adige, then countermanded it soon afterwards. Then he informed Alvinczy that he would not cross the Adige until the main force had been successful at Rivoli, because he thought the forces opposing him too strong, and that he might be cut off. In fact, his unwillingness to co-operate with Alvinczy was such that Thugut seriously questioned his loyalty.[27] Augereau was expecting the enemy to be more active, and informed Massena that the Austrians were going to cross the Adige below Legnago that night. Meanwhile, Bajalich received an order from Alvinczy to mount a serious attack on Verona, which it was hoped would induce the enemy to weaken his left.

That day, the 11th, the first two columns of the main Austrian army began their advance. Lusignan was faced with the almost Herculean task of leading his men along the top of the chain of mountain peaks (collectively known as Monte Baldo) that separates the Adige from the northern arm of Lake Garda, and runs parallel with them. In the winter, it was a featureless wasteland of snow and ice, the highest point of which lay ten miles north of Rivoli, and rose to the not inconsiderable height of 7,279 feet. In order to help in overcoming some of the probable difficulties, climbing-irons had been issued to Lusignan's pioneers, his advance-guard, and 400 men who were to march at the head of the column. Unfortunately, after setting off at daybreak, the column ran into insurmountable problems caused by the quantity of fresh snow, and was unable to continue its march on the highest ridges. The total lack of wood in the area also meant that the men would have frozen to death if they had tried to make camp on the crest, so Lusignan was forced to move down the slopes towards the lake, and halted two hours from Malcesine. The men were already suffering from exhaustion by this time, and although the bulk of the column stopped at 4 p.m., the last stragglers did not trail into the camp until 11 p.m. that night. Lipthay, with the second column, had been instructed to use a lower road, which ran between the mountain crest and the Adige, and consequently had a much easier march. By about 1 p.m. the head of this column had reached Artiglione, four miles north of Ferrara di Monte Baldo. Alvinczy was not the kind of man to avoid the hardships his men were suffering, and that evening he arrived at Artiglione himself. During the night, Fornésy, the commander of the 17th Light, warned Vial that the enemy was approaching. It would seem that the attack was not wholly unexpected, because according to Alberghini, the locals had previously noticed that the French guards had been doubled.

At daybreak (7 a.m.) on the 12th, Lusignan began his march again, and took a route that went further down the mountain towards Malcesine, then proceeded south along the lower slopes. At the same hour, the third Austrian column, under Köblös, left Belluno Veronese and climbed out of the Adige valley by way of a ravine. As they approached Ferrara di Monte Baldo, they gradually pushed back the French pickets. At 9 a.m., Köblös was already in a position to attack Ferrara, but the disposition for the operation stated that he and Lipthay were to wait until Lusignan had outflanked Ferrara before they began their frontal assault on its defences. However, as the morning wore on, and Köblös could still see no sign of either Lusignan or Lipthay, he decided at about 10 o'clock to attempt to take Ferrara on his own, then approach Madonna della Corona. After about three hours of fierce combat, during which the Austrians made great use of their mountain guns, they managed to capture the first entrenchments, just as Joubert arrived to take control of the defence. Under his steadying influence the French soon rallied, and the positions were recaptured. Lipthay's men arrived almost at the same moment, but rather than support Köblös's attack, their commander decided to follow instructions, and wait until Lusignan had appeared to the French rear. Eventually, darkness forced an end to the fighting, with the French still in solid possession of the defences.

At roughly the same time, about 4 p.m., Lusignan arrived in Sommavilla, which is almost opposite Ferrara, but on the other side of Monte Baldo. Aware of the fact that he was behind schedule, he tried to give at least some assistance to the other columns by sending a battalion of Frei-Corps Gyulay towards Ferrara by the perilous route over the highest peaks. With the rest of the column, he opted to make the detour right round the southern end of the mountain, which was much less risky and arduous, but was likely to take longer, unless the detached battalion met very great difficulties. His route took him by way of the hamlet of Lumini, and he then made his way round the southern flank of the mountain to the heights above Caprino, where he halted at 10 p.m. By this time, Lusignan had already lost 200 men in the snow, and despite having marched without pause all day, the column had not been able to reach its goal. This had had a knock-on effect on the operations of Lipthay and Köblös, who had also not achieved their objectives. In other words, 24 very precious hours had been lost at the very start of the offensive, which meant that the whole timetable was now running a day late. Schels, the Austrian officer-historian, makes very plain the lack of foresight in their planning – a fault that was to appear again at Austerlitz, when Weyrother was once again responsible for drafting the plans:

> In the disposition, the place to which each column was to continue its movement each day, and where they were to spend the night, was precisely prescribed. No special consideration was taken of the obstacles which the season and bad weather, or indeed enemy resistance, might create, but the infallible fulfilment of the instructions received was taken for granted. Foodstuffs and ammunition were only available with the troops for these precisely calculated times, and the former had to be carried by the men themselves during the most difficult movements for several days. In these circumstances the columns arrived on the 11th and 12th on Monte Baldo, which in that season was a truly terrifying mountain. Here it became clear that many assumptions in the operational plan were no longer relevant to reality. The troops had already exhausted their strength by the most strenuous marches through the deep snow, and by climbing the steep, trackless, rocky mountain. The burden of the supplies had become an unbearable load to them, and due to the increased consumption caused by the difficulties of movement, they had already exhausted their food supplies in the first couple of marches, without any consideration for the coming day, when they would go through areas that were scarcely inhabited, and bare of food.

Hunger must now also be joined to the remaining troubles, and the worn-out, unfed soldiers would then have to attack a rested enemy, who waited in a strong position.[28]

To these chilling revelations may be added the equally startling comments made by Thomas Graham:

> However much the General is to be commended for exposing himself to the inconveniences of such an undertaking I cannot think that it was prudent to adopt a plan which at this season it was more than probable a fall of snow might render totally impracticable, especially when the success of the plan was acknowledged to depend on the celerity of its execution ... It was unfortunate too that nobody at Head Quarters but myself ever had been on the Ground or knew anything of the Situation or Communications, except what was known very imperfectly from an indifferent plan by which the disposition of attack was made. Before they saw the Ravine of Ferrara they undervalued its strength, &, afterwards, thought it impossible to be forced by an attack in front, which however had succeeded on the 29th of July ...[29]

Alvinczy was forced to reassess the arrangements that had been made, and alter them on the hoof. In the evening, at 5 p.m., he issued an order to Quordanovich that the four most advanced battalions of V column, and the nearest battalions of IV column were to climb through the ravine of Belluno at daybreak with Ocskay, and join III column. The cavalry was to remain with V column in the valley.

At some time on the 12th, while these events were taking place in the mountains, Bonaparte arrived at the French HQ in Roverbella, having returned by way of Borgoforte. At this point, he was prepared to believe that the main enemy thrust was directed at the lower Adige, so he issued orders to the cavalry reserve to march on Legnago, and to Massena to hold himself ready to follow. He also informed Augereau that Joubert was 'very tranquil about his position: in any case, if he was beaten while we were at Legnago we would still have time'.[30] In other words, Bonaparte was intending to leave Joubert to fend for himself until the force on the lower Adige had been turned back, then march to Joubert's aid and defeat the other Austrian force. At the time these letters were written, Bonaparte still did not know that Bajalich had obeyed orders and attacked Massena's advance-guard that morning, and Bonaparte only received this information just after he set off for Verona. The attack made very little impression, and after eight hours of fighting, Bajalich fell back to Caldiero.

Many commanders might have seen such an attack as further evidence that the main area of danger was the lower Adige, but Bonaparte was not yet ready to commit himself, one reason being that he wanted to be sure that there was no Austrian force coming down the western side of Lake Garda. In the evening he ordered Massena to withdraw his division behind Verona to be able to march anywhere at will, and Rey to march to Valeggio with all speed. During the night, he received a report from Adjutant-General Duphot, who was at Legnago, that there were more than 12,000 of the enemy ranged against him. Since Joubert had reported that he had been able to contain the Austrian attack on Ferrara, this served to confirm the impression that the bulk of the Austrian forces were on the plains, rather than in the mountains. However, Bonaparte wanted more information, and at 9 a.m. on 13 January, he wrote to Joubert:

> I pray you to inform me, as soon as possible, if you think the enemy before you has more than 9,000 men. It is very necessary that I know if the attack they have made on you is a real attack, equal or superior to your forces, or if it is a secondary attack for deception.[31]

Bonaparte had to wait several hours before he received a report from Joubert, and in the meantime a great deal had happened. Alvinczy's orders to send more infantry had reached Quosdanovich at about midnight on the 12th, but seem to have been misunderstood. Within half an hour, Quosdanovich had issued instructions for Prince Reuss (V column) to relieve the infantry of IV column with a similar number of battalions, so that IV column's infantry could advance into the mountains. Despite Quosdanovich's promptness, it took an extraordinarily long time for these orders to be received and carried out. A little later, at 2 a.m., Lusignan received a report that there were many enemy camp-fires around Ferrara, and decided he would have to move in that direction to support the attack there. Later still, at about 4 a.m., while Lusignan was still resting his troops, Joubert was informed that Lusignan's column had got round behind him. This turning movement alone would have been enough to force him to abandon his position, but the fact that it had been carried out under such difficult conditions also suggested to him that he must be facing a major force which attached a great deal of importance to the capture of his defences. With this in mind, he made preparations to effect a retreat just before dawn.

From Madonna della Corona to Rivoli there were basically two routes available to Joubert. One was a road that ran down the valley of a small stream called the Tasso. Although the water-course was tiny, its valley was a wide feature, the western slopes of which were formed by the towering flanks of Monte Baldo. On the eastern side of the Tasso, the land sloped up to a rocky, undulating ridge, on the other side of which was an almost sheer drop of nearly 2,000 feet into the Adige valley. Joubert's other route lay along this ridge, which led directly to the Pontare. Laugier said that it took about three hours to come down from Madonna della Corona using the route down the valley, and that towards its end it was a 'stony and difficult road'[32] winding through terraces of vines. Having passed the villages of Pazzon and Porcino, it reached the flat land at the south-eastern foot of Monte Baldo near the villages of San Martino and Gamberon, about one and a half miles north of the Pontare. Rather than use this route, Joubert says that he retreated along the ridge, which would have given him the advantage of being able to see into the Adige valley and observe enemy movements there, as well as giving an uninterrupted view across the valley of the Tasso to the slopes of Monte Baldo. It also put a distance between him and any force attempting to take him in the rear from Monte Baldo.

The French followed the usual practice of leaving their camp-fires burning, and it was not until these began to die down that the Austrians realised their enemy had slipped away. Lusignan had begun his march at 5 a.m., and when the head of his column approached Ferrara some two hours later, just as it was getting light, they could see the hindmost French troops retiring along the opposite crest towards Rivoli, with II and III columns some way behind them. Lusignan knew he could do nothing to help, and therefore began to retrace his steps, stopping before Lumini for nearly two hours to rest and gather his scattered men, after which he made for Pesina. As the morning progressed, Joubert proceeded southwards untroubled by the Austrians, who could not catch up with his rearguard.

His route along the ridge took him to the chapel of San Marco, which stood perched on the cliffs about three-quarters of a mile north of the Pontare. Due west of the chapel, and 700 feet below it, a line of hills extended at right-angles from the ridge, then curved round in a complete semi-circle with a radius of about one and a half miles, at the centre of which was Rivoli. These hills were not particularly high, but were very steep-sided, being composed of morainic rubble, and they formed a natural rampart enclosing a flat area around the top of the Pontare. Graham described them as being much covered with woods. It was at San Marco and on the northern arm of the morainic hills that Joubert took up the defensive position that was to be the scene of the climactic battle of Bonaparte's first campaign.

Köblös approached San Marco at midday, and attacked it without success, then took up a position on the neighbouring heights. At the same time, Lipthay positioned his men behind Caprino, and at about 1 p.m., Lusignan arrived on the heights behind Pesina. In the meantime, Ocskay and Prince Reuss, who had not yet received their new orders from Quosdanovich, had been advancing southwards along the Adige valley towards the bottom of the Pontare. Reports of this movement naturally made Joubert concerned that he might be taken in the rear, added to which, at about 2 p.m., he perceived Lusignan's column in a position from which it could easily outflank his left wing. He therefore sent a detachment back towards Rivoli to guard his rear.

Joubert had already sent Bonaparte a long letter with very detailed reports of the positions and strength of his own units, and the forces of the enemy. Perhaps because he was new to his job, and did not want there to be any doubt about the situation, he was most emphatic in his statements:

> The report I have given you is exact. Be assured that the enemy will make every effort to throw me onto the blockade of Mantua or on Peschiera. I believe I see that his design is still to throw a corps behind me. He fears to attack me frontally. He saw yesterday what it cost him ... Send 4 or 5,000 infantry and two regiments of cavalry. Attack vigorously on my side and if, as I doubt not, we succeed, there will be no crossing of the Adige ... I think it would be as well to attack alternately on the two extremities, taking forces from the centre. Pardon me if I am long, but the movements of the enemy on Verona, and his reiterated attempts to trouble you and prevent you from taking help to the wings confirm me in my opinion.[33]

This missive reached Bonaparte in mid-afternoon, and it was precisely what he wanted to know. He reacted rapidly, and at 3 p.m. orders were sent to those farthest from the HQ. Sérurier, who had returned to command before Mantua, was told:

> The enemy's plan has finally been unmasked: he is marching with considerable forces on Rivoli. It is to be believed that General Wurmser will make a sortie ... The General-in-Chief is having part of Massena's division march to support General Joubert.[34]

Victor was ordered to march 'an hour after receiving the present order' and make for Villafranca. Another order, dated 5 p.m., commanded:

> General Massena will leave, with the 18th, 32nd and 75th demi-brigades, to take the left of General of Division Joubert. He will go in person, as soon as possible, to Rivoli, where the General-in-Chief is about to go by post, in order to arrange together the dispositions for tomorrow ... General Massena will have placed

in the orders of the demi-brigades which are leaving, that
tomorrow will be decisive, and that General Joubert, who has
obtained some success against the enemy, only awaits their arrival
to make a great number of prisoners and decide the fate of Italy.[35]

It was specified that the 18th Line, under Monnier, was not to go to Rivoli,
but to Garda, the intention being to block attempts to reach Peschiera. Rey
was also ordered to march to Castelnuovo, where he was to arrive at 2 a.m.

While Bonaparte was hurriedly issuing these orders, the forces around
Rivoli spent the afternoon and evening making cautious adjustments to
their positions. At 3.30 p.m., Lusignan received an order from Alvinczy to
move closer to Lipthay, and place his left wing behind Caprino. This can
hardly have been welcome to the exhausted troops, who could not make
camp until 8 p.m. On the French side, meanwhile, the continued Austrian
advance in the Adige valley made Joubert feel his position on the hills
before Rivoli was insecure, and at 4 p.m. he drew back to the flat ground
inside their circle. He also wrote to Bonaparte that he would have to evacuate the Rivoli position in the night if he did not receive contrary orders.
It was not until 10 p.m. that Bonaparte received this report, by which time
matters were well in hand, Massena's division having left an hour before.

In fact, although his overall position was certainly not sustainable
without help, at the time Joubert wrote his letter, his right was in less
danger than he thought. Unluckily for the Austrians, the new orders
from Quosdanovich did not reach Prince Reuss and Ocskay until the
afternoon. At about the same time as Joubert was falling back, therefore,
Ocskay also turned round, and began to march back towards Belluno.
From there he climbed up the ravine, and at 7 p.m. he reached the top,
ready to descend towards Rivoli behind II and III columns. In the
meantime, Prince Reuss had advanced to take Ocskay's place in the
Adige valley, and towards evening received orders to move nearer to the
bottom of the Pontare. By nightfall, his advance-guard had taken up a
position near the village of Canale.

When darkness fell, the locals were presented with a scene they were
unlikely to forget. Their priest, Alberghini, found himself impressed by
it, despite the anguish he felt at the presence of the armies:

It was truly a wonderful sight to see the many fires of the ... troops, which, starting from the hill called i Masi, and crossing all the hills in between as far as the ... orchards [of the *Marchese* Carlotti], did not leave the smallest space in which one did not see the sparkling of the flames. In particular, however, on the above-mentioned hill i Masi, where there was a large troop, and also in the said orchards, the fires were so large and close together that to see them they seemed those devices which are used to illuminate the churches on great occasions. Yes, it was a marvellous spectacle, but it caused incalculable damage, because many of the fields were completely devastated by the hatchets of the soldiers who spared no plant or tree. The French did the same around the Chapel of San Marco, on Trambasore and in other places where they were camped: but their fires were fewer in number.[36]

At about midnight, Alvinczy received a report that Joubert was expecting reinforcements, and ordered Ocskay to move a little nearer San Marco. Massena's division was in fact still some hours distant, but it was either at midnight (according to Joubert) or 2 a.m. (according to Bonaparte's own report) that the French commander-in-chief arrived in Rivoli, where he found Joubert in the church, writing his orders by candlelight.[37] They immediately went to inspect the enemy positions 'in excessive cold'.[38] Bonaparte remembered:

> The weather had cleared, and the moonlight was superb. [I] climbed the different heights and observed the lines of enemy fires. They filled the country between the Adige and Lake Garda, and the atmosphere was ablaze with them. One could easily distinguish five camps, each composed of a column ...[39]

It was simple to deduce that the Austrians intended to effect the junction of the two halves of their main force on the plateau of Rivoli, as they had done on previous occasions. It was also obvious that if they were permitted to do this before Massena's troops could arrive they would be sufficiently strong to overwhelm Joubert's division and drive it southwards. The remaining defensive positions in that direction were nowhere near as good as Rivoli, and in any case, trying to gather the troops to defend while being harried by a much larger and victorious force would not be easy. It was therefore crucial to prevent the concentration of the Austrian army for as long as possible, and this could only be done by defending the semi-circle of hills, San Marco and the Pontare.

Initially, there was only a single division of about 10,000 men to do this, but Bonaparte made intelligent use of his limited resources. In particular, he must have realised that the force in the Adige valley, though very large (V column actually had 8,000 men) could be held back by a much smaller number. This was because it was faced with a difficult climb up a very steep, narrow road that would only permit a few attackers to approach the defences at any one time. The core of these defences consisted of three entrenchments, provided with cannon, which fired down on the lower section of the roadway and the valley floor beyond it. Skirmishers could be placed on the bluffs to add their fire. Bonaparte therefore felt it was sufficient to leave the defence of this position to the 39th Line alone, which numbered only 978 men. This left some 9,000 men to oppose the first four columns, which amounted to seventeen battalions and 24 companies, or 16,000 men.

Fortunately for Bonaparte, Lusignan's column, now about 4,000 strong, rather than taking part in the first attack, was detailed to perform a long encircling movement that would completely by-pass the French left, and cut the road from Verona to Rivoli. To begin with, therefore, the bulk of Joubert's division was to find itself fighting about 12,000 men, which gave much more favourable odds. Moreover, they had a good position from which to do it, or would have when they had reversed the movement that Joubert had been forced to make before news of reinforcements arrived. Bonaparte recalled:

The [Austrian] outposts extended up to the first steps of the amphitheatre of Rivoli, to Trambasore, Zovo, Sarpelle, and the chapel of San Marco ... [I] ordered that the positions already occupied by the Austrian outposts be retaken, in order to be master of the heights on this side of the Tasso ...[40]

The amphitheatre and the heights that Bonaparte refers to are, of course, the morainic hills surrounding the top of the Pontare. Of the places he mentions here, Trambasore was on the semi-circle, just opposite Caprino, and Zovo was about 800 yards further east. This stretch of terrain was to the be the scene of some of the most critical moments of the forthcoming battle. Sarpelle was actually inside the line of hills, and lay only 650 yards north of the Pontare. The whole area around Sarpelle, as well as the hills north of it, were also to be the scene of dramatic incidents and ferocious combat. The Tasso, which was no more than a few feet wide, passed about half-way between Trambasore and Caprino, and curved away following the line of the semi circle.

At about 4 a.m., three hours before dawn, Vial's brigade, consisting of the 4th, 17th and 22nd Light, advanced past the top of the Pontare towards Monte Ceredello, the section of the semi-circle just north of Sarpelle. They were supported by the 33rd Line, led by Joubert himself. It had been arranged that the right wing of the division would be commanded by Joubert, the centre by Berthier, and the left would be taken by Massena. By about 5 a.m., Vial's men had taken the chapel of San Marco, which had been occupied by a few Croats, and advanced over the steep slopes of the ridge, driving the rest of the outposts back to the villages of San Giovanni and Gamberon. In the centre, the 14th Line took a position on Monte Ceredello, flanking the road that ran through a slight depression which separated Monte Ceredello from the rest of the semi-circle. The terrain which lay between this hill and Pazzon, where Alvinczy had his HQ, was described by Graham as having 'two or three other small villages & several large Houses, walled Gardens, & Vineyards, occupying the broken ground ...'[41] It was over this terrain that one of the battalions of the 14th shadowed the movement of Vial's brigade by following the line of the road northwards, and attacked the village of San Giovanni. On the left, the heights of Trambasore and Zovo were occupied by the 85th Line and the 29th Light respectively. Batteries of artillery had been placed before the demi-brigades, or in the case of the 29th, to its right, on the road. The history of the latter says: 'The 29th alone occupied such an extent of terrain, that the three battalions, although on the same line, were very distant from each other.'[42] Bonaparte's forces were obviously somewhat stretched.

The French advance gave rise to skirmishes along the whole front, and these became particularly serious on the ridge of San Marco. Destaing, the *chef* of the 4th Light, stated that his men got carried away and advanced too far beyond the chapel, running into the bulk of Köblös's column in the darkness. Years later, Bonaparte wrote in his memoirs:

> The combat was engaged a little earlier than one might have wanted, because of the position of the enemy line, which was very close. The successes of the right carried it perhaps a little too far ...[43]

Since Bonaparte was awaiting reinforcements, it would naturally have been useful to delay a full engagement until later, but the eagerness of the men set off an escalating combat that could not be stopped, and drew in ever more troops. Very soon, the 17th Light arrived to support the 4th, just in time to repel an Austrian assault.

On the other wing of the army, meanwhile, Lusignan set off about half an hour before dawn to make his long detour round the French left. 'Then, with the rising of the sun,' Alberghini observed, 'the nucleus of the [Austrian] army began a general attack.'[44] Lipthay, to the right of centre, had assembled near Caprino, and began to advance slowly towards Trambasore. In the centre itself, Ocskay, who had some good troops, including a combined grenadier battalion and one of IR Deutschmeister, found himself in a fierce fight with the 14th Line for the possession of the village of San Giovanni. High above them on the ridge, Köblös, who also had a combined grenadier battalion, as well as some companies of Mahony Jägers, subjected Vial's brigade to continual attacks, but without being able to dislodge him. Eventually, Joubert and the 33rd Line climbed up to join Vial, hoping to be able to push the right wing further forward. This proved impossible because the French centre could not advance the same distance to cover their left. Every attempt by Vial to gain ground was halted by the appearance of strong enemy forces on his flank.

This phase of the action continued for two hours, with no special advantage to either side, but it cost the French some significant casualties, as Sandos was fatally wounded, Fornésy grievously, and Destaing only slightly. Joubert also had his horse put out of action in the first half-hour of combat, and having no replacement to hand, he spent the rest of the day on foot. While the fighting was in progress, Massena's division arrived, as Thiébault described in his memoirs:

> At 8 or 9 a.m. only, we appeared on the plateau of Rivoli, and, as Joubert's division occupied the whole line, and the combat had already been heavily engaged along its whole length, the troops of Massena's division were placed in reserve to the left of the village ...[45]

The reinforcements were soon needed. By this time, Lipthay had managed to outflank the 85th Line through a ravine, and burst on it unexpectedly. We are told by the historian of the 29th Light:

> It was 9 a.m. when the 85th was attacked on its left. Then several battalions of Croats advanced on us and began a fusillade. The 3rd battalion of the 29th, which was closest, at the beginning made a very lively fire. However, the 85th had already abandoned its position. Its retreat was so precipitate that the enemy was already master of an eminence situated behind us. We therefore found ourselves placed between two fires. We resisted for a while, and lost many brave men ... We then retired in disorder on Rivoli ...[46]

Although Massena swiftly appeared on the scene and treated the fleeing men to a stream of invective, and even blows with the flat of his sabre, they were insufficient to halt the rush, and he found himself alone with

Thiébault and another ADC. Thiébault suggested it was time to be gone. 'He did not reply, but began to whistle while looking at the enemy skirmishers who were approaching us and crying "Prisoners! Prisoners!" Then, suddenly making up his mind, he took himself at a full gallop to the head of the troops he was waiting for.'[47] As the 32nd marched forward with grim determination, the 75th was sent to make its way round behind the enemy skirmishers. This tactic was successful, and by about 10 or 10.30 a.m., Trambasore was back in French hands, though this seems to have been partly because Lipthay had turned his main attention to the 14th.

Indeed, while Massena was leading his own division forward to plug the gap in the French line, the 14th, which was being commanded by Lebley, was subjected to the full force of the enemy's attack, both frontally and in the flank. It put up a heroic resistance, and managed to hold its main position for some time, but its advanced battalion was driven out of San Giovanni, and drew back from house to house, also making use of the hedges to slow the Austrian advance. At roughly the same time as the 85th had been attacked, Vial's brigade had also been forced to fall back a little by an enemy outflanking movement round a wood, and had noticed what was happening to the other parts of the French line. Destaing recalled:

> We had seen a rearward movement on our left, but it was not long in being repaired. The battery in front of our centre was heavily attacked and was not long in being captured, which also occasioned a disorder and a backward movement in this part. This took some of our troops on the crest of San Marco with it, and they fell back to the chapel.[48]

This withdrawal seems to have occurred at about the same time as Joubert, who had become concerned about the situation in the centre, was making his way down towards the 14th's position. He reported:

> Seeing that the left and the centre were in disorder, and that some enemy columns were to our rear, I left the right and went

to the centre. I saw General Berthier busy with the retreat. I had it made in order and sent to say that the chapel of San Marco was to be held. Vial had foreseen my wishes, and distinguished himself there.[49]

Joubert still seems to have been leading the 33rd Line at this time, and thanks to the stubborn defence of the 14th he was able to reach the plateau near Monte Ceredello safely. The 14th was drawn up there in battle order, and soon launched a counter-attack on Ocskay's men, who had taken the battery in front of them. An officer raised a cry of 'Fourteenth! Will you let them take your guns?'[50] which inspired a group of men to rush forward and seize them again. This abrupt reversal of fortune was entirely in keeping with the nature of the battle, which, in Joubert's words, consisted of 'ten hours of alternate charges and routs on both sides'.[51]

While battle was raging on the ridge and the semi-circle of hills, the Austrian forces in the Adige valley had also begun to lend their weight to the combat. Vukassovich had brought his artillery up to the flat land north of Ceraino, and from the left bank of the river had unleashed a heavy bombardment on the defences of the Pontare. Under cover of this, Prince Reuss's men had begun to make their way up the road, and were met with tremendous resistance by the 39th. 'After incredible efforts,' recounted Bonaparte, 'this [Austrian] infantry finally succeeded in capturing the defence works on the plateau.'[52] The 39th was forced back, which obliged the other French units to withdraw. Joubert wrote in his official report:

> Finally, a new disorder brought us back onto the road to Rivoli, to the entrenched plateau which had just been evacuated. Already the enemy was making his cavalry exit: already a column of 3,000 men coming from Canale took our entrenchments and brought up five pieces of cannon.[53]

Destaing commented: 'These circumstances necessitated a rapid evacuation of the crests of San Marco and the heights of San Martino [i.e., the semi-circle of hills].'[54] Almost at the same time, about 11 a.m. according

511

to the history of the 22nd Light, the French heard a double volley to their rear, on the road to Verona. It was Lusignan's column, which had finally reached its objective, and had taken a position on the southern side of the semi-circle, cutting the line of retreat to Verona and Peschiera. 'At this appearance, all looks turned towards General Bonaparte,' wrote Thiébault, 'but after a short inspection, he limited himself to saying calmly "They are ours."'[55]

Thiébault was not quite so sure about the situation, with good reason. At that moment Vial was hurriedly trying to extricate his men before they were cut off, with Köblös in hot pursuit. Ocskay was also taking advantage of the chaos to cannonade both the 39th and Vial's men with two guns he had captured. Before long, Köblös' men were filtering onto the flat land inside the semi-circle to the rear of the entrenchments that the 39th had abandoned, and penetrating south-westwards between these and Trambasore, where Massena was still in position. The head of V column, a squadron of Stabsdragoner followed by a battalion of IR Callenberg, arrived on the plateau at the top of the Pontare under heavy fire, while the rest of the troops pressed behind them. The Stabsdragoner moved forward, and three more squadrons moved up in their rear. 'It only needed an advance of few hundred paces, only the perseverance of half an hour ...',[56] commented Schels, and the French would be destroyed. 'The situation was desperate,' admitted Joubert.[57]

There was a glimmer of hope for the French, however. Sulkowski noted:

> Fortunately, the ravine which leads to the valley of the Adige goes a long way into the plain of Rivoli and where it comes out there is a house with a large enclosure. It is between this outlet and the enclosure that the road that goes to La Corona passes. All the fugitives ended up there, and it was easy to stop them.[58]

At this critical moment, Joubert encountered the Chief of Staff:

> Berthier, in a bad mood, told me that at least I should find a line to place my division. I reminded him that the general of division

was Bonaparte, and that day I only commanded the right of my division. That for the rest, only a good charge could save us.[59]

Elsewhere, he says he suggested that Berthier should take two squadrons of cavalry and charge 'on the plateau which dominates the road and where the infantry that had come from Corona was spreading out, while I, with the 14th and the other demi-brigades which had already rallied, charged the column arriving from Canale to prevent its junction with the enemy corps of battle ...'[60]

The fact that the Austrian troops that were coming down from the ridge and the hills had scattered and spread out was almost an open invitation to use cavalry against them, and it was gratefully accepted, though the French could only scrape together a small and motley collection of horsemen. According to Bonaparte's report, Leclerc (who commanded the 1st Cavalry) had been ordered to charge if the plateau were taken, and he also mentions that Lasalle was sent into the attack with 50 dragoons.[61] The total number of French cavalry involved is said by Schels to have been only 200 men. Thomas Graham was an anguished witness to the succeeding events:

I was with General Lipthay on the heights he had carried, & saw his uneasiness at the chance of a reverse by having his Right turned, which was unprotected: he received an order to advance immediately on Rivoli: it was fortunately countermanded before it could be executed. General Alvinczy himself came soon after upon the heights, instead of endeavouring to form a body there and above all to secure the Ridge next the Adige, the key of the Pass of Rivoli, He advanced towards the plain encouraging the men, who had begun to give way, to advance: he was soon left alone & being nearly surrounded was obliged to save himself: the men who still stood firm on the Ridge & the Heights, seeing the whole suite of the Commander galloping off concluded all was lost & took to their heels: this is the only way I can possibly account for the most stupid and absurd terror that the men were ever seized with ...[62]

In his journal, Graham adds a few extra details:

> The men especially of the 3rd and 4th columns, who had fought
> for near 5 hours with distinguished bravery, were much dispersed
> by the nature of the Ground; and, not having been collected &
> formed on the Heights and on the extremity of the Ridge, eagerly
> pursued the Enemy through some small woody enclosures into the
> Plain, where the foremost were attacked by a few Horsemen: these
> returning & calling out *French Cavalry*, a sudden panick spread like
> wildfire: no effort of the Officers nor of the Commander in Chief,
> who used every exertion & exposed himself much, had the smallest
> effect in rallying them: they fled in the utmost disorder & it was in
> vain to assure them that they were not pursued ...[63]

More by good luck than anything else, the French now found themselves completely relieved of pressure from one wing of the enemy army.
Moreover, the panic that had gripped the Austrian infantry was also to
assist Joubert in driving back the head of V column, because some of the
men belonging to III and IV columns had found themselves cut off by
the French cavalry, and chose to try to reach safety by way of the
Pontare. These carried off many of the troops that had reached the
plateau, and ran into the entrenchments sowing alarm and confusion,
thereby impeding all efforts at defence. At the same time, Joubert's men,
led by their general himself with musket in hand, lined the edge of the
ravine and began a plunging fire on the right flank of the troops on the
Pontare. On the other side of the ravine, the 39th returned to the attack
from the direction of Rivoli, while the French cavalry, having effected
the rout of one Austrian force, turned its attention to the head of V
column. Schels says that 'the French found little resistance',[64] as the
fugitives rushed into the tightly pressed ranks of infantry, cavalry and
artillery that were trying to climb up the narrow road of the Pontare,
and reduced them to disorder. Under fire from above, with no room to
deploy, and no place to rally the men, the Austrians were forced back to
the bottom of the valley, where Prince Reuss succeeded in regrouping
sufficiently to prevent a further French advance.

With the troops of II, III and IV columns in chaotic retreat towards their original positions on the far side of the Tasso, and V column hurled back in disorder from the plateau, the French were able to re-establish themselves on the northern arm of the semi-circle, on the ridge, and in the entrenchments of the Pontare. The manner in which the enemy had collapsed and fled made it look unlikely that there would be any renewal of the attacks on these positions for some time, which meant that the unfortunate Lusignan could now be dealt with at leisure. Lusignan realised that the bulk of the army had been driven back, but decided to try to hold his position, partly because he hoped to be able to assist with a second attempt to gain the plateau on the following day, as ordered by the Austrian disposition. In any case, for Lusignan to retreat would have brought swift and certain annihilation, but resisting until dark gave him some chance of survival. The French, however, proved to be too strong. In mid-afternoon, Lusignan's right wing was attacked by the 18th and one battalion of the 75th, some cavalry, and was bombarded by several 12pdr guns. Unable to sustain its position, it began an orderly withdrawal to a hill that was slightly farther back, where it held for an hour. Lusignan was eventually forced to move his right wing to join the left on the western side of the road to Verona, but also had to abandon this position when Rey's division finally arrived on the battlefield, and took him in the rear. Lusignan's men had mostly reached the limits of their endurance, and as they stumbled along the road to Pesina in gathering darkness, large numbers of them collapsed with fatigue, or could not keep up, and were made prisoner. The rapidly dwindling remnant found Pesina occupied by the French, and could only save themselves by striking into the mountains again.

As the fighting petered out, and Bonaparte assessed the results of the day's combat, he seems initially to have judged that Alvinczy had sustained a crushing blow from which he would not be able to recover. When he received a report during the evening which told him that Provera had actually stirred himself into activity and crossed the Adige that morning, Bonaparte must have taken the view that the greatest danger now lay on the lower Adige, and that he should switch his attention there. Accordingly, he made arrangements for Massena's division to march to support Augereau on the morning of the 15th, while he himself set off during the night to go and supervise operations against Provera. Before leaving, he gave Joubert instructions to attack Alvinczy in the morning, and gave him command of Rey's division as well as his own. However, it was not long before Bonaparte decided that he might have underestimated Alvinczy's power to restore order, and at 5 a.m. a letter was sent to Joubert from Castelnuovo making it very clear that there was still work to do before the northern flank could be considered secure:

> After having carefully reflected on the present situation of the different divisions of the army, the General-in-Chief thinks, General, that everything depends on the prompt occupation of La Corona. He would have returned to Rivoli himself, were it not for the confidence that he has in your talents and your sagacity in executing the overall dispositions that have just been made.[65]

The letter went on to authorise Joubert to retain for his reinforcement one of the demi-brigades that was supposed to march to support Augereau, in order to eliminate any risk that Joubert's attack might fail. Clearly, in Bonaparte's view, the battle of Rivoli was not quite over yet.

There was no doubt that Alvinczy was a determined man, and was not yet ready to give up. He spent the night making desperate attempts to reorganise, and issued orders for a new attack to be made on the 15th, but was not given the opportunity to carry it out. He was anticipated by Joubert, who had San Marco attacked by the 4th Light during the hours of darkness. As on the previous day, this combat escalated, and two hours before dawn, Vial's men found themselves fighting fiercely on the ridge. By daybreak, the French had gained control, and pushed the Austrians back northwards. Vial was supported by a single battalion, commanded this time by Baraguey d'Hilliers, which advanced on the flat land below him. However, like Bonaparte before him, Joubert could have done without too much action before reinforcements reached him. He admitted: 'This combat much disquieted me ... because there were large gaps in the line … and General Rey had not arrived.'[66] However, between 8 and 9 a.m., Rey's division appeared and took its place in the centre, which permitted Joubert to launch a concerted attack. Since his right and centre were being held up by the defences at San Martino, he sent Veaux with the 85th Line and 29th Light to outflank them via Caprino. They were to advance over the heights behind the village and try to reach Madonna della Corona, thus cutting the enemy line of retreat. The shaky and demoralised Austrian troops had lost much of their inclination to fight, and Joubert's well co-ordinated movements were too much for them. They were forced back, and when it was perceived that the French were outflanking them, the Austrians broke and fled. After that, there was nothing but a mad scramble for safety, sometimes quite literally, as a few desperate men took routes down the cliffs to the valley. As there was no organised opposition to their advance, the French resumed their positions at Madonna della Corona and Ferrara without difficulty. 'The success was beyond my expectations,'[67] Joubert told Bonaparte.

There was no more fighting near Rivoli after this, but there was still a small drama to be played out under the walls of Mantua before the attempt to relieve the fortress was completely over. At the same time as Joubert was driving Alvinczy back from Madonna della Corona, Provera's advance-guard reached Mantua, and came within a whisker of capturing San Giorgio. Since his hussars wore cloaks like those of the French 1st Hussars, they were nearly allowed to ride straight into the place unopposed, but a French sergeant became suspicious at their approach and gave the alarm just in time. Having failed to take San Giorgio, Provera was doomed, as the 5,000 men he then had at his disposal stood no chance against the combined forces of Sérurier, Victor, Guieu, Dugua and Massena, which Bonaparte had concentrated in the nearby area. Provera's attempt to link with Wurmser on the 16th, by capturing La Favorita and opening a way to the Citadel, was countered by seven times his number of men, and after a brief but ferocious action, he had to surrender with his entire division. 'So, here we are in the same positions as before!' Bonaparte wrote to Joubert on 17 January. 'M. Alvinczy cannot say the same.'[68]

NOTES

1. Napoleon. *Correspondance de Napoléon Ier publiée par ordre de l'empereur Napoléon III*. Paris, 1858–69, no. 1197.
2. Ibid., no. 1196.
3. Chevrier, E. *Le général Joubert d'après sa correspondance*. Paris, 1884, p. 62.
4. Napoleon. 1858–69, op. cit., no. 1196.
5. Ibid., no. 1208.
6. Chevrier, op. cit., p. 63.
7. Ibid., p. 62.
8. Ibid., p. 69.
9. Napoleon. 1858–69, op. cit., no. 1217.
10. Ibid., no. 1213.
11. Ibid., no. 1250.
12. Ibid., no. 1201.
13. Ibid., no. 1298.
14. Ibid., no. 1344.
15. Alberghini, G. B., don. *Gli austro-galli in val di Caprino (1796-1801) memoria storica*. Verona, 1880, p. 55.
16. Schels, J. B. 'Die Begebenheiten in und um Mantua vom 16 September 1796 bis 4 Februar 1797; nebst der Schlacht von Rivoli.' *Oesterreichische Militärische Zeitschrift*, Bd. 2; Bd. 3; Bd. 4 (1832), p. 269.
17. Aspinall-Oglander, C. *Freshly Remembered: The Story of Thomas Graham, Lord Lynedoch*. London, 1956, pp. 98-9.
18. Napoleon. *Correspondance inédite officielle et confidentielle de Napoléon Bonaparte: avec les cours étrangères, les princes, les ministres et les généraux français et étrangers, en Italie, en Allemagne, et en Egypte*. Paris, 1809, II, p. 376.
19. Schels, op. cit., p. 270.
20. Napoleon. 1858–69, op. cit., no. 1320.
21. Schels, op. cit., pp. 274–5.
22. Ibid., p. 277.
23. Ibid., pp. 121–35.
24. Ibid., p. 136. It is intriguing to note that this passage is followed quite closely in Massena's memoirs, but with one essential difference. The editor, General Koch, clearly states that his source for most of the detailed information regarding the 1796–7 campaign is Schels, but at times he makes strange use of it. Here he says that 'Alvinczy gave

instructions to the commanders of the various columns that were so obscure that those of the main columns did not know ...' etc. (See vol II, p. 281.) It remains to be seen whether this is a mistake or a wilful mistranslation intended to make the Austrian commander look foolish.

25. See Jomini, A.-H., baron. *Histoire critique et militaire des guerres de la Révolution.* Paris, 1820–24, IX, p. 262.

26. Laugier, J.-R. *Les cahiers du capitaine Laugier. – De la guerre et de l'anarchie, ou Mémoires historiques des campagnes et aventures d'un capitaine du 27me régiment d'infanterie légère par Jérome-Roland Laugier. Publiés d'après le manuscrit original par Léon G. Pélissier.* Aix, 1893, p. 128.

27. Vivenot, A., Ritter von. *Vertrauliche Briefe des Freiherrn von Thugut.* Vienna, 1872, II, pp. 10–11.

28. Schels, op. cit., pp. 241–2.

29. Holland Rose, J. 'Despatches of Colonel Thomas Graham on the Italian Campaign of 1796–1797.' *The English Historical Review*, 14 (1899), p. 323.

30. Napoleon. 1858–69, op. cit., no. 1373.

31. Ibid., no. 1377.

32. Laugier, op.cit., p. 117.

33. Chevrier, op. cit., p. 71.

34. Napoleon. 1858–69, op. cit., no. 1379.

35. Ibid., no. 1381.

36. Alberghini, op. cit., pp. 57–60.

37. Sulkowski also says midnight, while Berthier even says 11 p.m. Chevrier, op. cit., p. 80.

38. Ibid., p 72.

39. Napoleon. *Mémoires pour servir à l'histoire de France, sous le regne de Napoléon, écrits sous sa dictée à Sainte-Hélène, par les généraux qui ont partagé sa captivité.* Paris, 1829, II, p. 71.

40. Ibid., IV, p. 58.

41. Holland Rose, op. cit., p. 327.

42. Napoleon. 1829, op. cit., I, p. 447.

43. Ibid., IV, p. 59.

44. Alberghini, op. cit., p. 61.

45. Thiébault, P.-C. *Mémoires du général Baron Thiébault. Publiés sous les auspices de sa fille Mlle. Claire Thiébault d'après le manuscrit original par Fernand Calmettes.* Paris, 1895–96, II, p. 52.

46. Napoleon. 1829, op. cit., II, p. 447.
47. Thiébault, op. cit., II, p. 55.
48. Fabry, J. G. A. *Rapports historiques des régiments de l'armée d'Italie pendant la campagne de 1796–1797.* Paris, 1905, p. 321.
49. Massena, A. *Mémoires de Massena, rédigés d'après les documents qu'il a laissés et sur ceux du dépôt de la guerre et du dépôt des fortifications, par le général Koch.* Paris, 1848–50, II, p. 523.
50. Napoleon. 1858–69, op. cit., no. 1399.
51. Chevrier, op. cit., pp. 76–7.
52. Napoleon. 1829, op. cit., IV, p. 63.
53. Massena, op. cit., II, p. 523.
54. Fabry, op. cit., p. 322.
55. Thiébault, op. cit., II, p. 57.
56. Schels, op. cit., p. 17.
57. Massena, op. cit., II, p. 523.
58. Reinhard, M. *Avec Bonaparte en Italie; d'après les lettres inédites de son aide de camp Joseph Sulkowski.* Paris, 1946, p. 203.
59. Chevrier, op. cit., pp. 77–8.
60. Massena, op. cit., II, p. 523.
61. Napoleon. 1858–69, op. cit., no. 1399.
62. Holland Rose, op. cit., pp. 324–5.
63. Ibid., p. 328.
64. Schels, op. cit., p. 21.
65. Napoleon. 1858–69, op. cit., no. 1385. During the Empire, Napoleon gave the title 'Duke of Rivoli' to Massena, in recognition of his contribution to the victory. However, as Chevrier points out, it would seem that Joubert played the far more important role in the battle. Had Joubert still been alive, no one would have had more right to the title than he, the more so if one considers the great responsibility he was given on the second day of combat there.
66. Massena, op. cit., II, p. 524.
67. Napoleon. 1809, op. cit., II, p. 391.
68. Napoleon. 1858 69, op. cit., no. 1395.

19

AFTERMATH

Bonaparte's narrow victory at Rivoli and his capture of Provera meant that the fall of Mantua was inevitable. The only thing preventing an Austrian surrender was Wurmser's determination to spin out his provisions as long as possible. On 24 January, Alvinczy received a letter from Wurmser saying: 'he could feed his troops until 28 January, and that he would strive to hold on for a few days longer still'.[1] On the 29th (Scorza believes it was the 30th), however, Wurmser held a council of war with his senior generals, which came to the conclusion that it was no longer possible to defer making contact with the French and seeking terms for an honourable capitulation.

This was a somewhat delicate undertaking because the Austrians hoped to be able to obtain important concessions from the French, and did not want to give the impression of being desperate. Colonel Klenau was therefore sent on an errand to Roverbella, in the hope that the French might take the opportunity to broach the subject of a capitulation first. The French were no doubt expecting this, and Sérurier conveniently dropped the necessary hint. On the same day, Wurmser sent Bonaparte a note outlining his conditions, which included allowing the garrison to go free.

According to a version of events given in his memoirs, which Schels thinks is a complete fabrication, Bonaparte was present incognito at one of the meetings between Klenau and Sérurier, and spent half an hour writing his replies to Wurmser's demands, after which he made himself known to Klenau, who took the mostly negative answer back to Mantua.[2] Whatever the truth of this little anecdote, which is not mentioned in Austrian sources, it is certain that Bonaparte was not personally present for the rest of the negotiations. He was so confident of the eventual outcome that he saw no reason not to move on to the next task facing him, which was the continuation of the expedition against the Papal States, so hastily suspended three weeks before. 'I left my instructions with General Sérurier and I departed for Bologna,'[3] he told the Directory on 1 February.

Sérurier's instructions were to insist on the original offer that Bonaparte had made to Wurmser, namely that the Field Marshal, his generals and a detachment of specially selected men could go free, but the rest of the garrison would be made prisoner. In the face of total French inflexibility, Wurmser eventually had to agree to these terms, and the documents were signed on 2 February. On the 4th, the first Austrian troops filed out of the Citadel, and deposited their weapons on the glacis. Since the capitulation allowed them to return home, on condition that they did not serve against France until a similar number of French prisoners had been sent back, they then marched away eastwards to await exchange. They were followed by two more columns of men, which left on the 5th and 6th.

The fall of Mantua was really the end of effective Austrian resistance to the French in Italy, and the fighting that followed was little more than a short, anti-climactic coda to the main campaign. The Archduke Charles, the Emperor's brother, and probably the best Austrian general of his day, was appointed to command the army in Italy, but could do nothing to stave off defeat. The broken, weary and completely demoralised remnant of his forces showed little relish for action, and when Bonaparte recommenced operations against them in the middle of March he had no difficulty in forcing them to withdraw. The Tagliamento was crossed with ease, and by the end of the month Bonaparte had also crossed the mountains separating Italy from Austria. On the 31st, he sent a letter from Klagenfurt, appealing to the Archduke Charles to use his influence to persuade the Emperor to begin peace negotiations.

There was little else the Austrians could do. On 2 April, with Bonaparte's troops now 150 miles from Vienna and the army incapable of halting them, the Emperor decided to turn to diplomacy.[4] To begin with, Bonaparte agreed to a five-day cease-fire, starting on the 7th, which was later extended to the 20th. On the 15th, Bonaparte received the Austrian plenipotentiaries at Leoben. It did not take too long to hammer out a preliminary peace agreement, and this was signed on the 18th, in a pavilion standing in the garden of a house near Leoben. Bonaparte's first campaign as commander-in-chief was definitively over, one year and eight days after the Austrians had attacked his forces on the Riviera.

By any measure, his achievements during that year had been absolutely extraordinary. At its beginning, the French had been uneasily perched on the edge of the Ligurian mountains, and their previous commander had been talking of a retreat into Provence. Now they were masters of the whole of northern Italy, having defeated Piedmont in the space of a few days, driven and harried the Austrians for several hundred miles, and turned back four attempts to relieve Mantua. Every hostile power in Italy, including Naples and the Papal States, had been reduced to grudging, sometimes humiliating acquiescence. How had Bonaparte done it? It was a question that a writer, Antoine Arnault, asked Bonaparte himself when he met him in Italy:

> With few exceptions, he said, it is to the most numerous troops that victory is assured. The art of war therefore consists in finding oneself with superior numbers at the point where one wishes to fight. Is your army less numerous than that of the enemy? Do not leave the enemy time to unite his forces: surprise him in his movements, and moving rapidly on the various corps which you have had the art to isolate, arrange your manoeuvres in such a way that you can oppose your whole army to army divisions in every encounter. It is in this way that with an army half the strength of that of the enemy you will always be stronger than he on the field of battle. It is in this way that I successively annihilated the armies of Beaulieu, Wurmser, Alvinczy and Prince Charles.[']

It sounds simple, but of course if it had been simple, everyone would have done it. Bonaparte's remarkable achievement was to put the theories he had learned from books into practice. The factors that made this possible were many.

His incontestable superiority as a strategist was partly based on a profound knowledge of the geography and military history of the campaign area. Using this knowledge, he was able to analyse a military situation, calculate speeds and timings of marches, and exploit his formidable power to envisage and assess all the possible scenarios he might be faced with. As he himself once said, it was not genius that suggested what he should do, but reflection. His skill at thinking through the scenarios was such that he rarely, if ever, seems to have been taken completely by surprise, nor been at a loss as to what to do if his initial assessment proved to be at fault. He certainly made mistakes, but his ability to recover from them was far superior to that of his adversaries.

Making a correct analysis and coming up with a good plan was, of course, only a first step. This had to be followed by issuing clear instructions. Here, the clarity of Bonaparte's thought found natural expression in the precision of his orders, which Berthier turned into equally lucid written form.

This would not have been much use if the orders had not been obeyed, but most of Bonaparte's generals seem to have accepted his authority, though sometimes only grudgingly. Certainly, not all of them were eating out of the palm of his hand, and it is perceptible that during the course of the campaign Bonaparte began to build a team of subordinates who obviously had faith in him, and had the inclination and the ability to do what he asked. However, Bonaparte was extremely lucky both to have the raw material available that could be built into a good team, and to have a fair amount of freedom when it came to making appointments and giving promotion.

The interrelationship between Bonaparte and his army was crucial to the success of the campaign. Once again, he was very fortunate in the raw material he was given, which was well-suited to his methods. Especially important was the army's ability to move at speed, which he regularly exploited to embarrass his opponents. Moreover, there was a great deal of drive, initiative, intelligence, enthusiasm and flexibility among officers and soldiers. To a certain extent this was already there, and to some extent Bonaparte brought it out through his unrivalled ability to dominate and inspire men. As Thomas Graham noted in his report on Rivoli, Bonaparte's willingness to take great risks during that battle 'can only be accounted for by his confidence in the bravery of his troops & their implicit confidence in him'.[6] The campaign could be called a triumph of building and maintaining morale in the face of appalling difficulties of administration and supply.

A final factor was Bonaparte's almost incredible capacity for work. One of the first things that Berthier noted about his new commander was that 'he works a lot', which is not a comment that should be underestimated, given that it was made by a man who was said to be capable of working for days on end without any sleep at all. Periods of crisis would see Bonaparte racing everywhere, either by carriage or on horseback, inspecting, commanding, overseeing, cajoling and encouraging anyone and everyone. Even before a crisis was over, Bonaparte would move on to the next round of business as if rest were something that positively irritated him.

In the two centuries since it took place, the 1796–7 campaign has been largely overshadowed by the later triumphs of Austerlitz and Jena, not to mention the glitter of the Napoleonic Empire. In part, this may be because there were by then many people who were conscious that Napoleon was moulding the history of Europe, and were keen to record their involvement in the process, giving us an abundance of familiar accounts. The contribution of writers like Tolstoy should also not be forgotten. But were Austerlitz and Jena really greater achievements than Montenotte, the crossing of the Po, or Rivoli? This must be a matter of opinion, of course, but it is worth pointing out that in 1805 and 1806 Napoleon had various advantages that he did not have in 1796–7. For one thing, he controlled French policy and diplomacy and could call on the resources of the whole country. Moreover, he was a more experienced commander, and had an army that was much better prepared. If his earlier victories were not so comprehensive or decisive as the later ones, they were still remarkable examples of the skill of a novice commander in his mid-twenties, who possessed limited authority and limited resources, and was beset with many other difficulties. It is also arguable that the Italian campaign should not be judged on individual actions. Indeed, one of its most impressive features is the way that Bonaparte strung together a whole series of victories under varying conditions over the period of a whole year. Never again was Bonaparte to have such a sustained

THE ROAD TO RIVOLI

period of success in such difficult circumstances as he did in Italy. In many ways, it might be argued, the 1796–7 campaign was his finest achievement as a general.

NOTES

1. Schels, J. B. 'Die Begebenheiten in und um Mantua vom 16 September 1796 bis 4 Februar 1797; nebst der Schlacht von Rivoli.' *Oesterreichische Militärische Zeitschrift*, Bd. 2; Bd. 3; Bd. 4 (1832), p. 176.
2. See Napoleon. *Mémoires pour servir à l'histoire de France, sous le regne de Napoléon, écrits sous sa dictée à Sainte-Hélène, par les généraux qui ont partagé sa captivité*. Paris, 1829, III, pp. 464–6.
3. Napoleon. *Correspondance de Napoléon Ier publiée par ordre de l'empereur Napoléon III*. Paris, 1858–69, no. 1435.
4. There was a certain air of nervousness in Vienna. Thugut complained in a letter dated 6 April that Prince Starhemberg had issued instructions to some ministers and members of the Imperial family to pack and be ready to leave. See Vivenot, A., Ritter von. *Vertrauliche Briefe des Freiherrn von Thugut*. Vienna, 1872, II, p. 27.
5. Arnault, A. V. *Souvenirs d'un sexagénaire*. Paris, 1833, III, pp. 14–15.
6. Holland Rose, J. 'Despatches of Colonel Thomas Graham on the Italian Campaign of 1796–1797.' *The English Historical Review*, 14 (1899), p. 324.

BIBLIOGRAPHY

A. B., ed. *Histoire régimentaire et divisionnaire de l'armée d'Italie, commandé par le général Bonaparte. Historiques des demi-brigades, rédigés en vertu des ordres du général en chef Bonaparte, par les chefs de corps ou les conseils d'Administration, recueillis par A. B.* Paris, 1843

Abrantès, Duchess of. *Mémoires de Mme la duchesse d'Abrantès.* Paris, 1905–13

Abtheilung für Kriegsgeschichte des k. k. Kriegs-Archives, ed. *Feldzüge des Prinzen Eugen von Savoyen.* Vienna, 1876–92

Adlow, E. *Napoleon in Italy, 1796–1797.* Boston, 1948

Agnelli, G. 'An IV de la République française. Berthollet, Labillardière, Monge, Thouin, à Lodi.' *Revue des études napoléoniennes,* 45 (1939): 29–34

— 'La battaglia al ponte di Lodi e l'inizio della settimana napoleonica lodigiana.' *Archivio storico lombardo,* 60 (1933): 1–73

— 'Monumenti, lapidi, ricordi sparsi sull'itinerario della prima campagna napoleonica in Italia.' *Archivio storico lombardo,* s. 8, v. 5 (1954–55): 382–97

— 'Una piccola città lombarda durante la Repubblica Cisalpina (maggio 1796–aprile 1799).' *Archivio storico italiano,* s. 5, v. 24 (1899): 193–248

— 'Une inscription napoléonienne à Casalpusterlengo/Une nouvelle inscription napoléonienne à Lodi.' *Revue des études napoléoniennes,* 44 (1939): 116–17

Alberghini, G. B., Don. *Gli austro-galli in val di Caprino (1796–1801) memoria storica.* Verona, 1880

Amo, E. 'Battaglia di Ceva e della Pedaggera 16 aprile 1796. Compendio critico della prima fase delle operazioni militari della campagna di guerra del 1796, con particolare riferimento alle battaglie di Ceva e della Pedaggera.' *Bollettino della Società per gli Studi Storici, Archeologici ed Artistici della Provincia di Cuneo,* no. 58 (1968): 145–56

Amoretti, G., Gen., ed. *Cosseria 1796: guerra, popolazione, territorio.* Turin, 1996

Andréossy, A.-F. *Opérations des pontonniers français en Italie pendant les campagnes de 1795 à 1797.* Paris, 1843

Anon. *The Annual Register.* London, 1758–

Anon. *Biographie nationale de Belgique.* Brussels, 1866–1986

Anon. 'Bonaparte au combat de Montenotte (12 avril 1796), suivi des instructions de Martinel à Bagetti pour les aquarelles de Montenotte et Monte Legino.' *Le carnet de la sabretache,* 7 (1899): 350–71

Anon. *Briefe aus Italien. Ein Beitrag zur Geschichte und Charakteristik der Österreichischen Arméen in Italien in den Feldzügen, 1794–97.* Tübingen, 1798

Anon. 'Cronaca di Codevilla 1700–1809.' Codevilla, 1809?

Anon. *Der Grosse Brockhaus.* Leipzig, 1928

Anon. 'La générale La Harpe au Directoire.' *La nouvelle revue rétrospective,* 10 (1899): 370–4

Anon. 'Les Français en Allemagne.' *Carnet de la Sabretache,* X (1902): 139–41

Anon. 'Les généraux Bon et Duphot.' *La Révolution française,* 7 (1884): 41–4

Anon. *The New Encyclopædia Britannica.* Chicago, 1991

Anon. 'Tra il Pian Bombarda e Monte Negino Menard e Massena sconfiggono gli Austriaci.' In *Caironotizie,* 4–5. Cairo Montenotte, 1996

Anon. 'Une lettre du général Clarke au général Berthier (15 août 1796).' *La nouvelle revue rétrospective,* 10 (1899): 263–4

Anson, W. V., Capt. *The Life of John Jervis, Admiral Lord St Vincent.* London, 1913

Argan, G. C. 'Bonaparte in Italia. Dal Diario inedito della Marchesa Del Carretto. "Journal de ce qui est arrivé à Lesegno à l'occasion de l'invasion des François en Piemont. (Extrait des Mémoires écrites chaque jour par la Marquise Carret elle même)."' *La Cultura,* Jan–Mar (1932): 16–35

Arnault, A. V. *Biographie nouvelle des contemporains.* Paris, 1820–5

— *Souvenirs d'un sexagénaire.* Paris, 1833

Arndt, E. M. *Reisen durch einen Theil Teutschlands.* Leipzig, 1804

Arneth, A. *Geschichte Maria Theresias.* Vienna, 1863–79

Arrivabene, G., Count. *Memorie della mia vita, 1795–1859.* Florence, 1879

Aspinall-Oglander, C. *Freshly Remembered: The Story of Thomas Graham, Lord Lynedoch.* London, 1956

Augereau, P.-F.-C. 'Le général de division Augereau à ses frères d'armes.' (handbill). Verona, 1796

Augusta, J. M. 'Le sabre d'honneur du sergent Coujard.' *Revue des études napoléoniennes,* 43 (1936): 116–22

Bacler d'Albe, L.-A.-J. *Carte générale du théâtre de la guerre en Italie et dans les Alpes.* Milan, 1798

Balteau, J., and others, eds. *Dictionnaire de biographie française.* Paris, 1933–

Bapst, G., and 'W'. 'Le tambour d'Arcole.' *Intermédiaire des chercheurs et curieux,* 42 (1900): 18–21

Barnhart, L., ed. *The New Century Cyclopedia of Names.* New York, 1954

Barton, W. *Campagna Miravigliosa: or an Exact Journal of the Imperial Army's Advance into, and Incampments in Italy, under the command of Prince Eugene of Savoy.* London, 1702

Baur, S. *Allgemeines historisch-biographisch-literarisches Handwörterbuch aller merkwürdigen Personen, die in dem ersten Jahrzehnt des neunzehnten Jahrhunderts gestorben sind.* Ulm, 1816

Beamten des Kriegsarchivs, ed. *Inventar des Kriegsarchivs Wien, Publikationen des Österreichischen Staatsarchivs. II. Serie: Inventare Österreichische Archive: VIII.* Vienna, 1953

Bellcrive, J. A. B., de. *Histoire des campagnes de Monseigneur le duc de Vendosme.* Paris, 1715

Belletti, G. D. *Una missione Bellunese al generale Bonaparte nel 1797: con appendice di documenti inediti.* Belluno, 1898

Benotte, C., de la. 'Lavallette.' *Intermédiaire des chercheurs et curieux,* 41 (1900): 98

Benvenuti, M. 'Curioso documento.' *Archivio storico lombardo,* 9 (1882): 145–8

Bergadani, R. *Vittorio Amedeo III (1726–1796).* Turin, 1939

Bertaud, J.-P. *The Army of the French Revolution.* Princeton, 1988

Berthelot, P.-E.-M., and others, eds. *La grande encyclopédie.* Paris, 1887–1902

Bertrand, H. G., Gen. *Cahiers de Sainte-Hélène. Journal 1816–1817.* Paris, 1951

Besancenet, A., de, ed. *Le général Dommartin en Italie et en Egypte. Ordres de service. – Correspondances. 1786–1799.* Paris, 1880

— *Le portefeuille d'un général de la République. Une armée sous la Convention. Campagne de 1796–7. Coup d'Etat de fructidor. Armée d'Allemagne. Armée d'Angleterre.* Paris, 1877

— *Un officier royaliste au service de la République; d'après les lettres inédites du général Dommartin, 1786–1799.* Paris, 1876

Bianchi, N. *Storia della monarchia piemontese.* Rome, 1877–85

Bigarré, A.-J. *Mémoires du général Bigarré: aide de camp du roi Joseph, 1775–1813.* Paris, 1893

Birago, C., Gen. 'La difesa di Cosseria.' *Antologia italiana, Giornale di scienze lettere ed arti,* 2 (1847): 632–46

Blanning, T. C. W. *The Origins of the French Revolutionary Wars.* London, 1986

Blumer, M. L. 'La commission pour la recherche des objets de science et arts en Italie (1796–1797).' *La Révolution française,* 87 (1934): 62–88, 124–50, 222–59

Bodart, G. *Losses of Life in Modern Wars, Austria-Hungary; France.* Oxford, 1916

Bonaparte, J. *Mémoires et correspondance.* Paris, 1853–4

Borel, J. 'Bonaparte a Rivoli (1797). (Commentario iconografico).' *Rassegna storica del Risorgimento,* 23 (1936): 423–30

Bosco, U., and others, eds. *Dizionario enciclopedico italiano.* Rome, 1955–61

Botta, C. *Storia d'Italia dal 1789 al 1814.* unknown, 1824

Boursin, E., ed. *Dictionnaire de la Révolution Française.* Paris, 1893

Bouvier, F. *Bonaparte en Italie, 1796.* Paris, 1899

— 'La révolte de Pavie (23–26 mai 1796).' *Revue historique de la Révolution française,* 2; 3 (1911–12): 519–39; 72–89, 257–75, 424–46

— 'Le passage du Pô (7 mai 1796).' *Le carnet de la sabretache,* 7 (1899): 521–34

Brett-James, E. A. *General Graham, Lord Lynedoch.* London, 1959

Broglie, V.-F., de. *Correspondance inédite … Pour servir à l'histoire de la Guerre de Sept Ans.* Paris, 1903

Caldwell, R. J. *The Era of the French Revolution: A Bibliography of the History of Western Civilization, 1789–1799.* New York, 1985

Capra, C. *L'età rivoluzionaria e napoleonica in Italia, 1796–1815.* Turin, 1978

Carboneri, G. *La battaglia di Napoleone a Mondovì da ms. contemporaneo, con notizie sull'autore e dati illustrativi.* Mondovì, 1938

Carnot, Capt. 'La bataille de Lonato racontée par un témoin.' *Le carnet de la sabretache*, s. 2, v. 5 (1906): 557–60

Carnot, L.-N.-M. *Correspondance générale de Carnot.* Paris, 1892–1907

Caron, P. *Manuel pratique pour l'étude de la Révolution Française.* Paris, 1947

Caron, P., and others, eds. *Répertoire méthodique de l'histoire moderne et contemporaine de la France.* Paris, 1899–1914

Cary, J. 'Seat of the War in Italy. A Map of the Duchy of Mantua, the Territory of Verona and Surrounding Parts.' London, 1796

Casalis, G. *Dizionario geografico, storico-statistico-commerciale degli stati di S. M. il Re di Sardegna, compilato per cura del Prof Goffredo Casalis dottore di Belle Lettere, opera molto utile agli impiegati nei pubblici e privati Uffizi, a tutte le persone applicate al Foro della milizia, al Comercio e singolarmente agli amatori di cose patrie.* Turin, 1833–56

Catalano, F., Moscati, R., and Valsecchi, F., eds. *L'Italia nel Risorgimento* vol. 8, *Storia d'Italia.* Verona, 1964

Chabrol de Volvic, G. J. G. *Statistiques des provinces de Savone, d'Oneille, d'Acqui et de partie de la province de Mondovì, formant l'ancien département de Montenotte.* Paris, 1824

Chandler, D. G. *The Art of Warfare in the Age of Marlborough.* Staplehurst, 1990
— *The Campaigns of Napoleon.* London, 1966
— *Dictionary of the Napoleonic Wars.* London, 1979

Chandler, D. G., ed. *Napoleon's Marshals.* London, 1987

Charavay, E. 'Le général Joubert.' *La Révolution française,* 7 (1884): 460–4

Chevrier, E. *Le général Joubert d'après sa correspondance.* Paris, 1884

Chilosi, C., Oliveri, L., and Ferrando, L. *Bonaparte in Val Bormida. Paesi, paesaggi, campi di battaglia.* Millesimo, 1996

Chuquet, A. 'Une lettre de Desportes sur le général La Harpe, 19 novembre 1792.' *Annales révolutionnaires,* 1 (1908): 318–19

Ciampini, R. 'Nuovi documenti sulla prima campagna d'Italia (marzo–giugno 1796).' *Rivista italiana di studi napoleonici,* 9 (1970): 61–76

Ciravegna, M. 'La ritirata strategica dell'esercito piemontese dal 21 al 27 aprile del 1796.' *Rassegna storica del Risorgimento,* 29 (1942): 683–7

Clausewitz, C. P., von. *La campagne de 1796 en Italie.* Trans. Colin, J-L-A. Paris, 1899

Cleyet-Michaud, R. 'Un diplomate de la Révolution: François Cacault et ses plans de conquête de l'Italie (1793–1796).' *Revue d'histoire diplomatique*, 86 (1972): 308–32

Cohen, E. A., and Gooch, J. *Military Misfortunes: The Anatomy of Failure in War.* New York, 1990

Coiffier de Verseux, H. L., Baron. *Dictionnaire biographique et historique des hommes marquans de la fin du dix-huitième siècle.* London, 1800

Coignet, J.-R. *Les Cahiers du Capitaine Coignet.* Paris, 1883

Colbert, N. J. *Traditions et souvenirs ou Mémoires touchant le temps et la vie du général Auguste Colbert (1793–1809).* Paris, 1863–74

Colin, J.-L.-A. *Etudes sur la campagne de 1796–1797 en Italie.* Paris, 1898
— *L'éducation militaire de Napoléon.* Paris, 1900

Comeau de Charry, S. J. d., Baron. *Souvenirs des guerres d'Allemagne pendant la Révolution et l'Empire.* Paris, 1900

Comoli Mandracci, V. 'Paesaggio e guerra.' Paper presented at Cosseria 1796, guerra, popolazione, territorio, Cosseria 1996

Coniglio, G., ed. *Mantova; la storia.* Mantua, 1958–65

Conterno, G. 'Una cronaca inedita di èta napoleonica in val Bormida.' *Atti e Memorie della Società Savonese di Storia Patria,* XIX (1985): 110–24

Costa de Beauregard, C. A. *Un homme d'autrefois: souvenirs recueillis par son arrière-petit-fils.* Paris, 1879

Coston, F. G., Baron de. *Biographie des premières années de Napoléon Bonaparte.* Paris, 1840

Cottreau, G. 'Léon Aune, deuxième grenadier de France.' *Le carnet de la sabretache,* 3 (1895): 156–65

Cronin, V. *Napoleon.* London, 1990

Damamme, J.-C. *Lannes.* Paris, 1987

Dargenty, G. *Le Baron Gros, Les artistes célèbres.* Paris, 1887

Decker, C., von. *Der Feldzug in Italien in den Jahren 1796 und 1797, bearbeitet von C. von Decker, Major im Königlich preussischen General-stabe; mit einer Operations Karte, welche zugleich des Plan von Mantua und das Schlachtfeld von Rivoli enthält, und ein chronologisches Register.* Berlin & Posen, 1825

Delavoye, A. M. *Life of Thomas Graham, Lord Lynedoch.* London, 1880

Delhorbe, C.-R. 'Retouches à la biographie d'Amédée Laharpe.' *Revue historique vaudoise* (1959, 1964): 24–37, 105–56

Derrécagaix, V. B. *Le maréchal Berthier*. Paris, 1904

— *Nos campagnes au Tyrol. 1797–1799–1805–1809*. Paris, 1910

Desaix, L.-C.-A. *Journal de voyage du général Desaix, Suisse et Italie (1797)*. Paris, 1907

Desjardins, C.-L.-G. *Campagnes des Français en Italie, ou histoire militaire, politique et philosophique de la Révolution*. Paris, 1797–8

Desvernois, N. P. *Mémoires du général baron Desvernois ... d'après les manuscrits originaux, avec une introduction et des notes par A. Dufourcq. 1789–1815*. Paris, 1898

Di Renzo, L., and Salmoiraghi, A. *Aprile 1796*. Cairo Montenotte, 1996

Dixon, N. F. *On the Psychology of Military Incompetence*. London, 1979

Du Teil, J. *Rome, Naples et le Directoire. Armistices et traités 1796–1797*. Paris, 1902

Dubouloz-Dupas, F., and Folliet, A. *Le général Dupas (1761–1823). Italie, Egypte, Grande Armée (1792–1813)*. Paris, 1899

Duffy, C. J. *The Army of Frederick the Great*. London, 1974

— *The Army of Maria Theresa*. London, 1977

— *Austerlitz, 1805*. London, 1977

— *Fire and Stone: The Science of Fortress Warfare 1660–1860*. Newton Abbot, 1975

— *The Fortress in the Age of Vauban and Frederick the Great 1660–1789*. London, 1985

— *Frederick the Great*. London, 1985

— *The Military Experience in the Age of Reason*. London, 1987

— *Siege Warfare: The Fortress in the Early Modern World 1494–1660*. London, 1979

Dupont-Ferrier, G. 'Trois lettres inédites d'un caporal-fourrier aux armées des Alpes et d'Italie (1795–1797). Un récit nouveau de la bataille de Rivoli.' *Annuaire-bulletin de la société de l'histoire de France* (1929): 133–42

Dupuy, R. E., and Dupuy, T. N. *Encyclopedia of Military History*. London, 1970

Durieux, J. 'Bonaparte au pont d'Arcole.' *Revue des études napoléoniennes*, 2 (1912): 182–9

—'Le général Beyrand (1768–1796).' *Le carnet de la sabretache*, s. 3, v. 1 (1913): 557–68

— 'Les vingt-cinq cavaliers d'Arcole (17 novembre 1795 [sic]).' *Revue des études napoléoniennes*, 15 (1919): 225–34

Duval, C. 'La 19e demi-brigade à l'armée d'Italie (1793–1796) et le brigadier-général Dichat de Toisinge.' *Mémoires et documents publiés par la société savoisienne d'histoire et d'archéologie*, 36 (1897): 509–51

Elting, J. R. *Swords Around a Throne: Napoleon's Grande Armée.* London, 1989

Ersch, J. S., and Gruber, J. G., eds. *Allgemeine Encyclopädie.* Leipzig, 1818–1889

Esposito, V. J., and Elting, J. R. *A Military History and Atlas of the Napoleonic Wars.* London, 1964

Fabry, J. G. A. *Histoire de l'armée d'Italie (1796–1797).* Paris, 1900–14

— *Mémoires sur la campagne de 1796 en Italie.* Paris, 1905

— *Rapports historiques des régiments de l'armée d'Italie pendant la campagne de 1796–1797.* Paris, 1905

Fantelli, G. E. 'Spionaggio militare a Padova durante la prima campagna napoleonica in Italia (1796–1797).' *Bollettino del museo civico di Padova*, 49 (1960): 141–50

Fantin des Odoards, L. F. *Journal du Général Fantin des Odoards. Étapes d'un officier de la grande armée 1800–1830.* Paris, 1895

Ferrabino, A., and others, eds. *Dizionario biografico degli Italiani.* Rome, 1960–

Forrest, A. *Soldiers of the French Revolution.* Durham, 1990

Fournier, E. *L'ésprit dans l'histoire. Recherches et curiosités sur les mots historiques.* Paris, 1879

Foy, M. S., Gen. *Histoire de la guerre de la Péninsule sous Napoléon, précédé d'un tableau politique et militaire des puissances belligérantes ... publiés par Mme la Comtesse Foy.* Paris, 1827

Franceschetto, G. 'Il memoriale di P. A. Berti sugli anni 1796–1797.' *Bollettino del museo civico di Padova*, 50 (1961): 201–33

Gachot, E. *Histoire militaire de Massena. La première campagne d'Italie (1795–1798).* Paris, 1901

— 'Le siège de Cosseria, 13 avril 1796. Documents inédits.' *La nouvelle revue*, n.s., v. 12 (1901): 356–64

Gallavresi, G., and Laurani, F. 'L'invasione francese in Milano (1796). Da memorie inedite di Don Francesco Nava.' *Archivio storico lombardo*, s. 3, v. 18 (1902): 89–140, 318–60

Gandilhon, R., and Samaran, C., eds. *Bibliographie générale des travaux historiques et archéologiques publiés par les sociétés savantes de la France* vol. III. Paris, 1951

Garros, L. *Quel roman que ma vie! Itinéraire de Napoléon Bonaparte (1769–1821)*. Paris, 1947

Gerbaix di Sonnaz, C. A., de. 'Gli ultimi anni di regno di Vittorio Amedeo III re di Sardegna.' *Miscellanea di storia italiana*, 49 (1918): 271–452

Girault, P.-R. *Les campagnes d'un musicien d'état-major pendant la République et l'Empire, 1791–1810*. Paris, 1901

Glass, A. J., Col., ed. *Neuropsychiatry in World War II: Overseas Theatres*. Washington, 1973

Godechot, J. 'Le carnet de route du sergent Petitbon sur la campagne d'Italie de 1796–1797.' *Rivista italiana di studi napoleonici*, 15 (1978): 33–61

— *Les commissaires aux armées sous le Directoire*. Paris, 1937

Gonneville, A. O. l. H., de. *Souvenirs militaires*. Paris, 1875

Graham, J. M. *Memoir of General Lord Lynedoch*. Edinburgh, 1877

Grandin, F., ed. *Souvenirs historiques du capitaine Krettly, ancien trompette-major des guides d'Italie et d'Egypte*. Paris, 1839

Guglia, E. *Maria Theresia; ihr Leben und ihre Regierung*. Munich, 1917

Guibert, J.-A.-H., de. *Stratégiques*. Paris, 1977

Guichonnet, P. 'Henri Costa de Beauregard. Lettres de guerre à Madame de La Rive (1794–1796).' *L'histoire en Savoie*, n. spéc (1981): 61–4

Hanger, G., Col. *Colonel G. H. to all Sportsmen ... Above thirty years' practice in horses and dogs; how to feed and take care of them ... The rat-catching secret ... To breed ... pheasants ... On fowling-pieces ... To which is added, a plan for training ... a corps ... armed with a peculiar ... gun, etc.* London, 1814

Haythornthwaite, P. J. *Austrian Army of the Napoleonic Wars (1): Infantry, Men-at-Arms*. London, 1986

— *Austrian Army of the Napoleonic Wars (2): Cavalry, Men-at-Arms*. London, 1986

— *Austrian Specialist Troops of the Napoleonic Wars.* London, 1990

— *The Napoleonic Source Book.* London, 1990

Henri-Robert, J. *Dictionnaire des diplomates de Napoléon.* Paris, 1990

Heriot, A. *The French in Italy.* London, 1957

Hibbert, C. *The French Revolution.* London, 1982

Hirsching, F. C. G. *Historisch-literarisches Handbuch berühmter und denkwürdiger Personen, welche in dem 18. Jahrhunderte gestorben sind.* Leipzig, 1795

Hirtenfeld, J. *Der Militär-Maria-Theresien-Orden und seine Mitglieder. Nach authentischen Quellen bearbeitet von J. Hirtenfeld.* Vienna, 1857

Hoefer, D., ed. *Nouvelle biographie universelle/générale.* Paris, 1852–66

Holland Rose, J. 'Despatches of Colonel Thomas Graham on the Italian Campaign of 1796–1797.' *The English Historical Review,* 14 (1899): 111–24, 321–31

Horward, D. D. *The French Revolution and Napoleonic Collection at Florida State University: A Bibliographical Guide.* Tallahassee, 1973

Horward, D. D., ed. *Napoleonic Military History, A Bibliography.* London, 1986

Houdard, L. 'La situation sanitaire au siège de Mantoue.' *Revue des études napoléoniennes,* 31 (1930): 101–10

Hüffer, H. 'Ungedrückte Briefe Napoleons aus den Jahren 1796 und 1797 im Besitze des Haus-, Hof- und Staats-Archives in Wien.' *Archiv für Österreichische Geschichte,* 49 (1872): 267–95

Iung, T. *Bonaparte et son temps, 1769–1799, d'après les documents inédits.* Paris, 1880–1

Jackson, W. G. F., *Attack in the West.* London, 1953

James, W., Admiral Sir. *Old Oak, the Life of John Jervis, Earl of St Vincent.* London, 1950

Johnson, D. *The French Cavalry, 1792–1815.* London, 1989

— *Napoleon's Cavalry and its Leaders.* London, 1978

Joliclerc, F. X. *Joliclerc, volontaire aux armées de la Révolution: ses lettres (1793–1796).* Paris, 1905

Jomini, A.-H., Baron. *Histoire critique et militaire des guerres de la Révolution.* Paris, 1820–24

— *Histoire critique et militaire des guerres de la Révolution (Atlas).* Paris, 1825?

Jones, B. T., ed. *Napoleon's Army: The Military Memoirs of Charles Parquin.* London, 1987

Jones, C. *The Longman Companion to the French Revolution.* Harlow, 1988

Jourquin, J. *Dictionnaire des maréchaux du premier empire.* Paris, 1986

Keegan, J. *The Face of Battle.* London, 1976

— *The Mask of Command.* London, 1987

Kempeln, B. *Magyar Nemes Családok.* Buda, 1911–32

Kennedy, P. *The Rise and Fall of the Great Powers: Economic Change and Military Conflict from 1500 to 2000.* London, 1989

Kenyeres, Á., and others, eds. *Magyar Életrajzi Lexikon.* Buda, 1967–81

Köpeczi, B., ed. *Histoire de la Transylvanie.* Budapest, 1992

Kotarbinski, T., and others, eds. *Wielka Encyklopedia Powszechna Pwn.* Warsaw, 1968

Krebs, V. L., and Moris, H. *Campagnes dans les Alpes pendant la Révolution, d'après les archives des États-majors français et austro-sarde.* Paris, 1891–95

Kriegsgeschichtlichen Abteilung des k und k Kriegs-Archivs, ed. *Oesterreichischer Erbfolge-Krieg 1740–48. Nach den Feld-Acten und anderer authentischen Quellen bearbeitet in der Kriegsgeschichtlichen Abteilung des k und k Kriegs-Archivs, Geschichte der Kämpfe Oesterreichs.* Vienna, 1896–1914

Kriegsgeschichtlichen Abteilung des k. und k. Kriegsarchiv, ed. *Krieg gegen die Französische Revolution 1792–1797, Kriege unter der Regierung des Kaisers Franz.* Vienna, 1905

Kryn, J. *Le petit tambour d'Arcole.* Cadenet, 1987

Kurucz, G. *Guide to Documents and Manuscripts in Great Britain Relating to the Kingdom of Hungary from the Earliest Times to 1800.* London, 1992

Lachouque, H. *The Anatomy of Glory.* London, 1978

— *Napoléon, vingt ans de campagnes.* Paris, 1964

Laing, M. *Josephine and Napoleon.* London, 1973

Lambert, M. 'La mort du jeune Muiron, aide de camp de Bonaparte, à la bataille d'Arcole.' *Mémoires de la société d'émulation du département du Doubs,* s. 7, v. 2 (1897): 315–28

Landrieux, J. *Mémoires de l'adjudant-général Jean Landrieux, Chef d'état-major de la cavalerie de l'armée d'Italie, chargé du bureau secret, 1795–1797.* Paris, 1893

Langlois, V., Ch., and Stein, H. *Les archives de l'histoire de France, Manuels de bibliographie historique.* Paris, 1891

Las Cases, E.-A.-D.-M.-J. *Mémorial de Sainte-Hélène.* Paris, 1983

Laughton, J. K., ed. *Letters and Despatches of Horatio, Viscount Nelson, K. B., Duke of Bronte, Vice Admiral of the White Squadron.* London, 1886

Laugier, J.-R. *Les cahiers du capitaine Laugier. – De la guerre et de l'anarchie, ou Mémoires historiques des campagnes et aventures d'un capitaine du 27me régiment d'infanterie légère par Jérome-Roland Laugier. Publiés d'après le manuscrit original par Léon G. Pélissier.* Aix, 1893

Laurent de l'Ardèche, P. M. *Réfutation des mémoires du maréchal Marmont, duc de Raguse.* Paris, 1857

Lavallette, A.-M. C., Comte de. *Mémoires et souvenirs du comte Lavallette, aide de camp du général Bonaparte, conseiller-d'état et directeur-général des postes de l'Empire; publiés par sa famille et sur ses manuscrits.* Paris, 1831

Lazzari, A. 'Una relazione inedita del sacco di Lugo nel 1796.' *Studi romagnoli,* IV (1953): 37–49

Lecler, J.-A. 'Journal d'un lieutenant de sapeurs auxiliaires de l'armée des Alpes et de l'armée d'Italie, Jean-Antoine Lecler (septembre 1793 à juin 1796).' *Mémoires de la société des sciences naturelles et archéologiques de la Creuse,* 19 (1913): 95–145

Lees, F. *Wanderings on the Italian Riviera.* London, 1912

Lerda, A. 'Con il generale Stengel sulla piana di Cassanio il 21 aprile 1796.' *Bollettino della Società per gli Studi Storici, Archeologici ed Artistici della Provincia di Cuneo* (1980): 125–31

Lévy, A. *Napoléon intime.* Paris, 1893

Ligne, C. J., Prince de. *Mêlanges militaires, littéraires et sentimentaires.* Dresden, 1795-1802

Liliencron, R., von, and Wegele, F. X., eds. *Allgemeine Deutsche Biographie.* Leipzig, 1875–1912

Litta Biumi, A. *Della battaglia di Montenotte, con osservazioni strategiche politiche storiche, corredate di due tavole geografiche.* Milan, 1846

Lumbroso, A. *Cinque lettere di un ufficiale dell'esercito francese, aiutante generale nella battaglia di Lodi (1792-1796).* Modena, 1893

— *Il generale Dumas (da alcuni recenti scritti).* Turin, 1897

Lumbroso, A., ed. *Correspondance de Joachim Murat.* Turin, 1899

Lynn, J. A. *The Bayonets of the Republic*. Chicago, 1984

Macdonald, E. *Recollections of Marshal Macdonald*. Trans. Simeon, Stephen Louis. London, 1893

Magenta, C. 'L'insurrezione di Pavia nel 1796.' *Rivista storica italiana*, 1 (1884): 273–93

Magnaguti, A., Count. 'Napoléon à Mantoue.' *Revue des études napoléoniennes*, 30 (1930): 129–50

Manfredi, S. *L'insurrezione e il sacco di Pavia nel maggio, 1796: monografia storica documentata*. Pavia, 1900

Marbot, J.-B.-A.-M., Baron de. *The Memoirs of Baron de Marbot*. London, 1990

Marmont, A.-F.-L. V., de. *Mémoires du duc de Raguse de 1792 à 1832 imprimés sur le manuscrit original de l'auteur*. Paris, 1857

Martin, A., and Walter, G. *Catalogue de l'histoire de la Révolution française*. Paris, 1936–69

Massena, A. *Mémoires de Massena rédigés par le général Koch ('Atlas)*. Paris, 1848–50?

— *Mémoires de Massena, rédigés d'après les documents qu'il a laissés et sur ceux du dépôt de la guerre et du dépôt des fortifications, par le général Koch*. Paris, 1848–50

Masson, F., and Biagi, G. *Napoléon inconnu*. Paris, 1895

Mauvillon, E., de. *Histoire du Prince Eugène de Savoye*. Vienna, 1777

Melzi d'Eril, F. *Memorie, documenti, e lettere inedite di Napoleone I e di Beauharnais*. Milan, 1865

Michaud, ed. *Biographie universelle ancienne et moderne*. Paris, 1843–?

Mollo, J. *Uniforms of the Seven Years War 1756–63*. Poole, 1977

Monglond, A. *La France Révolutionnaire et Impériale: annales de bibliographie méthodique et description des livres illustrés*. Grenoble, 1933

Murat, J. *Les archives Murat. Inventaire*. Paris, 1967

— *Lettres et documents pour servir à l'histoire de Joachim Murat 1767–1815. Publiés par le prince Murat*. Paris, 1908–14

Naish, G. P. B., ed. *Nelson's Letters to his Wife, and other Documents, 1785–831*. London, 1958?

Napoleon. *Correspondance de Napoléon Ier publiée par ordre de l'empereur Napoléon III*. Paris, 1858–69

— *Correspondance inédite officielle et confidentielle de Napoléon Bonaparte: avec les cours étrangères, les princes, les ministres et les généraux français et étrangers, en Italie, en Allemagne, et en Egypte.* Paris, 1809

— *Lettres à Joséphine ... recueillies et commentées par J. Bourgeat.* Paris, 1941

— *Lettres d'amour à Joséphine.* Ed. Tourtier-Bonazzi, C. de. Paris, 1981

— *Lettres de Napoléon à Joséphine, réunies et prefacées par Léon Cerf.* Paris, 1928

— *Lettres inédites de Napoléon Ier. Collationées sur les textes et publiées par Léonce de Brotonne.* Paris, 1898

— *Mémoires pour servir à l'histoire de France, sous le regne de Napoléon, écrits sous sa dictée à Sainte-Hélène, par les généraux qui ont partagé sa captivité.* Paris, 1829

— *The Military Maxims of Napoleon, translated by Sir G. C. d'Aguilar.* London, 1987

— *Napoléon et Joséphine. Leur roman. Edition intégrale, revue, completée d'après les originaux et contenant de nombreux inédits des lettres de Napoléon et Joséphine (par Jean Savant).* Paris, 1960

— *Oeuvres.* Paris, 1822

— *Oeuvres complètes.* Stuttgart and Tubingen, 1822–3

— *Supplément à la correspondance de Napoléon Ier.* Paris, 1887

Oliveri, L. *Battaglie napoleoniche in Val Bormida (1793–1796).* Cairo Montenotte, 1996

— 'Chi era Filippo del Carretto ...' *alta Val Bormida,* XXV, no. 6 (1984): 3

— 'Invasione napoleonica: le testimonianze.' *Bollettino della Società per gli Studi Storici, Archeologici ed Artistici della Provincia di Cuneo,* 86 (1982): 149–65

— 'L'insorgenza antifrancese in Val Bormida durante il periodo napoleonico (1794–1815).' *Bollettino della Società per gli Studi Storici, Archeologici ed Artistici della Provincia di Cuneo,* 91, no. July–Dec (1984): 229–37

— 'La battaglia di Cosseria nelle testimonianze contemporanee.' *Bollettino storico-bibliografico subalpino,* LXX (1983): 165–77

— 'La resa di Cosseria (14 aprile 1796).' *alta Val Bormida,* XXV, no. 6 (1984): 3

— 'Napoleone in Val Bormida. Vicende di una comunità durante l'invasione francese (1794–1800).' *Bollettino storico-bibliografico subalpino,* LXXXIII, July–Dec (1985): 469–538

— 'Napoleone in Valbormida: la battaglia di Cosseria (13–14 aprile 1796).' *alta Val Bormida*, no. July (1989): 64

— 'Una comunità nella tempesta: la val Bormida durante l'invasione napoleonica 1792–1800.' *Bollettino della Società per gli Studi Storici, Archeologici ed Artistici della Provincia di Cuneo*, 82 (1980): 133–9

Oman, C. *Nelson*. London, 1967

Oppenheim, W. *Europe and the Enlightened Despots*. Ed. Randell, K., *Access to History*. London, 1990

— *Habsburgs and Hohenzollerns 1713–1786*. Ed. Randell, K., *Access to History*. London, 1993

P. K. 'Der überfall des Obersten Philipp Freiherrn von Vukassovich bei Dego 1796.' *Oesterreichische Militärische Zeitschrift*, 48 (1894): 281–90

Panigada, C. 'Pavia nel primo anno della dominazione francese dopo la Rivoluzione (maggio 1796–giugno 1797).' *Bollettino della Società Pavese di Storia Patria*, 10 (1910): 253–350

Pelleport, R *Souvenirs militaires et intimes du général vicomte de Pelleport, de 1793 à 1853*. Paris and Bordeaux, 1857

Petitfrère, C. *Le Général Dupuy et sa Correspondance (1792–1798)*. Paris, 1962

Petre, F. L. *Napoleon and the Archduke Charles*. London, 1909

Pezay, A.-F.-J. M., Marquis de. *Histoire des campagnes de M. le Maréchal de Maillebois en Italie pendant les années 1745 et 1746*. Paris, 1775

Phipps, R. W. *Armies of the First French Republic and the Rise of the Marshals of Napoleon I*. Oxford, 1926–39

Picard, J. J. E. *Bonaparte et Moreau*. Paris, 1905

Picri, G. *Napoleone e il dominio napoleonico nel Friuli*. Udine, 1942

Pierron, F., Gen. *Comment s'est formé le génie militaire de Napoléon Ier.* Paris, 1889

Pinelli, F. A. *Storia militare del Piemonte*. Turin, 1854–55

Piuma, Padre. *Récit historique de la campagne de Buonaparte en Italie, dans les années 1796 et 1797. Par un témoin oculaire*. London, 1808

Pommereul, F.-R.-J., de. *Campagne du général Buonaparte en Italie pendant les années IVe et Ve de la république française: par un officier général*. Paris, 1797

Quaini, M., ed. *La conoscenza del territorio Ligure fra Medio Evo ed età moderna*. Genoa, 1981

Rabel, A. *Le maréchal Bessières, duc d'Istrie.* Paris, 1903

Raggi, A. M. 'La campagna franco-austro-sarda del 1795 nelle lettere di un patrizio alessandrino.' *Rassegna storica del Risorgimento,* XLI (1954): 54–73

Rati, A. 'L'assedio napoleonico alla fortezza di Mantova dal giugno 1796 al febbraio 1797.' Paper presented at Guerre stati e città: Mantova e l'Italia padana dal secolo XIII al XIX, Mantua 1988

Rattier, J.-H. 'Campagne d'Italie (1796): notes d'un sergent-major.' *Revue rétrospective,* XX (1894): 217–88, 322–41

Reinhard, M. *Avec Bonaparte en Italie; d'après les lettres inédites de son aide de camp Joseph Sulkowski.* Paris, 1946

Rittersberg, J., Ritter von. *Biographien der ausgezeichnetsten verstorbenen und lebenden Feldherrn der k. k. Österreichischen Armée, aus der Epoche der Feldzüge 1788–1821 nebst Abbildungen.* Prague, 1829

Robinet, J. F. E., and others, eds. *Dictionnaire historique et biographique de la Révolution et de l'Empire 1789–1815.* Paris, 1899

Roederer, P.-L. *Oeuvres du comte P.-L. Roederer.* Paris, 1853–9

Rogers, H. C. B., Col. *Napoleon's Army.* London, 1974

Roguet, F. *Mémoires militaires du lieutenant général comte Roguet (François), colonel en second des grenadiers à pied de la Vieille Garde, pair de France.* Paris, 1862

Ronco, A. *Filippo Buonarroti e la rivoluzione in Liguria.* Genoa, 1982

— 'La battaglia di Loano.' *Il Secolo XIX,* 16 Sept 1995, 9

— 'La Rivoluzione Francese in Liguria.' *Il Secolo XIX,* 1992

— 'Un eroe per Napoleone.' *Il Secolo XIX,* 1996

Ross, S. T. *French Military History, 1661–1799. A Guide to the Literature.* New York, 1984

Rossi, G. C. 'Vittorio Amedeo III di Savoia nei dispacci inediti di un diplomatico portoghese (agosto 1789–giugno 1790).' *Rassegna storica del Risorgimento,* 39 (1952): 3–17

Rothenberg, G. E. *The Art of Warfare in the Age of Napoleon.* London, 1980

— *Napoleon's Great Adversaries: the Archduke Charles and the Austrian Army, 1792–1814.* London, 1982

— 'Nobility and Military Careers: the Habsburg Officer Corps, 1740–1914.' *Military Affairs,* XXXX, no. 4 (1976): 182–6

Rüstow, F. W. *Die ersten Feldzüge Napoleon Bonaparte's in Italien und Deutschland, 1796 und 1797.* Zurich, 1867

Sargent, H. H. *Napoleon Bonaparte's First Campaign. With Comments.* London, 1895

Schama, S. *Citizens.* London, 1989

Schels, J. B. 'Das Treffen am Mincio am 30 Mai, und die übrigen Kriegsereignisse in Italien, von der Mitte des Mai bis zu Anfang des Juli 1796.' *Oesterreichische Militärische Zeitschrift* Bd. 3; Bd. 4 (1827): 162–203, 98–320; 71–9

— 'Das Treffen an der Brenta, bei Bassano und Fontaniva, am 6 November 1796.' *Oesterreichische Militärische Zeitschrift* Bd. 3 (1828): 267–306

— 'Das Treffen bei Caldiero am 12 November 1796.' *Oesterreichische Militärische Zeitschrift* Bd. 2 (1828): 145–69

— 'Der Ueberfall von Brescia am 30 Juli 1796.' *Oesterreichische Militärische Zeitschrift* H. 9 (1812): 94–9

— 'Die Begebenheiten in und um Mantua vom 16 September 1796 bis 4 Februar 1797; nebst der Schlacht von Rivoli.' *Oesterreichische Militärische Zeitschrift,* Bd. 2; Bd. 3; Bd. 4 (1832): 161–93, 254–77; 115–44, 239–67; 3–61, 167–203

— 'Die Gefechte im tirolischen Etschtale, Anfangs November 1796.' *Oesterreichische Militärische Zeitschrift* Bd. 1 (1829): 115–53

— 'Die Gefechte in den Apenninen, bei Voltri, Montenotte, Millessimo, Cossaria und Dego, im April 1796.' *Oesterreichische Militärische Zeitschrift* Bd. 2 (1822): 123–217

— 'Die Kriegsereignisse in Italien vom 15 April bis 16 Mai 1796, mit dem Gefechte bei Lodi.' *Oesterreichische Militärische Zeitschrift* Bd. 2; Bd. 4 (1825): 195–231; 57–97

— 'Die Operationen des FM Grafen Wurmser am Ende Juli und Anfang August 1796, zum Ensatz von Mantua; mit der Schlacht bei Castiglione.' *Oesterreichische Militärische Zeitschrift,* Bd. 1; Bd. 2 (1830): 254–97; 41–81, 129–59

— 'Die Schlacht bei Arcole, am 15, 16 und 17 November 1796.' *Oesterreichische Militärische Zeitschrift,* Bd. 2 (1829): 35–103

— ' Die Treffen bei Rivoli am 17 und 21 November 1796.' *Oesterreichische Militärische Zeitschrift* Bd. 2 (1829): 151–91

— 'Die Vertheidigung von Mantua im Juni und Juli 1796.' *Oesterreichische Militärische Zeitschrift*, Bd. 1 (1830): 83–100, 15–52

— 'Die zweite Einschließung Mantuas, im August 1796, und gleichzeitige Ereignisse bei dem k. k. Heere unter dem FM Grafen Wurmser in Tirol und Vorarlberg.' *Oesterreichische Militärische Zeitschrift* Bd. 4 (1831): 251–95

— 'Die zweite Vorrückung des FM Grafen von Wurmser zum Entsatz von Mantua, im September 1796, mit den Treffen an der Etsch und Brenta bei Roveredo, Trient, Lavis, Primolano, Bassano, — dann bei Cerea, Castellaro, und vor Mantua.' *Oesterreichische Militärische Zeitschrift*, Bd. 1 (1832): 3–33, 111–64

Schlosser, F. C. *Geschichte des achtzehnten Jahrhunderts und des neunzehnten bis zum Sturze des französischen Kaiserreichs.* Heidelberg, 1836

Schuermanns, A. *Itineraire général de Napoléon 1er.* Paris, 1910?

Scorza, B. *Cronaca vissuta del duplice assedio di Mantova degli anni 1796 e 1797: le vicende di Mantova nel 1796.* Mantua, 1975

Ségur, P.-P., Count de. *Histoires et mémoires.* Paris, 1873

— *Mélanges.* Paris, 1873

Shennan, J. H. *International Relations in Europe, 1689–1789.* Ed. Evans, E. J. and King, P. D. *Lancaster Pamphlets.* London, 1995

Six, G. *Les généraux de la Révolution et de l'Empire.* Paris, 1948

— 'Un document intéressant sur l'origine de la campagne d'Italie de 1796.' *Revue des études napoléoniennes*, 45 (1939): 212–14

Smith, E., ed. *The Century Cyclopedia of Names.* London, 1894

Stagnon, G. 'Carta Corografica degli Stati di S. M. il Re di Sardegna data in luce dall'Ingegnere Borgonio nel 1683 corretta e accresciuta nell'anno 1772.' Turin, 1772

Stendhal (Marie-Henri Beyle). *La Chartreuse de Parme.* Paris, 1973

— *Mémoires d'un touriste.* Paris, 1854

— 'Souvenirs de Milan en 1796.' *La revue des Deux-mondes*, a. 25, s. 2, v. 11 (1855): 1128–36

— *Vie de Napoléon.* Paris, 1877

Stöckl, F. 'FZM Freiherr v. Beaulieu im Feldzuge in Italien 1796.' *Oesterreichische Militärische Zeitschrift* Bd. 61 (1900): 115–60

Thaon de Revel, I. *Mémoires sur la guerre des Alpes et les événements en*

Piémont pendant la domination française, tirés des papiers du comte Ignace Thaon de Revel. Turin, 1871

Thiébault, P.-C.-F.-A.-H.-D. *Mémoires du général Baron Thiébault. Publiés sous les auspices de sa fille Mlle. Claire Thiébault d'après le manuscrit original par Fernand Calmettes.* Paris, 1895–96

Thiers, L. A. *Atlas pour servir à l'intelligence des campagnes de la Révolution française.* Paris, 1846

Thiry, J. *Bonaparte en Italie 1796–97.* Paris, 1973

Thoumine, R. H. *Scientific Soldier: a life of General Le Marchant 1766–1812.* London, 1968

Tranie, J., and Carmigniani, J.-C. *Napoléon Bonaparte: la première campagne d'Italie.* Paris, 1990

Treccani, G., ed. *Enciclopedia italiana.* Milan, 1929–37

Trolard, E. *Pélerinage aux champs de bataille français d'Italie. De Montenotte au Pont d'Arcole.* Paris, 1893

Tuetey, L. *Catalogue général des manuscrits des bibliothèques publiques de France: Archives de la guerre.* Paris, 1912–20

— *Un général de l'armée d'Italie. Sérurier 1742–1819, d'après les archives de France et d'Italie.* Paris, 1899

Tulard, J. *Dictionnaire Napoléon.* Paris, 1987

Turotti, F. *Storia dell'armi italiane dal 1796 al 1814.* Milan, 1855

Vapereau, G., ed. *Dictionnaire universel des contemporains.* Paris, 1858

Vaublanc, V. M. V., Count de. 'Bonaparte et Carnot (1796).' *Revue rétrospective,* XII, no. Jan–July (1890): 400–2

— *Mémoires sur la Révolution de France et recherches sur les causes qui ont amené la Révolution de 1789 et celles qui l'ont suivie.* Paris, 1833

Vellay, F. 'Le château de Cosseria et le général Banel.' *Chercheurs et curieux,* 6 (1956): 65–7

Verri, P. *Lettere e scritti inediti di Pietro e Alessandro Verri.* Milan, 1881

Vigo-Roussillon, F. *Journal de campagne (1793–1837).* Paris, 1981

Vitale, V. 'I dispacci dei diplomatici genovesi a Parigi (1787–1793)' *Miscellanea di storia italiana,* 55 (1935): 1–680

Vivenot, A., Ritter von. *Thugut, Clerfayt und Wurmser. Original-Documente aus dem k. k. Haus-, Hof-, und Staats-Archiv und dem k. k. Kriegs-Archiv in Wien vom Juli 1794–Feb 1797.* Vienna, 1869

— *Vertrauliche Briefe des Freiherrn von Thugut.* Vienna, 1872

Vivenot, A., Ritter von, and Zeissberg, H., Ritter von. *Quellen zur Geschichte der Deutschen Kaiserpolitik Oesterreichs während der Französischen Revolutionskriege. 1790–1801.* Vienna, 1873–85

Watson, S. J. *By Command of the Emperor. A Life of Marshal Berthier.* London, 1957

Wilkinson, S. *The Rise of General Bonaparte.* Oxford, 1930

Wimpffen, M., von. 'Der Feldzug in Italien vom September 1796 bis Februar 1797.' *Oesterreichische Militärische Zeitschrift* Bd. 3 (1889): 189–213, 71–323

Woloch, I. *The French Veteran from the Revolution to the Restoration.* Chapel Hill, 1979

Wurzbach, C., von. *Biographisches Lexikon des Kaiserthums Oesterreich.* Vienna, 1856–91

Young, P., Brigadier. *Napoleon's Marshals.* Reading, 1973

Zuccagni-Orlandini, A. *Atlante illustrativo ossia raccolta dei principali monumenti italiani antichi, del medio evo e moderni e di alcune vedute pittoriche per servire di corredo alla corografia fisica storica e statistica dell'Italia.* Florence, 1845

— A. *Corografia fisica, storica e statistica dell'Italia e delle sue Isole, corredata di un Atlante di mappe geografiche e topografiche, e di altre tavole illustrative di Attilio Zuccagni-Orlandini, autore dell'Atlante toscano.* Florence, 1835–45

Zupko, R. E. *Italian Weights and Measures from the Middle Ages to the Nineteenth Century.* Philadelphia, 1981

INDEX

In most cases, the spellings of personal names are those given in standard biographical reference works, such as the *Dictionnaire de biographie française* and the *Biographisches Lexikon des Kaiserthums Oesterreich*. In other cases, when a person is not listed in such a work, the spelling given in the original source-material has been retained. (Sometimes different sources use different spellings, so it is necessary to make an arbitrary choice.) The spellings of place names are those to be found on the present-day maps of the Touring Club Italiano or the Istituto Geografico Militare Italiano.

A

Abbatucci, General Jacques-Pierre, Bonaparte's assessment, 412
Acqui, 85, 105, 113–15, 117, 138, 141, 149, 152, 167, 179, 195, 200, 212, 230, 231, 241, 244, 246, 249, 253, 263, 275, 277, 286–8
Adda River, 297, 302, 305–7, 310, 316
Adige River, 305, 329, 332–3, 348, 354–6, 360, 366, 377, 379–81, 388, 411, 416–20, 422–5, 427, 429, 432–3, 445, 448, 452, 454–5, 458–64, 466–74, 477, 491–7, 499, 500–6, 511–13, 515
Adrian, Colonel, 228, 316
Alberghini, Don Giovanni Battista, 443, 410, 485, 497, 504, 508
Alessandria, 30, 85–6, 89–90, 100, 104–5, 114, 131, 137–8, 141, 143, 148, 168, 179, 263, 274–5, 278, 282, 286–8, 291, 295, 322
Alps, 73, 76, 85, 88, 92, 94, 112, 123, 146, 156, 191, 422, 442
Alvinczy, General Baron Joseph (Jószef), 42, 371, 387, 406–7, 429, 440, 476–7

Arcole, 458–60, 462–3, 467, 470, 473, 475
Bassano, 443–50, 452, 454–5
Mantua, 486–7, 491–2, 521
Rivoli, 494, 496, 499, 500, 504–5, 507, 513, 515–16
American War of Independence, 54
Andréossy, Chef de Brigade Antoine-François, 291, 297, 299, 351, 367–8, 461
Apennines, 85–6, 103, 112, 197, 203, 209, 337
Arcole, 433, 438, 446, 458–76, 482, 485
Argenteau, General Count Eugène-Guillaume-Alexis Mercy d', 78, 90, 91, 110–11
Dego, 241–3, 246–8
Monte Negino, 208–9, 213
Montenotte, 200–2, 219–20, 222, 225–7, 230–1
troop movements, 150, 167–8, 177, 179, 188–9
Voltri, 194–5
armistices *see* peace negotiations
Arnault, Antoine Vincent, 523

art works *see* plunder
Artois, Count of, 73
Attems, Colonel Count, 314
Aubernon, Philippe, commissary, 117
Augereau, General Pierre-François-Charles, 118, 154, 190, 274, 288–9, 338, 355, 383, 458
Alba, 277
Arcole, 461–5, 468–72, 474–5
Bassano, 432, 448, 450–1, 454
Bologna, 370
Bonaparte's assessment, 412
Brescia, 388–9
Caldiero, 456
Castiglione, 391, 395–7, 399, 401
cease-fire, 286
Ceva, 258, 261, 264
character, 133
Cherasco, 275
Cosseria, 230, 240, 243, 245
crossing the Po, 288–9, 294–5, 298–300, 306–7
Legnago, 378, 434–5
Lodi, 309, 314, 337
looting, 274
losses in division, 230
Mantua, 361, 366–7, 435
Montebello, 381
Montenotte, 219, 221, 223

Montezemolo, 233–4,
249, 258
Montichiari, 384
Pavia, 338
Rivoli, 459, 494–6, 516
San Michele, 265–6
strength of division in
Italy, 127, 338
Tyrol, 409–10, 419,
422–3, 428–32, 447
Voltri, 196
Aune, Grenadier Léon, 311
Austria
and Piedmont, 74–5, 85,
89, 92, 111–12, 117,
119, 140
and Prussia, 18, 20, 111
relations with France, 19,
21, 101, 369
War of the First
Coalition, 15–16
Austrian Army, 33–45, 111,
132, 167, 258, 406–7,
411–12, 418–20, 442
army in Italy, 132; losses,
199, 215, 248
army regulations, 35–41
artillery, 38–9
Auxiliary Corps, 74, 135,
139, 161, 167, 186,
189, 219, 276, 286–7
Croats, 26, 34, 39, 89,
180, 188, 197–8, 202,
209, 213, 215, 238,
240–1, 247, 251, 260,
310–11, 314, 350,
372, 453, 464, 474,
507, 509
Frei-Corps, 34–5
Friuli Corps, 444–8, 450,
455, 456, 458, 475–6
Germans, 34
Grenzers, 35, 111, 202,
250, 442, 488
Hofkriegsrath, 38–40,
138, 371
Hungarians, 34
infantry, 35–8
officer corps, 39–45
reinforcements, 361
strength of army in Italy,
138, 184, 300, 366,
373, 379
titles of generals, 82n28
training, 37
Tyrol Corps, 444–7, 458,

475–6
Voltri, 194–5
Austrian Army Units
Garrison Regiments
1st Garrison Regiment,
329, 364
2nd Garrison
Regiment, 365,
406–7
Infantry Regiments
IR Alvinczy, 167, 186,
194–5, 197, 201–2,
209, 223, 225–8,
241, 247, 250, 302,
310, 350, 434, 449
IR Belgioioso, 235,
261, 310, 314, 364,
407
IR Brechainville, 167,
195, 350, 407
IR Callenberg, 512
IR De Vins, 382
IR Deutschmeister,
168, 241, 247, 418,
451, 473, 508
IR Erbach, 430
IR Erzherzog Anton,
168, 179, 195,
201–2, 209, 222,
225–7, 230, 241,
247, 364
IR Gemmingen, 407
IR Huff, 168, 350
IR Jordis, 168, 350,
353
IR Keuhl, 349, 350
IR Lattermann, 168,
171, 194, 350
IR Michael Wallis, 430
IR Nádasdy, 168, 171,
194, 250, 302, 310,
312, 314, 364, 424
IR Pellegrini, 167, 195,
201–2, 209, 213,
222, 225–6, 230,
241, 364, 407
IR Preiss, 167, 195,
222, 250, 364, 407,
425
IR Reisky, 168, 171,
194, 303, 350
IR Samuel Gyulay, 452
IR Splény, 449, 451,
463–4
IR Stein, 168, 195,
201–2, 209, 222,

224–6, 230–1, 241,
364, 407
IR Strassoldo, 168,
235, 310, 351–3,
355, 407
IR Terzi, 168, 171,
194–5, 222, 225–7,
241, 247, 310, 314,
365, 407
IR Thurn, 168, 302,
310, 314, 350, 355,
364, 407, 426
IR Toscana, 167, 195,
310, 350, 355
IR Wallis, 168, 350
IR Wenzel Colloredo,
168, 194, 350,
353–4, 407
IR Wilhelm Schröder,
168, 430
Cavalry Regiments
Erdödy Hussars, 138,
167, 195, 310, 350,
418, 430
Erzherzog Joseph
Hussars, 138, 168,
310, 350, 365, 407
Stabsdragoner, 365,
407, 512
Uhlans, 96, 138, 168,
171, 184, 194, 287,
302–3, 310, 315,
350–1, 361, 365
Wurmser Hussars, 382,
426
Frei-Corps Gyulay, 35,
89, 201–2, 213, 222,
235, 241, 329, 365,
407, 497
Grenz Regiments
Banal Grenzers, 407,
442
Carlstädter Grenzers,
167, 186, 194–5,
199, 202, 250,
310–11, 364–5,
406–7, 473
Szluiner Grenzers, 168,
171, 194, 198
Warasdiner Grenzers,
310, 364, 407, 468
Mahony Jägers, 382, 430,
508
Auxonne, 49, 65–6, 69
Avogadro di Valdengo,
Colonel Count, 246

INDEX

Azara, Don José Nicolás d',
369

B
Bacigalupo, Colonel, 90
Bajalich, General Baron
Adam, 361, 386, 401,
431, 491–2
Rivoli, 495–6, 500
Banel, General Pierre, 235,
237–8
Baraguey d'Hilliers, General
Louis, 52, 516
Barras, Jean-Nicolas-Paul-
François de, 81, 107,
109, 128
Bassano, 374, 417–19, 421,
426–30, 432, 440, 444,
448–51, 457, 491–2, 495
Beauharnais, General
Alexandre-François-Marie
de, 52, 109
Beaulieu, General Baron
Jean-Pierre de, 132–7,
179, 371–2
assessment of qualities,
360–1
Ceva, 263
defence of the Po, 286–8,
292–4, 296–305
Dego, 230–1, 241–2
Lodi, 275–8, 315–17
Lombardy, 347–9
Mantua defence, 321,
323, 330–3, 368
Milan, 328, 335
Mondovì, 260, 270
Montenotte, 219, 230
movements of army,
169–70, 174, 177,
185, 188
preparations for
campaign, 132–41,
143, 148–50, 160–1
strength of army, 138,
167
Voltri, 194, 199, 212
Beaumont, General Marc-
Antoine de la Bonninière,
Count de, 289, 313, 315,
319, 400
Belcredi, Marchese, 343
Bellegarde, Colonel
Chevalier de, 261
Belliard, Adjutant-General
Augustin-Daniel, 465

Beretta, Monsignor Count
Giovanni Antonio della,
317
Berthier, General Louis-
Alexandre, 144, 150, 172,
181, 187, 190, 241, 248,
324, 346
and the actress, 373
appearance, 143
armistice of Cherasco,
279–80
and Bonaparte, 143, 324,
412, 525
Castiglione, 399
Chief of Staff, 71, 130–1,
141, 152–3
Codogno, 304
Lodi, 314
Rivoli, 507, 511–13
supplies, 178, 183, 234
Tyrol, 447
Bertrand, General Henri-
Gratien, 322
Bessières, Captain Jean-
Baptiste, 355, 426
Beust, Colonel von, 348
Beyrand, General Martial,
261, 314, 395–6
Bigarré, General Auguste-
Julien, 34
Binasco, 342–3
Birago, Second Lieutenant
Cavaliere Carlo, 236–7,
239, 243
Blandin, Captain, 392
Bocchetta Pass, 86, 99, 115,
131, 144–5, 160–1,
170–1, 174, 176–7, 182,
184–5, 196, 212–13
Boiron, Grenadier Antoine,
227
Bologna, 236, 369–71, 489,
495, 522
Bon, General Louis-André,
435, 461–3
Bonaparte, Carlo (father of
NB), 62
Bonaparte, Joseph (brother
of NB), 49, 63, 72,
105–7, 183, 275
Bonaparte, Letizia (mother
of NB), 62
Bonaparte, Louis (brother of
NB), 449
Bonaparte, Marie-Anne
(sister of NB), 72

Bonaparte, Napoleon
LIFE
birth, 62
education, 63
marriage to Josephine,
128, 158, 175, 183
MEMOIRS, 96, 146
POLITICS
support of Revolution,
70, 107–8
Corsican politics, 76–7
arrested, 95
Paris Royalist uprising
quelled, 107–10
WAR
studies warfare, 16, 17,
48–9, 64–6, 123
military training, 63–9
siege of Toulon, 79–81
wounded, 80
artillery commander, 89,
95
conduct of the war, 93–4,
323–4
Italian campaign, 89–105
Topographical Bureau
Paris, 105–7
commander Army of the
Interior, 109
strategy in Italian
campaign, 113–19,
178, 283
commander Army of
Italy, 128, 337–8
inspirational leadership,
146–7, 282
losses at Voltri, 199–200
Piedmont campaign,
258–9, 265–75
Cherasco armistice
negotiations, 273–81
crossing the River Po,
206–307
Lodi, 309–17
Milan, 320, 331–42
Pavia, 342–5
crossing the River
Mincio, 346–56
Mantua, 362, 367–9, 374
Naples armistice, 368–9
Bologna, 369
armistice with Pope, 371
Florence, 371
Montichiari, 381, 389
Lonato, 393
Castiglione, 397–402

Tyrol, 408–31, 453–4
Mantua, 441–4
Bassano, 444–50
Arcole, 464–76
Rivoli, 499–512, 515–16
Mantua surrender, 521
peace with Austria, 522
military achievements,
523–5
Bonaparte, Pauline (sister of
NB), 140
Borghetto, 309, 346–54,
400–1
Bormida Rivers, 86, 89–90,
95–6, 98–9, 117, 120,
144, 150, 161, 169,
176–7, 182, 186, 188,
219, 234, 242–7, 252,
269, 288
Botta, Carlo, 134
Boudet, Sergeant, 465
Bourcet, Pierre-Joseph, 49,
66–8, 88–9, 219, 293
*Principes de la guerre de
montagnes*, 49, 69
Bouvier, Félix, 126, 211
Boyer, Adjutant-General
Pierre-François-Joseph,
290
Brabeck, General Baron
Adolph von, 444, 449,
451, 456, 462–4, 468
Brempt, General Baron,
260, 262–3
Brenta River, 366, 373,
416–17, 420, 424,
426–7, 429–31, 445,
447, 449–52, 455, 478
Brentano, General, 407
Brescia, 343, 346, 348–9,
379–85, 388–90, 392–3,
397, 399, 409, 415, 494
Bric Castlas, 203
Brigido, Colonel, 460, 462,
466, 469
Brissot de Warville, Jacques-
Pierre, 20–1
Broglie, Marshal Victor-
François Duke de, 48–9,
59n2
Brune, General Guillaume-
Marie-Anne, 108, 494
Brunswick-Lüneburg, Carl
Wilhelm Ferdinand,
Duke of, 72–3
Brunswick-Lüneburg,

Ferdinand, Prince of, 25
Buchmayer, Captain, 352
Buonaparte, Filippo, 371

C
Cacault, François, French
ambassador, 114
Cadibona (village), 157,
207–8, 221, 223, 225
Cadibona Pass *see* Colle di
Cadibona
Cairo (Montenotte), 90, 91,
95, 98, 105, 113, 120,
148, 150, 177, 179–80,
184–5, 187, 189, 195,
201, 204, 208, 221, 231,
233, 241, 243, 246, 249,
251–2, 254, 266, 288
Caldiero, 456, 460, 468,
470, 473, 477, 500
Calliano, 360, 366, 424–7,
449–50, 452–3, 455
Campbell, Colonel Sir Neil,
18
Canto d'Irles, General
Count Joseph, 330–1,
368, 376, 387, 398–9
Mantua, 406, 409, 417
Carnot, Lazare-Nicolas-
Marguerite, 106, 118,
120, 147, 306, 316, 482
campaign plans, 87, 92,
95, 114, 324–5
Mantua, 362
Carrère, Captain, 238
Carteaux, General Jean-
Baptiste François, 79–80
Casabianca, General
Raphaël, Bonaparte's
assessment, 412
Castiglione (delle Stiviere),
351, 382, 384, 391, 393,
395–9, 447, 457, 482
Causse, General Jean-
Jacques, 247, 252
Cavalcaselle, 401
Ceva, 87, 98–100, 103–5,
111, 113–19, 130, 139,
141, 143, 145, 148–9,
152, 159, 167, 169, 172,
176–8, 186, 219, 229,
233–4, 243, 248–9,
258–61, 263–6, 269,
278, 288, 329
Cervoni, General Jean-
Baptiste, 171, 212, 215,

314, 384, 399
Dego, 245, 247, 254
Montenotte, 224
Voltri, 196–8
Ceva, 105, 111, 113–19,
130, 149, 234, 243
siege, 248, 258–60
Chaffardon, Colonel Jean
Louis d'Oncieu, 271
Chambarlhac, Chef de
Brigade Jean-Jacques-
Antoine-François-Vital
de, 186
Charles, Archduke, 411,
417, 522
Chasseloup-Laubat, Chef de
Brigade François, Marquis
de, 148, 300, 367–8,
376, 441, 469
Chauvet, Félix-Joseph-
Antoine-François,
commissary, 109, 129,
141, 144, 156, 180–3
Cherasco, 259–60, 263,
275, 279–81, 286, 288
Chiese River, 333, 349, 378,
380–2, 385, 392, 394–5
citizens' army, 57
Clarke, General Henry-
Jacques-Guillaume, 241,
324, 489
Clerfayt, Field Marshal
Count Karl, 39, 42, 134
Coburg-Saalfeld, Field
Marshal Friedrich Josias,
Prince of, 133
Codogno, 301–4
Colle di Cadibona, 86, 98,
269
Colle di Nava, 87–9
Colle di Tenda, 75, 86–92,
99, 276, 278
Colin, Jean, 64, 69, 100
Colli-Marchi, General Baron
Michelangelo Alessandro,
78, 90–1, 95, 135, 161,
167, 233, 267, 353, 360,
371
Adige valley, 366
armistice of Cherasco,
274–8, 286
Ceva, 111, 249, 260, 263
character, 135
crossing the Po, 298
Dego, 242
Mantua, 333

Milan, 305
Mondovì, 270–1
Montezemolo, 237, 249
preparations for
campaign, 132,
135–40, 143, 148
San Michele, 265, 267–9
troop movements, 169,
177, 185–6, 188, 201,
219, 316, 355–6
Colli-Ricci, Colonel
Leonardo Antonio
Giuseppe Gaspare
Venanzio, 260
Colloredo, Count, 39, 91,
133
Colloredo, General, 42
Collot, Jean-Pierre,
commissary173, 182
Corsica, 63–4, 69–70, 72,
77, 99, 207
Corsini, Don Neri, Tuscan
ambassador, 126
Cosseria, 84, 230, 233, 235,
237–8, 243, 245, 248–9,
252, 263, 281, 483
Cossila, Piedmontese
ambassador, 160
Costa de Beauregard,
Colonel Joseph Henri,
110, 135–6, 139,
149–50, 160, 267, 281–2
Ceva, 111
Colli's Chief of Staff, 91,
140, 279
state of the French army,
159
Costa di Avignano, Vittorio
Gaetano, Cardinal
Archbishop of Turin, 273
Cronlse, Captain, 352
Cuneo, 75, 85, 88–9, 91–2,
99–100, 185, 270,
273–4, 278, 280, 282,
286, 288
Custine, General Adam
Philippe de, 75
Cuto, General Prince di,
348, 356
Czernin, Captain Count
(Wolfgang?), 303

D
Dallemagne, General
Claude, 289, 366, 374,
378, 384–5, 391–2, 483

crossing the Po, 295, 297,
301
Lonato, 385
Lodi, 311, 314
Mantua, 415, 441, 495
Daun, Field Marshal
Leopold Joseph Maria,
39–41, 132
Davidovich, General Baron
Paul, 378, 380–1, 383,
395–6, 400
Rivoli, 458–9, 462,
466–7, 470–2, 475–7
Seven Years War, 361
Tyrol, 417, 422–4,
426–9, 440, 446,
449–50, 452–3, 455
Davin, General Jean, 495
De La Chiusa, General
Marchese, 263
De Negri, Tuscan consul,
126
De Vins, General Baron
Joseph Nikolaus, 76,
77–8, 84, 88, 90, 92, 110
Debry or de Bry, Jean-
Antoine-Joseph, 107
Declaration of Pillnitz,
19–20
Dego, 89, 96–100, 144,
150, 157, 167–8, 179,
182, 185–6, 188, 195,
200–2, 221, 227, 229–1,
233–4, 237–8, 241–52,
254, 258, 263, 267, 274,
309, 311
Del Carretto di Camerano,
Colonel Marchese
Filippo Secondo
Antonio, 233, 235–6,
238, 240, 243
Del Carretto di Lesegno,
Marchesa Luisa, 263,
266, 269
Dellera, General, 88–9, 124,
272
Denniée, Antoine,
commissary, 420
Desaix, General Louis-
Charles-Antoine, 143,
156, 187, 207
Desenzano, 349, 380, 383,
385, 388, 390, 393–4
Despinoy, General
Hyacinthe-François-
Joseph, 280, 286, 335,

340–2, 345, 373, 378,
391–2
Bonaparte's assessment,
412–13
Brescia, 384–5, 388–9
Castelnuovo, 381
Castiglione, 397–400
Destaing, Chef de Brigade
Jacques-Zacharie, 253,
508–11
Desvernois, Lieutenant
Nicolas Philibert, 146–7,
302
Dichat de Toisinge, General
Chevalier Jean-Gaspard,
265–7, 271
Dietrichstein-Proskau-Leslie,
Colonel Franz Joseph
Johann, Prince, 41, 134
Dillon, General Théobald-
Hyacinthe, 71
Directory, 109, 112–16,
118–19, 127–9, 131,
141, 147, 159, 156, 167,
274–5, 286, 289, 295,
301, 304, 317, 321–5,
334–6, 345, 349, 352,
362, 366, 368–70,
373–4, 384–5, 399,
409–11, 414, 424, 441,
443, 445, 452, 457,
482–3, 485, 489, 522
Dolcè, 356, 360, 380–1,
476
Dommartin, General
Elzéard-Auguste Cousin
de, 79, 221, 230, 234,
271, 344, 425
Drake, Francis, British
diplomat, 160
Du Teil, General Baron
Jean-Pierre, 49, 65–6, 70
Du Teil, General Chevalier
Jean, 65–7, 94, 293
Dugommier, General
Jacques Coquille, *called*,
80
Dugua, General Charles-
François-Joseph, 494, 517
Dujard, General Chevalier
Jean-Lambert Marchal-,
77, 140, 172, 290, 300,
334
Dumas, General Thomas-
Alexandre, 448, 488, 495
Dumerbion or Du Merbion,

General Pierre Jadart, 91, 95, 98–9
Dumouriez, General Charles-François du Périer, 21, 72, 75, 77
Dupas, General Pierre-Louis, 313–14, 366
Duphot, Adjutant-General Mathurin-Léonard, 500
Dupont-Ferrier, Quartermaster-Corporal André, 124
Dupuy, Chef de Brigade Dominique-Martin, 251, 456–7
Duroc, Chef de Brigade Géraud-Christophe-Michel, 130, 446

E
Elliot, Bonaparte's aide, 469
Ertel, Captain, 352
Esterházy, General, 42
Estienne, Drummer André, 464–5, 469, 474
Eugene of Savoy, Prince, 16, 78, 123, 130, 348, 460

F
Fabry, Gabriel, 138, 145, 149, 189
Faipoult, Guillaume-Charles, ambassador, 141, 145, 173, 274–5, 287–8, 292
Ferdinand, Archduke, governor of Lombardy, 85, 93, 95, 305
Ferdinand, Grand Duke of Tuscany, 371
Ferrara (city), 370, 485
Ferrara di Monte Baldo, 493, 496–7, 499–502, 517
Fiorella, General Pascal-Antoine, 249, 264, 266–8, 271, 278, 286, 374, 398–400, 409, 471
Fontana, Matteo, 254
Fontaniva, 432, 449, 451
Fontbonne, General Alexandre-Louis de, 128
Fontenoy, battle of, 43
Fornésy, Chef de Brigade Henry-François, 207, 210, 214, 497, 509

Fort Urban, 370
Foy, General Sébastien-Maximilien, 55
France
    declares war on England, 76
    declares war on Holland, 76
    declares war on Spain, 76, 77
    invades Savoy, 73–5, 89
    natural frontiers, 73
    and Piedmont, 73–6, 90, 100, 137, 338
    relations with Austria, 19, 21, 369, 522
Franceschi, Adjutant-General Jean-Baptiste-Marie, 263, 299, 315
Francis II of Austria, 137, 141, 170–1, 174, 212, 440–3, 522
Frederick the Great, 17, 33, 45, 67, 72
Frederick William II of Prussia, 19
French Army, 47–59
    amalgame, 57, 127, 142, 148
    Army of the Alps, 91, 130, 322, 366
    Army of the Coasts of the Ocean, 408
    Army of the Interior, 109
    Army of Italy, 323, 338, 457
        achievements of campaign, 523–5
        artillery, 151, 290, 485
        Bonaparte as artillery commander, 89, 95
        Bonaparte as commander, 128, 337–8
        Bonaparte's assessment of condition, 482–6
        Bonaparte's strategy, 113–19, 178, 283
        cavalry, 150, 290
        defeat under Kellermann, 102
        execution of looters, 277, 291, 306
        pillaging, 268–9, 273–4, 277, 290, 306, 414
        plunder, 287–8, 306, 335–6
        problems, 100, 115,

        125–6, 144, 482–6
        staffs, 152, 159, 290
        strength, 127, 140, 373, 419–20, 448, 457–8
        supplies, 169, 173, 177, 183, 234, 320, 414
    Units
        1st Cavalry, 513
        1st Hussars, 150, 426, 517
        4th Light, 196, 227, 235, 252–3, 507–8, 516
        4th Line, 192n36, 196, 235, 238, 240, 262, 277, 284n6, 300–1, 355–6, 397–8, 400, 430–1, 462, 465, 472
        5th Dragoons, 150, 247, 344, 431
        5th Light, 430, 461, 462, 469, 472
        5th Line, 392
        7th Hussars, 146, 150, 302
        8th Dragoons, 150
        9th Dragoons, 472
        10th Chasseurs à Cheval, 150, 328
        11th Light, 195, 231, 238, 240, 262, 380
        12th Light, 461, 466
        13th Chasseurs à Cheval, 150
        14th Line (old), 300
        14th Line, 196, 507–8, 510–11, 513
        14th provisional, 246
        15th Line, 220
        15th Dragoons, 150, 344
        17th Light, 187, 195, 207–8, 210, 212, 214, 229, 246, 248, 251, 302, 304, 328, 400, 497, 507–8
        18th Light, 424
        18th Line, 131, 192n36, 196, 223, 237, 238–40, 252, 300, 336, 394, 424, 464, 503–4, 515
        20th Dragoons, 150
        21st Line, 126, 141
        22nd Chasseurs à

Cheval, 150, 247, 275, 396
22nd Light, 195, 507, 512
24th Chasseurs à Cheval, 150, 344
25th Chasseurs à Cheval, 150, 328
25th Line, 195, 290, 464
27th Light, 195, 300, 313, 341, 380, 429, 495
29th Light, 186, 196, 300, 313, 422, 507, 509, 517
32nd Line, 187, 190, 195, 207–8, 211, 212, 214, 223, 229, 232–3, 245–6, 250–3, 311–12, 331–2, 336, 341, 385, 393–4, 425, 474, 503, 510
33rd Line, 484, 507–8, 511
39th Line (old), 181, 192n36
39th Line, 196, 268, 454, 506, 511–12, 514
40th Line, 463, 469, 470, 472
45th Line, 151, 396
51st Line, 142, 176, 195–7, 199, 224, 229, 238, 247, 252–3, 300, 303–4, 308n19, 396, 400, 451, 461, 463–4, 466, 469 70, 472–3
55th Line, 195
69th Line (old), 181, 192n36
69th Line, 196, 396
75th Line, 142, 186, 190, 195–6, 198–9, 215, 223–4, 227, 229, 245, 247, 300, 304, 461, 466, 472, 503, 510, 515
85th Line, 196, 268, 449, 454, 471, 507, 509–10, 517
Army of the North

invades Netherlands, 70–1
Army of the Rhine, 369, 411, 415, 427
Army of the West, 101
artillery, 48–9
citizen soldiers, 49–53
citizens' army, 57–8
divisions, 47
Imperial Guard, 289, 355
La Fère artillery regiment, 64
levée en masse (conscription), 57, 77
officers, 51–3
patrie en danger, 54, 72
tactics, 48–9, 55–6
volunteer battalions, 54–7
French Revolution, 19
Bastille stormed, 69
execution of Robespierre, 94
Paris uprising, 107–10
Tuileries Palace stormed, 72

G
Galeazzini, Adjutant-General Pierre, 253
Gardanne, General Gaspard-Amédée, 353, 378, 474
Garessio, 90, 105, 113, 127, 149, 178, 183, 187, 190, 233, 234
Garnier, General Pierre-Dominique, 278
Bonaparte's assessment, 412
Garrau, Pierre-Anselme, commissioner, 322, 485
Gasparin, Thomas-Augustin de, 79
Gaultier de Kervéguen, General Paul-Louis, 140, 381
Bonaparte's assessment, 412
Gavasini, Lieutenant-Colonel Count Alois, 430–1, 462–3
Gavi, 115, 131, 141, 171, 173, 182, 370
Genoa, 62, 86–8, 94, 100–1, 103, 115, 127–31, 141, 145, 147–50, 156, 159,

160–1, 169–70, 172–4, 176, 181–4, 186, 191, 194, 196, 212, 223, 273–5, 278, 287–8, 368–9
Gherardini, Marquis, Austrian ambassador, 76, 80, 84, 88, 117, 160–1
Girola, Count Giovanni, 94
Giuseppi, Chef de Brigade, 231
Goethe, Johann Wolfgang von, 73
Goito, 346–7, 349, 351, 353, 380, 383, 386, 388, 391, 395, 397, 494
Graffen, General, 418
Graham, Colonel Thomas, 376, 411–13, 428
on the Austrian generals, 371–2, 407–8
Beaulieu, 360
Mantua, 407
official observer, 348
Rivoli, 499, 502, 507, 513–14, 524
Gribeauval, General Jean-Baptiste Vaquette de, 48
Gruardet, Captain Nicolas, 198
Guasco, Marchese Carlo, 100
Guibert, Jacques-Antoine-Hippolyte de, 59n2, 67
Essai général de tactique, 48–9, 65
Guieu, General Jean-Joseph, 249, 266–8, 271, 397–8, 483, 494, 517
Arcole, 464, 466
Lonato, 389
Salò, 378, 380, 382, 305, 392, 422
Guillaume, General Paul, 385, 420
Gummer, General, 348, 372, 378

H
Habbein, Lieutenant-Colonel, 213
Haller, Charles-Louis de, commissary, 486
Haquin, General Honoré-Alexandre, 339–41
Hauteville, Piedmontese foreign minister, 160

Henrici, General, 366, 372
Hercule, Lieutenant Joseph
    Damingue, 475
Hohenlohe, General Prince
    Friedrich von, 20
Hohenzollern-Hechingen,
    General Prince Friedrich
    Franz Xaver von, 354–5,
    366, 372, 379, 454, 467
    Arcole, 444
    Bassano, 449–50
    Caldiero, 456, 470
Hood, Admiral Samuel, 79
Hubner, Lieutenant-
    Colonel, 171
Humbourg, General, 174

I

Imperial Guard, 289, 355
Innsbruck, 329, 409–11,
    415, 420, 427
Italy
    campaign against Austria,
        90–105, 112
    as campaigning ground,
        15–16, 85–7
    anti-Jacobin riots in
        Lombardy, 338–43
Iuch, Major, 433

J

Josephine (Tascher de la
    Pagerie), 14, 52, 109,
    158, 175, 183, 336, 373
    marriage to Bonaparte,
        128
    in Milan, 373
    supposed pregnancy, 321
Joubert, General Barthélemy
    Catherine, 51, 75, 110,
    273, 282, 290
    Alessandria, 291
    Castiglione, 399–400
    Ceva, 261, 264
    Cosseria, 233–5, 238
    crossing the Po, 295
    Lodi, 316
    Mantua, 363
    Milan, 328, 332, 337
    Montenotte, 221
    Montezemolo, 249
    promotion, 483–4
    Rivoli, 366, 450, 494,
        497, 499–514, 516–17
    San Michele, 266
    Tyrol, 445, 450

Junot, Chef de Brigade
    Andoche, 81, 90, 94,
    106, 130, 183, 275, 394

K

Kaunitz, Prince Wenzel
    Anton, 40
Kellermann, General
    François Christophe de,
    72, 102, 104–5, 110,
    130, 152, 322, 324–5
    son captured, 382, 413
Kerpen, General, 168
Kienmayer, General Baron
    Michael, 43
Kilmaine, General Charles
    Edward Jennings, 309,
    338, 419
    Castelnuovo, 355, 381
    Castiglione, 396
    command of cavalry, 172,
        290
    crossing the Po, 295, 297,
        306
    Mantua, 366–7, 441, 448
    Milan, 332
    Peschiera, 349, 351–2,
        354
    Valeggio, 378
Kinsky, General Count
    (Franz Joseph?), 42
Klenau, Colonel Count
    Johann, 382, 386, 388,
    390, 392, 521
Köblös, General, 492, 497,
    502, 508, 512
Koch, General Jean-
    Baptiste-Frédéric, 211,
    518n24
Kray, General Baron Paul,
    42

L

La Bicocca, 167, 260, 263,
    265, 267–8, 270, 272
La Favorita, 367, 517
La Fère artillery regiment,
    64
La Harpe, General Amédée-
    Emmanuel-François de,
    98, 171, 173, 186, 190,
    275, 277
    cease-fire, 286
    Ceva, 258, 263–4
    crossing the Po, 288–9,
    295, 297–304

death, 304
Dego, 231, 246–7, 253
Monte Negino, 142,
    206–8
Montenotte, 220–1,
    224–6, 228, 230
Montezemolo, 233–4,
    249
Savona, 115
Tortona, 291
Voltri, 195
La Pedaggera, 167, 259–62
La Salcette, General Jean-
    Jacques-Bernardin Colaud
    de, 246–9, 251, 253
La Tour, General (Austrian),
    42
La Tour, General Sallier de
    (Piedmontese), 117, 140,
    279–80, 286
Lacy, Field Marshal Franz
    Moritz, 41, 135
Lafayette, General Marie-
    Joseph-Paul-Yves-Roch-
    Gilbert du Motier,
    Marquis de, 71, 77
Lallement, French
    ambassador, 335
Lambert, Jean-François,
    commissary, 183, 288
Lamberti, Count Giacomo,
    303
l'Ami, Lieutenant-Colonel
    de, 329
Lampugnani, Don Giovanni
    Battista, 317
Landrieux, Adjutant-
    General Jean, 308n19
Lannes, General Jean, 197,
    253, 295, 299, 301, 355
    Arcole, 463
    Bassano, 432
    captured, 382
    Lodi, 314
    Mantua, 366
    Pavia, 342, 344, 370
    Rivoli, 495
Lanusse, Adjutant-General
    François, 253, 297, 301,
    430, 457
Laporte or Delaporte,
    François-Sébastien-
    Christophe, 92
Laroche-Dubouscat, General
    Antoine, 60n5
Lasalle, Chef d'Escadron

Antoine Charles Louis,
51, 513
Lavis, 426–9, 448, 450
Lauer, General Baron Franz
von, 406, 416, 420
Laugier, Captain Jérôme-
Roland, 383, 389–90,
414, 501
Milan, 341
Rivoli, 495
Salo, 380
Tyrol, 422–3, 446, 453
Lavallette, Captain Antoine-
Marie Chamans, Count
de, 52
Lazary, General, 75
Le Marois, Captain Jean-
Léonor-François, 128,
130, 426
Lebley, General Claude-
Marie, 494, 510
Leclerc, General Victoire-
Emmanuel, 140, 494,
513
Leczeny, Lieutenant-
Colonel, 188, 222, 243,
250–2, 477
Legislative Assembly, 20
Legnago, 378, 388, 416,
432–4, 445, 450, 470,
472–3, 477, 491, 494–6,
499–500
Lejeune, General Baron
Louis-François, 143
Leoben, 522–3
Léon see Aune, Léon
Leopold II of Austria, 19,
21n2, 40
Lespinasse, General
Augustin, 485
Letourneur, Charles-Louis-
François-Honoré, 115
Liechtenstein, Field Marshal
Prince Joseph Wenzel
Laurenz, 38
Lilienberg, Lieutenant
Count Wenzel Vetter von,
196, 198
Lipthay, General Baron
Anton, 167, 174, 316,
333, 349, 355, 372, 379
Bassano, 444, 449, 451
Castiglione, 391, 395–6,
400
crossing the Po, 286–9,
294, 296–303, 305

relieved of command, 360
Rivoli, 492, 496, 502,
504, 508, 509–10, 513
Livorno, 130, 322–3, 368,
371, 483, 485
Loano, 37, 59, 92, 95, 110,
143, 149, 172, 202
battle of, 110–11
Lodi, 138, 168, 229, 302,
305–7, 309–12, 315–18,
320, 323, 337, 340–1,
366, 457, 465, 482
Lonato, 382, 384–6,
389–91, 393, 397
Loudon, General Baron
Johann Ludwig Alexander
von, 366, 372, 418, 447,
458, 492
Louis XVI, asks Assembly to
vote for war, 21
Luckner, Marshal Baron
Nicolas de, 71
Lusignan, Colonel Marquis
Franz Joseph, 378, 492,
496–8, 501–2, 504, 506,
508, 512, 515

M
Macquard, General
François, 92, 278, 448
Bonaparte's assessment,
412
Madonna della Corona,
196, 366, 379–80, 409,
450, 452, 455, 477, 493,
497, 501, 517
Maelcamp, Major Baron
Gustave, 170, 198, 333,
366, 394, 398
Voltri, 198, 333
Mahony, Colonel Count
William, 431
Maillebois, Marshal Jean-
Baptiste-François
Desmarets, Marquis de,
49, 88, 95, 98, 123, 259,
283, 294, 347–8
Malerat, Lieutenant, 238
Mantova see Mantua
Mantua, 76, 104, 106, 156,
282, 295, 297, 302, 305,
316, 321, 323, 329–31,
333, 335, 346–7, 349,
351, 355–6, 361–3,
367–70, 372–82, 384,
386–8, 391, 398–9, 401,

406–10, 415, 417, 419,
426, 428, 431–5,
438–42, 444–6, 448,
454, 458, 466, 471,
475–8, 482, 486–91,
494–5, 503, 517, 521–3
Marbot, General Baron
Jean-Baptiste-Antoine-
Marcellin de, 155
Marchand, Captain Jean-
Gabriel, 208
Marengo, 287
Maria Theresa of Austria, 17
reforms, 39–40
Marie-Antoinette of France,
19
Marmont, Chef de Brigade
Auguste-Frédéric-Louis
Viesse de, 81, 90–1,
101–2, 172, 240, 273,
280
Arcole, 467, 469, 482
Augereau, 155
Bonaparte's ADC, 109,
124
Castiglione, 400
Genoa, 94
Lodi, 309
Martinel, Chef d'Escadron,
198, 201, 203–5, 208–9,
226, 259–60, 262, 265,
272
Martonitz, Captain Baron
Andreas, 240, 260
Massari, Luigi, 319
Massena, General André,
51, 75, 153–4, 274
Army of Italy, 90, 92, 98,
115 18, 128, 131, 458
Alba, 286
Alessandria, 291
Arcole, 433, 461, 463–4,
468, 470, 472, 474–5
Bassano, 432, 448–9, 451
Borghetto, 354
Brescia, 388
Caldiero, 455–6
Castiglione, 391,
398–401
Cherasco, 275
Cosseria, 233–4, 241
crossing the Po, 288,
294–5, 298, 300,
306–7
Dego, 230–1, 238,
245–8, 251–2, 258

Lodi, 309, 313–14 .
Lonato, 385
Milan, 328, 331–2, 337
Monte Negino, 200, 206–7
Montenotte, 219–21, 223–6, 228, 232
Peschiera, 351, 383
preparations for war, 140–2, 144–6, 150, 153
Rivoli, 366, 377–8, 459, 494, 500, 503–5, 509–10, 516, 520n65
San Michele, 266
spies, 179, 184
strength of divisions, 127, 156–7, 289
troop movements, 169, 172, 175–6, 180, 187, 190
Tyrol, 408–10, 419, 421–5, 427, 429, 431–2, 447, 454
Verona, 360
Bonaparte's assessment, 412
Melas, General Baron Michael, 348, 350, 354–5, 366, 371–2, 378–9, 381, 383
Melzi d'Eril, Francesco, 320, 323
Ménard, General Philippe-Romain, 144, 157, 221, 223, 235, 253, 304, 307, 309, 317, 457
Menou, General Baron Jacques-François de, 108
Menzweig, Chef de Bataillon, 199
Mészáros, General Johann, 379–80, 391, 398–9, 407
Legnago, 388
Montebello, 383
Seven Years War, 361
Tyrol, 418, 423, 426, 429
Meynier, General Jean-Baptiste, 142, 273
Bonaparte's assessment, 412
Montezemolo, 233, 246
Voltri, 195
Milan, 74, 85, 115, 117, 119, 131, 277, 287, 292, 294–5, 305, 316, 320,

324, 328, 330–1, 334–43, 345, 368, 373, 379, 381, 383, 409, 412, 486, 495
Milhaud, Chef de Brigade Édouard-Jean-Baptiste, 431
Millesimo, 96, 98, 105, 179, 230, 233, 235, 240, 264, 457, 482
Miloradovics, Major Daniel von, 468, 476
Minkwitz, General, 379, 406, 439
Mincio River, 106, 124, 330, 331, 333, 346, 351–2, 354–5, 366, 383–7, 390–1, 395, 400–1, 406, 416–17, 435, 453, 483
Miollis, General Sextius-Alexandre-François, 495
Mirabeau, Honoré-Gabriel Riqueti, Count de, 36, 50
Mittrovsky, General Baron Anton, 378, 381, 383, 401, 447, 449, 458
Arcole, 460, 462–4, 467–8, 473, 475
Rivoli, 491–2
Modena, 76, 85, 287, 306, 335, 370, 485, 489
Mondovì, 87, 89, 98, 100, 117–18, 124, 139, 143, 167, 169, 177, 260, 270–2, 288
Monferrato, Duke of, 77
Monnier, Adjutant-General Jean-Charles, 251, 253, 290, 494, 504
Monte Baldo, 379, 381, 407, 409, 419, 458, 471, 488, 490, 493–4, 496–8, 501
Monte Castellazzo, 203, 222, 225–7
Monte Legino, 206
Monte Negino, 142, 149, 157, 203–4, 206, 208–9, 213, 220, 222, 224
Monteau, General, 495
Montenotte, 14, 104–5, 149, 174, 176, 185, 187, 188, 200–4, 208–9, 219, 221–3, 225–31, 234,

241–2, 246, 263, 388, 525
battle, 219–29
Montesquiou-Fezensac, General Anne-Pierre, Marquis de, 74–5
Montezemolo, 98, 104–5, 113–14, 167, 229–30, 233–5, 237, 241, 249, 258–9, 261
Moreau, General Jean-Victor-Marie, 369, 409–11, 417, 420, 427, 441
Moreau, Sergeant Jérôme, 210, 214
Moretti, Count Michele, 89, 111, 213
Mouton, Captain Georges, 196
Muiron, Chef de Brigade Jean-Baptiste, 80–1, 446, 465
Murat, General Joachim, 43, 108, 130, 183, 274, 280, 321, 354, 370, 457, 494
captured, 382
cease-fire, 286
library books, 123
Mantua, 374
Tyrol, 429, 431, 433

N
Naples, 17, 76, 138, 322–3, 362, 368–9, 523
armistice with France, 368–9
war against France, 76
Cavalry units
Napoli Dragoons, 350
Principe di Napoli, 350
Re di Napoli Dragoons, 351
Regina di Napoli, 350
Napoleon I, Emperor *see* Bonaparte, Napoleon
National Assembly, Military Committee, 50
Nelson, Commodore Horatio, 59, 124, 169, 191, 212, 368
Nesslinger, Lieutenant-Colonel, 226, 228
Nice, 73, 75, 77–9, 86–8, 90–2, 94–5, 98, 101,

104–5, 118, 124, 126–9,
141, 144, 147, 154, 169,
172, 174–5, 180, 183,
196, 278, 292
Nicoletti, General, 168,
310, 315, 348, 378, 397

O

Ocskay, General Baron
Joseph, 378, 388, 390,
392–4, 447, 458–9, 471,
477
Rivoli, 492, 494, 499,
502, 504–5, 508,
511–12
Salò blockade, 380, 382,
385–6
Oneglia, 75, 87–90, 95,
175, 177–8, 182
Ott, General Baron Peter
Karl, 378, 380, 388, 392,
394, 433–5
Mantua, 439
Ponte San Marco, 382,
385–6, 390

P

Paoli, Pasquale, 62, 69
Papal States, 85, 369, 487,
521, 523
Parma, 17, 76, 85, 287,
296–7, 306
Parquin, Captain Denis-
Charles, 60n5
Pavia, 132, 138, 140–1,
143, 168, 289, 292, 294,
296–8, 302, 305, 309,
334, 338–9, 341–5,
369–70
peace negotiations, 76,
111–12, 130, 273–5,
278, 286, 291–2, 306,
335, 338, 368–9, 371,
442, 489, 522
Pelleport, Lieutenant
Viscount Pierre de, 336
Pelletier, General, 384, 395
Peschiera, 333, 346–52,
354–5, 366, 378, 383,
385–6, 398, 401, 415,
420, 453, 476, 484,
493–4, 503–4, 512
Petitbon, Sergeant Jean,
240, 355, 383, 452, 462,
472–3
Piacenza, 17, 76, 185, 287,

294–8, 301–2, 307n10,
309, 461
Pico, French spy, 179, 184
Piedmont
armistice of Cherasco,
273–5, 278–82
and Austria, 74–5, 85,
89, 92, 111–12, 117,
119, 140
and France, 73–6, 90,
100, 137, 338
and Sicily, 16
Piedmontese army, 186,
258–61, 265–75
strategic plans, 148–50
strength of army, 138,
167
Infantry Regiments
Acqui, 261
Genevois, 261
La Marina, 233, 236,
241, 246
Mondovì, 261
Monferrato, 233, 235,
242, 248
Oneglia, 261
Piedmontese Free
Corps, 261
Royal Allemand, 261,
262
Royal Grenadiers, 261,
262
Savoy, 261
Stettler, 261
Susa, 233
Tortona, 261
Cavalry
Dragoons, 271
Pijon, General Jean-Joseph-
Magdelaine, 110, 142,
171, 206, 378, 381, 393,
419–5, 499, 457
pillaging, 75, 268–9, 273–4,
277, 290, 414
Pittoni, General Baron
Filippo, 145, 168, 170,
174, 185, 316, 348, 353,
378
Arcole, 444
defence of the Po, 296,
298
Novi, 171
Voltri, 194, 196–200
Piuma, Padre, 228
plunder, 287–8, 306, 335–6
Pizzighettone, 297, 302–3,

305, 307, 309, 310, 316,
337
Po River, 85–6, 94, 103,
138, 170, 181, 185, 203,
275, 286, 288–9,
291–301, 305–7, 309,
317, 324, 331, 333, 346,
351, 368–70, 373, 417,
449, 459, 489, 492, 495,
525
Pontare, 379–81, 471, 477,
493–4, 501–2, 504,
506–7, 511–12, 514–15
Pontécoulant, Louis-Gustave
de Doulcet, Count de,
102–3, 105
Pope, armistice with
Bonaparte, 371, 489
Provence, Count of, 73
Provera, General Marchese
Giovanni, 139, 161,
185–6, 188–9, 200–1
Arcole, 467–8, 473, 475
Bassano, 443–4, 446,
449, 451, 454
Caldiero, 456, 458
Cosseria, 233, 235–40,
243
Mantua, 517, 521
Montenotte, 219
Rivoli, 491–2, 495–6,
515
Prussia
and Austria, 18, 20, 111
War of the First
Coalition, 15–17, 72,
101

Q

Quenin, Adjutant-General
Jean, 238
Quosdanovich, General
Peter Vitus von, 361,
378–82, 385–98
Bassano, 444, 446–7,
452, 454, 458
Mantua, 406, 440
Rivoli, 494, 499, 500–2,
504
Tyrol, 418, 421, 426,
429–30, 431–2

R

Ramand, Lieutenant, 469
Rampon, Chef de Brigade
Antoine-Guillaume,

187–8, 207–8, 211, 214–15, 224, 414, 425
Rattier, Sergeant Jean-Henry, 224, 304, 396–7, 423, 430, 451
Arcole, 461, 469, 473
Reille, Captain Honoré-Charles-Michel-Joseph, 196
Reuss-Plauen, General Prince Heinrich, 378, 386, 390, 392, 394, 411
Brescia, 382
Rivoli, 492, 494, 500, 502, 504, 511, 514
Tyrol, 418–19, 422–3, 426
Revolutionary Army see French Army
Rey, General Antoine-Gabriel-Venance, 485, 494, 500, 504, 515
Ricord, Jean-François, 90, 92543
Ritter, François-Joseph, government commissioner, 115, 118
Riviera, 59, 85–9, 92, 94, 98, 100, 102, 127, 129, 139, 140, 159, 201, 203, 240, 288, 333, 523
Rivoli, 161, 207, 332, 360, 366, 377–81, 383, 409, 414, 419, 450, 452–3, 455, 458–9, 462, 466–7, 471, 475–7, 482–3, 486, 490–4, 496, 501–6, 509, 511–14, 516–17, 521, 524–5
Robert, General, 396, 472, 474
Robespierre, Augustin-Bon-Joseph de, 90, 92–4
Robespierre, Maximilien-François-Marie-Isidore de, 93–4
Rochambeau, Marshal Jean-Baptiste-Donatien de Vimeur, Count de, 71, 143
Roederer, Pierre-Louis, 69
Roguet, Captain François, 57, 211, 336, 340, 393, 466, 474
Rome, 369
Rondeau, Chef de Brigade

Gabriel, 226, 245, 251, 253
Rosales, Monsignor Giuseppe Ordegno di, 343–4
Roselmini, General, 168, 288–9, 292, 298, 310–11, 315,
Arcole, 444
Mantua, 333, 364
Rossbach, battle of, 18
Rovereto, 329, 346, 360, 366, 370, 376, 409, 416, 418, 421–5, 452–3, 455
Rukavina, General Baron Mathias, 141–2, 150, 167, 185–6, 188, 200,
Dego, 230–1, 242, 245
Lodi, 315
Mantua, 333, 351, 365, 374
Monte Negino, 200, 202, 207, 213, 215
Valeggio, 391
Rusca, General Jean-Baptiste, 179, 186, 189, 221, 241, 265, 338, 349, 378
crossing the Po, 291, 294
Lodi, 314
wounded, 380

S
Sahuguet d'Amarzit, General Jean-Joseph-François Léonard de, 409, 413
Mantua, 415, 419, 433–5, 441
Saint Marsan, Marquis de, 117
Saint-André, General Charles François Thaon de Revel, Count de, 75, 78
Saint-Hilaire, General Louis-Vincent-Joseph le Blond de, 150, 397, 422, 457
Saliceti, Antoine Christophe, 90, 118, 141, 290, 389
character, 159
control of troop movements, 322
government

commissioner with the army, 116, 229
Milan, 332
Mondovì, 272
Representative of French government, 79, 88, 94
request for loan for army, 128–9, 131
suspension of advance on Genoa, 156, 181
Voltri, 142, 144–5, 169
Salisch, Colonel, 364
Salò, 333, 349, 378–80, 382, 385–6, 388, 390–2, 394, 395, 419–20, 422, 494
San Giorgio (Mantua), 362, 365, 367, 375, 446, 517
San Michele, 265–70, 274, 427, 429, 448
Sandos, General, 494, 509
Saorgio, 75, 77–8, 88–92
Sardinia, King of see Victor Amadeus
Sauret, General Pierre Franconin, called, 366, 373, 378, 380, 384–5, 389–91, 409, 414
Bonaparte's assessment, 412, 483
Savona, 86–7, 95, 97–100, 103, 114–15, 126–8, 141–2, 145–6, 148, 153, 159, 175–6, 179, 188, 190, 194–5, 199–200, 203–4, 207–8, 212–13, 215, 220–21, 223–24, 229, 234, 269, 288
Savoy, 17, 73, 74–5, 78, 80, 87, 101, 104, 123, 313
Schels, Johann Baptist, 138, 189, 199, 213, 355, 494, 498, 512, 513–14
Schérer, General Barthélemy-Louis-Joseph, 99–100, 110, 112–19, 128–9, 131, 141, 144–5
praised by Bonaparte, 147
Seven Years War, 99
Schreiber, Captain Paul, 267
Schübirz, General Baron Anton, 168, 289, 298, 333, 372, 391, 396
Arcole, 467, 475
Bassano, 444, 451
Caldiero, 456

Castiglione, 395, 401
Codogno, 303
command of Auxiliary
  Corps, 276, 286
Lodi, 310, 315–16
Tyrol, 418, 426
Scorza, Baldassare, 363,
  367, 374–6, 387, 408,
  409, 438, 521
Mantua blockade, 438,
  521
Sebottendorf, General Baron
  Carl Philipp, 168, 174,
  348, 350, 372, 383, 395
defence of the Po, 287–9,
  296, 298, 301
Lodi, 305, 309–10,
  313–15
Mantua, 333, 366,
  379–81
Tyrol, 418, 421, 429
Villafranca, 353–5
Voltri, 194, 197, 200
Ségur, General Count
  Philippe-Paul de, 153,
  155, 199
Sérurier, General Jean-
  Mathieu-Philibert, 126,
  150, 157, 398
Bonaparte's assessment,
  412
Ceva, 248–9, 258, 263
character, 155
Cherasco, 275, 286
crossing the Po, 300, 309
Mantua, 156, 367–8,
  373–4, 378, 391,
  521–2
Montenotte, 219, 221,
  224
Montezemolo, 233–4,
  241
Rivoli, 503
San Michele, 265–8
strength of division in
  Italy, 127, 289, 338
troop movements, 177,
  183, 190, 291, 295,
  337
Voltri, 196
Servan de Gerbey, Joseph,
  59n2, 71
  Le soldat citoyen, 49
Serviez, General, 378, 495
Seulen, Lieutenant-Colonel,
  423, 447

Seven Years War, 18, 25, 33,
  39, 43, 99, 132, 135, 361
Sicily, and Piedmont, 16
Sillobod, Major, 171
Sola, Colonel Count, 302,
  407
Sornet, Adjutant-General,
  424
Soubise, Marshal Charles de
  Rohan, Prince of, 18, 372
Soulès, Chef de Bataillon,
  464–5
Spain, war against France,
  76, 77
Spiegel, General, 383,
  406–7
spies, 179, 184, 276, 335,
  345, 370, 409
Spork, General (Count
  Johann), 378, 392,
  394–5, 418–19, 424–5,
  427
Brescia, 382
Tyrol, 440, 447
Stengel, General Henry-
  Christian-Michel, 172,
  247, 252, 266, 271, 290
Stentsch, Colonel, 430
Sticker, Colonel, 467–8
Strassoldo, General Count
  Leopold, 74
Sturioni, Colonel, 365, 407
Suchet, Chef de Brigade
  Louis-Gabriel, 131, 239
Sucy de Clisson, Simone-
  Antoine-François-Marie
  de, commissary, 172–3
Sugny, Chef de Brigade, 172
Sulkowski, Captain Joseph,
  430–1, 438, 445, 451,
  456
Arcole, 462–3, 465, 474
Rivoli, 512
supply, 58, 99, 106, 111,
  118, 125, 129, 135, 141,
  144–5, 156, 172–3,
  177–8, 182–3, 234, 249,
  253–4, 268–9, 278, 288,
  305, 320, 335, 407, 408,
  414, 439, 442, 445, 446,
  450, 484, 485, 525

T
tactics
  cavalry, 28
  columns, 25–6

combat formations, 24–5
fortifications, 30–1
infantry, 24–7
sieges, 30–1
tambour d'Arcole *see*
  Estienne, André
Tanaro River, 86–7, 89–90,
  98, 103, 105, 113, 117,
  140, 169, 177, 186, 219,
  242, 248–9, 259, 265–6,
  269, 275, 288, 294
Tascher de la Pagerie, Marie-
  Josèphe-Rose *see*
  Josephine
Thiébault, Paul-Charles-
  François-Adrien-Henri-
  Dieudonné, 108, 129,
  154, 210, 509–10, 512
Thugut, Baron Johann
  Amadeus Franz, 38, 41,
  84, 91, 94, 112, 117,
  133–4, 140, 161, 372
Tornaforte, General Count
  Francesco Bruno di,
  260–1, 264–5
Tortona, 85–6, 114, 137–8,
  168, 171, 179, 263,
  274–5, 278, 280, 286–8,
  291–2, 295, 306, 322,
  324, 334, 345, 370, 417
Toulon, 77, 79–81, 94, 107,
  141, 160, 169, 368, 446
transport, 44, 104, 111,
  113, 141, 144, 147, 151,
  156, 173, 177, 183, 273,
  279, 281, 328, 330, 336,
  415, 420, 442
Trento, 104, 329, 335, 366,
  370, 409, 411, 415–16,
  418, 420–1, 423, 425–8,
  444–5, 448, 450
Trevor, John Hampden-,
  British ambassador, 60
Turchino Pass, 172, 174,
  179, 196–7
Turin, 73–6, 78, 85, 88, 91,
  114, 120, 130, 137, 139,
  140–1, 143, 160, 169,
  259–60, 266, 269–70,
  273–5, 277–8
Turkey, 106–7
Tuscany, 63, 322, 495
Tyrol, 71, 93–4, 104, 111,
  286, 305, 322, 329,
  331–2, 335, 346, 349,
  355, 366, 371–3, 375,

379, 384, 386, 401, 406,
408, 410–11, 415–17,
420, 426, 428, 440,
443–8, 450, 452, 458–9,
475–6, 488, 490–2

V

Valeggio sul Mincio,
347–51, 353–5, 378,
380, 383, 386, 388, 391,
398, 400, 500
Valence, General Cyrus-
Marie-Alexandre de
Timbrune, Count de, 64,
71
Valette, General, 378, 385,
391, 471
Vaublanc, Vincent-Marie
Viénnot, Count de, 102
Vaubois, General Claude-
Henri Belgrand, Count
de, 367, 370–1, 413–14,
419, 447, 458
Livorno, 371
replaced by Bonaparte,
483
Rivoli, 459, 467, 472
Tyrol, 2–9, 452–5, 475
Veaux, Chef de Brigade
Antoine-Joseph, 494, 517
Venice, 85, 316, 335, 370,
432
Verdier, General Jean-
Antoine, 395, 400,
462–3, 494
Verne, General, 463
Verona, 124, 360, 367,
377–80, 383, 407, 409,
415, 417, 419, 422–3,
427, 440, 448, 450,
454–9, 466–7, 475, 477,
491, 493–4, 496, 500,
503, 506, 512, 515
Verri, Count Pietro, 334
Vial, Adjutant-General
Honoré, 264, 299, 469,
494, 497
Rivoli, 507–10, 512, 516
Victor, General Claude
Perrin, *called*, 223, 252,
277, 378, 381, 424–5,
434, 457, 494, 503, 517
Victor Amadeus III, 73–4,
76, 78, 80, 85, 88, 90–2,
100–1, 104, 112, 114,
117, 130, 137, 141, 150

armistice negotiations,
273–4
Vignolle, Adjutant-General
Martin de, 128–9, 131,
144, 374, 465
Vigo-Roussillon, Sergeant
François, 190, 210–11,
215, 232, 250
Castiglione, 393
Lodi, 312, 314–15
Milan, 328, 336
Vincent, Lieutenant-Colonel
Baron Karl, 415, 489
Visconti, Monsignor
Filippo, Archbishop of
Milan, 342–3
Vital, General Count, 260–2
Volta, Alessandro Giuseppe
Antonio Anastasio, 344
Voltri, 142, 144–6, 148,
169–70, 172, 174,
176–7, 179–80, 184–90,
194–201, 212–13, 222,
242, 254
attack on, 194–215
Vukassovich, General Baron
Josef Philipp, 35, 179,
185–6, 188, 391, 471
defence of the Po, 286–9,
296, 298, 333
Dego, 242–3, 250–1, 253
Lodi, 311, 315
Mantua, 333, 364
Rivoli, 492, 494, 511
Tyrol, 418–19, 422–7,
447,Voltri, 197, 198,
213

W

Wallis, General Count
Olivier Remigius, 110,
132, 138
War of the Austrian
Succession, 17, 132
War of the Bavarian
Succession, 33, 135, 361
War of the First Coalition,
15, 19, 72
War of the Polish
Succession, 17
War of the Spanish
Succession, 16
warfare
alternative scenarios,
68–9
offensive operations, 67

writings on the theory of,
41, 48, 65
Wartensleben, General
Count Wilhelm Ludwig
Gustav, 42
weapons
artillery, 29–30
bayonets, 26
cannons, 29
lances, 27
muskets, 23–4, 441
swords, 26, 27
Weidenfeld, Colonel Baron
Karl Philippi von, 398,
401, 425
Wenckheim, General
(Count Joseph?), 127
Werneck, General Baron
Franz von, 42
Wetzel, Colonel (Baron
Karl?), 168, 297
Weyrother, Major Franz
von, 440, 491, 498
Wurmser, Field Marshal
Count Dagobert-
Sigismond de
Castiglione, 390–401
Mantua, 372–3, 376–81,
386–7, 415, 433–5,
438–48, 454, 471,
477, 486–7, 489–90,
517, 521
Mantua surrender, 521–2
Montebello, 432–3
Tyrol, 406, 411, 417–18,
421, 423, 426–9, 431,
434

Z

Zach, Colonel Baron Anton,
426